NATIONAL ACCOUNTS STATISTICS: STUDY OF INPUT-OUTPUT TABLES, 1970-80

UNITED NATIONS
NEW YORK, 1987

NOTE

Symbols of United Nations documents are composed of capital letters combined with figures.

The designations employed and the presentation of material in this publication do not imply the expression of any opinion whatsoever on the part of the Secretariat of the United Nations concerning the legal status of any country, territory, city or area or of its authorities, or concerning the delimitation of its frontiers or boundaries.

Where the designation "country" or "area" is used in the text, it covers, as appropriate, countries, territories, cities or areas.

ST/ESA/STAT/SER.X/7

UNITED NATIONS PUBLICATION

Sales No. E.86.XVII.15

03600

ISBN 92-1-161268-3

Inquiries should be directed to:

PUBLISHING DIVISION
UNITED NATIONS
NEW YORK, N.Y. 10017

PREFACE

An earlier version of this publication was circulated for comment to a number of experts in the field. Their contributions are incorporated in the present study.

Helpful contributions and suggestions were received from Pieter Al (Netherlands), Alfred Franz (Austria), Josef Richter (Austria), Bent Thage (Denmark) and Paula Young (United States of America).

CONTENTS

CONTENTS *(continued)*

Part Two

Statistical sources and compilation methods of selected countries

LIST OF TABLES

INTRODUCTION

1. The present publication is within the programme of publications on input-output by the Statistical Office of the United Nations Secretariat. This publication is the first attempt to study differences in concepts and methods used by various countries in their compilation of input-output tables. Recently, the United Nations Industrial Development Organization (UNIDO) published *Input-Output Tables for Developing Countries (1985)*. The next publication in the input-output programme will be the *Handbook of Input-Output Compilation and Analysis*.

2. The main objectives of the present publication and other United Nations publications on input-output are to give wider publicity to the availability of the input-output data of individual countries and to contribute to more internationally standardized input-output statistics, since, at present, international analysis and comparison are difficult because of a lack of standardization of individual country tables.

3. The first step in this standardization effort is to make explicit the incomparabilities between the input-output data of various countries. To that end, part one of this publication will summarize some major conceptual differences in methodology for data collection, classification, organization and treatment of many important economic transactions within the framework of input-output statistics. For comparison, recommendations of the System of National Accounts (SNA) are always summarized first so as to serve as background for illuminating concepts and methods utilized by country input-output practitioners. Part one is based on a survey of the tables of 53 countries.

4. Part two includes detailed information on various aspects of the analytical framework of the tables, and on statistical sources and compilation methods of 19 selected countries—only a sample of the 53 countries surveyed. The issues that will be dealt with are table presentations, valuation standards, classifications and units of classification, and treatment of selected transactions such as transactions in secondary products, non-marketed products and computation of financial services. Tables of other countries for which information on concepts, compilation methods and statistical sources are not yet available to the Statistical Office at a sufficiently detailed level will unfortunately have to be excluded. However, it is believed that a sufficiently diverse number of countries will be presented to cover many important concepts and compilation methods now in use.

5. In the description of the analytical framework, frequent reference is made to the SNA standards on input-output statistics, as defined in two United Nations publications: *A System of National Accounts,*[1] which will be referred to as the Blue Book, and *Input-Output Tables and Analysis.*[2] Those publications include the only available international

statistical standards for the field of input-output statistics.

6. It is hoped that through further studies on differences in concepts and compilation methods, a number of incomparabilities among countries and between countries and the SNA recommendations will gradually dissolve or at least narrow significantly.

7. Standardization in input-output statistics has become increasingly important as recent economic analysis and modelling have looked more seriously into international trade feedbacks within multinational and multi-sectoral models in understanding the economic growth process and vice versa; similarly, studies on economic implications of industrial structural changes, and of differences in industrial structures over time and across countries, also require statistical comparability or at least the knowledge of statistical incomparability so that appropriate analytical models can be developed. With the availability of a large number of country input-output tables, multinational and structural analysis becomes feasible. Nevertheless, the effort has still been made very difficult and its results face serious criticism because of international incomparability of sectoral and transactional flow definitions, classifications and methods of estimation.

8. The present study will attempt to review major economic and statistical concepts and compilation methods used by country input-output practitioners. These concepts and compilation methods are always contrasted with those recommended by SNA. Deviations from SNA recommendations are pointed out, but those deviations should in no way be understood in a negative sense. In fact, many deviations may be improvements over those recommended by the present SNA. This analysis of differences in concepts and in compilation methods among countries is critically necessary before any current SNA standards can be revised or new standards recommended. It is to be hoped that the present study will contribute to the international review of SNA standards currently being carried out by the United Nations, the Organisation for Economic Co-operation and Development (OECD), the European Economic Community (EEC), the International Monetary Fund (IMF), the World Bank and individual countries.

9. Part one will review concepts and country practices in valuation standards, statistical units and classification standards, treatment of secondary products, treatment of government expenditures, treatment of imports and exports and treatment of other selective transactions such as intra-establishment deliveries, imputed bank service charges, insurance services, rents, own-account production, and, finally, statistical sources, methods used for table construction and the comparison of the input-output structures of SNA and the System of Balances of the National Economy (MPS).

1

Part One

REVIEW OF CONCEPTS AND COMPILATION METHODS
USED IN INPUT-OUTPUT COUNTRY PRACTICES

I. VALUATION STANDARDS

10. The static input-output system in its simplest form is based on two important assumptions:

(a) Each sector in the system produces a single output, with a single input structure, that is, a single technique of production, and there is no substitution between input used by different sectors;

(b) The input into each sector is a linear fixed-coefficient production function only of the level of gross output of that sector; that is, the amount of each kind of input absorbed by any particular sector goes up or down in direct proportion to the increase or decrease in the gross output of that sector.

11. The above assumptions imply that transactions between sectors and final demand must be valued in as homogeneous a way as possible so that input-output coefficients that are designed to be technologically based are unaffected by tax and subsidy policies or by differences in types of economic transactions such as current business expenses, investments or personal consumption. For example, a quantity of goods can be valued differently if the goods sold to one type of buyer are subject to commodity taxes and to another type of buyer are not subject to taxes. In this example, the same producers' value, which includes indirect taxes minus subsidies, does not reflect the same value of materials absorbed in production. Commodity taxes also create heterogeneity problems in the valuation of different groups of commodities included in one sector. For example, if fuel oil and gasoline are included in the commodity group of petroleum products and if the tax rate is low on fuel oil and high on gasoline, then a dollar's worth of petroleum products at producers' values will represent a much smaller quantity in the case of transportation than it does in the case of industrial users whose purchases are mainly fuel oil.

12. For the reasons mentioned above, SNA suggests the use of approximate basic value in the valuation of input and output, a value concept aimed at measuring the production costs of goods and services before they are shipped out to the markets for consumption so that effects of tax and subsidy policies are eliminated. The term "approximate" implies that only the net indirect commodity taxes paid at the last stage are eliminated from the producers' values of input and output to get to the true basic values; indirect effects of indirect taxes in previous stages are not eliminated. Another value that can be used for input-output compilation is factor value. Factor values are equal to basic values minus all non-commodity indirect taxes.

13. The input-output table can also be constructed in other valuations, such as producers' values or purchasers' values. Producers' values are equal to basic values plus net commodity taxes (for example, commodity taxes minus subsidies). Purchasers' values are equal to producers' values plus distribution (trade and transportation) margins, the values that are actually paid by consumers. Assuming that valuation should be as homogeneous as possible, approximate basic values are preferable to producers' values, and producers' values are preferable to purchasers' values.

14. Within the above definitional framework, imports are valued in c.i.f., the value at the custom frontier of the importing country plus protective import duties for approximate basic values. For producers' value, both protective and net revenue-raising duties should be added to the c.i.f. values. Protective import duties are not for revenue raising or for discouraging consumption but aimed at putting domestic producers in a competitive position *vis-à-vis* foreign producers. They are based on the differences between c.i.f. values and domestic producers' values. The distinction between protective duties and non-protective duties is made by SNA to increase uniformity in valuation. SNA also recognizes that protective duties are small and present difficulties of definition (see para. 3.35 of the Blue Book). It seems that SNA has in mind only the actual protective duties but not the shadow protective duties that need to be imputed to increase uniformity in valuation.

15. On the basis of the most recent input-output tables compiled by countries since 1970, only 13 countries out of a total of 53 (one quarter) used basic or factor values. The majority of countries (34) used producers' values. Only a small number of countries used purchasers' values.

II. STATISTICAL UNITS AND CLASSIFICATION STANDARDS

16. The homogeneity assumption in input-output which should serve as the most important guideline in determining the statistical units used for data collection and the ways these statistical units are consolidated or deconsolidated and regrouped in defining industrial sectors requires that each activity produce only one homogeneous product and use only one homogeneous set of inputs.

17. Statistical units may be based on any of the following groupings: *(a)* a commodity grouping; *(b)* an establishment such as a factory, farm or mine, which is defined by SNA as an economic unit engaging under a single ownership or control in one or predominantly one kind of economic activity at a single physical location; *(c)* a grouping of activity units such as insurance, coal mining or construction, which involves one kind of economic activity without regard to ownership or physical location (the definition of activity or activity unit refers to a distinct technical process which is different from the SNA concept of activity, which is mainly a grouping of establishments engaging in one dominant type of activity); or *(d)* an institution such as a government agency or an enterprise, which might control more than one establishment and engage in more than one kind of activity. It would be perfect for input-output table compilation and analysis if each unit was involved in only one economic activity which produced only one type of commodity. However, none of the previously described groupings satisfies all the attributes of homogeneity required by input-output analysis.

18. Commodity grouping at the detailed level may not satisfy the attribute of a homogeneous product and many are unlikely to satisfy the attribute of a homogeneous set of inputs since an identical commodity can be produced by more than one technology, and so is represented by more than one set of inputs and/or one set of capital/output ratios. In this case, models based on more complex assumptions than those of the Leontief input-output table are needed. The complex models proposed by Von Neumann or used in linear programming may be alternatives. However, those optimization models, which assume a certain objective function, cannot be easily defined for the economy as a whole.

19. The establishment in the ideal form can be used to compile data on input of one kind of economic activity which results in one type of commodity output. However, in practice, a single establishment may engage in more than one kind of economic activity. In addition, present record-keeping practices usually do not allow separate compilation of output and input of differing classes of activity. Therefore, operationally, the establishment is defined by SNA as the combination of activities and resources directed by the singly owning or controlling entity towards the production of the most homogeneous group of goods and services, often at one location, but sometimes spread over a number of nearby sites, for which separate records are available that can provide the data concerning the production of those goods on services and the materials, labour and physical resources used in their production.

20. The dependence of the SNA operational definition of the establishment on the accounting practices of countries thus creates wide flexibility with regard to the coverage of the activity sectors in input-output tables and, as a consequence, reduces the comparability of input-output industrial structures over time and across countries.

21. It has become a common practice for many countries to classify agricultural sectors and mining sectors on the basis of commodity or activity groupings, construction on the basis of activity groupings, and financial services on the basis of enterprise (institutional) groupings. For manufacturing industries, a number of countries collected their data with the establishment as the statistical unit. According to a study by Alfred Franz[3] on practices of OECD countries in classification, almost 50 per cent of the countries used the establishment as the statistical unit, over 20 per cent used the enterprise and about 30 per cent used a combination of both the establishment and the enterprise as statistical units. While an establishment is classified to an industry on the basis of its characteristic (that is, principal) activity, it may contain a significant proportion of secondary products. Sometimes none of the commodities or activities makes up 50 per cent of the establishment's value added. An enterprise that usually contains more than one establishment may constitute a more diverse group of commodities or activities. As a consequence, an industry-by-industry input-output table compiled directly from the establishment or enterprise information will have to be highly aggregated to get away from the sectoring problem, when detailed information on input with respect to activity or commodity is not available for the reclassification of secondary products or activities. Of course, in this type of table, to the extent allowed by detailed information on input, some important secondary products are transferred by various methods to the industries where they are primary. The output of those secondary products can be transferred either alone or together with their associated input. (The treatment of secondary products will be discussed in detail in the following section.) The more highly aggregated tables will be less useful for analytical purposes when the composition of output or technologies within each input-output sector changes significantly.

22. Of the countries with tables compiled for the 1970s surveyed by the Statistical Office of the United Nations Secretariat, over 60 per cent adopted the conventional input-output framework on the basis of an industry-by-industry or a commodity-by-commodity classification. Nevertheless, countries with more resources and a great need for knowledge of narrowly defined industries spent more effort in separating out secondary products. Japan, even though adopting the conventional framework as discussed above, broke up establishment statistics into groupings of activities, each activity grouping associating with one commodity or a group of highly homogeneous commodities before being classified into input-output sectors. Japan considered its classification a commodity classification. The Netherlands adopted a method quite similar to that of Japan, but appar-

6

ently applied the transfer of secondary products on a more limited scale.

23. A growing number of countries adopted the double classifications in terms of both activities and commodities as recommended by SNA. Two separate matrices are formed. The absorption matrix represents the consumption of commodities by activities. The make matrix represents the production of commodity output by activities. Forty per cent of the countries surveyed have adopted this classification. The United States of America presented the output mix in the make matrix only after some secondary products or activities and their associated input were transferred to the industries where they are characteristic products.

24. Australia and Japan prepared the make and absorption matrices but used conventional methods to reclassify secondary products instead of mechanical methods such as those based on technology assumptions. However, the principal method used by Australia for the elimination of secondary products is appropriate aggregation. Some countries, such as the Federal Republic of Germany, used the enterprise instead of the establishment as the statistical unit in the classification of input-output activities. The United States identified some activities by institutional origins. It classified government enterprises that produce output similar to private industrial sectors into separate input-output sectors; for example, the sector of federal electric utilities and the sector of state and local utilities produce the same commodity as the industrial sector, namely, electric utilities. This treatment is applied because the government electric utilities sectors and the similar private sector have different sets of inputs in the absorption matrix owing to a different technology mix (for example, petroleum, coal, hydroelectric, nuclear), even though, on the basis of activities, electric generation produced by coal, for example, can be assumed to be technically the same whether it is produced by a private or a public firm. In the make matrix, electricity is treated as a secondary product of government electric utilities sectors (treated like institutions) that produce no characteristic product. This further identification of activities by institutional origin is useful in studying institutional differences and especially socio-economic differences (modern versus plantation-type technologies) between various production technologies.

25. Of the 53 countries surveyed by the Statistical Office, a growing number, including many developing countries, have been adopting the United Nations recommendation. The make and the absorption matrices have been used for deriving the commodity-by-commodity or industry-by-commodity input-output table for analytical purposes, but for some countries, the two matrices are also used for the purpose of presenting information as original data of actual groupings of enterprises. The bridging of the two types of input-output tables for two different purposes, that is, for data presentation and for input-output analysis, requires the integration of national accounts and input-ouput statistics. This is still made very difficult by the SNA use of dual classes of transactors, one in connection with flows of goods and services where the establishment is the statistical unit, and the other in connection with flows of finance where the enterprise is the statistical unit. This problem can only be eliminated or at least alleviated if statistics on output and the associated input for each activity unit (or at least establishments) can be identified with the enterprise where production takes place. The integration of national accounts and

input-output within the SNA framework has also been raised in the work towards the revision of SNA.[4,5]

26. According to the operational definition of SNA, an establishment may include other activities that cover a significant proportion of employment or value added. Those activities might include production of capital goods and other goods and services for own use, and also sold to other establishments, such as electricity, warehousing, container-making and wholesaling. Also, by the recommendation of the International Standard Industrial Classification of All Economic Activities (ISIC), ancillary activities in the form of central administration in support of two or more establishments in a multi-unit enterprise are to be allocated to the predominant kind of activity of the units they serve.[6]

27. All these practical rules have diluted the homogeneity property of the establishment unit in respect of both output and technology (input), which is essential for analytical purposes of input-output economics. Consequently, in order to compile an input-output table that better reflects the technical relationship of production processes, an establishment such as the statistical unit has to be further broken down into its constituent activities, each preferably producing a single commodity (good or service). In this case, an activity is the production unit at or below the establishment level at which its input structure can be technically separated from others. As such, an activity or a commodity is preferred to an establishment as the compilation unit for input-output analysis. The activity as a statistical unit in this sense is different from the activity concept used by SNA, where it is mainly used to define establishment groupings. The argument as outlined above does not deny the complexity or even the feasibility of separating activities within a service establishment producing diverse services both for own use and for sale. More research should be done in the area of service activities because of the increasingly important role of the service activities in an economy. For many developed countries up to 70 per cent of their employment is engaging the service activities.

28. To satisfy the homogeneity assumption, activities should be broken down to the most detailed level so that an activity can ideally be identified with the production of a single commodity. For example, construction can be broken down to many diverse activities such as the building of roads, bridges, residential housing, or the building of electricity facilities; each activity requires a quite different set of input. However, as already mentioned, in many instances an activity even at the most technically detailed level is identified as producing more than one commodity; then the dual classification in terms of both activity and commodity in the form of absorption and make matrices as recommended by SNA can be used. Where a commodity is produced by more than one activity, the issue cannot be easily resolved within the single input-output model, except by aggregating those different activities, which makes sense only if the market shares of the activities producing the same commodity were stable over time. To summarize, the establishment concept, even though having many defects, is closer to the activity concept and more homogeneous than the institution concept.

29. Institutional categories are not appropriate for defining an input-output sector for impact purposes. For example, an enterprise that might include many establishments must be separated into different activities. As another example, the public sector as an institution may be involved in the

production of many services to households, such as education and health services, or to business, such as electricity generation or even industrial commodity production. For the construction of input-output tables, it is recommended by SNA that public enterprises that produce commodities identical to those produced by private enterprises be separated out as separate activities and included together with similar private units.

30. In summary, as recommended by SNA, an establishment is used as the statistical unit for data collection for national account statistics. But for the construction of input-output statistics, the focus is on commodity and activity breakdown. Consequently, the Blue Book suggests that "data may be collected at a level below that of the establishment; engineering data may be available on inputs into certain commodities. But, as a rule, supplementary information of these kinds is incomplete and it is necessary to resort to some extent to mechanical means of effecting transfers [of secondary products] based on the application of mathematical methods (para. 3.16)."

III. TREATMENT OF SECONDARY PRODUCTS

31. Secondary products take many forms, as discussed in the Blue Book (para. 3.15). The most common form is a subsidiary product. A subsidiary product is produced in an establishment where another characteristic product is produced. But each product is produced by an entirely different technique of production or technology, and thus its input costs can be separated. For example, aero-engines made by a motor car establishment, and trade activity, construction and electricity produced by manufacturing plants are considered subsidiary products. Furthermore, the demand for the subsidiary product is also distinct from that of the characteristic product. Subsidiary products become the problem of secondary products mainly because of a lack of more detailed statistics owing to the application of the operational definition of the statistical unit, where more than one significant activity is included in an establishment.

32. Another form of secondary product is the by-product. In its simplest form, a by-product arises during the course of producing a primary commodity. Its output varies proportionally with the output of the primary commodity. Furthermore, very little additional input is required for its production. Examples of by-products include molasses produced in the sugar industry, scrap and waste in the non-ferrous establishments and sulphuric acid in basic metal smelting, and animal feed in whisky production.

33. The last form of secondary products, and the most complicated to deal with, is joint products. Joint products share a significant common cost. An example of joint products is milk and meat produced in the livestock industry. The common cost is the cost of reproducing and maintaining a herd of cows. In addition, each product requires a separate cost structure and can be produced to the extent allowed by the common cost on a separate scale, which depends on the demand for each product. Given that the input specific to each product is available, only the common costs need to be allocated.

34. Another example of joint products, which shows the complication of secondary products in an increasingly service-oriented society, is commodities produced in an establishment or enterprise that involve the significant common cost of central administration. Central administration includes such services as management, data processing and marketing, which require distinctly different input. The cost of central administration is classified in the establishment. This practice is accepted on the basis that these services are small and typically provided by the establishment. However, when some of the services are large and provided gradually at an increasing scale by other independent establishments, and when some of the services are both produced for own use and for sales, the conventional treatment should be re-examined.

35. The problem is also similar to problems of subsidiary products produced for own use such as electricity, construction and wholesaling. As those activities are typically provided by all similar establishments, the non-separation of the secondary products does not significantly bias analytical results. But as those activities are no longer all self-provided, and as the mix changes, the bias can be significant. It is for this reason that some countries have decided to transfer out those activities even though their products are not for sale. However, the rule is not so consistently applied. In the United States and Canadian tables, all construction in manufacturing either for sale or for own use are transferred out, but electricity is transferred out only if it is for sale.

36. The Blue Book discusses three distinct cases of secondary products and suggests the separation of output and the corresponding input with data collected below the level of the establishment (see para. 25 above), but the methods used for allocation, when necessary, are not discussed. When detailed data are not available, SNA suggests the use of either commodity technology or industry technology assumption for separation, without regard to the forms of secondary products. In practice, not many countries approached the problems of secondary products by devising methods specific to each type of secondary product. Some of the most commonly used methods are listed below. A comment on the shortcoming of each method is also provided. In general, there are two types of treatment of secondary products. The first one transfers only output, the second one transfers both input and output. Among the methods used in the second type of treatment, the method of redefinition, which transfers both input and output and requires detailed information of input used in producing secondary products, is the preferred method since no mathematical methods widely used at present are free of distortions for economic analysis. For the improvement of secondary product treatment and the devising of better methods, it is necessary to have overhead and common costs shown separately from costs specific to each activity within the establishment, and similarly to have overhead costs shown separately from costs specific to each establishment within an enterprise.

A. TRANSFER OF OUTPUT ALONE

37. Methods for transferring output only are not based on any economic assumptions. They are mainly used as mechanical devices for balancing flow tables. They create distortions in economic analysis and therefore are not recommended for treating significant secondary products. The Richard Stone method and the ESA method can be used only for by-products.

1. Transfer of secondary product as negative input (Richard Stone method)

38. This is a method of transferring output only and was adopted by Japan and Ireland for treating some special cases of secondary products. By this method, the secondary product is entered as negative input in the industry where it is produced. For example, if industry A produces a value of

TABLE 1. COMMODITY-BY-COMMODITY TABLE: NEGATIVE INPUT[a]

From \ To	A	B	Others	Total
A			90	90
B..........	-10		10	0
Others	100			100
Total........	90	0	100	190

[a] The example is taken from 1975 Input-Output Tables, Administrative Management Agency, the Government of Japan, 1979. A variation of this treatment is used by Ireland, where a positive value of the secondary product is not entered at the intersection of row B and column "others", but at row A and column A, thus leaving the total output value (primary and secondary) of producing sector column total unchanged, which is different from the Japanese method where only output of primary products is registered in the column and row totals. This method is applied only to by-products where no suitable sector exists to which by-products can be transferred.

100 in which 90 is commodity A, and 10 is commodity B, the treatment is as follows (see table 1).

39. Commodity B is entered as negative input in column A so that total input used in A is equal to total primary output of 90. Negative input of commodity B (minus 10) is then balanced by the consumption of B in other sectors. This treatment is appropriate in the case of by-products since it requires no associated input. One possible consequence might be that the output calculated using the Leontief inverse becomes negative when the demand for the primary product A is large and the demand for its secondary product is very small. But economically, it is defensible in the sense that it is a free good that is not fully used. This will not usually happen if there exists a separate industry producing it as a primary product. Another problem with this treatment is that the input structure of industry A is distorted. Consequently, an impact analysis of an economic project producing only commodity A will also be distorted unless commodity B is always equal to a fixed proportion of commodity A, that is, B is a by-product of A.

2. Transfer of secondary product as positive input (usually called simply the transfer method)

40. This is also an output transfer method. By this method, a secondary product is treated as if it were sold by the industry that produced it to the industry to which it is a primary product. This method is still in use in Japan to treat advertisement of newspapers but has been discarded by the United States after the publication of the 1967 Input/Output Table in which all secondary products were treated as if they were by-products.

41. In table 2, industry A sells a value of by-product B equal to 10 to industry B. The same example above is also used to describe the following method.

TABLE 2. COMMODITY-BY-COMMODITY TABLE: POSITIVE INPUT[a]

From \ To	A	B	Others	Total
A		10	90	100
B..........			10	10
Others	100			100
Total........	100	10	100	210

[a] Israel used a variation of this method in which only values of primary products are registered in each column and row total. Instead of entering 10 at the intersection of row B and column "others", -10 is entered at the intersection of row A and column A. In principle, the variation is similar to that of Ireland using the Richard Stone method (see table 1).

42. The same treatment is presented in a different manner in paragraph 3.13 of *Input-Output Tables and Analysis*. By that presentation, output of each sector includes not only its total output, but also the by-products produced elsewhere that are the same as the characteristic products produced by the sector. So, output of industry B contains commodity B produced as a secondary product in industry A, in addition to its own output which is made up of all commodities it produces. This method has many defects. The first one is that the input structure of industry B is distorted by the inclusion of a fictitious purchase. As a consequence, industry B is linked to industry A in such a way that an increase in demand for commodity B will lead to an increase in demand for commodity A, which is not always true. The second defect is that input of A is distorted if the proportion in which commodity B is produced within industry A changes. For example, in the 1967 United States table, printing (industry B) was a secondary product of the metal containers industry (industry A). Thus printing was treated as sold to the printing industry. The printing industry also produced advertising as a secondary product, which was treated as sold to the advertising industry. As a consequence of this treatment, an increase in the demand for advertising led indirectly to an increase in the demand for metal containers.

3. ESA method

43. In 1979 the Statistical Office of the European Communities (EUROSTAT) published recommendations for input-output statistics within the European System of Integrated Economic Accounts.[7] EUROSTAT recommended that secondary products not produced elsewhere be added to the characteristic product and treated as though they were the characteristic products. All other types of secondary products should be treated similarly in the following way.

TABLE 3. ESA TREATMENT OF SECONDARY PRODUCTS

From \ To	A	B	Others	Total uses
A				90
B..................				
Others				+10
Actual output	90+10			
Special row for transfers	-10	+10		
Distributed output for consumption	90	+10		

44. Group A produces both commodities A and B, and group B produces only commodity B. Actual output of A consists of commodity A, which is equal to 90, and commodity B, which is equal to 10. EUROSTAT recommends the creation of a special row treated similarly to a value added row where secondary products of group A, which is equal to 10 (commodity B), can be subtracted and transferred to group B. Thus, the inter-industrial coefficients will be based on the distributed output. This treatment, which is similar to the Richard Stone method, is legitimate only for by-products that are always produced when the primary

commodity is produced and not for subsidiary products or joint products the production scales of which are under the control of producers. EUROSTAT also does not differentiate three types of secondary products, as SNA does. The shortcomings of this treatment are that the input structure of an activity in group A, which has no secondary products, will be distorted. Similarly, input structure of B is also distorted. For example, the input coefficient of sector B is now equal to the input used by B, divided by total output value of sector B, plus 10, the value of secondary product transferred from A. When the table is as detailed as that of the United States (more than 500 sectors), the transfer of secondary products from sector A might reduce the distributed output of A to such an extent that the sum of input coefficients of A is much greater than 1, making the matrix inversion impossible.

45. All the input-output tables that are based on national tables and published by EUROSTAT for member countries follow the ESA recommendations.

B. TRANSFER OF OUTPUT AND INPUT

1. Redefinition

46. The term "redefinition" has been used by a number of countries to denote many different meanings in the treatment of secondary products. However, in the present study it will be used to denote the separation of output and input associated with secondary products so that they can be added to the output and input of the industry in which the secondary output is a primary or characteristic product. The input is either actual input or an input structure based on engineering data or from assuming that the input structure of the secondary commodity or activity is the same as that of a similar commodity or activity produced elsewhere—on which an independent set of input data in pure form is available. This method is the most attractive one in the treatment of secondary products and it is practised by a number of countries, such as Japan, the Netherlands and the United States. However, whenever the input associated with secondary products is not available, other assumptions are used. The first one is the commodity technology assumption and the second one is the industry technology assumption.

2. Commodity technology assumption

47. This transfer technique is based on the assumption that the secondary product or activity has the input structure of the same commodity or activity in the industry where it is produced as a primary product. This implies that its production process is technically separate from that of the characteristic product. While this assumption is similar to the assumption used in the redefinition method, there is no equivalent commodity or activity produced by another establishment as the sole commodity or activity to make possible the identification of its input. In addition, this method is formulated in a totally mechanical manner, so that no independent knowledge of input can be introduced, as was possible in the case of redefinition.

48. The commodity technology assumption requires the preparation of two separate matrices: a make and an absorp-

tion matrix. It also requires that the number of activities must be equal to the number of commodities. The most disappointing result of this convenient and elegant mathematically defined procedure is that very often it results in meaningless negative elements in the input-output coefficient matrix. This result is obtained when the input structure of the secondary product is, in practice, not the same as that of the characteristic product produced elsewhere, and the input which is transferred out is larger than the input that is actually consumed. Another shortcoming lies in the assumption that the number of commodities has to be equal to the number of activities.

3. Industry technology assumption

49. By the industry technology assumption, each industry has the same input requirements for any unit of output of any type. This implies that the input associated with each unit of secondary output can be separated and reclassified to the sector where it is produced as the characteristic product. Obviously, in order to aggregate into one sector the same commodity produced by different techniques of production and to maintain the fixed input coefficients of that commodity for economic analysis, another essential assumption is required, that is, the market share assumption. By this assumption, each industry has a fixed share of commodity market for the commodity it produces. The assumption of fixed market shares is not generally accepted by economists.[8] In addition, this assumption creates a merged matrix which is different from the matrix obtained by directly applying a price transformation on the basis of a new base-year price index, as pointed out by Raa, Chakraborty and Small.[9] The main reason for this is that the costs associated with either primary or secondary products should be the same as input structures for the two types of product, which are assumed to be identical, while the prices of these products are obviously different. In other words, on the cost side, the same commodity produced by different technologies is priced differently owing to differences in costs associated with each technology, while that commodity is valued uniformly by the weighted average of the costs of commodities produced by different technologies. This means that one of the assumptions in input-output, that cost is equal to price, is not satisfied.

4. Aggregation

50. Generally speaking, secondary production becomes a more serious problem when industries are narrowly defined. One method that is usually used to avoid or at least to reduce this problem is to aggregate the industries where these secondary products occur. For example, in the United States make table of 494 sectors, many industries produced a substantial amount of one secondary commodity which amounted to over 40 per cent of its industry output. In a few special cases, secondary products comprised almost 100 per cent of the industry output, such as advertising produced by radio and television broadcasting. When aggregated to the 85 sector level, most of the secondary commodity output was reduced to less than 10 per cent. A number of countries have resorted to this method to either a greater or lesser

extent. Australia and Fiji have deliberately used this technique in addition to other transfer methods such as redefinitions and transfer of output as positive input (in the case of Fiji). It is obvious that aggregation, rather than reducing heterogeneity, will create additional heterogeneity and serious distortion of analytical results when input structures of aggregated products are not similar, or if their market shares are not constant over time and space.

51. To summarize, it can be observed that widely diversified methods are still being used to treat secondary products. During the 1970s over 60 per cent of the countries surveyed still compiled industry-by-industry tables directly by using various methods for the treatment of secondary products. The methods used were not clearly described by many countries. Among the countries that seem to continue their traditional methods of compilation are Japan and the Netherlands. Japan compiled commodity-by-commodity tables even though it also compiled the make matrix; the Netherlands compiled industry-by-industry tables using mainly the redefinition method supplemented by other methods for output transfer only. For example, for some secondary products, Japan records the transfer of secondary products as negative input. Less than 40 per cent of the countries surveyed adopted the SNA recommendation to distinguish explicitly between make and absorption matrices. Most of the countries, namely, Brazil, Canada, Denmark, Finland, India, Sweden, the Union of Soviet Socialist Republics, the United Kingdom of Great Britain and Northern Ireland and the United States of America, used the industry technology assumption to merge the two matrices. Only two countries, the Federal Republic of Germany and Malaysia, relied mainly on the commodity technology assumption. Israel and South Africa used the method of transfer of output as positive input. The United States used that method until the 1967 input-output table. In 1972, the United States adopted the SNA recommendation but transferred some secondary products by redefinition before applying the industry technology assumption to obtain the merged input-output table. A few countries, such as Australia and Papua New Guinea, prepared the make and the absorption matrices but did not use those assumptions for mathematically deriving the merged table; instead, they prepared directly an industry-by-industry matrix either by redefining secondary products and their associated input or by aggregation. Papua New Guinea also did not attempt to reclassify all secondary products, but excluded rental income and own-account production of capital goods.

C.   INTRA-ESTABLISHMENT DELIVERIES

52. Intra-establishment deliveries are also part of the problem of secondary products, where products other than the characteristic product are also produced for own consumption. SNA adopts the convention that deliveries within the same establishment are to be omitted from the input-output framework, while deliveries between establishments should be included. In the context of the SNA definition of an establishment,[1] any production for own consumption within the establishment is omitted, but any sale to another establishment, although within the same enterprise (which is the legal entity that owns these establishments), must be recorded. However, owing to differences in practical definition of an establishment and difficulty in valuating intra-establishment deliveries, this recommendation has created incompatibility between the treatments of intra-establishment deliveries of different countries. For example, when a country adopts a practice whereby intra-sectoral transactions are included in the tables, it is unclear whether this includes intra-establishment deliveries, or only interestablishment deliveries within the same enterprise (a legal entity that might own more than one establishment). Some countries are explicit in their treatments; the Netherlands recorded intra-sectoral transactions by including only interestablishment deliveries within the same sector—as did the United States. Another question is whether intra-establishment deliveries among activity units should be included when an establishment is subdivided into separate activity units in the input-output table, such as construction activity by the railroads. In this case, adopted by the United States, intra-establishment deliveries between construction activity and railroad transportation activity are recorded in the input-output accounts. The input-output table of Japan, which is based on a commodity classification, also included, in principle, own-account production for intermediate consumption. The Federal Republic of Germany recorded intra-establishment as well as interestablishment consumption in the diagonal of the input-output table. But Papua New Guinea did not record any intra-sectoral deliveries, so that even market interestablishment deliveries were eliminated from the input-output accounts.

IV. TREATMENT OF GOVERNMENT EXPENDITURES

53. For the production, consumption and capital formation accounts which serve as the basis for the input-output system, SNA recommends that government activities be separated into two categories. The first category should encompass government establishments and similar units that are mainly engaged in selling the kinds of goods and services which are often produced by business establishments and that cover their costs fully or approximately through sales. It is recommended that those establishments be classified together with similar private establishments.

54. The second category—producers of government services—encompasses other government departments and activities which provide typical government services and also other services similar to private ones the costs of which are usually not covered by proceeds of sales. The latter include, among other things, educational, health and sanitary services. Also included are government activities engaged in providing services of a regulatory character, even though the fees may cover the full costs of operation, such as issuing passports, licences and administering driving tests.

55. Input-output statisticians of many countries do not generally follow the SNA recommendations in their decision to treat some government activities belonging to the second category. A large number treat them either as independent industries or include them with other private industries. For example, electricity produced and sold by the Government is included in the electricity sector, and health services produced by the Government are included in the health sector, regardless of whether they are provided free or not. The reason may be that the criteria for treating a government activity as an industry, whether its cost is fully or almost fully covered by the market prices, are not entirely applicable to input-output analysis. As input-output analysis is based on technical relationships, a government activity may be more usefully aggregated with private industry if they are technically similar and produce similar output.

56. Another SNA recommendation is to include purchases by producers of government services in intermediate rather than in final demand. Many countries do not implement this recommendation and continue to include the purchases in final demand in input-output tables. It seems that the crucial element in deciding to include purchases in intermediate or final demand is whether the government service is used as intermediate input by other sectors or not. For input-output analysis, if the government service is required as intermediate input by other sectors in the intermediate demand matrix, as was the case in the examples given in paragraph 55, then it must be treated as an industry in the intermediate demand matrix. But, if it is not required as intermediate input, then it can be treated either as intermediate demand or as final demand and the resulting input-output analysis will not be affected. However, later on it will be argued that one part of government expenditures should be treated as intermediate demand, and another part should be treated as government final demand when Petre's[10] ideas are to be incorporated.

57. The example below clarifies the differences in the presentation of the producers of government services (the first category) that are not required as input by other sectors in the intermediate demand matrix.

TABLE 4. PRESENTATION OF THE GOVERNMENT SECTOR AS INTERMEDIATE DEMAND

Gross output		Intermediate demand				Final demand
100		40	40	4		16
200		30	20	8		142
40	=	0	0	0	+	40[a]
Value added		30	140	28		
Gross input		100	200	40		

[a] Part of this expenditure can be allocated to non-government expenditure if the government services are sold directly to households.

58. In table 4, which corresponds to the SNA recommendation and is followed by Japan, Singapore, Thailand and other countries, sector 3 is the government sector which does not supply services to any other sector in the intermediate demand matrix. Thus, elements in row 3 of the intermediate demand matrix are all zeros. Total government expenditure is 40. This amount is spent in the intermediate demand on the output of sector 1 (4) and the output of sector 2 (8), and the rest is for paying wages and salaries to government employees (28) (see column 3 of the matrix of intermediate demand).

59. Other countries organize the table in a different manner, so that government expenditure, except wages and salaries, is treated completely as final demand (see table 5).

TABLE 5. PRESENTATION OF THE GOVERNMENT SECTOR AS FINAL DEMAND

Gross output		Intermediate demand				Final demand	
						Government	Non-government
100		40	40	0		4	16
200		30	20	0		8	142
28	=	0	0	0	+	28	0[a]
Value added		30	140	28			
Gross input		100	200	28			

[a] If there are government sales to households, this cell will have a positive value. This may also apply to sales to intermediate consumption.

60. With this new version, gross output of Government is composed of value added only. Total government expenditure is the sum of the government column in final demand. This version is used by Canada, the Netherlands, Sweden, the United Kingdom and the United States (Sweden, however, did not include value added for the government service sector in column 3). In both methods, the coefficients of other sectors will not be affected, and gross domestic product remains the same.

61. One final point that should be added to the country differences is the treatment of sales by Government of goods, such as second-hand goods, scrap materials, receipts of fees, incidental charges for government services, and receipts of rents (fees and charges are treated by SNA as non-commodity indirect taxes if paid by business). Some countries (Canada and the United States) subtract sales from government expenditures in the final demand column to arrive at a net concept of government expenditures in final demand. Other countries treat them as input (or cost) into industrial production activities or consumption of the household sector by creating a separate row in the input-output table. The Netherlands includes them in the intermediate and final demand matrix in the row of government sales of goods and services. The United Kingdom treats them similarly in a primary input row. In both countries, the total value of these sales is entered into the intersection of the row of government sector and the column of government expenditures as a negative value so that the sum of the column of government expenditure is net government expenditures. The indirect effect of the United Kingdom treatment, which records sales by Government as cost of production by other enterprises, is that government production can be generated by economic activities of other sectors. The Netherlands treatment is expected to have the same indirect effect as that of the United Kingdom. There seem to be shortcomings with both the Canada-United States method or the United Kingdom-Netherlands method of treatment of government sales. It is convenient to use the former method for government resales of goods and services, since they have already been counted in the consumption of the buyers in other sectors, and to use the latter method for new sales, fees and charges for government services, rents etc. It might therefore be important to differentiate between government resales of goods and government charges for its services.

62. Even though it is argued above that if producers of government services do not involve sales to intermediate demand then it is immaterial for input-output analysis whether this sector is treated as intermedite demand or final demand, it is still much better from the conceptual point of view (when Petre's ideas are taken into account) to treat producers of government services as intermediate demand. There are two types of government expenditures that should be called producers of government services. In the first type, the consumption of goods and services (as input) varies proportionally to total expenditure. An example of this type is the functioning of executive and legislative organs. Another type currently included by SNA in producers of government services is government consumption of goods and services for the benefit of households, for example, direct government purchases of goods and services that are distributed to households, such as food for the poor or for flood victims or indirect government purchases of goods and services to benefit households through reimbursement when households do not have freedom of choice, such as government medical insurance. This kind of expenditure, according to Petre, should not be treated as intermediate demand; it should be treated as final government consumption for the benefit of households. Applying the same reasoning, capital goods that are of exclusively military use should not be treated as government intermediate consumption as recommended by SNA.

V. TREATMENT OF IMPORTS AND EXPORTS

A. VALUATION

63. According to the SNA recommendations, imports should be valued at the prices of goods at the border of the importing country, which may be termed the port value. This is the c.i.f. value of imports plus protective import duties which aim to put the domestic producer in a competitive position *vis-à-vis* foreign producers. Other duties aimed at raising revenues or discouraging consumption are excluded (see the Blue Book, para. 3.35). The c.i.f. value of imports consists of the value of goods when leaving the exporting country, including freight charges and insurance charges. Exports, according to SNA, should be valued f.o.b. the point of consignment for export, that is, at the same price at which domestic products are valued, excluding freight and insurance charges.

64. Countries generally follow these recommendations, except for the coverage of freight and insurance charges for services provided by domestic shipping and insurance companies, which SNA recommends be treated as exports of transportation and insurance services. Many countries that follow the balance of payments as a basis for estimating exports and imports do not include these services in exports or in imports.

65. For exports, in many cases, when the exporter is not the original producer, f.o.b. value includes domestic trade and transportation margins; these margins should be deducted from export values in order to express exports at producers' prices. The margins are also treated as exports. This was the procedure followed by Canada.

66. In cases where exports are subsidized by the Government, values of exports must also be adjusted to the producers' values, as was done by Israel. Export data include discounts and commissions to agents abroad; these costs should also be deducted.

67. In most countries that utilize the SNA concept of GDP, service exports do not include factor income payments (compensation, interest, dividend, etc.) to and from abroad in the input-output table, which deals only with domestic production. This treatment differs from the treatment in the balance of payments. The United States differs from most countries by creating the rest-of-the-world sector in order to account for output produced outside the United States but accruing to United States residents, and discount output produced in the United States but accruing to foreign residents. The sum of the value added sector in the United States table is gross national product (GNP) instead of GDP. The input into this sector, which is net factor income only, consists of (a) net compensation of employees (compensation paid to United States residents minus compensation paid to foreigners) and (b) net receipts of income on foreign investment (investment income received from abroad minus income paid to foreigners).

68. Personal consumption expenditure (PCE), according to SNA, does not include expenditures at home by foreign travellers, foreign residents working for foreign Governments and international organizations, and by foreign workers. These expenditures are to be classified as exports. Israel explicitly netted out these expenditures, item by item, from PCE and added them to the export column. The United States, however, treated all these expenditures as one balancing item. It created a dummy sector called "rest of the world" and entered these expenditures as one negative item (-3524.4) at the intersection of the PCE column and the rest of the world row. At the same time, it entered the same value as a positive item in the export column (see table 6). Similarly treated are government sales to abroad when these sales could not be readily classified by commodity. Purchases by producers of the United States of factors of production owned by residents of foreign countries are treated as imports.

69. According to the SNA, input-output reflects production within the territory, including foreign production. Within this framework, factor payments (employees' compensation and investment earnings) from abroad to national residents are not counted as payments to some implicit exports of services provided by residents, while factor payments to foreigners working in the countries are considered as domestic output; and not as imports of services. Most countries follow this treatment. The United States, however, adopts the GNP concept, which is equal to GDP plus net factor payments. Its treatment of factor payments is the reverse of that defined by SNA. Net payments from abroad are considered exports of domestic products. Net factor payment (6918.1 in table 6) is entered at the intersection of the

TABLE 6. UNITED STATES PRESENTATION OF THE "REST OF THE WORLD" SECTOR. 1977

	Others	Rest of the world	Personal consumption expenditure	Exports	Imports	Federal Government
Others		0				
Rest of the world	0	0	-3524.4	3524.4	-3521.2	-203.3
				3521.1		
				203.3		
				6918.1		
Value added	GDP	6918.1				

15

value added row and the rest of the world column. It is treated as value added generated by the rest of the world sector. Simultaneously, it is also treated as exports so the same value is recorded as exports by the rest of the world sector.

B. Principles used for export and import classification

70. SNA recommends two principles in recording imports and exports. The first principle is border crossing. According to this principle, goods are included in imports and exports only if they physically cross the border. The second principle is change of ownership, on the basis of which goods that do not pass the border but are sold to foreign entities are still considered as exports. Although SNA overall adopts the ownership principle, it allows the border-crossing principle to operate on merchandise exports and imports so that, item by item, they will correspond with international trade statistics. Only an overall adjustment item is introduced to align the total value of exports or imports of merchandise based on the border-crossing to the change of ownership principle. Certain countries, such as Canada, tried to adjust each value of merchandise trade in conformity with the change of ownership principle; most countries do not.

71. The second principle recommended by SNA is the use of general trade principles in recording foreign trade. By this principle, and in conjunction with the first principle, goods that are physically passing the border are recorded in foreign trade, even if they are only passing through free zones and national customs entrepôts owned by residents, without being processed and without change of ownership. This SNA principle is also not accepted by many countries that rely on the special trade principle, which excludes from foreign trade all re-exports and re-imports.

C. Distinction and classification of competitive and complementary imports

72. Commodities can be divided into two main classes: competitive and complementary. The supply of competitive commodities may come either from domestic production or imports. Complementary commodities do not have domestic substitutes and cannot be produced domestically. They can only come from imports. SNA recommends that a distinction be made between the two classes of commodities so that aggregation of commodity categories would not result in input/output analysis of an assumed link between an increase in the demand of the aggregated commodity and domestic production of complementary commodities.

73. Operationally, imports of complementary commodities are distributed over their users in either one or more than one row of complementary imports. Complementary imports by sectors are relatively easy to identify, for example, coffee beans imported by a coffee products industry and rubber by a rubber products industry, for a few countries such as France, the United Kingdom and the United States, which do not produce them.

74. Competitive imports are by definition perfect substitutes of domestic products. They have been presented by countries in the input-output table in two different ways.

1. Variant A. Imports classified by commodities

75. By this method, the import of a competitive commodity is used to increase total supply of that commodity to the domestic economy. Thus, the commodity is distributed to its users without indicating its source of supply (domestic or foreign). Imports of competitive commodities can be presented in an additional row to the make matrix and as a negative column in the use matrix in final demand columns. Imports of complementary imports are presented in one or more rows showing the total or breakdown by type of goods of complementary imports by each consumption sector. This method presents input as it is technically required. However, it is not suitable to study the impact of a certain level of final demand on imports, as one is forced to assume that each sector will require the same proportion of imports. The advantage, however, is that this method requires no more information than is available in foreign trade statistics. It is also more acceptable for countries with low imports.

2. Variant B. Separate tables for imported and domestic products

76. This method requires the most information. Commodity input in each sector is divided into two parts: one domestically produced part and one imported part. Information can also be arranged into two separate tables: one for domestic input and the other for imported competitive and complementary input. The sum of the two tables is the table of technically required input, which is similar to that of variant A.

77. In this variant, the assumption should not automatically be made that domestic input coefficients and import coefficients are constant. While input-output economics assumes that technical coefficients are constant in the short run, the relative use of either domestic or imported input may change since, even in the short run, it depends on the relative competitiveness of foreign and domestic prices.

78. Up to the time of the present report, more and more countries (a little over 50 per cent of the countries surveyed) have adopted variant B. Such countries include: Australia, Austria, Denmark, Federal Republic of Germany, Israel, Italy, Japan, Kenya, Lebanon, Malaysia, Mexico, Netherlands, Norway, Papua New Guinea, Republic of Korea, Singapore, Sweden, Thailand, United Kingdom, and Yugoslavia. Some of these countries, such as Israel, Japan, the Netherlands and the United Kingdom, have actually collected or at least tried to separate imports from domestic input on the basis of an examination of statistical sources of supply and demand. Others, such as Australia and Denmark, have simply estimated the import matrix by assuming that users draw on domestic and foreign sources in the same proportion ascertained in the total for each commodity. However, Denmark applied this assumption at a 1000 commodity-detailed level before aggregation. The import proportion of each commodity category of an input-output account will not be equal after aggregation. This method is obviously preferred to the application of the assumption after aggregation. Many other countries are, however, unclear in their description of how their import matrices are derived. In any case, it is certain, as described by Israel, that value judgement and assumptions have been extensively used to supplement statistical sources of supply and demand of imports, even in countries that used statistical sources extensively.

VI. TREATMENT OF OTHER SELECTED TRANSACTIONS

A. VALUE ADDED

79. SNA recommends the separation of value added into at least four categories: (*a*) compensation of employees, which includes wages and salaries, and other employers' contributions, such as contributions to social securities, private pension, casualty insurance, life insurance and similar schemes, other payments in kind and other imputed contributions that benefit only employees; (*b*) consumption of fixed capital; (*c*) indirect taxes and subsidies; (*d*) operating surplus, which is estimated residually as the excess of value added over the three other components. By definition, only establishments whose output is valued at market prices can have operating surplus; wherever output is valued at cost, such as producers of government services, operating surplus is zero. Most countries make no distinction between market and non-market value added. Papua New Guinea, however, separated non-market value added from market value added.

B. PRIVATE FINAL CONSUMPTION

80. Private final consumption expenditure includes all consumption expenditure made by households plus some "attributable" consumption paid for by other sectors. These attributions include consumption expenditures indirectly provided through a non-government third party, fully or partially paid by the Government and with the condition that the consumers are free to choose the service and its provider. Goods and services provided directly to households by the Government should be considered government intermediate demand, not private final consumption.

81. Private final consumption excludes expenditures at home by foreign travellers, foreign residents working for foreign Governments and international organizations and expenditures at home by foreign workers. According to SNA, these expenditures should be treated as exports. The United States did not net out these expenditures by selling sectors but by a negative balancing of items in the rest of the world sector (see para. 68 above).

82. To illuminate the discussion of the SNA revision, it is relevant to bring in the criticism of Petre of the present SNA treatment of consumption. Petre objects to the SNA criteria which state that: (*a*) any direct government purchase of goods and services should be treated as intermediate consumption of producers of government services even though the government merely pays for and/or distributes these goods and services to the households, and is not involved in the transformation of intermediate input into different goods and services, for example, government purchase of goods to distribute to the poor or flood victims; (*b*) any indirect government purchase of goods and services for the benefit of households should be treated as intermediate consumption of producers of government services if households do not have the freedom to determine the conditions under which consumption takes place, or treated as private final con-

sumption if households do have the freedom of choice, for example, reimbursement of medical insurance. Both of these cases, according to Petre, should be treated as government final consumption for the benefit of households. In this situation, depending on the objective of analysis, the government final consumption for the benefit of households can be aggregated to the private final consumption to obtain total household consumption.

C. GROSS FIXED CAPITAL FORMATION

83. Gross fixed capital formation consists of outlays on additions to fixed assets reduced by net sales (sales less purchases) of similar second-hand and scrapped goods of industries, producers of government services and of private non-profit services serving households. SNA recommends the separation of private and government fixed capital formation. However, for the government sector, all capital goods that are of exclusively military use are allocated in SNA to government intermediate consumption. Of the goods that have a combined civilian-military use, only construction and improvement of family dwellings are allocated to gross capital formation (see para. 62 above).

84. Work in progress is partly allocated in SNA to gross fixed capital formation and partly to changes in stocks. Included in gross fixed capital formation is work in progress in construction projects such as dwellings, factories and commercial buildings, roads, dams and ports. Included in changes in stocks is work in progress in heavy machinery. Many countries also differ from SNA in this matter by including work in progress in heavy machinery in gross fixed capital formation, while others, particularly EEC countries following the ESA recommendation, exclude from gross fixed capital formation work in progress in civilian construction, as long as no buyer has been found.

85. All expenditures on research and development are included in intermediate consumption. However, exploitation costs for oil and mineral deposits are included in gross fixed capital formation if mineral deposits are found. This latter SNA recommendation was violated by many oil-producing countries, following the practice of oil companies to include only the expenditures in gross fixed capital formation after a decision on oil exploitation is made. This practice is also the ESA recommendation.

86. Another issue that creates wide differences between the SNA recommendations and country practice is whether user or owner principles should be used in the classification of capital. SNA recommends that the owner principle be used. However, as capital tends to be reported with the users, countries predominantly adopted the user principle throughout their classification. Some countries combined both principles in their classification. In Japan, the user criterion is used in most instances, except for leased computer equipment, cars and other goods for business use and personal use which are classified by the owner principle.

D. TREATMENT OF IMPUTED BANK SERVICE CHARGES

87. For most producers, gross output is measured by the amounts explicitly charged to users, but in the case of banks and similar financial intermediaries, there are also service charges that are implicit in the interest paid to depositors and the interest received from borrowers. A depositor may receive less than the "pure" interest as a result of a deduction of an implicit charge for a financial service. Similarly, a borrower may have to pay more than the "pure" interest including an implicit charge for a financial service;* this is different from the treatment of sale and personal finance companies where SNA recommends that interest be treated as transfer and service charges as gross output. Because of difficulty in allocating imputed service charges, SNA treats both interest and imputed service charges as transfer for the economy as a whole. Table 7 shows that imputed service charges do not change the sum of total values added. The imputed bank service charges of domestic banks and other financial institutions are calculated to be equal to the difference between interest received on deposits and interest paid. The imputed service charges are then treated as intermediate consumption of a fictitious financial sector, which has no output and therefore a negative value added has to be added to counterbalance the imputed intermediate consumption. This treatment is aimed at avoiding the difficulty of allocating imputed service charges to specific intermediate and final consumers. By this treatment, the sum total of values added of all sectors is not affected by the introduction of total imputed service charges which are not allocated to either intermediate consumption of various users of bank services or to final demand users.

TABLE 7. SNA METHOD FOR TREATING IMPUTED BANK SERVICE CHARGES

	Others	Bank and financial sector	Fictitious dummy financial sector	Gross output
Bank and financial sector .	b		a	a+b
Gross input (intermediate input + value added).........		b		
Adjustment to value added			a	–a
Adjusted gross input		a+b	0	

88. The recommended treatment can be used only as a device for balancing the flow matrix. The method does not work for analytical purposes, since with the output of the fictitious financial sector equal to zero, input-output coefficients for this sector will be of infinite values. In addition, the SNA method unfortunately eliminates the important linkage between industrial and household activities to the activity of banks and similar financial intermediaries. In order to use input-output tables for analytical purposes, most countries using the SNA method transferred this fictitious sector to final demand (such as Denmark) or to outside the

---

*If i is the pure interest, r_p is the interest paid on loans and S_p is implicit service charge on loans, r_r is the interest received on deposits and S_r is implicit service charge on deposits, then:

$$r_p = i + S_p$$
$$r_r = i - S_r$$
$$\text{then: } S_p + S_r = r_p - r_r$$

intermediate input-output framework (which is analytically similar to transfer to final demand) as is done by France, the the Federal Republic of Germany, Israel, Kenya, Malaysia, Mexico and Norway. The Netherlands treatment before 1982 (see table 8) differed slightly by recording imputed service charges with a minus sign in the value-added section of the banking and financial services column and thus reducing gross bank input and output to the explicit bank service charges only. Since 1982, the Netherlands has adopted the SNA treatment as presented in table 7. Sweden, similarly, aggregated the fictitious dummy financial sector into the bank and financial sector. In this way, the implicit service charge is recorded at the diagonal of the bank and financial sector. The treatments of both the Netherlands and Sweden distort the technical input structure of the financial sector.

89. Some other countries have attempted to resolve the problem in an entirely different manner but more satisfactorily for analytical purposes. They used various methods to distribute imputed service charges, as calculated above, directly to intermediate and final demand sectors. The United States distributed them to different sectors in proportion only to non-interest cash deposits held by those sectors in the banks and financial institutions on the assumption that the largest depositors were the chief beneficiaries of the services for which these imputed charges were payment. Japan distributed service charges to both non-interest cash depositors in proportion to their non-interest cash deposits and to borrowing sectors in proportion to their loans. Imputed service charges "purchased" by non-interest-bearing depositors are taken to be equal to the interest that they should have obtained if they had "ordinary" interest-bearing deposits. The difference between total imputed service charges and charges imputed to non-interest cash deposits is the total imputed service charges to borrowers. Canada carried the imputation further on the basis of both non-interest and interest-bearing deposits, and also loans. The difference between the interest paid to depositors and the "pure" interest (which is higher than the former) is the service charge "purchased" by depositors. Similarly, the interest received by banks from their borrowers is higher than the "pure" interest; the difference should be the imputed service charge on the borrowers. Australia allocated imputed service charges first on the basis of total interest received from three broad institutional categories, then allocated the subtotals to producing units according to their output.

90. Compared to the SNA treatment, the allocation of imputed bank service charges directly to intermediate and final demand would increase gross domestic product to the extent that they are allocated to final demand, and shift gross domestic product from other industries to the banks.

TABLE 8. NETHERLANDS METHOD OF TREATING IMPUTED BANK SERVICE CHARGES BEFORE 1982

	Others	Bank and financial sector	Gross output
Bank and financial sector	b		b
Gross input (intermediate input + value added)		a+b	
Adjustment to value added		–a	
Adjusted gross input............		b	

a: Imputed bank service charges.
b: Explicit bank service charges.

E. Insurance services

91. Output of insurance services includes output of insurance services performed by insurance carriers and those of insurance agents and brokers. As output of insurance agents and brokers has a minor value in most countries, it is often neglected or measured by value added only. Output of insurance services performed by insurance carriers, including casualty insurance, life insurance and pension funds, are measured in SNA by imputing service charges.

92. With respect to casualty insurance, the service charge is equal to the difference between the premiums received and the claims paid. This service charge is to be included in intermediate consumption of producers or in final consumption by households. It is allocated in proportion to the amount of premiums paid.

93. With respect to life insurance, the service charge is equal to the excess between the premiums received over the sum of the claims paid and the net additions to the actuarial reserves, but excluding the interest on these reserves which accrues to policy holders. It is treated as part of final consumption by households. The service charge for pension funds is taken by SNA as equal to the administrative expenses of those funds. They are allocated to various classes of households in proportion to their contribution to the fund.

94. Most countries have adopted SNA methods of measurement for casualty insurance and pension funds; however, many of them have differed from SNA in their methods of measuring output of life insurance. They often approach it from the operating cost side. For the United States, service charges for life insurance are taken as the actual expenses on goods and services of life insurance companies plus an imputed net property income including (a) imputed interest, which is the difference between interest and dividends received and the total of interest paid, (b) dividends paid and profits. Its output does not cover any of the transactions with foreign consumers. Similar to the United States, although slightly different, Australia measured it by the actual expenses of life insurance companies and gross operating surplus. (It is unclear whether gross operating surplus was equated to gross profits, since gross operating surplus as a residual cannot be measured without the knowledge of gross output.)

F. Scrap, used and second-hand goods

95. SNA recommends an additional commodity category for second-hand goods, scraps and wastes represented by a row in the input-output table. These scraps and wastes are not the same as new scraps and wastes which are secondary products of the manufacture of commodities. The output generated in the case of transactions in scrap and second-hand goods is measured by the dealers' margins and other distribution costs (trade and transportation), which are equal to the difference between sellers' net receipts and buyers' full payments. This output will add to the supply of commodities during the period of account. For imported second-hand goods and scrap, the entire c.i.f. value of these goods (that is, purchasers' value excluding dealers' and distribution margins) should be added to the supply of commodities. Most countries have adopted the SNA recommendation; however, there are differences in the incorporation of the net concept in the input-output table.

96. In the United States table, the treatment of output of scrap and second-hand goods does follow the SNA recommendation even though it is included in the trade sector. The value of transactions of scrap and second-hand goods is separated into a trade margin, which includes dealers' margin and other transaction margins, and a producers' value. In the absorption matrix, these producers' values are shown to be purchased as input by intermediate users; however, in the final demand sectors, apart from purchases being entered as positive values, sales mostly from gross capital stock, inventories and imports are entered as negative values; sales from households to households are cancelled out. Net value of this row must be, therefore, equal to the output of scrap and second-hand goods supplied by industries, which is recorded as secondary products in the make matrix. For the derivation of the merged tables, output of scrap and second-hand goods is assumed to be proportional to industry output. Trade margins of scrap and second-hand goods are treated similarly to the traditional trade margins.

97. In the Australian industry-by-industry table, only the value of scrap and second-hand goods, excluding the dealers' margins, is shown to be consumed by industries in the value added quadrant, while sales by final buyers are being recorded as negative entries and purchases as positive entries. As a consequence, the total value of the scrap and second-hand goods is zero. Trade margins for those goods which include dealers' margins and other distribution margins are shown as purchased separately. The input consumed by producers of those margins is treated as input to the trade sector. Japan included only distribution and dealers' margins as part of the trade sector, and did not identify transactions in scrap and second-hand goods.

98. Some countries, such as Spain, have adopted the ESA recommendation and used the gross concept of valuation by creating a sector called recovery sector, which has an output equal to the total value of scrap and second-hand goods (which is recorded in the value added quadrant) and the expenditures on demolition and on the processing and treatment of demolition materials and recovered non-durable goods (which are recorded in the column of the recovery sector). The row of the recovery sector records sales of demolition materials and recovered goods to intermediate users, and net purchases (purchases less sales) to final users such as Government, non-profit institutions and households.

G. Treatment of rent

99. Rent payments by an industry for the use of structures, machinery and equipment are treated differently from rent payments for the use of land, patents, trademarks and copyrights. The former are to be included as intermediate or final consumption and net rent is treated as operating surplus of the owner. In this case, the ownership principle is applied. However, the user principle is applied to rent payments in respect of land and royalties in order to avoid the problem of dealing with the owner's production account. For the latter case, part of the gross land rent, which covers land taxes and maintenance paid by the owner, is recorded in the production account of the user of land as indirect taxes and intermediate consumption respectively, as though the user incurs these costs directly. Operating surplus of the owner is included in value added of the user. This means that the production accounts of the renter and the owner of land are

aggregated into the same input-output sector. Because of these different treatments, rents inclusive of structures and equipment must be separated from rents in respect of land. Where the breakdown is not feasible, at least real estate taxes must be segregated according to the SNA recommendation. This recommendation, however, is not followed by many countries.

100. A special form of rents that needs to be discussed is leasing. There are two types of leases: operating leases and financial leases. Operating leases are generally short term and normally require the owner of the good to be responsible for its repairs and maintenance. Financial leases are generally long-term contracts, whereby the lessee incurs all costs of maintenance and repairs. The lessor or owner of the good acts more like the financier between the lessee and the supplier of the good. The present SNA does not differentiate between the two types of leasing. However, it has been suggested that only operating leases which should be treated as rents; goods under financial leases should be classified as owned by the users.

101. It is recommended that rents be imputed for owner-occupied dwellings, including dwellings owned by private non-profit institutions and family dwellings owned by the Government and dwellings furnished free to employees by employers, which should be valued at the market rent of the same facilities. Market rents may also be approximated by operating, maintenance, repair outlays and other charges, including insurance, taxes, mortgage interests, imputed interest on the owner's equity, and capital consumption. Its gross output and costs are to be included in the real-estate industry.

H. OWN-ACCOUNT (NON-MONETARY) PRODUCTION

102. Own-account activities or subsistence production by households produce goods and services for their own use or for barter without involving any monetary transactions. These activities include all production and processing of primary products for consumption, and all production for fixed capital formation. For example, households not only grow, hunt and fish for their own food, but often repair their own houses, make their own furniture, mill their grains, make their own utensils; groups of individuals also co-operate in building huts, roads, bridges etc. As these activities are a major source of the economic well-being in developing countries and may also contribute considerably to investments in infrastructures, SNA recommends that they be included in the production boundary. However, SNA excludes the service of housewives and other family members, including household maintenance, recreation and schooling.

103. Most developing countries have developed estimates of output and of their corresponding input for these activities and included them in input-output accounts. Almost all of them, such as the Islamic Republic of Iran, Israel, Mexico and Zambia, included own-account estimates of output and of their corresponding input, together with similar output of marketed sectors. Papua New Guinea also aggregated market and non-market production of a commodity into one sector, but at the same time separated gross output into market and non-market components for private final demand and private fixed capital formation. In the input side, it also disaggregated the two components of value added, that is, compensation and operating surplus, into market and non-market components.

VII. STATISTICAL SOURCES

104. The basic information utilized by a majority of countries in constructing their input-output tables included the following: censuses of agriculture, mining, manufacturing, construction, wholesale and retail trade, services, and transportation, and other statistical sources such as annual economic surveys, taxation statistics, employment and income statistics, statistics on government finance and foreign trade, as well as annual reports of various economic sectors such as utilities, telecommunication, financial institutions, and non-profit organizations and special surveys such as surveys of capital formation and surveys of household consumer expenditures. These sources provide estimates of output, wages and salaries, employment, government expenditures, capital formation, and private final consumption.

105. Data on input obtained from the censuses and surveys are almost always collected only for materials consumed in manufacturing industries and sometimes in agriculture. This information is supplemented by special *ad hoc* surveys on services consumed by manufacturing industries, and on materials and services consumed by most of the services sectors for which information is not available from the census sources. The data on services consumed are therefore much less reliable than the data on materials consumed.

106. Data on distribution margins (trade and transportation) are usually estimated by type of commodity and then distributed in proportion to the value of commodity consumed. In some cases, these gross allocations are supplemented by specific data that are collected through special surveys or through expert knowledge.

VIII. METHODS FOR TABLE CONSTRUCTION

107. Broadly speaking, benchmark input-output tables[11] are compiled for the year for which census data on output and input are available, usually at intervals of 5 to 10 years. These benchmark tables might be updated during the interval years by mathematical methods, of which the most prominent is the RAS method, which uses supplementary data on value added for all sectors, more detailed input and output information for some sectors and final demand information, from statistics on annual production, income, employment, taxes, government expenditures, foreign trade etc. In Norway, the Netherlands and Australia no clear-cut benchmark tables are compiled. Those countries gradually, but on an annual basis, update part of their data base. Norway and Denmark seem to go furthest in compiling their annual input-output tables as an integral core of their efforts to compile annual national accounts statistics, and constant price estimates by commodity-flow methods.

108. In the compilation work, control totals are first established for every commodity and economic activity, and for every industrial sector, including the identification of primary and secondary products. Estimates of intermediate demand for goods and services as input and value added are then made. Estimates of value added as residuals can be compared with value added independently estimated. As supplementary data, estimates of intermediate demand of goods and services are also obtained through market surveys of sales of commodities to various users which must be subject to inventory adjustment. In general, many transactions in the use tables are represented by two estimates; one is calculated as input purchased, usually in purchasers' price; and the other is calculated as output based on sales of a given product, usually in producer's prices. These two estimates have to be reconciled through various *ad hoc* methods, including plausibility checks based on industrial experts' advice, reports of trade data and engineering specifications, continuity checks with figures of preceding years or preceding tables, and reliability checks that depend on the survey coverage and the method used in obtaining the estimates. Finally, the tables have to be balanced. Methods for final balancing are more or less arbitrary, either distributing the residuals proportionally to input of a sector or by the RAS method if a previous table is available, or by other more sophisticated methods. Table balancing is still more an art than a science, though based on careful experts' value judgements. For benchmark tables, the values that have to be somewhat arbitrarily balanced are usually small in value.

IX. COMPARISON OF THE SYSTEM OF BALANCES OF THE NATIONAL ECONOMY AND THE SYSTEM OF NATIONAL ACCOUNTS

109. The System of Balances of the National Economy (MPS)[12] is the system developed on the Marxist theory of social production and adopted by the member States of the Council for Mutual Economic Assistance (CMEA). Economic activities are divided into two groups or spheres: the sphere of material production and the non-material sphere. The sphere of material production consists of activities that engage in the production of goods, the final results of which are means of production and consumer goods. It also includes material services—transport, trade, storage and communication services—that are necessary for the production of material goods. Included in the sphere of material production are agriculture, forestry, construction, industry, transport and commmunications serving activities of material production, trade, restaurants, and other branches of material production such as publishing houses, motion picture studios, telegraphic agencies and press agencies. The sphere of non-material production includes all activities that render services to the population in order to satisfy certain personal and collective needs. It includes activities rendering services in housing, hotels, utilities, personal services, education, health, sports, culture, other government services and defence.

110. According to MPS, global product (equivalent to gross output in SNA) and national income are only produced in the material production sphere. The non-material sphere creates neither product nor income, but merely utilizes goods and material services to render non-material services and to redistribute national income to the sectors that do not engage in material production. On the basis of the framework described above, input-output tables in MPS present only activities producing goods and material services and the consumption of those goods and material services in the matrix of intermediate demand. The consumption of goods and material services in the activities rendering non-material services are included in final demand.

111. Also included in final demand are net fixed capital formation, changes in stocks and exports. Included in the quadrant of newly created value (equivalent to the SNA quadrant of value added) are wages and salaries, profits, turnover taxes and other indirect taxes, enterprise contributions to social insurance, other deductions to various types of funds, and other expenditures on non-material services such as bank service charges, insurance premiums, other administrative and business costs. MPS also includes depreciation as cost of production in intermediate demand (for this reason, net instead of gross fixed capital formation is entered in final demand), while SNA treats depreciation as a value added component.

112. The basic difference between MPS and SNA in the input-output framework lies in the treatment of non-material services. SNA includes the activities rendering non-material services in the sphere of production, while MPS considers them unproductive. To show the difference between SNA

and MPS input-output tables, illustrative examples of the two systems are presented in tables 9 and 10 below. Table 9 shows the SNA input-output structure and table 10 presents the MPS input-output structure. These tables abstract from categories such as exports, imports and capital formation. The important differences between MPS and SNA are that (*a*) non-material services consumed as input by sectors of goods and material services in the SNA table, which are equal to 20, are moved down to the newly created value quadrant in the MPS table, and (*b*) the consumption of goods and material services by the non-material sphere, which is equal to 10 in the SNA table, is moved to the final demand quadrant in the MPS table. Gross output and global output for sectors goods and material services are defined similarly in the MPS and SNA tables.

TABLE 9. SNA INPUT-OUTPUT STRUCTURE

	Intermediate demand		
	Goods and material services	Non-material services	Final demand: households
Goods and material services........	50	10	40
Non-material services........	20	30	90
Value added	30	100	
Gross output......	100	140	

TABLE 10. MPS INPUT-OUTPUT STRUCTURE

	Intermediate demand: goods and material services	Final demand	
		Material goods and services by non-material sphere	Households
Goods and material services ...	50	10	40
Newly created value	50		
Global value	100		

113. At present, all input-output tables of CMEA member States published by the Economic Commission for Europe (ECE) are presented in a format similar to table 10. The unit of classification adopted by MPS is the enterprise which is based primarily on units performing the same kind of economic activity. If an enterprise carries on more than one type of economic activity, it might be considered to consist of two or more activities, each belonging to its respective branch if they exist as separate, independent reporting units. Non-material activities in the enterprise are also subject to segregation. Repairs, procurement and marketing serving the productive process of the enterprise are not segregated as separate establishments.

114. Trade and transport margins are treated in the same manner as in SNA. Imports of goods and material services are also similarly treated as in SNA. Competitive imports are either aggregated into or separated from domestic input. Complementary imports are included in the quadrant below the quadrant of intermediate demand. A foreign-trade productive activity is incorporated in the quadrant of intermediate demand, which covers as output foreign trade margins which include expenditures on materials and wages as well as profits and other components of newly created value. The row of the sector contains trade margins which are proportional to the utilization of foreign trade by various activities. This means that, for sectors using imports, import margins must be included separately as cost of production, and export margins are included in the table at the intersection of the export column and the foreign-trade activity row.

NOTES

[1] *A System of National Accounts*, Studies in Methods, Series F, No. 2, Rev.3 (United Nations publication, Sales No. E.69.XVII.3).

[2] *Input-Output Tables and Analysis*, Series F, No. 14, Rev.1 (United Nations publication, Sales No. E.73.XVII.11).

[3] Alfred Franz, *A Survey of the Statistical Units Underlying the Basic Data Used to Compile the National Accounts of OECD Countries*, Meeting of National Accounts Experts, May 1984.

[4] See "Considerations on revising input-output concepts in SNA and ESA", Working Party on National Accounts and Balances, Conference of European Statisticians, Geneva, March 1986 (CES/WP.22/83).

[5] See "Dual sectoring in national accounts", Working Party on National Accounts and Balances, Conference of European Statisticians, Geneva, March 1986 (CES/WP.22/84).

[6] See *Indexes to the International Standard Industrial Classification of All Economic Activities*, Series M, No. 4, Rev.2, Add.1 (United Nations publication, Sales No. E.71.XVII.8).

[7] Statistical Office of the European Communities, *European System of Integrated Economic Accounts (ESA)*, 2nd edition (Luxembourg, 1979).

[8] It is possible to defend the assumption on the basis that, as the market changes, other market shares will be introduced for the compilation of an input-output coefficient table. But this possibility defeats the purpose of input-output since basically it is based on technological relationships, and a study on as complicated a matter as market shares is highly unreliable, time-consuming and must rely on many other economic analyses.

[9] See T. T. Raa, D. Chakraborty, J. A. Small, "An alternative treatment of secondary products in input-output analysis", *The Review of Economics and Statistics*, vol. LXVI, No. 1, February 1984, pp. 88-97.

[10] See Jean Petre, *The Treatment in the National Accounts of Goods and Services for Individual Consumption, Produced, Distributed or Paid for by the Government* (Gouvieux, France, International Association for Research in Income and Wealth, August 1981).

[11] Benchmark tables are still important in the sense that (*a*) they are based on the most complete set of data at more or less the same year and (*b*) they are also based on the year in which economic development of a country is generally normal, that is, without severe business fluctuations; however, the second condition is rarely satisfied by intention.

[12] See *Basic Principles of the System of Balances of the National Economy*, Studies in Methods, Series F, No. 17 (United Nations publication, Sales No. E.71.XVII.10); see also *Comparisons of the System of National Accounts and the System of Balances of the National Economy, Part One, Conceptual Relationships*, Studies in Methods, Series F, No. 20 (United Nations publication, Sales No. E.77.XVII.6).

Part Two

STATISTICAL SOURCES AND COMPILATION METHODS
OF SELECTED COUNTRIES

I. AUSTRALIA

A. General information

The present report is based on *Australian National Accounts and Input-Output Tables 1974-1975* (advance release), *Australian National Accounts and Input-Output Tables 1974-75* (preliminary release), *Australian National Accounts and Input-Output Tables 1978-79,* published by the Australian Bureau of Statistics.

Input-output tables for Australia have been compiled for the years 1958/59, 1962/63, 1968/69, 1974/75, 1977/78 and 1978/79 by the Australian Bureau of Statistics. An annual series of input/output tables started in 1977/78. The 1958/59 tables were experimental. The basic methodology used to compile the 1962/63 and 1968/69 tables was the same for both tables but substantially improved source data were available for the 1968/69 tables. The tables for 1974/75, 1977/78, and 1978/79 were compiled according to a different methodology which involves estimating summary aggregates (industry output, primary input and final demand) and some intermediate input from basic data sources and then estimating the remaining intermediate input using a modified RAS procedure. The new methodology has enabled Australia to compile input-output tables annually and has significantly reduced the time lag between the reference period and publication.

Final published tables were aggregated into 108 sectors. The tables basically become industry-by-industry tables, since information on commodity input was not normally available. Even though the absorption and make matrices were prepared, industry-by-industry tables were compiled by redefining secondary products and aggregation; commodity-technology and industry-technology assumptions were not used to merge the two types of tables.

Input-output tables have not been used systematically in compiling annual estimates of aggregate national income and expenditure, mainly because they have become available well after the national accounts estimates were published. However, they have been used to check past estimates. In the future it is intended to use their results as bench-mark data from which national accounts estimates can be obtained. At present, there are differences between the input-output and national accounts estimates of primary input and final demand. Those differences have generally been mainly due to the use of different statistical sources and classification systems. However, the differences are within acceptable bounds.

The Australian input-output table differs from the SNA recommendations on input-output in *(a)* the treatment of activities of private non-profit institutions, *(b)* the treatment of producers of government services, *(c)* the treatment of imputed bank services, and *(d)* the breakdown of value added.

B. Analytical framework

1. *Tables and derived matrices available*

The following basic tables are compiled:

   (i)   Absorption matrix

   (ii)   Make matrix
   (iii)   Import matrix
   (iv)   Table of reconciliation of transactions valued at basic values and at purchasers' prices
   (v)   Wholesale trade margins
   (vi)   Retail trade margins
   (vii)   Road transport margins
 (viii)   Railway and other transport margins
   (ix)   Water transport margins
   (x)   Air transport margins
   (xi)   Marine insurance margins
   (xii)   Restaurants, hotels and clubs margins
 (xiii)   Commodity taxes less subsidies

On the basis of these tables, the following derived matrices are calculated:

   (i')   Industry-by-industry input-output table
   (ii')   Input coefficients
   (iii')   Inverse matrix
   (iv')   Total requirements of primary input for $100 of final demand
   (v')   Total requirements of primary input for each category of final demand

Since 1968/69, basic tables (i) through (xiii) (except (iv)) are compiled at a level of disaggregation of 108 commodity x 108 industry sectors. One dummy sector, business expenses, is also included in the 1968/69 and 1974/75 tables. In table (iv), gross output of each commodity group in purchasers' values is disaggregated into approximate basic values, commodity taxes and margins. This disaggregation is also presented for total intermediate demand and for each category of final demand.

A special feature of table (i) is that it includes the reconciliation of row and column totals. Since column totals refer to industry output while row totals refer to commodity output, both values differ by the amount of secondary production. Therefore in table (i) two additional columns are presented, one recording the amount of commodities that are primary to the corresponding industry but are produced in other industries, and another recording (with a minus sign) the amount of secondary products produced by the corresponding industry. This reconciliation is only presented in the preliminary publication of the table.

The margin tables [(v) through (xiii)] provide information on margins which supplements that contained in table (iv). They follow the structure of table (i) so that each element in the margin table shows the margin applying to the transaction described in the corresponding position in table (i).

Matrix (i') is derived from basic tables (i), (ii) and (iii) by redefinition and aggregation. Two versions of matrix (i') are calculated, one in which only domestically produced input is recorded in intermediate consumption and final demand (characterized as the table of direct allocation of competitive imports), and another in which competitive imports are distributed together with domestic output (characterized as the table of indirect allocation of competitive imports). Matrices (ii′) and (iii′) are based on matrix (i′). Therefore, two versions of these matrices are also compiled. The meaning of coefficients in matrices (ii′) and (iii′) varies according to the version of (i′) on which they are based. For example, in the inverse matrix based on a direct allocation of competing imports, each coefficient shows the total requirements of domestic production of each industry needed to meet $100 value of final demand for domestic production; in the inverse matrix based on an indirect allocation of competing imports, each coefficient shows the total requirements for domestic production of each industry required to meet $100 of final demand assuming a 0 value of competitive imports.

Since 1968/69, matrices (i′) through (iii′) are compiled at two levels of aggregation of intermediate sectors, namely, 108 x 108 and 28 x 28.

2. *Valuation*

Basic tables (i) and (ii) and derived matrices (i′), (ii′) and (iii′) are valued at approximate basic values, that is, at the value at which commodity flows leave the producers before commodity taxes are charged. Commodity taxes are recorded in a separate row in table (i), (i′) and (ii′) and are charged to the purchasing sector. Commodity taxes include all customs duties levied on imported commodities, as well as excise taxes levied on goods when they are produced domestically. They also include subsidies paid to all producers of services. In table (iv), total intermediate use and final demand categories are also valued at purchaser's prices. Because tables are valued at approximate basic values, margins have only been applied to those commodities that have actually passed through the margin industries. Imports are valued c.i.f. and exports are valued f.o.b.

3. *Statistical units and classification standards*

Commodities are the statistical units used in rows of tables (i), (iii) and (iv) and in the columns of table (ii). The statistical unit adopted for columns of tables (i) and (iii), for rows in table (ii) and for rows and columns of derived matrices (i′), (ii′) and (iii′) is the establishment.

Establishments are generally classified according to the Australian Standard Industrial Classification (ASIC), except in cases where the characteristics of input-output analysis required some redefinition of secondary production. The classification of commodities is an industry-of-origin classification and is based on ASIC. That is, each commodity group includes those commodities that are mainly produced by a given industry, and any establishment producing mainly that type of commodity is allocated to that industry.

The classification of the intermediate consumption quadrant differs from the SNA recommendations in that (*a*) no distinction is made between services provided by private non-profit institutions and those provided by industry, (*b*) output of producers of government services is recorded together with the same kind of services provided by industries and (*c*) the imputed bank service charges are allocated directly to using industries since 1977/78.

The breakdown and definition of value added and final demand follow the SNA recommendations with one exception: consumption of fixed capital is not disaggregated from operating surplus. In addition to the disaggregation of gross fixed capital formation into private and public components, gross fixed capital formation by the government sector is separated into capital formation by public enterprises and that of general government services.

In addition to showing all imports routed directly to users in the imports table, a distinction is made between competing and complementary imports, as recommended in SNA. In practice, all imports for which insufficient information is available to enable them to be classified to an industry-of-origin specific input-output commodity classification item are treated as complementary. Also, since 1977/78, imports that in principle are complementary and that are identified as having a value of less than $10 million at the Australian import commodity classification item level are not treated as complementary. Complementary imports are allocated directly to the using industries. Regarding the allocation of competing imports, two alternative procedures have been followed. In the absorption table and one version of derived matrices (i′), (ii′) and (iii′), competing imports are indirectly allocated; that is, they are classified by commodity and distributed to intermediate and final users together with domestic output. In the other version of matrices (i′), (ii′) and (iii′), competing imports are directly allocated. In the imports table, imports are cross-classified by commodity and industry of destination. Competing imports are allocated to each consuming sector by the same proportion established by the import proportion for the total supply of each commodity. The allocation was carried on at the detailed working matrices of 1,500 commodities and 108 industries.

4. *Treatment and presentation of selected transaction*

In cases where an industry has significant secondary production which has a different pattern of input from the primary activity of the industry, and where it is practicable, the secondary production and the associated input are transferred to the sectors to which they are primary. Transfers are made by redefining the sectors involved. Major redefinitions include: trading activities of mining and manufacturing, which are reallocated to wholesale and retail trade; manufacturing activities of wholesalers and retailers, which are redefined to appropriate manufacturing industries and repair activities of wholesalers and retailers; and the most significant cases of capital formation on own account, which are allocated to the construction or the appropriate manufacturing industry. Separate commodity flows are not recognized for intra-establishment activity such as own-account transport activity of manufacturers. Accordingly, this activity is not recorded as secondary production and subject to redefinition.

Sales of second-hand goods are lumped together in a "sales by final buyers" row. Transactions in second-hand goods are recorded along this row as net transfers to the industry or final demand category, buying them from the final demand category in which the purchase by the current seller was originally recorded. For example, the purchase of a used car by a household from a private enterprise is recorded as a positive entry in the private consumption column and as a negative entry in the private gross fixed capital formation column. At basic values, the row total of "sales by final buyers" has a 0 value: any margins involved in these transactions are recorded as paid by purchasers.

Scrap generated in the production process is excluded from "sales by final buyers" and treated as any other secondary product of the industry producing it.

Waste products having no positive economic value, such as sewage, contaminated water or poisonous gases resulting from manufacturing processes, are not defined as commodities and, as such, are excluded from the output of the industry producing them. Any costs incurred in the disposal or purification of the products are treated as input to the industry incurring the costs.

Non-market production and the corresponding input are recorded in the relevant industrial sector of the table. Non-market production mainly includes: (a) food consumed by farmers which is produced on their own farm; (b) mineral exploration expenditure on non-production leases; (c) imputed rental value of occupied privately owned dwellings; and (d) capital work done for own use, or for rental or for lease.

Since 1974/75, the output of industries is defined gross, that is, it includes intra-sectoral consumption. It also includes own consumption of those secondary products that have not been reallocated.

Output of the financial, trade and transportation sectors is generally defined and distributed as recommended in SNA, except since the 1977/78 table, in which imputed bank service charges are allocated directly to using industries. First, these charges are allocated to the institutional sectors of general government and financial institutions, to the combined sectors of corporate trading enterprises and households, and to the real estate industry on the basis of the proportion of total interest paid by each sector to financial enterprises. The remainder is allocated to the producing units of each relevant sector.

C. Statistical Sources and Compilation Methodology

Intermediate input was estimated by applying the modified RAS method. This methodology involves: (a) estimating from basic data sources the summary aggregates (industry output, primary input and final demand), (b) estimating intermediate input for which basic data are available, (c) extrapolating the remaining intermediate input using the preceding tables in the series, (d) modifying those estimates for which evidence exists suggesting that the extrapolated values can be significantly improved upon by using additional basic data (modifications are applied to individual cells or to complete rows and columns) and (e) re-estimating the unmodified intermediate input by applying the method described in (c) with the additional constraints imposed by the modified estimates. Extrapolation is based on highly disaggregated working matrices including 108 industries and 1,600 commodities.

For the 1974/75 final tables, approximately 28 per cent of all intermediate input (in terms of value) was modified. For the 1977/78 preliminary tables, approximately 18 per cent was modified. For 1978/79, over 20 per cent of the intermediate input (other than the imputed bank service charge) to manufacturing industries was estimated from basic data.

1. Gross output and intermediate consumption

In agriculture, the value of output is the ex-farm or local value, which is estimated by valuing quantities of the various products, the quantities being obtained mainly from the annual agricultural census and the agricultural finance survey. The value of containers, such as bags and cases, has

been added where appropriate to the local value of output, to bring the treatment of rural industries into line with that of manufacturing industries. The output of forestry and logging includes the value of forest products and government and private current expenditure on management of forest resources. The information came partly from the Australian Bureau of Statistics collections and partly from the reports of public authorities. The output of fishing, trapping and hunting is the local value of the relevant products.

Output of the mining, manufacturing, electricity and gas sectors was based on data collected in the relevant economic censuses supplemented by periodic extensions of those censuses to obtain additional details from a small number of additional respondents. The census data include: sales and transfers out of goods of own production, plus change in stocks of finished goods and work-in-progress; margins on merchanted goods; capital work on own account; and other operating income. The following corrections were made on these original estimates: (a) trading activity was redefined to the wholesale trade and retail trade industries as appropriate. In the redefinition, it is assumed that percentage margins earned by the mining, manufacturing, and electricity and gas industries on trade activities were similar to those earned by wholesalers and retailers dealing in similar goods, and that the input structure of trade activities was also similar to that of the wholesale and retail industries; (b) capital work on own account was also transferred to the construction sector, provided that it represented a large amount of output, the activity was primary to another industry, and sufficient information was available on its associated input; and (c) revenue items of a non-operating nature included under "other operating income" were deducted. Data on (b) and (c) were obtained from special inquiries carried out for this purpose.

Non-trading activities of the trade sector were transferred to the sectors to which they are primary on the basis of periodic economic censuses, the 1973/74 retail census and other sources. After separation of non-trading activities, the gross margin on goods sold was estimated in total and by commodity groups. The margin on individual commodities was estimated by references to the results of the periodic economic censuses and surveys of the wholesale and retail trade industries and results of supplementary investigations and by reference to the supply of commodities at basic values and usage at purchasers' prices. Wholesale or retail margins are estimated for about 800 input-output commodities within 78 input-output commodity groups. The estimates of wholesale and retail margins at commodity level are subject to a measure of approximation because the number of individual wholesale and retail commodities distinguished in the censuses and supplementary investigations was necessarily limited and it was difficult to match those commodities with input-output commodities.

Output of the construction industry is based on building statistics, surveys of capital expenditure, and accounts of public authorities. The results of the 1978/79 construction industry survey were also taken into account.

Output of rail, pipeline, air and water transportation was obtained from the reports of the enterprises concerned. The estimate of output of the road transport industry was built up from information on primary input, motor vehicle running costs, miscellaneous other costs, revenue for services provided and data collected in the periodic surveys of motor vehicle usage conducted by the Australian Bureau of Statistics. There was insufficient information on the type of goods

29

carried by each mode of transport and the estimates of transport margin by commodity are approximate.

The communication industry covers in particular Australia Post, Telecom and the Overseas Telecommunications Commission. Estimates of output were based on the published accounts of those bodies, plus unpublished information made available by the enterprises.

Data on the finance and insurance services was made available from the Australian Bureau of Statistics data and the Reserve Bank. For real estate and business services there is little information, and output estimates are built up from the input side by adding together estimates of primary input and use of commodities primary to those industries.

Data on public administration and defence are based on public accounts. They are collected on a cash rather than on an accrual basis and therefore they are not consistent with estimates for other industries.

Estimates on health, education and welfare services are based on public accounts, for the public component of the sector; on estimates of final and intermediate consumption of those services, for the private trading enterprise component of the sector; and on intermediate input, wages, salaries and supplements, and indirect taxes, for producers of private non-profit services to households.

Data on entertainment, restaurants, hotels and clubs and personal services were collected from a wide variety of sources, including the 1968/69, 1973/74 and 1979/80 census data, public accounts, reports of the Australian Broadcasting Control Board, and other published reports.

2. *Value added*

Data on primary input are obtained, whenever possible, from the Australian Bureau of Statistics integrated economic censuses or surveys.

Integrated economic census or survey data on wages, salaries and supplements were substantially complete for the industries covered but several adjustments had to be made as a result of investigations into other expenses of industries, which were found to include certain elements of wages and salaries (e.g., directors' fees, long-service leave etc.). For industries not covered in the economic censuses, the wages estimates were based on payroll tax statistics and other sources used in the national accounts.

Gross operating surplus of industries included in the integrated economic censuses or surveys has been estimated as a residual, after subtracting from the value of output all intermediate input, indirect taxes and wages, salaries and supplements. In the light of investigations into other income and other expenses of industries, adjustments were made to the census and survey figures to exclude elements of non-operating income (such as interest, dividends, profit on sale of assets) and to add back elements of non-operating expenses (such as income tax, bad debts written off).

Good information was available for net customs duties, both in total and by commodity. Comprehensive information is also available for the total value of commodity taxes less subsidies. Other commodity taxes are sometimes levied on easily distinguishable commodities (e.g., excise on beer, sales tax on motor vehicles) and there is no allocation problem. In other cases, it is difficult to relate available commodity statistics to the description of commodities subject to various rates of tax, and the allocation of such taxes to commodities and using sectors is inevitably subject to a degree of approximation.

Good figures of total collections of indirect taxes n.e.c. were available but there was little information on the distribution by industry. Apart from sales tax, the only taxes reported specifically (although in total only) in the integrated economic censuses and surveys were land tax, local government rates and payroll tax. For industries not covered by the censuses and surveys, even this information was not available. Payroll tax was allocated to industries in proportion to wages and salaries. Motor vehicle taxes were first pro-rated between persons and business on the basis of the Motor Vehicle Usage Survey 1971, and the business part was allocated to industries in proportion to motor vehicle running expenses. Other indirect taxes in this group were allocated to industries on various bases. Sometimes the nature of the tax would determine the allocation (e.g., road maintenance tax was allocated entirely to industry road transport). In some other cases information on indirect taxes was obtained in the course of investigating industries' input. The relatively small remainder of indirect taxes n.e.c. was allocated to industries on the basis of the nature of the tax.

3. *Final demand and imports*

Estimates of private final consumption expenditure are based largely on retail sales, supply of consumer goods, output of services, information about revenues of public enterprises and general government, and estimates of the actual and imputed rent of dwellings. Estimates by industry of origin are based partly on the commodity dissection of retail sales provided by retail censuses and partly on the supply of consumer goods.

Estimates of government final consumption expenditure are based on the accounts of public authorities and additional information supplied by those bodies.

Estimates of private gross fixed capital expenditure are based on a variety of sources, including building statistics, a regular Australian Bureau of Statistics survey of private capital expenditure, and taxation statistics. To some extent the total estimate for this category depends on the output of goods and services not absorbed by other final demand categories or intermediate usage, and the classification by commodity relies to a considerable extent on this method. Estimates of public gross fixed capital formation are based on the accounts of public authorities and additional information supplied by those bodies.

The major stock-owning industries are covered by the economic censuses, and information for other industries is available from a regular survey by the Australian Bureau of Statistics of private stockholdings, taxation statistics and public authority accounts. However, those sources do not provide a sufficient dissection of stocks by commodity. The allocation of the increase in book value of stocks to industry of origin was therefore made by inference (but not by automatic apportionment) from the categories of goods sold in the case of wholesalers and retailers and the finished goods of producers, and from the categories of input in the case of materials. Increase in stocks is valued by deducting stock valuation adjustment from the increase in book value of stocks, as in national income and expenditure. Estimates of the stock valuation adjustment by commodity group required similar inferences in relation to the level of stocks, assumptions about valuation practices and reliance on selected information on commodity prices.

Exports are based on foreign trade and balance-of-payments statistics. They include re-exports for which the corresponding import is included in the row of competing imports. The commodity detail provided in foreign trade and balance-of-payments statistics is used to classify exports into commodities. Since 1977/78, the value of exports includes the value of freight supplied by Australian residents carriers on imports.

Imports of goods are based on foreign trade recorded imports adjusted to an input-output cost, insurance and freight (c.i.f.) valuation basis and a balance-of-payments scope, coverage and timing basis. Foreign trade imports recorded on a cost, insurance, freight and exchange (c.i.f.e.) transactions value basis are adjusted to exclude the value of exchange.

AUSTRALIA
INPUT-OUTPUT TABLES
1978-79

Source: *Australian National Accounts and Input-Output Tables 1978-1979*, Australian Bureau of Statistics.

TABLE 4 RECONCILIATION OF FLOWS AT BASIC VALUES AND AT PURCHASERS PRICES BY COMMODITY GROUP 1978-79
INDIRECT ALLOCATION OF COMPETING IMPORTS, RECORDING INTRA-INDUSTRY FLOWS
($ MILLION)

COMMODITY GROUP	INTERMEDIATE USAGE				FINAL CONSUMPTION EXPENDITURE PRIVATE			
	BASIC VALUES	COMMODITY TAXES	MARGIN	PURCHASERS PRICES	BASIC VALUES	COMMODITY TAXES	MARGIN	PURCHASERS PRICES
01.01 SHEEP	636.4	21.9	114.2	772.5	18.2	-	-	18.2
01.02 CEREAL GRAINS	725.6	-24.6	159.1	860.1	16.2	-0.3	4.1	20.0
01.03 MEAT CATTLE	1,933.9	2.3	190.4	2,126.6	28.5	-	-	28.5
01.04 MILK CATTLE AND PIGS	794.1	-.1	50.0	844.1	1.7	-	-	1.7
01.05 POULTRY	217.3	-.1	22.1	239.3	183.3	-8.3	57.1	232.1
01.06 OTHER AGRICULTURE	1,055.1	3.6	132.9	1,191.6	635.6	-9.1	386.1	1,012.5
02.00 SERVICES TO AGRICULTURE	324.1	-.6	-	323.5	7.7	-	-	7.7
03.00 FORESTRY AND LOGGING	228.8	-.6	37.4	265.6	9.8	-.4	7.6	17.0
04.00 FISHING AND HUNTING	156.7	-	25.2	181.9	117.8	-	62.8	180.5
11.01 FERROUS METAL ORES	221.5	-	61.1	282.6	-	-	-	-
11.02 NON-FERROUS METAL ORES	1,132.0	-	115.4	1,247.5	.1	-	-	-
12.00 COAL, OIL AND GAS	2,343.9	1,208.3	190.4	3,742.6	23.0	-1.8	8.6	29.8
14.00 OTHER MINERALS	547.8	-	310.0	857.8	.8	-	.6	1.5
16.00 SERVICES TO MINING NEC	361.4	-	-	361.4	-	-	-	-
21.01 MEAT PRODS	841.7	-	93.8	935.5	2,545.4	-1.4	1,039.5	3,583.5
21.02 MILK PRODS	426.6	17.6	61.4	505.6	1,003.4	22.2	445.3	1,470.9
21.03 FRUIT, VEGETABLE PRODS	94.7	-.4	19.1	113.4	509.3	-1.7	246.5	754.1
21.04 MARGARINE,OILS,FATS NEC	234.6	-	31.5	266.4	232.0	-	70.3	302.4
21.05 FLOUR MILL, CEREAL PRODS	286.3	-	26.0	312.3	198.9	.6	80.3	279.7
21.06 BREAD, CAKES, BISCUITS	73.3	-	8.9	82.3	825.7	-.1	352.1	1,177.7
21.07 CONFECTIONERY ETC PRODS	68.6	-.1	18.4	86.9	310.9	43.7	247.3	601.9
21.08 OTHER FOOD PRODS	739.6	22.6	109.3	871.5	923.8	12.4	355.7	1,291.9
21.09 SOFT DRINKS,CORDIALS ETC	120.7	-	10.9	131.5	353.4	38.5	154.5	546.4
21.10 BEER AND MALT	82.5	-	26.8	109.3	540.4	1,041.8	1,019.4	2,601.7
21.11 OTHER ALCOHOL. BEVERAGES	65.8	28.3	19.4	113.4	331.2	320.9	294.2	946.3
22.01 TOBACCO PRODS	26.5	44.8	5.5	76.8	359.1	724.8	233.6	1,317.6
23.01 COTTON GINNING ETC	163.1	-	34.1	197.2	-	-	-	-
23.02 MAN-MADE FIBRES, ETC	607.7	-.7	154.3	761.4	49.1	-	37.4	86.5
23.03 COTTON FABRICS,ETC	412.9	-	102.1	514.9	252.4	-	188.5	440.9
23.04 WOOL,WORSTED FABRICS ETC	124.5	-	39.4	164.0	62.1	.6	45.8	108.4
23.05 TEXTILE FINISHING	208.5	-.3	79.5	287.6	139.0	-.2	125.0	263.9
23.06 FLOOR COVERINGS ETC	95.1	-	22.9	118.0	227.4	4.0	117.7	349.1
23.07 OTHER TEXTILE PRODS	211.7	-	52.7	264.4	66.3	1.5	37.7	105.5
24.01 KNITTING MILLS	232.1	-	53.3	285.3	356.3	-.1	296.6	652.8
24.02 CLOTHING	266.9	-	23.2	290.1	1,464.6	-.1	1,137.5	2,602.0
24.03 FOOTWEAR	124.8	-	21.4	146.3	353.2	-	327.9	681.1
25.01 SAWMILL PRODS	924.2	-.4	226.1	1,150.7	17.0	-	12.6	29.6
25.02 VENEERS,MFD. WOOD BOARDS	255.3	-.7	85.6	340.1	15.6	-	14.0	29.6
25.03 JOINERY, WOOD PRODS NEC	607.5	2.0	151.9	761.4	73.2	4.3	61.6	139.1
25.04 FURNITURE AND MATTRESSES	170.1	1.8	36.3	208.2	587.6	8.7	404.5	1,000.8
26.01 PULP, PAPER, PAPERBOARD	975.5	1.6	109.7	1,086.8	8.3	8.0	17.3	33.6
26.02 BAGS AND CONTAINERS	616.7	-.4	41.5	658.2	.4	-	.3	.7
26.03 PAPER PRODS NEC	178.6	-	45.7	224.7	59.6	17.8	71.0	148.3
26.04 PUBLISHING, PRINTING	862.3	-4.9	139.9	997.3	350.9	-6.8	453.4	797.5
26.05 PRINTING, STATIONERY ETC	1,138.2	94.4	109.8	1,342.4	86.0	23.6	62.4	172.0
27.01 CHEMICAL FERTILISERS	468.0	-56.8	97.0	508.2	12.0	-	8.8	20.9
27.02 OTHER BASIC CHEMICALS	2,116.3	9.4	250.2	2,375.9	.7	.1	.3	1.2
27.03 PAINTS	342.4	-	44.4	386.8	5.7	-	7.0	12.7
27.04 PHARMACEUTICALS ETC	498.0	3.5	266.6	768.1	230.5	.7	481.6	712.7
27.05 SOAP, OTHER DETERGENTS	113.0	-	11.3	124.2	254.5	25.9	127.8	408.2
27.06 COSMETICS ETC	36.5	-	11.9	48.4	191.4	54.9	225.3	471.6
27.07 OTHER CHEMICAL PRODS	389.8	10.0	71.7	471.5	38.6	14.3	28.9	81.9
27.08 PETROLEUM, COAL PRODS	2,529.2	412.9	887.1	3,829.2	966.4	427.6	500.2	1,894.1
28.01 GLASS AND GLASS PRODS	366.5	6.0	45.7	418.3	41.3	8.0	41.9	91.2
28.02 CLAY PRODS, REFRACTORIES	506.0	-	114.1	620.1	48.2	2.8	60.0	111.0
28.03 CEMENT	239.0	-	65.9	304.9	.9	-	.7	1.5
28.04 READY MIXED CONCRETE	446.9	-	113.3	560.2	-	-	-	-
28.05 CONCRETE PRODS	345.6	-	104.2	449.8	.8	-	.7	1.4
28.06 NON-METALLIC MIN. PRODS	428.1	-	79.7	507.8	5.1	-.1	5.1	10.1
29.01 BASIC IRON AND STEEL	3,351.3	-.1	300.5	3,651.7	3.7	-.1	1.8	5.4
29.02 NON-FERROUS METALS ETC	1,576.2	-1.3	112.2	1,687.1	15.4	-	2.4	17.8

34

	INTERMEDIATE USAGE				FINAL CONSUMPTION EXPENDITURE PRIVATE			
COMMODITY GROUP	BASIC VALUES	COMMODITY TAXES	MARGIN	PURCHASERS PRICES	BASIC VALUES	COMMODITY TAXES	MARGIN	PURCHASERS PRICES
31.01 STRUCTURAL METAL PRODS	1,066.9	-0.1	101.1	1,168.0	30.0	–	6.1	36.1
31.02 SHEET METAL PRODS	929.5	-.1	95.8	1,025.1	52.5	0.6	32.9	86.0
31.03 OTHER METAL PRODS	1,476.6	9.1	184.5	1,670.2	128.2	51.1	136.1	315.4
32.01 MOTOR VEHICLES ETC	2,420.7	92.6	371.6	2,884.9	1,856.8	444.6	841.4	3,142.8
32.02 SHIPS AND BOATS	198.1	-.1	1.9	199.9	53.7	8.0	22.4	84.1
32.03 RAILWAY ROLLINGSTOCK ETC	249.0	–	.1	249.1	14.7	–	.2	14.9
32.04 AIRCRAFT	494.0	–	3.9	498.0	–	–	–	–
33.01 SCIENTIFIC EQUIP. ETC	316.6	13.6	94.0	424.1	287.2	57.5	185.3	529.9
33.02 ELECTRONIC EQUIP.	882.4	8.6	216.0	1,107.0	546.8	158.9	336.2	1,041.9
33.03 HOUSEHOLD APPLIANCES	368.3	3.4	58.0	429.8	667.5	20.2	298.5	986.2
33.04 OTHER ELECTRICAL EQUIP.	1,113.4	5.9	216.9	1,336.3	116.7	5.2	80.2	202.0
33.05 AGRICULTURAL MACHINERY	83.2	–	22.8	106.0	.4	–	.4	.9
33.06 CONSTRUCT. MACHINERY ETC	277.4	–	95.7	373.0	.7	–	.2	.9
33.07 OTHER MACHINERY ETC	1,053.5	-1.6	211.4	1,263.3	76.0	.3	42.9	119.2
34.01 LEATHER PRODS	207.1	–	23.0	230.1	101.6	4.4	96.3	202.3
34.02 RUBBER PRODS	618.6	12.5	222.4	853.5	159.9	54.1	151.1	365.1
34.03 PLASTIC, RELATED PRODS	1,497.6	.8	136.9	1,635.3	198.1	13.6	133.8	345.6
34.04 SIGNS, WRITING EQUIP.	176.0	24.4	32.8	233.2	14.3	10.6	32.7	57.6
34.05 OTHER MANUFACTURING	161.3	–	28.9	190.2	390.6	97.3	315.4	803.4
36.01 ELECTRICITY	2,520.8	23.0	–	2,543.8	987.3	15.7	–	1,003.0
36.02 GAS	173.9	5.4	–	179.4	188.1	5.9	–	194.0
37.01 WATER,SEWERAGE,DRAINAGE	1,108.4	1.5	–	1,110.4	42.7	–	–	42.7
41.01 RESIDENTIAL BUILDING	502.8	–	–	502.8	–	–	–	–
41.02 OTHER CONSTRUCTION	649.3	–	–	649.3	–	–	–	–
47.01 WHOLESALE TRADE	5,352.3	–	-4,994.8	357.5	3,206.0	–	-3,205.1	.8
48.01 RETAIL TRADE	457.8	–	-311.2	146.6	8,257.3	–	-8,120.7	136.7
49.01 MECHANICAL REPAIRS	673.2	–	–	673.2	1,148.0	–	–	1,148.0
49.02 OTHER REPAIRS	413.4	–	–	413.4	269.6	–	–	269.4
51.01 ROAD TRANSPORT	2,497.5	–	-1,971.7	525.8	1,291.6	-10.8	-556.4	724.4
52.01 RAILWAY, OTHER TRANSPORT	1,077.7	.1	-509.1	568.7	305.7	-.4	-82.1	221.2
53.01 WATER TRANSPORT	724.1	.1	-292.1	432.1	146.1	-.1	-47.1	99.0
54.01 AIR TRANSPORT	825.9	–	-53.5	772.4	1,112.3	-.1	-47.6	1,064.6
56.01 COMMUNICATION	1,883.0	–	–	1,883.0	925.0	–	–	925.0
61.01 BANKING	2,129.1	37.1	–	2,166.2	535.2	22.9	–	558.1
61.02 NON-BANK FINANCE	1,988.6	–	–	1,988.6	358.2	–	–	358.2
61.03 INVESTMENT ETC	184.2	–	–	184.2	163.0	–	–	163.0
61.04 INSURANCE ETC	807.8	98.1	-19.3	886.6	900.5	30.4	-8.1	922.7
61.05 OTHER BUSINESS SERVICES	6,139.5	–	–	6,139.5	367.9	-.5	–	367.9
61.06 OWNERSHIP OF DWELLINGS	3.6	–	–	3.6	10,132.5	–	–	10,132.0
71.01 PUBLIC ADMINISTRATION	361.0	–	–	361.0	136.1	–	–	136.1
72.01 DEFENCE	–	–	–	–	–	–	–	–
81.01 HEALTH	61.5	–	–	61.5	2,960.3	–	–	2,960.3
82.01 EDUCATION,LIBRARIES,ETC	142.3	–	–	142.3	400.3	–	–	400.3
83.01 WELFARE ETC SERVICES	381.2	–	–	381.2	728.4	–	–	728.4
91.01 ENTERTAINMENT ETC	837.9	14.3	-3.0	855.2	1,278.6	382.0	10.2	1,670.7
92.01 RESTAURANTS,HOTELS,CLUBS	352.9	–	-11.8	341.1	2,573.9	–	-1,058.1	1,515.8
93.01 PERSONAL SERVICES	128.3	–	–	128.3	749.9	–	–	749.9
T1 INTERMEDIATE USAGE	81,636.8	2,150.0	-98.0	83,688.5	59,025.3	4,148.6	-434.2	62,739.8
P1 WAGES, SALARIES, SUPPS	55,411.7	–	–	55,411.7	–	–	–	–
P2 GROSS, OPERATING SURPLUS	38,628.2	–	–	38,628.2	–	–	–	–
P3 COMMODITY TAXES (NET)	2,150.0	-2,150.0	–	–	4,150.6	-4,150.6	–	–
P4 INDIRECT TAXES NEC (NET)	3,825.8	–	–	3,825.8	–	–	–	–
P5 SALES BY FINAL BUYERS	245.3	–	66.0	311.3	343.9	1.9	434.2	780.0
P6A COMPLEMENTARY IMPORTS CIF	731.3	–	32.0	763.2	567.5	–	–	567.5
P7A DUTY ON P6A	–	–	–	–	–	–	–	–
T2 AUSTRALIAN PRODUCTION	182,629.0	–	–	182,629.0	64,087.3	–	–	64,087.3
P6B+C COMPETING IMPORTS CIF	15,865.4	–	–	15,865.4	–	–	–	–
P7B+C DUTY ON 6B+C	1,133.7	–	–	1,133.7	–	–	–	–
T3 TOTAL USAGE	199,628.1	–	–	199,628.1	64,087.3	–	–	64,087.3

TABLE 4 RECONCILIATION OF FLOWS AT BASIC VALUES AND AT PURCHASERS PRICES BY COMMODITY GROUP 1978-79 - CONTINUED
INDIRECT ALLOCATION OF COMPETING IMPORTS, RECORDING INTRA-INDUSTRY FLOWS
($ MILLION)

COMMODITY GROUP	FINAL CONSUMPTION EXPENDITURE GOVERNMENT				GROSS FIXED CAPITAL EXPENDITURE PRIVATE			
	BASIC VALUES	COMMODITY TAXES	MARGIN	PURCHASERS PRICES	BASIC VALUES	COMMODITY TAXES	MARGIN	PURCHASERS PRICES
01.01 SHEEP	-	-	-	-	-	-	-	-
01.02 CEREAL GRAINS	-	-	-	-	-	-	-	-
01.03 MEAT CATTLE	-	-	-	-	-	-	-	-
01.04 MILK CATTLE AND PIGS	-	-	-	-	-	-	-	-
01.05 POULTRY	-	-	-	-	-	-	-	-
01.06 OTHER AGRICULTURE	83.0	-	-	83.0	-	-	-	-
02.00 SERVICES TO AGRICULTURE	30.7	-	-	30.7	28.5	-	-	28.5
03.00 FORESTRY AND LOGGING	5.7	-	-	5.7	-	-	-	-
04.00 FISHING AND HUNTING	-	-	-	-	-	-	-	-
11.01 FERROUS METAL ORES	-	-	-	-	-	-	-	-
11.02 NON-FERROUS METAL ORES	-	-	-	-	-	-	-	-
12.00 COAL, OIL AND GAS	-	-	-	-	-	-	-	-
14.00 OTHER MINERALS	-	-	-	-	-	-	-	-
16.00 SERVICES TO MINING NEC	23.4	-	-	23.4	-	-	-	-
21.01 MEAT PRODS	-	-	-	-	-	-	-	-
21.02 MILK PRODS	-	-	-	-	-	-	-	-
21.03 FRUIT, VEGETABLE PRODS	-	-	-	-	-	-	-	-
21.04 MARGARINE,OILS,FATS NEC	-	-	-	-	-	-	-	-
21.05 FLOUR MILL, CEREAL PRODS	-	-	-	-	-	-	-	-
21.06 BREAD, CAKES, BISCUITS	-	-	-	-	-	-	-	-
21.07 CONFECTIONERY ETC PRODS	-	-	-	-	-	-	-	-
21.08 OTHER FOOD PRODS	-	-	-	-	-	-	-	-
21.09 SOFT DRINKS,CORDIALS ETC	-	-	-	-	-	-	-	-
21.10 BEER AND MALT	-	-	-	-	-	-	-	-
21.11 OTHER ALCOHOL. BEVERAGES	-	-	-	-	-	-	-	-
22.01 TOBACCO PRODS	-	-	-	-	-	-	-	-
23.01 COTTON GINNING ETC	-	-	-	-	-	-	-	-
23.02 MAN-MADE FIBRES, ETC	-	-	-	-	.1	-	-	.1
23.03 COTTON FABRICS ETC	-	-	-	-	1.0	-	0.3	1.2
23.04 WOOL,WORSTED FABRICS ETC	-	-	-	-	.2	-	.1	.3
23.05 TEXTILE FINISHING	-	-	-	-	-	-	-	-
23.06 FLOOR COVERINGS ETC	-	-	-	-	34.3	-	15.0	49.3
23.07 OTHER TEXTILE PRODS	-	-	-	-	11.6	-	2.6	14.2
24.01 KNITTING MILLS	-	-	-	-	1.2	-	.3	1.5
24.02 CLOTHING	-	-	-	-	7.7	-	1.6	9.3
24.03 FOOTWEAR	-	-	-	-	-	-	-	-
25.01 SAWMILL PRODS	-	-	-	-	1.4	-	.3	1.7
25.02 VENEERS,MFD. WOOD BOARDS	-	-	-	-	-	-	-	-
25.03 JOINERY, WOOD PRODS NEC	-	-	-	-	34.4	-	8.4	42.8
25.04 FURNITURE AND MATTRESSES	-	-	-	-	135.0	-	30.7	165.7
26.01 PULP, PAPER, PAPERBOARD	-	-	-	-	-	-	-	-
26.02 BAGS AND CONTAINERS	-	-	-	-	-	-	-	-
26.03 PAPER PRODS NEC	-	-	-	-	-	-	-	-
26.04 PUBLISHING, PRINTING	-	-	-	-	8.8	-0.2	3.5	12.1
26.05 PRINTING, STATIONERY ETC	-	-	-	-	-	-	-	-
27.01 CHEMICAL FERTILISERS	-	-	-	-	-	-	-	-
27.02 OTHER BASIC CHEMICALS	-	-	-	-	5.5	-	.6	6.1
27.03 PAINTS	35.6	-	-	35.6	-	-	-	-
27.04 PHARMACEUTICALS ETC	-	-	-	-	-	-	-	-
27.05 SOAP, OTHER DETERGENTS	-	-	-	-	-	-	-	-
27.06 COSMETICS ETC	-	-	-	-	-	-	-	-
27.07 OTHER CHEMICAL PRODS	-	-	-	-	-	-	-	-
27.08 PETROLEUM, COAL PRODS	-	-	-	-	-	-	-	-
28.01 GLASS AND GLASS PRODS	-	-	-	-	.1	-	-	.1
28.02 CLAY PRODS, REFRACTORIES	-	-	-	-	2.6	-	.7	3.3
28.03 CEMENT	-	-	-	-	-	-	-	-
28.04 READY MIXED CONCRETE	-	-	-	-	1.6	-	.5	2.1
28.05 CONCRETE PRODS	-	-	-	-	8.6	-	2.4	11.0
28.06 NON-METALLIC MIN. PRODS	-	-	-	-	6.4	-	.6	7.0
29.01 BASIC IRON AND STEEL	-	-	-	-	4.3	-	.6	4.8
29.02 NON-FERROUS METALS ETC	-	-	-	-	-	-	-	-

FINAL CONSUMPTION EXPENDITURE GOVERNMENT · GROSS FIXED CAPITAL EXPENDITURE PRIVATE

COMMODITY GROUP	FINAL CONSUMPTION EXPENDITURE GOVERNMENT				GROSS FIXED CAPITAL EXPENDITURE PRIVATE			
	BASIC VALUES	COMMODITY TAXES	MARGIN	PURCHASERS PRICES	BASIC VALUES	COMMODITY TAXES	MARGIN	PURCHASERS PRICES
31.01 STRUCTURAL METAL PRODS	-	-	-	-	150.6	-	14.5	165.1
31.02 SHEET METAL PRODS	-	-	-	-	227.9	-	27.5	255.4
31.03 OTHER METAL PRODS	-	-	-	-	239.2	-	18.3	257.6
32.01 MOTOR VEHICLES ETC	-	-	-	-	1,472.9	132.5	317.9	1,923.2
32.02 SHIPS AND BOATS	-	-	-	-	50.5	2.3	4.2	56.9
32.03 RAILWAY ROLLINGSTOCK ETC	-	-	-	-	19.1	-	.1	19.1
32.04 AIRCRAFT	-	-	-	-	142.4	-	1.5	144.0
33.01 SCIENTIFIC EQUIP. ETC	-	-	-	-	97.1	15.2	30.1	142.4
33.02 ELECTRONIC EQUIP.	-	-	-	-	45.7	6.5	7.2	59.4
33.03 HOUSEHOLD APPLIANCES	-	-	-	-	174.5	.2	26.2	200.9
33.04 OTHER ELECTRICAL EQUIP.	-	-	-	-	273.3	3.2	46.8	323.2
33.05 AGRICULTURAL MACHINERY	-	-	-	-	423.6	-5.5	121.4	539.5
33.06 CONSTRUCT. MACHINERY ETC	-	-	-	-	477.7	-	173.7	651.5
33.07 OTHER MACHINERY ETC	-	-	-	-	1,685.5	-3.7	329.1	2,010.9
34.01 LEATHER PRODS	-	-	-	-	1.1	-	.2	1.3
34.02 RUBBER PRODS	-	-	-	-	3.8	-	.8	4.6
34.03 PLASTIC, RELATED PRODS	-	-	-	-	30.5	-	2.4	32.9
34.04 SIGNS, WRITING EQUIP.	-	-	-	-	13.0	-	.4	13.3
34.05 OTHER MANUFACTURING	-	-	-	-	3.3	-	.8	4.1
36.01 ELECTRICITY	66.2	-	-	66.2	-	-	-	-
36.02 GAS	-	-	-	-	-	-	-	-
37.01 WATER,SEWERAGE,DRAINAGE	-	-	-	-	-	-	-	-
41.01 RESIDENTIAL BUILDING	-	-	-	-	4,772.0	-	-	4,772.0
41.02 OTHER CONSTRUCTION	-	-	-	-	3,817.2	-1.8	-	3,815.4
47.01 WHOLESALE TRADE	-	-	-	-	732.2	-	-694.2	38.0
48.01 RETAIL TRADE	-	-	-	-	319.7	-	-296.7	23.0
49.01 MECHANICAL REPAIRS	-	-	-	-	45.0	-	-	45.0
49.02 OTHER REPAIRS	-	-	-	-	16.0	-	-	16.0
51.01 ROAD TRANSPORT	142.6	-	-	142.6	122.4	-	-114.4	8.0
52.01 RAILWAY, OTHER TRANSPORT	31.4	-	-	31.4	45.9	-	-41.9	4.0
53.01 WATER TRANSPORT	3.3	-	-	3.3	25.6	-	-25.6	-
54.01 AIR TRANSPORT	87.1	-	-	87.1	21.7	-	-21.7	-
56.01 COMMUNICATION	9.1	-	-	9.1	9.2	-	.8	10.0
61.01 BANKING	-	-	-	-	-	-	-	-
61.02 NON-BANK FINANCE	-	-	-	-	2.0	-	-	2.0
61.03 INVESTMENT ETC	4.0	-	-	4.0	-	-	-	-
61.04 INSURANCE ETC	.4	-	-	.4	2.3	-	-2.3	-
61.05 OTHER BUSINESS SERVICES	-	-	-	-	914.7	-	-	914.7
61.06 OWNERSHIP OF DWELLINGS	68.6	-	-	68.6	-	-	-	-
71.01 PUBLIC ADMINISTRATION	3,615.6	-	-	3,615.6	35.7	-	-	35.7
72.01 DEFENCE	2,532.0	-	-	2,532.0	-	-	-	-
81.01 HEALTH	3,272.3	-	-	3,272.3	-	-	-	-
82.01 EDUCATION,LIBRARIES,ETC	5,061.9	-	-	5,061.9	-	-	-	-
83.01 WELFARE ETC SERVICES	1,781.7	-	-	1,781.7	-	-	-	-
91.01 ENTERTAINMENT ETC	500.2	-	-	500.2	2.2	-	6.0	8.3
92.01 RESTAURANTS,MOTELS,CLUBS	2.9	-	-	2.9	-	-	-	-
93.01 PERSONAL SERVICES	12.2	-	-	12.2	-	-	-	-
T1 INTERMEDIATE USAGE	17,369.5	-	-	17,369.5	16,709.2	149.4	-	16,858.6
P1 WAGES, SALARIES, SUPPS	-	-	-	-	-	-	-	-
P2 GROSS OPERATING SURPLUS	-	-	-	-	-	-	-	-
P3 COMMODITY TAXES (NET)	-	-	-	-	149.4	-149.4	-	-
P4 INDIRECT TAXES NEC (NET)	-4.6	-	-	-4.6	336.7	-	-	336.7
P5 SALES BY FINAL BUYERS	-	-	-	-	-391.8	-	-	-391.8
P6A COMPLEMENTARY IMPORTS CIF	-	-	-	-	-	-	-	-
P7A DUTY ON P6A	-	-	-	-	-	-	-	-
T2 AUSTRALIAN PRODUCTION	17,364.9	-	-	17,364.9	16,803.5	-	-	16,803.5
P6B+C COMPETING IMPORTS CIF	-	-	-	-	-	-	-	-
P7B+C DUTY ON 6B+C	-	-	-	-	-	-	-	-
T3 TOTAL USAGE	17,364.9	-	-	17,364.9	16,803.5	-	-	16,803.5

TABLE 4   RECONCILIATION OF FLOWS AT BASIC VALUES AND AT PURCHASERS PRICES BY COMMODITY GROUP 1978-79 - CONTINUED
INDIRECT ALLOCATION OF COMPETING IMPORTS; RECORDING INTRA-INDUSTRY FLOWS
($ MILLION)

COMMODITY GROUP	GROSS FIXED CAPITAL EXPENDITURE PUBLIC ENTERPRISES				GROSS FIXED CAPITAL EXPENDITURE GENERAL GOVERNMENT			
	BASIC VALUES	COMMODITY TAXES	MARGIN	PURCHASERS PRICES	BASIC VALUES	COMMODITY TAXES	MARGIN	PURCHASERS PRICES
01.01 SHEEP	--	--	--	--	--	--	--	--
01.02 CEREAL GRAINS	--	--	--	--	--	--	--	--
01.03 MEAT CATTLE	--	--	--	--	--	--	--	--
01.04 MILK CATTLE AND PIGS	--	--	--	--	--	--	--	--
01.05 POULTRY	--	--	--	--	--	--	--	--
01.06 OTHER AGRICULTURE	--	--	--	--	--	--	--	--
02.00 SERVICES TO AGRICULTURE	--	--	--	--	--	--	--	--
03.00 FORESTRY AND LOGGING	--	--	--	--	55.2	--	--	55.2
04.00 FISHING AND HUNTING	--	--	--	--	--	--	--	--
11.01 FERROUS METAL ORES	--	--	--	--	--	--	--	--
11.02 NON-FERROUS METAL ORES	--	--	--	--	--	--	--	--
12.00 COAL, OIL AND GAS	--	--	--	--	--	--	--	--
14.00 OTHER MINERALS	--	--	--	--	--	--	--	--
16.00 SERVICES TO MINING NEC	--	--	--	--	--	--	--	--
21.01 MEAT PRODS	--	--	--	--	--	--	--	--
21.02 MILK PRODS	--	--	--	--	--	--	--	--
21.03 FRUIT, VEGETABLE PRODS	--	--	--	--	--	--	--	--
21.04 MARGARINE,OILS,FATS NEC	--	--	--	--	--	--	--	--
21.05 FLOUR MILL, CEREAL PRODS	--	--	--	--	--	--	--	--
21.06 BREAD, CAKES, BISCUITS	--	--	--	--	--	--	--	--
21.07 CONFECTIONERY ETC PRODS	--	--	--	--	--	--	--	--
21.08 OTHER FOOD PRODS	--	--	--	--	--	--	--	--
21.09 SOFT DRINKS,CORDIALS ETC	--	--	--	--	--	--	--	--
21.10 BEER AND MALT	--	--	--	--	--	--	--	--
21.11 OTHER ALCOHOL. BEVERAGES	--	--	--	--	--	--	--	--
22.01 TOBACCO PRODS	--	--	--	--	--	--	--	--
23.01 COTTON GINNING ETC	0.8	--	0.2	1.0	6.6	--	1.7	8.3
23.02 MAN-MADE FIBRES, ETC	1.3	--	.3	1.6	6.4	--	1.7	8.1
23.03 COTTON FABRICS ETC	.5	--	.1	.6	.9	--	.3	1.2
23.04 WOOL,WORSTED FABRICS ETC	--	--	--	--	--	--	--	--
23.05 TEXTILE FINISHING	--	--	--	--	.8	--	.3	1.1
23.06 FLOOR COVERINGS ETC	2.3	--	.3	2.6	8.7	--	1.3	10.0
23.07 OTHER TEXTILE PRODS	.8	--	.2	1.0	1.1	--	.3	1.4
24.01 KNITTING MILLS	--	--	--	--	.3	--	.1	.4
24.02 CLOTHING	.9	--	.2	1.1	.1	--	.1	.1
24.03 FOOTWEAR	--	--	--	--	--	--	--	--
25.01 SAWMILL PRODS	--	--	--	--	--	--	--	--
25.02 VENEERS,MFD. WOOD BOARDS	7.5	--	2.0	9.5	--	--	--	--
25.03 JOINERY, WOOD PRODS NEC	8.2	--	1.9	10.0	--	--	--	--
25.04 FURNITURE AND MATTRESSES	--	--	--	--	36.7	--	8.5	45.2
26.01 PULP, PAPER, PAPERBOARD	--	--	--	--	--	--	--	--
26.02 BAGS AND CONTAINERS	--	--	--	--	--	--	--	--
26.03 PAPER PRODS NEC	--	--	--	--	--	--	--	--
26.04 PUBLISHING, PRINTING	.7	--	.3	1.0	10.6	-0.2	4.0	14.4
26.05 PRINTING, STATIONERY ETC	--	--	--	--	--	--	--	--
27.01 CHEMICAL FERTILISERS	--	--	--	--	--	--	--	--
27.02 OTHER BASIC CHEMICALS	--	--	--	--	--	--	--	--
27.03 PAINTS	--	--	--	--	--	--	--	--
27.04 PHARMACEUTICALS ETC	--	--	--	--	--	--	--	--
27.05 SOAP, OTHER DETERGENTS	--	--	--	--	--	--	--	--
27.06 COSMETICS ETC	--	--	--	--	--	--	--	--
27.07 OTHER CHEMICAL PRODS	--	--	--	--	--	--	--	--
27.08 PETROLEUM, COAL PRODS	--	--	--	--	--	--	--	--
28.01 GLASS AND GLASS PRODS	--	--	--	--	--	--	--	--
28.02 CLAY PRODS, REFRACTORIES	.2	--	--	.2	3.3	--	.6	3.9
28.03 CEMENT	--	--	--	--	--	--	--	--
28.04 READY MIXED CONCRETE	--	--	--	--	--	--	--	--
28.05 CONCRETE PRODS	--	--	--	--	--	--	--	--
28.06 NON-METALLIC MIN. PRODS	--	--	--	--	--	--	--	--
29.01 BASIC IRON AND STEEL	--	--	--	--	--	--	--	--
29.02 NON-FERROUS METALS ETC	--	--	--	--	--	--	--	--

COMMODITY GROUP

	GROSS FIXED CAPITAL EXPENDITURE PUBLIC ENTERPRISES				GROSS FIXED CAPITAL EXPENDITURE GENERAL GOVERNMENT			
	BASIC VALUES	COMMODITY TAXES	MARGIN	PURCHASERS PRICES	BASIC VALUES	COMMODITY TAXES	MARGIN	PURCHASERS PRICES
31.01 STRUCTURAL METAL PRODS	18.9	-	1.8	20.7	12.7	-	2.5	15.2
31.02 SHEET METAL PRODS	2.3	-	.2	2.5	7.2	-	1.6	8.8
31.03 OTHER METAL PRODS	8.3	-	1.1	9.4	52.8	-	1.3	54.1
32.01 MOTOR VEHICLES ETC	101.9	-	4.2	106.1				
32.02 SHIPS AND BOATS	64.8	-7.6	-	57.3	5.1	-0.6	-	4.5
32.03 RAILWAY ROLLINGSTOCK ETC	120.4	-	.4	120.9				
32.04 AIRCRAFT	118.2	-	1.5	119.7	10.8	-	.1	10.9
33.01 SCIENTIFIC EQUIP. ETC	9.1	-	2.9	12.0	33.2	-	10.3	43.5
33.02 ELECTRONIC EQUIP.	110.8	-.1	27.2	137.8	72.2	-.1	23.1	95.2
33.03 HOUSEHOLD APPLIANCES	2.5	-	.4	2.9	4.2	-	.8	5.0
33.04 OTHER ELECTRICAL EQUIP.	141.4	-	25.3	166.8	7.4	-	1.8	9.2
33.05 AGRICULTURAL MACHINERY	1.7	-	.5	2.2	2.6	-	.7	3.3
33.06 CONSTRUCT. MACHINERY ETC	79.8	-	25.5	105.5	18.7	-	8.0	26.7
33.07 OTHER MACHINERY ETC	180.1	-	35.5	215.6	28.7	-	6.1	34.8
34.01 LEATHER PRODS	.1	-	-	.1	.2	-	.1	.3
34.02 RUBBER PRODS	.1	-	-	.1	.5	-	.1	.6
34.03 PLASTIC, RELATED PRODS	.3	-	-	.3				
34.04 SIGNS, WRITING EQUIP.					1.4	-	.6	2.0
34.05 OTHER MANUFACTURING	.1	-	-	.1	3.9	-	1.0	4.9
36.01 ELECTRICITY								
36.02 GAS								
37.01 WATER, SEWERAGE, DRAINAGE								
41.01 RESIDENTIAL BUILDING	280.8	-	-	280.8	9.0	-	-	9.0
41.02 OTHER CONSTRUCTION	2,957.6	-	-	2,957.6	3,385.0	-	-	3,385.0
47.01 WHOLESALE TRADE	106.5	-	-106.5	-	65.4	-	-65.4	-
48.01 RETAIL TRADE	1.6	-	-1.6	-				
49.01 MECHANICAL REPAIRS								
49.02 OTHER REPAIRS								
51.01 ROAD TRANSPORT	13.5	-	-13.5	-	7.7	-	-7.7	-
52.01 RAILWAY, OTHER TRANSPORT	4.2	-	-4.2	-	1.2	-	-1.2	-
53.01 WATER TRANSPORT	2.2	-	-2.2	-	.8	-	-.8	-
54.01 AIR TRANSPORT	3.9	-	-3.9	-	1.6	-	-1.6	-
56.01 COMMUNICATION								
61.01 BANKING								
61.02 NON-BANK FINANCE								
61.03 INVESTMENT ETC								
61.04 INSURANCE ETC	.4	-	-.4	-	.1	-	-.1	-
61.05 OTHER BUSINESS SERVICES	47.9	-	-	47.9				
61.06 OWNERSHIP OF DWELLINGS								
71.01 PUBLIC ADMINISTRATION								
72.01 DEFENCE								
81.01 HEALTH								
82.01 EDUCATION,LIBRARIES,ETC								
83.01 WELFARE ETC SERVICES								
91.01 ENTERTAINMENT ETC								
92.01 RESTAURANTS,HOTELS,CLUBS								
93.01 PERSONAL SERVICES								
T1 INTERMEDIATE USAGE	4,402.6	-7.7	-	4,394.9	3,863.8	-.9	-	3,863.0
P1 WAGES, SALARIES, SUPPS								
P2 GROSS OPERATING SURPLUS (NET)					-.9	-	-	-.9
P3 COMMODITY TAXES (NET)	-7.7	7.7	-	-	-	.9	-	-
P4 INDIRECT TAXES NEC (NET)								
P5 SALES BY FINAL BUYERS	-197.7	-	-	-197.7	-37.1	-	-	-37.1
P6A COMPLEMENTARY IMPORTS CIF								
P7A DUTY ON P6A								
T2 AUSTRALIAN PRODUCTION	4,197.1	-	-	4,197.1	3,825.9	-	-	3,825.9
P6+C COMPETING IMPORTS CIF					-.9			
P7B+C DUTY ON 6B+C								
T3 TOTAL USAGE	4,197.1	-	-	4,197.1	3,825.9	-	-	3,825.9

TABLE 4 RECONCILIATION OF FLOWS AT BASIC VALUES AND AT PURCHASERS PRICES BY COMMODITY GROUP 1978-79 - CONTINUED

INDIRECT ALLOCATION OF COMPETING IMPORTS; RECORDING INTRA-INDUSTRY FLOWS
($ MILLION)

COMMODITY GROUP	INCREASE IN STOCKS				EXPORTS OF GOODS AND SERVICES			
	BASIC VALUES	COMMODITY TAXES	MARGIN	PURCHASERS PRICES	BASIC VALUES	COMMODITY TAXES	MARGIN	PURCHASERS PRICES
01.01 SHEEP	-119.9	-10.0	-10.0	-139.8	1,156.4	88.5	86.6	1,331.5
01.02 CEREAL GRAINS	826.2	-47.9	205.9	984.2	812.2	31.9	204.3	1,048.3
01.03 MEAT CATTLE	2.8	-	.3	3.1	12.0	-	1.2	13.2
01.04 MILK CATTLE AND PIGS	-	-	-	-	.1	-	.1	.2
01.05 POULTRY	-	-	-	-	11.2	-1.4	1.9	11.6
01.06 OTHER AGRICULTURE	66.5	-1.2	15.5	80.9	114.2	2.0	32.0	148.2
02.00 SERVICES TO AGRICULTURE	-1.5	-	-.6	-2.1	1.3	-	.2	1.5
04.00 FORESTRY AND LOGGING	-15.6	-	-3.6	-19.1	94.5	-	17.3	111.9
11.01 FERROUS METAL ORES	-27.0	-	-7.2	-34.3	772.6	-	230.8	1,003.4
11.02 NON-FERROUS METAL ORES	-74.4	-	-8.2	-82.6	526.6	-	68.1	594.7
12.00 COAL, OIL AND GAS	24.2	3.3	4.1	31.6	1,300.0	123.8	262.2	1,686.0
14.00 OTHER MINERALS	-1.9	-	-2.3	-4.1	78.3	-	34.7	113.0
16.00 SERVICES TO MINING NEC	-	-	-	-	-	-	-	-
21.01 MEAT PRODS	-22.1	-	-.1	-22.2	1,964.4	1.6	253.2	2,219.2
21.02 MILK PRODS	-7.3	-.3	.7	-6.9	244.1	-36.2	36.9	244.7
21.03 FRUIT, VEGETABLE PRODS	-9.5	-	1.0	-8.5	53.8	-.2	12.0	65.6
21.04 MARGARINE,OILS,FATS NEC	-2.2	-	.5	-1.7	14.4	-	2.1	16.5
21.05 FLOUR MILL, CEREAL PRODS	-.4	-	.2	-.2	88.5	-	13.3	101.8
21.06 BREAD, CAKES, BISCUITS	6.6	-	.8	7.4	7.3	-	.9	8.2
21.07 CONFECTIONERY ETC PRODS	.6	-	.9	1.5	12.0	.1	3.3	15.3
21.08 OTHER FOOD PRODS	9.3	-	1.7	11.1	533.1	-	81.3	614.5
21.09 SOFT DRINKS,CORDIALS ETC	-3.0	-	.2	-2.8	8.1	-	.7	8.8
21.10 BEER AND MALT	-1.3	-	.4	-.9	42.0	-	13.6	55.6
21.11 OTHER ALCOHOL. BEVERAGES	9.3	-	1.8	11.1	7.0	-	1.5	8.5
22.01 TOBACCO PRODS	1.9	8.8	.6	11.3	231.0	4.3	49.4	284.7
23.01 COTTON GINNING ETC	-3.2	-	-.3	-3.2	5.4	-	1.3	6.7
23.03 MAN-MADE FIBRES, ETC	4.3	-	1.2	5.5	6.5	-	1.5	8.0
23.03 COTTON FABRICS ETC	1.4	-	.4	1.8	2.2	-	.6	2.8
23.04 WOOL,WORSTED FABRICS ETC	.3	-	-	.3	5.2	-	.7	5.9
23.05 TEXTILE FINISHING	4.2	-	.9	5.1	4.9	-	1.3	6.2
23.06 FLOOR COVERINGS ETC	3.8	-	.6	4.4	1.4	-	.3	1.7
23.07 OTHER TEXTILE PRODS	10.8	-	-1.3	9.5	10.4	-	1.9	12.3
24.01 KNITTING MILLS	9.3	-	1.1	10.4	3.2	-	.5	3.7
24.02 CLOTHING	-	-	-	-	-	-	-	-
24.03 FOOTWEAR	-	-	-	-	-	-	-	-
25.01 SAWMILL PRODS	-22.7	.1	-4.9	-27.5	95.9	-	11.5	107.4
25.02 VENEERS,MFD. WOOD BOARDS	-5.2	-	-1.5	-6.7	1.8	-	.6	2.4
25.03 JOINERY, WOOD PRODS NEC	-1.7	-	-.2	-1.9	2.4	-	.6	3.0
25.04 FURNITURE AND MATTRESSES	3.6	-	1.0	4.6	2.0	-	.5	2.5
26.01 PULP, PAPER, PAPERBOARD	4.7	-.1	.9	5.5	18.4	-	2.0	20.4
26.02 BAGS AND CONTAINERS	9.1	-	.4	9.5	1.3	-	-	1.3
26.03 PAPER PRODS NEC	-4.3	-	-1.7	-6.0	4.3	-	1.0	5.3
26.04 PUBLISHING, PRINTING	9.5	-	.7	10.2	21.0	-.3	7.1	27.8
26.05 PRINTING, STATIONERY ETC	-	-	-	5.8	4.0	-	1.1	5.1
27.01 CHEMICAL FERTILISERS	-9.1	-	.8	-8.3	1.9	-	.4	2.3
27.02 OTHER BASIC CHEMICALS	-.5	-	1.8	1.3	113.3	-	14.5	127.8
27.03 PAINTS	1.5	-	.1	1.6	5.1	-	.7	5.8
27.04 PHARMACEUTICALS ETC	5.0	-	3.5	8.5	41.1	-	22.5	63.6
27.05 SOAP, OTHER DETERGENTS	-1.2	-	.2	-1.0	9.6	-	1.0	10.6
27.06 COSMETICS ETC	-2.8	-	-1.1	-3.9	4.2	-	1.3	5.5
27.07 OTHER CHEMICAL PRODS	-.5	-	.2	-.3	19.9	-	3.3	23.2
27.08 PETROLEUM, COAL PRODS	61.2	15.9	24.2	101.2	333.2	26.7	107.8	467.7
28.01 GLASS AND GLASS PRODS	-5.8	-	.9	-4.9	7.6	-	1.3	8.9
28.02 CLAY PRODS, REFRACTORIES	-6.4	-	.4	-6.0	6.0	-	1.4	7.4
28.03 CEMENT	.2	-	.1	.3	2.6	-	.7	3.3
28.04 READY MIXED CONCRETE	.1	-	-	.1	-	-	-	-
28.05 CONCRETE PRODS	3.4	-	1.1	4.5	-	-	-	-
28.06 NON-METALLIC MIN. PRODS	-3.9	-	-	-3.9	16.8	-	4.3	21.1
29.01 BASIC IRON AND STEEL	-78.2	-	3.8	-74.4	535.5	-	50.0	585.5
29.02 NON-FERROUS METALS ETC	-78.4	-.2	5.8	-72.6	1,560.6	-.3	157.8	1,718.1

COMMODITY GROUP

Commodity Group	Stocks Basic Values	Stocks Commodity Taxes	Stocks Margin	Stocks Purchasers Prices	Exports Basic Values	Exports Commodity Taxes	Exports Margin	Exports Purchasers Prices
31.01 STRUCTURAL METAL PRODS	20.3	-	1.1	21.4	13.3	-	1.3	14.6
31.02 SHEET METAL PRODS	17.9	-	2.0	19.9	12.0	-	1.2	13.2
31.03 OTHER METAL PRODS	-9.5	-	-3.3	-12.8	62.6	-	10.0	72.6
32.01 MOTOR VEHICLES ETC	71.1	-	13.0	84.1	130.2	-	8.6	138.8
32.02 SHIPS AND BOATS	-6.3	-0.1	.2	-6.2	35.9	-2.2	.3	34.0
32.03 RAILWAY ROLLINGSTOCK ETC	6.8	-	-	6.8	7.3	-	-	7.3
32.04 AIRCRAFT	.6	-	-	.6	47.1	-	.3	47.4
33.01 SCIENTIFIC EQUIP. ETC	2.4	-	-1.9	.5	69.0	-	20.9	90.0
33.02 ELECTRONIC EQUIP.	9.8	-	5.2	15.0	27.1	-	6.2	33.3
33.03 HOUSEHOLD APPLIANCES	4.9	-	.8	5.7	31.9	-	5.0	36.9
33.04 OTHER ELECTRICAL EQUIP.	32.6	-	4.0	36.5	46.6	-	9.6	56.1
33.05 AGRICULTURAL MACHINERY	-11.5	-	-3.4	-14.9	30.8	-	8.8	39.6
33.06 CONSTRUCT. MACHINERY ETC	-31.0	-	-3.6	-34.6	21.4	-	8.1	29.5
33.07 OTHER MACHINERY ETC	-22.5	-	-4.4	-26.9	110.6	-	22.9	133.6
34.01 LEATHER PRODS	-2.7	-	-	-2.6	45.6	-	4.0	49.6
34.02 RUBBER PRODS	1.8	-	2.8	4.6	5.5	-	1.3	6.8
34.03 PLASTIC, RELATED PRODS	5.2	-	1.3	6.5	41.1	-	3.7	44.8
34.04 SIGNS, WRITING EQUIP.	.6	-	.7	1.2	3.8	-	1.0	4.8
34.05 OTHER MANUFACTURING	-14.9	-	-2.3	-17.1	36.7	-	16.7	53.3
36.01 ELECTRICITY	-	-	-	-	8.8	-	-	8.8
36.02 GAS	-	-	-	-	-	-	-	-
37.01 WATER, SEWERAGE, DRAINAGE	-	-	-	-	2.4	-	-	2.4
41.01 RESIDENTIAL BUILDING	-	-	-	-	-	-	-	-
41.02 OTHER CONSTRUCTION	-	-	-	-	-	-	-	-
47.01 WHOLESALE TRADE	158.2	-	-158.2	-	1,008.3	-	-1,008.3	-
48.01 RETAIL TRADE	-	-	-	-	-	-	-	-
49.01 MECHANICAL REPAIRS	-	-	-	-	-	-	-	-
49.02 OTHER REPAIRS	-	-	-	-	2.5	-	-	2.5
51.01 ROAD TRANSPORT	47.4	-	-47.4	-	312.2	-	-310.9	1.4
52.01 RAILWAY, OTHER TRANSPORT	46.9	-	-46.9	-	391.2	-	-391.2	-
53.01 WATER TRANSPORT	5.1	-	-5.1	-	1,324.0	.4	-240.5	1,083.8
54.01 AIR TRANSPORT	-.6	-	.6	-	530.5	-	-6.1	524.4
56.01 COMMUNICATION	-	-	-	-	47.2	-	-	47.2
61.01 BANKING	-	-	-	-	-	-	-	-
61.02 NON-BANK FINANCE	-	-	-	-	76.8	-	-	76.8
61.03 INVESTMENT ETC	-	-	-	-	43.3	-	-	40.7
61.04 INSURANCE ETC	.4	-	-.4	-	-	2.4	-	-
61.05 OTHER BUSINESS SERVICES	-	-	-	-	61.7	-	-5.0	61.7
61.06 OWNERSHIP OF DWELLINGS	-	-	-	-	-	-	-	-
71.01 PUBLIC ADMINISTRATION	-	-	-	-	-	-	-	-
72.01 DEFENCE	-	-	-	-	-	-	-	-
81.01 HEALTH	-	-	-	-	28.0	-	-	28.0
82.01 EDUCATION,LIBRARIES,ETC	-	-	-	-	-	-	-	-
83.01 WELFARE ETC SERVICES	-	-	-	-	18.6	-	-	18.6
91.01 ENTERTAINMENT ETC	-	-	-	-	36.6	.7	.9	38.2
92.01 RESTAURANTS,HOTELS,CLUBS	-	-	-	-	17.3	-	-	17.3
93.01 PERSONAL SERVICES	-	-	-	-	1.7	-	-	1.7
T1 INTERMEDIATE USAGE	993.7	-31.7	-2.0	959.9	15,626.7	241.4	-19.0	15,849.2
P1 WAGES, SALARIES, SUPPS	-	-	-	-	-	-	-	-
P2 GROSS OPERATING SURPLUS	-	-	-	-	-	-	-15.4	-
P3 COMMODITY TAXES (NET)	-31.7	31.7	-	-	241.4	-241.4	15.4	-
P4 INDIRECT TAXES NEC (NET)	10.1	-	-	10.1	-	-	-	-
P5 SALES BY FINAL BUYERS	19.0	-	2.0	21.1	32.0	-	3.6	35.6
P6A COMPLEMENTARY IMPORTS CIF	-	-	-	-	.1	-	-	.1
P7A DUTY ON P6A	-	-	-	-	-	-	-	-
T2 AUSTRALIAN PRODUCTION	991.1	-	-	991.1	15,900.3	-	-15.4	15,884.8
P6B+C COMPETING IMPORTS CIF	-	-	-	-	815.9	-	15.4	831.4
P7B+C DUTY ON 6B+C	-	-	-	-	-	-	-	-
T3 TOTAL USAGE	991.1	-	-	991.1	16,716.2	-	-	16,716.2

TABLE 4 RECONCILIATION OF FLOWS AT BASIC VALUES AND AT PURCHASERS PRICES BY COMMODITY GROUP 1978-79 - CONTINUED

INDIRECT ALLOCATION OF COMPETING IMPORTS, RECORDING INTRA-INDUSTRY FLOWS

($ MILLION)

COMMODITY GROUP	TOTAL FINAL DEMAND				TOTAL SUPPLY			
	BASIC VALUES	COMMODITY TAXES	MARGIN	PURCHASERS PRICES	BASIC VALUES	COMMODITY TAXES	MARGIN	PURCHASERS PRICES
01.01 SHEEP	1,054.8	78.5	76.6	1,209.9	1,691.2	100.4	190.7	1,982.3
01.02 CEREAL GRAINS	1,654.7	-16.3	414.2	2,052.6	2,380.3	-40.9	573.3	2,912.7
01.03 MEAT CATTLE	43.4	-	1.4	44.8	1,977.3	2.3	191.8	2,171.4
01.04 MILK CATTLE AND PIGS	1.8	-	-	1.8	795.9	-	50.0	845.9
01.05 POULTRY	194.5	-9.8	59.0	243.7	411.8	-9.9	81.1	483.0
01.06 OTHER AGRICULTURE	816.3	-8.2	433.6	1,241.6	1,871.4	-4.6	566.4	2,433.2
02.00 SERVICES TO AGRICULTURE	90.9	-.4	7.3	90.9	414.9	-1.0	44.8	414.9
03.00 FORESTRY AND LOGGING	124.0	-	76.6	130.9	352.8	-.1	101.7	396.5
04.00 FISHING AND HUNTING	202.4	-	223.6	278.9	359.1	-	284.7	460.8
11.01 FERROUS METAL ORES	745.6	-	-	969.1	967.1	-	-	1,251.8
11.02 NON-FERROUS METAL ORES	452.3	-.1	59.9	512.1	1,584.3	-.1	175.4	1,759.6
12.00 COAL, OIL AND GAS	1,347.2	125.3	274.9	1,747.5	3,691.1	1,333.6	465.3	5,490.1
14.00 OTHER MINERALS	77.3	-	33.0	110.3	625.0	-	343.1	968.1
16.00 SERVICES TO MINING NEC	23.4	-	-	23.4	384.8	-	-	384.8
21.01 MEAT PRODS	4,487.8	.2	1,292.6	5,780.6	5,329.4	.2	1,386.4	6,716.1
21.02 MILK PRODS	1,240.2	-14.4	482.9	1,708.7	1,666.8	3.2	544.4	2,214.3
21.03 FRUIT, VEGETABLE PRODS	553.6	-2.0	259.6	811.2	648.3	-2.3	278.7	924.6
21.04 MARGARINE,OILS,FATS NEC	244.3	-.6	72.8	317.1	479.2	-	104.4	583.6
21.05 FLOUR MILL, CEREAL PRODS	287.0	-	93.8	381.4	573.3	.6	119.8	693.7
21.06 BREAD, CAKES, BISCUITS	839.7	-.1	353.8	1,193.3	913.0	-.1	362.7	1,275.6
21.07 CONFECTIONERY ETC PRODS	323.5	43.6	251.5	618.7	392.1	43.5	269.9	705.6
21.08 OTHER FOOD PRODS	1,466.2	12.6	438.7	1,917.5	2,205.8	35.5	548.0	2,789.0
21.09 SOFT DRINKS,CORDIALS ETC	364.5	38.5	155.4	558.4	485.2	38.5	166.2	689.9
21.10 BEER AND MALT	581.1	1,041.8	1,033.4	2,656.4	663.6	1,041.8	1,060.3	2,765.7
21.11 OTHER ALCOHOL. BEVERAGES	347.5	320.9	297.6	966.0	413.3	349.2	317.0	1,079.5
22.01 TOBACCO PRODS	364.7	737.9	234.7	1,337.3	391.2	782.7	240.2	1,414.1
23.01 COTTON GINNING ETC	227.7	-	53.7	281.5	390.8	-	87.9	478.7
23.02 MAN-MADE FIBRES, ETC	62.1	-	41.2	103.3	669.9	-.7	195.5	864.7
23.03 COTTON FABRICS ETC	272.0	-	193.4	465.3	684.8	-	295.4	980.3
23.04 WOOL,WORSTED FABRICS ETC	67.4	.6	47.2	115.1	191.9	.6	86.6	279.1
23.05 TEXTILE FINISHING	140.0	-.2	125.4	265.3	348.5	-1.5	204.9	552.9
23.06 FLOOR COVERINGS ETC	279.3	4.0	135.4	418.7	374.4	4.0	158.3	536.7
23.07 OTHER TEXTILE PRODS	88.9	1.5	42.9	133.3	300.6	1.5	95.6	397.7
24.01 KNITTING MILLS	363.0	-.1	297.9	660.8	395.1	-.1	351.2	946.2
24.02 CLOTHING	1,494.4	-	1,139.9	2,634.3	1,761.3	-	1,163.1	2,924.4
24.03 FOOTWEAR	367.1	.1	329.8	696.9	491.9	-	351.3	843.2
25.01 SAWMILL PRODS	90.1	-.1	19.3	109.5	1,014.3	.5	245.5	1,260.3
25.02 VENEERS,MFD. WOOD BOARDS	12.2	-.3	13.2	25.4	267.4	-.8	98.8	365.5
25.03 JOINERY, WOOD PRODS NEC	116.4	4.3	72.5	193.2	723.9	6.4	224.4	954.6
25.04 FURNITURE AND MATTRESSES	773.1	8.7	447.0	1,228.8	943.2	10.5	483.1	1,437.0
26.01 PULP, PAPER, PAPERBOARD	31.4	7.9	20.1	59.4	1,007.0	9.5	129.8	1,146.3
26.02 BAGS AND CONTAINERS	16.7	.7	.7	11.5	627.4	-	42.2	669.6
26.03 PAPER PRODS NEC	39.5	17.8	70.4	147.7	238.1	18.2	116.0	372.4
26.04 PUBLISHING, PRINTING	397.5	-7.5	468.6	858.5	1,259.8	-12.5	608.5	1,855.8
26.05 PRINTING, STATIONERY ETC	99.5	23.6	64.2	187.4	1,237.8	118.0	174.0	1,529.7
27.01 CHEMICAL FERTILISERS	4.8	.1	10.0	14.8	472.7	-56.8	107.0	523.3
27.02 OTHER BASIC CHEMICALS	119.1	.1	17.3	136.5	2,235.4	9.5	267.1	2,512.4
27.04 PAINTS	16.9	.7	7.8	24.7	359.4	-	52.1	411.5
27.05 PHARMACEUTICALS ETC	312.1	.7	507.6	820.3	810.1	4.1	774.2	1,588.4
27.05 SOAP, OTHER DETERGENTS	262.9	25.9	129.0	417.8	375.9	25.9	140.3	542.0
27.06 COSMETICS ETC	192.8	54.9	225.6	473.3	229.3	54.9	237.5	521.7
27.07 OTHER CHEMICAL PRODS	58.0	14.4	32.2	104.6	447.8	24.4	119.9	576.1
27.08 PETROLEUM, COAL PRODS	1,360.9	470.1	632.2	2,463.1	3,890.0	883.0	1,519.3	6,292.3
28.01 GLASS AND GLASS PRODS	46.7	8.0	44.6	95.3	413.2	14.1	90.4	517.6
28.02 CLAY PRODS, REFRACTORIES	50.4	2.8	62.5	115.7	556.3	2.8	176.6	735.8
28.03 CEMENT	3.6	-	1.5	5.1	242.6	-	67.4	310.0
28.04 READY MIXED CONCRETE	.1	-	-	.1	447.0	-	113.3	560.3
28.05 CONCRETE PRODS	6.2	-	2.4	8.6	351.8	-	106.7	458.4
28.06 NON-METALLIC MIN. PRODS	26.6	-.1	11.7	38.3	454.7	-.1	91.4	546.0
29.01 BASIC IRON AND STEEL	544.8	-.1	56.3	600.9	3,896.0	-.2	356.8	4,252.6
29.02 NON-FERROUS METALS ETC	1,302.1	-.5	166.7	1,668.2	3,078.3	-1.9	278.8	3,355.3

COMMODITY GROUP

COMMODITY GROUP	TOTAL FINAL DEMAND				TOTAL SUPPLY			
	BASIC VALUES	COMMODITY TAXES	MARGIN	PURCHASERS PRICES	BASIC VALUES	COMMODITY TAXES	MARGIN	PURCHASERS PRICES
31.01 STRUCTURAL METAL PRODS	233.1	-	24.8	257.9	1,300.1	-0.1	125.9	1,425.9
31.02 SHEET METAL PRODS	325.4	0.6	66.3	392.2	1,254.8	0.5	162.0	1,417.3
31.03 OTHER METAL PRODS	436.1	51.1	163.7	650.9	1,912.7	60.2	348.2	2,321.2
32.01 MOTOR VEHICLES ETC	3,685.6	577.1	1,186.4	5,449.1	6,106.3	669.7	1,557.9	8,333.9
32.02 SHIPS AND BOATS	203.9	-.3	27.1	230.6	401.9	-.4	29.0	430.5
32.03 RAILWAY ROLLINGSTOCK ETC	153.6	-	.5	154.2	402.7	-	.6	403.4
32.04 AIRCRAFT	333.8	-	3.6	337.4	827.8	-	7.6	835.4
33.01 SCIENTIFIC EQUIP. ETC	497.9	72.6	247.7	818.3	814.5	86.2	341.6	1,242.4
33.02 ELECTRONIC EQUIP.	812.4	165.2	405.1	1,382.7	1,694.8	173.8	621.1	2,489.7
33.03 HOUSEHOLD APPLIANCES	885.6	20.4	331.5	1,237.6	1,253.9	23.8	389.6	1,667.3
33.04 OTHER ELECTRICAL EQUIP.	617.9	8.4	167.6	793.9	1,731.3	14.4	384.5	2,130.2
33.05 AGRICULTURAL MACHINERY	447.6	-5.5	128.3	570.5	530.8	-5.5	151.2	676.5
33.06 CONSTRUCT. MACHINERY ETC	567.4	-3.4	212.1	779.4	844.8	-5.0	307.7	1,152.5
33.07 OTHER MACHINERY ETC	2,058.5		432.1	2,487.2	3,112.0	-5.0	643.5	3,750.5
34.01 LEATHER PRODS	146.0	4.4	100.5	251.0	353.1	4.4	123.5	481.1
34.02 RUBBER PRODS	171.6	54.1	156.1	381.8	790.2	66.6	378.6	1,235.3
34.03 PLASTIC, RELATED PRODS	275.2	13.6	141.2	430.1	1,772.8	14.4	278.2	2,065.4
34.04 SIGNS, WRITING EQUIP.	33.1	10.6	35.3	79.0	209.1	35.0	68.1	312.1
34.05 OTHER MANUFACTURING	419.7	97.3	331.7	848.7	581.0	97.3	360.6	1,038.9
36.01 ELECTRICITY	996.1	15.7	-	1,011.8	3,516.9	38.7	-	3,555.6
36.02 GAS	188.1	5.9	-	194.0	362.0	11.4	-	373.4
37.01 WATER,SEWERAGE,DRAINAGE	111.3	-	-	111.3	1,219.9	1.5	-	1,221.4
41.01 RESIDENTIAL BUILDING	5,061.9	-	-	5,061.9	5,564.6	-	-	5,564.6
41.02 OTHER CONSTRUCTION	10,159.8	-1.8	-	10,158.0	10,809.1	-1.8	-	10,807.3
47.01 WHOLESALE TRADE	5,276.6	-	-5,237.8	38.8	10,629.0	-	-10,232.6	396.4
48.01 RETAIL TRADE	8,578.7	-	-8,419.0	159.7	9,036.5	-	-8,730.2	306.3
49.01 MECHANICAL REPAIRS	1,193.0	-	-	1,193.0	1,866.2	-	-	1,866.2
49.02 OTHER REPAIRS	287.9	-	-	287.9	701.4	-	-	701.4
51.01 ROAD TRANSPORT	1,937.4	-10.8	-1,050.3	876.3	4,435.0	-10.8	-3,022.1	1,402.1
52.01 RAILWAY, OTHER TRANSPORT	826.6	-.4	-567.6	258.6	1,904.3	-.3	-1,076.7	827.3
53.01 WATER TRANSPORT	1,507.1	-.4	-321.3	1,186.1	2,231.2	.5	-613.5	1,618.2
54.01 AIR TRANSPORT	1,756.6	-.1	-80.4	1,676.1	2,582.6	-.2	-133.9	2,448.5
56.01 COMMUNICATION	981.2	-	-	981.2	2,864.2	-	-	2,864.2
61.01 BANKING	544.5	23.6	-	568.1	2,673.6	60.7	-	2,734.3
61.02 NON-BANK FINANCE	360.2	-	-	360.2	2,348.8	-	-	2,348.8
61.03 INVESTMENT ETC	243.8	-	-	243.8	428.1	-	-	428.1
61.04 INSURANCE ETC	947.3	32.8	-16.3	963.8	1,755.3	130.8	-35.8	1,850.4
61.05 OTHER BUSINESS SERVICES	1,460.8	-.5	-	1,460.8	7,600.3	-.5	-	7,600.3
61.06 OWNERSHIP OF DWELLINGS	10,132.5	-	-	10,132.0	10,136.1	-	-	10,135.6
71.01 PUBLIC ADMINISTRATION	3,787.4	-	-	3,787.4	4,148.4	-	-	4,148.4
72.01 DEFENCE	2,560.0	-	-	2,560.0	2,560.0	-	-	2,560.0
81.01 HEALTH	6,232.6	-	-	6,232.6	6,294.0	-	-	6,294.0
82.01 EDUCATION,LIBRARIES,ETC	5,462.3	-	-	5,462.3	5,604.6	-	-	5,604.6
83.01 WELFARE ETC SERVICES	2,528.6	-	-	2,528.6	2,909.7	-	-	2,909.7
91.01 ENTERTAINMENT ETC	1,817.6	382.7	17.1	2,217.3	2,655.5	397.0	20.0	3,072.5
92.01 RESTAURANTS,HOTELS,CLUBS	2,594.1	-	-1,058.1	1,536.0	2,947.0	-	-1,069.9	1,877.1
93.01 PERSONAL SERVICES	763.9	-	-	763.9	892.2	-	-	892.2
T1 INTERMEDIATE USAGE	117,991.0	4,499.1	-455.3	122,034.8	199,628.1	6,649.1	-553.3	205,723.9
P1 WAGES, SALARIES, SUPPS	-	-	-	-	55,411.7	-	-	55,411.7
P2 GROSS OPERATING SURPLUS	-	-	-	-	38,628.2	-	-	38,628.2
P3 COMMODITY TAXES (NET)	4,501.1	-4,501.1	-	-	6,651.0	-6,651.0	-	-
P4 INDIRECT TAXES NEC (NET)	336.7	-	-	336.7	4,162.5	-	-	4,162.5
P5 SALES BY FINAL BUYERS	-245.3	1.9	437.8	194.4	-	1.9	503.8	505.7
P6A COMPLEMENTARY IMPORTS CIF	586.7	-	2.1	588.7	1,317.9	-	34.0	1,351.9
P7A DUTY ON P6A	-	-	-	-	-	-	-	-
T2 AUSTRALIAN PRODUCTION	123,170.1	-	-15.4	123,154.7	305,799.4	-	-15.4	305,783.9
P6B+C COMPETING IMPORTS CIF	815.9	-	15.4	831.4	16,681.4	-	15.4	16,696.8
P7B+C DUTY ON 6B-C	-	-	-	-	1,133.7	-	-	1,133.7
T3 TOTAL USAGE	123,986.0	-	-	123,986.0	323,614.1	-	-	323,614.1

TABLE 11. INDUSTRY BY INDUSTRY FLOW MATRIX 1978-79

DIRECT ALLOCATION OF COMPETING IMPORTS, BASIC VALUES, RECORDING INTRA-INDUSTRY FLOWS, 28 INDUSTRIES
($ MILLION)

	USAGE	1	2	3	4	5	6	7	8	9
SUPPLY										
1	AGRICULTURE	678.4	3.7	0.3	3,341.5	1,023.5	170.5	295.5	0.1	2.1
2	FORESTRY,FISHING,HUNTING	15.5	6.9	18.0	17.1	124.5	.1	.1	.1	125.5
3	MINING	1.6	1.0	637.1	4.3	6.5	1.1	1.2	–	.7
4	MEAT AND MILK PRODS	47.3	4.3	2.8	893.1	145.8	1.4	.3	.9	.9
5	OTHER FOOD PRODS	312.5	22.1	9.5	83.2	693.5	89.1	2.0	.4	1.4
6	BEVERAGES, TOBACCO PRODS	5.2	.2	17.1	11.7	6.8	125.2	.8	.6	2.1
7	TEXTILES	10.4	3.9	2.7	4.9	9.9	5.3	364.9	282.5	55.2
8	CLOTHING AND FOOTWEAR	1.7	1.9	1.6	7.1	1.8	.6	7.6	318.0	1.2
9	WOOD,WOOD PRODS ETC	5.0	4.1	11.0	2.8	.8	3.2	.4	2.4	466.9
10	PAPER,PRINTING ETC	45.5	1.0	13.6	88.7	81.7	81.4	9.7	13.0	25.8
11	CHEMICALS	432.4	4.5	53.7	24.5	31.8	12.3	49.7	16.0	55.3
12	PETROLEUM AND COAL PRODS	184.4	36.4	91.6	18.1	19.5	7.4	4.7	3.4	15.1
13	NON-METALLIC MIN. PRODS	.5	3.0	-9.1	32.0	14.5	69.4	.1	.1	13.0
14	BASIC METALS AND PRODS	5.2	.8	56.6	2.3	9.1	2.0	4.0	.6	58.4
15	FABRICATED METAL PRODS	5.4	4.2	40.4	60.0	164.2	181.9	.8	1.4	26.5
16	TRANSPORT EQUIP.	4.7	9.7	11.2	3.4	1.2	.7	.3	.2	1.3
17	OTHER MACHINERY ETC	35.4	14.2	129.1	4.6	4.5	1.9	1.1	.4	4.6
18	MISCELL. MANUFACTURING	7.7	11.7	32.9	99.4	92.9	43.8	6.3	112.0	49.5
19	ELECTRICITY, GAS, WATER	142.2	2.3	158.0	64.7	49.1	32.0	25.8	10.8	28.9
20	CONSTRUCTION	18.4	4.9	30.3	13.2	8.3	3.9	2.4	1.2	5.1
21	WHOLESALE, RETAIL TRADE	229.3	35.8	128.4	296.3	236.4	115.0	189.3	179.9	169.3
22	REPAIRS	115.5	22.4	45.6	21.9	15.1	5.1	.9	.6	6.7
23	TRANSPORT, COMMUNICATION	229.6	18.0	208.7	360.0	204.5	67.2	54.9	45.7	116.9
24	FINANCE, PROPERTY ETC	197.8	25.2	384.0	219.4	139.4	66.2	36.8	37.5	94.5
25	OWNERSHIP OF DWELLINGS	.3	.1	.2	.1	.2	.1	.2	.1	.1
26	PUBLIC ADMIN., DEFENCE	11.6	.8	3.7	20.9	8.4	3.6	2.5	1.3	5.5
27	COMMUNITY SERVICES	82.9	1.4	30.9	14.0	8.4	5.1	2.7	1.9	3.5
28	RECREATION. ETC SERVICES	14.9	.8	17.9	23.3	73.6	31.3	4.6	12.3	11.0
T1	INTERMEDIATE USAGE	2,841.3	245.1	2,146.0	5,732.8	3,175.9	1,126.9	1,069.3	1,043.1	1,347.1
P1	WAGES, SALARIES, SUPPS	855.8	195.9	1,332.7	860.1	862.8	323.6	369.1	673.1	692.0
P2	GROSS OPERATING SURPLUS	5,357.7	173.0	2,495.9	231.1	420.8	273.5	134.0	166.3	331.6
P3	COMMODITY TAXES (NET)	5.0	8.8	49.6	21.6	-4.3	42.5	23.0	1.4	6.4
P4	INDIRECT TAXES (NET)	174.3	19.0	72.2	52.3	45.6	22.5	17.2	28.2	31.1
P5	SALES BY FINAL BUYERS	–	–	1.0	–	–	–	1.6	–	–
P6A	COMPLEMENT. IMPORTS CIF	.3	.3	4.1	12.0	127.4	3.5	3.1	4.3	5.0
P7A	DUTY ON P6A	–	–	–	–	–	–	–	–	–
P6B+C	COMPETING IMPORTS CIF	162.1	40.0	257.3	82.4	184.3	79.7	335.4	281.1	195.9
P7B+C	DUTY ON P6B+C	4.7	3.7	13.8	4.9	5.8	13.4	18.4	28.6	13.3
T2	AUSTRALIAN PRODUCTION	9,401.3	685.8	6,372.6	6,997.4	4,818.3	1,855.7	1,971.1	2,226.1	2,622.5

	10	11	12	13	14	15	16	17	18	19	20
1	0.2	0.7	–	–	0.2	0.1	0.2	0.2	11.5	0.2	0.8
2	26.8	2.2	–	0.5	.3	.1	.2	.2	.2	1.3	21.3
3	7.7	25.7	656.3	226.8	1,415.8	2.0	1.6	6.0	46.9	373.3	168.0
4	1.6	35.8	.1	.7	.9	.8	1.7	1.4	42.1	.8	6.2
5	6.4	50.7	.2	2.2	13.4	1.9	4.0	3.4	2.2	2.6	9.0
6	3.3	4.3	.2	1.9	2.7	2.9	8.9	4.4	1.5	3.4	14.3
7	7.5	1.6	.3	2.0	8.2	14.8	22.7	8.8	100.7	.4	22.2
8	2.7	.9	–	.8	.8	1.6	2.5	2.4	1.3	1.8	23.8
9	2.8	6.2	.2	1.4	5.0	17.4	18.8	42.9	5.2	2.6	875.4
10	723.4	74.9	1.0	31.9	8.5	31.5	36.6	69.3	32.1	8.2	24.1
11	84.5	736.2	31.5	44.9	68.3	55.5	53.4	88.0	323.2	16.9	182.7
12	20.8	56.6	174.1	30.5	120.3	14.2	5.9	16.3	10.9	84.8	171.7
13	.6	30.9	–	190.1	55.8	12.6	13.2	15.5	6.0	8.4	1,523.4
14	10.3	59.4	2.1	40.2	1,418.7	1,242.0	297.1	662.2	26.4	9.2	429.0
15	6.0	46.5	.1	7.3	40.4	326.0	176.2	187.0	26.1	37.5	1,380.8
16	1.3	1.7	.3	21.2	2.8	8.2	1,021.5	13.7	.8	1.5	14.7
17	16.5	6.3	.5	7.1	18.9	35.5	71.6	457.8	4.5	27.1	897.7
18	40.2	101.7	.9	5.6	11.0	34.0	110.6	115.6	255.4	5.8	223.5
19	41.0	86.2	10.3	88.2	204.7	38.8	33.0	44.4	35.7	1,004.5	56.3
20	9.0	9.1	.5	8.3	3.0	5.6	5.3	7.3	5.8	24.2	11.8
21	129.8	199.3	66.8	63.3	188.7	133.9	142.5	320.1	145.1	57.9	830.9
22	6.4	5.6	.1	6.5	3.1	6.2	3.3	12.0	2.2	6.6	57.0
23	134.1	150.2	45.0	225.9	320.1	104.3	113.8	147.7	78.6	118.2	611.8
24	177.0	136.5	21.3	89.8	97.4	130.4	188.1	194.8	81.7	322.2	587.0
25	.2	.2	–	.2	.1	.1	.1	.2	.2	.1	.1
26	7.9	6.4	.7	4.5	7.7	7.2	11.9	9.4	3.4	9.7	38.2
27	6.5	5.6	1.0	5.7	5.3	4.8	7.4	9.8	3.0	5.2	17.5
28	31.2	91.3	1.1	10.5	6.3	15.9	20.9	37.0	12.9	12.0	21.8
T1	1,505.4	1,935.0	1,014.9	1,118.2	4,028.5	2,248.0	2,373.1	2,477.6	1,265.4	2,146.3	8,221.9
P1	1,125.6	697.9	98.4	558.2	1,218.6	1,102.4	1,491.5	1,704.6	667.2	1,281.3	4,626.9
P2	488.5	448.0	92.6	305.2	721.9	433.1	286.5	458.2	261.8	1,548.6	2,259.7
P3	26.3	21.1	1,184.7	4.2	18.4	7.9	9.2	17.3	10.6	-10.6	36.2
P4	55.3	40.0	9.5	33.2	46.1	44.9	56.0	57.9	31.2	78.5	240.7
P5	8.5	–	–	1.1	211.4	6.1	3.9	4.0	.2	–	.4
P6A	6.7	97.4	8.5	3.8	12.1	6.6	9.1	11.5	48.8	3.7	30.1
P7A	–	–	–	–	–	–	–	–	–	–	–
P6B+C	502.5	511.1	869.1	161.5	276.2	203.0	900.0	756.8	282.1	92.8	854.1
P7B+C	18.9	9.8	.3	3.4	8.5	13.7	73.3	51.6	19.7	3.2	66.8
T2	3,737.7	3,760.2	3,278.0	2,188.8	6,541.7	4,065.8	5,202.5	5,539.5	2,587.0	5,143.7	16,336.7

TABLE 11. INDUSTRY BY INDUSTRY FLOW MATRIX 1978-79

DIRECT ALLOCATION OF COMPETING IMPORTS, BASIC VALUES, RECORDING INTRA-INDUSTRY FLOWS, 28 INDUSTRIES
($ MILLION)

	USAGE	21	22	23	24	25	26	27	28
	SUPPLY								
1	AGRICULTURE	1.0	0.2	1.6	2.3	-	6.7	8.9	30.8
2	FORESTRY,FISHING,HUNTING	.3	.1	6.8	1.2	-	.1	1.0	.2
3	MINING	20.7	-	44.6	3.0	1.0	8.9	12.1	9.7
4	MEAT AND MILK PRODS	14.1	.7	4.6	14.3	-	1.9	24.0	14.3
5	OTHER FOOD PRODS	21.4	1.4	10.5	17.5	2.1	5.6	41.8	17.1
6	BEVERAGES, TOBACCO PRODS	22.3	2.5	12.7	13.7	-	7.1	18.5	6.8
7	TEXTILES	12.6	1.1	57.3	3.1	.5	8.6	31.4	37.4
8	CLOTHING AND FOOTWEAR	11.2	3.7	21.1	7.0	.2	18.1	73.2	8.0
9	WOOD,WOOD PRODS ETC	53.4	.2	16.1	4.0	38.4	36.9	79.8	15.3
10	PAPER,PRINTING ETC	912.8	7.6	178.1	241.1	3.5	186.9	188.4	141.4
11	CHEMICALS	20.8	5.3	24.4	57.2	72.2	32.9	217.3	53.6
12	PETROLEUM AND COAL PRODS	133.1	7.4	624.7	35.9	4.6	· 26.0	60.3	34.4
13	NON-METALLIC MIN. PRODS	35.1	3.2	4.7	3.5	27.3	4.0	12.2	10.5
14	BASIC METALS AND PRODS	10.3	.9	8.0	3.6	56.9	19.6	8.4	3.2
15	FABRICATED METAL PRODS	112.6	11.3	40.6	17.1	67.1	50.0	60.1	42.7
16	TRANSPORT EQUIP.	58.8	232.9	653.3	2.1	.5	111.8	9.8	5.4
17	OTHER MACHINERY ETC	51.2	67.1	85.3	32.2	27.0	90.7	87.4	86.0
18	MISCELL. MANUFACTURING	210.3	14.0	166.5	15.9	10.6	49.6	78.0	32.8
19	ELECTRICITY, GAS, WATER	141.1	35.8	117.3	267.4	531.7	155.4	220.6	198.4
20	CONSTRUCTION	107.7	.8	171.4	48.7	502.5	133.6	94.9	19.6
21	WHOLESALE, RETAIL TRADE	376.3	197.5	661.8	208.2	45.0	137.0	396.7	176.2
22	REPAIRS	322.8	1.5	269.3	50.3	.4	19.7	41.5	29.4
23	TRANSPORT, COMMUNICATION	804.1	48.8	683.2	512.8	16.9	316.4	395.9	181.0
24	FINANCE, PROPERTY ETC	1,916.1	77.5	570.4	1,410.1	1,258.3	632.8	1,001.6	370.6
25	OWNERSHIP OF DWELLINGS	-	.1	.2	.2	-	-	.1	.1
26	PUBLIC ADMIN., DEFENCE	47.1	6.5	49.6	26.4	1.7	8.6	47.2	10.3
27	COMMUNITY SERVICES	66.8	3.3	29.2	89.5	.8	54.7	96.6	33.9
28	RECREATION. ETC SERVICES	173.2	2.5	62.2	190.3	.1	49.3	69.9	249.5
T1	INTERMEDIATE USAGE	5,657.3	733.9	4,575.2	3,278.5	2,669.3	2,172.9	3,377.4	1,818.2
P1	WAGES, SALARIES, SUPPS	7,815.4	944.0	4,891.9	4,821.7	-	3,807.8	9,869.0	2,524.3
P2	GROSS OPERATING SURPLUS	5,554.1	535.5	1,872.4	4,943.1	6,544.2	-	1,014.2	1,276.6
P3	COMMODITY TAXES (NET)	139.1	53.2	315.8	56.9	53.6	-.1	55.7	26.5
P4	INDIRECT TAXES NEC (NET)	553.2	43.0	303.9	624.9	787.5	33.1	85.3	239.0
P5	SALES BY FINAL BUYERS	-	-	-	-	-	-	3.1	4.0
P6A	COMPLEMENT. IMPORTS CIF	46.0	3.1	9.5	31.2	-	221.2	9.6	12.3
P7A	DUTY ON P6A	-	-	-	-	-	-	-	-
P6B+C	COMPETING IMPORTS CIF	326.5	204.6	832.5	192.0	72.1	479.6	414.6	272.3
P7B+C	DUTY ON P6B+C	16.3	12.1	26.6	6.5	5.3	-	12.3	15.2
T2	AUSTRALIAN PRODUCTION	20,108.0	2,529.5	12,827.8	13,954.9	10,132.0	6,714.5	14,841.2	6,188.5

		T4 INTERM USAGE	Q1 FINAL CONS EXPEND PVTE	Q2 GOVT	Q3 GROSS FIXED CAPITAL EXPEND PVTE	Q4 PUB ENT	Q5 GEN GOVT	Q6 INCR IN STOCKS	Q7 EXPORTS	T5(Q1-Q7) FINAL DEMAND	T6 TOTAL SUPPLY
	1	5,581.2	854.7	82.7	-	-	-	776.2	2,106.4	3,820.0	9,401.3
	2	370.5	116.1	35.5	28.5	-	55.2	-15.9	95.8	315.3	685.8
	3	3,683.6	26.9	23.4	10.7	26.3	5.7	-81.6	2,677.5	2,689.0	6,372.6
	4	1,262.8	3,547.3	.2	6.0	2.4	1.6	-28.7	2,205.3	5,734.5	6,997.3
	5	1,427.2	2,650.7	1.0	13.3	3.0	.7	10.2	712.3	3,391.1	4,818.3
	6	301.3	1,478.1	-	4.2	.9	.2	9.4	61.5	1,554.3	1,855.7
	7	1,080.7	577.9	-	33.8	4.0	14.2	4.4	256.1	890.4	1,971.1
	8	522.7	1,658.7	.1	8.3	.8	.3	19.8	15.2	1,703.3	2,226.0
	9	1,718.5	607.5	1.0	159.1	15.9	35.4	-18.0	103.2	904.0	2,622.5
	10	3,261.9	354.7	.4	27.8	8.1	7.7	23.3	53.9	475.9	3,737.8
	11	2,849.1	673.4	32.9	8.7	2.7	.6	-12.2	205.2	911.2	3,760.2
	12	2,012.9	895.5	-	.8	1.2	.2	47.6	319.5	1,265.1	3,278.0
	13	2,098.9	40.8	.2	20.5	2.2	3.8	-12.2	34.4	89.9	2,188.8
	14	4,446.4	19.0	-	70.9	13.2	9.3	-99.9	2,082.8	2,095.3	6,541.7
	15	3,120.1	171.5	.4	568.6	44.9	20.9	34.1	105.3	945.7	4,065.8
	16	2,194.8	1,341.8	.1	1,126.4	208.1	42.1	69.2	219.9	3,007.7	5,202.5
	17	2,266.1	983.7	.2	1,668.9	237.9	55.8	-1.2	328.0	3,273.3	5,539.4
	18	1,938.4	465.9	.2	47.2	1.4	4.1	-2.9	132.7	648.6	2,587.0
	19	3,824.7	1,237.6	66.1	-	-	.1	-	15.2	1,319.0	5,143.7
	20	1,256.6	13.7	2.5	8,518.6	3,178.8	3,366.8	-.1	.2	15,080.5	16,337.1
	21	6,056.5	11,627.1	8.2	1,060.5	108.3	66.0	158.6	1,022.7	14,051.4	20,107.9
	22	1,077.7	1,388.7	-	60.6	-	-	-	2.5	1,451.8	2,529.5
	23	6,314.5	3,318.0	248.6	214.5	23.9	11.2	98.9	2,598.0	6,513.2	12,827.7
	24	10,464.9	2,289.9	66.1	916.7	44.2	.1	.4	172.7	3,490.1	13,955.0
	25	3.6	10,128.4	-	-	-	-	-	-	10,128.4	10,132.0
	26	362.9	141.2	6,147.2	35.7	-	-	-	28.1	6,352.2	6,715.1
	27	599.7	4,107.0	10,113.9	.2	.1	-	-	20.2	14,241.4	14,841.1
	28	1,247.4	4,382.3	504.4	2.1	-	-	-	52.2	4,941.0	6,188.5
	T1	71,344.7	55,098.7	17,335.6	14,612.7	3,928.3	3,702.2	979.7	15,626.7	111,283.9	182,629.0
	P1	55,411.7	-	-	-	-	-	-	-	-	55,411.7
	P2	38,628.2	-	-	-	-	-	-	-	-	38,628.2
	P3	2,150.0	4,150.6	-	149.4	-7.7	-.9	-31.7	241.4	4,501.1	6,651.1
	P4	3,825.7	-	-	336.7	-	-	-	-	336.7	4,162.4
	P5	245.3	343.9	-4.6	-391.8	-197.7	-37.1	10.1	32.0	-245.3	-
	P6A	731.3	567.5	-	-	-	-	-	19.0	586.7	1,317.9
	P7A	-	-	-	-	-	-	-	-	-	-
	P6B+C	9,821.9	3,496.8	34.0	1,891.6	445.4	161.6	14.2	815.9	6,859.5	16,681.4
	P7B+C	470.2	429.8	-	204.9	28.9	-	-.1	-	663.5	1,133.7
	T2	182,629.0	64,087.3	17,364.9	16,803.5	4,197.1	3,825.9	991.1	16,716.2	123,986.0	306,614.9

45

	SUPPLY	USAGE	1	2	3	4	5	6	7	8	9
1	AGRICULTURE	689.4	3.8	0.3	3,343.3	1,042.3	220.6	297.0	0.1	3.4
2	FORESTRY,FISHING,HUNTING	15.5	6.9	18.0	17.8	133.8	.1	.1	.1	127.5
3	MINING	4.4	1.0	641.4	4.3	7.1	1.1	1.2	-	.7
4	MEAT AND MILK PRODS	47.7	4.3	2.9	912.2	146.9	1.5	.3	1.0	1.0
5	OTHER FOOD PRODS	313.9	22.2	9.7	88.0	763.3	91.0	2.2	.4	1.5
6	BEVERAGES, TOBACCO PRODS	5.7	.3	17.6	12.1	6.9	132.6	.8	.6	2.2
7	TEXTILES	13.6	5.4	5.5	6.5	10.9	6.9	664.4	513.3	70.8
8	CLOTHING AND FOOTWEAR	2.3	2.7	2.3	9.9	2.4	.8	14.3	358.2	1.5
9	WOOD,WOOD PRODS ETC	5.1	4.8	14.0	3.3	.9	3.4	.4	2.8	580.2
10	PAPER,PRINTING ETC	58.3	1.1	15.6	93.9	94.2	85.0	11.1	13.4	27.4
11	CHEMICALS	499.9	5.6	75.7	31.4	61.0	15.2	84.3	22.8	83.4
12	PETROLEUM AND COAL PRODS	199.4	39.8	104.6	24.7	25.4	9.2	6.6	3.8	17.4
13	NON-METALLIC MIN. PRODS	.6	3.0	9.7	33.7	15.2	72.3	.2	.1	22.7
14	BASIC METALS AND PRODS	5.3	.8	66.2	2.4	9.4	2.1	4.0	.6	65.0
15	FABRICATED METAL PRODS	6.3	6.0	47.0	62.2	166.2	184.9	.9	1.6	31.1
16	TRANSPORT EQUIP.	7.3	10.9	16.0	3.6	1.3	.8	.3	.2	1.4
17	OTHER MACHINERY ETC	70.7	36.9	264.6	9.8	13.5	5.7	4.2	.9	12.3
18	MISCELL. MANUFACTURING	10.5	20.0	46.5	120.3	115.3	53.6	8.6	138.7	59.5
19	ELECTRICITY, GAS, WATER	142.4	2.3	158.5	64.8	49.2	32.0	25.9	10.9	29.0
20	CONSTRUCTION	18.4	4.9	30.3	13.2	8.3	3.9	2.4	1.2	5.1
21	WHOLESALE, RETAIL TRADE	229.3	35.8	128.4	296.3	236.4	115.0	189.3	179.9	169.3
22	REPAIRS	115.7	22.4	45.8	21.9	15.1	5.2	.9	.6	6.7
23	TRANSPORT, COMMUNICATION	236.4	19.3	243.0	364.6	208.3	68.4	56.6	48.0	121.3
24	FINANCE, PROPERTY ETC	200.3	25.4	400.7	221.1	142.3	68.5	37.5	38.2	95.9
25	OWNERSHIP OF DWELLINGS	.3	.1	.2	.1	.2	.1	.2	.1	.1
26	PUBLIC ADMIN., DEFENCE	11.6	.8	3.7	20.9	8.4	3.6	2.5	1.3	5.5
27	COMMUNITY SERVICES	82.9	1.4	31.0	14.1	8.4	5.1	2.7	1.9	3.5
28	RECREATION. ETC SERVICES	15.1	.8	18.2	23.5	73.7	31.6	4.6	12.3	11.0
T1	INTERMEDIATE USAGE	3,008.2	288.8	2,417.1	5,820.1	3,366.0	1,220.1	1,423.1	1,352.8	1,556.3
P1	WAGES, SALARIES, SUPPS	855.8	195.9	1,332.7	860.1	862.8	323.6	369.1	673.1	692.0
P2	GROSS OPERATING SURPLUS	5,357.7	173.0	2,495.9	231.1	420.8	273.5	134.0	166.3	331.6
P3	COMMODITY TAXES (NET)	5.0	8.8	49.6	21.6	-4.3	12.5	23.0	1.4	6.4
P4	INDIRECT TAXES NEC (NET)	174.3	19.0	72.2	52.3	45.6	22.5	17.2	28.2	31.1
P5	SALES BY FINAL BUYERS	-	-	1.0	-	-	-	1.6	-	-
P6A	COMPLEMENT. IMPORTS CIF	.3	.3	4.1	12.0	127.4	3.5	3.1	4.3	5.0
P7A	DUTY ON P6A	-	-	-	-	-	-	-	-	-
T2	AUSTRALIAN PRODUCTION	9,401.3	685.8	6,372.6	6,997.4	4,818.3	1,855.7	1,971.1	2,226.1	2,622.5
P6B+C	COMPETING IMPORTS CIF	130.0	26.3	927.0	45.3	425.7	109.4	903.5	446.6	351.1
P7B+C	DUTY ON P6B+C	11.4	.2	.1	.8	11.2	4.6	79.0	141.8	29.4
T3	TOTAL USAGE	9,542.7	712.3	7,299.7	7,043.5	5,255.3	1,969.6	2,953.7	2,814.4	3,003.0

	10	11	12	13	14	15	16	17	18	19	20
1	0.2	0.8	-	-	0.2	0.1	0.2	0.2	11.6	0.2	0.9
2	27.2	3.9	-	0.5	.3	.1	.2	.2	.8	1.3	21.4
3	9.4	48.9	1,483.2	267.8	1,434.3	2.0	1.7	5.8	49.1	373.8	170.3
4	1.6	36.5	.1	.7	1.0	.8	1.8	1.4	42.7	.8	6.4
5	6.6	64.7	.3	2.3	15.3	2.0	4.1	3.5	2.4	2.7	9.4
6	3.4	4.3	.2	2.0	2.8	2.9	9.0	4.4	1.5	3.5	14.3
7	28.3	2.4	.8	5.7	11.6	26.4	36.3	14.8	156.5	.6	29.3
8	3.5	1.3	-	1.1	1.9	2.0	3.3	3.1	1.5	2.4	33.6
9	2.8	7.5	.2	1.6	5.7	19.7	21.2	45.5	5.9	2.9	1,019.8
10	1,122.7	85.3	1.3	35.1	9.7	32.8	38.6	75.0	39.3	9.2	28.2
11	106.7	1,146.0	46.3	106.9	106.9	71.6	62.5	135.3	464.9	28.8	221.2
12	25.4	70.0	199.7	43.7	174.3	16.2	7.3	17.9	12.9	122.6	189.1
13	.9	32.5		214.7	76.7	22.7	22.3	28.2	7.9	9.4	1,625.6
14	12.6	63.3	2.2	44.5	1,528.3	1,352.6	327.5	718.2	28.0	10.2	488.7
15	6.5	47.7	.1	7.9	44.9	355.0	208.8	222.4	31.0	45.7	1,493.0
16	1.3	1.7	.3	21.3	3.0	8.3	1,772.1	15.3	.8	1.5	15.9
17	47.5	13.1	1.2	9.6	29.5	52.9	134.7	1,036.1	7.8	50.9	1,208.4
18	56.1	124.4	1.0	7.8	21.6	44.2	161.9	163.4	328.4	8.2	312.1
19	41.1	86.4	10.3	88.4	205.2	38.9	33.1	44.5	35.8	1,007.5	56.4
20	9.0	9.1	.5	8.3	3.0	5.6	5.3	7.3	5.8	24.2	11.8
21	129.8	199.3	66.8	63.3	188.7	133.9	142.5	320.1	145.1	57.9	830.9
22	6.5	5.6	.1	6.5	3.1	6.2	3.3	12.1	2.2	6.6	57.1
23	138.3	155.2	45.3	230.8	326.6	108.2	117.4	155.8	82.7	121.3	626.0
24	183.2	139.8	21.4	91.5	99.1	132.4	190.9	198.7	83.0	323.0	594.1
25	.2	.2	-	.2	.1	.1	.1	.2	.2	.1	.1
26	7.9	6.4	.7	4.5	7.7	7.2	11.9	9.4	3.4	9.7	38.2
27	6.5	7.9	1.0	5.8	5.3	4.8	7.5	9.8	3.0	5.2	17.5
28	42.0	91.6	1.1	10.6	6.4	16.0	21.0	37.3	13.0	12.1	22.5
T1	2,026.8	2,455.9	1,884.3	1,283.1	4,313.2	2,464.7	3,346.4	3,286.0	1,567.3	2,242.2	9,142.8
P1	1,125.6	697.9	98.4	558.2	1,218.6	1,102.4	1,491.5	1,704.6	667.2	1,281.3	4,626.9
P2	488.5	448.0	92.6	305.2	721.9	433.1	286.5	458.2	261.8	1,548.6	2,259.7
P3	26.3	21.1	1,184.7	4.2	18.4	7.9	9.2	17.3	10.6	-10.6	36.2
P4	55.3	40.0	9.5	33.2	46.1	44.9	56.0	57.9	31.2	78.5	240.7
P5	8.5	-	-	-	1.1	211.4	6.1	3.9	4.0	.2	.4
P6A	6.7	97.4	8.5	3.8	12.1	6.6	9.1	11.5	48.8	3.7	30.1
P7A	-	-	-	-	-	-	-	-	-	-	-
T2	3,737.7	3,760.2	3,278.0	2,188.8	6,541.7	4,065.8	5,202.5	5,539.5	2,587.0	5,143.7	16,336.7
P6B+C	775.3	1,184.4	549.3	286.1	403.9	398.7	2,297.0	4,154.0	947.4	11.2	-
P7B+C	23.7	26.4	.4	23.8	21.3	44.7	325.4	258.5	130.9	-	-
T3	4,536.7	4,971.1	3,827.8	2,498.7	6,967.0	4,509.2	7,824.9	9,951.9	3,665.4	5,154.9	16,336.7

TABLE 14. INDUSTRY BY INDUSTRY FLOW MATRIX 1978-79
INDIRECT ALLOCATION OF COMPETING IMPORTS, BASIC VALUES, RECORDING INTRA-INDUSTRY FLOWS, 28 INDUSTRIES
($ MILLION)

	USAGE	21	22	23	24	25	26	27	28
	SUPPLY								
1	AGRICULTURE	1.0	0.2	1.8	2.4	–	6.8	9.0	50.5
2	FORESTRY,FISHING,HUNTING	.3	.1	6.9	1.4	–	.1	1.1	.2
3	MINING	20.8	–	44.8	3.0	1.0	9.0	12.1	9.7
4	MEAT AND MILK PRODS	14.2	.7	4.8	14.5	–	1.9	24.7	14.3
5	OTHER FOOD PRODS	22.9	1.5	11.3	18.0	2.1	5.8	45.8	17.5
6	BEVERAGES, TOBACCO PRODS	22.5	2.5	13.0	15.1	–	10.9	18.6	6.8
7	TEXTILES	16.2	1.5	74.8	3.5	.5	13.3	47.2	56.9
8	CLOTHING AND FOOTWEAR	14.6	4.2	27.6	9.0	.3	22.6	95.0	10.6
9	WOOD,WOOD PRODS ETC	59.9	.2	16.9	4.1	44.2	40.1	87.2	16.2
10	PAPER,PRINTING ETC	939.7	8.4	185.8	257.9	4.5	213.5	261.4	147.6
11	CHEMICALS	25.9	6.2	33.4	91.6	78.9	50.9	248.3	69.0
12	PETROLEUM AND COAL PRODS	143.9	13.3	822.7	45.6	5.0	30.5	65.7	42.9
13	NON-METALLIC MIN. PRODS	37.2	5.5	7.2	4.7	39.1	5.0	27.5	23.4
14	BASIC METALS AND PRODS	10.6	.9	8.1	3.6	66.1	20.9	8.7	3.3
15	FABRICATED METAL PRODS	131.0	13.6	45.7	19.6	76.4	68.3	80.9	59.3
16	TRANSPORT EQUIP.	82.1	324.2	767.0	2.8	.5	343.7	11.2	6.3
17	OTHER MACHINERY ETC	62.8	171.8	151.9	103.5	41.0	180.7	221.6	227.1
18	MISCELL. MANUFACTURING	291.6	19.3	237.1	21.3	19.6	62.0	120.6	46.5
19	ELECTRICITY, GAS, WATER	141.4	35.9	117.6	267.8	531.9	155.8	221.0	198.8
20	CONSTRUCTION	107.7	.8	171.4	48.7	502.5	133.6	94.9	19.6
21	WHOLESALE, RETAIL TRADE	376.3	197.5	661.8	208.2	45.0	137.0	396.7	176.2
22	REPAIRS	323.9	1.5	269.4	50.4	.4	19.8	41.6	29.4
23	TRANSPORT, COMMUNICATION	881.3	49.9	1,027.1	540.0	17.0	359.8	427.8	190.0
24	FINANCE, PROPERTY ETC	1,982.3	78.6	584.8	1,430.9	1,268.4	644.9	1,009.5	379.6
25	OWNERSHIP OF DWELLINGS	–	.1	.2	.2	–	–	.1	–
26	PUBLIC ADMIN., DEFENCE	47.1	6.5	49.6	26.4	1.7	8.6	47.2	10.3
27	COMMUNITY SERVICES	67.0	3.3	29.3	90.0	.8	54.7	96.7	34.0
28	RECREATION. ETC SERVICES	176.3	2.5	63.0	193.1	.1	52.5	82.4	259.6
T1	INTERMEDIATE USAGE	6,000.1	950.6	5,434.4	3,477.1	2,746.7	2,652.5	3,804.3	2,105.8
P1	WAGES, SALARIES, SUPPS	7,815.4	944.0	4,891.9	4,821.7	–	3,807.8	9,869.0	2,524.3
P2	GROSS OPERATING SURPLUS	5,554.1	535.5	1,872.4	4,943.1	6,544.2	–	1,014.2	1,276.6
P3	COMMODITY TAXES (NET)	139.1	53.2	315.8	56.9	53.6	-.1	55.7	26.5
P4	INDIRECT TAXES NEC (NET)	553.2	43.0	303.9	624.9	787.5	33.1	85.3	239.0
P5	SALES BY FINAL BUYERS	–	–	–	–	–	–	3.1	4.0
P6A	COMPLEMENT. IMPORTS CIF	46.0	3.1	9.5	31.2	–	221.2	9.6	12.3
P7A	DUTY ON P6A	–	–	–	–	–	–	–	–
T2	AUSTRALIAN PRODUCTION	20,108.0	2,529.5	12,827.8	13,954.9	10,132.0	6,714.5	14,841.2	6,188.5
P6B+C	COMPETING IMPORTS CIF	–	2.1	1,153.9	234.4	–	–	4.3	98.3
P7B+C	DUTY ON P6B+C	–	–	–	–	–	–	–	.1
T3	TOTAL USAGE	20,108.0	2,531.6	13,981.7	14,189.4	10,132.0	6,714.5	14,845.5	6,286.9

	T4 INTERM USAGE	Q1 FINAL CONS PVTE	Q2 EXPEND GOVT	Q3 GROSS FIXED CAPITAL EXPEND PVTE	Q4 PUB ENT	Q5 GEN GOVT	Q6 INCR IN STOCKS	Q7 EXPORTS	T5(Q1-Q7) FINAL DEMAND	T6 TOTAL SUPPLY
1	5,686.4	891.2	83.0	–	–	–	775.7	2,106.4	3,856.2	9,542.6
2	385.9	127.6	36.3	28.5	–	55.2	-17.1	95.8	326.4	712.3
3	4,607.8	27.0	23.4	10.7	26.3	5.7	-78.7	2,677.5	2,692.0	7,299.7
4	1,286.7	3,570.5	.2	6.0	2.4	1.6	-29.1	2,205.3	5,756.8	7,043.5
5	1,530.2	2,988.9	1.0	13.3	3.0	.7	5.9	712.3	3,725.0	5,255.2
6	316.3	1,575.2	–	4.2	.9	.2	11.2	61.5	1,653.3	1,969.6
7	1,823.7	790.4	–	45.3	5.8	24.0	8.4	256.1	1,130.0	2,953.7
8	631.9	2,131.4	.1	10.5	.9	.4	23.9	15.2	2,182.5	2,814.4
9	2,016.3	681.0	1.0	173.1	16.8	37.8	-26.2	103.2	986.6	3,003.0
10	3,896.0	510.9	.4	31.3	8.3	12.1	24.0	53.9	640.8	4,536.8
11	3,980.5	742.4	35.8	11.5	2.7	.6	-7.5	205.2	990.6	4,971.1
12	2,479.5	964.8	–	.8	1.2	.2	61.5	319.7	1,348.3	3,827.7
13	2,348.0	97.8	.2	23.7	2.3	4.8	-12.6	34.4	150.7	2,498.7
14	4,853.7	20.0	–	71.9	13.2	9.3	-84.0	2,082.8	2,113.2	6,966.9
15	3,464.0	226.4	.4	612.7	46.7	24.7	29.1	105.3	1,045.2	4,509.2
16	3,420.8	1,928.0	.1	1,716.4	400.2	70.0	69.5	219.9	4,404.1	7,824.9
17	4,170.6	1,711.6	.2	3,072.0	512.1	165.8	-8.3	328.0	5,781.3	9,951.9
18	2,620.0	850.0	.2	64.1	1.7	6.4	-9.8	132.7	1,045.4	3,665.4
19	3,832.8	1,240.6	66.1	–	–	.1	–	15.2	1,322.1	5,154.9
20	1,256.6	13.7	2.5	8,518.6	3,178.8	3,366.8	-.1	.2	15,080.5	16,337.1
21	6,056.5	11,627.1	8.2	1,060.5	108.3	66.0	158.6	1,022.7	14,051.4	20,107.9
22	1,079.7	1,388.7	–	60.7	–	–	–	2.5	1,451.9	2,531.6
23	6,966.4	3,801.1	267.6	214.5	23.9	11.2	98.9	2,598.0	7,015.2	13,981.6
24	10,665.7	2,316.9	66.1	920.5	47.1	.1	.4	172.7	3,523.7	14,189.4
25	3.6	10,128.4	–	–	–	–	–	–	10,128.4	10,132.0
26	362.9	141.2	6,147.2	35.7	–	–	–	28.1	6,352.2	6,715.1
27	601.2	4,109.0	10,114.7	.2	.1	–	–	20.2	14,244.2	14,845.4
28	1,294.0	4,423.7	514.6	2.4	–	–	–	52.2	4,992.9	6,286.8
T1	81,636.8	59,025.3	17,369.5	16,709.2	4,402.6	3,863.8	993.7	15,626.7	117,990.9	199,628.1
P1	55,411.7	–	–	–	–	–	–	–	–	55,411.7
P2	38,628.2	–	–	–	–	–	–	–	–	38,628.2
P3	2,150.0	4,150.6	–	149.4	-7.7	-.9	-31.7	241.4	4,501.1	6,651.1
P4	3,825.7	–	–	336.7	–	–	–	–	336.7	4,162.4
P5	245.3	343.9	-4.6	-391.8	-197.7	-37.1	10.1	32.0	-245.3	–
P6A	731.3	567.5	–	–	–	–	19.0	.1	586.7	1,317.9
P7A	–	–	–	–	–	–	–	–	–	–
T2	182,629.0	64,087.3	17,364.9	16,803.5	4,197.1	3,825.9	991.1	15,900.2	123,170.1	305,799.0
P6B+C	15,865.4	–	–	–	–	–	–	815.9	815.9	16,681.4
P7B+C	1,133.7	–	–	–	–	–	–	–	–	1,133.7
T3	199,628.1	64,087.3	17,364.9	16,803.5	4,197.1	3,825.9	991.1	16,716.2	123,986.0	323,614.1

47

KEY BETWEEN THE AGGREGATED (28) INDUSTRY CLASSIFICATION
AND THE DISAGGREGATED (108) INDUSTRY CLASSIFICATION

1.	Agriculture	01.01	Sheep
		01.02	Cereal grains (including oilseeds n.e.c.)
		01.03	Meat cattle
		01.04	Milk cattle and pigs
		01.05	Poultry
		01.06	Other agriculture
		02.00	Services to agriculture
2.	Forestry, fishing and hunting	03.00	Forestry and logging
		04.00	Fishing and hunting
3.	Mining	11.01	Ferrous metal ores
		11.02	Non-ferrous metal ores
		12.00	Coal, oil and gas
		14.00	Other minerals
		16.00	Services to mining n.e.c.
4.	Meat and milk products	21.01	Meat products
		21.02	Milk products
5.	Other food products	21.03	Fruit and vegetable products
		21.04	Margarine and oils and fats n.e.c.
		21.05	Flour mill and cereal food products
		21.06	Bread, cakes and biscuits
		21.07	Confectionery and cocoa products
		21.08	Other food products
6.	Beverages and tobacco products	21.09	Soft drinks, cordials and syrups
		21.10	Beer and malt
		21.11	Other alcoholic beverages
		22.01	Tobacco products
7.	Textiles	23.01	Cotton ginning, wool scouring and top making
		23.02	Man-made fibres, yarns and broadwoven fabrics
		23.03	Cotton yarns, broadwoven fabrics, narrow woven, elastic and household textiles
		23.04	Worsted and woollen yarns and broadwoven fabrics
		23.05	Textile finishing
		23.06	Textile floor coverings, felt and felt products
		23.07	Other textile products
8.	Clothing and footwear	24.01	Knitting mills
		24.02	Clothing
		24.03	Footwear
9	Wood, wood products and furniture (except sheet metal)	25.01	Sawmill products
		25.02	Veneers and manufactured wood boards
		25.03	Joinery and wood products n.e.c.
		25.04	Furniture and mattresses
10.	Paper, paper products, printing and publishing	26.01	Pulp, paper and paperboard
		26.02	Bags, fibreboard containers
		26.03	Paper products n.e.c.
		26.04	Publishing; printing and publishing
		26.05	Paper stationery; printing and bookbinding; printing trade services n.e.c.
11.	Chemicals	27.01	Chemical fertilisers
		27.02	Other basic chemicals
		27.03	Paints
		27.04	Pharmaceutical and veterinary products; pesticides
		27.05	Soap and other detergents
		27.06	Cosmetics and toilet preparations
		27.07	Other chemical products
12.	Petroleum and coal products	27.08	Petroleum and coal products

13.	Non-metallic mineral products	28.01	Glass and glass products
		28.02	Clay products and refractories
		28.03	Cement
		28.04	Ready mixed concrete
		28.05	Concrete products
		28.06	Other non-metallic mineral products
14.	Basic metals and products	29.01	Basic iron and steel
		29.02	Basic non-ferrous metals and products
15.	Fabricated metal products	31.01	Structural metal products
		31.02	Sheet metal products
		31.03	Other metal products
16.	Transport equipment	32.01	Motor vehicles and parts and transport equipment n.e.c.
		32.02	Ships and boats
		32.03	Railway rolling stock and locomotives
		32.04	Aircraft
17.	Other machinery and equipment	33.01	Photographic, professional and scientific equipment
		33.02	Electronic equipment
		33.03	Refrigerators, household appliances and water heating systems
		33.04	Other electrical equipment
		33.05	Agricultural machinery
		33.06	Construction machinery and materials handling equipment
		33.07	Other machinery and equipment
18.	Miscellaneous manufacturing	34.01	Leather products
		34.02	Rubber products
		34.03	Plastic and related products
		34.04	Signs and advertising displays; writing and marking equipment
		34.05	Other manufacturing
19.	Electricity, gas and water	36.01	Electricity
		36.02	Gas
		37.01	Water, sewerage and drainage
20.	Construction	41.01	Residential building construction
		41.02	Other construction
21.	Wholesale and retail trade	47.01	Wholesale trade
		48.01	Retail Trade
22.	Repairs	49.01	Mechanical repairs
		49.02	Other repairs
23.	Transport, storage and communication	51.01	Road transport
		52.01	Railway transport, other transport and storage
		53.01	Water transport
		54.01	Air transport
		56.01	Communication
24.	Finance, property and business services	61.01	Banking
		61.02	Non-bank finance
		61.03	Investment and services to finance and investment
		61.04	Insurance and services to insurance
		61.05	Other business services
25.	Ownership of dwellings	61.06	Ownership of dwellings
26.	Public administration and defence	71.01	Public administration
		72.01	Defence
27.	Community services	81.01	Health
		82.01	Education, museum and library services
		83.01	Welfare and religious institutions and other community services
28.	Recreational, personal and other services	91.01	Entertainment and recreational services
		92.01	Restaurants, hotels and clubs
		93.01	Personal services

II. CHILE

A. General information

The present report is based on *Matriz de Insumo-Producto de la Economía Chilena 1977,* published by the Social Accounting Department of the National Bureau of Planning (ODEPLAN).

The latest input-output table available refers to 1977, and was compiled by ODEPLAN. This was the second table compiled in the country, the first one referring to the year 1962. Major differences between the 1962 and 1977 input-output tables include: (*a*) different classification systems; (*b*) inclusion of the government sector in the final demand sector only (1962); (*c*) treatment of the financial system; (*d*) treatment of import taxes; (*e*) treatment of trade margins on imports; (*f*) more narrow scope of the transfer of secondary production in the 1962 table; and (*g*) basing of the 1962 table on the old version of the United Nations System of National Accounts.

One purpose of compiling the 1977 input-output table was to establish a coherent accounting framework which will form the basis of a new series of national accounts, with 1977 as the reference year.

Major deviations of the Chilean input-output table from the SNA recommendations on input-output include: (*a*) no make matrix is compiled; (*b*) no valuation of transactions at approximate basic values is available; (*c*) activities of private non-profit institutions are not recorded separately; (*d*) disaggregation of value added; (*e*) treatment of imports; (*f*) treatment of secondary products; (*g*) definition of output of the transportation sector; (*h*) definition of output of the financial sector, and (*i*) definition of output of the insurance sector.

B. Analytical framework

1. *Tables and derived matrices available*

Data are presented in three basic tables:

(i) Absorption table of total flows at purchasers' prices;

(ii) Absorption table of domestic flows at purchasers' prices;

(iii) Imports absorption matrix.

On the basis of these data, the following derived matrices were compiled:

(i') Technical coefficients based on table (i);

(ii') Technical coefficients based on table (ii);

(iii') Technical coefficients based on table (iii);

(iv') Coefficients of distribution based on table (i);

(v') Coefficients of distribution based on table (ii);

(vi') Coefficients of distribution based on table (iii);

(vii') Inverse matrix based on table (i).

All basic tables and derived matrices compiled are presented at a level of disaggregation of 67 x 67 intermediate sectors. In addition, a more aggregated version of tables (i),

(ii) and (iii), with 20 intermediate sectors, was also compiled.

2. *Valuation standards*

All transactions were valued at purchasers' prices. However, information was also compiled on distribution margins and commodity taxes so that a valuation at approximate basic values can be made available at a later stage. Direct imports are valued c.i.f. plus import duties. Indirect imports, that is, imports through foreign trade channels, are valued at the total cost of purchase by the enterprise, which includes internal charges and distribution margins. Exports are valued f.o.b.

(a) *Statistical units and classification standards*

The industry was generally adopted as statistical unit, owing to lack of data at the establishment level. Exceptions to this approach were: (*a*) the agriculture, livestock and forestry sectors, which were defined on a commodity basis, and (*b*) the trade and private construction sectors, which were defined on an activity basis.

A modified version of ISIC was adopted as the classification system. Deviations from this system include:

(*a*) At the division level. (i) The copper mining sector includes smelting, alloying and refining of copper ores, unlike ISIC, which classifies those processes in the manufacturing division. Lack of data at a more disaggregate level prevented the adoption of the ISIC criterion. (ii) Repair services were assigned to the manufacturing or personal services divisions according to whether major or minor repairs (respectively) were involved. (iii) Sanitary services were included in electricity, gas and water, rather than in community, social and personal services.

(*b*) At the major group level. Livestock activities were disaggregated from ISIC major group 111 and recorded separately; copper and salt mining were treated as separate sectors; and ownership of dwellings was recorded separately.

The classification of the intermediate consumption quadrant differs from SNA recommendations on input-output in that the activities of private non-profit institutions are recorded together with those referring to enterprises. The activities of producers of government services, including public education and health, were recorded in the intermediate consumption quadrant, as recommended in SNA.

The SNA presentation of value added was disaggregated as follows: compensation of employees was classified into wages, salaries and employers' contribution to social security and similar schemes; indirect taxes were classified into taxes on value added, taxes on production and other indirect taxes; and operating surplus was divided into that of corporations and net incomes of the self-employed. Components of value added were defined as in SNA.

Final demand was disaggregated as in SNA. Private consumption was defined on a national basis. Therefore, it includes expenditure by domestic households on the domestic and foreign markets, and excludes direct purchases in the domestic market by non-resident households. Government consumption was defined as in SNA, that is, it includes the value of goods and services produced for its own use. Investment was defined as the sum of domestic supply of capital goods during the period plus imports of capital goods, adjusted for change of stocks of capital goods imported. Exports included tourism expenditure in the country and expenditure on the domestic market by diplomats.

Contrary to the SNA recommendations, no distinction was made in the Chilean input-output table between competitive and complementary imports. All imports have been cross-classified by origin and destination in the import matrix.

(b) *Treatment and presentation of selected transactions*

Owing to lack of data, secondary products were not in all instances transferred to their characteristic sectors. However, efforts were made to reallocate secondary output belonging to different ISIC divisions. Special attention was given to trade and building rental activities carried out by enterprises other than trade dealers and real estate agencies, since those activities constituted the bulk of secondary production. Both types of secondary output were recorded as fictitious sales to the characteristic industries, that is, they were recorded as input into the trade and real estate sectors (respectively) from the sectors having those activities as secondary production. Lack of information prevented the corresponding transfer of input. In the case of large mining enterprises, except for copper mining and the industrial subsector of the fishing sector, the reallocation of both output and intermediate input corresponding to their manufacturing activities was possible, on the basis of data provided by the enterprises themselves. Similarly, the construction of plants carried out by electricity and water supply industries was transferred to the construction sector, together with their associated input. In other cases, such as the ship repair activities carried out by the fishing sector and electricity produced for own consumption, neither output nor input could be reallocated.

Scrap sales were included in the trade sector. They were recorded as secondary trade activity of the corresponding sector (in the case of scrap generated by the mining, energy and transport sectors), or as part of direct trade (i.e., transaction of used goods) in the case of second-hand goods mainly consumed by households.

Non-monetary output and its associated input are recorded together with the monetary components in the corresponding input-output sector. Major types of non-monetary production covered include: (*a*) own consumption of agriculture products; (*b*) payments in kind; (*c*) imputed rents of owner-occupied dwellings; (*d*) own account gross fixed capital formation; and (*e*) own account repairs and input used and produced in the same establishment.

Intra-sector consumption is recorded in the main diagonal of the absorption table and therefore it is included in the gross output of each input-output sector.

Gross output of the trade sector was defined as the sum of: (*a*) trade margins on agriculture, fishing and manufacturing products; (*b*) direct trade, that is, that referring to transac-

tions of used goods; (*c*) trade margins on imports; (*d*) commissions received from abroad for trade services; and (*e*) trade margins that are part of the secondary activities of enterprises included in other input-output sectors. The first component was estimated by comparison of gross output of the corresponding sector valued at producers' and purchasers' prices.

Gross output of the transportation sector includes only the activity of enterprises mainly engaged in providing transportation services. The remaining transportation activities are recorded as part of the gross output of the enterprises carrying out transportation activities as secondary production.

As recommended in SNA, a distinction was made between actual and imputed charges for financial services, the latter being equal to the excess of property income received by banks on loans and other investments over the interest they paid out on deposits. Only the former were distributed among the intermediate sectors of the table. All imputed charges were recorded as the single input of a fictitious sector ("banking imputations"), whose value added was set equal to the value of those imputed charges with a minus sign. Lack of data prevented the exclusion from those imputed charges of interest received from investment of the bank's own funds, as recommended in SNA.

Gross output of the insurance sector includes: (*a*) premiums for insurance against risk (lack of data prevented the valuation of premiums net of claims, as recommended in SNA); (*b*) life insurance premiums minus net additions to actuarial reserves during the year (this value differs from that recommended in SNA in that claims are not deducted); (*c*) commissions received by agents acting as intermediaries between insurance companies and policyholders.

C. Statistical sources and compilation methodology

Data collection is mainly based on regular sources, special surveys carried out for the purpose of compilation of the input-output table and the preliminary results of the 1977 Agriculture and Livestock Census and the 1976 Manufacturing Census.

1. *Gross output, intermediate consumption and value added*

(a) *Agriculture, livestock and forestry*

Data on agriculture, livestock and forestry were obtained as indicated in the following paragraphs.

The physical volume of the various commodities produced was estimated on the basis of census data, and an analysis of their sectoral destination was carried out to get a balance of demand and supply in physical terms. The supply of the various commodities was valued at their representative producers' prices, defined as those prevailing in the most usual location of delivery by the producer. Demand was valued at the corresponding purchasers' prices, defined as those at which the final transaction took place (excluding value-added taxes). The commercialization channels, seasonal factors, and quality, variety and destination of the quantities demanded of each commodity were taken into account to estimate the purchasers' prices representative of each demand transaction. These data allowed for the estimation of gross output for each one of the three sectors mentioned, that is, agriculture, livestock and forestry.

An estimate of the total physical quantities of each intermediate input consumed by all three sectors was then obtained. This estimate is based on sales data provided by the corresponding producers. The total was then allocated among the three sectors according to the characteristics of their respective main products. A detailed analysis of the uses of each main intermediate input was thus carried out. This analysis made possible the valuation of intermediate input at the representative sales prices to producers. Representative prices were selected taking into account such factors as quality, variety, commercialization channels, and specific destination of each input. Finally, tax on value added was charged so as to obtain a value estimate of intermediate input at purchasers' prices.

The components of value added were estimated as follows: employment was estimated on the basis of number of man-days needed in the production process. This total was disaggregated by occupational category to determine the man-days corresponding to remunerated work. This disaggregation was based on the results of the Occupational Survey of the National Institute of Statistics and the preliminary results of the Agriculture and Livestock Census. Average wages and salaries per day (including payments in kind) were provided by the results of the survey. The total value of employers' contribution to social security and similar schemes was provided by the relevant institutions and was allocated among sectors in proportion to their level of wages and salaries. Net indirect taxes were provided by data compiled for the government sector. Depreciation was estimated by applying coefficients of the useful life of each kind of capital good to the value of the stock of the corresponding type of goods. The operating surplus was estimated as residual.

In the agricultural sector, the lack of correspondence between the calendar and the agricultural years presented an additional problem. It was decided to refer data to the calendar year, which implies that adjustments had to be made for intermediate input of products harvested in years other than 1977.

The large variety of existing agricultural products also presented a problem. This was dealt with by first classifying all products into "main" and "other" categories, and then extrapolating to the "other" category the data estimated for the "main" group.

Information on agriculture prices was obtained from the National Institute of Statistics, Empresa de Comercio Agrícola, Oficina de Planificación Agrícola and marketing studies of the agricultural enterprises carried out by a consulting firm.

(b) Fishing

In the fishing sector, a distinction was made between the traditional and industrial fishing subsectors, based mainly on the size of the vessels with which the fishing activity was carried out. Data on intermediate and final input of the traditional subsector were obtained through surveys conducted for this purpose. Total physical gross output of this subsector and its evaluation at beach prices were obtained from the Fishing Yearbook of the División de Protección Pesquera.

Special surveys were also carried out to collect data on physical gross output, beach prices, intermediate input and primary input of the industrial subsector. The surveyed units were also required to provide separate data on their extractive and manufacturing activities. Data on the sectoral distribution of the physical output of each species were provided by the Agriculture and Livestock Service. The main problem encountered was the influence of regional and destination factors in the prevailing beach prices. To allow for these differences, a distinction was made in the total catch of each fishing area between fish sold for fresh consumption and that sold for further processing. The assumption was made that the output of the traditional sector was mainly sold for fresh consumption, and that the difference between this output and total demand for fresh consumption was provided by the industrial sector. Similarly, in regions where total output of the industrial subsector was inferior to the amount processed, the traditional subsector was assumed to cover the difference. Fish sold for further processing was valued at regional beach prices for industrial fishing. Sales for fresh consumption in each area were further disaggregated into direct sales, which were valued at regional beach prices for traditional fishing, and sales through trade dealers, on the basis of information collected by the surveys. Finally, sales through trade dealers were classified according to the regional location of the final transaction, and were valued according to the retail prices prevailing in Santiago when no information on zonal retail prices was available. A zero trade margin was assumed for direct sales to consumers and for fish sold for further processing, since those sales do not go through distribution channels. Trade margins on the remaining transactions were estimated as the ratio between gross output valued at purchasers' and at producers' prices.

(c) Mining and quarrying

The characteristic gross output of the mining sector was obtained as the sum of domestic sales, exports and stock variation. Changes in stocks were estimated as the difference between sales and production, both measured in physical terms, and were valued at market prices. Secondary output consists mainly of services provided gratis to employees. Intermediate sales were obtained by deducting from gross output the supply of final demand. Data were obtained from surveys and from the accounts of mining establishments.

(d) Manufacturing

In the manufacturing sector, for purposes of data collection, industries were stratified into three groups according to their levels of employment. Data on industries belonging to strata 1 and 2 (i.e., industries with less than 9 and between 10 and 49 employees, respectively) were obtained from the annual reports to the Rol Industrial de la Dirección de Industria y Comercio. This source provides detailed estimates on raw material and products by type of enterprise. The monthly estimates were then inflated into annual estimates. Trend, seasonality and variation of each sector's wholesale price index were taken into account in the adjustment. For stratum 3 (i.e., industries with over 50 employees), data from the same source were supplemented with the results of the annual Industrial Survey of the National Institute of Statistics and with data obtained directly from the industries.

Gross output of the manufacturing sector was estimated from sales data (including indirect taxes) adjusted for variation of stocks of finished and in-process goods. Main statistical sources used were records on tax on value added for several months of 1977, classified by ISIC four-digit industrial subsector. These data were extrapolated for the entire year, taking into account trend values, seasonal variations and changes in the wholesale price index of the corresponding industrial subsectors. Total sales, which include those subject to value-added tax as well as those exempt from it, were divided into three strata on the basis of their proportion in the sample, and were also compared with the results of the 1967 Industrial Census and the 1977 Industrial Survey. Gross output of each stratum was determined on the basis of the sample ratio between gross value of output and sales.

Intermediate input of the manufacturing sector data was estimated on the basis of purchases. Adjustments were made to take into account variations of raw material inventory changes. Estimates for each stratum were obtained by expanding the corresponding sample estimates by a factor equal to the ratio gross output of the universe/gross output of the sample. Those estimates were checked against data on corresponding production by the agriculture, fishing, mining and other relevant sectors. Self-consumption was valued at producers' prices. Value-added data were estimated according to the same procedure used for intermediate input.

Each one of the products obtained in the sampled industries was classified by destination into final consumption, intermediate consumption and capital goods, and into goods for the domestic market or goods for exports. To avoid distortions, changes in stocks of finished and in-process goods were proportionally allocated to domestic and export sales. This classification of commodities by destination was based on the results of the Industrial Survey of the National Institute of Statistics, the 1978 Family Budget Survey, balance-of-payments data, direct inquiries and the analysis of compatibilization of supply and demand for each input-output sector. The producers' and purchasers' prices corresponding to the main destination of each good were determined through marketing surveys and direct inquiries to the enterprises. This analysis required the estimation of the percentages of total output distributed directly and through trade channels. Producers' prices were defined as the average price of cash sales.

(e) Electricity, gas and water

Data on output, input and distribution of output of the electricity, gas, water and sanitary services sectors were obtained from the accounts, balances, budgets, and direct information of the institutions that produce, supervise and/or control those activities. Electrical energy output excludes energy production by enterprises for their own use, except in the case of electricity generated by large copper mining enterprises. Estimates of the input structure took into account the marked differences between the hydraulic and thermal technological processes. Waterworks output excludes production by enterprises for their own consumption and sanitary services.

(f) Construction

Because of the wide variety of works included in the construction sector, this sector was disaggregated into five sub-sectors: housing, non-residential buildings, engineering works, repairs and demolitions. An additional distinction was made in the first three subsectors mentioned between works that are carried out by the public and private sectors. For public works, total expenditure in construction was known and the cost structure was estimated as follows: (a) data on total expenditure for each public-sector project in 1977 were obtained from the institutions and enterprises in charge of the projects; (b) the most representative projects of each institution were selected; (c) the budget(s), unit prices and other data for each project were obtained from the relevant institutions; (d) each item of the budget was disaggregated into physical quantities and unit prices; (e) the expenditure on intermediate consumption and value added was assigned to the corresponding sectors of the input-output table; (f) this expenditure was valued in terms of the price index corresponding to the first semester of 1977; different deflators were used for each specific product; (g) the cost structure thus obtained was applied to the actual expenditures of the institution on each project.

Data for works in the first two subsectors of the construction sector carried out by private enterprises were compiled by a consulting firm on the basis of municipal building licences. Licences were first grouped into different typologies, and an analysis was made of the intermediate input, value added and market price of each of them. Gross output was estimated as the sum of the products of market price and total area constructed of each type. Market prices were provided by the real estate classified announcements published in newspapers. Area constructed of each type was estimated by applying an estimated expenditure-time curve to the area of each type initiated each month in each "comuna". Intermediate input and value added were estimated by first defining a set of unitary construction items (for example, 1 square metre of masonry), and then determining the physical quantities and prices of the corresponding input. Adjustments were made for areas constructed without license on the basis of research carried out in the years around 1977.

Repairs include only those carried out by enterprises belonging to the construction sector. Housing repairs were estimated by applying to the physical stock of housing units a set of physical repair coefficients mainly determined on the basis of technological considerations.

In order to determine the output of demolitions, a coefficient was obtained for the Santiago "comuna", expressing the ratio of demolitions to total stock of housing units. A coefficient equal to half of that obtained for Santiago was assumed for the entire country, since, on average, housing units outside Santiago were of more recent construction.

(g) Trade, restaurants and hotels

Data on output, intermediate input and value added of the trade sector were obtained from special surveys and other *ad hoc* information. The available data did not allow for the disaggregation of trade margins between those corresponding to wholesale and retail trade.

Gross output of restaurants and hotels was estimated as the sum of demand for those services by individuals, the intermediate sector, general government and tourists on the basis of data provided mainly by the 1978 Households Survey, and the results of a survey of tourism hotels carried out by the Instituto Nacional de Estadística and the Servicio Nacional de Turismo. The input structure was obtained as a weighted average of the cost structure of restaurants, tourism hotels and other hotels, which were provided by surveys carried out for this purpose.

(h) Transportation

Data for the transportation sector were mainly obtained from general balances, budgets and surveys of transportation firms and special analyses carried out for this purpose. Intermediate consumption data were obtained directly from consumption, rather than purchases, data. This consumption was disaggregated into that of domestic or imported origin mainly on the basis of the currency in which the transaction took place. The interrelationships existing among this sector's enterprises were taken into account to avoid double counting. International freight by Chilean companies was recorded as sales abroad, to obtain data consistent with those of the balance of payments.

(i) Services

The finance sector included the institutions forming part of the monetary system and other financial institutions such as savings banks, the stock exchange etc. Data on this sector and on the insurance sector were obtained from sample surveys.

The real estate sector includes real estate agents and societies and owners of real estate. The universe of the sector was obtained from sources such as tax records, National Confederation of Real Estate Agents, Association of Incorporated Enterprises and telephone books. Data were obtained from sampling surveys and tax records.

The business services sector covers the activities described in the corresponding major group of ISIC. Gross output and cost structure were obtained from surveys of the enterprises representative of each type of service. Intermediate and primary input were estimated by applying to the gross output of the different activities their corresponding cost structures.

The 1978 Family Budget Survey and the 1970 Housing and Population Census were the basic data sources used for the estimation of gross output of the housing ownership sector. Gross output was estimated as the product of average rent paid per household and total number of households in the country. The result was compared to other available information, such as tax records. Intermediate input includes repairs, insurance, commissions paid to real estate agents, maintenance expenditures etc.

Activities of the education, health and services sector include those of major division 9 of ISIC except for sanitary services and public administration and defence services. Gross output was generally measured by the amount of gross receipts (in the case of private industries) and by the amount of current expenditures (in the case of public health and education services and of similar services provided by private non-profit institutions). The following data sources were used: balance sheets and budgets of the relevant institutions; sampling surveys; physical and financial data of public institutions with centralized information such as the National Association of Education, the National Association of Incorporated Enterprises etc.; and tax records.

Gross output of the public administration and defence sector includes the small percentage of output represented by market sales such as rental of real estate, sale of publica-

tions, veterinarian services etc. The cost structure of these market sales was estimated separately on the basis of data gathered for the industries having these activities as main production. Data were obtained from the analytical report of the Controller's Office, budgets of public institutions, and the Office of Government Supplies. Lack of data prevented the estimation of depreciation charges, which were usually treated as current expenditure. The positive entries recorded in the depreciation and operating surplus rows of the sector correspond mainly to those referring to the market sales mentioned above.

2. Final demand

Data on final demand categories were obtained in the following ways. Private consumption was estimated from the results of the 1978 Family Budget Survey, and from the analysis involved in the process of compatibilization of demand and supply of each input-output sector. Government consumption was estimated as the sum of government services produced for its own consumption recorded in the public education, public health and public administration and defence sectors. Domestic investment data were obtained directly from the accounts of industries included in the construction, mining and agriculture sectors; the analysis of destination of output of the manufacturing sectors; and imported capital goods adjusted for stock changes. Variation of stocks of finished and in-process goods was estimated from information available for each sector of the table; variation of stocks of raw materials was estimated as the residual obtained in the process of balancing supply and demand of each sector; change of stock of imported goods was determined exogenously, assuming an average turnover period of 30 to 60 days. Data on exports of goods were based on customs data and information from the main exporting sectors. Exports of services were estimated on the basis of central bank data. Tourism expenditure was estimated through a special survey, and expenditure by foreign diplomats was estimated also on the basis of survey information.

The basic statistical sources used in the estimation of imports were the imports registry, tax records and customs data. The first and second sources mentioned provided a classification of imports of goods by origin and destination. On the basis of those data, a preliminary c.i.f. imports matrix was calculated, which was then disaggregated into direct imports and imports-through-trade matrices, so as to make these data comparable to those provided by customs and the balance of payments. Customs data provided information on import duties paid by sector of origin. Aggregate value taxes were then estimated for both matrices. Imports of services by sector of origin were based on statistics on invisible trade provided by the central bank. Their allocation to demand sectors was done on the basis of the nature of the services.

CLASSIFICATION OF INPUT-OUTPUT TABLES FOR 1977

(Translation of rows and sector of origin)
1 Agricultural production
2 Agricultural livestock production
3 Agricultural services
4 Forestry and logging
5 Fishing
6 Copper mining
7 Iron ore mining

(Translation of rows and sector of origin)

8 Saltpetre mining
9 Crude petroleum and natural gas
10 Coal mining
11 Quarrying
12 Other mining
13 Food manufacturing
14 Beverage industry
15 Tobacco manufacturing
16 Manufacturing of textiles
17 Manufacturing of wearing apparel
18 Manufacturing of leather and leather products
19 Manufacturing of footwear
20 Manufacturing of wood and cork
21 Manufacturing of furniture and fixtures
22 Manufacturing of paper and paper products
23 Printing, publishing and allied industries
24 Industrial chemicals
25 Other chemical products
26 Petroleum refineries
27 Petroleum and coal products
28 Rubber products
29 Plastic products
30 Pottery, china and earthware
31 Glass and glass products
32 Other non-metallic mineral products
33 Iron and steel basic industries
34 Non-ferrous metal basic industries
35 Metal products
36 Manufacturing of machinery except electrical machinery
37 Manufacture of electrical machinery
38 Transport equipment
39 Manufacture of professional and other equipment
40 Other manufacturing industries
41 Electricity
42 Gas
43 Waterworks and supply
44 Construction
45 Wholesale and retail trade
46 Restaurants and hotels
47 Rail transport

48 Freight, transport by road
49 Passenger transport
50 Water transport
51 Air transport
52 Other transport services
53 Communication
54 Financial institutions
55 Insurance
56 Real estate
   A. Business services
57 Ownership of dwellings
58 Public education
59 Private education
60 Public health
61 Private health
62 Recreational services
63 Repair services
64 Laundries
65 Miscellaneous services
66 Public administration and defence
67 Imputed bank services

Intermediate input
Value added
Wages
Salaries
Employers' contributions
Total remunerations
Indirect taxes
Subsidies
Consumption of fixed capital
Operating surplus
Gross production value (producers' values)
Gross production value (purchasers' values)

(Translation of columns and sector of receipt)

1-67   Identical to rows 1-67 above

Total intermediate sales
Private consumption
Government consumption
Gross fixed capital formation
Increase in stocks
Exports
Total final demand
Total demand: domestic and imported

For tables, see end of volume.

III. FEDERAL REPUBLIC OF GERMANY

A. General information

The present report is based on *Input-Output-Tabellen 1975*, published by Statistisches Bundesamt in Reihe 2 of Fachserie 18 on national accounts.

The input-output table described here refers to 1975, and was compiled by the Federal Statistical Office. Previously, input-output tables had been prepared for 1965, 1970 and 1974 by the same office. A similar methodology was applied to the 1970, 1974 and 1975 tables. However, the 1975 table deviates from previous tables in that it contains detailed information on supply and demand of energy in value as well as in energy units (joule).

The input-output tables are fully integrated within the national accounts system. Both sets of estimates use similar concepts and definitions and are generally consistent with each other, although certain differences exist because of the special characteristics of the input-output tables.

The main deviations of the German input-output table from the SNA recommendations include: (*a*) commodity taxes are not recorded separately; (*b*) breakdown of final demand; and (*c*) treatment of imports.

B. Analytical framework

1. *Tables and derived matrices available*

Data are presented in the following main basic tables:

(i)   Input-output table of total transactions valued at producers' prices;

(ii) Input-output table of domestic production valued at producers' prices;

(iii) Imports table;

(iv) Final demand for domestic products and imports valued at purchasers' prices;

(v)   Final demand for domestic products valued at purchasers' prices;

(vi) Final demand for imports;

(vii) Table of energy input classified by type of energy source and sector using them, expressed in quantity terms;

(viii) Table of energy input classified by type of energy source and sector using them, expressed in value terms.

On the basis of these data the following derived matrices were compiled:

(i')   Technical coefficients based on table (i);

(ii') Technical coefficients based on table (ii);

(iii') Inverse matrix based on table (ii);

(iv') Technical coefficients expressed in terms of tera-joule per million deutsche mark (DM) of output and of value of energy input per DM of output value, based on tables (vii) and (viii).

All basic tables (except for energy tables) are presented at a level of aggregation of 60 x 60 intermediate sectors.

2. *Valuation standards*

Producers' prices are defined to include taxes net of subsidies. Purchasers' prices are defined to be equal to producers' prices plus distribution margins. Exports are valued f.o.b. Imports are valued c.i.f. plus import duties in the producers' prices tables, and c.i.f. plus import duties plus distribution margins in the tables valued at purchasers' prices. Contrary to the SNA recommendations, commodity taxes are not recorded separately and therefore no valuation at approximate basic values can be derived.

3. *Statistical units and classification standards*

Input-output sectors are classified according to branches, which are defined as in the classification system of the European Community. That is, a branch groups all production units sharing a common input structure and producing a homogeneous group of commodities. For this purpose, establishments are divided into two or several homogeneous production units. Auxiliary services of the establishment, such as administration, stocks management, repairs etc., are included partly with the main activity and partly with the secondary activities of the establishment.

Branches are classified according to a national system of classification, which is based on the especial version of the General Industrial Classification of Economic Activities used by the European Communities for their input-output tables (NACE/CLIO). Deviations from NACE/CLIO are mainly due to attempts made at reconciliation of the branch-based classification of economic activities used for the input-output table with the industry-based classification of economic activities used in the national accounts. The national classification system used for input-output tables (SIO) is revised every year. The input-output table described in the present report is based on the 1975 version of the system.

The intermediate consumption quadrant generally follows the SNA recommendations on input-output. Thus, the activities of private non-profit institutions are recorded in a separate sector of this quadrant and the activities of producers of government services are also recorded in a separate sector of the intermediate consumption quadrant, and include public health and education services.

The breakdown of final demand differs from the SNA recommendations in that gross fixed capital information is subdivided into the buildings and equipment subsectors. It should also be noted that since total investment (i.e., gross fixed capital formation plus change in stocks) gross of the deductible value added tax in the input-output table, an entry equal to deductible value added tax (with a minus sign) on investment is recorded at the intersection of the value added and final demand quadrant, so as to obtain total investment valued at producers' prices net of deductible value added tax. Private consumption has been defined on a domestic basis, that is, it includes purchases of goods and services made by foreigners in the Federal Republic of Germany and excludes consumption abroad by German nationals.

Value added has been defined and disaggregated as recommended in SNA. Contrary to the SNA recommendations, no distinction is made in the German input-output table between competitive and complementary imports. In the input-output table of total transactions (table (i)), all imports were classified according to the input-output sector to which they characteristically belonged, and were then distributed together with domestic production to intermediate and final demand categories. In the input-output table of domestic production (table (ii)), input imported by each input-output sector was recorded in a row which was added to domestic input of the sector. In addition, all imports were classified by sector of origin and destination in the imports table (table (iii)).

4. Treatment and presentation of selected transactions

The problem of secondary production was dealt with by defining input-output sectors in terms of the branch concept used in the classification system of the European Community. Since the original data were obtained from institutional units (i.e., enterprises), some preliminary work on transfer of secondary products was required to arrive at the definition of input-output sectors. This work was carried out on the basis of a commodity technology assumption, that is, the assumption was made that commodities had the same input structure in all industries in which they are produced.*

Non-market output (such as imputed rent of owner-occupied dwellings, commodities consumed by the same units that produce them etc.) and its associated input were recorded together with the corresponding market transactions in the corresponding input-output sectors.

Intra-sector consumption was recorded in the main diagonal of the input-output table. It includes non-market deliveries among different production units belonging to the same input-output sector as well as intra-production units deliveries.

Output of the financial sector was defined as recommended in SNA, that is, it includes the difference of interest earned over interest paid. Also, as recommended in SNA, imputed financial charges were distributed by means of an "imputed bank services" dummy sector.

C. Statistical sources and compilation methodology

Data compilation is mainly based on regular sources, of which the production statistics used to obtain the national accounts estimates are the most important.

The following methodology is used to estimate the input-output table. Production statistics used for the national accounts estimates provide control totals and basic information on selected cells of the input-output table. Gaps in this information are filled in by a combination of the input and output methods, that is, by estimation of the cost structure and distribution of output of the input-output sectors. Since the combined application of these two methods does not generally result in equal row and column totals, a recon

ciliation of results is required. This work involves a preliminary analysis of the level of accuracy to be assigned to each cell's estimates, and the weakest estimates are then corrected on the basis of additional information available on why particular estimates appear to be incorrect. The remaining differences are dealt with by means of an error balancing computer program which applies an iteration process to arrive at a balance between row and column totals.

1. Gross output and intermediate consumption

Gross output estimates are based on the production data of the national accounts. Since these data are compiled using the enterprise as statistical unit while input-output sectors are defined in terms of branches, the estimation of gross output of each input-output sector requires the transfer of secondary products, which is carried out on the basis of a breakdown of sector output into 60 commodity groups. Other main adjustments of the national accounts data to input-output concepts include: (a) the addition of the production of commodities of the enterprises for their own use and (b) the reduction of the market value of the trade transactions by the delivered costs of the goods.

Estimates of intermediate consumption are mainly based on company records. The use of special intermediate input not covered by this source is obtained from four yearly cost structure surveys, which provide information on composition of input for wholesale and retail trade, restaurants and hotels, communications and special professional services. Data on manufacturing are obtained from annual cost structure surveys carried out since 1975. For agriculture, data are mainly based on information provided by the Ministry of Agriculture. In the case of energy (to which special attention is given in the German input-output tables), data were obtained from the energy balances estimated by the Statistical Office of the European Community and the working group for energy balances. In addition, official statistics on production and foreign trade of energy and special studies on gas, electricity and oil production and consumption were used. Data on output and use of energy were available for 40 six-digit SIO positions in value as well as in quantity terms.

Gaps in the information provided by the sources mentioned in the above paragraph were filled in with data provided by the output method, which were available at a level of detail of 3,000 commodities defined at the six-digit level of SIO.

2. Value added

Gross value added was generally calculated as the difference between total gross output and intermediate input. Data on the categories of value added are mainly based on cost structure statistics, reports of individual enterprises and finance statistics regarding allocation of consumption tax and subsidies.

3. Final demand and imports

Data on final demand categories are compiled at the six-digit level of classification of the national system of classification used for input-output tables. Estimates are obtained at both producers' and purchasers' prices.

Estimates on private consumption are mainly based on available data on retail business sales to private households, the Trade Census of 1969, the Income Expenditure Surveys

---

*See C. Stahmer: "Connecting national accounts and input-output tables in the Federal Republic of Germany," in: J. Skolka, ed., *Compilation of Input-Output Tables*, (Berlin-Heidelberg-New York, 1982).

of 1969 and 1973, and the results of monthly surveys of selected households.

Estimates on final government consumption are taken directly from the uses accounts sub-system of the national accounts.

Estimates on gross fixed capital formation are mainly obtained according to the commodity flow method. They are mainly based on the quarterly production statistics used in the national accounts and foreign trade statistics. The detailed commodity breakdown provided by these statistics allows for a high level of accuracy in the distribution of gross fixed capital formation among input-output sectors. Basic data are available at producers' and c.i.f. respectively f.o.b. prices. To arrive at a valuation in purchasers' prices, use is made of available data on trade and transportation margins, value added tax and import duties.

Estimates of changes in stocks are mainly obtained from the national accounts, and are allocated to input-output sectors on the basis of data available on changes in stocks by commodity groups held by producers and traders.

Exports and imports estimates are obtained from the foreign trade statistics and the balance-of-payments statistics.

CLASSIFICATION OF INPUT-OUTPUT TABLES FOR THE FEDERAL REPUBLIC OF GERMANY
(Translation of rows)

Input/output sector	Industry
1	Agricultural products
2	Forestry and fish products
3	Electricity, steam and hot water
4	Gas
5	Water
6	Coal and coal mining products
7	Mining products (except coal, crude petroleum and natural gas)
8	Crude petroleum and natural gas
9	Chemical products and fissile materials
10	Mineral oil products
11	Plastic products
12	Rubber products
13	Stone, sand and clay
14	Fine ceramic ware
15	Glass and glass products
16	Iron and steel
17	Non-ferrous metals, non-ferrous semi-finished products
18	Casting products (foundries)
19	Drawing products and cold rolling products
20	Structural products of steel and light metals and rail vehicles
21	Machinery
22	Office and electronic data processing machinery and equipment
23	Road vehicles
24	Watercrafts
25	Aircrafts and space vehicles
26	Electro-technical products
27	Fine mechanical and optical products, watches and clocks
28	Electrical products
29	Musical instruments, toys, sports equipment, jewellery etc.
30	Lumber
31	Products of wood
32	Pulp, wood pulp, paper and paperboard
33	Paper and paperboard products
34	Printing products
35	Leather, leather products and shoes
36	Textiles
37	Apparel
38	Food
39	Beverages
40	Tobacco products
41	Surface engineering and underground engineering
42	Completion services
43	Wholesaling services and recycling
44	Retailing services
45	Rail transportation
46	Water transportation (shipping, waterways, ports)
47	Postal and telecommunication services
48	Other transportation or communication services
49	Banking services
50	Insurance services (except social security)
51	Real estate services
52	Market services of hotels, restaurants and residences
53	Cultural, research and publishing services
54	Market health and veterinary services
55	Other market services
56	Public administration services (on all territorial levels)
57	Social security services
58	Services of non-profit organizations and household services
59	Intermediate goods and services (input cols. 1-59); final use of products (col. 60)
60	Non-deductible value added tax excluding sales tax
61	Same as No. 59, but including non-deductible sales tax
62	Amortizations
63	Taxes at production stage, excluding subsidies
64	Income from employment
65	Income from entrepreneurship and property
66	Gross value added at market prices
67	Production value
68	Imports of similar goods at c.i.f.
69	Total value of goods

(Translation of columns)

Input/output sector	Final use of goods
1-59	Identical to rows 1-59
60	Private consumption, domestic
61	Government consumption
62	Investments for equipment
63	Investment for construction
64	Change of stocks
65	Exports of products and services
66	Total
67	Total use of goods

FEDERAL REPUBLIC OF GERMANY
INPUT-OUTPUT TABLES
1980

Source: *Input-Output Tabellen 1980*, Statistisches Bundesamt, Wiesbaden, Federal Republic of Germany.

LFD. NR.	VERWENDUNG / AUFKOMMEN	INPUT DER				
		ERZG. V. PRODUKTEN DER LAND-WIRTSCHAFT	ERZG. V. PROD. DER FORSTWIRT-SCHAFT. FISCHEREI USW.	ERZG. U. VERTLG. V. ELEKTRI-ZITAET DAMPF. WARMWASSER	ERZG. U. VERTLG. V. GAS	GEW. U. VERTLG. V. WASSER
		1	2	3	4	5

OUTPUT NACH GUETERGRUPPEN (ZEILE 1 BIS 58)

1	PRODUKTE DER LANDWIRTSCHAFT	8595	685	.	.	.
2	PRODUKTE DER FORSTWIRTSCHAFT. FISCHEREI USW.	24	60	.	.	.
3	ELEKTRIZITAET. DAMPF. WARMWASSER	748	160	2977	18	135
4	GAS	16	17	3869	42	5
5	WASSER	106	3	.	3	5
6	KOHLE. ERZEUGNISSE DES KOHLENBERGBAUS	2	.	10091	489	1
7	BERGBAUERZEUGNISSE (OHNE KOHLE. ERDOEL. ERDGAS)	279	17	.	.	.
8	ERDOEL. ERDGAS	.	.	168	10332	.
9	CHEMISCHE ERZEUGNISSE. SPALT- U. BRUTSTOFFE	4210	177	784	13	45
10	MINERALOELERZEUGNISSE	3721	662	2412	629	33
11	KUNSTSTOFFERZEUGNISSE	5	19	51	.	3
12	GUMMIERZEUGNISSE	280	25	5	1	.
13	STEINE U. ERDEN. BAUSTOFFE USW.	207	18	25	3	4
14	FEINKERAMISCHE ERZEUGNISSE	24	2	13	1	.
15	GLAS U. GLASWAREN	19	1	3	1	1
16	EISEN U. STAHL	16	26	524	124	74
17	NE-METALLE. NE-METALLHALBZEUG	.	.	6	7	5
18	GIESSEREIERZEUGNISSE	.	.	1	5	3
19	ERZEUGNISSE DER ZIEHEREIEN. KALTWALZWERKE USW.	643	30	102	26	23
20	STAHL- U. LEICHTMETALLBAUERZEUGN.. SCHIENENFAHRZEUGE	37	8	593	49	102
21	MASCHINENBAUERZEUGNISSE	891	56	497	40	120
22	BUEROMASCHINEN. ADV-GERAETE U. -EINRICHTUNGEN	.	.	2	4	.
23	STRASSENFAHRZEUGE	464	68	37	15	3
24	WASSERFAHRZEUGE	.	24	1	.	.
25	LUFT- U. RAUMFAHRZEUGE	.	.	7	.	1
26	ELEKTROTECHNISCHE ERZEUGNISSE	289	33	630	2	26
27	FEINMECHANISCHE U. OPTISCHE ERZEUGNISSE. UHREN	3	24	27	41	9
28	EBM-WAREN	111	29	24	.	4
29	MUSIKINSTRUMENTE. SPIELWAREN. SPORTGERAETE. SCHMUCK USW.	2	.	4	1	.
30	HOLZ	34	11	16	1	1
31	HOLZWAREN	197	12	3	.	7
32	ZELLSTOFF. HOLZSCHLIFF. PAPIER. PAPPE	3	11	1	2	2
33	PAPIER- U. PAPPEWAREN	59	40	57	7	8
34	ERZEUGNISSE DER DRUCKEREI U. VERVIELFAELTIGUNG	150	38	23	7	3
35	LEDER. LEDERWAREN. SCHUHE	16	1	.	.	.
36	TEXTILIEN	17	22	21	8	3
37	BEKLEIDUNG	2	7	11	.	.
38	NAHRUNGSMITTEL (OHNE GETRAENKE)	8811	13	2	.	.
39	GETRAENKE	43	31	11	2	.
40	TABAKWAREN	2	.	14	7	.
41	HOCH- U. TIEFBAULEISTUNGEN U.AE.	206	33	220	1	134
42	AUSBAULEISTUNGEN	272	35	440	13	110
43	DIENSTLEISTUNGEN DES GROSSHANDELS U.AE.. RUECKGEWINNUNG	794	79	338	44	10
44	DIENSTLEISTUNGEN DES EINZELHANDELS	309	12	26	4	1
45	DIENSTLEISTUNGEN DER EISENBAHNEN	303	50	601	39	4
46	DIENSTLEISTUNGEN D. SCHIFFAHRT. WASSERSTRASSEN. HAEFEN	67	1	170	10	.
47	DIENSTLEISTUNGEN D. POSTDIENSTES U. FERNMELDEWESENS	84	15	73	.	12
48	DIENSTLEISTUNGEN DES SONSTIGEN VERKEHRS	1386	312	191	30	12
49	DIENSTLEISTUNGEN DER KREDITINSTITUTE	29	6	19	15	2
50	DIENSTLSTG. D. VERSICHERUNGEN (OH. SOZIALVERSICHERUNG)	298	41	105	18	59
51	DIENSTLEISTUNGEN D. GEBAEUDE- U. WOHNUNGSVERMIETUNG	6	4	16	12	2
52	MARKTBESTIMMTE DIENSTLSTG. D. GASTGEWERBES U. D. HEIME	13	25	18	2	5
53	DIENSTLEISTUNGEN D. WISSENSCHAFT U. KULTUR U. D. VERLAGE	45	8	55	6	4
54	MARKTBESTIMMTE DIENSTLSTG. D. GESUNDH.- U. VETERINAERWES.	633	28	24	.	.
55	SONSTIGE MARKTBESTIMMTE DIENSTLEISTUNGEN	880	86	597	84	174
56	DIENSTLEISTUNGEN DER GEBIETSKOERPERSCHAFTEN	261	13	131	34	24
57	DIENSTLEISTUNGEN DER SOZIALVERSICHERUNG	.	.	.	.	.
58	DIENSTLSTG. D. PRIV.ORG.OH.ERWERBSZWECK. HAEUSL.DIENSTE	43	20	.	1	.
59	VORLEISTUNGEN DER PRODUKTIONSBEREICHE (SP.1 BIS 59) BZW. LETZTE VERWENDUNG VON GUETERN (SP.60 BIS 66) OHNE UMSATZSTEUER	35657	3220	26036	12193	1263
60	NICHTABZUGSFAEHIGE UMSATZSTEUER	.	.	.	.	.
61	VORLEISTUNGEN DER PRODUKTIONSBEREICHE (SP.1 BIS 59) BZW. LETZTE VERWENDUNG VON GUETERN (SP.60 BIS 66) EINSCHL. NICHTABZUGSFAEHIGER UMSATZSTEUER	35657	3220	26036	12193	1263
62	ABSCHREIBUNGEN	8512	530	8184	901	1060
63	PRODUKTIONSSTEUERN ABZUEGL. SUBVENTIONEN	-744	-11	3132	396	328
64	EINKOMMEN AUS UNSELBSTAENDIGER ARBEIT	2871	3627	10762	1416	1491
65	EINKOMMEN AUS UNTERNEHMERTAETIGKEIT UND VERMOEGEN	13843	1546	3502	3232	1376
66	BRUTTOWERTSCHOEPFUNG ZU MARKTPREISEN	24482	5592	25580	5945	4255
67	PRODUKTIONSWERT	60139	8812	51616	18138	5518
68	EINFUHR GLEICHARTIGER GUETER ZU AB-ZOLL-PREISEN	26656	3586	921	.	1
69	GESAMTES AUFKOMMEN AN GUETERN	86795	12398	52537	18138	5519

62

PRODUKTIONSBEREICHE

GEW. V. KOHLE H.V. ERZEUG-NISSEN DES KOHLEN-BERGBAUS	GEW. V. BERGBAU-ERZEUGN. (OH. KOHLE, ERDOEL ERDGAS)	GEW. V. ERDOEL ERDGAS	H.V. CHEMISCHEN ERZEUGN. SPALT- U. BRUT-STOFFEN	H.V. MINERAL-OELERZEUG-NISSEN	H.V. KUNST-STOFF-ERZEUG-NISSEN	H.V. GUMMI-ERZEUG-NISSEN	GEW. V. STEINEN U. ERDEN H.V. BAU-STOFFEN USW.	H.V. FEINKERA-MISCHEN ERZEUG-NISSEN	H.V. GLAS U. GLASWAREN	LFD. NR.
6	7	8	9	10	11	12	13	14	15	
10	.	.	393	10	86	5	20	1	5	1
125	1	.	62	10	9	489	44	.	.	2
1396	174	45	4986	549	434	172	986	66	237	3
167	131	181	1503	17	45	44	555	114	191	4
72	1	2	196	13	22	21	52	7	27	5
7311	.	.	953	5	2	14	336	2	10	6
254	934	7	729	14	2	1	42	5	13	7
.	10	455	108	43641	4	3	44	8	13	8
243	28	5	44524	614	8206	1652	1021	155	440	9
227	34	6	7660	9063	260	179	1632	78	353	10
85	3	2	1767	51	3254	120	138	30	157	11
135	10	3	132	37	101	315	48	2	25	12
135	12	11	402	4	10	57	6836	163	166	13
1	1	.	200	3	3	.	41	7	21	14
1	2	3	382	6	469	.	29	3	1377	15
424	17	63	212	35	25	4	221	8	2	16
56	2	1	1655	10	12	15	187	109	42	17
25	2	3	90	44	108	20	44	.	16	18
230	30	76	46	110	279	284	138	8	53	19
782	23	99	349	323	32	8	40	2	41	20
1957	77	104	1906	272	467	119	1126	55	103	21
4	.	.	110	9	2	4	20	5	4	22
31	3	7	59	51	57	47	447	15	72	23
.	.	.	.	.	.	.	2	.	.	24
.	.	.	.	.	.	.	.	.	.	25
738	28	41	374	108	153	35	104	13	52	26
61	5	16	234	12	23	5	3	1	3	27
152	4	3	1527	28	584	29	127	14	68	28
3	.	.	13	8	9	7	.	1	.	29
42	2	3	52	6	80	21	52	.	1	30
8	.	3	55	18	98	8	79	17	63	31
5	.	2	776	18	144	23	104	21	16	32
10	45	2	1868	31	190	38	462	32	137	33
13	7	3	370	11	59	84	138	62	46	34
38	.	.	2	4	4	14	2	.	2	35
24	1	.	126	16	413	287	32	8	31	36
22	.	.	30	6	6	5	13	.	1	37
3	.	.	1624	27	103	2	14	.	.	38
11	1	3	299	28	14	1	23	3	2	39
.	.	.	17	12	5	1	12	.	1	40
962	2	2	61	5	9	4	2	.	37	41
262	8	12	92	87	65	21	24	12	28	42
228	23	2	2006	1137	509	265	1085	31	263	43
20	.	.	112	31	26	5	38	3	42	44
241	12	2	860	141	140	48	215	11	33	45
66	4	.	239	209	19	4	146	8	9	46
161	24	4	1165	29	249	67	160	16	41	47
203	61	203	2859	2500	491	147	1433	126	199	48
15	2	8	34	8	16	4	25	2	4	49
18	8	29	249	8	88	31	121	7	24	50
20	8	8	180	5	102	21	280	1	16	51
66	4	18	977	89	236	65	294	23	45	52
121	9	7	484	36	113	70	178	28	49	53
.	.	.	28	2	.	.	11	.	.	54
1032	86	103	7555	939	1723	628	2625	200	428	55
90	5	4	940	78	179	23	116	8	24	56
.	.	.	.	.	.	.	.	.	.	57
2	.	.	96	1	.	.	2	.	.	58
18308	1844	1551	93728	60533	19739	5539	21967	1491	5033	59
.	.	.	.	.	.	.	.	.	.	60
18308	1844	1551	93728	60533	19739	5539	21967	1491	5033	61
1440	329	380	6142	1155	1463	585	2834	217	563	62
-1874	44	50	1029	19366	236	53	526	29	117	63
10318	745	451	27605	1557	8113	4174	9588	1995	2979	64
794	-66	3003	2818	-1046	2243	329	1927	288	683	65
10678	1052	3884	37594	21032	12055	5141	14875	2529	4342	66
28986	2896	5435	131322	81565	31794	10680	36842	4020	9375	67
1509	5256	52867	29964	25289	4031	3074	3785	1643	1797	68
30495	8152	58302	161286	106854	35825	13754	40627	5663	11172	69

LFD. NR.	VERWENDUNG / AUFKOMMEN	H.V. EISEN U. STAHL	H.V. NE-METALLEN, NE-METALL-HALBZEUG	H.V. GIESSEREI-ERZEUG-NISSEN	INPUT DER — H.V. ERZEUGN. DER ZIEHE-REIEN, KALTWALZ-WERKE USW.	H.V.STAHL-U. LEICHT-METALLBAU-ERZEUGN., SCHIENEN-FAHRZG.
		16	17	18	19	20
	OUTPUT NACH GUETERGRUPPEN (ZEILE 1 BIS 58)					
1	PRODUKTE DER LANDWIRTSCHAFT	5	.	1	1	1
2	PRODUKTE DER FORSTWIRTSCHAFT, FISCHEREI USW.	-	-	8	2	-
3	ELEKTRIZITAET, DAMPF, WARMWASSER	2087	1833	398	450	70
4	GAS	959	133	110	249	29
5	WASSER	142	36	33	53	5
6	KOHLE ERZEUGNISSE DES KOHLENBERGBAUS	4934	159	215	10	31
7	BERGBAUERZEUGNISSE (OHNE KOHLE, ERDOEL, ERDGAS)	2483	2031	68	7	-
8	ERDOEL, ERDGAS	56	9	7	20	2
9	CHEMISCHE ERZEUGNISSE, SPALT- U. BRUTSTOFFE	358	1356	416	242	183
10	MINERALOELERZEUGNISSE	814	211	187	284	247
11	KUNSTSTOFFERZEUGNISSE	74	13	29	88	227
12	GUMMIERZEUGNISSE	5	11	76	17	28
13	STEINE U. ERDEN, BAUSTOFFE USW.	1122	33	345	147	50
14	FEINKERAMISCHE ERZEUGNISSE	19	3	2	32	120
15	GLAS U. GLASWAREN	58	1	2	59	177
16	EISEN U. STAHL	63080	42	1043	7626	3342
17	NE-METALLE, NE-METALLHALBZEUG	656	12457	1345	719	624
18	GIESSEREIERZEUGNISSE	975	59	1056	200	397
19	ERZEUGNISSE DER ZIEHEREIEN, KALTWALZWERKE USW.	1035	100	127	3838	1954
20	STAHL- U. LEICHTMETALLBAUERZEUGN., SCHIENENFAHRZEUGE	10	13	17	-	961
21	MASCHINENBAUERZEUGNISSE	461	139	126	271	1228
22	BUEROMASCHINEN, ADV-GERAETE U. -EINRICHTUNGEN	15	7	7	2	9
23	STRASSENFAHRZEUGE	73	117	10	51	31
24	WASSERFAHRZEUGE	3	-	-	-	-
25	LUFT- U. RAUMFAHRZEUGE	-	-	-	-	-
26	ELEKTROTECHNISCHE ERZEUGNISSE	537	108	102	70	406
27	FEINMECHANISCHE U. OPTISCHE ERZEUGNISSE, UHREN	75	45	59	86	140
28	EBM-WAREN	247	75	59	289	984
29	MUSIKINSTRUMENTE, SPIELWAREN, SPORTGERAETE, SCHMUCK USW.	2	3	3	6	-
30	HOLZ	28	14	8	29	110
31	HOLZWAREN	54	59	73	50	76
32	ZELLSTOFF, HOLZSCHLIFF, PAPIER, PAPPE	26	12	6	20	29
33	PAPIER- U. PAPPEWAREN	58	11	8	14	21
34	ERZEUGNISSE DER DRUCKEREI U. VERVIELFAELTIGUNG	29	19	13	38	31
35	LEDER, LEDERWAREN, SCHUHE	-	1	9	2	-
36	TEXTILIEN	2	3	3	11	-
37	BEKLEIDUNG	1	2	1	5	4
38	NAHRUNGSMITTEL (OHNE GETRAENKE)	26	-	1	-	2
39	GETRAENKE	49	5	4	5	3
40	TABAKWAREN	25	9	1	2	1
41	HOCH- U. TIEFBAULEISTUNGEN U.AE.	82	18	13	11	4
42	AUSBAULEISTUNGEN	24	10	41	83	28
43	DIENSTLEISTUNGEN DES GROSSHANDELS U.AE., RUECKGEWINNUNG	2952	1264	957	1003	715
44	DIENSTLEISTUNGEN DES EINZELHANDELS	74	3	8	9	30
45	DIENSTLEISTUNGEN DER EISENBAHNEN	863	91	70	276	147
46	DIENSTLEISTUNGEN D. SCHIFFAHRT, WASSERSTRASSEN, HAEFEN	85	16	14	13	13
47	DIENSTLEISTUNGEN D. POSTDIENSTES U. FERNMELDEWESENS	146	46	49	264	147
48	DIENSTLEISTUNGEN DES SONSTIGEN VERKEHRS	1068	269	174	497	461
49	DIENSTLEISTUNGEN DER KREDITINSTITUTE	4	5	7	19	21
50	DIENSTLSTG. D. VERSICHERUNGEN (OH. SOZIALVERSICHERUNG)	61	34	36	77	69
51	DIENSTLSTG. D. GEBAEUDE- U. WOHNUNGSVERMIETUNG	34	24	20	320	62
52	MARKTBESTIMMTE DIENSTLSTG. D. GASTGEWERBES U. D. HEIME	327	79	68	113	348
53	DIENSTLEISTUNGEN D. WISSENSCHAFT U. KULTUR U. D. VERLAGE	165	69	89	186	145
54	MARKTBESTIMMTE DIENSTLSTG. D. GESUNDH.- U. VETERINAERWES.	-	-	-	1	-
55	SONSTIGE MARKTBESTIMMTE DIENSTLEISTUNGEN	1404	568	737	839	1001
56	DIENSTLEISTUNGEN DER GEBIETSKOERPERSCHAFTEN	215	66	36	120	128
57	DIENSTLEISTUNGEN DER SOZIALVERSICHERUNG	-	-	-	-	-
58	DIENSTLSTG. D. PRIV.ORG.OH.ERWERBSZWECK, HAEUSL.DIENSTE	2	-	-	-	-
59	VORLEISTUNGEN DER PRODUKTIONSBEREICHE (SP.1 BIS 59) BZW. LETZTE VERWENDUNG VON GUETERN (SP.60 BIS 66) OHNE UMSATZSTEUER	88089	21691	8297	18826	14842
60	NICHTABZUGSFAEHIGE UMSATZSTEUER	-	-	-	-	-
61	VORLEISTUNGEN DER PRODUKTIONSBEREICHE (SP.1 BIS 59) BZW. LETZTE VERWENDUNG VON GUETERN (SP.60 BIS 66) EINSCHL. NICHTABZUGSFAEHIGER UMSATZSTEUER	88089	21691	8297	18826	14842
62	ABSCHREIBUNGEN	2517	831	780	1266	564
63	PRODUKTIONSSTEUERN ABZUEGL. SUBVENTIONEN	73	62	50	295	128
64	EINKOMMEN AUS UNSELBSTAENDIGER ARBEIT	10996	3307	6372	9227	7115
65	EINKOMMEN AUS UNTERNEHMERTAETIGKEIT UND VERMOEGEN	-680	190	363	2366	2325
66	BRUTTOWERTSCHOEPFUNG ZU MARKTPREISEN	12906	4390	7565	13154	10132
67	PRODUKTIONSWERT	100995	26081	15862	31980	24974
68	EINFUHR GLEICHARTIGER GUETER ZU AB-ZOLL-PREISEN	11125	15309	500	2475	1139
69	GESAMTES AUFKOMMEN AN GUETERN	112120	41390	16362	34455	26113

PRODUKTIONSBEREICHE

H.V. MASCHINENBAUERZEUGNISSEN	H.V. BUEROMASCHINEN ADV·GERAETEN U. ·EINRICHTUNGEN	H.V. STRASSENFAHRZEUGEN	H.V. WASSERFAHRZEUGEN	H.V. LUFT· U. RAUMFAHRZEUGEN	H.V. ELEKTROTECHNISCHEN ERZEUGNISSEN	H.V. FEINMECHANISCHEN U. OPTISCHEN ERZEUGN. UHREN	H.V. EBMWAREN	H.V.MUSIKINSTRUM. SPIELW. SPORTGER.. SCHMUCK USW.	BEARB. V. HOLZ	LFD. NR.
21	22	23	24	25	26	27	28	29	30	

3	3	26	3	2	35	1	7	8	9	1
2	12	1	·	·	·	23	·	23	3491	2
560	77	926	48	33	524	64	218	28	216	3
1·7	12	161	12	11	60	6	58	2	15	4
69	7	57	11	4	57	11	44	4	4	5
20	·	35	·	1	7	2	2	·	6	6
2	·	2	·	·	5	·	27	·	·	7
9	1	11	1	1	5	·	4	·	2	8
828	5·	1709	65	26	1793	201	725	280	278	9
1112	79	771	48	49	829	137	376	61	215	10
1599	217	2525	94	41	2759	382	728	193	54	11
805	10	2926	5	3	347	29	126	26	12	12
200	31	437	45	11	177	2	51	30	30	13
19	2	8	·	1	193	16	18	·	25	14
57	10	886	10	3	632	247	147	31	10	15
4018	141	4956	566	77	1013	55	3413	22	15	16
2347	113	989	14	249	5070	627	2907	657	6	17
4129	121	4095	88	61	1024	133	564	14	2	18
3975	187	4858	93	51	1554	245	1460	132	9	19
621	3	45	144	1	15	18	16	·	5	20
21597	211	2724	1076	61	2009	153	627	12	111	21
8	855	147	83	3	293	16	8	3	2	22
708	15	24475	18	3	39	10	9	3	16	23
5	2	1	132	11	·	11	1	·	·	24
·	1	·	·	1604	12	·	·	·	·	25
5858	1194	6234	404	17·	16605	581	608	72	29	26
697	36	874	275	179	247	2275	143	36	·	27
1000	83	1963	96	43	1104	111	1239	82	29	28
56	5	17	·	·	16	8	92	581	·	29
177	3	204	42	6	239	21	238	73	1403	30
275	20	205	35	23	146	25	263	68	9	31
141	144	137	2	1	239	28	154	73	44	32
171	11	98	·	1	560	65	213	36	34	33
276	150	212	4	8	256	188	82	167	23	34
21	3	17	1	·	5	12	12	12	4	35
56	7	953	18	10	46	26	100	51	8	36
9	10	26	4	·	2	4	3	3	·	37
21	·	2	·	·	20	1	9	1	6	38
15	4	29	2	3	2·	7	18	2	3	39
18	1	11	1	2	14	2	5	2	2	40
59	27	59	·	·	6	3	9	4	21	41
74	56	85	4	1	18	8	66	17	13	42
1588	330	4424	176	126	1712	415	761	466	272	43
164	20	153	9	6	137	40	34	9	24	44
315	14	599	28	5	169	19	175	17	88	45
63	·	47	1	·	36	1	9	2	4	46
986	53	638	38	4	492	198	280	62	47	47
1669	102	1821	86	43	1144	277	631	176	346	48
103	22	74	2	1	50	15	32	4	8	49
413	2	446	18	9	80	41	53	9	38	50
322	33	176	3	69	443	36	174	15	4	51
1574	97	632	22	105	1319	150	478	66	66	52
798	41	694	26	19	317	81	231	27	29	53
22	11	18	·	·	25	4	17	·	·	54
6322	1456	5938	381	318	5464	974	2134	476	235	55
665	9	379	20	262	243	67	109	10	22	56
·	·	·	·	·	·	·	·	·	·	57
1	1	6	·	·	3	1	1	·	·	58
66739	6106	79942	4254	3722	49630	8074	19909	4148	7344	59
·	·	·	·	·	·	·	·	·	·	60
66739	6106	79942	4254	3722	49630	8074	19909	4148	7344	61
4157	1420	5781	219	275	4118	697	1401	253	471	62
952	136	1017	-207	12	261	284	368	92	59	63
45619	3432	39354	2501	2982	41456	7571	12394	2342	1837	64
3523	174	3008	-349	178	5279	2522	2753	369	492	65
54251	5162	49160	2164	3447	51114	11074	16916	3056	2859	66
120990	11268	129102	6418	7169	100744	19148	36825	7204	10203	67
16104	5771	14853	751	6400	21290	4743	6304	5438	4011	68
137094	17039	143955	7169	13569	122034	23891	43129	12642	14214	69

		INPUT DER			
LFD. NR.	VERWENDUNG / AUFKOMMEN	H.V. HOLZWAREN	H.V. ZELLSTOFF, HOLZ-SCHLIFF, PAPIER, PAPPE	H.V. PAPIER- U. PAPPE-WAREN	H.V. ERZEUGN. DER DRUCKEREI U.VERVIEL-FAELTIGUNG	H.V. LEDER, LEDER-WAREN, SCHUHEN
		31	32	33	34	35

OUTPUT NACH GUETERGRUPPEN (ZEILE 1 BIS 58).

1	PRODUKTE DER LANDWIRTSCHAFT	38	23	25	5	-
2	PRODUKTE DER FORSTWIRTSCHAFT, FISCHEREI USW.	34	425	18	-	37
3	ELEKTRIZITAET, DAMPF, WARMWASSER	169	977	125	157	30
4	GAS	3	157	29	20	3
5	WASSER	6	17	8	15	4
6	KOHLE, ERZEUGNISSE DES KOHLENBERGBAUS	2	71	-	2	2
7	BERGBAUERZEUGNISSE (OHNE KOHLE, ERDOEL, ERDGAS)	-	-	-	-	-
8	ERDOEL, ERDGAS	-	13	2	2	-
9	CHEMISCHE ERZEUGNISSE, SPALT- U. BRUTSTOFFE	761	752	721	1250	296
10	MINERALOELERZEUGNISSE	576	516	139	175	89
11	KUNSTSTOFFERZEUGNISSE	1604	26	468	88	460
12	GUMMIERZEUGNISSE	32	3	10	12	71
13	STEINE U. ERDEN, BAUSTOFFE USW.	77	50	14	4	-
14	FEINKERAMISCHE ERZEUGNISSE	12	2	8	2	13
15	GLAS U. GLASWAREN	381	3	-	-	3
16	EISEN U. STAHL	22	4	21	2	1
17	NE-METALLE, NE-METALLHALBZEUG	-	1	2	1	1
18	GIESSEREIERZEUGNISSE	1	2	2	1	-
19	ERZEUGNISSE DER ZIEHEREIEN, KALTWALZWERKE USW.	413	29	64	23	28
20	STAHL- U. LEICHTMETALLBAUERZEUGN., SCHIENENFAHRZEUGE	6	26	3	-	-
21	MASCHINENBAUERZEUGNISSE	214	312	145	139	46
22	BUEROMASCHINEN, ADV-GERAETE U. -EINRICHTUNGEN	2	1	7	86	2
23	STRASSENFAHRZEUGE	233	27	40	53	7
24	WASSERFAHRZEUGE	-	-	-	-	-
25	LUFT- U. RAUMFAHRZEUGE	-	-	-	-	-
26	ELEKTROTECHNISCHE ERZEUGNISSE	170	78	30	46	10
27	FEINMECHANISCHE U. OPTISCHE ERZEUGNISSE, UHREN	3	-	-	4	20
28	EBM-WAREN	1252	4	207	96	206
29	MUSIKINSTRUMENTE, SPIELWAREN, SPORTGERAETE, SCHMUCK USW.	3	-	12	38	25
30	HOLZ	4888	63	14	7	7
31	HOLZWAREN	2790	36	11	7	35
32	ZELLSTOFF, HOLZSCHLIFF, PAPIER, PAPPE	92	4540	4521	3955	34
33	PAPIER- U. PAPPEWAREN	122	161	2448	431	60
34	ERZEUGNISSE DER DRUCKEREI U. VERVIELFAELTIGUNG	166	3	344	833	8
35	LEDER, LEDERWAREN, SCHUHE	74	1	12	3	1345
36	TEXTILIEN	853	19	75	17	62
37	BEKLEIDUNG	4	1	3	-	49
38	NAHRUNGSMITTEL (OHNE GETRAENKE)	13	1	98	1	435
39	GETRAENKE	5	2	4	6	3
40	TABAKWAREN	5	1	1	4	1
41	HOCH- U. TIEFBAULEISTUNGEN U.AE.	42	6	2	-	4
42	AUSBAULEISTUNGEN	10	7	11	21	7
43	DIENSTLEISTUNGEN DES GROSSHANDELS U.AE., RUECKGEWINNUNG	950	1141	431	539	295
44	DIENSTLEISTUNGEN DES EINZELHANDELS	43	14	15	27	95
45	DIENSTLEISTUNGEN DER EISENBAHNEN	95	90	63	74	17
46	DIENSTLEISTUNGEN D. SCHIFFAHRT, WASSERSTRASSEN, HAEFEN	5	16	7	8	1
47	DIENSTLEISTUNGEN D. POSTDIENSTES U. FERNMELDEWESENS	362	37	130	256	142
48	DIENSTLEISTUNGEN DES SONSTIGEN VERKEHRS	849	498	481	485	99
49	DIENSTLEISTUNGEN DER KREDITINSTITUTE	22	10	15	12	7
50	DIENSTLSTG. D. VERSICHERUNGEN (OH. SOZIALVERSICHERUNG)	121	49	65	39	9
51	DIENSTLEISTUNGEN D. GEBAEUDE- U. WOHNUNGSVERMIETUNG	68	24	61	122	48
52	MARKTBESTIMMTE DIENSTLSTG. D. GASTGEWERBES U. D. HEIME	370	50	71	166	123
53	DIENSTLEISTUNGEN D. WISSENSCHAFT U. KULTUR U. D. VERLAGE	197	54	51	239	54
54	MARKTBESTIMMTE DIENSTLSTG. D. GESUNDH.- U. VETERINAERWES.	1	-	-	-	-
55	SONSTIGE MARKTBESTIMMTE DIENSTLEISTUNGEN	1724	350	1010	1145	265
56	DIENSTLEISTUNGEN DER GEBIETSKOERPERSCHAFTEN	92	43	64	43	20
57	DIENSTLEISTUNGEN DER SOZIALVERSICHERUNG	-	-	-	-	-
58	DIENSTLSTG. D. PRIV.ORG.OH.ERWERBSZWECK, HAEUSL.DIENSTE	1	-	-	4	-
59	VORLEISTUNGEN DER PRODUKTIONSBEREICHE (SP.1 BIS 59) BZW. LETZTE VERWENDUNG VON GUETERN (SP.60 BIS 66) OHNE UMSATZSTEUER	19978	10736	12112	10665	4579
60	NICHTABZUGSFAEHIGE UMSATZSTEUER					
61	VORLEISTUNGEN DER PRODUKTIONSBEREICHE (SP.1 BIS 59) BZW. LETZTE VERWENDUNG VON GUETERN (SP.60 BIS 66) EINSCHL. NICHTABZUGSFAEHIGER UMSATZSTEUER	19978	10736	12112	10665	4579
62	ABSCHREIBUNGEN	1118	691	646	1128	245
63	PRODUKTIONSSTEUERN ABZUEGL. SUBVENTIONEN	287	53	116	209	58
64	EINKOMMEN AUS UNSELBSTAENDIGER ARBEIT	10322	2148	3973	8832	2585
65	EINKOMMEN AUS UNTERNEHMERTAETIGKEIT UND VERMOEGEN	3276	595	326	1711	984
66	BRUTTOWERTSCHOEPFUNG ZU MARKTPREISEN	15003	3487	5061	11880	3872
67	PRODUKTIONSWERT	34981	14223	17173	22545	8451
68	EINFUHR GLEICHARTIGER GUETER ZU AB-ZOLL-PREISEN	3773	7155	1272	1210	5744
69	GESAMTES AUFKOMMEN AN GUETERN	38754	21378	18445	23755	14195

DM

PRODUKTIONSBEREICHE

H.V. TEXTILIEN	H.V. BEKLEIDUNG	H.V. NAHRUNGS-MITTELN (OHNE GETRAENKE)	H.V. GETRAENKEN	H.V. TABAKWAREN	HOCH- U. TIEFBAU U.AE.	AUSBAU	LEISTG. DES GROSS-HANDELS U.AE., RUECKGE-WINNUNG	LEISTG. DES EINZEL-HANDELS	LFD. NR.
36	37	38	39	40	41	42	43	44	
1388	96	49458	2026	1140	10	2	237	26	1
3	861	1337	21	2	137	33	12	58	2
507	63	922	155	22	539	126	979	2642	3
134	5	295	47	5	19	11	184	270	4
40	5	159	67	2	121	19	128	146	5
13	.	67	10	.	8	5	6	13	6
.	.	59	.	.	1	.	6	3	7
10	.	25	4	.	.	.	.	.	8
3219	195	998	296	122	303	1431	185	146	9
459	252	2015	474	121	1840	672	2948	1673	10
177	293	1080	231	30	3711	3206	132	191	11
65	22	78	27	3	152	130	352	111	12
2	.	13	1	2	19633	1295	54	50	13
.	.	3	3	1	144	1552	3	3	14
3	.	645	732	1	321	471	4	13	15
7	2	35	.	1	2116	360	114	120	16
1	.	4	.	.	514	271	7	7	17
.	3	5	1	.	639	291	27	2	18
4	10	1	1	20	1797	333	7	55	19
3	6	9	.	.	1788	1818	16	7	20
425	89	393	217	89	630	1481	35	299	21
18	2	6	11	12	28	3	509	367	22
74	21	328	185	49	233	137	510	574	23
.	.	.	.	.	.	.	.	3	24
.	.	.	.	.	.	.	1	3	25
33	44	70	21	11	1358	2474	351	342	26
3	.	10	.	.	25	7	85	34	27
57	158	1309	681	61	1007	2867	236	66	28
3	20	13	.	1	26	8	142	74	29
.	3	5	31	10	3253	1864	.	72	30
3	33	134	93	25	1480	2903	163	119	31
37	23	95	20	30	50	23	455	189	32
216	86	1276	356	185	64	269	608	404	33
87	96	735	232	79	129	72	585	2316	34
58	246	5	.	.	11	3	9	3	35
9:23	6996	22	10	3	37	80	191	43	36
6	879	6	2	1	10	4	1	24	37
46	29	23229	1228	7	15	6	50	39	38
5	2	395	2074	15	31	10	170	30	39
6	2	33	14	78	19	17	206	54	40
1	2	13	5	1	3545	.	149	164	41
20	19	71	99	.	1772	1942	295	290	42
798	1417	3665	791	95	3109	1086	2683	529	43
227	88	435	81	3	165	164	62	63	44
74	40	788	68	24	460	125	160	87	45
7	1	112	5	1	233	10	158	162	46
230	311	431	125	2	840	183	1680	886	47
449	319	3732	886	64	2786	1602	3088	960	48
23	10	33	5	3	200	66	435	134	49
73	22	203	44	10	896	195	890	316	50
47	110	222	75	19	275	63	2649	6383	51
258	415	244	127	22	325	41	2959	267	52
223	108	370	117	40	204	260	983	970	53
.	.	13	1	.	48	7	50	25	54
1178	1465	2913	1337	601	4037	3074	9009	4058	55
83	82	504	106	45	849	93	439	219	56
.	.	.	.	.	.	.	.	.	57
1	.	2	.	.	.	.	.	.	58
19927	14551	99025	13147	3058	61943	33165	35397	26104	59
.	.	. .	.	.	.	.	.	.	60
19927	14551	99025	13147	3058	61943	33165	35397	26104	61
1303	377	3653	1589	289	4005	1055	5450	5901	62
185	133	-404	4037	11034	1244	622	-1302	3441	63
9193	6996	17109	4992	998	47671	19100	48891	43822	64
1339	1763	13310	212	1	15121	13652	26893	22254	65
12020	9269	33668	10830	12322	68041	34429	79732	75418	66
31947	23820	132693	23977	15380	129984	67594	115129	101522	67
16873	9506	20230	3153	442	4987	18	2804	.	68
48820	33326	152923	27130	15822	134971	67612	117933	101522	69

LFD. NR.	VERWENDUNG / AUFKOMMEN	LEISTG. DER EISEN- BAHNEN	LEISTG. DER SCHIFF- FAHRT, WASSER- STRASSEN, HAEFEN	LEISTG. DES POST- DIENSTES U. FERN- MELDE- WESENS	LEISTG. DES SONSTIGEN VERKEHRS	LEISTG. DER KREDIT- INSTITUTE
		45	46	47	48	49

OUTPUT NACH GUETERGRUPPEN (ZEILE 1 BIS 58):

LFD. NR.	AUFKOMMEN	45	46	47	48	49
1	PRODUKTE DER LANDWIRTSCHAFT	.	9	.	10	7
2	PRODUKTE DER FORSTWIRTSCHAFT, FISCHEREI USW.	.	.	1	2	7
3	ELEKTRIZITAET, DAMPF, WARMWASSER	1094	37	371	191	586
4	GAS	7	6	83	67	83
5	WASSER	.	6	.	33	38
6	KOHLE, ERZEUGNISSE DES KOHLENBERGBAUS	30	2	3	1	1
7	BERGBAUERZEUGNISSE (OHNE KOHLE, ERDOEL, ERDGAS)	.	.	.	8	.
8	ERDOEL, ERDGAS	.	.	.	.	.
9	CHEMISCHE ERZEUGNISSE, SPALT- U. BRUTSTOFFE	54	19	52	342	59
10	MINERALOELERZEUGNISSE	723	2077	308	5292	406
11	KUNSTSTOFFERZEUGNISSE	7	1	3	23	4
12	GUMMIERZEUGNISSE	10	9	6	592	1
13	STEINE U. ERDEN, BAUSTOFFE USW.	12	1	28	55	.
14	FEINKERAMISCHE ERZEUGNISSE	30	.	3	3	.
15	GLAS U. GLASWAREN	25	.	9	2	1
16	EISEN U. STAHL	298	23	23	331	.
17	NE-METALLE, NE-METALLHALBZEUG	4	.	.	4	.
18	GIESSEREIERZEUGNISSE	48	.	5	12	.
19	ERZEUGNISSE DER ZIEHEREIEN, KALTWALZWERKE USW.	80	5	20	64	1
20	STAHL- U. LEICHTMETALLBAUERZEUGN., SCHIENENFAHRZEUGE	241	69	15	228	.
21	MASCHINENBAUERZEUGNISSE	89	8	22	133	17
22	BUEROMASCHINEN, ADV-GERAETE U. -EINRICHTUNGEN	21	3	58	45	25
23	STRASSENFAHRZEUGE	53	17	46	2225	16
24	WASSERFAHRZEUGE	.	388	.	116	.
25	LUFT- U. RAUMFAHRZEUGE	14	29	.	558	.
26	ELEKTROTECHNISCHE ERZEUGNISSE	143	10	382	300	380
27	FEINMECHANISCHE U. OPTISCHE ERZEUGNISSE, UHREN	2	1	11	46	9
28	EBM-WAREN	10	23	21	328	29
29	MUSIKINSTRUMENTE, SPIELWAREN, SPORTGERAETE, SCHMUCK USW.	7	7	1	185	4
30	HOLZ	2	2	5	.	.
31	HOLZWAREN	6	1	19	12	14
32	ZELLSTOFF, HOLZSCHLIFF, PAPIER, PAPPE	8	1	10	47	64
33	PAPIER- U. PAPPEWAREN	27	10	35	254	39
34	ERZEUGNISSE DER DRUCKEREI U. VERVIELFAELTIGUNG	229	53	357	652	524
35	LEDER, LEDERWAREN, SCHUHE	43	3	.	16	.
36	TEXTILIEN	46	16	32	56	10
37	BEKLEIDUNG	14	2	34	29	9
38	NAHRUNGSMITTEL (OHNE GETRAENKE)	.	189	.	289	9
39	GETRAENKE	4	43	1	47	8
40	TABAKWAREN	1	4	.	57	3
41	HOCH- U. TIEFBAULEISTUNGEN U.AE.	112	8	16	197	27
42	AUSBAULEISTUNGEN	64	2	165	313	186
43	DIENSTLEISTUNGEN DES GROSSHANDELS U.AE., RUECKGEWINNUNG	174	186	77	590	74
44	DIENSTLEISTUNGEN DES EINZELHANDELS	19	13	7	50	12
45	DIENSTLEISTUNGEN DER EISENBAHNEN	35	15	281	87	15
46	DIENSTLEISTUNGEN D. SCHIFFAHRT, WASSERSTRASSEN, HAEFEN	23	2836	16	1407	16
47	DIENSTLEISTUNGEN D. POSTDIENSTES U. FERNMELDEWESENS	79	59	259	1214	1057
48	DIENSTLEISTUNGEN DES SONSTIGEN VERKEHRS	435	266	171	5200	339
49	DIENSTLEISTUNGEN DER KREDITINSTITUTE	10	11	40	97	56006
50	DIENSTLSTG. D. VERSICHERUNGEN (OH. SOZIALVERSICHERUNG)	175	115	48	1634	2
51	DIENSTLEISTUNGEN D. GEBAEUDE- U. WOHNUNGSVERMIETUNG	37	10	119	895	614
52	MARKTBESTIMMTE DIENSTLSTG. D. GASTGEWERBES U. D. HEIME	70	67	24	1795	760
53	DIENSTLEISTUNG D. WISSENSCHAFT U. KULTUR U. D. VERLAGE	22	45	19	195	214
54	MARKTBESTIMMTE DIENSTLSTG. D. GESUNDH.- U. VETERINAERWES.	30	9	12	64	36
55	SONSTIGE MARKTBESTIMMTE DIENSTLEISTUNGEN	442	492	269	2081	5503
56	DIENSTLEISTUNGEN DER GEBIETSKOERPERSCHAFTEN	43	17	31	596	136
57	DIENSTLEISTUNGEN DER SOZIALVERSICHERUNG	.	.	.	.	.
58	DIENSTLSTG. D. PRIV.ORG.OH.ERWERBSZWECK, HAEUSL.DIENSTE	.	.	5	.	.
59	VORLEISTUNGEN DER PRODUKTIONSBEREICHE (SP.1 BIS 59) BZW. LETZTE VERWENDUNG VON GUETERN (SP.60 BIS 66) OHNE UMSATZSTEUER	5152	7225	3523	29070	67353
60	NICHTABZUGSFAEHIGE UMSATZSTEUER	.	64	337	.	778
61	VORLEISTUNGEN DER PRODUKTIONSBEREICHE (SP.1 BIS 59) BZW. LETZTE VERWENDUNG VON GUETERN (SP.60 BIS 66) EINSCHL. NICHTABZUGSFAEHIGER UMSATZSTEUER	5152	7289	3860	29070	68131
62	ABSCHREIBUNGEN	3546	1221	6978	5817	1859
63	PRODUKTIONSSTEUERN ABZUEGL. SUBVENTIONEN	-5200	119	21	-607	2264
64	EINKOMMEN AUS UNSELBSTAENDIGER ARBEIT	12524	2946	17770	19069	23645
65	EINKOMMEN AUS UNTERNEHMERTAETIGKEIT UND VERMOEGEN	-1678	538	6635	12015	-31246
66	BRUTTOWERTSCHOEPFUNG ZU MARKTPREISEN	9192	4824	31404	36294	-3478
67	PRODUKTIONSWERT	14344	12113	35264	65364	64653
68	EINFUHR GLEICHARTIGER GUETER ZU AB-ZOLL-PREISEN	485	3678	261	4263	496
69	GESAMTES AUFKOMMEN AN GUETERN	14829	15791	35525	69627	65149

DM

PRODUKTIONSBEREICHE

LEISTG. DER VERSI-CHERUNGEN (OHNE SO-ZIALVER-SICHERUNG)	VERMIETUNG VON GEBAEUDEN UND WOHNUNGEN	MARKTBEST. LEISTG. DES GAST-GEWERBES U. DER HEIME	LEISTG. DER WISSEN-SCHAFT U. KULTUR U. DER VERLAGE	MARKTBEST. LEISTG.DES GESUNDH.- U. VETE-RINAER-WESENS	SONSTIGE MARKTBEST. DIENST-LEISTUNGEN USW.	LEISTG. DER GEBIETS-KOERPER-SCHAFTEN	LEISTG. DER SOZIALVER-SICHERUNG	LEISTG.DER PRIV. ORG. OH. ER-WERBSZWECK. HAEUSL. DIENSTE	LFD. NR.
50	51	52	53	54	55	56	57	58	
21	182	3132	30	128	405	1256	191	336	1
2	1422	162	70	178	659	62	2	130	2
241	65	974	143	264	907	2764	84	1043	3
32	8	75	24	60	167	679	42	56	4
25	2563	118	13	28	118	613	28	62	5
.	.	4	2	2	6	304	2	5	6
.	1C	1	.	.	3	.	.	.	7
.	.	.	.	.	.	.	.	.	8
137	38	382	670	1715	3441	3233	7686	1117	9
158	591	822	240	457	1433	4119	272	511	10
5	.	47	33	19	143	374	90	18	11
5	9	46	94	259	382	421	109	89	12
.	4	26	.	29	90	346	.	95	13
.	.	137	3	36	55	52	.	2	14
.	.	272	20	376	134	102	.	4	15
9	22	4	15	.	191	25	.	1	16
.	.	.	1	.	3	85	.	.	17
.	.	.	7	.	102	.	.	.	18
3	4	1	2	.	55	164	.	.	19
2	60	2	1	7	61	204	.	71	20
38	33	48	31	3	315	1087	.	1	21
132	.	115	74	24	152	727	208	.	22
58	49	77	86	97	843	3041	107	91	23
.	.	.	3	.	54	294	.	10	24
.	.	.	1	.	30	2386	.	130	25
379	296	173	339	119	2694	3756	156	86	26
99	127	20	90	3045	239	1030	2167	67	27
99	58	233	253	37	1080	1775	69	45	28
23	16	16	7	2	225	302	68	23	29
12	2	36	2	5	6	15	22	10	30
11	112	36	7	21	342	400	14	23	31
29	.	15	254	10	257	693	116	25	32
96	57	146	451	39	669	587	228	86	33
174	36	174	8155	74	612	1199	58	144	34
.	.	.	22	103	92	38	50	17	35
56	23	171	143	157	868	461	83	178	36
31	18	106	57	53	197	267	47	85	37
13	2	6831	98	119	1157	1968	444	1279	38
30	16	5284	151	5	906	131	79	880	39
27	19	2885	50	.	75	.	.	1	40
59	1988	19	86	20	100	3703	.	76	41
98	6793	2	34	23	351	2277	111	82	42
116	48	2547	512	957	1350	2370	1054	518	43
19	3	438	111	41	210	226	2772	39	44
9	6	106	18	12	62	579	164	27	45
1	3	28	1	2	106	36	1	29	46
776	17	407	770	273	850	2946	584	165	47
216	149	1265	480	503	1470	1922	585	473	48
606	867	90	32	22	265	419	52	188	49
372	834	148	260	317	1102	750	25	66	50
32	11	1438	214	697	1098	2123	118	130	51
250	142	146	1043	91	2944	2440	288	256	52
503	293	294	1590	178	3646	2619	250	133	53
15	23	7	10	209	67	2948	33924	13	54
8162	3346	1278	1524	1956	15470	7955	377	1478	55
151	3734	104	73	221	747	392	15547	169	56
.	.	.	.	.	.	30	.	.	57
.	.	3	195	407	457	8746	12260	.	58
13332	24686	30891	18555	13003	49460	77441	80534	10563	59
842	1719	.	22	872	512	6681	2076	647	60
14174	26405	30891	18577	13875	49972	84122	82610	11210	61
556	39996	2582	1873	3500	7086	8961	300	2550	62
2722	919	951	-400	-22	6202	229	10	20	63
10484	1864	10442	5364	8026	30759	153318	9240	24630	64
88	56134	6229	8300	21438	67455	.	.	.	65
13850	98913	20204	15137	32942	111502	162508	9550	27200	66
28024	125318	51095	33714	46817	161474	246630	92160	38410	67
221	561	2797	1079		10670	100	.	.	68
28245	125879	53892	34793	46817	172144	246730	92160	38410	69

69

MILL.

LFD. NR.	AUFKOMMEN / VERWENDUNG	INPUT DER PRODUKTIONSBEREICHE ZUSAMMEN	LETZTE	
			PRIVATER VERBRAUCH IM INLAND	STAATS-VERBRAUCH
		59	60	61

OUTPUT NACH GUETERGRUPPEN (ZEILE 1 BIS 58):

LFD. NR.	AUFKOMMEN	59	60	61
1	PRODUKTE DER LANDWIRTSCHAFT	70096	14527	.
2	PRODUKTE DER FORSTWIRTSCHAFT, FISCHEREI USW.	10061	1321	.
3	ELEKTRIZITAET, DAMPF, WARMWASSER	37378	14346	.
4	GAS	11404	6091	.
5	WASSER	5449	.	.
6	KOHLE, ERZEUGNISSE DES KOHLENBERGBAUS	25204	1206	.
7	BERGBAUERZEUGNISSE (OHNE KOHLE, ERDOEL, ERDGAS)	7013	130	.
8	ERDOEL, ERDGAS	54970		.
9	CHEMISCHE ERZEUGNISSE, SPALT- U. BRUTSTOFFE	100251	15435	.
10	MINERALOELERZEUGNISSE	61727	38149	.
11	KUNSTSTOFFERZEUGNISSE	27172	2580	.
12	GUMMIERZEUGNISSE	8650	1747	.
13	STEINE U. ERDEN, BAUSTOFFE USW.	32645	2655	.
14	FEINKERAMISCHE ERZEUGNISSE	2843	1494	.
15	GLAS U. GLASWAREN	8149	1099	.
16	EISEN U. STAHL	94931	.	.
17	NE-METALLE, NE-METALLHALBZEUG	31794	165	.
18	GIESSEREIERZEUGNISSE	14428	.	.
19	ERZEUGNISSE DER ZIEHEREIEN, KALTWALZWERKE USW.	24880	101	.
20	STAHL- U. LEICHTMETALLBAUERZEUGN., SCHIENENFAHRZEUGE	9000	.	.
21	MASCHINENBAUERZEUGNISSE	44935	999	.
22	BUEROMASCHINEN, ADV-GERAETE U. -EINRICHTUNGEN	4262	414	.
23	STRASSENFAHRZEUGE	36231	38432	.
24	WASSERFAHRZEUGE	1062	182	.
25	LUFT- U. RAUMFAHRZEUGE	4777	27	.
26	ELEKTROTECHNISCHE ERZEUGNISSE	49856	9649	.
27	FEINMECHANISCHE U. OPTISCHE ERZEUGNISSE, UHREN	12860	4647	.
28	EBM-WAREN	22375	3443	.
29	MUSIKINSTRUMENTE, SPIELWAREN, SPORTGERAETE, SCHMUCK USW.	2089	5562	.
30	HOLZ	13253	43	.
31	HOLZWAREN	10799	19076	.
32	ZELLSTOFF, HOLZSCHLIFF, PAPIER, PAPPE	17778	527	.
33	PAPIER- U. PAPPEWAREN	13697	2688	.
34	ERZEUGNISSE DER DRUCKEREI U. VERVIELFAELTIGUNG	20636	500	.
35	LEDER, LEDERWAREN, SCHUHE	2336	8910	.
36	TEXTILIEN	21734	16179	.
37	BEKLEIDUNG	2116	27338	.
38	NAHRUNGSMITTEL (OHNE GETRAENKE)	48401	91070	.
39	GETRAENKE	10979	15848	.
40	TABAKWAREN	3730	11187	.
41	HOCH- U. TIEFBAULEISTUNGEN U.AE.	12339	.	.
42	AUSBAULEISTUNGEN	17074	2590	.
43	DIENSTLEISTUNGEN DES GROSSHANDELS U.AE., RUECKGEWINNUNG	51677	29275	.
44	DIENSTLEISTUNGEN DES EINZELHANDELS	6795	94727	.
45	DIENSTLEISTUNGEN DER EISENBAHNEN	9157	4005	.
46	DIENSTLEISTUNGEN D. SCHIFFAHRT, WASSERSTRASSEN, HAEFEN	6487	333	.
47	DIENSTLEISTUNGEN D. POSTDIENSTES U. FERNMELDEWESENS	20621	14606	.
48	DIENSTLEISTUNGEN DES SONSTIGEN VERKEHRS	48689	14201	.
49	DIENSTLEISTUNGEN DER KREDITINSTITUTE	60236	4680	.
50	DIENSTLSTG. D. VERSICHERUNGEN (OH. SOZIALVERSICHERUNG)	11270	16790	.
51	DIENSTLEISTUNGEN D. GEBAEUDE- U. WOHNUNGSVERMIETUNG	20118	104874	.
52	MARKTBESTIMMTE DIENSTLSTG. D. GASTGEWERBES U. D. HEIME	23078	28430	.
53	DIENSTLEISTUNGEN D. WISSENSCHAFT U. KULTUR U. D. VERLAGE	18001	13561	.
54	MARKTBESTIMMTE DIENSTLSTG. D. GESUNDH.- U. VETERINAERWES.	38336	8481	.
55	SONSTIGE MARKTBESTIMMTE DIENSTLEISTUNGEN	127886	27800	.
56	DIENSTLEISTUNGEN DER GEBIETSKOERPERSCHAFTEN	28924		205770
57	DIENSTLEISTUNGEN DER SOZIALVERSICHERUNG	30	11500	92130
58	DIENSTLSTG. D. PRIV.ORG.OH.ERWERBSZWECK, HAEUSL.DIENSTE	22221	16199	.
59	VORLEISTUNGEN DER PRODUKTIONSBEREICHE (SP.1 BIS 59) BZW. LETZTE VERWENDUNG VON GUETERN (SP.60 BIS 66) OHNE UMSATZSTEUER	1504890	751770	297900
60	NICHTABZUGSFAEHIGE UMSATZSTEUER	14550	62800	.
61	VORLEISTUNGEN DER PRODUKTIONSBEREICHE (SP.1 BIS 59) BZW. LETZTE VERWENDUNG VON GUETERN (SP.60 BIS 66) EINSCHL. NICHTABZUGSFAEHIGER UMSATZSTEUER	1519440	814570	297900
62	ABSCHREIBUNGEN	173320		
63	PRODUKTIONSSTEUERN ABZUEGL. SUBVENTIONEN	53100		
64	EINKOMMEN AUS UNSELBSTAENDIGER ARBEIT	840710		
65	EINKOMMEN AUS UNTERNEHMERTAETIGKEIT UND VERMOEGEN	304330		
66	BRUTTOWERTSCHOEPFUNG ZU MARKTPREISEN	1371460		
67	PRODUKTIONSWERT	2890900		
68	EINFUHR GLEICHARTIGER GUETER ZU AB-ZOLL-PREISEN	378370		
69	GESAMTES AUFKOMMEN AN GUETERN	3269270		

DM

VERWENDUNG VON GUETERN					GESAMTE VERWENDUNG VON GUETERN	LFD. NR.
ANLAGEINVESTITIONEN		VORRATS-VERAEN-DERUNG	AUSFUHR VON WAREN UND DIENST-LEISTUNGEN	ZUSAMMEN		
AUS-RUESTUNGEN	BAUTEN					
62	63	64	65	66	67	
.	.	-464	2636	16699	86795	1
.	321	.	695	2337	12398	2
.	.	.	813	15159	52537	3
.	.	39	604	6734	18138	4
.	.	.	70	70	5519	5
.	.	372	3713	5291	30495	6
.	.	3	1006	1139	8152	7
.	.	906	2426	3332	58302	8
.	.	894	44706	61035	161286	9
.	.	1983	4995	45127	106854	10
.	.	114	5959	8653	35825	11
.	.	354	3003	5104	13754	12
.	16	2203	3108	7982	40627	13
.	.	33	1293	2820	5663	14
.	.	74	1850	3023	11172	15
.	.	703	16486	17189	112120	16
.	419	545	8467	9596	41390	17
881	.	103	950	1934	16342	18
.	4900	242	4732	9575	34455	19
3772	9424	87	3830	17113	26113	20
38815	374	-1067	53038	92159	137094	21
7240	.	334	4789	12777	17039	22
21207	.	700	47385	107724	143955	23
1796	.	2845	1284	6107	7169	24
992	.	2850	4923	8792	13569	25
23652	2996	3792	32089	72178	122034	26
2740	.	-2273	5917	11031	23891	27
4678	1030	17	11586	20754	43129	28
435	.	829	3726	10553	12642	29
.	.	-99	1017	961	14214	30
5326	372	83	3098	27935	38754	31
.	.	348	2725	3600	21378	32
.	.	269	1791	4748	18445	33
.	.	100	2519	3119	23755	34
.	.	1402	1547	11859	14195	35
420	.	525	9962	27086	48820	36
.	.	9	3863	31210	33326	37
.	.	-900	13952	104522	152923	38
.	.	-281	584	16151	27130	39
.	.	269	636	12092	15822	40
.	115471	.	7161	122632	134971	41
.	47941	.	47	50538	67612	42
12168	.	193	24620	66256	117933	43
.	.	.	.	94727	101522	44
263	.	44	1360	5672	14829	45
.	.	65	8906	9304	15791	46
.	.	.	298	14904	35525	47
1345	.	255	5137	20938	69627	48
.	.	.	233	4913	65149	49
.	.	.	185	16675	28245	50
.	.	.	887	105761	125879	51
.	.	.	2384	30814	53892	52
.	.	.	1231	16792	34793	53
.	.	.	.	8481	46817	54
.	10586	.	5872	44258	172144	55
.	.	.	536	217806	246730	56
.	.	.	.	92130	92160	57
.	.	.	.	16180	38410	58
125730	193450	18900	376630	1764380	3268270	59
2140	16660		300	81900	96450	60
127870	210110	18900	376930	1846280	3365720	61
						62
						63
						64
						65
						66
						67
						68
						69

IV. GREECE

A. GENERAL INFORMATION

The present report is based on the *Input-Output Table of the Greek Economy Year 1970*, published in 1978 by the Center of Planning and Economic Research of the Ministry of Co-ordination.

Input-output tables for Greece have been compiled for the years 1954, 1958, 1960 and 1970. The present report refers to the latest table available, that is, the 1970 table.

The economic magnitudes recorded in the table are similar to those used in SNA except that indirect taxes on domestic production recorded in the input-output table include custom duties on domestically produced petroleum, sugar and malt products, and exclude stamp duties paid on wages and salaries. This accounting procedure results in lower indirect taxes on imports and higher direct taxes being recorded in the input-output table than in SNA.

Main deviations of the Greek input-output table and the SNA recommendations on input-output include: (*a*) treatment of public health and education services; (*b*) treatment of activities of private non-profit institutions; (*c*) disaggregation of value added; (*d*) treatment of imports; (*e*) distribution of output of banking services; (*f*) definition of output of the transportation sector; (*g*) commodity taxes are not separately recorded and therefore no valuation at approximate basic values can be derived.

B. ANALYTICAL FRAMEWORK

Only an input-output table valued at producers' prices was compiled. No derived matrices are available. The input-output table is presented at a level of disaggregation of 36 intermediate sectors.

1. *Valuation standards*

All transactions are valued at producers' prices, which are defined as factor costs plus net indirect taxes. Imports are valued c.i.f. plus import duties. Exports are valued at producers' prices, that is, payments for trade, transportation and insurance services were deducted from their f.o.b. values.

2. *Statistical units and classifications*

The classification system used in the input-output table is mainly based on the official statistical classification of sectors of economic activity of the National Statistical Service of Greece, which generally takes the establishment as the basic statistical unit. However, the treatment of secondary products adopted results in an input-output table of the commodity-by-commodity type.

The classification of the intermediate consumption quadrant differs from the SNA recommendations on input-output in that: (*a*) included in the intermediate sector as public services are public educational and health services, government services of administration and defence, local authorities

services and local insurance services; (*b*) the activities of private non-profit institutions are not recorded separately, but are included with similar activities carried out by private enterprises.

Final demand is disaggregated according to the SNA recommendations. Final demand components are also defined as in SNA. Private consumption is defined on a domestic basis.

The breakdown of value added is as follows: (*a*) compensation of employees is disaggregated into wages and salaries and employers' contributions to social security; (*b*) net indirect taxes are disaggregated into those referring to domestic and import commodities (other than import duties) and (*c*) depreciation and operating surplus are recorded together under "other income".

Imports are classified by commodity in a separate row which is added to domestic output of the corresponding sector to yield total supply. Contrary to the SNA recommendations, no distinction is made between complementary and competitive imports.

3. *Treatment and presentation of selected transactions*

A distinction was made between secondary products, that is, products obtained in an establishment mainly dedicated to the fabrication of other products, and by-products, that is, those products that are technologically linked to the production of the principal product of the establishment. Secondary products, as well as their corresponding input, were transferred to the sector in which they are principal products, whenever the proportion of their output in the total output of the sector in which they were produced was significant. By-products, however, were recorded in the same sector that produced them.

Intermediate inputs produced by the same sector that used them were recorded as part of the output of that sector. Non-monetary output and its associated input are recorded together with the monetary components in the corresponding input-output sector. Intra-sector consumption is recorded in the main diagonal of the table and therefore is included in the output of each input-output sector.

Gross output of the banking sector was defined as the difference between interests received on credits granted minus interests paid on deposits, plus actual commissions and receipts for services. This definition is in agreement with the SNA recommendations. However, contrary to the SNA recommendations, output of this sector was distributed to each sector of intermediate and final demand. The distribution was done indirectly, in the process of compilation of the column entries of each production sector, and, in the case of final demand sectors, on the basis of statistical data available on use of financial services by these sectors.

Gross output of the transportation sector includes only services provided by public transport equipment. Services provided by privately owned transport equipment are included in the output of the input-output sector to which the equipment belongs. This treatment of transportation services is not in agreement with the SNA recommendations on input-output.

Intermediate input and value added of the government sector were recorded in the intermediate consumption and value added quadrants, respectively, of the table, as recommended in SNA. Foreign exchange receipts and payments classified in the Balance of International Payments of the Bank of Greece as "foreign missions" and "government expenditures", respectively, were included in the input-output table as public services.

C. Statistical sources and compilation methodology

Data collection is mainly based on regular sources, annual surveys of mining and manufacturing and special studies conducted for the purpose of compilation of the input-output tables.

Owing to the nature of the available statistical material, compilation of the 1970 input-output table was carried out in two successive stages. At the first stage, intermediate input and output (at market prices) were computed for each production sector. At the second stage, trade margins and transportation costs were calculated for the intermediate output and the final demand products, and the allocation of output to intermediate sectors of the table was calculated on the basis of column information; very rarely was direct information on row entries available.

1. Gross output, intermediate consumption and value added

(a) Agriculture, livestock, forestry and fishing

The primary data used in filling the column entries of the agriculture, livestock, forestry and fishing sectors were those available at the National Accounts Division of the Ministry of Co-ordination regarding quantities and values of production, as well as current expenditures on the various input. In certain cases (mainly when the current expenditure concerned a group of commodities classified in different sectors, such as the expenditure for the maintenance of buildings and machines), the results of special studies based on statistical material selected by the Ministry of Agriculture, the Agricultural Bank of Greece, and certain other organizations were used.

(b) Mining

The compilation of the columns and rows of the mining sectors has been based almost entirely on the statistical data of the National Statistical Service of Greece, in particular on the data of the Annual Statistical Survey for Mining (coal mining, iron mining, quarries, salterns) for 1970 and on the 1970 Foreign Trade Statistics. Supplementary data provided by the National Accounts Division have also been used, especially concerning output going to final demand and adjustment of the total gross production value of quarries.

The input into this sector was calculated as follows: for industrial establishments covered by the survey, input was computed by classifying expenditures by sector of origin. Regarding iron-mining establishments not covered in the survey, input was calculated by multiplying the total gross

production value by technological coefficients derived on the basis of sample data selected by the National Statistical Service for its Annual Industrial Survey. In those cases in which the basic data were not provided in the required analysis, auxiliary statistical sources, such as the Ministry of Commerce and the Ministry of Industry, were consulted.

(c) Manufacturing

To compute input and total gross production values for each manufacturing sector of the table, the following sources were used: for data on the activities of private industrial establishments (except handicraft), the Annual Industrial Survey for 1970; for data on public industrial establishments, the National Budget, estimates made by the National Accounts Division of the value added of handicraft industries, and special studies conducted on the basis of a small sample with regard to the value of packing and other materials used. Those studies were applied in breaking down certain input recorded in the Annual Industrial Survey, thus facilitating their classification by sector of origin.

Regarding the coverage of activities of private industrial establishments (except handicraft), it should be noted that the Annual Industrial Survey presents several deficiencies regarding its suitability as a source of data for the input-output table: (a) it does not provide statistical information on the processing of raw and auxiliary materials for the production of products belonging to other sectors of the economy; (b) it does not provide analyses of the sectoral expenditures for the value of packing materials consumed, the value of privately owned transport equipment and the value of miscellaneous consumable materials; (c) establishments with less than 20 employees are investigated by means of a sampling (rather than census) method and, although the magnitudes obtained by inference from a sample are considered to approximate satisfactorily the broad aggregates, they seem less reliable when a more detailed sectoral breakdown is adopted.

Total gross output of each manufacturing sector (except handicraft) was estimated by adding to the output estimate provided by the Annual Industrial Survey (after the separation of secondary products) the value of raw and auxiliary materials processed by the sector on account of the non-manufacturing sectors of the economy. This latter value was obtained by applying the technical coefficient of the corresponding manufacturing sector to the amount of the receipts acquired by it for work performed on the account of the non-manufacturing sectors of the economy.

Estimates of intermediate input used by manufacturing enterprises fully covered by the Annual Industrial Survey were provided directly from the survey results, and were simply classified according to sector of origin. Expenditures by these enterprises on packing materials and on the use of privately owned transport means, for which the survey only provides aggregate value estimates, were classified by sector of origin on the basis of technological coefficients taken from the ad hoc studies mentioned above and the input column of the public transportation subsector, respectively.

Estimates of intermediate input used by the remaining manufacturing enterprises covered by the Annual Industrial Survey were separated by sector of origin on the basis of the technological coefficients obtained in the survey for the establishments included in the sample. The allocation by sector of origin of packing materials and privately owned transport means used by these remaining manufacturing enterprises followed the same method described above.

The gross production value of handicraft was estimated by applying to the estimate of value added of handicraft obtained by the National Accounts Division the technological coefficient between value added and gross production. This technological coefficient was taken from the corresponding relationship estimated in the Annual Industrial Survey for small establishments, which can be assumed to be closely related to handicraft. The same procedure was adopted to estimate total intermediate input of the handicraft sector. This total was disaggregated by sector of origin by applying to it the relevant technological coefficient estimates for the manufacturing establishments included in the Annual Industrial Survey on a sampling basis.

Allocation of manufacturing output to exports was calculated by classifying the exported industrial products according to the sectors that produced them as principal products.

(d) Construction

Gross output of the construction sector was computed by adding the current expenses of the production sectors for the repair and maintenance of buildings and other plants (as derived from the compilation of the respective columns) and the expenditures on consumption and investment made for every type of construction. Prices of building and other construction work were provided by the National Statistical Service of Greece. Input for construction carried out by the Ministry of Public Works was obtained from the technical coefficients estimated by this institution for machinery, materials and labour. Input for the construction carried out by the Public Power Corporation and the Hellenic Telecommunications Organization was obtained from special analysis carried out by those institutions. Input of residential construction, hotels and road construction (59 per cent of the total construction work for 1970) was calculated on the basis of technological coefficients constructed from data taken from a special study of the National Statistical Service. Input of shop construction (about 16 per cent of the total construction work) was calculated on the basis of the technical coefficients for residential construction, adjusted as necessary. Finally, the input of all other types of construction was calculated on the basis of: (a) the technical coefficients for those types of construction previously discussed that have similar cost structures or (b) appropriate combinations of these technical coefficients and those provided by the Ministry of Public Works.

(e) Electricity, gas, water

Input of these sectors was calculated directly from data provided by the National Accounts Division, the results of special questionnaires sent to various enterprises of the sector and data in the annual balance sheets of those enterprises concerning some unspecialized group of operational expenses.

(f) Transportation, storage, communications

Data on output and input of railway and air transport, metropolitan electric railways, train cars, and the loading and unloading of ships were estimated directly. Input and output of transportation services provided by urban and inter-urban buses were estimated indirectly from data provided by the National Statistical Service on gross receipts and total number of buses in circulation. The calculation was made on the basis of kilometres run by, and kilometric cost rates of, every urban and inter-urban bus.

Output and input estimates of the remaining subsectors of the transportation sector were estimated indirectly as indicated in the following four paragraphs.

Output and input estimates of sea transport were computed on the basis of both recent and old data collected by means of a special questionnaire forwarded to a sampling of sea transport firms. These data were processed together with data on the number of passengers transported by ship and motor car, the number of tons of freight transported by ship on the Mediterranean Sea and the average freight rate of passengers, cars and goods (by lines).

The gross production value of the subsector for tourist buses was estimated by adding the input values, computed on the basis of the technological coefficients of the subsector for passenger transportation by buses, to the gross value added of the subsector, as estimated in SNA. Regarding the subsector that deals with the transportation of goods by truck, the total gross production value was estimated by adding the input values, calculated on the basis of technological coefficients derived from special studies of the Ministry of Transportation and the General Confederation of Professional Drivers of Greece and related to the kilometric cost of public-use trucks, to the gross value added of the subsector, as given in SNA.

The gross production value of the subsector for passenger transport by taxis was estimated on the basis of average kilometres run and frequency of dropping the taxi flag. The data came from a special study made by the Ministry of Communications. The input values were computed by using technological coefficients for the gross production value, derived from the processing of data concerning the kilometric cost rate of the transport means used by passengers. These data were provided by studies made at the Ministry of Communications and the General Confederation of Professional Drivers of Greece.

The value of output of transport services going to private consumption, public consumption and investment was estimated on the basis of a special processing of both the data available at the National Accounts Division and the data (from the balance of payments) available at the Bank of Greece. Total intermediate output was computed by subtracting the value of final uses from the gross value of production plus the value of imported transportation services.

The total gross production value and the input values of the communications sector were calculated directly on the basis of data derived from special questionnaires of the National Accounts Division sent to the Hellenic Telecommunications Organization and to the Greek post offices. Supplementary statistical data were used to compute the above-mentioned values for those groups of expenditures that could not be broken down. These data were taken either from budgets and balance sheets or from the enterprises directly. On the other hand, the values of intermediate output, including the values of the imported services of the sector, were calculated indirectly from the estimated input of the production sectors, on the basis of technological coefficients.

(g) *Trade*

Gross output of the trade sector was estimated as follows: first, the total value of distribution services, that is, trade and transportation margins, was estimated for each intermediate and final demand sector on the basis of gross average rates. The gross rates were calculated according to (*a*) gross trade profits determined according to certain rules enacted by the market-inspection police and/or (*b*) percentage relation between producers' prices and market prices (in wholesale or retail trade, according to circumstances, and for products for which producers' and market prices were available). Secondly, trade margins were separated from total distribution margins through the use of a percentage rate computed according to information obtained about the relative expenses of certain individual products and the input-output tables of countries with an economic structure similar to that of Greece. The sums of the trade margins so obtained for each intermediate sector and the trade margins corresponding to final demand sectors, obtained from data available at the National Accounts Division, constituted the estimate of total output of the trade sector. Input values of the sector were calculated on the basis of the technological coefficients taken from the 1965 Italian input-output table. This approach to the estimation of the trade sector data was adopted because of the large numbers, wide dispersion and extreme variety of the commercial establishments in the Greek economy.

(h) *Services*

Gross output of the private services sectors was generally determined as the sum of input values and value added of each subsector, as calculated by the National Accounts Division. Intermediate input was estimated on the basis of technical coefficients derived either by means of special studies or by applying the input structure of other known relevant subsectors (e.g., the cost structure of private clinics and hospitals was taken from the cost structure of public hospitals).

All values related to public services were computed by means of a special processing of the analytical data available at the National Accounts Division concerning: (*a*) the bal-ance sheets of the receipts and expenditures recorded in the State budget; (*b*) special extrabudgetary accounts; (*c*) the accounts of local authorities; (*d*) social insurance magnitudes; and (*e*) other legal entities at public law. In some cases, particularly when certain groups of expenditures could not be allocated by production sector of origin, supplementary studies were undertaken. With regard to the classification of goods used by the same production sector in which they are produced, information available at the State level, as well as data available at the National Statistical Service concerning the duty-free goods imported by the State, were used.

2. *Final demand and imports*

The allocation of each sector's output to final demand categories has been estimated directly and separately according to final demand sectors (i.e., private and public consumption, fixed capital investments and exports), on the basis of data available at the National Accounts Division and the Foreign Trade Statistics Bulletin (regarding exports). The figures for changes in stocks resulted as residuals by subtracting the total value of intermediate uses from each sector's total supply. Owing to the use of this method of calculation, magnitudes for change in stocks also include statistical differences and/or possible calculation errors.

With respect to imports and exports, the statistical data used in the calculation of the commodity transactions were provided mainly by the customs statistics of the National Statistical Service of Greece on the foreign trade of the country. Those statistics give the quantities and values of imported and exported goods, with a separate analysis for each product. Statistics on payments, from the Balance of International Transactions of the Bank of Greece, as well as data from the Ministry of Commerce, were used to supplement the analysis and to compute the values of those commodities that either do not get through customs or do not get recorded in the statistics of the Service because their customs declaration was not presented during the surveyed year. Additionally, data on the receipts and payments for services (except the services of the production factors) provided to and by the rest of the world, as well as data on the expenditures of Greeks abroad and foreign tourists at home, were taken from the Balance of International Payments of the Bank of Greece.

GREECE
INPUT-OUTPUT TABLES
1970

Source: *Input-Output Table of the Greek Economy Year 1970.* Center of Planning and Economic Research of the Ministry of Co-ordination.

ΚΛΑΔΟΙ SECTORS		1 Γεωργία, δασοκομία, άλιεία Agriculture, forestry, fishing	2 Όρυχεῖα, λατομεῖα καί άλυκαί Mining, quarrying and salt-works	3 Μεταποίησις Manufacturing	4 Κατασκευαί Constructions	5 Ήλεκτρισμός, φωταέριον καί ὕδωρ Electricity, gas and water	6 Μεταφοραί Transportation	7 Ἐπικοινωνίαι (περιλαμβανομένων τηλεοράσεως καί ραδιοφωνίας) Communications (incl. TV and radio broadcasts)	8 Ἐνοικιάσεις κατοικιῶν Dwellings
Γεωργία, δασοκομία, άλιεία Agriculture, forestry, fishing	1								
	T	8.626.513	—	26.355.500	297.080	—	25.200	—	—
	D	7.881.374	—	24.973.293	108.958	—	25.200	—	—
	M	745.139	—	1.382.207	188.122	—	—	—	—
Όρυχεῖα, λατομεῖα καί άλυκαί Mining, quarrying and salt-works	2								
	T	41.160	34.163	4.818.674	2.197.265	558.294	—	—	—
	D	41.160	—	1.562.397	2.015.380	552.875	—	—	—
	M	—	34.163	3.256.277	181.885	5.419	—	—	—
Μεταποίησις Manufacturing	3								
	T	6.502.317	855.006	60.772.525	21.779.604	526.370	7.379.244	125.049	—
	D	5.873.828	660.877	43.681.909	18.038.526	522.767	5.877.752	93.389	—
	M	628.489	194.129	17.090.616	3.741.078	3.603	1.501.492	31.660	—
Κατασκευαί Constructions	4								
	T	173.934	27.421	219.803	—	62.724	19.000	13.969	804.000
	D	173.934	27.421	219.803	—	62.724	19.000	13.969	804.000
	M	—	—	—	—	—	—	—	—
Ήλεκτρισμός, φωταέριον καί ὕδωρ Electricity, gas and water	5								
	T	220.434	186.633	2.124.820	150.708	91.875	266.236	33.154	—
	D	220.434	186.633	2.124.820	150.708	91.875	266.236	33.154	—
	M	—	—	—	—	—	—	—	—
Μεταφοραί Transportation	6								
	T	1.457.442	97.368	3.605.313	1.108.475	57.954	553.391	79.656	—
	D	1.457.442	97.368	3.605.313	1.108.475	57.954	523.391	79.656	—
	M	—	—	—	—	—	30.000	—	—
Ἐπικοινωνίαι (περιλαμβανομένων τηλεοράσεως καί ραδιοφωνίας) Communications (incl. TV and radio broadcasts)	7								
	T	29.298	12.109	263.872	172.189	12.979	75.294	23.270	—
	D	29.298	12.109	263.872	172.189	12.979	75.294	23.270	—
	M	—	—	—	—	—	—	—	—

Ἐνοικιάσεις κατοικιῶν Dwellings	8	T D M	- - -	- - -	- - -	- - -	- - -	- - -	- - -	- - -
Ὑπηρεσίαι Services	9	T D M	1.488.290 1.488.290 -	127.470 127.470 -	10.712.499 10.712.499 -	2.127.093 2.127.093 -	484.723 484.723 -	2.067.532 2.067.532 -	60.565 60.565 -	21.000 21.000 -
Σύνολον ἐνδιαμέσων εἰσροῶν Total intermediate inputs	(1 ∕ 9) 10 $\dot{U}$	T D M	18.539.388 17.165.760 1.373.628	1.340.170 1.111.878 228.292	108.873.006 87.143.906 21.729.100	27.832.414 23.721.329 4.111.085	1.794.919 1.785.897 9.022	10.385.897 8.854.405 1.531.492	335.663 304.003 31.660	825.000 825.000 -
Μισθοί καί ἡμερομίσθια Wages and salaries	11 W	T D M	3.858.610	2.026.581	16.928.556	11.848.001	1.520.329	8.201.680	2.164.560	-
Ἐργοδοτικαί εἰσφοραί Social security contributions	12 S^s	T D M	531.772	353.123	2.644.925	1.726.972	242.402	1.047.975	276.773	-
Λοιπά εἰσοδήματα Other income	13 Π	T D M	41.261.577	1.160.697	31.769.992	9.441.679	3.388.925	6.407.659	1.531.174	21.098.994
Ἔμμεσοι φόροι - Ἐπιδοτήσεις Indirect taxes - Subsidies	14 (Tind-Sub)	T D M	-696.000	214.000	18.081.559	2.723.172	299.256	2.371.617	326.817	324.198
Φόροι ἐπί τῶν εἰσαγωγῶν Taxes on imports	15 T^{cd}	T D M	-	-	-	-	-	-	-	-
Προστιθεμένη ἀξία εἰς τιμάς συντελεστῶν παραγωγῆς Value-added at factor cost	(11 ∫ 13) 16 V^{fc}	T D M	45.651.959	3.540.401	51.343.473	23.016.652	5.151.656	15.657.314	3.972.507	21.098.994
Προστιθεμένη ἀξία εἰς ἀγοραίας τιμάς Value-added at market prices	(14 ∫ 16) 17 V^{mp}	T D M	44.955.959	3.754.401	69.425.032	25.739.824	5.450.912	18.028.931	4.299.324	21.423.192
Ἀκαθάριστος ἀξία παραγωγῆς εἰς τιμάς παραγωγοῦ Gross domestic output at producer prices	(10 + 16) 18 X^{PP}	T D M	64.191.347	4.880.571	160.216.479	50.849.066	6.946.575	26.043.211	4.308.170	21.923.994

SECTORS / ΚΛΑΔΟΙ		1 Γεωργία, δασοκομία, ἁλιεία / Agriculture, forestry, fishing	2 Ὀρυχεῖα, λατομεῖα καί ἁλυκαί / Mining, quarrying and salt-works	3 Μεταποίησις / Manufacturing	4 Κατασκευαί / Constructions	5 Ἠλεκτρισμός, φωταέριον καί ὕδωρ / Electricity, gas and water	6 Μεταφοραί / Transportation	7 Ἐπικοινωνίαι (περιλαμβανομένων τηλεοράσεως καί ραδιοφωνίας) / Communications (incl. TV and radio broadcasts)	8 Ἐνοικιάσεις κατοικιῶν / Dwellings
Ἀναλλοίωτος ἀξία παραγωγῆς εἰς τιμάς ἐργοστασίου (14+18) / Gross domestic output at work prices	19 χ^wp	T	63.495.347	5.094.571	178.298.038	53.572.238	7.245.831	28.414.828	4.634.987	22.248.192
		D								
		M								
Εἰσαγωγαί εἰς ἀξίαν cif / Imports in cif value	20 M^cif	T	2.812.583	3.256.021	44.595.493	8.000	14.000	916.850	107.000	-
		D								
		M								
Δασμοί καί φόροι ἐπί τῶν εἰσαγωγῶν / Taxes and custom duties on imports	21 T^cd	T	544.674	72.224	9.810.793	-	-	-	-	-
		D								
		M								
Σύνολον εἰσαγωγῶν καί δασμῶν (20+21) / Total of imports and custom duties	22 M	T	3.357.257	3.328.245	54.406.286	8.000	14.000	916.850	107.000	-
		D								
		M								
Συνολική προσφορά (19+22) / Total supply	23 Z	T	66.852.604	8.422.816	232.704.324	53.580.238	7.259.831	29.331.678	4.741.987	22.248.192
		D								
		M								

		9 Ὑπηρεσίαι / Services	10 (7÷9) Σύνολον ἐνδιαμέσων ἐκροῶν / Total intermediate outputs	11 Ἰδιωτική κατανάλωσις Cp / Private consumption	12 Δημοσία κατανάλωσις Cg / Public consumption	13 Ἀκαθάριστοι ἐπενδύσεις παγίου κεφαλαίου Ι / Gross fixed capital formation	14 Αὐξομειώσεις ἀποθεμάτων J / Changes in stocks	15 Ἐξαγωγαί ἀγαθῶν καί ὑπηρεσιῶν E / Exports of goods and services	16 (11÷15) Συνολική τελική ζήτησις F / Total final demand
Γεωργία, δασοκομία ἀλιεία / Agriculture, forestry, fishing	1 T	453.490	35.757.783	28.590.071	37.240	—	400.353	2.067.157	31.094.821
	D	453.490	33.442.315	27.607.978	29.652	—	348.245	2.067.157	30.053.052
	M	—	2.315.468	982.093	7.588	—	52.108	—	1.041.789
Ὀρυχεῖα, λατομεῖα καί ἅλυκαί / Mining, quarrying and salt-works	2 T	10.018	7.659.574	—	2	—	-427.678	1.190.918	763.242
	D	10.018	4.181.830	—	—	—	-274.907	1.187.648	-912.741
	M	—	3.477.744	—	2	—	-152.771	3.270	-149.499
Μεταποίησις / Manufacturing	3 T	7.735.232	105.675.347	75.023.051	5.002.261	18.922.263	11.570.258	16.511.144	127.028.977
	D	6.904.645	81.653.593	63.059.663	3.090.796	5.241.240	8.787.341	16.465.305	96.644.345
	M	830.587	24.021.654	11.963.388	1.911.465	13.681.023	2.782.917	45.839	30.384.632
Κατασκευαί / Constructions	4 T	422.533	1.743.384	289.018	1.767.964	48.979.872	350.000	450.000	51.836.854
	D	422.533	1.743.384	286.196	1.762.786	48.979.872	350.000	450.000	51.828.854
	M	—	—	2.822	5.178	—	—	—	8.000
Ἠλεκτρισμός, φωταέριον καί ὕδωρ / Electricity, gas and water	5 T	1.800.703	4.874.563	1.922.539	462.729	—	—	—	2.385.268
	D	1.800.703	4.874.563	1.908.539	462.729	—	—	—	2.371.268
	M	—	—	14.000	—	—	—	—	14.000
Μεταφοραί / Transportation	6 T	1.196.773	8.156.372	16.516.584	1.279.427	519.513	—	2.859.782	21.175.306
	D	1.196.773	8.126.372	15.645.017	1.264.144	519.513	—	2.859.782	20.288.456
	M	—	30.000	871.567	15.283	—	—	—	866.850
Ἐπικοινωνίαι (περιλαμβανομένων τηλεοράσεως καί ραδιοφωνίας) / Communications (incl. TV and radio broadcasts)	7 T	1.132.834	1.721.845	2.780.912	172.230	—	—	67.000	3.020.142
	D	1.132.834	1.721.845	2.680.912	165.230	—	—	67.000	2.913.142
	M	—	—	100.000	7.000	—	—	—	107.000

ΚΛΑΔΟΙ / SECTORS

Ἐνοικιάσεις κατοικιῶν Dwellings	8	T D M	– – –	– – –	22.248.198 22.248.198 –	– – –	– – –	– – –	– – –	22.248.198 22.248.198 –
Ὑπηρεσίαι Services	9	T D M	5.171.978 4.483.978 688.000	22.261.150 21.573.150 688.000	59.015.008 58.047.377 967.631	28.621.642 26.763.632 1.858.010	2.241.331 2.241.331 –	355.000 355.000 –	6.841.929 6.583.929 258.000	97.074.910 93.991.269 3.083.641
Σύνολον ἐνδιαμέσων εἰσροῶν (1/9) Total intermediate inputs	10 Ü	T D M	17.923.561 16.404.974 1.518.587	187.850.018 157.317.152 30.532.866	206.385.381 191.483.880 14.901.501	37.343.495 33.538.969 3.804.526	70.662.979 56.981.956 13.681.023	12.247.933 9.565.679 2.682.254	29.987.930 29.680.821 307.109	356.627.718 321.251.305 35.376.413
Μισθοί καί ἡμερομίσθια Wages and salaries	11 W	T D M	42.649.280	89.197.597						
Ἐργοδοτικαί εἰσφοραί Social security contributions	12 S^s	T D M	2.426.845	9.250.787						
Λοιπά εἰσοδήματα Other income	13 Π	T D M	46.567.317	162.620.020						
Ἔμμεσοι φόροι – Ἐπιδοτήσεις (Tind-Sub) Indirect taxes – Subsidies	14	T D M	5.997.416	29.642.035						
Φόροι ἐπί τῶν εἰσαγωγῶν Taxes on imports	15 T^{cd}	T D M	10.429.444	10.429.444						
Προστιθεμένη ἀξία εἰς τι-μάς συντελεστῶν παραγωγῆς (11/13) Value-added at factor cost	16 V^{fc}	T D M	91.643.442	261.076.404						
Προστιθεμένη ἀξία εἰς ἀγοραίας τιμάς (14/16) Value-added at market prices	17 V^{mp}	T D M	108.070.302	301.147.883						
Ἀκαθάριστος ἀξία παραγω-γῆς εἰς τιμάς παραγωγοῦ (10+16) Gross domestic output at producer prices	18 X^{pp}	T D M	109.567.003	448.926.422						

ΚΛΑΔΟΙ SECTORS		Υπηρεσίαι Services 9	Σύνολον ἐνδιαμέσων ἐκροῶν Total intermediate outputs U (1/9) 10	Ἰδιωτική κατανάλωσις Private consumption Cp 11	Δημοσία κατανάλωσις Public consumption Cg 12	Ἀκαθάριστοι ἐπενδύσεις παγίου κεφαλαίου Gross fixed capital formation I 13	Αὔξησις ἀποθεμάτων Changes in stocks L 14	Ἐξαγωγαί ἀγαθῶν καί ὑπηρεσιῶν Exports of goods and services E 15	Συνολική τελική ζήτησις Total final demand F (11/15) 16
Ἀναδρομιστος δεξία παραγωγῆς (14+18) εἰς τιμάς ἐργοστασίου Gross domestic output at work prices	T D M	115.564.419	478.568.457						
19 X^wp									
Εἰσαγωγαί εἰς ἀξίαν cif Imports in cif value	T D M	3.769.888	55.479.835						
20 M^cif									
Δασμοί καί φόροι ἐπί τῶν εἰσαγωγῶν Taxes and custom duties on imports	T D M	1.753	10.429.444						
21 T^cd									
Σύνολον εἰσαγωγῶν καί δασμῶν (20+21) Total of imports and custom duties	T D M	3.771.641	65.909.279						
22 M									
Συνολική προσφορά Total supply (19+22)	T D M	119.336.060	544.477.736						
23 Z									

	17 (10+16) Συνολική ζήτησις Total demand						
ΚΛΑΔΟΙ SECTORS	Z						
Γεωργία, δασοκομία, ἁλιεία Agriculture, forestry, fishing 1	T 66.852.604 D 63.495.347 M 3.357.257						
Ὀρυχεῖα, λατομεῖα καί ἁλυκαί Mining, quarrying and salt-works 2	T 8.422.816 D 5.094.571 M 3.328.245						
Μεταποίησις Manufacturing 3	T 232.704.324 D 178.298.038 M 54.406.286						
Κατασκευαί Constructions 4	T 53.580.238 D 53.572.238 M 8.000						
Ἠλεκτρισμός, φωταέριον καί ὕδωρ Electricity, gas and water 5	T 7.259.831 D 7.245.831 M 14.000						
Μεταφοραί Transportation 6	T 29.331.678 D 28.414.828 M 916.850						
Ἐπικοινωνίαι (περιλαμβανομένων τηλεοράσεως καί ραδιοφωνίας) Comunications (incl. TV and radio broadcasts) 7	T 4.741.987 D 4.634.987 M 107.000						

84

Ενοικιάσεις κατοικιών Dwellings	8	T D M	22.248.198 22.248.198 —							
Ὑπηρεσίαι Services	9	T D M	119.336.060 115.564.419 3.771.641							
Σύνολον ἐνδιαμέσων εἰσροῶν (1/9) Total intermediate inputs	10 ὑ	T D M	544.477.736 478.568.457 65.909.279							

85

V. INDONESIA

A. GENERAL INFORMATION

The present report is based on the *Input-Output Table for Indonesia, 1980, volume I,* published in 1984 by the Indonesian Central Bureau of Statistics.

Input-output tables for Indonesia have been published for 1971, 1975 and 1980. The 1980 tables differ from the previous tables in that domestically produced goods and services are separated from imported goods and services. The most detailed tables for 1980 are prepared in terms of 340 commodities by 170 industries. These matrices are then aggregated to 66 by 66 and then to 19 by 19 industry-by-industry tables. No make matrix is compiled. Activities of non-profit institutions are not recorded separately.

B. ANALYTICAL FRAMEWORK

1. *Tables and derived matrices available*

The following basic tables are compiled:

(i) Transaction tables in purchasers' prices and producers' prices;
(ii) Import tables by origin and destination in purchasers' prices and producers' prices;
(iii) Tables of trade margins;
(iv) Tables of transport margins;
(v) Total workers by sectors.

On the basis of these tables, the following tables are derived:

(i') Input coefficient tables in purchasers' prices and producers' prices;
(ii') Import coefficients in purchasers' prices and producers' prices;
(iii') Transport coefficient matrices;
(iv') Trade coefficient matrices;
(v') Leontief inverse matrices in purchasers' prices and producers' prices.

2. *Valuation standards*

The Indonesian input-output tables are valued at both purchasers' prices and producers' prices, which differ from the SNA recommendation of using the approximate basic values.

In the tables valued at producers' values, exports are valued at producers' values and imports are valued at equivalent producers' prices, which are equal to c.i.f. prices plus import duty and sales tax on import goods. However, in the tables valued at purchasers' prices, exports are valued at f.o.b. prices but imports are valued at equivalent purchaser's prices.

In the tables valued at purchasers' prices, trade and transport costs for distributing goods to the consumers are not included, gross input is only expressed in producers' prices. The input coefficients in the tables in purchasers' values are then calculated in terms of input per unit value of the goods and services in producers' prices.

3. *Treatment and presentation of selected transactions*

Four kinds of secondary products are differentiated: by-products, subsidiary products, scraps and wastes. By-products are included in the sectors where they are produced. Subsidiary products and their associated input are transferred out and included in the sectors where similar products are produced. Scraps and wastes, which are defined as unused raw materials, intermediate goods and finished goods created during a production process, are included in the sectors where they are produced.

C. STATISTICAL SOURCES AND COMPILATION METHODOLOGY

Agriculture includes, in addition to the values of its output, the activities of simple product processing using traditional tools such as paddy handpounding, coffee and maize roasting and unskinning, cassava chipping, rubber smoking, coconut oil extracting, brown sugar producing, wood saving, and fish salting and drying. The output of this sector is estimated by multiplying the product output with its producers' prices. Market prices are used to estimate producers' prices when the latter type is not available by deducting from the former type trade and transport margins. The input structures are estimated by multiplying input coefficients with the output of each commodity. Data on input coefficients, trade and transport margins are collected by special surveys conducted by the Central Bureau of Statistics.

Mining and quarrying includes all activities in mining, quarrying, evaporating etc. of natural deposits for the purpose of obtaining solids, liquids and gases. The transformation of natural gas into liquefied natural gas and its condensates is also included. However, further processing, such as splitting, melting and refining, research, preparation of mining facilities and refining of water, is not included. The output of the sector is obtained by multiplying output with its producers' price. Producers' prices of export commodities are assumed to be equal to their export prices. (This is not a reasonable assumption, since it ignores domestic trade and transport costs.) The input structure of the sector is estimated by multiplying its output with its input coefficients which are obtained by special surveys. The final results are obtained by reconciling estimated input and output.

Manufacturing covers all production activities that transform raw materials or semi-finished goods into new products. Also included are service sectors that support manufacturing. Output and input data of manufacturing activities are based on the 1980 annual survey of large and medium manufacturing establishments and the 1979 annual survey of small-scale manufactures and handicrafts conducted by the Central Bureau of Statistics. Others are obtained directly from reports of the concerned establishments. Output and input are calculated separately for large, medium, small and handicraft manufacturing. Characteristics and secondary products of each establishment are identified and the latter type is transferred out. Input structures are estimated by output with their input coefficients.

The output of electricity, gas and water supply includes electric power produced by estates, mining, manufacturing and other sectors except those produced for own consumption. The gas sector covers the production and distribution of utility gas for sales. Water supply also includes both production and distribution.

The construction sector includes new construction, extension, alteration and repairs of residential and non-residential buildings, irrigation projects and bridges, electric plants, gas and water pipe installation, harbours, sport fields, transport and communication networks and terminals, sewers etc., both for civilian and military purposes. Output is defined as the value of works put in place. Value of land is excluded.

In trade, restaurants and hotels, restaurants cover gross sale values and exclude food and refreshment, which are included as part of the service package rendered by hotels, trains, ships and airplanes. The output of restaurants is calculated by multiplying the number of workers employed by per worker average output. The output of hotels is computed by multiplying the number of hotel beds by per bed average output. Input structures are calculated by multiplying the input coefficients of each activity by the value of its output. Trade margins are estimated based on the commodity flow approach by summing up trade margins gained for each flow.

In transport and communication, the output of road transport is calculated by multiplying the total number of vehicles by type by their corresponding output per vehicle. The output of sea transport by type is computed by multiplying the total number of freight or passengers by average fee per ton of cargo or per passenger. The output of inland water transport is computed as the product of the number of vessels and the average output per vessel. Air output is obtained by summing up all sales of national airlines. The output of services associated with transport by type is obtained by multiplying indicators of production such as number of vehicles, vessels, aircraft, passengers or cargo weight by the fee or average cost of each service. Input is either supplied directly by the establishments or through surveys.

Banks and other financial institutions include banking and activities of other financial institutions, insurance services, real estate and business services. Output of banking includes service imputations as recommended by SNA, and is provided by the Bank of Indonesia. The output of other trading banks, rural banks, credit co-operatives, money changers etc. is estimated as a proportion of the output of banking. The output of life and non-life insurance is the difference between premiums received and claims paid. Net additions

to the actuarial services are not included and interest on the reserves accruing to policy holders is not excluded, as recommended by SNA. The output of residential rents is obtained by using per capita values of household expenditures on house rents, taxes and home maintenance. The output of non-residential leasing is obtained by multiplying the number of real estate enterprises by their average output. The output of business service is computed by multiplying the average output per worker by the total number of workers.

Other sources such as government services, community services, recreational services, repair services and personal services rely on government data, the Population Census of 1980 and surveys.

SECTOR CLASSIFICATION OF INDONESIAN INPUT-OUTPUT TABLES, 1980

Input/output sector	Industry
1	Paddy
2	Other food crops
3	Other agricultural crops
4	Livestock and livestock products
5	Forestry
6	Fishery
8	Food, beverage and tobacco
7	Mining and quarrying
9	Other industries
10	Oil refinery
11	Electricity, gas and water supply
12	Construction
13	Trade
14	Restaurant and hotel
15	Transport and communication
16	Financing, real estate, business services
17	Public administration and defence
18	Other services
19	Unspecified sector
190	Total intermediate input
201	Wages and salaries
202	Operating surplus
203	Depreciation
204	Indirect taxes
205	Subsidies
209	Gross value added
210	Total input
301	Private consumption expenditures
302	Government consumption expenditures
303	Gross fixed capital formation
304	Change in stocks
305	Exports of goods
306	Exports of services
309	Total final demand
310	Total demand
401	Imports of goods
402	Import sales taxes
403	Import duties
404	Subsidies
405	Imports of services
409	Total imports
501	Wholesale trade margins
502	Retail trade margins
503	Transport costs
509	Total trade margins and transport costs
600	Total input
700	Total supply

INDONESIA
INPUT-OUTPUT TABLES
1980

Source: *Input-Output Table for Indonesia, 1980, Vol.1,*
Indonesian Central Bureau of Statistics.

TABLE 16. TRANSACTION TABLE AT PURCHASER'S PRICES, 19 x 19
(MILLION RUPIAHS)

Sector	1	2	3	4	5	6	7	8
1	63192.1	1064813.2	0.0	6122.0	0.0	0.0	0.0	2263720.9
2	0.0	144808.2	1501.3	10948.1	0.0	591.6	0.0	463453.4
3	0.0	464.5	705968.3	11249.4	0.0	0.0	0.0	1128981.5
4	5903.4	18882.0	5394.0	571340.0	0.0	258.0	0.0	31118.0
5	292.0	2336.1	10914.9	1268.9	45488.5	10916.2	145.6	4091.5
6	0.0	0.0	0.0	288.6	0.0	108256.6	0.0	44758.3
7	0.0	0.0	1.5	160.1	0.0	4789.4	418772.7	10191.6
8	0.0	0.0	6.5	97432.2	0.0	10473.1	9.0	406392.4
9	200071.9	98578.3	185704.0	10263.0	42582.3	50246.8	414662.7	172914.0
10	174.6	395.7	20789.1	1301.0	24191.1	16231.5	71969.4	44929.1
11	0.0	0.0	4181.3	550.5	2710.3	582.8	746.7	13516.2
12	2463.6	7917.2	20702.8	4176.0	18542.8	1936.4	66525.5	5623.3
13	0.0	0.0	0.0	0.0	0.0	0.0	0.0	0.0
14	0.0	0.0	2639.7	758.4	2297.6	593.8	59245.0	11305.6
15	195.4	1213.2	6154.2	108.7	4652.0	422.0	40912.4	9992.8
16	27444.2	10614.2	38232.1	11822.6	28506.3	11869.0	422614.5	52402.7
17	0.0	0.0	0.0	0.0	0.0	0.0	0.0	0.0
18	1353.7	970.2	42303.9	2164.2	44440.8	1350.6	109168.1	7881.3
.19	0.0	0.0	0.0	0.0	0.0	0.0	0.0	0.0
190	301090.9	1350992.8	1044493.6	729953.7	213211.7	218515.8	1604771.6	4671272.6
201	630498.2	409228.6	694445.1	289304.6	242465.8	126057.9	333662.6	449521.2
202	2431988.3	2514941.7	1588269.5	873422.0	1042828.0	626858.8	11746361.2	822866.4
203	39998.5	35534.9	99270.2	19717.2	113888.1	33591.7	342773.7	228103.6
204	32645.1	7617.6	28644.9	8525.6	12918.6	6081.7	16667.3	312940.7
205	0.0	0.0	0.0	0.0	0.0	0.0	0.0	-62953.0
209	3135130.1	2967322.8	2410629.7	1190969.4	1412100.5	792590.1	124436734.8	1750478.9
210	3436221.0	4318315.6	3455123.3	1920923.1	1625312.2	1011105.9	14061506.4	6421751.5

Table 16 (Continued)

Sector	9	10	11	12	13	14	15	16
1	1938.5	0.0	0.0	18949.8	10.1	0.0	0.0	0.0
2	1794.6	0.0	0.0	0.0	152.7	106916.4	147.0	0.0
3	187257.0	0.0	0.0	173.5	114.2	69474.4	10.5	0.0
4	35695.1	0.0	0.0	0.0	0.0	288062.7	4273.4	0.0
5	281641.6	27.0		636621.5	147.6	11969.2	1324.6	0.0
6	123.8	0.0	0.0	0.0	0.0	85659.5	164.5	0.0
7	385393.6	1378052.3	3933.1	546089.9	189.0	2.5	1012.7	1.4
8	285531.6	0.0	0.0	0.0	0.0	442535.4	8844.1	1204.2
9	4385971.1	44124.6	38934.3	2863074.0	84839.6	66072.9	173908.1	56526.9
10	114942.1	1561.0	139456.4	716649.8	46345.2	48706.9	455512.0	6579.9
11	46785.1	16776.5	73232.9	6072.8	35618.1	56317.1	16462.6	17534.0
12	15701.3	6291.3	15969.5	12784.4	37076.8	27466.1	61364.7	160319.4
13	0.0	0.0	0.0	0.0	0.0	0.0	0.0	0.0
14	14284.1	29305.3	2755.8	27258.4	53638.8	4485.6	33774.0	23366.2
15	17193.2	13914.3	3416.4	12465.5	104774.2	14082.4	335779.4	43587.3
16	68608.7	31541.9	6961.2	102417.7	223386.3	53397.1	136658.5	70824.2
17	0.0	0.0	0.0	0.0	0.0	0.0	0.0	0.0
18	17088.9	7492.0	8216.8	7698.9	58701.1	22860.6	429663.6	37710.0
19	9.3	0.0	0.0	0.0	0.0	8417.2	7638.1	0.0
190	5602959.6	1529086.2	292876.4	4950256.2	644993.7	1306426.0	1666537.8	417653.5
201	901259.9	32415.2	85250.0	1347383.0	909938.7	275572.4	720428.6	360207.5
202	2159402.9	361874.6	111009.2	948516.5	5144322.5	556473.7	1035836.9	1793864.4
203	311222.0	61610.1	33560.8	161378.4	156547.1	98519.0	418630.2	163733.3
204	-127570.0	0.0	780.9	125148.0	213454.3	78106.2	35827.4	36601.5
205	-372300.0	-361874.6	0.0	0.0	-6935599.4	0.0	0.0	0.0
209	3127154.8	94025.3	230600.9	2582425.9	5730663.2	1008671.3	2210723.1	2354406.7
210	8730114.4	1623111.5	523477.3	7532682.1	6375656.9	2315097.3	3877260.9	2772060.2

91

Table 16 (Continued)

Sector	304	303	302	301	190	19	18	17
1	115750.6	0.0	0.0	0.0	3418932.0	0.0	185.4	0.0
2	3078.6	0.0	0.0	4593307.1	758670.3	0.0	28357.0	0.0
3	55173.4	2654.2	10123.2	897526.9	2105470.6	0.0	1777.3	0.0
4	99878.2	0.0	0.0	1147502.7	988933.4	0.0	28006.8	0.0
5	5658.6		0.0	246638.3	1008537.9	0.0	1352.7	0.0
6	0.0	0.0	0.0	1140585.7	245571.3	0.0	6322.0	0.0
7	903296.7	0.0	0.0	64727.6	2748590.1	0.0	0.3	0.0
8	26196.3	0.0	3525.9	6797751.2	1026243.3	0.0	30814.8	0.0
9	192221.0	3699999.2	429152.5	3378742.3	9816471.7	0.0	927997.2	0.0
10	-56594.5	0.0	70442.2	530011.6	1740997.0	0.0	31262.2	0.0
11	0.0	0.0	25161.8	144981.8	362473.0	0.0	71386.1	0.0
12	0.0	6847092.4	175780.1	0.0	509809.6	0.0	44948.5	0.0
13	0.0	0.0	0.0	0.0	0.0	0.0	0.0	0.0
14	0.0	0.0	327282.0	1777625.9	281717.8	0.0	16009.5	0.0
15	0.0	0.0	148662.8	1345791.9	636706.8	0.0	28043.4	0.0
16	0.0	0.0	108531.9	1582354.9	1386885.9	0.0	89584.7	0.0
17	0.0	0.0	2468094.2	0.0	0.0	0.0	0.0	0.0
18	0.0	0.0	1084763.9	1903640.4	923195.0	0.0	124130.3	0.0
19	0.0	0.0	296155.0	43664.2	16064.6	0.0	0.0	0.0
190	1344658.9	10549745.8	5147675.5	25596852.5	27975270.3	0.0	1430178.2	0.0
201					11667415.7	0.0	1515086.9	2344689.5
202					34419174.8	0.0	663068.2	0.0
203					26178825.2	0.0	176341.7	123404.7
204					1116382.9	0.0	72853.1	0.0
205					-1490727.0	0.0	0.0	0.0
209					48330071.6	0.0	2427349.9	2468094.2
210					76305361.9	0.0	3857528.1	2468094.2

Table 16 (Continued)

Sector	305	306	309	310	401	402	403	404
1	0.0	0.0	115750.6	3534682.6	0.0	0.0	0.0	0.0
2	36001.9	0.0	4632387.6	5391057.9	-142561.3	-3163.1	-7862.0	0.0
3	1382312.3	0.0	2345135.8	4450606.4	-181492.7	-2718.3	-3933.2	0.0
4	13544.7	0.0	1263579.8	2252513.2	-7413.8	-354.0	-783.9	0.0
5	1028389.8	0.0	1280686.7	2289224.6	-710.3	-34.8	-120.3	0.0
6	132937.1	0.0	1273522.8	1519094.1	-542.9	-56.0	-122.9	0.0
7	1133003.4	0.0	12301027.7	15049617.8	-695989.2	-733.7	-857.5	0.0
8	119170.8		6946644.2	7972887.5	-655498.2	-9780.8	-16652.0	0.0
9	829356.2	20029.6	8549500.8	18365972.5	-5812417.4	-156909.8	-370053.1	0.0
10	772673.4	349780.6	1316532.7	3057529.7	-1265980.1	-3475.6	-4934.7	0.0
11	0.0	0.0	170143.6	532616.6	0.0	0.0	0.0	0.0
12	0.0	0.0	7022872.5	7532682.1	0.0	0.0	0.0	0.0
13	0.0	59170.2	0.0	0.0	0.0	0.0	0.0	0.0
14	0.0		2164078.1	2445795.9	0.0	0.0	0.0	0.0
15	0.0		1844235.3	2480942.1	0.0	0.0	0.0	0.0
16	0.0	30321.0	1721207.8	3108093.7	-217799.9	-2.4	-6.2	0.0
17	0.0	0.0	2468094.2	2468094.2	0.0	0.0	0.0	0.0
18	504.2	0.0	2988908.5	3912103.5	-2526.8	-239.4	-512.4	0.0
19	54967.0	0.0	394786.2	410850.8	-74052.5	-32.1	-61.8	0.0
190	15702860.8	459301.4	58799094.9	86774365.2	-9086985.1	-177500.0	-405900.0	0.0

93

Table 16 (Continued)

Sector	405	409	501	502	503	509	600	700	Sector
1	0.0	0.0	-89627.8	0.0	-8833.8	-98461.6	3436221.0	3534682.6	1
2	0.0	-153586.4	-356956.7	-440507.5	-121691.7	-919155.9	4318315.6	5391057.9	2
3	0.0	-188144.2	-569486.3	-70346.0	-167506.6	-807338.9	3455123.3	4450606.4	3
4	0.0	-8551.7	-181790.9	-90344.0	-50903.5	-323038.4	1920923.1	2252513.2	4
5	0.0	-865.4	-551225.0	-6573.1	-105248.9	-663047.0	1625312.2	2289224.6	5
6	0.0	-721.8	-272499.6	-172779.3	-61987.5	-507266.4	1011105.9	1519094.1	6
7	0.0	-697580.4	-230818.8	-12846.1	-66866.1	-310531.0	14041506.4	15049617.8	7
8	0.0	-681931.0	-356288.4	-293222.6	-219694.0	-869205.0	6421751.5	7972887.5	8
9	-42407.9	-6381788.2	-2270125.0	-341053.3	-642891.6	-3254069.9	8730114.4	18365972.5	9
10	0.0	-1304390.4	142193.5	-147253.7	-124967.6	-130027.8	1623111.5	3057529.7	10
11	0.0	0.0	0.0	-9139.3	0.0	-9139.3	523477.3	532616.6	11
12	0.0	0.0	0.0	0.0	0.0	0.0	7532682.1	7532682.1	12
13	0.0	0.0	4791592.0	1584064.9	0.0	6375656.9	6375656.9	0.0	13
14	-130698.6	-130698.6	0.0	0.0	0.0	0.0	2315097.3	2445795.9	14
15	-174272.5	-174272.5	0.0	0.0	1570591.3	1570591.3	3877260.9	2480942.1	15
16	-118225.0	-336033.5	0.0	0.0	0.0	0.0	2772060.2	3108093.7	16
17	0.0	0.0	0.0	0.0	0.0	0.0	2468094.2	2468094.2	17
18	-51296.8	-54575.4	0.0	0.0	0.0	0.0	3857528.1	3912103.5	18
19	-281737.4	-355883.8	-54967.0	0.0	0.0	-54967.0	0.0	410850.8	19
190	-798638.2	-10469023.3	0.0	0.0	0.0	0.0	76305341.9	86774365.2	190

94

TABLE 17. TRANSACTION TABLE AT PRODUCEP'S PRICES, 19 x 19

(MILLION RUPIAHS)

Sector	1	2	3	4	5	6	7	8
1	61432.8	1035167.7	0.0	5940.4	0.0	0.0	0.0	2200694.9
2	0.0	133184.3	1316.7	9448.0	0.0	507.6	0.0	435144.0
3	0.0	420.7	589918.8	10186.3	0.0	0.0	0.0	938635.8
4	5673.1	18072.0	5122.9	503658.9	0.0	241.6	0.0	27874.4
5	235.0	1886.6	8809.7	1013.3	44625.2	8593.7	111.4	3087.7
6	0.0	0.0	0.0	227.3	0.0	80387.0	0.0	32945.8
7	0.0	0.0	0.9	78.3	0.0	2343.9	418739.0	5783.7
8	0.0	0.0	6.2	81995.1	0.0	8624.4	8.0	353563.4
9	178059.4	87804.5	156898.0	8454.7	35145.3	44351.5	390602.4	140048.0
10	239.3	584.1	20346.7	1321.2	23378.0	14981.1	74165.2	43595.4
11	0.0	0.0	4181.3	550.5	2710.3	582.8	746.7	13516.2
12	2463.6	7917.2	20702.8	4176.0	18542.8	1936.4	66525.5	5623.3
13	8577.5	40948.6	81402.7	65078.9	6957.0	32171.2	13299.8	312507.9
14	0.0	0.0	2639.7	758.4	2297.6	593.8	59245.0	11305.6
15	15612.3	13422.7	72611.2	23079.6	6608.4	9981.2	49546.0	86662.5
16	27446.2	10614.2	38232.1	11822.6	28506.3	11869.0	422614.5	52402.7
17	0.0	0.0	0.0	0.0	0.0	0.0	0.0	0.0
18	1353.7	970.2	42303.9	2164.2	44440.8	1350.6	109168.1	7881.3
19	0.0	0.0	0.0	0.0	0.0	0.0	0.0	0.0
190	301090.9	1350992.8	1044493.6	729953.7	213211.7	218515.8	1604771.6	4671272.6
201	630498.2	409228.6	694445.1	289304.6	242465.8	126057.9	333662.6	449521.2
202	2431988.3	2514941.7	1588269.5	873422.0	1042828.0	626858.8	11743631.2	822866.4
203	39998.5	35534.9	99270.2	19717.2	113888.1	33591.7	342773.7	228103.6
204	32645.1	7617.6	28644.9	8525.6	12918.6	6081.7	16667.3	312940.7
205	0.0	0.0	0.0	0.0	0.0	0.0	0.0	-62953.0
209	3135130.1	2967322.8	2410629.7	1190969.4	1412100.5	792590.1	12436734.8	1750478.9
210	3436221.0	4318315.6	3455123.3	1920923.1	1625312.2	1011105.9	14041506.4	6421751.5

Table 17 (Continued)

Sector	16	15	14	13	12	11	10	9	Sector
1	0.0	0.0	0.0	9.7	18384.2	0.0	0.0	1881.4	1
2	0.0	125.6	93532.9	129.8	0.0	0.0	0.0	1586.3	2
3	0.0	8.4	60540.3	103.4	169.5	0.0	0.0	177231.9	3
4	0.0	3805.6	259468.3	0.0	0.0	0.0	0.0	33983.9	4
5		1021.1	8624.4	103.6	445292.2		21.8	198341.9	5
6	0.0	126.4	68711.3	0.0	0.0	0.0	0.0	109.4	6
7	0.6	831.1	2.3	92.5	307537.5		1377281.5	362003.6	7
8	958.4	7397.3	375566.0	0.0	0.0	3903.2	0.0	23643.9	8
9	44484.1	164138.7	52369.9	68786.3	2149466.5	35668.9	36793.0	3810017.1	9
10	6391.7	424264.9	47731.4	44438.9	649604.5	127914.0	1462.9	124746.7	10
11	17534.0	16462.6	56317.1	35618.1	6072.8	73232.9	16776.5	46785.1	11
12	160319.4	61364.7	27466.1	37076.8	12784.4	15969.5	6291.3	15701.3	12
13	8158.8	19770.1	115269.3	11577.3	1003915.1	11086.8	6492.3	494575.8	13
14	23366.2	33774.0	4485.6	53638.8	27258.4	2755.8	29305.3	14284.1	14
15	47906.1	359487.1	51666.2	111331.1	219654.5	7167.3	15627.7	212360.3	15
16	70824.2	136658.5	53397.1	223386.3	102417.7	6961.2	31541.9	68608.7	16
17	0.0	0.0	0.0	0.0	0.0	0.0	0.0	0.0	17
18	37710.0	429663.6	22860.6	58701.1	7698.9	8216.8	7492.0	17088.9	18
19	0.0	7638.1	8617.2	0.0	0.0	0.0	0.0	9.3	19
190	417653.5	1666537.8	1306426.0	644993.7	4950256.2	292876.4	1529086.2	5602959.6	190
201	360207.5	720428.6	275572.4	909938.7	1347383.0	85250.0	32415.2	901259.9	201
202	1793864.4	1035836.9	556473.7	5144322.5	9485516.5	111009.2	361874.6	2159402.9	202
203	163733.3	418630.2	98519.0	156547.1	161378.4	33560.8	61610.1	311222.0	203
204	36601.5	35827.4	78106.2	213454.3	125148.0	780.9	0.0	127570.0	204
205	0.0	0.0	0.0	-693599.4	0.0	0.0	-361874.6	-372300.0	205
209	2354406.7	2210723.1	1008671.3	5730663.2	2582425.9	230600.9	96025.3	31271154.8	209
210	2772060.2	3877260.9	2315097.3	6375656.9	7532682.1	523477.3	16231111.5	8730116.4	210

Table 17 (Continued).

Sector	17	18	19	190	301	302	303	304
1	0.0	180.0	0.0	3323691.1	0.0	0.0	0.0	112529.9
2	0.0	24848.3	0.0	699823.5	3737635.0	0.0	0.0	2745.9
3	0.0	1552.2	0.0	1778767.3	687372.1	9256.2	0.0	48817.4
4	0.0	25196.8	0.0	883097.5	942566.2	0.0	2216.7	88938.4
5	0.0	925.8	0.0	722693.4	169645.2	0.0	0.0	4820.3
6	0.0	5483.8	0.0	187991.0	720817.3	0.0	0.0	0.0
7	0.0	0.2	0.0	2478598.3	25575.7	0.0	0.0	903285.0
8	0.0	27767.1	0.0	879529.8	6092561.3	3015.7	0.0	24013.3
9	0.0	739493.0	0.0	8142581.3	2620116.0	357138.9	3171200.8	145013.4
10	0.0	33343.0	0.0	1638509.0	579846.8	68132.5	0.0	-55326.3
11	0.0	71386.1	0.0	362473.0	135842.5	25161.8	6847092.4	0.0
12	0.0	44948.5	0.0	509809.6	0.0	175780.1	467310.3	0.0
13	0.0	155766.4	0.0	2387555.5	2668382.4	52804.4		54279.8
14	0.0	16009.5	0.0	281717.8	1777625.9	327282.0	61925.6	
15	0.0	69562.5	0.0	1372286.7	1907206.6	17158.9		15541.8
16	0.0	89584.7	0.0	1386885.9	1582354.9	108531.9	0.0	0.0
17	0.0	0.0	0.0	0.0	0.0	2468094.2	0.0	0.0
18	0.0	124130.3	0.0	923195.0	1903640.4	1084763.9	0.0	0.0
19	0.0	0.0	0.0	16064.6	43664.2	296155.0		0.0
190	0.0	1430178.2	0.0	27975270.3	25594852.5	5147675.5	10549745.8	1344658.9
201	2344689.5	1515086.9	0.0	11667415.7				
202	0.0	663068.2	0.0	34419174.8				
203	123404.7	176341.7	0.0	2617825.2				
204	0.0	72853.1	0.0	1116382.9				
205	0.0	0.0	0.0	-1490727.0				
209	2468094.2	2427349.9	0.0	48330071.6				
210	2468094.2	3857528.1	0.0	76305341.9				

Table 17 (Continued)

Sector	305	306	309	310	401	402	403	604	Sector
1	0.0	0.0	112529.9	3436221.0	0.0	0.0	0.0	0.0	1
2	31697.6	0.0	3772078.5	4471902.0	-142561.3	-3163.1	-7862.0	0.0	2
3	111054.5	0.0	1864500.2	3643267.5	-181492.7	-2718.3	-3933.2	0.0	3
4	12656.0	0.0	1046377.3	1929474.8	-7413.8	-354.0	-783.9	0.0	4
5	729018.7	0.0	903486.2	1626177.6	-710.3	-34.8	-120.3	0.0	5
6	103019.4	0.0	8238836.7	1011827.7	-542.9	-56.0	-122.9	0.0	6
7	11331627.8	0.0	12260488.5	14739086.8	-695989.2	-733.7	-857.5	0.0	7
8	104562.4	0.0	62224152.7	71036082.5	-655498.2	-9780.8	-16652.0	0.0	8
9	655822.6	20029.6	6969321.3	15111902.6	-5812417.4	-156909.8	-370053.1	0.0	9
10	696339.9	0.0	1288992.9	2927501.9	-1295980.1	-3475.6	-4934.7	0.0	10
11	0.0	0.0	161004.3	523477.3	0.0	0.0	0.0	0.0	11
12	0.0	0.0	70228872.5	75326682.1	0.0	0.0	0.0	0.0	12
13	745324.5	0.0	3988101.4	6375656.9	0.0	0.0	0.0	0.0	13
14	0.0	59170.2	2164078.1	2445795.9	0.0	0.0	0.0	0.0	14
15	173233.2	349780.6	26792466.7	4051533.4	0.0	0.0	0.0	0.0	15
16	0.0	30321.0	1721207.8	3108093.7	-217799.9	-2.4	-6.2	0.0	16
17	0.0	0.0	24680094.2	24680094.2	0.0	0.0	0.0	0.0	17
18	504.2	0.0	29889908.5	39121035.5	-2526.8	-239.4	-512.4	0.0	18
19	0.0	0.0	339819.2	3555883.8	-74052.5	-32.1	-61.8	0.0	19
190	15702860.8	459301.4	58799094.9	86774365.2	-9086985.1	-177500.0	-405900.0	0.0	190

98

Table 17 (Continued)

Sector	405	409	501	502	503	509	600	700	Sector
1	0.0	0.0	0.0	0.0	0.0	0.0	3436221.0	3436221.0	1
2	0.0	-153586.4	0.0	0.0	0.0	0.0	4318315.6	4471902.0	2
3	0.0	-188144.2	0.0	0.0	0.0	0.0	3455123.3	3643267.5	3
4	0.0	-8551.7	0.0	0.0	0.0	0.0	1920923.1	1929474.8	4
5	0.0	-865.4	0.0	0.0	0.0	0.0	1625312.2	1626177.6	5
6	0.0	-721.8	0.0	0.0	0.0	0.0	1011105.9	1011827.7	6
7	0.0	-697580.4	0.0	0.0	0.0	0.0	14041506.4	14739086.8	7
8	0.0	-681931.0	0.0	0.0	0.0	0.0	6421751.5	7103682.5	8
9	-42607.9	-6381788.2	0.0	0.0	0.0	0.0	8730114.4	15111902.6	9
10	0.0	-1306390.4	0.0	0.0	0.0	0.0	1623111.5	2927501.9	10
11	0.0	0.0	0.0	0.0	0.0	0.0	5234177.3	5234177.3	11
12	0.0	0.0	0.0	0.0	0.0	0.0	7532682.1	7532682.1	12
13	0.0	0.0	0.0	0.0	0.0	0.0	6375656.9	6375656.9	13
14	-130698.6	-130698.6	0.0	0.0	0.0	0.0	2315097.3	2445795.9	14
15	-174272.5	-174272.5	0.0	0.0	0.0	0.0	3877260.9	4051533.6	15
16	-118225.0	-336033.5	0.0	0.0	0.0	0.0	2772060.2	3108093.7	16
17	0.0	0.0	0.0	0.0	0.0	0.0	2468094.2	2468094.2	17
18	-51296.8	-54575.4	0.0	0.0	0.0	0.0	3857528.1	3912103.5	18
19	-281737.4	-355883.8	0.0	0.0	0.0	0.0	0.0	355883.8	19
190	-798638.2	-10469023.3	0.0	0.0	0.0	0.0	76305341.9	86774365.2	190

99

TABLE 18. IMPORTS AT PURCHASER'S PRICES, 19 x 19

(MILLION RUPIAHS)

Sector	1	2	3	4	5	6	7	8
1	0.0	1788.7	0.0	0.0	0.0	0.0	0.0	0.0
2	0.0	0.0	0.0	0.0	0.0	0.0	0.0	128510.9
3	0.0	0.0	146.1	19.0	0.0	0.0	0.0	73598.7
4	0.0	0.0	0.0	2280.4	0.0	0.0	0.0	111.3
5	0.0	0.0	0.0	0.0	0.0	0.0	0.0	0.0
6	0.0	0.0	0.0	0.0	0.0	0.0	0.0	4.1
7	0.0	0.0	0.0	0.0	0.0	0.0	22.0	131.0
8	0.0	0.0	0.0	0.0	0.0	0.0	74353.1	33452.9
9	38043.5	15778.1	34650.8	13867.6	1493.8	1227.7	66471.6	51878.0
10	59.8	164.3	15767.7	160.2	21183.0	13438.7	0.0	31944.4
11	0.0	0.0	0.0	799.8	0.0	0.0	0.0	0.0
12	0.0	0.0	0.0	0.0	0.0	0.0	0.0	0.0
13	0.0	0.0	57.2	2.9	111.3	0.0	3210.0	347.6
14	0.0	0.0	44.0	0.6	66.5	0.0	737.8	622.5
15	0.0	0.0	0.0	0.0	0.0	0.0	0.0	0.0
16	0.0	0.0	0.0	0.0	0.0	0.0	259931.2	0.0
17	0.0	0.0	0.0	0.0	0.0	0.0	0.0	0.0
18	0.0	0.0	0.0	0.0	0.0	0.0	0.0	0.0
19	0.0	0.0	0.0	0.0	0.0	0.0	0.0	0.0
190	38103.3	17731.1	50665.8	17130.5	22854.6	14666.4	404725.7	320601.4

Table 18 (Continued)

Sector	9	10	11	12	13	14	15	16
1	0.0	0.0	0.0	0.0	0.0	0.0	0.0	0.0
2	0.0	0.0	0.0	0.0	0.0	1421.4	0.0	0.0
3	122983.0	0.0	0.0	0.0	0.0	380.5	0.0	0.0
4	509.0	0.0	0.0	0.0	0.0	988.3	0.0	0.0
5	1369.6	0.0	0.0	1.9	0.0	1.7	0.0	0.0
6	4.0	0.0	0.0	0.0	0.0	127.8	0.0	0.0
7	47279.5	635880.0	0.0	4570.4	0.0	0.0	90.3	0.0
8	7843.0	0.0	0.0	0.0	0.0	41247.0	0.0	0.0
9	2703247.9	13719.2	3397.6	1131605.1	11743.4	5552.6	27129.6	2659.7
10	80065.2	1337.0	54818.6	33747.6	42722.4	20426.5	424857.3	3024.2
11	0.0	0.0	0.0	0.0	0.0	0.0	0.0	0.0
12	0.0	0.0	0.0	0.0	0.0	0.0	0.0	0.0
13	0.0	0.0	0.0	0.0	0.0	0.0	0.0	0.0
14	492.5	1817.2	105.7	1032.0	3220.6	140.0	1466.4	1395.2
15	563.1	736.2	169.5	254.8	11112.7	105.0	58546.7	1120.4
16	0.0	0.0	0.0	3819.0	18158.3	1754.1	18518.6	8766.5
17	0.0	0.0	0.0	0.0	0.0	0.0	0.0	0.0
18	0.0	0.0	0.0	0.0	0.0	0.0	0.0	904.3
19	9.3	0.0	0.0	0.0	0.0	8417.2	7638.1	0.0
190	2964366.1	653489.6	58491.4	1175030.8	86957.4	80562.1	538247.0	17870.3

Table 18 (Continued)

Sector	304	303	302	301	190	19	18	17
1	0.0	0.0	0.0	0.0	0.0	0.0	0.0	0.0
2	3078.5	0.0	0.0	39915.4	131721.0	0.0	0.0	0.0
3	4757.3	0.0	0.0	3142.0	197127.3	0.0	0.0	0.0
4	0.3	2654.2	0.0	3777.4	3889.0	0.0	0.0	0.0
5	0.0	0.0	0.0	105.1	1373.2	0.0	0.0	0.0
6	0.0	0.0	0.0	1169.6	135.9	0.0	0.0	0.0
7	23190.2	0.0	0.0	0.0	687973.2	0.0	0.0	0.0
8	2247.3	0.0	0.0	622841.9	96782.2	0.0	371.7	0.0
9	132656.6	2590995.1	119221.1	379579.5	4414499.7	0.0	297859.4	0.0
10	-10782.2	0.0	59373.3	248323.1	830281.2	0.0	19453.1	0.0
11	0.0	0.0	0.0	0.0	0.0	0.0	0.0	0.0
12	0.0	0.0	0.0	0.0	0.0	0.0	0.0	0.0
13	0.0	0.0	14261.1	102231.9	14205.6	0.0	807.0	0.0
14	0.0	0.0	6056.9	93818.1	74397.5	0.0	317.7	0.0
15	0.0	0.0				0.0		0.0
16	0.0	0.0	15057.0	9528.8	311447.7	0.0	500.0	0.0
17	0.0	0.0	0.0	0.0	0.0	0.0	0.0	0.0
18	0.0	0.0	1188.6	14124.8	39262.0	0.0	38357.7	0.0
19	0.0	0.0	296155.0	43666.2	16064.6	0.0	0.0	0.0
190	155148.0	2593649.3	511313.0	1562221.8	6819160.1	0.0	357666.6	0.0

102

Table 18 (Continued)

Sector	305	306	309	310	401	402	403	404	Sector
1	0.0	0.0	0.0	0.0	0.0	0.0	0.0	0.0	1
2	0.0	0.0	42993.9	174714.9	-142561.3	-3163.1	-7862.0	0.0	2
3	0.0	0.0	7899.3	205026.6	-181492.7	-2718.3	-3933.2	0.0	3
4	0.0	0.0	6431.9	10320.9	-7413.8	-354.0	-783.9	0.0	4
5	0.0	0.0	105.1	1478.3	-710.3	-34.8	-120.3	0.0	5
6	0.0	0.0	1169.6	1305.5	-542.9	-56.0	-122.9	0.0	6
7	0.0	0.0	23190.2	711163.4	-695989.2	-733.7	-857.5	0.0	7
8	0.0	0.0	625089.2	721871.4	-655498.2	-9780.8	-16652.0	0.0	8
9	0.0	0.0	3222452.3	7636952.0	-5812417.4	-156909.8	-370053.1	0.0	9
10	0.0	0.0	296914.2	1127195.4	-1295980.1	-3475.6	-4934.7	0.0	10
11	0.0	0.0	0.0	0.0	0.0	0.0	0.0	0.0	11
12	0.0	0.0	0.0	0.0	0.0	0.0	0.0	0.0	12
13	0.0	0.0	116493.0	130698.6	0.0	0.0	0.0	0.0	13
14	0.0	0.0	99875.0	174272.5	0.0	0.0	0.0	0.0	14
15	0.0	0.0						0.0	15
16	0.0	0.0	24585.8	336033.5	-217799.9	-2.6	-6.2	0.0	16
17	0.0	0.0	0.0	0.0	0.0	0.0	0.0	0.0	17
18	0.0	0.0	15313.4	54575.4	-2526.8	-239.4	-512.4	0.0	18
19	0.0	0.0	339819.2	355883.8	-74052.5	-32.1	-61.8	0.0	19
190	0.0	0.0	4822332.1	11641492.2	-9086985.1	-177500.0	-405900.0	0.0	190

Table 18 (Continued)

Sector	405	409	501	502	503	509	600	700	Sector
1	0.0	0.0	0.0	0.0	0.0	0.0	0.0	0.0	1
2	0.0	-153586.4	-12369.2	-5074.6	-3684.7	-21128.5	0.0	174714.9	2
3	0.0	-188144.2	-13012.2	-196.8	-3673.4	-16882.4	0.0	205026.6	3
4	0.0	-8551.7	-1501.2	-108.0	-160.0	-1769.2	0.0	10320.9	4
5	0.0	-865.4	-484.2	-1.5	-127.2	-612.9	0.0	1478.3	5
6	0.0	-721.8	-317.9	-218.9	-46.9	-583.7	0.0	1305.5	6
7	0.0	-697580.4	-9675.3	0.0	-3907.7	-13583.0	0.0	711163.4	7
8	0.0	-681931.0	20228.3	-18651.2	-41517.5	-39940.4	0.0	721871.4	8
9	-42407.9	-6381788.2	-961211.6	-59609.4	-234342.8	-1255163.8	0.0	7636952.0	9
10	0.0	-1304390.4	321618.1	-77569.5	-66853.6	177195.0	0.0	1127195.4	10
11	0.0	0.0	0.0	0.0	0.0	0.0	0.0	0.0	11
12	0.0	0.0	0.0	0.0	0.0	0.0	0.0	0.0	12
13	0.0	0.0	656725.2	161429.9	354313.8	818155.1	0.0	-818155.1	13
14	-130698.6	-130698.6	0.0	0.0	0.0	0.0	0.0	130698.6	14
15	-174272.5	-174272.5	0.0	0.0	0.0	354313.8	0.0	-180061.3	15
16	-118225.0	-336033.5	0.0	0.0	0.0	0.0	0.0	336033.5	16
17	0.0	0.0	0.0	0.0	0.0	0.0	0.0	0.0	17
18	-51296.8	-54575.4	0.0	0.0	0.0	0.0	0.0	54575.4	18
19	-281737.4	-355883.8	0.0	0.0	0.0	0.0	0.0	355883.8	19
190	-798638.2	-10469023.3	0.0	0.0	0.0	0.0	0.0	10469023.3	190

104

TABLE 19. IMPORTS AT PRODUCER'S PRICES, 19 x 19

(MILLION RUPIAHS)

Sector	1	2	3	4	5	6	7	8
1	0.0	0.0	0.0	0.0	0.0	0.0	0.0	0.0
2	0.0	1080.0	0.0	0.0	0.0	0.0	0.0	123861.9
3	0.0	0.0	127.7	16.6	0.0	0.0	0.0	60958.2
4	0.0	0.0	0.0	1838.2	0.0	0.0	0.0	105.3
5	0.0	0.0	0.0	0.0	0.0	0.0	0.0	0.0
6	0.0	0.0	0.0	0.0	0.0	0.0	0.0	2.7
7	0.0	0.0	0.0	0.0	0.0	0.0	17.4	85.8
8	0.0	0.0	0.0	11278.8	0.0	0.0	0.0	27337.3
9	33149.1	13836.4	30421.8	103.4	1091.1	1131.9	65188.6	43071.9
10	145.5	401.6	16927.3	940.8	20698.7	12925.0	70068.1	34133.4
11	0.0	0.0	0.0	0.0	0.0	0.0	0.0	0.0
12	0.0	0.0	0.0	0.0	0.0	0.0	0.0	0.0
13	0.0	0.0	57.2	2.9	111.3	0.0	3210.0	347.6
14	0.0	0.0	44.0	0.6	66.5	0.0	737.8	622.5
15	0.0	0.0	0.0	0.0	0.0	0.0	0.0	0.0
16	0.0	0.0	0.0	0.0	0.0	0.0	259931.2	0.0
17	0.0	0.0	0.0	0.0	0.0	0.0	0.0	0.0
18	0.0	0.0	0.0	0.0	0.0	0.0	0.0	0.0
19	0.0	0.0	0.0	0.0	0.0	0.0	0.0	0.0
190	33296.6	15318.0	47578.0	16181.3	21967.6	14056.9	399153.1	290526.6

Table 19 (Continued)

Sector	9	10	11	12	13	14	15	16
1	0.0	0.0	0.0	0.0	0.0	0.0	0.0	0.0
2	0.0	0.0	0.0	0.0	0.0	873.8	0.0	0.0
3	120028.7	0.0	0.0	0.0	0.0	307.6	0.0	0.0
4	436.2	0.0	0.0	0.0	0.0	821.6	0.0	0.0
5	806.7	0.0	0.0	1.3	0.0	1.0	0.0	0.0
6	2.6	0.0	0.0	0.0	0.0	71.5	0.0	0.0
7	-34380.8	635851.2	0.0	3994.3	0.0	0.0	70.6	0.0
8	6407.4	11442.6	0.0	0.0	0.0	35985.8	0.0	0.0
9	2351547.2	1250.6	2552.9	884039.5	8824.9	3866.2	26655.6	2030.0
10	99846.1	0.0	53520.0	44088.4	42789.1	23003.5	407580.3	3090.2
11	0.0	0.0	0.0	0.0	0.0	0.0	0.0	0.0
12	0.0	0.0	0.0	0.0	0.0	0.0	0.0	0.0
13	0.0	0.0	0.0	0.0	0.0	0.0	0.0	0.0
14	492.5	1817.2	105.7	1032.0	3220.6	140.0	1466.4	1395.2
15	563.1	736.2	169.5	254.8	11112.7	105.0	58546.7	1120.4
16	0.0	0.0	0.0	3819.0	18158.3	1754.1	18518.6	8766.5
17	0.0	0.0	0.0	0.0	0.0	0.0	0.0	0.0
18	0.0	0.0	0.0	0.0	0.0	0.0	0.0	904.3
19	9.3	0.0	0.0	0.0	0.0	8417.2	7638.1	0.0
190	2614520.6	651097.8	56348.1	937229.3	84105.6	75347.3	520476.3	17306.6

Table 19 (Continued)

Sector	17	18	19	190	301	302	303	304
1	0.0	0.0	0.0	0.0	0.0	0.0	0.0	0.0
2	0.0	0.0	0.0	125815.7	25024.9	0.0	0.0	2745.8
3	0.0	0.0	0.0	181438.8	2462.2	0.0	0.0	4243.2
4	0.0	0.0	0.0	3201.3	3133.4	0.0	2216.7	0.3
5	0.0	0.0	0.0	809.0	56.4	0.0	0.0	0.0
6	0.0	0.0	0.0	76.8	645.0	0.0	0.0	0.0
7	0.0	0.0	0.0	674400.1	0.0	0.0	0.0	23180.3
8	0.0	949.7	0.0	81959.0	598253.4	86051.3	0.0	1718.6
9	0.0	229187.7	0.0	3708140.8	255873.7	58821.7	2213634.6	118087.8
10	0.0	22841.3	0.0	854249.9	400740.0	0.0	0.0	-9421.2
11	0.0	0.0	0.0	0.0	0.0	0.0	0.0	0.0
12	0.0	0.0	0.0	0.0	0.0	0.0	0.0	0.0
13	0.0	0.0	0.0	0.0	0.0	0.0	0.0	0.0
14	0.0	807.0	0.0	16205.6	102231.9	14261.1	0.0	0.0
15	0.0	317.7	0.0	74397.5	93818.1	6056.9	0.0	0.0
16	0.0	500.0	0.0	311447.7	9528.8	15057.0	0.0	0.0
17	0.0	0.0	0.0	0.0	0.0	0.0	0.0	0.0
18	0.0	38357.7	0.0	39262.0	14124.8	1188.6	0.0	0.0
19	0.0	0.0	0.0	16064.6	43664.2	296155.0	0.0	0.0
190	0.0	292961.1	0.0	6085468.8	1549556.8	477591.6	2215851.3	140554.8

Table 19 (Continued)

Sector	404	403	402	401	310	309	306	305	Sector
1	0.0	0.0	0.0	0.0	0.0	0.0	0.0	0.0	1
2	0.0	-7862.0	-3163.1	-142561.3	153586.4	27770.7	0.0	0.0	2
3	0.0	-3933.2	-2718.3	-181492.7	188144.2	6705.4	0.0	0.0	3
4	0.0	-783.9	-354.0	-7413.8	8551.7	5350.4	0.0	0.0	4
5	0.0	-120.3	-34.8	-710.3	865.4	56.4	0.0	0.0	5
6	0.0	-122.9	-56.0	-542.9	721.8	645.0	0.0	0.0	6
7	0.0	-857.5	-733.7	-695989.2	697580.4	23180.3	0.0	0.0	7
8	0.0	-16652.0	-9780.8	-655498.2	681931.0	599972.0	0.0	0.0	8
9	0.0	-370053.1	-156909.8	-5812417.4	6381788.2	2673647.4	0.0	0.0	9
10	0.0	-4934.7	-3475.6	-1295980.1	1304390.4	450140.5	0.0	0.0	10
11	0.0	0.0	0.0	0.0	0.0	0.0	0.0	0.0	11
12	0.0	0.0	0.0	0.0	0.0	0.0	0.0	0.0	12
13	0.0	0.0	0.0	0.0	0.0	0.0	0.0	0.0	13
14	0.0	0.0	0.0	0.0	130698.6	116493.0	0.0	0.0	14
15	0.0	0.0	0.0	0.0	174272.5	99875.0	0.0	0.0	15
16	0.0	-6.2	-2.4	-217799.9	336033.5	24585.8	0.0	0.0	16
17	0.0	0.0	0.0	0.0	0.0	0.0	0.0	0.0	17
18	0.0	-512.4	-239.4	-2526.8	54575.4	15313.4	0.0	0.0	18
19	0.0	-61.8	-32.1	-76052.5	355883.8	339819.2	0.0	0.0	19
190	0.0	-405900.0	-177500.0	-9086985.1	10469023.3	4383554.5	0.0	0.0	190

108

Table 19 (Continued)

Sector	405	409	501	502	503	509	600	700	Sector
1	0.0	0.0	0.0	0.0	0.0	0.0	0.0	0.0	1
2	0.0	-153586.4	0.0	0.0	0.0	0.0	0.0	153586.4	2
3	0.0	-188144.2	0.0	0.0	0.0	0.0	0.0	188144.2	3
4	0.0	-8551.7	0.0	0.0	0.0	0.0	0.0	8551.7	4
5	0.0	-865.4	0.0	0.0	0.0	0.0	0.0	865.4	5
6	0.0	-721.8	0.0	0.0	0.0	0.0	0.0	721.8	6
7	0.0	-697580.4	0.0	0.0	0.0	0.0	0.0	697580.4	7
8	0.0	-681931.0	0.0	0.0	0.0	0.0	0.0	681931.0	8
9	-42407.9	-6381788.2	0.0	0.0	0.0	0.0	0.0	6381788.2	9
10	0.0	-1304390.4	0.0	0.0	0.0	0.0	0.0	1304390.4	10
11	0.0	0.0	0.0	0.0	0.0	0.0	0.0	0.0	11
12	0.0	0.0	0.0	0.0	0.0	0.0	0.0	0.0	12
13	0.0	0.0	0.0	0.0	0.0	0.0	0.0	0.0	13
14	-130698.6	-130698.6	0.0	0.0	0.0	0.0	0.0	130698.6	14
15	-174272.5	-174272.5	0.0	0.0	0.0	0.0	0.0	174272.5	15
16	-118225.0	-336033.5	0.0	0.0	0.0	0.0	0.0	336033.5	16
17	0.0	0.0	0.0	0.0	0.0	0.0	0.0	0.0	17
18	-51296.8	-54575.4	0.0	0.0	0.0	0.0	0.0	54575.4	18
19	-281737.4	-355883.8	0.0	0.0	0.0	0.0	0.0	355883.8	19
190	-798638.2	-10469023.3	0.0	0.0	0.0	0.0	0.0	10469023.3	190

VI. ISLAMIC REPUBLIC OF IRAN

A. GENERAL INFORMATION

The present report is based on the *Iran Input-Output Table for 1352, Methodology and Tentative Estimates*, published by the Statistical Centre of the Islamic Republic of Iran.

Three input-output tables have been compiled for the Islamic Republic of Iran. The first table, with 10 intermediate sectors, refers to 1965 and was constructed by the Ministry of Economy. Another table, with 25 intermediate sectors, was compiled for the year 1969 by the Bank Markazi. The latest table, described in the present report, refers to 1973. Contrary to previous tables, the input-output table of 1973 is mainly based on Iranian statistics, rather than on the adoption of ratios from tables constructed for other countries.

The input-output estimates of gross output, total intermediate and value added of most sectors agree closely with, and are often based on, the corresponding national accounts estimates presented in the breakdown of gross domestic product by industrial origin. However, minor differences exist owing to the more recent information used in the input-output table and to minor changes in definitions. Furthermore, the national accounts estimate of value added includes the rent paid by business, which in the input-output table is deducted as a part of intermediate input.

The major discrepancies between the Iranian input-output table and the SNA recommendations on input-output refer to the following aspects: (*a*) treatment of the government sector; (*b*) recording of the activities of private non-profit institutions; (*c*) the use of a dummy sector to allow for statistical discrepancies between totals of rows and columns; (*d*) the breakdown of value added and final demand; (*e*) treatment of imports; (*f*) treatment of secondary production; (*g*) treatment of the financial sector. Furthermore, commodity taxes are not reported separately and therefore no valuation of the table at basic values can be derived.

B. ANALYTICAL FRAMEWORK

1. *Tables and derived matrices available*

The basic information is presented in one absorption table valued at producers' prices. On the basis of this table, the following derived matrices were compiled:

(i') Input coefficients;

(ii') Input coefficients of medium-scale manufacturing establishments, which are defined as those employing 10 to 99 persons;

(iii') Input coefficients of large manufacturing establishments, which are defined as those employing 100 or more persons;

(iv') Inverse matrix, presenting total input requirements per rial of delivery of final demand.

All tables and matrices are compiled at a disaggregation level of 59 x 59 intermediate sectors

2. *Valuation standards*

Producers' prices are defined as the cost of the goods as they leave the factory. They include indirect taxes net of subsidies and exclude transportation and trade margins. Imports are valued c.i.f. Exports of goods and services other than crude oil are valued f.o.b. Exports of crude oil are valued at approximate actual selling prices. Contrary to the SNA recommendations, commodity taxes are not separated out and therefore no valuation at basic approximate values can be derived.

3. *Statistical units and classification standards*

The establishment is the statistical unit adopted for rows and columns of the input-output table and derived matrices.

Establishments are generally classified according to ISIC, with two main exceptions: (*a*) ISIC major group "Public administration and defence" has been replaced by a "government industry" sector which, covers all government services; and (*b*) ISIC major group "Domestic services" has been excluded from the ISIC division "Personal and household services" and has been recorded as a separate input-output sector "Household industry".

The structure of the intermediate consumption quadrant differs from the SNA recommendations in three aspects: (*a*) intermediate input of the government services sector is recorded in the final demand quadrant; (*b*) no distinction is made between industry activities and the activities of the private non-profit institution; and (*c*) an "unallocated input" sector is set up to balance estimation errors in rows and columns.

Government services have been disaggregated into a productive sector (government industry) and a final demand sector (public consumption). Output of the government industry sector is defined as equal to total compensation of government employees and is distributed in its entirety to the public consumption category of final demand. Purchases of intermediate input by the government sector are recorded in the public consumption category of final demand. This treatment of the activity of producers of government services does not agree with the SNA recommendations.

The breakdown of value added differs from the SNA recommendations in that consumption of fixed capital is not disaggregated from operating surplus. The breakdown and definition of final demand follows the SNA recommendations, except for the inclusion of military construction in gross fixed capital formation.

Imports were classified by commodity and distributed together with domestic production to intermediate and final demand sectors. Total imports of each sector were recorded in a column of the final demand quadrant, which was deducted from total demand to obtain gross domestic product of the commodities of each input-output sector. Contrary to the SNA recommendations, no distinction is made between competitive and complementary imports.

4. Treatment and presentation of selected transactions

Information was collected on secondary products produced by medium-scale and large-scale manufacturing establishments, but time constraints precluded any attempt to transfer secondary output and its associated input to their corresponding characteristic sectors. This is contrary to the SNA recommendations.

Non-monetary production (such as own consumption of agricultural products and imputed housing rents) and its corresponding input have been covered. Non-monetary production is included in the output of each intermediate sector of the input-output table.

Output is defined gross, that is, it includes intra-sectoral consumption of all types of products.

Contrary to the SNA recommendations, output of financial institutions is defined to include only actual service charges, that is, the excess of interest earned over interest paid is excluded. As a consequence, the estimate of value added other than compensation of employees for this sector is negative. Output of the sector was allocated to intermediate and final demand sectors in proportion to the sectors' gross output, except in cases where information was available on actual values of commissions and other charges paid to banks.

C. STATISTICAL SOURCES AND COMPILATION METHODOLOGY

Data collection is mainly based on regular sources, as well as on the Agriculture, Organized Mines and Manufacturing Censuses of 1973 and special surveys and research projects carried out for the purpose of the compilation of the input-output table.

1. Gross ouput and intermediate consumption

(a) Agriculture, forestry, fishing

Estimates of output of the crops sector (i.e., grains, industrial crops and other crops) were obtained from the results of the Agriculture Census of 1973, conducted by the Statistical Centre of the Islamic Republic of Iran, supplemented by the information obtained from the Ministry of Agriculture and Natural Resources and other government agencies. Those estimates were systematically cross checked against the results of the household budget survey for 1973 (adjusted for imports, exports and non-household consumption) and, where necessary, correction and adjustments were made to ensure internal consistency within the national accounting framework. Where direct information was lacking, estimation of physical production was derived on the basis of yields per hectare and the total area under cultivation, while output value estimation was obtained by multiplying the volume of physical production by unit prices (farm-gate prices).

Intermediate input for the production of crops consists of water, seeds, chemical and animal fertilizers, pesticides and machinery. Water cost for each irrigated crop was estimated on the basis of irrigated area (based on plan organization data) and water consumption. Expenditures on seeds were estimated on the basis of information for different crops available in *Estimates of Value Added in Agriculture, and*

Preliminary Estimate of National Accounts, published by the Statistical Centre. For all types of fertilizers, the required information regarding total use was obtained from the Chemical Fertilizers' Company, and the Ministry of Agriculture and Natural Resources. On the basis of data on the consumption of fertilizers per hectare and the total area under each crop, estimates were made for the total use of fertilizers per crop. In the case of pesticides and insecticides, the wide variety of brands used for different crops made it rather difficult to obtain reliable estimates. Expenditures on this input by crop group were calculated on the basis of various assumptions concerning the amount used per hectare of different crops and the total area under every crop, as well as the available information on the total domestic production and imports of such items. For expenditures on the use of agricultural machinery, the following procedure was used. Information on the numbers of tractors, combines and tillers was extracted from the agricultural census; then, on the basis of studies undertaken by the Ministry of Agriculture, it was assumed that the cost of using one tractor equals the cost of utilizing five tillers. Detailed information, on an hourly basis, on the various expenses (fuel etc.) involved in using different agricultural machineries was obtained from the Ministry of Agriculture. Then, on the basis of the total number of machines of each type of machinery, the average number of hours that each type is used annually and the hourly costs of utilization, total expenditures by type of machinery were estimated. The costs of utilizing traditional types of capital goods were estimated on the basis of information provided by experts in the Ministry of Agriculture.

Gross output of the livestock sector was based on national accounts estimates. Input of grains, fodder, secondary crops, and vaccines and medicines were estimated separately on the basis of the specific information available. For the remaining input, the required information was obtained mainly through interviews with experts, and estimates were made on the basis of quantities involved and unit prices.

For output of fishing in rivers and lakes, use was made of the number of fishing permits and the average number of fish catches per permit, the average weight of fish and the relevant unit prices. For fishing in the Caspian Sea and the Persian Gulf, all the required information on output and unit prices was obtained from the two government-owned fishing companies. In both cases, in line with the situation in countries similar to the Islamic Republic of Iran, intermediate expenditures were estimated at 6 per cent of the total value of production.

(b) Mining

Data collection for the crude petroleum and natural gas sector was complicated by the unavailability of sets of comparable data in terms of the Iranian calendar years, and by the fact that crude petroleum is undertaken by several different companies which do not follow any standard reporting procedures. Since all companies use the Gregorian calendar years, data required for the Iranian year 1352 were obtained by combining data for the last nine-months of 1973 and the first quarter of 1974.

Gross output of crude petroleum and natural gas was estimated by multiplying the volume of production in barrels by the cost of production per barrel, and adding the profits of the National Iranian Oil Company, the National Iranian Gas

Company and government revenues from oil and gas. Information on production cost, including intermediate consumption and value added (excluding profits) is based on information provided by experts of the National Iranian Oil Company. The breakdown of intermediate consumption by ISIC code was also obtained through interviews with experts of the Oil Company.

The main source of information used for the mining sector was the Census of Organized Mines conducted by the Statistical Centre in co-operation with the Ministry of Industries and Mines. Census information on intermediate input was assigned to appropriate ISIC codes as follows:

(a) The value of purchased electricity was assumed to be insignificant and was therefore disregarded;

(b) Contractual, laboratory, research and exploratory services were classified under business services;

(c) Input of explosives and chemicals was disaggregated on the basis of information extracted from the questionnaires used in the Census of Organized Mines;

(d) Rent for buildings was allocated to the real estate sector;

(e) The same treatment was accorded to royalties;

(f) Other payments were allocated to the "unallocated input" row;

(g) Intermediate consumption of other fuels by the metal ore mining industry was assumed to be produced by the hunting, forestry and fishing sector.

Regarding the unorganized mining sector (i.e., mines without a licence or operating permit), the only data available were those provided by the Ministry of Industries and Mines on value of gross output and value added. Intermediate consumption was obtained as the difference between those two values, and was assumed to be produced by the following sectors: hunting, forestry and fishing; petrochemicals; petroleum refineries; machinery manufacturing; real estate; machinery and equipment rental and leasing, and transport. Relative shares of those sectors in intermediate consumption were estimated on the basis of interviews conducted with experts of the Ministry of Industries and Mines.

(c) *Manufacturing*

Information on the manufacturing sector, except for hand-made carpets, is based on the results of the 1973 Manufacturing Census conducted by the Statistical Centre. Completed questionnaires were available for 3,781 manufacturing establishments, of which 493 had 100 or more employees and 3,288 had between 10 and 99 employees. Firms with fewer than 10 employees, defined as small establishments, were not covered by the census and were not taken into account in the input-output table. It is for this reason that row and column number 37, "Handicrafts and small-scale manufacturing", were left blank. Should data for those small establishments become available later they can be accommodated in the table.

The census forms for each ISIC group were first separated into those for large-scale and those for medium-scale establishments, the former having 100 or more employees, the latter between 10 and 99. In view of the fact that large establishments, despite their smaller number, accounted for most of the output and value added of all firms, the returns of all large establishments were tabulated. Where firms supplied

incomplete data on their intermediate input (usually regarding raw material input), it was generally assumed that their technological input structure resembled that of firms in the same code for which complete information was available. Thus, for large-scale firms, total output was multiplied by the input structure of firms in the same code supplying complete information to obtain estimated intermediate purchases for the full number of large firms in the code.

For the medium-sized firms, the procedure was different. To begin with, a sample of questionnaire returns was drawn for each ISIC group, varying from about 10 to 20 per cent of the total number, the fraction generally being larger for the industries (codes) with fewer firms and never under five. The selection process was essentially random but fully completed and, therefore, usable returns were favoured. From the sample for each activity category, the average input pattern was calculated and applied to the total production of all firms within the code to obtain the values of all input, intermediate and primary. Where production figures for non-sampled firms were lacking, they were estimated using the average output employment ratio of similar firms providing complete data.

At a later stage in the work, the Department of Industrial and Trade Statistics of the Statistical Centre obtained or estimated data on production and/or employment, for firms which had failed to respond to the initial census inquiry.

In the case of only one industry, non-ferrous metal basic industries, it was necessary to refer to sources other than the census questionnaires. Owing to the absence of information for one large public enterprise, use was made of a study of the aluminium industry by the Statistical Centre to obtain the input coefficients for the firm in question and gross output was obtained from a budgetary source.

Three types of output were tabulated from the census questionnaire: the primary output of each firm, the secondary output and the output of capital goods. In a few cases where no production figure was recorded on the census form, production was approximated by calculating average monthly employment and multiplying that figure by average production per employee (average labour productivity) of firms in the same code for which production and employment figures were available. Estimated and actual production figures were then added, by code, to provide a comprehensive total.

Intermediate input was tabulated separately for the sample of medium-scale firms and for those large-scale firms that provided complete information. Each input was assigned an ISIC code. Since the breakdown of raw material input as reported in the census forms varied from firm to firm, that input was individually coded by members of the Department of Financial Statistics and National Accounts; these outlays on raw material input that could not be identified were grouped together as unallocated input.

Handmade carpets were not covered by the Manufacturing Census. Information for this sector was mainly obtained from that available for other years and from interviews with experts in the field.

(d) *Electricity, water supply*

Since published information proved to be inadequate, the main statistical sources used for data on electricity were the records and accounts of the regional electricity authorities, which were obtained from the General Department for the Supervision of the Electricity Authorities of the Ministry of Energy. For the output allocation and input structure of the electricity industry, the detailed cost and sales accounts of the electricity authorities were used. Information on the physical production of electricity was obtained from the published reports of the Ministry of Energy, which covered gross output of electricity produced in the public sector as well as in the private sector. The output value of electricity produced by the private sector was estimated using the average prices for the public sector's production. Similarly, the input structure of the public sector's production of electricity was extrapolated to cover the intermediate consumption of the entire industry. Most of the output of the private sector was self-consumed.

Information on the water sector was mainly obtained from the actual budgetary transactions of public companies and government affiliated profit-making enterprises as prepared by the Plan and Budget Organization. A distinction was made between the organized and unorganized water subsectors, since the latter only provides water for agricultural purposes and, in addition, unorganized water is supplied through wells, ghanats and springs and no actual transactions take place. Information on the unorganized subsector was mainly obtained through personal interviews with authorities at the Ministry of Energy, especially the Department of Underground Water Resources. Output of water was allocated on the basis of information provided by household budget surveys and financial balance sheets of municipalities, which provide water primarily for drinking and household uses. Intermediate input of the organized water subsector is mainly obtained from the Actual Budget Accounts of Public Companies. In the case of the unorganized subsector, estimates of intermediate input were made for wells only, since the other two sources (i.e., ghanats and springs) do not make use of intermediate input. Intermediate input of wells consists of fuel and spare parts, and estimates were derived on the basis of production figures and cost composition of wells.

(e) Construction

Information on the construction sector was mainly obtained from the survey of Construction Activities of the Private Sector in Urban Areas during the first six months of 1973, the Sample Survey of Construction Activity in Rural Areas in 1972, the analysis of government sector accounts and interviews with various consulting engineers and construction companies.

(f) Trade

Output of the trade sector was distributed on the assumption that percentage mark-ups on commodity groups are uniform for all buyers. The commodity composition of trade was estimated from the results of the Internal Trade Statistics published by the Ministry of Economy. The pattern so obtained was then applied to total output of the trade sector as estimated in the national accounts. The intermediate input structure was obtained from the Survey of the Distributive Trades Sector in Rasht and was applied to total input of the trade sector as estimated in the national accounts. Results for the wholesale and retail sectors were reported separately.

(g) Transport and communication

Estimates of output and intermediate input of the transportation sector were obtained from the national accounts figures, National Iranian Railways Statistics, Iran Air, various shipping companies, and police department data on total number of buses and taxis. Transport margins to the purchasing industries were estimated by pro-rating total transport margins over the producing sectors on the basis of their production of goods and services.

Owing to lack of reliable data, the input structure of the communication, insurance and real estate sectors was taken from the corresponding estimates in the United States input-output table. Total output of the communication sector was obtained by applying the United States ratio of gross output to value added to the value added estimate of the sector for the Islamic Republic of Iran. The distribution of output of the insurance sector was based on the results of the Survey of Insurance Companies and Representatives of Iran. Total output of this sector was obtained as the sum of the sector's row entries. Total output of the real estate and rentals sector was obtained as the sum of estimates of residential gross rent—obtained in the Household Expenditure Survey—and rents paid by sectors other than households, estimated in industry surveys.

(h) Services

Information on the banking and restaurants and hotels sectors was derived from national accounts estimates and *ad hoc* surveys. According to Iranian sources, input-output estimates for both sectors should be considered as tentative.

Data on services sectors were provided by national accounts estimates and the Household Budget Survey. The structure of intermediate input of the business services, machinery rental and leasing and other social services sectors was obtained from an informal survey of business services establishments carried out for this purpose by the Statistical Centre. Intermediate input of most of the remaining service sectors was obtained by applying the corresponding United States input-output estimates to total output as estimated in the national accounts. The structure of intermediate input of personal and household services other than repairs was assumed to be equal to that of the retail trade, estimated through the Survey of the Distributive Trades Sector in Rasht.

2. Value added

Except for agricultural sectors, in which value added was estimated as the difference between total output and intermediate consumption, value added was generally estimated directly. As a rule, data on labour costs and total value added were obtained from the same statistical sources used for the estimation of output and intermediate input, and value added other than labour cost was obtained as a residual.

Indirect taxes include those on domestic transactions and import duties. Taxes on domestic transactions include mainly those on petroleum products, locally produced vehicles and alcoholic beverages, with the balance distributed over five other products. Classification according to input-output codes was straightforward except for a miscellaneous group which made up less than 1 per cent of the total; those taxes were assigned to other manufacturing industries. Import duties consist of customs duties, commercial profit taxes on imports and import registration fees. A breakdown of customs plus commercial profit taxes into some 4,000 items is available in a computer printout of the Ministry of Economic Affairs and Finance. Since items are listed according to a code, which is the same as that used for foreign trade statistics, those statistics were used to identify the items concerned. Except in a small number of cases, the customs codes were readily matched with the industries of the input-output table. Similar information was lacking, however, for import registration fees, which together account for 30 per cent of total import duties. Those fees were, therefore, distributed in proportion to other import duties and added to customs duties and commercial profit taxes to give a breakdown of all import duties. Subsidies are treated as negative indirect taxes and were estimated on the basis of information provided by the Plan and Budget Organization.

3. *Final demand and imports*

Data on private consumption were mainly based on the results of several household expenditure surveys carried out in the country. However, there is strong evidence that the survey approach leads to underestimation of aggregate consumption and, in fact, a positive statistical discrepancy was found between the value added and final demand estimates. This statistical discrepancy was added as an unallocated item in the column of private consumption. Consideration was given to pro-rating the statistical discrepancy over the itemized consumption expenditures but the procedure was disregarded since in many cases it led to an excess of total final demand over total supply.

Information on consumption by the government sector is based mainly on national accounts estimates derived from the Plan and Budget Organization. The breakdown of government expenditures was mainly based on the records of the Foreign Transactions Company, which was found to be involved in the purchase of a substantial fraction of the goods and materials consumed by the Government.

Gross fixed capital formation was estimated as the sum of imports, domestic production and new construction including major additions and renovations. Imports of machinery and other capital equipment, consumer durable types of goods (i.e., items purchased by business and Government), and selected intermediate types of goods of a capital nature (such as chassis, engines and other major motor vehicle parts) were mainly obtained from the *Foreign Trade Statistics of Iran,* published by the Ministry of Economic Affairs and Finance, and from the police department files of motor registrations and the Household Budget Survey. Domestic production of capital goods was derived as an integral part of the processing of the Manufacturing Census. The construction component of gross fixed capital formation excludes total current outlays on construction by sectors other than the private and public sectors.

Owing to the lack of information, estimates of inventory changes could only be prepared for the livestock and manufacturing sectors. In the case of livestock, the estimate refers to the value of change in livestock numbers as determined in the sources described above. For the manufacturing sector, the figures measure the value of the change over the one-year period in question in the stocks of finished goods, as reported in the Manufacturing Census.

Exports and imports of commodities were based on the *Foreign Trade Statistics of Iran.* For the conversion of the Standard International Trade Classification (SITC) code used in that source to the ISIC code used in the input-output table, use was made of the *Classification of Commodities by Industrial Origin,* published by the United Nations. Estimates on service imports and exports were provided by balance-of-payments specialists of the Bank Markazi.

IRAN
INPUT-OUTPUT TABLES
1352

Source: *Iran Input-Output Table for 1352, Methodology and Tentative Estimates,* Statistical Center of the Islamic Republic of Iran.

•••
TABLE 1- IRAN INPUT-OUTPUT TABLE   (MILLION RIALS)
•••

	1	2	3	4	5	6	7	8	9	10	11	12
1)GRAIN.	4809	..	..	6960	..	..	..	..	..	35881	83	..
2)INDUSTRIAL CROPS.	..	151	..	..	..	..	..	..	..	28685	14	931
3)OTHER CROPS.	..	..	3172	24430	..	..	..	..	..	1055	240	..
4)LIVESTOCK.	1012	2355	4993	2720	..	..	..	..	..	1499	..	..
5)HUNT.+ FISH.+ FORESTRY.	..	..	..	..	..	..	..	5	10	5455	..	..
6)COAL MINING.	..	..	..	..	..	..	..	1	..	65	..	..
7)CRUDE PETROLEUM.	..	..	..	..	..	..	..	..	..	..	..	..
8)METAL ORE MINING.	..	..	..	..	..	..	..	..	..	..	..	..
9)OTHER MINING.	..	..	..	..	..	..	..	..	..	68	..	..
10)FOOD MFG.	..	..	..	8481	..	..	494	..	..	20806	672	..
11)BEVERAGES.	..	..	..	..	..	..	..	..	..	37	..	..
12)TOBACCO MFG.	..	..	..	..	..	..	..	..	..	..	..	65
13)TEXTILES.	..	126	..	..	..	..	..	..	..	..	167	..
14)HAND-MADE CARPETS.	..	..	..	..	..	..	..	..	..	..	..	..
15)WEARING APPAREL.	..	..	..	..	..	..	..	..	..	..	..	..
16)LEATHER PRODUCTS.	..	..	..	..	..	..	..	..	..	..	..	..
17)FOOTWEAR.	..	..	..	..	..	..	..	..	..	..	..	..
18)WOOD+WOOD PRODUCTS.	..	..	..	..	..	..	..	..	..	..	..	..
19)FURNITURE+FIXTURES.	..	..	..	..	..	..	..	..	..	..	..	..
20)PAPER+PAPER PRODUCTS.	..	..	..	..	..	..	..	..	..	2	1	94
21)PRINTING+PUBLISHING.	..	..	..	..	..	..	..	..	..	..	..	..
22)INDUSTRIAL CHEMICALS.	1767	1421	1901	3881	..	3	..	17	9	1382	28	..
23)OTHER CHEMICALS.	..	..	..	..	..	27	..	117	121	5	..	..
24)PETROLEUM REFINERIES.	1952	135	380	..	..	21	..	68	87	979	132	12
25)MISC.PETROLEUM PRODUCTS.	..	..	..	..	..	..	..	..	..	4	..	..
26)RUBBER+PLASTICS.	..	..	..	..	..	..	..	..	..	..	25	..
27)POTTERY.	..	..	..	..	..	..	..	..	..	..	..	..
28)GLASS PRODUCTS.	..	..	..	..	..	..	..	..	..	..	..	..
29)NON-MET.MINERAL PROD.	..	..	..	..	..	..	..	..	..	..	..	..
30)IRON AND STEEL.	..	..	..	..	..	..	..	..	..	..	..	..
31)NON-FER.BASIC METAL.	..	..	..	..	..	..	..	..	..	..	..	..
32)FABRIC.METAL PRODUCTS.	4139	285	807	..	..	..	..	..	..	..	95	..
33)NON-ELEC.MACHINERY.	..	..	..	..	..	13	1888	25	33	258	72	5
34)ELECTRICAL MACHINERY.	..	..	..	..	..	..	..	..	..	..	..	..
35)TRANSPORTATION EQUIP.	..	..	..	..	..	..	..	..	..	..	..	..
36)PROFESS.+ SCIEN.EQUIP.	..	..	..	..	..	..	..	..	..	..	..	..
37)SMALL SCALE MFG. (1)	..	..	..	..	..	..	..	..	..	..	..	..
38)ELECTRICITY.	..	..	..	..	..	..	..	5	2	737	30	11
39)WATER.	1235	1870	3983	..	..	..	..	..	..	..	..	..
40)PRIVATE CONSTRUCTION.	..	..	..	..	..	..	..	..	..	116	16	6
41)PUBLIC CONSTRUCTION.	..	..	..	..	..	..	..	..	..	..	..	..
42)WHOLESALE TRADE.	142	55	136	606	..	1	47	2	2	1260	21	14
43)RETAIL TRADE.	184	82	135	1881	..	1	174	4	4	4353	155	22
44)RESTAURANTS.	..	..	..	..	..	..	..	..	..	..	..	..
45)HOTELS.	..	..	..	..	..	..	..	..	..	..	..	..
46)TRANSPORTATION.	880	332	865	3349	..	4	138	15	17	6839	78	90
47)COMMUNICATION.	..	..	..	..	..	..	..	2	2	95	10	8
48)FINANCIAL INSTITUT. (2)	159	88	221	340	..	2	200	9	24	754	26	35
49)INSURANCE.	..	..	..	..	..	61	..	71	28	488	36	16
50)REAL ESTATE+RENTALS.	..	..	..	..	..	7	470	66	156	236	3	23
51)BUSINESS SERVICES.	..	..	..	..	..	28	..	75	17	83	114	6
52)MACH.+ EQUIP.RENTALS.	..	..	..	..	..	..	..	11	83	266	82	..
53)EDUCATION.	..	..	..	..	..	..	80	..	..	..	..	..
54)MEDICAL+HEALTH.	..	..	..	..	..	..	1460	..	..	..	..	..
55)SOCIAL SERVICES.	..	..	..	..	..	..	460	..	..	..	..	..
56)RECREAT.+ CULT.SERVICES.	..	..	..	..	..	..	..	..	..	..	..	..
57)HOUSEHOLD SERVICES.	..	..	..	..	..	..	..	..	..	..	..	..
58)HOUSEHOLD INDUSTRY.	..	..	..	..	..	..	..	..	..	..	..	..
59)GENERAL GOVERMENT.	..	..	..	..	..	..	..	..	..	..	..	..
60)UNALLOCATED INPUTS.	-777	-354	-1088	-629	617	21	3970	113	121	6729	990	603
61)INTERMEDIATE INPUTS.	15502	6545	15505	52019	617	189	9380	606	717	118135	3092	1942
62)COMPENSATION.	..	..	..	..	..	315	12400	719	..	4476	600	1101
63)OTHER VALUE ADDED.	40033	20754	52577	52607	13706	94	688700	1590	6723	115225	1799	7802
64)TOTAL FACTOR PAYMENTS.	40033	20754	52577	52607	13706	409	701100	2309	6723	119701	2399	8903
65)NET INDIRECT TAXES.	-5755	8	1233	1569	-2	..	..	..	..	-1862	2643	154
66)VALUE ADDED (M.P.).	34278	20762	53810	54176	13704	409	701100	2309	6723	117839	5042	9057
67)TOTAL INPUTS (F.C.).	55535	27299	68082	104626	14323	598	710480	2915	7440	237836	5491	10845
68)TOTAL INPUTS (M.P.).	49780	27307	69315	106195	14321	598	710480	2915	7440	235974	8134	10999

SOURCE: STATISTICAL CENTER OF IRAN, DEPARTMENT OF FINANCIAL STATISTICS AND NATIONAL ACCOUNTS.

1)SECTOR EXCLUDED FOR LACK OF DATA.
2)EXCLUDES IMPUTED SERVICE INCOME.

TABLE 1- IRAN INPUT-OUTPUT TABLE (MILLION RIALS)

	49	50	51	52	53	54	55	56	57	58	59	60
1)GRAIN.	..	..	..	..	..	..	..	..	..	..	..	..
2)INDUSTRIAL CROPS.	1348	..	..	..	..	22	..	..	..	1551	..	..
3)OTHER CROPS.	..	..	..	..	..	..	..	..	..	51	..	..
4)LIVESTOCK.	1405	3376	..	2410	..	..	..	..	..	538	..	..
5)HUNT.+ FISH.+ FORESTRY.	..	..	..	..	..	256	..	..	..	154	..	..
6)COAL MINING.	16	..	..	..	..	..	..	..	..	..	10	..
7)CRUDE PETROLEUM.	..	..	..	..	..	..	..	..	..	..	..	278
8)METAL ORE MINING.	..	..	..	..	..	..	..	1	..	..	1	..
9)OTHER MINING.	..	..	..	3	..	..	..	..	..	4	656	1
10)FOOD MFG.	3	..	..	1	..	..	..	68	..	10	..	..
11)BEVERAGES.	..	..	..	..	..	..	..	2	..	..	..	..
12)TOBACCO MFG.	..	..	..	..	..	..	..	..	..	..	..	..
13)TEXTILES.	19687	1056	1562	9	157	4	73	..	1	25	..	..
14)HAND-MADE CARPETS.	..	..	..	..	..	..	..	..	..	..	..	..
15)WEARING APPAREL.	..	..	..	..	..	..	..	..	..	..	..	..
16)LEATHER PRODUCTS.	..	..	..	..	254	..	..	..	..	..	..	..
17)FOOTWEAR.	..	..	..	..	..	..	..	..	..	..	..	..
18)WOOD+WOOD PRODUCTS.	..	..	..	1	5	353	114	36	..	3	..	..
19)FURNITURE+FIXTURES.	..	..	..	..	..	..	..	..	..	..	..	..
20)PAPER+PAPER PRODUCTS.	3	..	..	6	1	..	..	3082	403	15	..	..
21)PRINTING+PUBLISHING.	..	..	..	..	..	..	..	..	..	..	..	..
22)INDUSTRIAL CHEMICALS.	2028	146	..	96	252	12	30	35	100	2837	5528	258
23)OTHER CHEMICALS.	3	..	..	8	..	..	3	..	..	96	65	..
24)PETROLEUM REFINERIES.	392	184	5	13	4	14	3	11	9	44	67	53
25)MISC.PETROLEUM PRODUCTS.	..	..	..	..	..	..	..	..	..	123	..	..
26)RUBBER+PLASTICS.	155	..	3	13	430	5	10	12	..	..	..	..
27)POTTERY.	..	..	..	..	..	..	..	..	..	..	..	..
28)GLASS PRODUCTS.	..	..	..	..	..	..	..	..	..	1	..	..
29)NON-MET.MINERAL PROD.	1	..	..	2	..	..	..	..	..	..	2	..
30)IRON AND STEEL.	..	..	..	7	..	..	2	..	..	..	..	155
31)NON-FER.BASIC METAL.	..	..	..	..	..	..	..	437	..	..	81	..
32)FABRIC.METAL PRODUCTS.	..	..	3	19	7	22	10	..	3	6	..	..
33)NON-ELEC.MACHINERY.	71	..	1	4	3	6	1	11	11	30	153	11
34)ELECTRICAL MACHINERY.	..	..	..	..	..	..	..	..	7	..	..	..
35)TRANSPORTATION EQUIP.	18	..	9	..	..	..	..	..	..	..	..	..
36)PROFESS.+ SCIEN.EQUIP.	1	..	8	3	..	..	..	..	25	52	..	..
37)SMALL SCALE MFG. (1)	..	..	..	..	..	..	..	..	..	..	..	..
38)ELECTRICITY.	478	160	..	9	26	15	5	15	28	50	199	23
39)WATER.	..	..	..	..	..	..	..	..	..	..	..	..
40)PRIVATE CONSTRUCTION.	44	..	2	3	4	21	1	2	4	23	25	..
41)PUBLIC CONSTRUCTION.	..	..	..	..	..	..	..	..	..	..	..	..
42)WHOLESALE TRADE.	516	70	36	35	18	27	10	43	7	64	72	5
43)RETAIL TRADE.	3410	213	265	29	85	32	22	94	13	98	143	10
44)RESTAURANTS.	..	..	..	..	..	..	..	..	..	..	..	..
45)HOTELS.	..	..	..	..	..	..	..	..	..	..	..	..
46)TRANSPORTATION.	1709	375	105	223	77	314	101	255	37	391	430	27
47)COMMUNICATION.	40	1	3	3	2	3	2	6	4	29	6	4
48)FINANCIAL INSTITUT. (2)	182	42	9	14	9	12	3	25	9	49	48	46
49)INSURANCE.	536	8	21	11	9	18	12	14	72	109	71	9
50)REAL ESTATE+RENTALS.	55	..	29	3	8	9	10	3	34	20	11	5
51)BUSINESS SERVICES.	21	480	5	..	20	1	..	13	..	500	1	17
52)MACH.+ EQUIP.RENTALS.	59	..	2	3	10	7	3	2	2	50	16	10
53)EDUCATION.	..	..	..	..	..	..	..	..	..	..	..	..
54)MEDICAL+HEALTH.	..	..	..	..	..	..	..	..	..	..	..	..
55)SOCIAL SERVICES.	..	..	..	..	..	..	..	..	..	..	..	..
56)RECREAT.+ CULT.SERVICES.	..	..	..	..	..	..	..	..	..	..	..	..
57)HOUSEHOLD SERVICES.	..	..	8	..	..	..	..	..	..	..	..	..
58)HOUSEHOLD INDUSTRY.	..	..	..	..	..	..	..	..	..	..	..	..
59)GENERAL GOVERMENT.	..	..	..	..	..	..	..	..	..	..	..	..
60)UNALLOCATED INPUTS.	4251	-42	92	212	230	69	32	242	243	1967	722	313
61)INTERMEDIATE INPUTS.	36430	6069	2168	3237	1610	1223	447	4410	1011	8688	8106	1225
62)COMPENSATION.	7191	1719	289	207	460	221	87	338	667	897	1017	267
63)OTHER VALUE ADDED.	7746	5310	171	727	666	1698	145	1019	1036	2730	3234	626
64)TOTAL FACTOR PAYMENTS.	14937	7029	460	934	1126	1919	232	1357	1703	3627	4251	893
65)NET INDIRECT TAXES.	5537	..	63	14	7	609	120	2037	31	2939	2759	12399
66)VALUE ADDED (M.P.).	20474	7029	523	948	1133	2528	352	3394	1734	6566	7010	13292
67)TOTAL INPUTS (F.C.).	51367	13098	2628	4171	2736	3142	679	5767	2714	12315	12357	2118
68)TOTAL INPUTS (M.P.).	56904	13098	2691	4185	2743	3751	799	7804	2745	15254	15116	14517

SOURCE: STATISTICAL CENTER OF IRAN, DEPARTMENT OF FINANCIAL STATISTICS AND NATIONAL ACCOUNTS.

1)SECTOR EXCLUDED FOR LACK OF DATA.
2)EXCLUDES IMPUTED SERVICE INCOME.

TABLE 1- IRAN INPUT-OUTPUT TABLE   (MILLION RIALS)

	25	26	27	28	29	30	31	32	33	34	35	36
1)GRAIN.	..	..	..	..	..	..	..	..	..	..	..	..
2)INDUSTRIAL CROPS.	..	61	..	..	..	..	..	2	..	..	..	..
3)OTHER CROPS.	..	..	..	..	..	..	..	..	..	..	..	..
4)LIVESTOCK.	..	..	..	..	8	..	..	..	..	..	..	..
5)HUNT.+ FISH.+ FORESTRY.	..	..	..	..	184	..	..	..	..	..	..	..
6)COAL MINING.	..	..	..	..	4	4	..	34	27	..	..	..
7)CRUDE PETROLEUM.	..	..	..	..	..	..	..	..	..	..	..	..
8)METAL ORE MINING.	..	..	1	1	26	..	376	22	..	..	..	..
9)OTHER MINING.	4	..	61	98	3492	..	..	38	..	37	..	2
10)FOOD MFG.	..	..	..	..	..	..	..	..	..	..	..	..
11)BEVERAGES.	..	..	..	..	..	..	..	..	..	..	..	..
12)TOBACCO MFG.	..	..	..	..	..	..	..	..	..	..	..	..
13)TEXTILES.	6	245	..	..	467	..	..	29	..	..	..	17
14)HAND-MADE CARPETS.	..	..	..	..	..	..	..	..	..	..	..	..
15)WEARING APPAREL.	..	..	..	..	..	..	..	..	..	..	..	..
16)LEATHER PRODUCTS.	..	76	..	..	..	..	..	..	..	..	..	..
17)FOOTWEAR.	..	..	..	..	..	..	..	..	..	..	..	..
18)WOOD+WOOD PRODUCTS.	..	4	..	..	4	..	..	6	26	1	22	..
19)FURNITURE+FIXTURES.	..	..	..	..	..	..	..	..	..	..	9	..
20)PAPER+PAPER PRODUCTS.	5	2	..	..	2	..	..	14	..	6	9	..
21)PRINTING+PUBLISHING.	..	..	6	..	..	..	..	..	..	..	..	..
22)INDUSTRIAL CHEMICALS.	1	495	..	147	65	..	..	94	465	389	286	10
23)OTHER CHEMICALS.	..	1233	..	..	7	..	..	74	..	825	..	11
24)PETROLEUM REFINERIES.	3	91	..	91	1266	12	52	91	139	99	51	2
25)MISC.PETROLEUM PRODUCTS.	9	55	..	1	..	..	1	2	..	4	..	..
26)RUBBER+PLASTICS.	..	2273	..	..	5	..	..	173	640	160	54	8
27)POTTERY.	..	..	..	..	54	..	..	6	..	4	..	..
28)GLASS PRODUCTS.	..	..	..	230	..	5	..	8	..	45	72	..
29)NON-MET.MINERAL PROD.	..	7	..	2	1191	7	..	..	..	..	..	2
30)IRON AND STEEL.	..	22	..	5	151	3139	..	2968	5376	1694	847	14
31)NON-FER.BASIC METAL.	..	38	..	46	1	28	4421	1443	1306	3992	1653	90
32)FABRIC.METAL PRODUCTS.	..	25	..	..	..	..	..	609	1092	33	255	84
33)NON-ELEC.MACHINERY.	1	22	..	9	171	14	19	69	861	..	9887	4
34)ELECTRICAL MACHINERY.	..	5	..	11	..	108	..	48	304	2289	12	..
35)TRANSPORTATION EQUIP.	..	..	..	..	..	..	..	..	..	..	..	..
36)PROFESS.+ SCIEN.EQUIP.	..	1	..	..	19	..	..	49	4	9	..	..
37)SMALL SCALE MFG. (1)	..	..	..	..	..	..	..	..	..	..	..	..
38)ELECTRICITY.	..	68	2	33	967	2	41	87	177	95	49	81
39)WATER.	..	..	..	..	1	..	..	..	..	..	..	..
40)PRIVATE CONSTRUCTION.	..	..	1	16	80	20	6	27	23	18	4	1
41)PUBLIC CONSTRUCTION.	..	..	..	..	..	..	..	..	..	..	..	..
42)WHOLESALE TRADE.	..	56	1	11	137	41	54	67	133	182	255	3
43)RETAIL TRADE.	1	149	6	203	311	83	107	151	260	358	699	8
44)RESTAURANTS.	..	..	..	..	..	..	..	..	..	..	..	..
45)HOTELS.	..	..	..	..	..	..	..	..	..	..	..	..
46)TRANSPORTATION.	2	309	6	43	535	122	192	233	457	458	808	10
47)COMMUNICATION.	1	9	..	3	47	2	3	18	52	21	10	..
48)FINANCIAL INSTITUT. (2)	..	34	4	10	80	55	26	45	103	85	132	10
49)INSURANCE.	1	53	3	18	394	8	22	116	243	118	17	6
50)REAL ESTATE+RENTALS.	..	28	..	12	50	2	8	61	72	25	20	2
51)BUSINESS SERVICES.	..	25	..	8	74	..	..	89	299	258	15	2
52)MACH.+ EQUIP.RENTALS.	1	12	..	2	406	10	25	47	100	52	26	9
53)EDUCATION.	..	..	..	..	..	..	..	..	..	..	..	..
54)MEDICAL+HEALTH.	..	..	..	..	..	..	..	..	..	..	..	..
55)SOCIAL SERVICES.	..	..	..	..	..	..	..	..	..	..	..	..
56)RECREAT.+ CULT.SERVICES.	..	..	..	..	..	..	..	..	..	..	..	..
57)HOUSEHOLD SERVICES.	..	..	..	..	..	..	..	..	..	..	..	..
58)HOUSEHOLD INDUSTRY.	..	..	..	..	..	..	..	..	..	..	..	..
59)GENERAL GOVERMENT.	..	..	..	..	..	..	..	..	..	..	..	..
60)UNALLOCATED INPUTS.	2	1271	9	204	3408	140	88	1882	2003	3950	5009	21
61)INTERMEDIATE INPUTS.	36	6670	99	1204	13609	3802	5440	8601	14161	15204	20200	399
62)COMPENSATION.	27	934	13	351	4322	210	534	1478	2001	2206	1254	80
63)OTHER VALUE ADDED.	57	1913	74	735	6687	1267	1602	2841	9064	2994	9864	137
64)TOTAL FACTOR PAYMENTS.	84	2847	87	1086	11009	1477	2136	4319	11065	5200	11118	217
65)NET INDIRECT TAXES.	..	1115	1222	792	606	11885	733	1094	6949	6287	10166	2338
66)VALUE ADDED (M.P.).	84	3962	1309	1878	11615	13362	2869	5413	18014	11487	21284	2555
67)TOTAL INPUTS (F.C.).	120	9517	186	2290	24618	5279	7576	12920	25226	20404	31318	616
68)TOTAL INPUTS (M.P.).	120	10632	1408	3082	25224	17164	8309	14014	32175	26691	41484	2954

SOURCE: STATISTICAL CENTER OF IRAN, DEPARTMENT OF FINANCIAL STATISTICS AND NATIONAL ACCOUNTS.

1)SECTOR EXCLUDED FOR LACK OF DATA.
2)EXCLUDES IMPUTED SERVICE INCOME.

TABLE 1- IRAN INPUT-OUTPUT TABLE   (MILLION RIALS)

	37	38	39	40	41	42	43	44	45	46	47	48
1)GRAIN.	..	..	..	..	123	..	..	..	..	..	..	..
2)INDUSTRIAL CROPS.	..	..	..	..	..	..	..	..	..	..	..	..
3)OTHER CROPS.	..	..	..	..	..	..	..	739	251	1039	..	..
4)LIVESTOCK.	..	..	..	..	..	..	..	..	..	..	..	..
5)HUNT.+ FISH.+ FORESTRY.	..	..	..	..	..	..	..	..	..	..	..	..
6)COAL MINING.	..	..	..	..	..	..	..	..	..	..	..	..
7)CRUDE PETROLEUM.	..	..	..	..	..	..	..	..	..	..	..	..
8)METAL ORE MINING.	..	..	..	..	..	..	..	..	..	..	..	..
9)OTHER MINING.	..	..	..	6726	17119	..	..	..	..	..	..	..
10)FOOD MFG.	..	..	..	..	..	..	..	4878	1419	580	..	36
11)BEVERAGES.	..	..	..	..	..	..	..	1430	456	..	..	104
12)TOBACCO MFG.	..	..	..	..	..	..	..	..	..	..	..	..
13)TEXTILES.	..	..	..	..	..	..	..	..	..	..	..	..
14)HAND-MADE CARPETS.	..	..	..	..	..	..	..	..	..	..	..	..
15)WEARING APPAREL.	..	..	..	..	..	..	..	..	..	614	2	63
16)LEATHER PRODUCTS.	..	..	..	..	..	..	..	..	..	..	..	..
17)FOOTWEAR.	..	..	..	..	..	..	..	..	..	..	..	..
18)WOOD+WOOD PRODUCTS.	..	..	..	4316	1035	..	..	..	..	..	..	..
19)FURNITURE+FIXTURES.	..	..	..	..	..	..	..	..	..	..	..	1
20)PAPER+PAPER PRODUCTS.	..	12	49	1283	683	9	49	176	202	..	41	371
21)PRINTING+PUBLISHING.	..	..	21	..	..	..	..	..	..	519	1	147
22)INDUSTRIAL CHEMICALS.	..	..	4	566	455	..	..	..	..	..	1	..
23)OTHER CHEMICALS.	..	358	..	..	..	..	..	84	151	..	..	20
24)PETROLEUM REFINERIES.	..	2060	4343	..	..	14	230	307	522	10765	55	33
25)MISC.PETROLEUM PRODUCTS.	..	21	..	1164	3182	..	..	214	..	..	..	..
26)RUBBER+PLASTICS.	..	12	..	..	..	..	..	..	..	5100	10	..
27)POTTERY.	..	..	..	773	491	..	..	..	..	..	..	..
28)GLASS PRODUCTS.	..	..	..	1375	519	..	..	..	..	..	..	..
29)NON-MET.MINERAL PROD.	..	..	..	16575	20182	..	..	..	..	..	..	..
30)IRON AND STEEL.	..	..	..	10526	11647	..	..	..	..	..	..	..
31)NON-FER.BASIC METAL.	..	..	..	..	..	..	..	..	..	..	5	..
32)FABRIC.METAL PRODUCTS.	..	36	223	6938	4327	..	..	..	..	..	1	12
33)NON-ELEC.MACHINERY.	..	29	195	..	..	..	..	..	..	..	..	57
34)ELECTRICAL MACHINERY.	..	..	..	1997	1330	..	..	..	..	218	102	101
35)TRANSPORTATION EQUIP.	..	..	..	..	..	..	..	..	..	13401	65	39
36)PROFESS.+ SCIEN.EQUIP.	..	..	..	..	..	16	97	..	29	..	1	97
37)SMALL SCALE MFG. (1)	..	..	..	..	..	..	..	..	..	..	..	..
38)ELECTRICITY.	..	626	188	..	..	31	931	194	334	311	65	158
39)WATER.	..	43	63	..	..	10	118	51	334	207	33	9
40)PRIVATE CONSTRUCTION.	..	82	..	..	..	24	374	389	278	..	262	171
41)PUBLIC CONSTRUCTION.	..	..	..	..	..	..	..	..	..	..	..	..
42)WHOLESALE TRADE.	..	6	8	1794	1866	..	3	104	34	402	7	22
43)RETAIL TRADE.	..	11	33	4185	3422	1	6	1119	339	1407	12	199
44)RESTAURANTS.	..	..	21	..	..	..	..	..	..	..	..	..
45)HOTELS.	..	..	..	..	..	..	..	..	..	..	3	48
46)TRANSPORTATION.	..	166	312	6262	4628	3	25	284	131	2125	19	66
47)COMMUNICATION.	..	23	36	..	..	113	642	31	277	863	68	404
48)FINANCIAL INSTITUT. (2)	..	32	13	409	389	64	325	51	41	393	15	31
49)INSURANCE.	..	29	48	20	82	18	29	92	55	1857	62	44
50)REAL ESTATE+RENTALS.	..	..	..	..	..	150	1300	133	403	1514	172	702
51)BUSINESS SERVICES.	..	..	350	..	..	9	120	..	..	407	160	645
52)MACH.+ EQUIP.RENTALS.	..	12	..	597	652	13	46	..	..	..	..	206
53)EDUCATION.	..	..	..	..	..	..	..	..	..	..	4	..
54)MEDICAL+HEALTH.	..	..	..	..	..	..	..	..	..	..	..	110
55)SOCIAL SERVICES.	..	..	228	..	..	..	..	..	..	..	4	110
56)RECREAT.+ CULT.SERVICES.	..	..	..	..	..	..	..	..	111	..	1	43
57)HOUSEHOLD SERVICES.	..	..	..	..	..	17	306	..	..	..	..	..
58)HOUSEHOLD INDUSTRY.	..	..	..	..	..	..	..	..	..	..	..	..
59)GENERAL GOVERMENT.	..	..	..	..	..	..	..	..	..	..	..	..
60)UNALLOCATED INPUTS.	..	..	-123	201	-471	-19	-777	-51	180	2785	161	337
61)INTERMEDIATE INPUTS.	..	3558	6012	65707	71660	473	3823	10224	5547	44506	1331	4387
62)COMPENSATION.	..	9845	2747	18471	23027	985	4074	947	646	19213	4040	15098
63)OTHER VALUE ADDED.	..	8875	3346	43639	27255	19080	95331	4609	6729	60099	3355	-10011
64)TOTAL FACTOR PAYMENTS.	..	18720	6093	62110	50282	20065	99405	5556	7375	79312	7395	5087
65)NET INDIRECT TAXES.	..	-20	-270	..	..	-410	-1451	..	..	-843	-285	..
66)VALUE ADDED (M.P.).	..	18700	5823	62110	50282	19655	97954	5556	7375	78469	7110	5087
67)TOTAL INPUTS (F.C.).	..	22278	12105	127817	121942	20538	103228	15780	12922	123818	8726	9474
68)TOTAL INPUTS (M.P.).	..	22258	11835	127817	121942	20128	101777	15780	12922	122975	8441	9474

SOURCE: STATISTICAL CENTER OF IRAN, DEPARTMENT OF FINANCIAL STATISTICS AND NATIONAL ACCOUNTS.

1)SECTOR EXCLUDED FOR LACK OF DATA.
2)EXCLUDES IMPUTED SERVICE INCOME.

TABLE 1- IRAN INPUT-OUTPUT TABLE   (MILLION RIALS)

	49	50	51	52	53	54	55	56	57	58	59	60
1)GRAIN.	..	..	..	..	..	..	..	..	..	..	..	9021
2)INDUSTRIAL CROPS.	..	..	..	..	..	..	..	..	..	..	..	-13857
3)OTHER CROPS.	..	..	..	..	..	..	..	..	..	..	..	-9014
4)LIVESTOCK.	..	..	..	..	..	..	..	..	..	..	..	77685
5)HUNT.+ FISH.+ FORESTRY.	..	..	..	..	..	..	..	..	..	..	..	2385
6)COAL MINING.	..	..	..	..	..	..	..	..	..	..	..	444
7)CRUDE PETROLEUM.	..	..	13	1	..	..	6	..	..	..	..	154724
8)METAL ORE MINING.	..	..	..	..	..	..	..	..	..	..	..	1085
9)OTHER MINING.	..	..	..	..	..	..	..	..	..	..	..	-19761
10)FOOD MFG.	2	..	..	..	53	75	..	..	..	..	..	-21672
11)BEVERAGES.	2	..	..	..	..	..	..	..	..	..	..	4819
12)TOBACCO MFG.	..	..	..	..	..	..	..	..	..	..	..	1322
13)TEXTILES.	..	..	..	..	..	..	..	..	..	..	..	28158
14)HAND-MADE CARPETS.	..	..	..	..	..	..	..	..	..	..	..	-3805
15)WEARING APPAREL.	2	..	..	..	..	..	..	..	..	..	..	-21615
16)LEATHER PRODUCTS.	..	..	..	..	..	..	..	..	..	..	..	3317
17)FOOTWEAR.	..	..	..	..	..	..	..	..	..	..	..	-6701
18)WOOD+WOOD PRODUCTS.	..	..	..	..	..	..	..	..	..	..	..	-1228
19)FURNITURE+FIXTURES.	..	..	..	..	..	..	..	..	..	..	..	440
20)PAPER+PAPER PRODUCTS.	12	..	208	15	35	49	92	..	158	..	..	-3487
21)PRINTING+PUBLISHING.	10	..	..	..	50	70	..	3	..	..	..	-471
22)INDUSTRIAL CHEMICALS.	..	..	..	..	9	13	..	5	299	..	..	-3815
23)OTHER CHEMICALS.	1	166	..	..	116	163	..	..	86	..	..	2191
24)PETROLEUM REFINERIES.	3	341	..	..	29	40	..	..	279	..	..	-53977
25)MISC.PETROLEUM PRODUCTS.	..	..	..	..	..	..	..	..	..	..	..	-4567
26)RUBBER+PLASTICS.	..	..	..	..	9	13	..	..	140	..	..	4415
27)POTTERY.	..	..	..	..	..	..	..	..	..	..	..	951
28)GLASS PRODUCTS.	..	..	..	..	..	..	..	..	25	..	..	3276
29)NON-MET.MINERAL PROD.	..	..	..	..	..	..	..	..	60	..	..	-6267
30)IRON AND STEEL.	..	..	..	..	..	..	..	..	..	..	..	18789
31)NON-FER.BASIC METAL.	..	..	..	..	..	..	..	..	..	..	..	-4271
32)FABRIC.METAL PRODUCTS.	1	..	..	..	..	..	..	..	195	..	..	-2567
33)NON-ELEC.MACHINERY.	..	..	..	..	..	..	..	..	..	..	..	-4757
34)ELECTRICAL MACHINERY.	6	..	..	..	..	..	..	..	109	..	..	11646
35)TRANSPORTATION EQUIP.	..	..	..	..	..	..	..	..	490	..	..	-15524
36)PROFESS.+ SCIEN.EQUIP.	8	..	..	..	64	90	..	11	86	..	..	-4906
37)SMALL SCALE MFG. (1)	..	..	..	..	..	..	..	..	..	..	..	..
38)ELECTRICITY.	3	130	46	3	159	222	20	87	428	..	..	5400
39)WATER.	2	..	10	1	43	60	4	1	113	..	..	17
40)PRIVATE CONSTRUCTION.	14	5410	..	..	143	199	..	9	329	..	..	-14
41)PUBLIC CONSTRUCTION.	..	..	..	..	..	..	..	..	..	..	..	..
42)WHOLESALE TRADE.	1	2	2	..	5	8	1	..	31	..	..	729
43)RETAIL TRADE.	13	4	5	..	59	82	2	3	79	..	..	8362
44)RESTAURANTS.	..	..	..	..	..	..	..	..	..	..	..	11668
45)HOTELS.	..	156	..	..	..	..	..	..	..	..	..	12393
46)TRANSPORTATION.	3	33	14	1	22	31	6	1	121	..	..	30373
47)COMMUNICATION.	7	130	..	..	90	125	..	6	611	..	..	2200
48)FINANCIAL INSTITUT. (2)	8	195	28	2	4	6	9	1	16	..	..	2488
49)INSURANCE.	-4	1769	31	2	37	51	14	9	120	..	..	-4167
50)REAL ESTATE+RENTALS.	34	2081	576	41	570	796	253	76	1346	..	..	-470
51)BUSINESS SERVICES.	15	1418	4	..	140	196	2	36	182	..	..	-762
52)MACH.+ EQUIP.RENTALS.	..	..	..	..	..	..	..	..	39	..	..	-2245
53)EDUCATION.	..	..	..	..	20	29	..	..	..	..	..	-133
54)MEDICAL+HEALTH.	..	..	..	..	45	63	..	..	..	..	..	-1714
55)SOCIAL SERVICES.	2	..	..	..	..	..	..	..	..	..	..	-800
56)RECREAT.+ CULT.SERVICES.	..	..	..	..	..	..	..	155	..	..	..	-80
57)HOUSEHOLD SERVICES.	2	..	57	4	63	88	25	..	271	..	..	3830
58)HOUSEHOLD INDUSTRY.	..	..	..	..	..	..	..	..	..	..	..	..
59)GENERAL GOVERMENT.	..	..	..	..	..	..	..	..	..	..	..	..
60)UNALLOCATED INPUTS.	14	1400	72	6	267	375	34	-45	922	..	..	..
61)INTERMEDIATE INPUTS.	169	13235	1066	76	2035	2844	468	358	6534	..	..	..
62)COMPENSATION.	648	..	3384	242	3184	3076	1852	582	7367	1698	149907	..
63)OTHER VALUE ADDED.	4161	97988	4480	320	7584	10402	360	1446	12480	..	..	..
64)TOTAL FACTOR PAYMENTS.	4809	97988	7864	562	10768	13478	2212	2028	19847	1698	149907	..
65)NET INDIRECT TAXES.	..	..	-79	..	..	-37	..	..	..	..	..	..
66)VALUE ADDED (M.P.).	4809	97988	7785	562	10768	13441	2212	2028	19847	1698	149907	..
67)TOTAL INPUTS (F.C.).	4978	111223	8930	638	12803	16322	2680	2386	26381	1698	149907	..
68)TOTAL INPUTS (M.P.).	4978	111223	8851	638	12803	16285	2680	2386	26381	1698	149907	..

SOURCE: STATISTICAL CENTER OF IRAN, DEPARTMENT OF FINANCIAL STATISTICS AND NATIONAL ACCOUNTS.

1)SECTOR EXCLUDED FOR LACK OF DATA.
2)EXCLUDES IMPUTED SERVICE INCOME.

TABLE 1- IRAN INPUT-OUTPUT TABLE   (MILLION RIALS)

	INT.OUTP.	PRIV.CONS.	PUBL.CONS.	CAP.FORM.	INVENT.	EXPORTS.	IMPORTS.	FINAL DEM.	TOT.OUTPUT
1)GRAIN.	56877	74	..	..	..	31	-7202	-7097	49780
2)INDUSTRIAL CROPS.	18908	..	..	..	..	8515	-116	8399	27307
3)OTHER CROPS.	21964	41845	1182	..	..	6220	-1897	47351	69315
4)LIVESTOCK.	97900	8362	..	..	1730	127	-1925	8295	106195
5)HUNT.+ FISH.+ FORESTRY.	8448	5724	..	..	..	1875	-1726	5873	14321
6)COAL MINING.	636	313	..	..	..	1	-322	-8	598
7)CRUDE PETROLEUM.	155022	..	..	..	..	575640	-20182	555458	710480
8)METAL ORE MINING.	1513	..	..	..	..	1436	-34	1402	2915
9)OTHER MINING.	8546	..	..	..	..	315	-1421	-1106	7440
10)FOOD MFG.	15906	200819	8131	..	22254	5193	-16329	220068	235974
11)BEVERAGES.	6849	623	561	..	200	2	-101	1285	8134
12)TOBACCO MFG.	1387	10014	..	..	-135	1	-268	9612	10999
13)TEXTILES.	51759	13644	763	..	2144	2828	-14263	5115	56904
14)HAND-MADE CARPETS.	-3805	11270	..	..	..	5792	-159	16903	13098
15)WEARING APPAREL.	-20934	21115	2644	..	96	327	-557	23625	2691
16)LEATHER PRODUCTS.	3647	188	..	..	375	64	-90	538	4185
17)FOOTWEAR.	-6701	8844	508	..	60	37	-6	9444	2743
18)WOOD+WOOD PRODUCTS.	4697	511	..	..	829	31	-2317	-946	3751
19)FURNITURE+FIXTURES.	451	103	92	182	2	..	-31	348	799
20)PAPER+PAPER PRODUCTS.	3601	115	9499	..	81	14	-5506	4203	7804
21)PRINTING+PUBLISHING.	356	2179	951	..	13	2	-756	2389	2745
22)INDUSTRIAL CHEMICALS.	21019	10089	25	..	339	809	-17027	-5765	15254
23)OTHER CHEMICALS.	5931	15349	965	..	196	1070	-8394	9185	15116
24)PETROLEUM REFINERIES.	-28493	14771	4294	..	31	24212	-297	43010	14517
25)MISC.PETROLEUM PRODUCTS.	211	..	347	..	-1	14	-451	-91	120
26)RUBBER+PLASTICS.	13665	1375	3294	35	453	721	-8911	-3033	10632
27)POTTERY.	2279	16	..	..	1	68	-957	-871	1408
28)GLASS PRODUCTS.	5555	488	..	..	138	28	-3127	-2473	3082
29)NON-MET.MINERAL PROD.	31764	..	530	..	741	159	-7970	-6540	25224
30)IRON AND STEEL.	55341	..	..	..	461	42	-38680	-38177	17164
31)NON-FER.BASIC METAL.	9271	2602	..	..	177	868	-4608	-962	8309
32)FABRIC.METAL PRODUCTS.	16662	3646	4559	5235	29	477	-16795	-2648	14014
33)NON-ELEC.MACHINERY.	9177	..	3595	57944	587	77	-39205	22998	32175
34)ELECTRICAL MACHINERY.	18292	8019	7125	12703	355	137	-19940	8399	26691
35)TRANSPORTATION EQUIP.	-1502	9137	15645	34077	5803	553	-22229	42986	41484
36)PROFESS.+ SCIEN.EQUIP.	-4239	1243	6474	5472	125	118	-6239	7193	2954
37)SMALL SCALE MFG. (1)	..	..	..	..	..	..	..	..	..
38)ELECTRICITY.	12731	7375	2128	..	..	..	-17	9527	22258
39)WATER.	8208	3086	541	..	..	..	..	3627	11835
40)PRIVATE CONSTRUCTION.	8133	..	..	119684	..	..	..	119684	127817
41)PUBLIC CONSTRUCTION.	..	..	5171	116771	..	..	..	121942	121942
42)WHOLESALE TRADE.	9152	6117	1431	2827	..	601	..	10976	20128
43)RETAIL TRADE.	33093	52022	6192	7605	..	2865	..	68684	101777
44)RESTAURANTS.	11689	5958	..	..	..	..	-1867	4091	15780
45)HOTELS.	12600	2189	..	..	..	..	-1867	322	12922
46)TRANSPORTATION.	64451	34831	11866	7613	..	4214	..	58524	122975
47)COMMUNICATION.	6012	1096	1333	..	..	..	..	2429	8441
48)FINANCIAL INSTITUT. (2)	7410	772	1292	..	..	..	..	2064	9474
49)INSURANCE.	2791	1103	1014	..	..	70	..	2187	4978
50)REAL ESTATE+RENTALS.	11105	99800	318	..	..	..	..	100118	111223
51)BUSINESS SERVICES.	5073	178	3605	..	..	..	-5	3778	8851
52)MACH.+ EQUIP.RENTALS.	616	5	17	..	..	..	..	22	638
53)EDUCATION.	..	12803	..	..	..	..	..	12803	12803
54)MEDICAL+HEALTH.	-32	16322	..	..	..	..	-5	16317	16285
55)SOCIAL SERVICES.	..	2680	..	..	..	..	..	2680	2680
56)RECREAT.+ CULT.SERVICES.	230	2386	..	..	..	1	-231	2156	2386
57)HOUSEHOLD SERVICES.	4671	21782	..	..	..	1	-73	21710	26381
58)HOUSEHOLD INDUSTRY.	..	1698	..	..	..	..	..	1698	1698
59)GENERAL GOVERMENT.	..	..	149907	..	..	..	..	149907	149907
60)UNALLOCATED INPUTS.	-147560	147580	..	..	..	..	-71027	147580	..
61)INTERMEDIATE INPUTS.	..	..	..	..	..	..	..	..	632311
62)COMPENSATION.	..	..	..	..	..	..	..	..	317414
63)OTHER VALUE ADDED.	..	..	..	..	..	..	..	..	1465481
64)TOTAL FACTOR PAYMENTS.	..	..	..	..	..	..	-50300	..	1732595
65)NET INDIRECT TAXES.	..	..	..	..	..	..	..	..	64295
66)VALUE ADDED (M.P.).	..	..	..	..	..	..	..	..	1847190
67)TOTAL INPUTS (F.C.).	..	..	..	..	..	..	..	..	2415206
68)TOTAL INPUTS (M.P.).	632311	812462	256001	370149	37084	645597	-395430	1847190	2479501

SOURCE: STATISTICAL CENTER OF IRAN, DEPARTMENT OF FINANCIAL STATISTICS AND NATIONAL ACCOUNTS.

1)SECTOR EXCLUDED FOR LACK OF DATA.
2)EXCLUDES IMPUTED SERVICE INCOME.

123

VII. ISRAEL

A. General information

The present chapter is based on *Input-Output Tables 1975/76*, Special Series, No. 625, *Input-Output Tables 1977/78* and *Input-Output Tables 1980/81*, published by the Central Bureau of Statistics.

Input-output tables for Israel have been compiled for the year 1958, and for budget years 1965/66, 1968/69, 1972/73, 1975/76 and 1977/78.* The first two tables were compiled by the research division of the Bank of Israel. The remaining tables have been compiled by the Central Bureau of Statistics. A similar methodology was applied to all tables except the one for 1958. However, tables for 1972/73 and 1975/76 are not directly comparable to those for previous years because of differences in the classification system adopted. The 1975/76 table was obtained by updating the results of 1972/73 according to the modified RAS method. The tables for 1977/78 were based on complete and comprehensive information. The 1980/81 tables were an updating of the detailed tables of 1977/78. The main differences between the 1977/78 tables and previous tables are:

(*a*) A distinction is made between competitive and complementary imports. Competitive imports are recorded together with domestic production in the intermediate consumption quadrant, while complementary imports are recorded in a row of the value added quadrant;

(*b*) The activities of producers of government services and of private non-profit institutions are recorded in the intermediate consumption quadrant;

(*c*) Changes in stocks of raw materials are recorded in the final demand quadrant, so that from 1977/78 the transaction matrix contains use of input rather than purchases of input.

Input-output estimates differ from those obtained in the national accounts for various reasons, such as differences in definitions adopted and in estimating techniques, various imputations made in the input-output tables and the need to reconcile total uses and resources of each sector in the input-output table. However, most of these differences are within reasonable limits. The greatest discrepancies refer to subsidies, taxes, private consumption and exports, the input-output estimates of which exceed those of the national accounts by 46.4 per cent, 9.3 per cent, 5.4 per cent and 5.0 per cent, respectively. (This information was based on *Input-Output Tables 1975/76*.) Adjustments made to adapt the input-output estimates of private final consumption to those provided by the national accounts are described below.

The main differences between the Israeli input-output tables, beginning with the 1977/78 tables, and the SNA recommendations on input-output are as follows: (*a*) the introduction of a dummy sector to account for the distribution of "general use" input; (*b*) the breakdown and coverage of final demand and value added; (*c*) treatment of secondary production; and (*d*) no separate "make" and absorption tables

are compiled. The following analysis is based on *Input-Output Tables 1977/78*.

B. Analytical framework

1. *Tables and derived matrices available*

Two basic tables are compiled:
(i) Input-output tables of domestic production at approximate basic values;
(ii) Import matrix.

In addition, the following main derived matrices are presented:
(i′) Input coefficients based on (i);
(ii′) Inverse matrix based on (i′);
(iii′) Input coefficients of imports, based on (ii);
(iv′) Inverse matrix of imports, based on (iii′);
(v′) Total coefficients for primary input, based on tables (i′) and (ii′). This matrix shows the total or accumulated primary input composition of the output of each input-output sector. Primary input recorded in the table includes: value added (excluding wages), wages, subsidies on domestic production, taxes on imports, subsidies on imports, imports c.i.f., and imports including net taxes.

All tables and derived matrices compiled for 1977/78 are presented at four different levels of aggregation of the intermediate sectors: 6 x 6, 12 x 12, 43 x 43 and 92 x 92, and 187 x 187 (unpublished).

2. *Valuation standards*

All tables are valued at producers' values, including subsidies but excluding trade and transportation margins and commodity taxes. Imports are valued c.i.f. and exports are valued at domestic market prices, which are obtained by adjusting for subsidies, that is, by adding f.o.b. to their value, the difference between the sum that would have been received, had exports been evaluated at domestic prices, and the f.o.b. price. This valuation of exports ensures that equal values in the table represent equal quantities, whether the product was sold abroad or in Israel. It seems that exports in market prices are then adjusted to obtain producers' values.

3. *Statistical units and classification standards*

The establishment is the statistical unit adopted for rows and columns in all tables compiled, except for the imports table, the rows of which are defined in terms of commodities.

Establishments are classified according to the 1970 Standard Industrial Classification of All Economic Activities issued by the Central Bureau of Statistics of Israel, with slight modifications in instances where this classification did not meet the requirements of input-output analysis.

The structure of the intermediate consumption quadrant

---

*The budget year in Israel extends from April through March.

differs from the SNA recommendations in the following aspect. A dummy sector—"general expenditures"—is set up to record unspecified input such as packing materials, office supplies and travel expenditures, as well as errors and omissions. This sector forms part of the services sector in the input-output tables compiled at the 31, 12 and 6 levels of aggregation of intermediate sectors.

The breakdown and definition of categories of value added and final demand generally follow the SNA recommendations, with the following exceptions: (a) final consumption of private non-profit and public institutions is recorded in a separate column of the final demand quadrant, which is defined as final purchases of institutions, less exports and sales to domestic enterprises; (b) consumption of fixed capital is not shown separately from operating surplus; (c) compensation of employees includes imputed wages of the self-employed; (d) taxes and subsidies on domestic production are recorded separately from those levied on imports; and (e) taxes on domestic production include "artificial taxes and subsidies", that is, corrections introduced to compensate for the price discrimination that exists in the sales of some commodities (such as water and electricity) and for the adjustment of export prices.

Private consumption is defined on a national basis, that is, it includes the consumption of Israeli residents abroad and excludes the consumption of foreigners in Israel.

In the input-output table of domestic production (table (i)), complementary imports are classified by industry in a separate row of the value added quadrant and competitive imports are classified by type of commodities in a final demand column. In addition, imports are cross-classified by commodity and destination in the import matrix (table (ii)).

4. Treatment and presentation of selected transactions

Secondary products are recorded as an imputed sale from the industry producing them to the industry of which they are characteristic. In addition, and to avoid double counting of these products, the imputed sale is deducted from the intra-sector consumption of the industry of which these products are characteristic. Contrary to the SNA recommendations, input associated with the production of secondary products is not transferred.

Non-characteristic input used and produced within the same sector has been generally recorded in the output of the input-output sector to which they characteristically belong. Therefore, use of this input is recorded as a fictional transaction from the characteristic input-output sector to the sector using them.

Non-monetary production (such as home consumption on the farms and seeds for field crops) and its corresponding input have been covered. Non-monetary production is included in the output of each intermediate sector of the input-output table.

Output of each sector is defined gross, that is, it includes intra-sector consumption of characteristic as well as secondary products.

Output of the trade, transportation and financial services is defined and distributed as recommended in SNA. The dummy sector recording total imputed banking services forms part of the dummy "general expenditures" sector of the input-output tables compiled at the 40 x 40 level of aggregation.

Data collection is mainly based on regular statistical sources, on the 1977/78 Industry and Crafts Survey, the 1977/78 Survey of Trade and Services, the 1977 Tourism Survey, the 1977/78 Survey of Hotel Expenditures, the 1977 Survey of Trucks, the 1977/78 Import Destination Survey, and other statistical sources.

1. Gross output and intermediate consumption

Gross output data were generally obtained from regular statistical sources.

Agricultural output was estimated from the *Statistical Abstract* series published by the Central Bureau of Statistics. Data on cultivated areas and yields are collected through annual censuses, supplemented by information received from production boards and other sources. Estimates of value of agricultural production are obtained by multiplying the various quantities of production by the prices received by farmers at the first delivery point. The main sources of data regarding input are as follows: analysis of balance sheets of farms and various organizations; financial reports of the government and local authorities; surveys of distribution and production boards; and data on water consumption provided by the Water Commission.

Industrial output estimates were based on the results of the 1977/78 Industry and Crafts Survey. Those results were also adjusted to include the output of small establishments (i.e., those employing fewer than five persons), and to include own-account transportation in establishment vehicles and other adjustments. For input-output tables, data were especially collected from some of their general costs.

Output data of the construction industry are based mainly on the value of investment in structures and site works estimated regularly by the National Accounts Division of the Central Bureau of Statistics. The sources of these estimates are the area under construction and the cost per square metre for construction, and the reports of construction companies and institutions that ordered construction works. Input was based on surveys of costs.

Data on the output of the electricity sector are based on the profit and loss statement of the Israel Electric Corporation and on general figures of the East Jerusalem Electric Company. Output also includes independent production of electricity in industries such as petroleum and sugar refining, paper and mining and quarrying.

Output of the water sector comprises two main components: the Mekorot Company, which supplies about 60 per cent of consumption, and smaller producers such as kibbutz and moshav settlements, various associations and private companies. Output of Mekorot is based on its profit and loss statement. For the remaining producers, output was estimated on the basis of a survey covering 9 per cent of the population of those producers.

Output of the transportation sector includes five components:

(a) Buses and ports, the revenues of which were obtained from company reports;

(b) Truck transportation. Output of hired trucks is based on the 1977 Survey of Trucks. Imputed revenue was added for trucks transporting on own account. It was based on the expenditures for such trucks, according to the Survey, with the addition of imputed interest and depreciation;

(*c*) Transport in pipes, sea transport, air transport and air services. Output was assessed on the basis of company financial reports;

(*d*) Storage. Output was determined as the product of the ratio of wages to revenue in the Dagon Company and total wages in this branch according to data of the Transportation Division of the Bureau of Statistics;

(*e*) Taxis and transport services, n.e.c. Output of these branches was estimated according to data on wages, private consumption and company reports.

The main source for the estimate of the output and input of the commerce sector was the 1977/78 Survey of Trade and Service. Extrapolation to 1975/76 was done according to the percentage change in the value of sales of organized retailers and wholesalers between 1975/76 and 1976/77—according to the regular series published by the Bureau. As the trade survey does not include small businesses that employ between one and four persons, an estimate was made of the output of this group. It was based on the product of the number of persons employed in the reporting year and the output per employed person in the group with the fewest employees in the survey (businesses with five or six employees). Extrapolation to 1975/76 for the small businesses was according to the same ratio employed in the organized retail trade.

Output of the banking and financial sectors is based on the balance sheets and financial statements obtained mainly from the Bank of Israel, profit and loss statements of non-commercial institutions etc. Output is defined as the sum of commissions and imputed service charges, which is equal to the difference between interest paid and interest received. The treatment of imputed service charges followed the SNA recommendation by creating a dummy sector characterized as "undistributed sector".

Output of the insurance sector was estimated on the basis of data published by the Central Bureau of Statistics and the Ministry of Finance. Input data came from company reports. Data on social insurance funds are based on *Insurance in Israel—1977*, published by the Bureau of Statistics. It seems that the output of life insurance was calculated in the same way as casualty insurance, contrary to the SNA recommendations.

Output and input of the business, legal and personal services sector was estimated from the Survey of Trade and Services conducted by the Input-Output Unit. The personal service sector was characterized by the large share of the self-employed (60 per cent) for whom values were imputed.

The output of the Broadcasting Authority was defined as the total expenditures of the Authority and was determined from its annual report. The output of private medical and educational services was based on the general survey of trade and services; similarly, output data for art and culture services, domestic services and services for institutions and kibbutzim were adapted from sample surveys by the Central Bureau of Statistics.

Output data for restaurants, cafés and other eating and drinking places do not include expenditures on food, which is included in private expenditure on food. Imputed output was also included for the self-employed, making up 38 per cent of the total output. Purchased input and value added were also accordingly imputed. In hotels and other lodging places, output was estimated according to revenue data in the Survey of Tourism, undertaken by the Bureau. It covered recommended hotels only. For the remainder, an impu-

tation was made in collaboration with the Bureau's Internal Trade and Services Section. It should be noted that income from food services, already included in the private consumption expenditure estimate of expenditures on food, was deducted from total revenue.

2. *Value added*

Data on wages and other value added in the manufacturing sector were obtained from the 1977/78 Industry and Crafts Survey. Wages and employment of most of the agricultural sectors were estimated from national insurance data and the results of the Labor Force Survey, respectively. Revenue was estimated as the product of the number of the self-employed and their imputed average daily wage, which was assumed to be 15 per cent higher than the average for wage earners. Total labour costs were obtained as the sum of those two components. From this total, wages paid in the citrus, cotton, dairy and the broiler and egg sub-branches of poultry—which were directly estimated—were subtracted.

Data on indirect taxes on domestic production were mainly obtained from the national accounts, the report of the Customs and Excise Department of the Ministry of Finance on charges and collection of purchase tax and excise duties in 1977/78, and the Industry and Crafts Survey for 1977/78. Taxes, which are usually calculated as a fixed percentage of the price of the product and paid at the producer level (such as purchase tax, excise duties etc.), were allocated according to the principle that the purchasing branch pays the tax. Import taxes were obtained from the 1977/78 foreign trade tables.

Subsidies are divided into four types: subsidies on domestic production, imports, exports and imputed subsidies to offset the artificial taxes. Subsidies on domestic production were recorded according to national accounts data and were derived from reports of the Accountant General. Subsidies on goods and services (group A) for agriculture, bakeries, transportation etc. were allocated on the principle that the purchasing branch receives support that is proportional to its purchases. Subsidies on water were allocated only to the agricultural branches. Those on electricity were allocated to the industrial branches and subsidies on fuel were mainly allocated to electricity generators and cement production. Subsidies provided by the Ministry of Agriculture, according to the output of the various branches, and grants and transportation rebates were divided by purchasing branch on the basis of information provided by the Financial Department of the Ministry of Transport. Subsidies on domestic production in loans to establishments (group B) include two parts: subsidy in export credits and subsidy on operating capital and investments. Subsidies in exports require the inflation of branch output and value added compared to those obtained by surveys. Supports for operating and investments are not allocated to individual branch but to the "undistributed branch" for lack of data. Data on import subsidies for staple products were taken from foreign trade data on imports by purchasing branch and from the government accounts. They refer to products such as sugar, meat and wheat for which the Government is the sole importer and fixes local market prices that are lower than the import costs. Export subsidies include export premiums according to the related value added of the product in foreign currency.

3. Final demand and imports

Private consumption data were collected from the National Accounts Division and are based on the Family Expenditure Survey of 1975/76. Tax and subsidy estimates obtained from this computation were updated on the basis of national accounts data on tax collection and actual subsidy payments. Other adjustments to the national accounts estimates of private consumption include:

(*a*) Deduction of consumption in Israel by foreigners. Data on consumption of tourists, foreign diplomats and workers were taken from the national accounts estimates and added to exports of goods and services;

(*b*) Addition of consumption of Israelis abroad. Tourism consumption abroad was taken from the balance of payments. The estimates of consumption of Israeli representatives abroad were calculated as 60 per cent of their salaries as reported by the Accountant General for the fiscal year 1972/73. The estimate of consumption of sailors and pilots was done by taking the foreign currency salary in the airlines and shipping companies, and from that sum the wages of foreign sailors and pilots were deducted.

Data on gross fixed capital formation were taken mainly from the National Accounts Division. Changes in the stocks of industrial finished goods and goods in progress were estimated on the basis of the results of the Industry and Crafts Survey of 1977/78 and national accounts data. In agriculture, commerce, diamonds and the oil refining industry, as well as for staple commodities, estimates of changes in inventories were based on national accounts figures. Since changes in stocks were estimated on the basis of data for the beginning and the end of the year, it was necessary to carry out an adjustment to express values at average annual prices. Price indices employed were the wholesale price indices for industrial goods. The stock adjustment was based on national accounts data.

Data on exports of goods were obtained from the Foreign Trade Section of the Central Bureau of Statistics, which estimates quarterly figures in United States dollars. The dollar values were translated into Israeli pounds by an average quarterly exchange rate. A list of export subsidies classified by selling sector was also produced. The following adjustments were made to the figures obtained:

(*a*) Addition of export subsidies and imputed taxes on exempt imported goods brought in for the production of export goods;

(*b*) Deduction of agents' commissions paid abroad;

(*c*) Revaluation of export prices in terms of domestic prices required that an artificial tax on exports be added on exports to keep gross profit, a component of an enlarged value added equal to the true profit reported by the establishments;

(*d*) Addition of exports to Judaea, Samaria and Gaza. From the Bureau's belt survey, export data were totalled by branch of origin according to the Standard Industrial Classification of All Economic Activities. Owing to the relatively low reliability of the survey's data for individual commodities or groups of commodities, a number of adjustments were made to the data at the stage of matching resources and uses;

(*e*) Deduction of the value of returned exports, which was obtained from the Foreign Trade Section by branch of origin. It is noteworthy that diamonds represent 90 per cent of all returns;

(*f*) Addition of consumption by foreigners in Israel (tourists, foreign legations, visitors or workers from the administered territories), which was estimated on the basis of balance-of-payments data.

Export of services was estimated from detailed balance-of-payments figures produced by the Balance-of-Payments Section of the Bureau.

Imports were estimated on the basis of customs data, detailed by customs items (c.i.f. value of imports, plus value of duties and other taxes on each good). The main steps taken to obtain the imports table (table (ii)) were as follows:

(*a*) Classification of goods by selling sector based on the 1977/78 classification;

(*b*) Classification of goods by type of use. This was done in a manner similar to that of 1972/73. Goods designated for consumption (according to the classification of the Foreign Trade Section of the Bureau) were separated by computer from those used as input and classified by their sector of origin;

(*c*) Classification of importers of goods by purchasing sector was carried out for those goods defined as input in the various branches of production or goods divided between investments and consumption or investments and input etc.

In the first stage, importers that imported goods for their own production needs were classified. It was assumed that their imports were destined to the sector into which the importer was classified and not meant to be sold or transferred to other sectors. With respect to the goods imported by indirect importers to be sold to a number of purchasing sectors, their destinations were the target of a special survey by the Central Bureau of Statistics.

The following main adjustments of the import estimates obtained were introduced:

(*a*) Addition of imports from the administered territories of Judaea, Samaria and Gaza, as measured by the special belt survey conducted by the Bureau on a regular basis and published quarterly;

(*b*) Returned imports were deducted by purchasing branch on the basis of foreign trade statistics;

(*c*) Goods imported by Israeli importers and sold directly to the administered territories without further processing (e.g., wheat) were deducted from both imports to Israel and exports to the administered territories;

(*d*) Shipments by tourists and diplomats were deducted from imports for private consumption;

(*e*) Addition of direct defence imports, which were not registered by the customs authorities;

(*f*) Imports of services were added to the total imports of the economy on the basis of balance-of-payments data. For purposes of the input-output tables, they were classified by branch of origin and of purchase.

4. Uses and resources balancing

Balancing uses and resources of each branch relied mainly on:

(*a*) Adjustment of purchases of imports and their allocation among purchasing branches. The reasons for this emphasis on import data are: inconsistencies in the classification of imported goods, which differed from the classification by industry, and the allocation of indirect imports on the basis of proportionality or individual judgements;

(*b*) Adjustment of industrial output because of the fact that the 1977/78 Industry and Crafts Survey was an updated sample drawn in 1968 and thus created a large difference between revenue from the old sample and that based on the new sample;

(c) Adjustments through comparison between export data of manufacturing branches with a high proportion of output for exports from the Central Survey. In a number of cases large differences were found;

(d) Adjustment of private consumption according to the 1979/80 Family Consumption Survey.

ISRAEL
INPUT-OUTPUT TABLES
1977-78

Source: *Input-Output Tables 1977/88*, Israel Central
Bureau of Statistics.

מיליוני ש', במחירים שוטפים

7	6	5	4	3	2	1	שימושי ביניים(א) / קונים / מוכרים
1.6	.1	58.0	757.7	4.1	0	117.1	1. חקלאות, ייעור ודיג
6.1	13.9	.6	15.6	21.1	84.7	1.4	2. כרייה, חציבה ומינרלים אל-מתכתיים
51.6	88.2	36.8	88.3	235.3	63.4	138.7	3. כימיקלים, גומי ופלסטיק
.2	.1	2.8	416.1	27.4	0	368.6	4. מזון, משקאות וטבק
12.1	4.8	546.1	2.5	22.3	1.5	14.9	5. טקסטיל, הלבשה ועור
40.9	883.0	17.2	74.4	72.1	32.1	24.4	6. מתכת, מכונות, ציוד חשמלי ואלקטרוני
261.5	24.6	18.1	31.9	26.7	5.8	37.6	7. עץ, נייר, דפוס הוצאה לאור ושונות
16.0	5.5	0	0	0	0	0	8. יהלומים
4.9	·12.4	7.2	8.5	6.3	4.3	.1	9. בינוי
13.1	32.3	17.3	24.8	39.0	22.9	141.0	10. חשמל ומים
17.8	57.3	8.4	67.0	63.2	24.4	21.3	11. תחבורה וקשר
77.5	164.5	62.7	108.2	69.4	33.7	61.6	12. מסחר ושירותים
503.2	1,286.6	775.2	1,595.1	586.8	272.9	926.7	מוצרי ביניים - סך הכל
232.8	536.2	164.9	488.2	1,244.5	32.6	60.1	יבוא, כולל מסים נטו - סך הכל, מזה
166.7	402.2	98.3	435.4	1,132.4	25.0	50.6	- יבוא סי"ם
-2.4	-9.4	-3.3	-34.3	-4.2	-.3	-1.5	- ספיכות ליבוא
68.4	143.4	69.8	87.1	116.3	8.0	11.0	- מסים על יבוא
45.2	59.4	60.8	19.8	26.0	26.1	22.4	מסים על תפוקה מקומית
-2.7	-3.5	-4.4	-161.9	-6.0	-8.6	-67.0	תמיכות למפוקה מקומית
317.9	1,068.3	316.9	279.1	266.3	152.3	511.4	שכר עבודה (ב)
154.7	325.4	145.2	197.3	225.9	102.4	497.2	ערך מוסף (פרט לשכר)
1,251.1	3,272.4	1,458.5	2,417.5	2,343.4	577.8	1,950.8	תשומות - סך כולל

(א) הספרות שבמגדירי הטורים הם מספרי הענפים המופיעים במגדירי השורות במטאבה.

(ב) כולל זקיפה לפועסקים שאינם שכירים.

| 250.8 | 1,020.9 | 292.4 | 268.6 | 260.3 | 147.6 | 234.4 | - שכ"ע שכירים |
| 67.1 | 47.4 | 24.5 | 10.5 | 5.9 | 4.7 | 277.0 | - שכ"ע זקוף לעצם |

TABLE 1.- INPUT OUTPUT 1977/78 - TRANSACTION

IS million - Current Prices

	Intermediate uses(a)					
Purchasers Sellers	סך הכל Total	12	11	10	9	8
1. Agriculture, forestry and fishing	949.8	6.0	0	0	5.3	0
2. Mining, quarrying and non-metallic mineral products	476.7	17.1	1.5	2.2	312.4	0
3. Chemicals, rubber and plastic products	1,828.6	383.1	326.9	314.9	101.4	.1
4. Food, beverages and tobacco	834.5	5.5	9.1	0	4.7	0
5. Textiles, clothing and leather	667.8	59.8	1.8	0	1.9	0
6. Metals, machinery, electrical and electronic equipment	2,434.4	847.7	50.6	9.5	379.1	3.3
7. Wood, paper, printing, publishing and miscellaneous	842.2	317.1	6.4	1.7	110.8	.1
8. Diamonds	21.4	0	0	0	0	0
9. Construction	279.6	221.3	8.5	4.7	1.1	.2
10. Electricity and water	466.7	68.1	13.1	87.3	5.8	2.1
11. Transport and communication	1,238.3	355.6	533.3	3.4	86.4	.3
12. Commerce and services	3,757.9	2,649.4	328.9	30.0	163.2	8.7
INTERMEDIATE PRODUCTS - TOTAL	13,797.8	4,930.8	1,280.1	453.7	1,172.1	14.7
Imports, incl. net taxes - total, thereof:	6,091.4	2,037.2	23.1	10.7	74.7	1,186.6
- Import C.i.f.	5,138.5	1,666.5	15.5	9.4	29.2	1,107.3
- Subsidies on imports	-68.5	-4.3	-3.4	-.2	-5.3	0
- Taxes on imports	1,021.5	375.0	11.0	1.5	50.8	79.2
Taxes on domestic production	1,045.1	629.1	95.4	7.5	53.3	.1
Subsidies on domestic production	-1,188.1	-818.9	-29.9	-81.3	-3.6	-.1
Wages (b)	7,243.5	2,303.2	885.0	127.5	937.7	77.9
Value added (excl. wages)	4,688.1	1,678.0	543.5	110.6	270.0	437.8
INPUTS - GRAND TOTAL	31,677.9	10,759.3	2,797.2	628.9	2,504.2	1,716.8

(a) Figures in column headings are the code numbers of the branches which are presented in the rows.

(b) Incl. imputation for non-employees.

- Wages of employees	5,948.7	1,600.2	735.1	127.5	937.7	73.2
- Imputation for non-employees	1,294.8	702.9	150.0	0	0	4.7

ליח 1 -. (המשך)

Changes in products stocks	Fixed domestic capital formation	General government consumption	Consumption of non-profit institutions	Private consumption	קונים / מוכרים
					שימושים סופיים
5.8	38.9	0	0	474.7	חקלצות, ייעור ודיג .1
-17.3	2.3	0	0	24.3	כרייה, חציבה ומינרליים אל-מתכח .2
17.6	5.4	0	0	263.7	כימיקלים, גומי ופלסטיק .3
-4.0	0	0	0	1,360.1	מזון, משקאות וטבק .4
5.9	2.4	0	0	525.1	טקסטיל, הלבשה ועור .5
-23.7	588.3	0	0	192.7	מתכת, מכונות, ציוד חשמלי ואלקטרוני .6
-2.5	75.9	0	0	304.1	עץ, נייר, דפוס הוצאה לאור ושונים .7
211.4	0	0	0	0	יהלומים .8
0	2,155.6	0	0	69.1	בינוי .9
0	0	0	0	156.3	חשמל ומים .10
0	33.7	0	0	634.7	מתבורה וקשר .11
1.0	38.5	3,830.4	323.5	2,688.7	מסחר ושירותים .12
194.2	2,941.0	3,830.4	323.5	6,693.6	מוצרי ביניים - סך הכל
14.7	578.3	0	0	503.3	יבוא, כולל מסים נטו - סך הכל, מזה
14.2	410.0	0	0	102.3	יבוא סים -
-.1	-25.4	0	0	-8.0	חמיכום ליבוא -
.6	193.7	0	0	408.9	מסים על יבוא -
5.6	166.6	0	0	1,179.8	מסים על תפוקה מקומית
-1.4	0	0	0	-183.4	תמיכות לתפוקה מקומית
0	0	2,254.0	911.5	60.0	שכר עבודה(ב)
0	0	22.9	8.5	1,204.5	ערך מוסף (פרט לשכר)
213.1	3,685.9	6,107.3	1,243.6	9,457.8	תשומות - סך כולל
0	0	2,254.0	911.5	60.0	שכ"ע שכירים -
0	0	0	0	0	שכ"ע זקיף לעצם -

(ב) כולל זקיפה לפועסקים שאינם שכירים.

TABLE 1.- (Cont'd.)

Purchasers / Sellers	סך הכל Grand total	פחות יבוא מחתרה	Final uses		
			שימושים סופיים- סך הכל Final uses - total	יצוא כולל פמיכות Exports, incl. subsidies	השינוי במלאי חומרים Changes in raw material stocks
1. Agriculture, forestry and fishing	1,950.8	-146.8	1,147.8	638.7	-10.3
2. Mining, quarrying and non-metallic mineral products	577.8	-63.1	164.2	157.3	-2.4
3. Chemicals, rubber and plastic products	2,343.4	-345.6	860.4	578.1	-4.3
4. Food, beverages and tobacco	2,417.5	-222.5	1,805.6	449.1	.3
5. Textiles, clothing and leather	1,458.5	-201.3	992.0	457.3	1.3
6. Metals, machinery, electric and electronic equipment	3,272.4	-941.1	1,779.1	1,029.2	-7.4
7. Wood, paper, printing, publishing and miscellaneous	1,251.1	-205.5	614.4	242.3	-5.4
8. Diamonds	1,716.8	0	1,695.4	1,484.5	-.4
9. Construction	2,504.2	0	2,224.7	0	0
10. Electricity and water	628.9	-1.1	163.3	7.0	0
11. Transport and communication	2,797.2	-517.7	2,076.5	1,409.2	-1.1
12. Commerce and services	10,759.3	-693.0	7,694.4	812.9	-.5
INTERMEDIATE PRODUCTS - TOTAL	31,677.9	-3,337.7	21,217.8	7,265.5	-30.5
Imports, incl. net taxes - total, thereof:	10,887.1	3,337.7	1,457.9	0	361.6
- Import c.i.f.	9,365.7	3,337.7	889.5	0	363.1
- Subsidies on imports	-143.0	0	-74.4	0	-40.9
- Taxes on imports	1,664.3	0	642.8	0	39.5
Taxes on domestic production	2,491.5	0	1,446.5	97.1	-2.6
Subsidies on domestic production	-2,103.6	0	-915.5	-730.7	0
Wages (b)	10,469.1	0	3,225.5	0	0
Value added (excl. wages)	6,028.2	0	1,340.1	104.2	0
INPUTS - GRAND TOTAL	59,450.3	0	27,772.3	6,736.2	328.5
(b) Incl. imputation for non-employees.					
- Wages of employees	9,174.3	0	3,225.5	0	0
- Imputation for non-employees	1,294.8	0	0	0	0

VIII. JAPAN

A. GENERAL INFORMATION

The present description is based on the *1975 Input-Output Tables* (English summary), Administrative Management Agency, Government of Japan, March 1979, and the *1980 Input-Output Tables*, March 1984, which used the same methods and concepts as the 1975 tables.

Input-output tables for Japan have been compiled every five years since 1955. They are the result of the joint work of several agencies and ministries co-ordinated by the Administrative Management Agency of the Government of Japan. A similar methodological framework has been adopted for all tables, except for those referring to 1955. The present report describes the latest tables available, those for 1975 and 1980.

Although input-output tables are integrated with the national accounts, estimates obtained in both sets differ slightly owing to different computation procedures. Also, the national accounts system differs in the following aspects from the input-output tables: (*a*) private final consumption expenditure outside the household sector is distinguished as a separate category in the input-output tables, while such expenses are treated as intermediate consumption in the national accounts; (*b*) imputed banking services are allocated in the input-output tables to different intermediate and final demand categories, while in the national accounts such imputed service charges have been deducted in one amount from GDP in conformity with the SNA recommendations; (*c*) the classification of economic activities in the national accounts differs slightly from the SNA recommended ISIC breakdown, that is, the breakdown in the input-output tables is based on the four-digit level of ISIC, but does not follow the ISIC aggregates.

There are several differences between the input-output tables of the Government of Japan and the SNA recommendations on input-output with regard to the treatment of transactions, the definition of concepts and also the presentation of the tables. These concern the inclusion in final consumption expenditure of a separate category for consumption outside households, which affects the size of GDP; the presentation and treatment of secondary production; trade and transport margins in the table valued at purchasers' prices; the distribution of imputed banking services; the classification of imports; and the introduction of two dummy sectors. Also, the allocation of government services and private non-profit services to economic activity categories is different from what is recommended in SNA. Finally, all tables are valued in producers' or purchasers' prices and no attempt has been made to separate commodity taxes to arrive at approximate basic values for the goods and services flows, as recommended in SNA.

B. ANALYTICAL FRAMEWORK

1. *Tables and derived matrices available*

The following tables with basic information are available:

(i) Input-output table in producers' prices;
(ii) Input-output table in purchasers' prices;
(iii) Make matrix;
(iv) Matrix of domestic trade margins;
(v) Matrix of domestic transport margins;
(vi) Matrix of imported goods and services;
(vii) Input-output table of selected goods in values and quantities (this refers to the input-output table in producers' prices);
(viii) Table of number of persons engaged, classified by type of work (self-employed, unpaid family workers, paid directors, employees etc.) and economic activity of employment; the table also includes information on per capita compensation of employees, again classified by economic activity;
(ix) Table on hours worked, classified by economic activity of employment;
(x) Table on number of employees, classified by occupations and economic activity of employment;
(xi) Table on gross fixed capital formation, classified by types of capital goods and economic activity of destination; this table is further broken down into public and private capital formation.

On the basis of the basic table, the following derived tables have been elaborated:

(i') Matrix of input coefficients of components of intermediate consumption (including imports) and value added to gross output per sector;
(ii') Table of inverse input coefficients; this table actually consists of three subtables, that is, one referring to domestic produced goods and services, a second one covering imported goods and services and a third one referring to the total of domestic production and imports;
(iii') Table of total domestic production required for final demand, classified by final demand categories and economic activities; this table consists of three subtables, that is, one presenting the actual values of total production, a second one showing the ratio of total production to the actual value of final demand and a third one showing the distribution ratios of total production between the final demand categories;
(iv') Table on total imports required for final demand, classified by final demand categories and economic activities; similar to table (iii'), this table consists of three subtables that present, respectively: actual values, ratio between total value of imports and final demand and distribution ratios of total imports between final demand categories;
(v') Table on total value added induced by final demand, classified by final demand categories and economic activities; similar to tables (iii') and (iv'), this table also includes three subtables that present, respectively: actual value, ratios between

total value of final demand and distribution ratios of total value added between final demand categories;

(vi') Table presenting direct import coefficients of total supply, total imports coefficients of exports and of the subtotal of the remaining final demand categories and total value added coefficients of total final demand. All coefficients are presented in a breakdown by economic activity categories. This table summarizes the information of tables (iv') and (v').

In the presentation of the tables, three levels of aggregation have been applied: 72 x 72, 164 x 164 and 551 row sectors by 406 column sectors. The basic tables, (i) to (vi), except table (iii), are available in all three levels of aggregation. The derived matrices, (i') to (vi'), are only available in two levels of aggregation, that is, 72 x 72 and 164 x 164. Table (iii), the make matrix, is presented in a modified version of the aggregation levels, which includes 98 x 98 categories. The remaining supporting basic tables, (vii) to (xi), are generally classified in the breakdown of 72 economic activity categories, except table (viii), which is presented for the 72, 164 and 456 categories.

With regard to the basic tables, there is additional detail presented in a separate table on the trade and transport margins. This table includes for each element of the input table the link between the valuation in producers' and purchasers' prices. The additional detail included for each element is a breakdown of the trade margins by wholesale and retail trade, and of the transport margins by modes of transport. This information refers to the level of aggregation of 164 x 164.

A special feature of the Japanese input-output tables, which should be pointed out for a better understanding of the table presentation, is the integration of the input-output presentation with a presentation of total supply and demand of goods and services. Total demand, which is reflected in the columns of intermediate consumption and final demand, is followed by columns that present total supply. In the input-output table valued at producers' prices, total supply includes columns for domestic products, imports and import taxes. In the table valued at purchasers' prices, total supply is obtained by adding the columns of domestic products, imports and import taxes, trade and transport margins and, owing to their special treatment in this table, scrap and by-products.

2. *Valuation standards*

As indicated above, the input-output tables are valued in producers' as well as in purchasers' prices. Producers' prices are defined as average shipment prices. Though there are differences between the shipment prices over time between different locations and also owing to institutional differences, an average unit price has been applied to all commodity flows, which is calculated by dividing the value of domestic production of each commodity by the quantities produced. Differences between the actual and the average unit prices are recorded in a separate row and column as statistical discrepancies. The purchasers' price is derived from the uniform producers' price by adding distribution margins for trade and transport. Producers' prices of exports are defined as their f.o.b. value less distribution margins that occur between the producing establishment and the export port. Purchasers' prices of exports are based on the f.o.b. value. Imports are valued c.i.f. in both types of valuations; import duties and import commodity taxes, other than those related to the distribution process, are recorded in separate columns of input-output tables (i) and (ii). Other commodity taxes are not separated out, so that a valuation in approximate basic values neither is included nor can be derived.

3. *Statistical units and classification standards*

In the input-output tables and also in the matrices of domestic trade and transport margins and of imported goods and services, data are classified by commodity groupings in the rows and activity categories in the columns. In the make matrix the activity categories are in the rows and the commodity groupings in the columns. The unit of classification of the activity breakdown is more refined than establishment units, in the sense that the units of production are as close as possible to producing only one type of commodity.

Commodities and activities are classified according to the Japanese Basic Sector Classification, which provides a six-digit breakdown for activities and a seven-digit breakdown for commodities. The classification is designed in such a manner that each basic sector of the input-output table (6 and 2 digits) corresponds to the four-digit level of ISIC.

The structure and classification of the intermediate consumption quadrant differs from the SNA recommendations in four respects. The first one concerns the classification of government services such as health and education, which in the Japanese table are recorded together with the same type of services provided by private producers. (However, health, education and other social services provided by the Government are distinguished from private services in the basic classification.) Public administration broken down by central and local in two columns of the intermediate consumption quadrant then covers the remaining part of producers of government services. A second deviation is the inclusion of a dummy sector for office supplies, packing materials, own-account transport, real estate renting etc., which channels groups of commodities commonly used in industrial sectors whose precise commodity composition is not known. The third deviation is the inclusion of a sector for activities n.e.c., which is introduced to account for estimation errors and other statistical discrepancies in both rows and columns. Finally, activities of private non-profit institutions are not recorded separately.

The breakdown and definition of value added and final demand deviate from the SNA recommendations as follows. Final demand includes a separate final demand item, known as consumption outside households. This refers to the reimbursement of travelling expenses, expenses for amenities at work and other employers' welfare and social expenditures paid by enterprises. To match the inclusion of a separate column in final demand, an extra row has been inserted for value added in addition to the traditional components of value added. Both value added and final demand are therefore higher in the Japanese input-output table than they would have been according to the SNA recommendations. Since information on consumption outside households is reflected in a separate row and column, the coverage of the remaining value added and final demand components has not been affected and the SNA concepts can be derived from the presentation. In fact, the SNA concept of gross domestic product is explicitly recorded in the input-output table in producers' prices in the row "Gross domestic products" and in the column "Gross domestic expenditures".

Final household consumption expenditures are defined on a national basis. Direct expenditures abroad and in the domestic market by, respectively, residents and non-residents are incorporated with imports and exports of goods and services. However, in the 164 x 164 table, such expenses are recorded separately as subcategories of imports and exports respectively, entitled "direct purchase imports" and "direct purchase exports". Therefore, the domestic concept of private final consumption expenditure can also be obtained from the table.

In addition to the SNA requirements of a commodity breakdown of imports, the Japanese input-output publication presents a cross-classification of imports by type of commodities and activity and final demand categories of destination. The distinction between competitive and complementary imports is reflected in the commodity breakdown. Some commodity groups in imports concern only competitive imports (barley, wheat, soybean, log, coking coal, anthracite, iron, ore, crude petroleum, cleaned rice and refined sugar) and others refer only to complementary imports (coffee bean and cocoa bean, spices, corn and kaoliang, as well as rubber and cotton).

4. *Treatment and presentation of selected transactions*

Although the activity unit closely resembles the commodity unit, that is, in most instances produces one type of commodity only, some secondary production remains. Varying treatments have been applied to this problem in the input-output tables. In the table in producers' prices (table (i)), two types of treatment can be distinguished. By-products and scrap generated in the production process are entered as negative input in the column of the economic activity that produces such products and are assigned to the row sector to which they characteristically belong. A second method applies to advertisement services, which are recorded as positive input in the column of the sector that characteristically produces such services and in the row sector that actually produces them. A third method is adopted in the table in purchasers' prices (table (ii)). There, by-products and scrap are entered as negative input in the column of the sector that generates those products and in a separate row that records all secondary products together. In other words, by-products and scrap are separately identified as a total for each sector, without distinguishing between the products involved. As the purchasers' price table includes a confrontation of supply and demand, by-products and scrap have been included in a separate column where they are classified by sectors to which they characteristically belong. The three methods of transferring secondary production refer only to the transfer of gross output. Contrary to the SNA recommendations, no attempt has been made to transfer the input that corresponds to the secondary output.

The gross output concept is close to that of SNA. It includes non-marketed production of agricultural products and foodstuffs that are consumed and produced in the household sector. The gross output and corresponding input have been included in the appropriate intermediate sector of the

input-output table. The diagonal elements of the tables include the intra-sectoral consumption of industries, only as far as data are available. Included are, among others, agricultural products consumed in agriculture itself (seed rice, seeds etc.), finance transactions between financial institutions and motor vehicle parts that are used in the assembly of motor vehicles by the same industry. Also included in the diagonal are characteristic products produced and consumed by the same producing unit, not, however, secondary products.

Gross output includes the imputed value of rent for owner-occupied dwellings and dwellings supplied by employers. The rent is estimated on the basis of the average market price of rented houses. Gross output and input are included in a separate sector, known as house rents.

Domestic output of financial services is defined in conformity with SNA, that is, the imputed value of banking services is equal to the difference between interest received on loans and paid on deposits, and the imputed value of life and casualty insurance is equal to total premiums received, less claims paid, less net additions to the actuarial reserved. The distribution, however, is different. Banking services are imputed to current depositors on the basis of their average current deposit holdings, using an interest rate that is paid to ordinary depositors. The remaining amount of the total imputed service charge is then prorated to the intermediate and final demand sectors on the basis of their average amounts of loans outstanding.

Gross output of trade includes domestic trade margins (table (iv)) and the following other components:

(*a*) Trade margins on second-hand goods, which are traded between or within the categories of intermediate consumption or final demand. In accordance with the SNA recommendations, these margins are always separately recorded from the actual transactions in second-hand goods;

(*b*) Some trade services supplied by foreign agencies, which are not included in the c.i.f. values of imported goods. These are the so-called "charges of agencies" in the balance-of-payments statistics. This component is separately presented in the intersection of the import column with the wholesale trade row in the input-output tables (tables (i) and (ii));

(*c*) The trade services supplied by Japanese trading companies either for the import of goods or other services that are not directly related to the goods imported, but form a part of the "charges of agencies". These services are recorded as a part of exports in the row of wholesale trade;

(*d*) The remaining international trade services that are supplied by foreign trade companies in connection with either imports or exports. These services are not separately identified in the table, either because such services are already included in the c.i.f. value of imports, or because they relate to exports, in which case they are not to be included at all, since exports are valued f.o.b.

In the input-output table in purchasers' prices, the row for the trade sector includes only the additional components of the trade output mentioned above. The domestic trade margins are recorded as part of total supply in the above-mentioned integration of the input-output table with a presentation of total supply and demand. In the table in producers' prices, the domestic trade margins are distributed in the trade row to the sectors of destination of the goods on which they are levied, in accordance with SNA. The treatment of the other components of the trade output is the same as in the table in purchasers' prices.

The treatment of transport services is similar to that of trade services. Also, in this case a distinction is made between the domestic transport margins included in the transport margins matrix (table (v)) and the total output of transport services. The additional transport services components concern the transport cost involved in the course of production for the transport of raw materials, of goods to wholesale markets etc.; the transport fees for furniture, parcels, mail and soil to be moved; and the transport of passengers. As these additional transport components do not form part of the difference between producers' and purchasers' values, they are not included in the transport margins matrix. In the input-output table in purchasers' prices, they are the only components that are included in the transport row. The transport margins are not included there, but are covered in a separate column forming part of the total supply as in the case of the trade margins. The treatment of the transport output in the table in producers' prices conforms to the SNA recommendations, in the sense that the transport margins are allocated to the intermediate and final demand of destination of the goods on which they are levied, while the remaining transport components are allocated to the sectors that pay for such services.

C. Statistical sources and compilation methodology

Data collection is based on existing regular sources as well as on results of special surveys conducted for the specific purpose of compiling input-output tables. Two estimates were obtained for each cell of the table: one from the input and one from the output side. Both estimates were then reconciled into a single figure. Furthermore, a third estimate was obtained by applying the 1975 input coefficients to the 1980 gross output data adjusted for inflation. This estimate was used for reference purposes only.

1. Gross output and intermediate consumption

Data on the agricultural sector are obtained from regular sources such as crop statistics and statistics on agricultural costs and from household expenditure services. In addition, there are such administrative sources as the statistics on national forestry and the monthly report of the food administration. Special surveys were also conducted on 1,000-2,000 samples for the purpose of compilation of the 1980 input-output table by the Ministry of Agriculture, Forestry and Fisheries. These mainly included input surveys that covered the breakdown of expenses in particular agricultural and related activities such as those of agricultural engineering enterprises, exploitation of privately owned forests, baby silkworm breeding industry, activities concerning cultures in sea and inland waters, and trade activity in agricultural products.

Data on capital, number of employees, production, sales and cost ratios per subactivity of mining were collected through a special survey of the mining industry, conducted by the Ministry of International Trade and Industry for the specific purpose of compilation of the 1980 input-output tables.

The major part of the data on the manufacturing sector is

provided by the 1980 Census of Manufactures and Trade Statistics. The census information is supplemented by other surveys, such as the Current Production Survey of the Ministry of International Trade and Industry and surveys conducted by industrial associations, such as the ones for the confection and chemical industries. The 1975 census has a 100 per cent coverage, using different questionnaires for establishments with 30 employees or more, 29 employees or less, and head offices. The Current Production Survey is conducted on a commodity basis and has a coverage of 85 per cent of the value of the commodities produced in each industry of the two-digit level of the Japanese Standard Industrial Classification.

The main regular data sources of construction statistics are the monthly statistics on construction materials and the statistics on building works started. The Ministry of Construction also conducted special surveys for 1980 input-output tables, including: input survey of building expenses, survey of construction ordered by the Government, input survey of civil engineering expenses etc.

Trade data are mainly obtained from monthly statistics on commerce. Special surveys were conducted by the Ministry of International Trade and Industry. These include a trade margin survey with wholesalers, which collected data on origin of purchases and destination of sales per item, details on sales expenses and rough margins per item, and a commodity distribution survey conducted with producers which included information per item and per region on production, own consumption and shipments.

The Ministry of Transportation conducted several surveys that were specifically designed for the 1980 input-output table. Of these, the road facilities and light car utilization surveys included information on the industries and commodities that use those road and car facilities. Another survey of freight income of coastal ships covered freight income per item; and input surveys of transportation in general covered trucking and warehousing and local public transportation facilities.

Most data for services were collected through special surveys. These included input surveys of 1,000 service establishments and a survey of local industries with regard to the composition of their financial expenses. Both surveys were conducted by the Economic Planning Agency. In addition, the Ministry of Health and Welfare conducted special surveys of the pharmaceutical, health, public welfare and environmental hygienic industries, which provided information on their operating expenses.

2. Value added, final demand and imports

Independent information available on value added concerns employment data provided by the monthly labour statistics. Benchmark information on employment is obtained from the population census. Employment data for specific sectors were obtained in the survey of services industries' labour expenses, conducted by the Ministry of Labour and through earlier-mentioned special input surveys of particular industries.

Household expenditure statistics and farm household expenditure information are the main independent sources for the estimation of private final consumption expenditure. Independent information on public and private capital formation was collected through a special survey for the compilation of the capital matrix, which was conducted by the Ministry of International Trade and Industry with the producers of fixed assets. It contained information on the production, own consumption and shipment of fixed assets.

Import and export statistics were provided in commodity detail that made it possible to rearrange those data to conform to the Japanese Basic Sector Classification of the input-output tables.

JAPAN
INPUT-OUTPUT TABLES
1980

Source: *1980 Input-Output Tables*, Administrative Management Planning, Government of Japan.

Table II-1 Input-Output Table at Producers' Prices (13 Sectors)

			Intermediate Demand												
			01	02	03	04	05	06	07	08	09	10	11	12	13
Intermediate Input	01	Agriculture, Forestry & Fishery	20119	54	126431	855	0	0	0	10	28	11923	0	0	125
	02	Mining	1	46	155558	11126	20238	0	0	1	3	84	0	0	704
	03	Manufacturing	35743	2703	1027004	207368	31048	20257	163	116929	13125	114849	6747	19682	36772
	04	Construction	739	84	5442	597	2789	22084	1113	2162	2173	4708	0	19	442
	05	Electricity, Gas & Water	776	649	52866	5030	4029	7453	335	6899	4418	20148	0	156	2979
	06	Commerce, Finance Insurance & Real Estate	7217	1605	140864	41987	10548	58153	513	36360	2120	45328	3430	1994	11800
	07	Real Estate Rent	141	145	6045	3101	573	20457	0	5450	593	10189	0	62	1028
	08	Transportation & Communication	5334	6088	53615	23342	4160	44008	185	40015	7272	23861	237	634	8205
	09	Public Services	0	0	0	0	0	0	0	0	0	0	0	0	2448
	10	Services	164	222	54291	18758	3558	35065	985	9982	6216	39348	0	159	5553
	11	Office Supplies	143	26	4733	422	320	2040	4	729	437	1555	0	26	0
	12	Packing	1265	2	23181	0	0	2689	0	204	3	10	0	0	103
	13	Others	1904	534	39354	6500	1459	14415	155	4888	58	10693	23	66	0
	73	Sub-total	735417	12158	1689384	319086	78723	226621	3452	223629	36446	282696	10437	22797	70158
Gross Value Added	74	Consumption Outside Households	1123	781	39448	12862	1426	21034	189	5998	3664	13652	0	145	1542
	75	Compensation of Employees	14149	5252	362898	133306	25083	274008	2923	111441	88459	284261	0	3637	0
	77	Operating Surplus	54835	4589	138237	49950	19762	248114	35068	8032	0	74248	0	2208	4497
	78	Depreciation of Fixed Capital	17514	2957	92496	22144	16729	97043	3320	26960	3900	33219	0	127	0
	79	Indirect Taxes	4566	643	82001	5804	6553	33944	2830	4885	284	21752	0	35	461
	80	Subsidies	-4619	-367	-7935	-578	-770	-9058	0	-8399	0	-1503	0	0	-2479
	87	Sub-total	87567	13854	707144	233488	68783	665085	44330	148916	96307	425629	0	6152	4020
	95	Total Domestic Products	161114	206012	2396528	552574	147505	891706	47783	372545	132752	708326	10437	28949	74178
Ref.	99	Gross Domestic Products	86444	13073	667696	220626	67357	644051	44141	142919	92642	411977	0	6008	2478
	98	Net Domestic Products at Factor Cost	68984	9841	501135	193256	44845	522122	37991	119473	88459	358509	0	5845	4497

| Sub-total | Final Demand | | | | | | | 83 | Imports | | | 95 | Ref. |
73	74	75	77	78	80	81	82		84	85	Sub-total		99
159545	1088	41891	0	1830	-2896	753	42665	202211	-40489	-608	-41096	161114	482
187762	0	52	0	0	2018	196	2265	190028	-159039	-4477	-164015	26012	-161750
1632391	18370	378946	0	200971	20616	277633	896536	2528927	-124883	-7516	-132399	2396528	745766
42352	0	0	0	510222	0	0	510222	552574	0	0	0	552574	510222
105739	40	34836	6874	0	0	43	41794	147532	-27	0	-27	147505	41726
361918	9462	463924	0	43509	1137	21186	539219	901136	-9430	0	-9430	891706	520326
47783	0	0	0	0	0	0	0	47783	0	0	0	47783	0
216955	1214	129690	2736	2903	283	37345	174170	391125	-18581	0	-18581	372545	154376
2448	0	2427	127878	0	0	0	130305	132752	0	0	0	132752	130305
174301	71689	367686	100796	0	0	1101	541273	715573	-7248	0	-7248	708326	462336
10437	0	0	0	0	0	0	0	10437	0	0	0	10437	0
27456	0	1493	0	0	0	0	1493	28949	0	0	0	28949	1493
80048	0	0	0	0	-2126	7177	5051	85099	-10900	-21	-10921	74178	-5870
3049133	101863	1420944	236284	759435	19032	345434	2884993	5934126	-370597	-13121	-383718	5550408	2399412

101863
1305417
649539
316409
163757
-35710
2501275
5550408
2399412
1954956

Column Codes are:

74 Consumption Expenditures Outside Households
75 Consumption Expenditures of Households
77 Consumption Expenditures of General Government
78 Gross Domestic Fixed Capital Formation
80 Increase in Stocks
81 Exports
82 Sub-total
83 Total Demand
84 Imports
85 Customs Duties
95 Total Domestic Products
99 Gross Domestic Expenditures

Table II-2 Input-Output Table at Purchasers' Prices (13 Sectors)

		01	02	03	04	05	06	07	08	09	10	11	12	13
Intermediate Input	01 Agriculture, Forestry & Fishery	20479	62	139264	979	–	–	–	12	47	17422	0	0	125
	02 Mining	1	54	163205	13980	21208	–	–	2	3	92	0	0	775
	03 Manufacturing	41391	3496	1129834	246801	33214	28011	219	138494	15209	144491	10411	22237	44225
	04 Construction	739	84	5442	597	2789	22084	1113	2162	2173	4706	0	19	442
	05 Electricity, Gas & Water	776	649	52866	5030	4029	7453	335	6899	4418	20148	0	156	2979
	06 Commerce, Finance Insurance & Real Estate	2781	812	41321	6401	8448	49020	441	15365	214	11892	0	17	4467
	07 Real Estate Rent	141	145	6045	3101	573	20457	–	5450	593	10189	0	62	1028
	08 Transportation & Communication	3484	5994	24114	15570	2910	43287	179	38730	7066	20590	0	45	8014
	09 Public Services	–	–	–	–	–	–	–	–	–	–	0	0	2448
	10 Services	164	222	54291	18758	3558	35065	985	9982	6216	39348	0	159	5553
	11 Office Supplies	143	26	4733	422	320	2040	4	729	437	1555	0	26	0
	12 Packing	1265	2	23181	–	–	2689	–	204	3	10	0	0	103
	13 Others	2181	611	45088	7447	1672	16515	177	5600	66	12251	26	76	0
	73 Sub-total	73547	12158	1689384	319086	78723	226621	3452	223629	36446	282694	10437	22797	70158
Gross Value Added	74 Consumption Outside Households	1123	781	39448	12862	1426	21034	189	5998	3664	13652	0	145	1542
	75 Compensation of Employees	14149	5252	362898	133306	25083	274008	2923	111441	88459	284261	0	3637	0
	77 Operating Surplus	54835	4589	138237	59950	19762	248114	35068	8032	–	74248	0	2208	4497
	78 Depreciation of Fixed Capital	17514	2957	92496	22144	16729	97043	3320	26960	3900	33219	0	127	0
	79 Indirect Taxes	4566	643	82001	5804	6553	33994	2830	4885	284	21752	0	35	461
	80 Subsidies	-4619	-367	-7935	-578	-770	-9058	–	-8399	–	-1503	0	0	-2479
	87 Sub-total	87567	13854	707144	233488	68783	665085	44330	148916	96307	425629	0	6152	4020
	95 Total Domestic Products	161114	26012	2396528	552574	147505	891706	47783	372545	132752	708326	10437	28949	74178

146

Sub-total	Final Demand							83	Imports			89	90	Ref.
73	74	75	77	78	80	81	82	83	84	85	Sub-total	89	90	95
178390	1922	70807	0	1830	-2843	886	72603	250993	-40489	-608	-41096	-42350	-6433	161114
199322	0	61	0	0	2177	248	2486	201807	-159039	-4977	-164015	-5231	-6549	26012
1858033	27555	581636	0	245061	21824	294629	1170705	3028738	-124883	-7516	-132399	-448107	-51705	2396528
42352	0	0	0	510222	0	0	510222	552574	0	0	00	0	0	552574
105739	40	34836	6874	0	0	43	41794	147532	-27	0	-27	0	0	147505
141180	0	244896	0	2321	0	5815	253032	394212	-9430	0	-9430	506924	0	891706
47783	0	0	0	0	0	0	0	47783	0	0	0	0	0	47783
169983	658	117102	2736	0	0	34489	154984	324968	-18581	0	-18581	0	66158	372545
2448	0	2427	127878	0	0	0	130305	132752	0	0	0	0	0	132752
174301	71689	367686	100796	0	0	1101	541273	715573	-7248	0	-7248	0	0	708326
10437	0	0	0	0	0	0	0	10437	0	0	0	0	0	10437
27456	0	1493	0	0	0	0	1493	28949	0	0	0	0	0	28949
91711	0	0	0	0	-2126	8222	6096	97807	-10900	-21	-10921	-11237	-1471	74178
3049133	101863	1420944	238284	759435	19032	345434	2884993	5934126	-370597	-13121	-383718	0	0	5550408

101863
1305417
649539
316409
163757
-35710
2501275
5550508

Column Codes are:

74 Consumption Expenditures Outside Households
75 Consumption Expenditures of Households
77 Consumption Expenditures of General Government
78 Gross Domestic Fixed Capital Formation
80 Increase in Stocks
81 Exports
82 Sub-total
83 Total Demand
84 Imports
85 Customs Duties
89 Trade Margins
90 Domestic Transportation Fees for Goods
95 Total Domestic Products

AGGREGATED SECTOR CLASSIFICATION

Intermediate Sector

164 Aggregated Group Classification		72 Aggregated Major Group Classification	
Code	Name of Sector	Code	Name of Sector
0011	Field crops	01	Agricultural products
0012	Vegetables		
0013	Fruits		
0014	Edible farm products (except elsewhere classified)		
0015	Inedible farm products		
0016	Livestock	02	Livestock and sericulture
0017	Sericulture		
0020	Agricultural services	03	Agricultural services
0211	Forest tree nurseries	04	Forestry and logging
0212	Other forestry		
0220	Logging		
0410	Ocean and coastal fishery products	05	Fishery products
0430	Inland water fishery products		
1101	Coal	06	Coal
1210	Iron ore	07	Metal mining
1220	Non-ferrous ore		
1301	Crude petroleum	08	Crude petroleum and natural gas
1302	Natural gas		
1410	Ceramic clay	09	Other non-metal mining

164 Aggregated Group Classification		72 Aggregated Major Group Classification	
Code	Name of Sector	Code	Name of Sector
1420	Stone quarrying	09	Other non-metal mining
1990	Other non-metal mining		
2011	Slaughtering	10	Slaughtering, preparing & preserving meat and dairy products
2012	Meat prepared and preserved		
2020	Dairy products		
2030	Vegetables and fruits canned and preserved	(Aggregated into 13)	
2040	Seafood preserved	11	Seafood preserved
2050	Grain mill products	12	Grain mill products
2060	Bread and confectionery	13	Other food products
2070	Sugar		
2091	Other food products		
2092	Prepared animal food	14	Prepared animal food
2110	Liquor and alcoholic beverages	15	Beverages
2140	Soft drinks and carbonated drinks		
2200	Tobacco	16	Tobacco
2301	Raw silk (including spun silk yarn)	17	Fiber yarn
2302	Cotton yarn		
2303	Woollen yarn		
2304	Hemp yarn		
2305	Rayon yarn		
2306	Other synthetic fiber yarn		

164 Aggregated Group Classification		72 Aggregated Major Group Classification	
Code	Name of Sector	Code	Name of Sector
2311	Silk and artificial silk fabric	18	Fabric and other ready-made textile goods
2312	Cotton and rayon fabric		
2313	Synthetic fiber fabric		
2314	Woollen fabric		
2315	Hemp fabric		
2316	Yarn and fabric dyeing and finishing (entrusted process-ing only)		
2320	Knitted fabric	19	Knitted fabric
2390	Other ready-made textile goods	20	Other ready-made textile goods
2410	Footwear (except rubber made)	21	Apparel and accessories
2430	Apparel and accessories		
2510	Lumber, plywood and chips	22	Lumber and wood products
2520	Other wood products		
2600	Furniture and fixtures	23	Furniture and fixtures
2711	Pulp	24	Pulp and paper
2712	Paper		
2720	Paper products	25	Paper products
2800	Printing and publishing	26	Printing and publishing
2910	Leather and fur	27	Leather and leather products
2930	Leather products (except leather accessories)		
3000	Rubber products	28	Rubber products

164 Aggregated Group Classification		72 Aggregated Major Group Classification	
Code	Name of Sector	Code	Name of Sector
3111	Inorganic basic chemicals	29	Basic chemicals
3112	Organic basic chemicals (except petrochemicals)		
3113	Organic basic petrochemicals	30	Basic petrochemicals
3115	Chemical fiber materials	31	Chemical fiber materials
3116	Synthetic fiber materials		
3117	Plastic	32	Plastic
3118	Chemical manures and pesticides	33	Chemical manures and pesticides
3119	Other basic chemicals	(Aggregated into 29.)	
3130	Paint, varnish and lacquer	34	Other chemical products
3191	Medicine		
3192	Other chemical products		
3210	Petroleum refinery products	35	Petroleum refinery products
3291	Coal products	36	Coal products
3310	Clay products for construction	37	Non-metallic mineral products
3320	Glass and glass products		
3330	Pottery, china and earthenware		
3340	Cement		
3390	Other non-metallic mineral products		
3411	Pig iron	38	Iron and steel materials
3412	Iron scrap		
3413	Ferro alloy		
3414	Steel ingot		
3415	Hot-rolled steel	39	Basic iron and steel products

151

164 Aggregated Group Classification		72 Aggregated Major Group Classification	
Code	Name of Sector	Code	Name of Sector
3416	Steel pipes and tubes	39	Basic iron and steel products
3417	Cold-finished and plated steel		
3418	Iron and steel casting and forging	40	Iron and steel casting and forging
3421	Non-ferrous metal materials	41	Non-ferrous metal materials
3422	Copper rolling	42	Basic non-ferrous metal products
3423	Aluminum rolling		
3429	Other basic non-ferrous metal products		
3501	Metal products for construction	43	Metal products
3502	Other metal products		
3601	Motors and boilers	44	General machinery
3602	Machine tools and metallic working machinery		
3603	Industrial machinery		
3604	General industrial machinery and equipments		
3605	Office machinery		
3606	Other general machinery		
3701	Heavy electric machinery	45	Electric machinery and appliances
3702	Household electric appliances	46	Light electric appliances
3703	Electronic computers and accessories		
3704	Other light electric appliances		
3705	Electric wires and cables	(Aggregated into 42)	
3810	Ships and their repairing	48	Other transport equipments
3820	Railroad equipments		
3830	Motor vehicles	47	Motor vehicles

164 Aggregated Group Classification		72 Aggregated Major Group Classification	
Code	Name of Sector	Code	Name of Sector
3840	Motor vehicle repairing	47	Motor vehicles
3850	Motorcycles and bicycles		
3860	Aircraft	(Aggregated into 48)	
3890	Other transport equipments		
3910	Scientific, measuring and medical instruments	49	Precision instruments
3920	Photographic and optical instruments		
3930	Watches and clocks		
3990	Other industrial products	50	Other industrial products
4001	New residential building construction	51	Building construction
4002	New non-residential building construction		
4003	Building repairing	52	Building repairing
4004	Public utility construction	53	Civil engineering
4009	Other construction		
5110	Electric power supply	54	Electric power supply
5120	Gas supply	55	Gas supply (including steam and hot water supply)
5130	Steam and hot water supply		
5200	Water supply	56	Water supply (including sanitary service)
5300	Sanitary service		
6110	Wholesale trade	57	Commerce
6120	Retail trade		
6200	Financial service	58	Financial and insurance services
6300	Insurance service		

164 Aggregated Group Classification		72 Aggregated Major Group Classification	
Code	Name of Sector	Code	Name of Sector
6401	Real estate agencies	59	Real estate dealing
6402	House rent		
6403	Real estate rent	60	Real estate rents
7110	National railway transport	61	Transport (excluding self-transport)
7120	National railway electric train transport (passengers)		
7121	Local railway and tramway transport		
7122	Road transport (passengers)		
7123	Self-road transport (passengers)	62	Self-transport
7131	Road transport (freight)	(Aggregated into 61)	
7132	Self-road transport (freight)	(Aggregated into 62)	
7142	Road transport facility services	(Aggregated into 61)	
7150	Ocean transport		
7160	Coastal and inland water transport		
7170	Air transport		
7190	Other transport services		
7200	Storage facility services		
7300	Communication	63	Communication
8101	Public administration (central)	64	Public administration
8102	Public administration (local)		
8210	School education and research	65	Education

154

164 Aggregated Group Classification		72 Aggregated Major Group Classification	
Code	Name of Sector	Code	Name of Sector
8211	Self-education	65	Education
8212	Social education and other education		
8213	Research	66	Research
8214	Self-research		
8220	Health	67	Health and social insurance
8250	Social insurance		
8290	Other public services	68	Other public services
8300	Services to establishments	69	Other services
8302	Rent services		
8400	Amusement services		
8410	Broadcasting		
8501	Drinking and eating places		
8509	Other services to households		
8600	Office supplies	70	Office supplies
8700	Packing	71	Packing
9000	Activities not elsewhere classified	72	Activities not elsewhere classified
9099	Total of intermediate sectors	73	Total of intermediate sectors

164 Aggregated Group Classification		72 Aggregated Major Group Classification	
Code	Name of Sector	Code	Name of Sector
9110	Consumption expenditures outside households (column)	74	Consumption expenditures outside households (column)
9121	Consumption expenditures of households	75	Consumption expenditures of households
9122	Consumption expenditures of private non-profit institutions		
9130	Consumption expenditures of general government	77	Consumption expenditures of general government
9141	Gross domestic fixed capital formation (government)	78	Gross domestic fixed capital formation (government)
9142	Gross domestic fixed capital formation (private)	79	Gross domestic fixed capital formation (private)
9150	Increase in stocks	80	Increase in stocks
9211	Exports	81	Exports
9212	Exports (direct purchase)		
9300	Total final demand	82	Total final demand
9350	Total demand	83	Total demand
9411	(Less) Imports	84	(Less) Imports
9412	(Less) Imports (direct purchase)		
9420	(Less) Customs duties	85	(Less) Customs duties

Final Demand Sector (continued)

164 Aggregated Group Classification		72 Aggregated Major Group Classification	
Code	Name of Sector	Code	Name of Sector
9430	(Less) Commodity taxes on imported goods	86	(Less) Commodity taxes on imported goods
9450	(Less) Total imports	87	Total imports
9500	Total of final demand sectors	88	Total of final demand sectors
9510	Trade margins (wholesale trade)	89	Trade margins
9520	Trade margins (retail trade)		
9610	Domestic transportation fees for goods (national railways)	90	Domestic transportation fees for goods
9620	Domestic transportation fees for goods (local railways)		
9630	Domestic transportation fees for goods (road)		
9640	Domestic transportation fees for goods (coastwise and inland water)		
9650	Domestic transportation fees for goods (air transport)		
9660	Domestic transportation fees for goods (warehousing)		
9700	Domestic products (Gross outputs)	95	Domestic products (Gross outputs)

Value Added Sector

164 Aggregated Group Classification		72 Aggregated Major Group Classification	
Code	Name of Sector	Code	Name of Sector
9110	Consumption expenditures outside households (row)	74	Consumption expenditures outside households (row)
9311	Wages and salaries	75	Compensation of employees
9312	Contribution of employers to social insurance		
9313	Other payments and allowances		
9412	Operating surplus	77	Operating surplus
9420	Depreciation of fixed capital	78	Depreciation of fixed capital
9430	Indirect taxes (except customs duties)	79	Indirect taxes (except customs duties)
9440	(Less) Current subsidies	80	(Less) Current subsidies
9500	Total gross value added	87	Total gross value added
9700	Domestic produces (Gross outputs)	95	Domestic products (Gross outputs)

IX. KENYA

A. GENERAL INFORMATION

The present report is based on *Input-Output Tables for Kenya 1976,* published by the Central Bureau of Statistics of the Ministry of Economic Planning and Community Affairs in October 1979, and on *Sources and Methods Used for the National Accounts of Kenya,* published by the Central Bureau of Statistics of the Ministry of Finance and Planning in December 1977.

Input-output tables for Kenya have been compiled approximately every five years since 1967 by the Central Bureau of Statistics of Kenya, with technical assistance provided by the Chr. Michelsen Institute of Bergen, Norway. The latest table available refers to 1976. A similar basic methodology has been followed in the compilation of the 1967, 1971 and 1976 tables. In fact, the 1976 table has been obtained by updating the 1971 table according to a special variant of the RAS method developed by the Chr. Michelsen Institute. The only difference between the 1971 and 1976 tables refers to the number of intermediate sectors, which in the 1976 table has been increased from 30 to 37. The new sectors are formed by disaggregating government services into five sectors and by setting up petroleum products, water supply and communications as separate sectors; the non-monetary sectors of previous tables have been replaced by a separate traditional sector which excludes all agricultural activities and includes non-monetary output of forestry, fishing, building and construction and ownership of dwellings. All output of this traditional sector is assumed to be produced and consumed by the same units.

Consistency checks were made between the figures used in the input-output tables and the corresponding aggregates in the national accounts. For some sectors, recent revisions effected in the national accounts were incorporated in the input-output tables. However, national accounts figures published in the 1979 Economic Survey included other revisions carried out after the aggregates for the input-output tables had been finalized so that minor differences still remain between the aggregates of the two sources. These differences mainly affect private final consumption, which was estimated as a residual in the input-output tables. Further, imports in the input-output tables are net of re-exports, whereas those published in the national accounts include the value of goods imported but subsequently re-exported.

The main discrepancies between the Kenya input-output table and the SNA recommendations on input-output include: (*a*) the inclusion of two dummy sectors; (*b*) treatment of the activities of private non-profit institutions; (*c*) treatment of the public sector health and education services; (*d*) disaggregation of final demand in tables (ii) and (iii); (*e*) breakdown of value added; (*f*) treatment of imports; (*g*) treatment of by-products and scrap; (*h*) no separate information on commodity taxes is recorded.

B. ANALYTICAL FRAMEWORK

1. *Tables and derived matrices available*

The following basic tables were compiled:
   (i) Input-output table of total flows valued at producers' prices;
   (ii) Input-output table of domestic flows valued at producers' prices;
   (iii) Import matrix;
   (iv) End-use analysis of imports. This table is a more condensed version of the final demand quadrant of table (iii) and identifies separately, within the same classification, the distribution of import duties with respect to end uses.

On the basis of the data mentioned above, the following derived matrices were compiled:
   (i') Technical coefficients based on table (i);
   (ii') Technical coefficients based on table (ii);
   (iii') Technical coefficients based on table (iii);
   (iv') Inverse matrix based on table (i');
   (v') Inverse matrix based on table (ii');
   (vi') Inverse matrix based on table (iii')

It should be noted that different assumptions underlie inverse matrix (iv') and inverse matrices (v') and (vi'). In matrix (iv') products are assumed to be identical regarding their use as intermediate products, no matter whether they are domestically produced or imported. Imports constitute a mere expansion of the existing domestic production of a particular commodity, that is, the assumption is made that it is always possible to expand production without any adverse effects on the balance of payments. However, the adverse effects on the balance of payments are made explicit in the case of inverse matrices based on tables (v') and (vi'). For those tables, unit increases in final demand for domestic products are assumed to be met in fixed proportions from increased domestic production (matrix v') and from increased imports (matrix vi').

All basic tables and derived matrices are presented at a level of disaggregation of 37 x 37 intermediate sectors.

2. *Valuation standards*

All basic tables are valued at producers' prices. Producers' prices are defined to exclude distribution margins, which are treated as payments for services rendered by the distribution sectors. Imports are valued c.i.f., plus import duties. Exports are valued at ex-factory prices, which are obtained by deducting estimated distribution margins from their f.o.b. prices. Contrary to the SNA recommendations, commodity taxes are not recorded separately.

3. *Statistical units and classification standards*

The establishment is the statistical unit adopted for all columns of tables (i), (ii) and (iii), and commodities are the statistical units adopted for the rows of all tables mentioned above.

The overall classification of input-output sectors adopted generally follows ISIC, except for minor variations.

The classification of the intermediate consumption quadrant differs from the SNA recommendations in that:

(a) Two dummy sectors are included in the table, namely, ownership of business premises and unspecified. Output of the unspecified sector includes commodity flows for which there are few reliable data, as well as the imputed service charges of financial institutions;

(b) No distinction is made between activities of the industries and activities of private non-profit institutions;

(c) Health and education services provided by the Government are distributed together with the same kind of services provided by private industries.

Intermediate and primary input of the dummy sectors is incorporated into the structure of production of the remaining sectors of the table and therefore all entries in the columns of those sectors are zero. It should also be noted that, since total output of the non-dummy sectors includes gross earnings from rental and unspecified activities, while deliveries from those sectors exclude deliveries from the dummy sectors, a discrepancy should appear in the total of rows and columns of all sectors of the table except for the dummy sectors. However, this discrepancy is not shown in the table because private consumption of each input-output sector has been estimated as a residual. The resulting overestimation of total private consumption is compensated by recording negative entries in the private consumption of the dummy sectors.

Final demand is disaggregated according to the SNA recommendations in table (i). However, in tables (ii) and (iii), private consumption is combined with changes in stocks to form a single column.

The breakdown of value added adopted differs from that recommended in SNA in that operating surplus is disaggregated into profits and interest paid. Other categories of value added are defined as in SNA.

Imports are classified by commodity and distributed together with domestic production in table (i). In addition, imports are cross-classified by origin and destination in table (iii). In table (iii), imports are defined net of re-exports and therefore no exports column is recorded in this table. Contrary to the SNA recommendations, no distinction is made between complementary and competitive imports.

4. *Treatment and presentation of selected transactions*

Efforts were made to reallocate secondary activities of the establishments to their corresponding characteristic sectors, but only in those cases in which establishments engaged 50 or more employees in those activities. By-products, that is, secondary products technologically linked to the production of characteristic products, and scrap generated in the production process were not transferred to their characteristic sectors.

Non-monetary output and its corresponding input are generally recorded together with monetary output and input in the corresponding input-output sectors, except in the case of forestry, fishing, building and construction, and ownership of dwellings. For the latter sectors, non-monetary output is

included in a separate sector known as the traditional sector.

Output is generally defined on a gross basis, that is, it includes intra-sector consumption of characteristic and non-characteristic goods and services.

Output of the financial sector is defined and distributed as recommended in SNA. The corresponding dummy sector showing the value of imputed service charges is incorporated into the unspecified sector.

Output of the government services sectors includes the activities of the central Government and of firms with 50 per cent or more of their capital owned by the Government. These activities are recorded in the intermediate consumption quadrant. Activities of the East African Community corporations and of firms that are 50 per cent or less owned by the Government are recorded together with similar activities carried out by private enterprises. This procedure is in agreement with the SNA recommendations. The value of output and corresponding input of the East African Community corporations has been allocated among the partner States in proportion to the value of output obtained in each partner State.

5. *Statistical sources and compilation methodology*

The 1976 input-output table was obtained by updating the 1971 table according to a special variant of the RAS method. This model has been developed solely to estimate the elements of the intermediate consumption quadrant. All primary input and final uses, as well as the row and column totals of intermediate uses, are treated by the program as exogenous variables. Information on statistical sources and compilation methodology of these exogenous variables is given below. The elements of the intermediate consumption quadrant of the basic year (that is, the corresponding elements of the 1971 input-output table) are also exogenous variables of the program. However, the decision to expand the number of intermediate sectors in the 1976 input-output table required an extensive reaggregation exercise of the unpublished 59 sectors of the basic 1971 table.

The basic assumption on which the RAS model relies may be summarized as follows. All variations that have affected the matrix of intermediate uses between the base year and the updating year are on the whole the results of certain uniform price and volume changes and these can be represented by simple price and volume indices. The price effect index is assumed to represent the price increase (or decrease) which has affected the intermediate uses of products originating from each sector. The price effects are assumed to vary between the sectors of origin, but to be uniform within each sector of origin, that is, all products that a sector delivers to other sectors are subject to one and the same price effect. The volume effect index is assumed to represent the increase (or decrease) in the volume of each sector's production. As in the previous case, the volume effects are assumed to vary between production sectors but to be uniform within each production sector, that is, all intermediate goods and services that the sector uses in its production process are affected by one and the same volume effect.

The basic assumption just described implies that, in general, the model assumes the non-existence of substitution between different intermediate production factors. However, the model does not entirely exclude the possibility of introducing substitution effects. Such effects are incorporated into the model by a predefinition mechanism. The application of this mechanism is limited by the access to relevant data, and the modest breakdown of intermediate uses by type of goods. Apart from the agricultural sector, which is fully determined exogenously, only the manufacturing sector's uses of transport services and water are based on direct knowledge of elements. In addition to those direct predefinitions, some elements have been adjusted between successive runs of the RAS program.

The values of the volume and price indices are not known *a priori,* and their estimation, which in practice may prove to be quite difficult, is not carried out by the program. This, however, is of no importance, since the above-mentioned assumption of individual but uniform price and volume effects provides enough information for the calculation of the one set of values of the elements of the intermediate consoumption quadrant that conforms to those assumptions.

The Kenyan input-output tables are three-dimensional, that is, each element of the intermediate consumption quadrant is split between use of imports and use of domestic products. Row and column totals are, however, calculated according to the modified RAS method for the total dimension only, that is, for the aggregate of imports and domestic products.

The disaggregation of the total supply matrix into two matrices for imports and domestic production is carried out as follows. Deliveries of imports to intermediate and final demand sectors are based mainly on the end-use analysis of the imports matrix (table (iv)) and the domestic elements are calculated as residuals. In cases where no information is available on end-use totals of table (iv), import matrix elements are estimated from the elements of the total supply matrix (table (i)) on the assumption that the 1971 import fractions, adjusted for import price effects, still hold.

The assumption concerning the relative constancy of import fractions implies that this model assumes no substitution between imports and domestic products. However, the program does not entirely rule out the possibility of introducing substitution effects, for it would be a rare case, indeed, if no such changes in production techniques occurred over the years. Such changes, whether they be due to substitution, new production lines etc., are incorporated into the model by a predefinition mechanism. The predefinition mechanism may also, if the necessary data are available, be used to give special treatment of the largest or most important of the intermediate uses, thereby increasing the quality of the final results.

The calculations of both the technical and the full input coefficients are computerized. These calculation routines are incorporated with the main RAS program in a complete updating program package. Hence, all calculations of elements and coefficients may be carried out directly when all the exogenous variables are given.

6. *Gross output, intermediate consumption and value added*

(a) *Agriculture, forestry and fishing*

Total agricultural output includes: (*a*) sales of crops, fruits and vegetables to marketing boards, co-operatives and processing factories; (*b*) home-grown seed; (*c*) output sold in local markets, home consumed, fed to livestock, and output given free to employees; (*d*) growth in immature permanent crops; and (*e*) land improvement.

The Annual Survey of Employees and Self-employed Persons is the source of information on wages and salaries paid by the agriculture sector. Subtraction of wages and salaries from total value added yields the operating surplus, including consumption of fixed capital. Total value added is estimated as the difference between value of output and intermediate consumption.

As mentioned above, the traditional sector covers non-monetary output of forestry, fishing, building and construction and ownership of dwellings. This output is estimated as indicated in the following paragraphs.

Firewood, poles and posts are the products of non-monetary output of forestry. Production of firewood is based on the number of rural households outside pastoral areas, the estimated number of working days a year devoted to collecting firewood (currently assumed to be 42 working days per year) and the opportunity cost of such labour. The opportunity cost, that is, the wage rate available in alternative employment, is taken as the wage rate for casual female labour on small farms and settlement schemes based on data obtained from the 1971/72 Census of Small Farms. This wage rate is assumed to rise at the same rate as that for large farms, obtained from the Annual Survey of Employees and Self-employed Persons. Intermediate consumption is, of course, nil.

Non-monetary output of fishing consists of fishing undertaken for own consumption. The value of this output, in the absence of any information, is arbitrarily put at 10 per cent of that of monetary output of fishing. Value added is the same as value of output since no input is consumed in this production.

Non-monetary output of building and construction consists of "hut" building, that is, all traditional residential buildings outside the boundaries of municipal and local authority areas. Value of this non-monetary output is taken to be equal to the product of new huts built and building costs. These data are taken from a special study undertaken in 1967. Input consists of posts and poles from forestry output and input from the manufacturing sector. The former is put at 9 per cent of the value of output and the latter at 10 per cent. These percentages are based on *ad hoc* inquiries. Subtraction of intermediate consumption from the value of total output provides the estimate of value added.

Non-monetary output of ownership of dwellings consists of actual and imputed rental of huts. Few, if any, huts in rural areas are in fact rented. An imputed rental for owner-occupied huts has therefore to be derived indirectly. The imputed rental, it is assumed, must be sufficient to account for maintenance costs and consumption of fixed capital, and still yield a "normal" return on capital, that is, on the current value of the stock of huts. Maintenance costs are assumed to be equal to 25 per cent of the value of new huts constructed. Consumption of fixed capital is estimated as being equal to the aggregate value of all traditional dwellings that are replaced during the year. The interest on capital is estimated at an assumed rate of return based on the rate of interest offered on post office deposit accounts of 4 per cent.

Total output of the forestry sector includes that obtained by the Forestry Department of the Kenyan Public Sector and forestry activities of private firms. A special problem exists with regard to the measurement of the forestry output by the

Forestry Department. In countries where planting has been going on regularly for some time, the value of output can be satisfactorily measured by the value of trees felled. But in Kenya, where many of the forests—which take 35 years to mature—are newly planted, this does not seem appropriate. If the value of output is measured solely by the value of trees felled, then for a newly planted forest the value of output will be nil for 34 years and a large figure in the thirty-fifth year when the trees are felled. To avoid this, the value of output of forests planted and maintained by the Forestry Department is measured not only by the value of timber—both mature trees and thinnings—felled, but also by the value of the increase in standing timber or "work in progress". Included too in the value of output of the Forestry Department are expenditures on new planting and royalties, except outlays on new planting of trees during the current year.

Each year the Forestry Department supplies information on the distribution of its planted forests by years to maturity. From this information it is possible at any given time to make an estimate of the increase in the number of hectares of planted forests detailed by "vintage". The physical increase, or decrease, so obtained for each "vintage" in terms of hectares is then valued. A discount factor of 8 per cent is applied to the value of timber on one mature hectare to obtain the then current value of immature timber on a hectare of planted forest for all the "vintages" to the year of maturity. This enables the value of the physical increase in each "vintage" to be calculated.

Information on the forestry activities in the planted and natural forests of large farms is similarly lacking. Estimates, however, of the acreage of planted and of natural forests are available. For planted forests, the acreage is multiplied by an assumed annual offtake of 200 cubic feet per acre to obtain an estimate of the value of the annual offtake. The prices obtained from the Forestry Department are used to value this annual offtake. A similar method is used for natural forests. A base year figure on the value of the offtake per acre was estimated by the Forestry Department. The value of intermediate consumption of large farms for forestry is included with their intermediate consumption for agriculture. Their total intermediate consumption is allocated between agriculture and forestry in proportion to the value of output from those activities.

Output estimates of logging within the forestry reserves are based on licences issued by the Forestry Department to private firms. Information on the number of persons so employed is supplied by the Forestry Department. The total wage bill is derived by multiplying this number by the average wage for casual labour in sawmills obtained from the Annual Survey of Employees and Self-employed Persons. The ratio of the value of output to the wage bill, and that of intermediate consumption to the wage bill, were calculated from an *ad hoc* inquiry. Those ratios are applied to the current wage bill to obtain the required estimates of the value of output and intermediate consumption. A similar method is applied to obtain estimates for logging outside forestry reserves.

The Fisheries Department provides estimates on the value and quantities of the commercial catches brought on shore at the various landing points on both inland waters and the sea. The value of other marine products is added to obtain the total value of output. Input consists of nets, cork and glass buoys, diesel fuel, and the cost of repair and maintenance of boats. The cost of nets is obtained from import figures and

from output figures on local production. These are duly adjusted to purchaser prices by adding import duty and transport and distribution margins. The quantity of diesel fuel used is taken as a fixed percentage of the value of output at constant prices; this figure is then raised in line with the rise in the price of diesel fuel. Maintenance and repair costs are obtained by multiplying the estimated average cost per boat by the number of boats. The average cost per boat is increased annually in line with the landed prices of imported paint.

(b) *Mining and quarrying*

The Annual Survey of Mining and Quarrying is the main source of data for this sector. The survey covers all establishments with 50 or more employees, and a 25 per cent sample of establishments with 20 to 49 employees. Information on the value of output, intermediate consumption and value added is obtained. Comparable information for establishments with 5 to 19 employees was obtained in the 1972 Census of Industry. The output of those small-sized establishments is calculated on the assumption that the rate of growth of their output is the same as that of establishments with 20 to 49 employees. The Annual Survey of Employees and Self-employed Persons provides information on salaries and wages of establishments with under 20 employees. This information, together with the assumption that the ratios of the other components of value added to labour costs remain as in the census year, enables an estimate of value added to be made. Intermediate consumption for those small-sized establishments is the difference between the value of output and value added.

(c) *Manufacturing*

The manufacturing sector consists of three main categories of establishments: urban and large rural private establishments, small rural private establishmnets and public establishments. The latter include parastatal bodies undertaking enterprise activities in the manufacturing sector, manufacturing enterprises in which the public sector has a majority holding in their equity capital, enterprise activities of the central Government and local authorities using technological processes similar to those used by the private sector, and the manufacturing activities of the East African Community corporations that occur in Kenya.

Data on urban and large rural private establishments are obtained from the 1972 Census of Industry, which fully covered all manufacturing establishments with five or more employees in urban areas and all large establishments in rural areas that are included in the *Directory of Industries* of the Central Bureau of Statistics. In addition, a 25 per cent sample of urban establishments with fewer than five employees was also covered in the census. From each establishment covered in the census, information was obtained concerning details on sales, the value of increase in stocks of manufactured but unsold goods, the changes in stocks of raw materials and work in progress, intermediate consumption, labour costs, the consumption of fixed capital, the number of employees etc. The information obtained from the census is updated through the Annual Survey of the Manufacturing Industry. This survey covers all establishments employing 50 or more persons and a 25 per cent sample of the establishments employing 20 to 49 persons. The survey collects information similar to that obtained from the census. Hence, for establishments in these size groups, estimates can be made of the value of output, intermediate consumption and value added and its components. For establishments with under 20 employees, which were covered in the census but are not covered in the annual survey, it is assumed that the annual percentage increase in the value of their output is the same as that for establishments with 20 to 49 employees. The Annual Survey of Employees and Self-employed Persons provides the wage bill for such establishments. A further assumption made is that the other components of value added, for establishments with under 20 employees, have the same ratio to their labour costs as in the census year. Intermediate consumption of those establishments is obtained as a residual, that is, as the difference between the estimated value of output and value added.

Benchmark data on small rural private manufacturing, except the manufacture of indigenous beers, were obtained from the Survey of Small-scale Rural Enterprises, held in 1972, which included information on sales and the value of input. These data were updated with an index of gross domestic output of the traditional economy. Benchmark estimates of output and production of indigenous beer were based on the results of the Central Province Household Survey undertaken in 1963, which indicated that an average of 10 shillings per household per week was spent on traditional alcoholic beverages. Multiplication of that figure by the number of rural households provided an estimate of the value of output. Intermediate consumption was assumed to be equal to 25 per cent of the value of output. The number of persons engaged in making beer was derived from the estimated volume of production and an assumed production of 780 gallons per person a year. An average price of 50 cents a pint was used to calculate the volume of output. Only 20 per cent of the persons engaged in the industry were assumed to be paid employees. The average wage of casual employees in agriculture—obtained from the Annual Survey of Employees and Self-employed Persons—was used to calculate the labour cost of paid employees. Subtraction of that figure from value added provided an estimate of operating surplus. As with other sectors and activities, the consumption of fixed capital is included in the operating surplus. These various estimates—of the value of output, intermediate consumption and labour costs—are extrapolated annually in line with the index of the estimated gross domestic product of the traditional economy mentioned above. The estimates for this subsector are of poor quality and may be too low. Household surveys recently undertaken will, it is hoped, give some clues on the extent of this underestimation.

The required information for parastatal bodies and for firms with a majority holding of equity capital by the public sector are obtained directly from the enterprises themselves, and that for the Government Printer and the Ministry of Works from the published accounts of the central Government. The Ministry of Works also supplies supplementary information on an annual basis. The sources of information on the East African Community corporations are their annual reports and the data provided by answers to a special national accounts questionnaire, which they complete each year.

(d) Construction

Data on building and construction of the private sector are taken from the 1972 Census of Industry, which covered all establishments of building and construction contractors em-

ploying five or more persons and a 25 per cent sample of those employing fewer than five persons. Detailed information is given in the census about value of output, intermediate consumption, labour costs, and other aggregates related to production. There is always a possibility of duplication in the information on production supplied by the contractors, as contractors subcontract out work to other contractors. Information on the value of work subcontracted was specifically obtained by the census to obviate this. In addition, each year the survey of building contractors collects information similar to that collected in the census from all contractors with 50 or more employees, and from a 25 per cent sample of contractors with 20 to 49 employees. Accordingly, for contractors in these size groups, estimates can be made of the value of output, intermediate consumption, value added, and the components of value added. For contractors having under 20 employees, it is assumed that the percentage change in the value of their output since the census year is the same as that of contractors with 20 to 49 employees. The wage bill of these small contractors is supplied by the Annual Survey of Employees and Self-employed Persons. The assumption is also made that the other components of their value added remain in the same ratio to their labour costs as in the census year. Intermediate consumption for these small contractors is obtained as the difference between the estimates of the value of output and value added. Also included is the value of residential and non-residential building and other construction work undertaken on large farms as reported in the annual census of large farms. Excluded from the latter is the value of building work undertaken on large farms by contractors to avoid double counting. It was assumed that, of the total building and construction work undertaken on large farms, 14 per cent was contracted out. This figure is based on an *ad hoc* inquiry made with large farms. Expenditure by large farms on maintenance of building and construction works is assumed to be 10 per cent of their annual own-account expenditure on building and construction. Labour costs are estimated as being equal to 20 per cent of the value of own-account construction. This figure is based on the proportion of contractors' labour costs to the value of output for similar construction work. Intermediate consumption of large farms is calculated as the difference between their value of output and labour costs, that is, the assumption is made that operating surplus is nil.

Data on the public subsector of the building and construction sector are obtained as follows. The East African Power and Lighting Company annually provides the information needed on the value of its own-account building and construction activities. The source of information for the Ministry of Works is the accounts of the central Government, supplemented by special information from the Ministry of Works itself. The value of output—equal to total expenditures on goods and services and personal emoluments—is obtained from the recurrent and development accounts. The value of output is then broken down by economic activity into the value of manufacturing output, the value of building and construction and the value of new purchases of machinery and equipment. This is done by allocating all recognizable expenditure to one of these categories and prorating the headquarters expenditure on personal emoluments and other non-specific expenditures in proportion to the value of the expenditures already allocated. From the value of building and construction so derived is deducted the value of building and construction work contracted out in order to obtain the value of output on own account. To this value of output of own-account building are added two imputed values, namely, the employer's contribution to pensions and the value of consumption of fixed capital. The latter is based on the average replacement cost of lorries and road building equipment during the previous three years. Further, an analysis of the relevant expenditures, together with some additional prorations, enables the value of output to be split between expenditures on residential and non-residential building, on the one hand, and on roads and other construction works, on the other. The estimates of the value of own-account building and construction work undertaken by the Forestry Department are made from the information supplied annually by the Department. All local authorities are requested to supply annual information on the value of residential and non-residential buildings and other construction work undertaken and labour costs. Maintenance expenditure is assumed to be equal to 10 per cent of the value of such capital expenditure. The two together give the total value of output of building and construction by local authorities. The value of work contracted out is estimated at 56.8 per cent of the value of output; this is deducted from the total output to obtain the value of output of own-account work. This percentage deduction is based on an *ad hoc* inquiry. Intermediate consumption is calculated as the difference between the value of own-account output and labour costs. No imputations are made for the consumption of fixed capital.

The value of output so derived obviously needs to tie in with the estimate of capital expenditures on building and construction obtained from the expenditure side. In fact, there always is a discrepancy. The first step in eliminating the discrepancy is to estimate the maintenance component in the value of output of building and construction, since it is impossible for building contractors and others engaged in this activity to subdivide realistically their output into its maintenance and capital formation components. Hence, alternative means are adopted to estimate the maintenance component. The value of maintenance on residential buildings is taken to be equal to the maintenance input into ownership of dwellings. Maintenance expenditure on roads and non-residential buildings owned by the central Government is obtained from its accounts. The only missing estimate then left to be computed is the value of maintenance on private non-residential buildings, which is assumed to be equal to 2 per cent of the estimated replacement cost on those buildings. The various estimates of maintenance—on residential and non-residential buildings and on other construction works—are then added to obtain the overall estimate of the value of maintenance. This estimate of maintenance is added to the estimate of capital formation in buildings and construction works obtained from the expenditure side. The estimates of capital formation from the expenditure side are adopted since they are believed to be more reliable than those from the production side. The final step is to revise the original estimates of intermediate consumption and value added. These are multiplied by the ratio of the revised value of the output of building and construction to their original value.

(e) *Electricity, water supply*

All data on the electricity sector—value of output, intermediate consumption, personal emoluments, consumption of fixed capital etc.—are provided by the two enterprises undertaking generation and distribution of electricity in the country.

In the monetary economy, the collection, processing and distribution of water is mainly a public sector activity undertaken by the Ministry of Water Development, the Mombasa Water Supply, the Mombasa Pipeline Board, and by the water departments of various local authorities. A small amount of activity is also undertaken by private enterprises. The relevant information on the operation of the public sector institutions and enterprises engaged in this activity is readily available from their published accounts. The private concerns are covered by the Annual Survey of Employees and Self-employed Persons, from which information about their total labour costs is obtained. It is assumed that the ratios of the value of output and of intermediate consumption to labour costs prevailing for the water departments of municipal councils are also relevant to those private concerns. For the traditional economy, the value of output is based on the number of rural households outside pastoral areas, the estimated number of woman-hours per household spent a year in drawing water and the opportunity cost of such labour. The alternative to drawing water is taken to be farm work, and the average wage for casual adult females working on small farms and settlement schemes—the same rate as used for firewood collection—is taken to measure the opportunity cost. Since intermediate consumption is irrelevant, value added equals the value of output. The imputation is only made for rural households living in non-pastoral areas, since in pastoral areas no alternative employment is thought to exist.

(f) *Trade, hotels, cafés, restaurants*

Data on wholesale and retail trade (other than petrol and oil products) were obtained from the 1971 Survey of Distribution, the National Accounts Questionnaire and the annual Trade Report of the East African Customs and Excise Department. The annual estimates of output and value added are based on the breakdown of expenditure of trade enterprises in four categories of throughputs, namely, domestic manufactured goods, domestic agricultural products, imports from Uganda and the United Republic of Tanzania and imports from the rest of the world. Estimates are calculated as follows. First, the ratio of each throughput to its total domestic production or import are estimated for the base year. These ratios are then applied to the relevant 1976 totals of flows of goods to obtain the value of each of these throughputs in that year. Next, these 1976 values are aggregated and the aggregate is adjusted for the value of the change in stocks in 1976 obtained from the quarterly Business Expectations Enquiry. The base year ratio of value added to the value of aggregate throughputs is then applied to the adjusted value of aggregate throughputs for 1976 to provide an estimate of value for that year. This estimate is then subdivided into its components—personal emoluments and operating surplus—using the proportion composition of the base year. Finally, output is estimated using the base year ratio of value added to output. These calculations are all based on the assumption that the base year ratios remain unchanged.

Data on wholesale distribution of petroleum and oil products are provided directly by the small number of firms engaged in this activity. For the firms engaged in retail distribution of petrol and oil products, base year figures on the value of their output, intermediate consumption, value added, and the components of value added were obtained from the 1971 Survey of Distribution. The base year estimate of value added is extrapolated forward on the basis of the value of petroleum and oil products entering the Kenya market in 1976. This is estimated as the sum of the total value of imports of final products, plus domestic production, less the value of transfers to Uganda and to the United Republic of Tanzania, plus import duties and sales tax on the value of products entering the Kenya market. Value added is subdivided into its components on the assumption that the composition of value added remains proportionally the same as in the base year. Similarly, output is estimated on the assumption that the ratio of the value of output to value added remains the same as in the base year.

The 1975 Survey of Services provided the benchmark information on cafés and restaurants in urban areas and also for the larger cafés and restaurants in rural areas. The data were analysed separately for hotels, restaurants and cafés with 50 or more employees, 20 to 49 employees, and zero to 19 employees; and the value of output, intermediate consumption, value added and the wage bill were determined for each size class. The Annual Survey of Employees and Self-employed Persons provides figures on the wage bill in 1976. Again, 1975 base year ratios—of the wage bill to value added and of value added to the value of output—for each size class are applied to the 1976 wage bill to estimate the relevant aggregate for that year.

(g) Transport, storage, communication

Data on railway, ocean and coastal water, inland water, and air transport are obtained directly from the public and private enterprises engaged in those activities. Data on urban, suburban and inter-urban highway passenger transport are mainly obtained from an annual survey of firms with 20 or more employees operating taxis, minibuses and passenger-carrying utility vans. For each type of vehicle, figures are obtained on the value of output, intermediate consumption and labour costs. Ratios of the value of output and intermediate consumption to labour costs are then calculated and these are applied to the estimated labour costs of unsurveyed firms in each category. Again, estimates of these labour costs are derived from the number of such vehicles registered, the number of operators per vehicle, and an average wage rate supplied by the Annual Survey of Employees and Self-employed Persons. The numbers of operators per taxi, minibus and lorry are put at 1.04, 1.10 and 1.40, respectively. Those averages are based on information collected in a benchmark inquiry a few years ago. The sum of the value of the surveyed and unsurveyed firms, and similarly of their intermediate consumption, provides the needed estimates for the activity. Value added is derived as the difference between the value of output and intermediate consumption. Beforehand, however, 25 per cent of the labour costs of the unsurveyed enterprises is deducted form the total labour costs of all enterprises to take account of the number of operators thought to be self-employed. It is this adjusted labour cost that is deducted from value added to obtain the operating surplus. An almost identical method is applied to obtain the estimates of output and value added of private enterprises engaged in freight transport by road.

Data on supporting services to water and air transport provided by local offices of foreign enterprises are obtained through an annual questionnaire. Ratios of the value of output and intermediate consumption to their labour costs are calcualted from it. Those ratios are then applied to the estimated labour costs of the unsurveyed offices, which are obtained from the Annual Survey of Employees and Self-employed Persons. The local offices of foreign shipping lines are treated as agents of their foreign principals. Accordingly, value added consists of wages and salaries only. Consumption of fixed capital is assumed to be insignificant in value.

All private booking and travel agencies with 20 or more employees are covered in an annual survey that provides information on their operations. The usual ratios of the value of output and intermediate consumption to labour costs are calculated and then applied to the labour costs of the unsurveyed firms obtained from the Annual Survey of Employees and Self-employed Persons.

The required information on storage and warehousing enterprises with 20 or more employees in this activity is obtained directly. The estimates on the operations of the smaller enterprises are derived by applying the usual ratios, calculated from the information supplied by the large enterprises, to their labour costs obtained through the Annual Survey of Employees and Self-employed Persons. Data on the communication sector are provided by the East African Posts and Telecommunications Corporations, by far the largest contributor to the value added of this activity.

(h) Services

Data on financial institutions, insurance, real estate and business services are obtained from the following sources: special questionnaires circulated among commercial banks by the central bank, the Annual Survey of Employees and Self-employed Persons, income tax statistics, the annual survey of insurance companies, and the 1975 Survey of Services, the results of which are extrapolated forward in line with the ratio of the 1976 labour bill to that of 1975.

The ownership of dwellings sector is subdivided into two subsectors—monetary and traditional—to facilitate the computation of output, intermediate consumption and value added. Output of the monetary sector is provided by the results of an annual rent survey. Rental values of owner-occupied dwellings are considered to be equal to the average rent paid on equivalent rented properties in the same locality. Intermediate consumption of this monetary sector covers maintenance expenditures, which are put at 10 per cent of aggregate rental for privately owned dwellings and 5 per cent for those owned by the central Government, municipalities and the East African Community. Non-monetary output for owner-occupied huts was described above.

Data on the social and personal services sector are obtained from the 1975 Survey of Services, which provides information on salaries and wages, employment, intermediate consumption and capital expenditures. These data are updated to 1976 by multiplying, on a service-by-service basis, the 1975 estimates by the ratio of the 1976 wage bill to that in 1975. Information on the 1976 wage bill is provided by the Annual Survey of Employees and Self-employed Persons. Data on services in the rural sector were based on the 1972 Survey of Small-scale Rural Enterprises, which are updated to 1976 on the assumption that their rate of growth is two thirds of that of the corresponding activities in urban areas.

Government services cover general administration, education, health and defence. General administration includes the National Social Security Fund as well as the Government Agricultural Service, while education and health also embrace the private enterprises engaged in those fields. The main sources of information are the accounts of the central Government, local authorities, the East African Community (general fund services) and the relevant statutory boards.

The value of output of government services is mainly for the Government's own use, and to that extent is included in general government consumption. Some part, however, is used by industry as intermediate consumption or is purchased by households and therefore included as private consumption. Households, for example, make purchases of education and health services.

7. *Final demand*

Gross fixed capital formation is classified by sector of origin. The end-use analysis of imports provides estimates of imports of capital goods. The locally produced element of capital formation is estimated from details of production of various commodities. The value of land improvement, plantation development and increase in cattle herds is included, while the increase in forest reserves is treated as an addition to stocks.

The total value of private consumption is derived as the residual when all other end-use categories and intermediate deliveries have been calculated. Sector-specific information has been made available for the changes in stocks through special studies. However, it has not been possible to undertake satisfactory breakdowns of these figures into imported and domestically produced goods mainly because of the possibility that changes of opposite signs in these two categories may occur in the same sector. Therefore, in the imports and domestic production tables, changes in stocks are recorded together with private consumption. In the table on the total supply of goods and services, joint estimates of sector-specific private consumption and intermediate use are derived residually after the other components of end uses have been completed. The allocation of each sector's output to each one of these two categories has been made possible by combining all relevant information from published and unpublished sources. For a few sectors, however, the allocation was based on the nature of the sector's products.

The Annual Trade Report and the balance-of-payments estimates are the sources of information for exports and imports. Exports are reduced from f.o.b. values to ex-factory prices by deducting estimated distribution margins, which are obtained on the basis of survey results.

For tables, see end of Volume.

X. MALAYSIA

A. GENERAL INFORMATION

The present report is based on *Input-Output Tables, Malaysia*, published by the Department of Statistics.

Input-output tables for Malaysia have been compiled for the years 1960, 1965, 1970 and 1978. The first two tables are not directly comparable to the one referring to 1970, mainly because the general limitations of the statistical data then available limited the detail at which those tables could be compiled. The present report refers to the 1978 table.

The adoption by Malaysia of the new System of National Accounts for the years 1969 onward greatly simplified the compilation of the 1970 and 1978 input-output tables, since the new series of Malaysian national accounts are based on the commodity flow approach. Discrepancies between the input-output estimates and those reported in SNA are very minor and generally the result of rounding.

The main discrepancy between the Malaysian table and the SNA recommendations on input-output is the breakdown of value added.

B. ANALYTICAL FRAMEWORK

1. *Tables and derived matrices available*

The following basic tables were compiled:

  (i)   Absorption matrix at approximate basic values;
  (ii) Make matrix at approximate basic values;
  (iii) Input-output table of the commodity-by-commodity type valued at approximate basic values. This table is obtained as described below;
  (iv) Input-output table of the industry-by-industry type valued at approximate basic values.
  (v)   Imports matrix;
  (vi) Table of commodity taxes on domestic products;
  (vii) Table of commodity taxes on imports;
  (viii) Tables of trade margins on domestic commodities and on imported commodities.

The maximum size of the tables is governed by the national accounts classification framework. This classification distinguishes a total of 750 commodities that are the characteristic output of 105 sectors. For internal working purposes, all tables produced were of this size. However, for reasons related to computation, time and resource constraints, these were aggregated to a 60 x 60 sector table size.

2. *Valuation standards*

All transactions as shown in the tables are valued at approximate basic values. Taxes levied on commodities are shown in row entries of tables (i), (ii) and (iii), as well as in tables (v) and (vi). Hence, any operations requiring the use of producers' values can be met simply by adding up the corresponding cells in the relevant tables. Exports are valued f.o.b. and imports are valued c.i.f.

3. *Statistical units and classification standards*

Since much of the basic statistics available for the compilation of the input-output table provide information on the destination of output to main purchasers of commodities, commodities were the basic statistical units adopted for rows and columns of all tables, except for columns of table (i) and rows of table (ii), in which the establishment is the basic statistical unit.

All production activities were originally classified into 105 sectors, which are based on ISIC. The output of those sectors was then classified into 750 commodity groups, which were defined so as to meet as closely as possible the fundamental input-output assumptions of homogeneity and proportionality.

The classification of value added differs from the SNA recommendations in that only salaries and wages are disaggregated from total value added.

Adopting the SNA recommendations, distinction was made between competitive and complementary imports. All imports had to be regarded as complementary because of major problems associated with their classification into those two categories. Imports were recorded in a row of tables (i) and (ii), and were also cross-classified by origin and destination in table (iv).

4. *Treatment and presentation of selected transactions*

Outputs of secondary products were transferred to their corresponding characteristic sectors on the basis of the information provided by the make matrix. Their corresponding inputs were transferred on the basis of the industry technology assumption.

The activities of the producers of government services were treated as recommended in SNA, that is, those activities were recorded in the intermediate consumption quadrant of the table.

Output of the financial sector was defined and distributed as recommended in SNA. A dummy sector—"imputed bank service charges"—was included in the intermediate consumption quadrant of the table to record the imputed service charges of this sector.

Non-monetary output and its corresponding input were generally recorded together with monetary output and input in the corresponding input-output sector.

Output was generally defined on a gross basis, that is, it includes intra-sector consumption of goods and services.

MALAYSIA
INPUT-OUTPUT TABLES
1978

Source: *Input-Output Tables, Malaysia, 1978,*
Department of Statistics, Malaysia.

JADUAL 1.1 – MATRIKS 'MAKE' PADA NILAI–NILAI ASAS, 1978. KOMODITI X AKTIVITI (RIBU RINGGIT)

Table 1.1 – Make Matrix At Basic Values, 1978. Commodity x Activity (Thousand Ringgit)

COL / ROW	1 OTH AGRIC	2 RUBBER PLN	3 OIL PALM	4 LIVESTOCK	5 FORESTRY	6 FISHING	7 PETROL MIN	8 DAIRY PROD	9 VEG FRUIT	10 OIL & FATS
1 OTH AGRIC	1633639.	0.	0.	0.	0.	0.	0.	0.	0.	151.
2 RUBBER PLN	0.	1253582.	0.	0.	0.	0.	0.	0.	0.	0.
3 OIL PALM	0.	0.	831909.	0.	0.	0.	0.	0.	0.	0.
4 LIVESTOCK	0.	0.	0.	933774.	0.	0.	0.	0.	0.	0.
5 FORESTRY	0.	0.	0.	0.	1766114.	0.	0.	0.	0.	0.
6 FISHING	0.	0.	0.	0.	0.	1626970.	0.	0.	0.	0.
7 PETROL MIN	0.	0.	0.	0.	0.	0.	4084051.	0.	0.	0.
8 DAIRY PROD	0.	0.	0.	0.	0.	0.	0.	772597.	4710.	0.
9 VEG FRUIT	0.	0.	0.	0.	0.	0.	0.	1048.	384208.	0.
10 OIL 4 FATS	0.	0.	937906.	0.	0.	0.	0.	242.	7559.	2600688.
11 GRAIN MILL	113141.	0.	0.	0.	0.	0.	0.	0.	0.	0.
12 BAKER COMP	0.	0.	0.	0.	0.	0.	0.	0.	130.	620.
13 OTH FOODS	10321.	0.	0.	0.	0.	0.	0.	659.	11871.	523.
14 ANMAL FEED	0.	0.	0.	0.	0.	0.	0.	6618.	34194.	1117.
15 BEVERAGES	0.	0.	0.	0.	0.	0.	0.	0.	0.	0.
16 TOBACCO	0.	0.	0.	0.	0.	0.	0.	5338.	1006.	25.
17 TEXTILES	0.	0.	0.	0.	0.	0.	0.	0.	0.	0.
18 WEARNG APL	0.	0.	0.	0.	0.	0.	0.	0.	0.	0.
19 SAWMILLS	0.	0.	0.	0.	0.	0.	0.	0.	0.	0.
20 FURN FIXT	0.	0.	0.	0.	0.	0.	0.	0.	0.	0.
21 PAPER PPRT	0.	0.	0.	0.	0.	0.	0.	8.	0.	12.
22 INDST CHEM	0.	0.	0.	0.	0.	0.	0.	0.	0.	26.
23 PAINTS ETC	0.	0.	0.	0.	0.	0.	0.	0.	0.	26.
24 OT CHM PRD	0.	0.	0.	0.	0.	0.	0.	0.	0.	0.
25 PETROL PRD	0.	0.	0.	0.	0.	0.	0.	2152.	24083.	2296.
26 RUBBER PRO	0.	1033246.	0.	0.	0.	0.	0.	0.	0.	0.
27 RUBBER PRD	0.	0.	0.	0.	0.	0.	0.	0.	0.	505.
28 PLSTIC PRD	0.	0.	0.	0.	0.	0.	0.	0.	0.	0.
29 GLASS PROD	0.	0.	0.	0.	0.	0.	0.	0.	0.	0.
30 CEMENT	0.	0.	0.	0.	0.	0.	122.	0.	0.	0.
31 N METALLIC	0.	0.	0.	0.	0.	0.	0.	0.	0.	0.
32 BASIC MTL	0.	0.	0.	0.	0.	0.	0.	0.	0.	0.
33 OTH METAL	0.	0.	0.	0.	0.	0.	0.	0.	0.	0.
34 N ELEC MAC	35.	535.	6587.	0.	0.	0.	0.	0.	0.	0.
35 ELECT MACH	0.	0.	0.	0.	0.	0.	0.	0.	0.	0.
36 MOTOR VEH	1.	150.	0.	0.	0.	0.	0.	0.	0.	0.
37 OTH TRANSP	0.	0.	0.	0.	0.	0.	0.	0.	0.	10.
38 C MFG PROD	0.	0.	0.	0.	0.	0.	0.	0.	0.	0.
39 ELECTRCITY	0.	0.	0.	0.	0.	0.	0.	0.	0.	0.
40 WATER	0.	0.	0.	0.	0.	0.	134.	0.	64.	217.
41 CNSTRCTION	5129.	11975.	11711.	0.	0.	0.	0.	0.	0.	1667.
42 TRADE	0.	0.	0.	0.	0.	0.	11.	3120.	536.	1667.
43 HOTEL ETC	0.	0.	0.	0.	0.	0.	11.	442.	4094.	6315.
44 TRANSPORT	0.	0.	0.	0.	0.	0.	0.	0.	0.	0.
45 COMMUNICAT	0.	0.	0.	0.	0.	0.	1253.	0.	65.	684.
46 FINANCE	0.	0.	0.	0.	0.	0.	0.	0.	0.	0.
47 INSURANCE	0.	0.	0.	0.	0.	0.	0.	0.	0.	0.
48 DWELLINGS	0.	0.	0.	0.	0.	0.	0.	0.	0.	0.
49 BUSIN SERV	0.	0.	0.	0.	0.	0.	438.	275.	564.	73.
50 PRIV EDUC	0.	0.	0.	0.	0.	0.	258.	70.	85.	1402.
51 PR HEALTH	0.	0.	0.	0.	0.	0.	0.	0.	0.	0.
52 CULT SERV	0.	0.	0.	0.	0.	0.	0.	0.	0.	0.
53 REPAIR VEH	0.	0.	0.	0.	0.	0.	0.	0.	0.	0.
54 PERSON SER	0.	0.	0.	0.	0.	0.	0.	0.	0.	0.
55 PUB ADMIN	0.	0.	0.	0.	0.	0.	0.	0.	0.	0.
56 GOV EDUC	0.	0.	0.	0.	0.	0.	0.	0.	0.	0.
57 GOV HEALTH	0.	0.	0.	0.	0.	0.	0.	0.	0.	0.
58 O GOV SERV	0.	0.	0.	0.	0.	0.	0.	0.	0.	0.
59 PRI NP SER	0.	0.	0.	0.	0.	0.	0.	0.	0.	0.
60 OTHER SERV	0.	0.	0.	0.	0.	0.	0.	0.	0.	0.
61 MISCELLAN	0.	0.	0.	0.	0.	0.	0.	0.	0.	0.
62 GROSS OUTP	1733868.	2375508.	1790011.	933774.	1766114.	1626970.	4086267.	792569.	473159.	2616153.

JADUAL 1.1 – MATRIKS 'MAKE' PADA NILAI–NILAI ASAS, 1978. KOMODITI X AKTIVITI (RIBU RINGGIT) – SAMB.

Table 1.1 – Make Matrix At Basic Values, 1978. Commodity x Activity (Thousand Ringgit) – Cont'd.

COL	11 GRAIN MILL	12 BAKER CONF	13 OTH FOODS	14 ANMAL FEED	15 BEVERAGES	16 TOBACCO	17 TEXTILES	18 WEARNG APL	19 SAWMILLS	20 FURN FIXT
ROW										
1 OTH AGRIC	0.	0.	65.	0.	0.	0.	0.	0.	0.	0.
2 RUBBER PLN	0.	0.	0.	0.	0.	0.	0.	0.	0.	0.
3 OIL PALM	0.	0.	0.	0.	0.	0.	0.	0.	0.	0.
4 LIVESTOCK	0.	0.	25.	0.	0.	0.	0.	0.	0.	0.
5 FORESTRY	0.	0.	0.	0.	0.	0.	0.	0.	78119.	0.
6 FISHING	0.	0.	0.	0.	0.	0.	0.	0.	0.	0.
7 PETROL MIN	0.	0.	0.	0.	0.	0.	0.	0.	0.	0.
8 DAIRY PROD	0.	195.	288.	0.	0.	0.	0.	0.	0.	0.
9 VEG FRUIT	0.	7275.	1946.	0.	2757.	0.	0.	0.	0.	0.
10 OIL A FATS	2163.	681.	246.	0.	0.	0.	0.	0.	0.	0.
11 GRAIN MILL	425829.	7732.	2041.	2130.	0.	0.	0.	0.	0.	0.
12 BAKER CONF	0.	117597.	11385.	0.	181.	0.	0.	0.	0.	0.
13 OTH FOODS	206.	863.	542775.	0.	220.	0.	9604.	0.	0.	0.
14 ANMAL FEED	0.	0.	0.	327033.	0.	0.	0.	0.	0.	0.
15 BEVERAGES	0.	37.	2647.	0.	291647.	0.	0.	0.	0.	0.
16 TOBACCO	0.	0.	0.	0.	0.	514774.	0.	0.	0.	0.
17 TEXTILES	0.	0.	0.	0.	0.	0.	965394.	55822.	0.	244.
18 WEARNG APL	0.	0.	0.	0.	0.	0.	196.	385268.	0.	0.
19 SAWMILLS	0.	0.	0.	0.	0.	0.	0.	0.	1647931.	5066.
20 FURN FIXT	1.	0.	0.	8.	11.	11.	32.	25.	3189.	127598.
21 PAPER PRNT	0.	0.	0.	0.	0.	63.	263.	96.	144.	0.
22 INDST CHEM	0.	0.	0.	0.	0.	2816.	0.	0.	0.	0.
23 PAINTS ETC	0.	0.	0.	0.	0.	0.	0.	0.	0.	0.
24 OT CHM PRD	0.	117.	5651.	0.	0.	0.	0.	0.	0.	0.
25 PETROL PRD	0.	0.	0.	0.	0.	0.	0.	0.	0.	0.
26 RUBBER PRD	41.	0.	0.	0.	0.	0.	0.	0.	0.	0.
27 RUBBER PRD	0.	0.	0.	0.	101.	0.	0.	0.	0.	538.
28 PLSTIC PRO	0.	0.	0.	0.	0.	0.	0.	784.	0.	166.
29 GLASS PROD	0.	0.	0.	0.	0.	0.	0.	0.	0.	0.
30 CEMENT	0.	0.	0.	0.	0.	0.	0.	0.	0.	0.
31 N METALLIC	0.	0.	0.	0.	0.	0.	0.	0.	75.	0.
32 BASIC MTL	0.	0.	0.	0.	0.	0.	0.	0.	20.	1454.
33 OTH METAL	0.	0.	0.	0.	0.	0.	0.	0.	0.	0.
34 N ELIC MAC	31.	0.	6.	2.	2.	0.	276.	317.	288.	0.
35 ELECT MACH	0.	0.	0.	0.	0.	0.	0.	0.	0.	0.
36 MOTOR VEH	1.	0.	0.	0.	1.	11.	43.	38.	54.	3.
37 OTH TRANSP	0.	0.	0.	0.	0.	0.	0.	0.	0.	0.
38 O MFG PROD	0.	0.	0.	0.	0.	0.	0.	30.	103.	15.
39 ELECTRCITY	0.	0.	263.	0.	0.	0.	0.	0.	378.	0.
40 WATER	0.	0.	0.	0.	0.	0.	0.	0.	0.	0.
41 CNSTRCTION	1920.	464.	977.	242.	923.	180.	688.	344.	11625.	1121.
42 TRADE	3998.	773.	1673.	4143.	1088.	6158.	3230.	1494.	8148.	1220.
43 HOTEL ETC	0.	0.	0.	0.	20.	0.	0.	0.	0.	0.
44 TRANSPORT	218.	0.	4.	42.	20.	0.	45.	289.	12101.	36.
45 COMMUNICAT	0.	0.	0.	0.	0.	0.	0.	0.	0.	0.
46 FINANCE	0.	0.	0.	0.	0.	0.	0.	0.	0.	0.
47 INSURANCE	0.	0.	0.	0.	0.	0.	0.	0.	0.	0.
48 DWELLINGS	217.	137.	301.	20.	51.	186.	209.	117.	2499.	358.
49 BUSIN SERV	296.	193.	237.	24.	65.	18.	777.	21.	1090.	84.
50 PRIV EDUC	0.	0.	0.	0.	0.	0.	0.	0.	0.	0.
51 PR HEALTH	0.	0.	0.	0.	0.	0.	0.	0.	0.	0.
52 CULT SERV	0.	0.	0.	0.	0.	0.	0.	0.	0.	0.
53 REPAIR VEH	0.	0.	0.	0.	0.	0.	0.	0.	0.	0.
54 PERSON SER	0.	0.	0.	0.	0.	0.	0.	0.	0.	0.
55 PUB ADMIN	0.	0.	0.	0.	0.	0.	0.	0.	0.	0.
56 GOV EDUC	0.	0.	0.	0.	0.	0.	0.	0.	0.	0.
57 GOV HEALTH	0.	0.	0.	0.	0.	0.	0.	0.	0.	0.
58 O GOV SERV	0.	0.	0.	0.	0.	0.	0.	0.	0.	0.
59 PRI NP SER	0.	0.	0.	0.	0.	0.	0.	0.	0.	0.
60 OTHER SERV	0.	0.	0.	0.	0.	0.	0.	0.	0.	0.
61 MISCELLAN	0.	0.	0.	0.	0.	0.	0.	0.	0.	0.
62 GROSS OUTP	434907.	336124.	663732.	333344.	297087.	524182.	979757.	444645.	1765764.	137896.

JADUAL 1.1 – MATRIKS 'MAKE' PADA NILAI-NILAI ASAS, 1978. KOMODITI X AKTIVITI (RIBU RINGGIT) – SAMB.

Table 1.1 – Make Matrix At Basic Values, 1978. Commodity x Activity (Thousand Ringgit) – Cont'd.

COL / ROW	21 PAPER PRNT	22 INDST CHEM	23 PAINTS ETC	24 OT CHM PRD	25 PETROL PRD	26 RUBBER PRO	27 RUBBER PRD	28 PLSTIC PRD	29 GLASS PROD	30 CEMENT
1 OTH AGRIC	0.	0.	0.	0.	0.	0.	0.	0.	0.	0.
2 RUBBER PL	0.	0.	0.	0.	0.	0.	0.	0.	0.	0.
3 OIL PALM	0.	0.	0.	0.	0.	0.	0.	0.	0.	0.
4 LIVESTOCK	0.	0.	0.	0.	0.	0.	0.	0.	0.	0.
5 FORESTRY	0.	1519.	0.	184.	0.	0.	0.	0.	0.	0.
6 FISHING	0.	0.	0.	0.	0.	0.	0.	0.	0.	0.
7 PETROL MIN	0.	2144.	0.	0.	0.	0.	0.	0.	1869.	491.
8 DAIRY PROD	0.	0.	0.	0.	0.	0.	0.	0.	0.	0.
9 VEG FRUIT	0.	0.	0.	0.	0.	0.	0.	0.	0.	0.
10 OIL & FATS	0.	0.	0.	837.	0.	0.	0.	0.	0.	0.
11 GRAIN MILL	0.	0.	0.	0.	0.	0.	0.	0.	0.	0.
12 BAKER CONF	17.	0.	0.	1088.	0.	0.	0.	0.	0.	0.
13 OTH FOODS	0.	0.	0.	0.	0.	0.	0.	314.	0.	0.
14 ANMAL FEED	0.	0.	0.	0.	0.	0.	0.	779.	0.	0.
15 BEVERAGES	0.	0.	0.	0.	0.	0.	0.	0.	0.	0.
16 TOBACCO	0.	0.	0.	0.	0.	0.	0.	1260.	0.	0.
17 TEXTILES	0.	0.	0.	0.	0.	0.	0.	7872.	0.	0.
18 WEARNG APL	0.	0.	0.	0.	0.	0.	1233.	0.	0.	0.
19 SAWMILLS	39.	29.	0.	824.	0.	0.	0.	51.	0.	0.
20 FURN FIXT	173.	15.	0.	0.	0.	37.	0.	32.	0.	0.
21 PAPER PRNT	546511.	0.	0.	2048.	0.	0.	0.	0.	0.	0.
22 INDST CHEM	0.	389623.	0.	5811.	252.	4208.	0.	15393.	0.	0.
23 PAINTS ETC	0.	0.	134537.	1509.	0.	0.	0.	0.	0.	1142.
24 OT CHM PRD	1414.	5782.	54.	154765.	407.	0.	0.	0.	0.	0.
25 PETROL PRD	0.	1741.	227.	130.	1625948.	0.	0.	0.	0.	0.
26 RUBBER PRO	0.	0.	0.	0.	0.	1438959.	0.	0.	0.	0.
27 RUBBER PRD	0.	0.	0.	33.	0.	0.	523851.	17.	0.	0.
28 PLSTIC PRD	3565.	792.	0.	0.	0.	0.	2751.	275729.	0.	0.
29 GLASS PROD	0.	112.	0.	0.	0.	0.	0.	2.	215378.	0.
30 CEMENT	0.	2011.	0.	0.	0.	0.	7.	0.	96.	207265.
31 N METALLIC	0.	0.	0.	0.	0.	0.	0.	0.	217.	0.
32 BASIC MTL	0.	0.	0.	0.	0.	0.	14.	0.	0.	0.
33 OTH METAL	0.	0.	0.	0.	0.	0.	27.	0.	0.	0.
34 N ELEC MAC	518.	631.	6.	29.	0.	73.	0.	71.	144.	0.
35 ELECT MACH	0.	1773.	0.	0.	0.	0.	147.	171.	0.	0.
36 MOTOR VEH	0.	57.	8.	0.	0.	111.	0.	1655.	0.	0.
37 OTH TRANSP	0.	0.	0.	0.	0.	0.	0.	799.	0.	0.
38 O MFG PROD	315.	0.	0.	0.	0.	0.	27.	494.	0.	0.
39 ELECTRICITY	0.	65.	0.	0.	0.	17.	0.	0.	0.	0.
40 WATER	0.	0.	0.	0.	0.	0.	0.	0.	0.	0.
41 CNSTRCTION	3145.	2552.	0.	512.	3386.	579.	519.	281.	1728.	0.
42 TRADE	2410.	3691.	731.	4909.	2146.	11134.	7200.	1707.	1075.	101.
43 HOTEL ETC	0.	0.	0.	0.	0.	0.	0.	0.	0.	0.
44 TRANSPORT	44.	477.	0.	66.	8.	28.	99.	4.	756.	2.
45 COMMUNICAT	0.	0.	0.	0.	0.	0.	0.	0.	0.	0.
46 FINANCE	0.	0.	0.	0.	0.	0.	0.	0.	0.	0.
47 INSURANCE	0.	0.	0.	0.	0.	0.	0.	0.	0.	0.
48 DWELLINGS	330.	323.	41.	421.	16.	170.	266.	537.	1094.	0.
49 BUSIN SERV	14652.	957.	75.	125.	0.	59.	95.	99.	135.	36.
50 PRIV EDUC	0.	0.	0.	0.	0.	0.	0.	0.	0.	0.
51 PH HEALTH	0.	0.	0.	0.	0.	0.	0.	0.	0.	0.
52 CULT SERV	0.	0.	0.	0.	0.	0.	0.	0.	0.	0.
53 REPAIR VEH	0.	0.	0.	0.	0.	0.	0.	0.	0.	0.
54 PERSON SER	0.	0.	0.	0.	0.	0.	0.	0.	0.	0.
55 PUB ADMIN	0.	0.	0.	0.	0.	0.	0.	0.	0.	0.
56 GOV EDUC	0.	0.	0.	0.	0.	0.	0.	0.	0.	0.
57 GOV HEALTH	0.	0.	0.	0.	0.	0.	0.	0.	0.	0.
58 O GOV SERV	0.	0.	0.	0.	0.	0.	0.	0.	0.	0.
59 PRI NP SER	0.	0.	0.	0.	0.	0.	0.	0.	0.	0.
60 OTHER SERV	0.	0.	0.	0.	0.	0.	0.	0.	0.	0.
61 MISCELLAN	0.	0.	0.	0.	0.	0.	0.	0.	0.	0.
62 GROSS OUTP	554202.	415370.	105440.	174790.	1632263.	1455371.	535926.	307269.	222892.	209037.

JADUAL 1.1 – MATRIKS 'MAKE' PADA NILAI–NILAI ASAS, 1978. KOMODITI X AKTIVITI (RIBU RINGGIT) – SAMB.

Table 1.1 – Make Matrix At Basic Values, 1978. Commodity x Activity (Thousand Ringgit) – Cont'd.

COL ROW	31 N METALLIC	32 BASIC MTL	33 OTH METAL	34 N ELEC MAC	35 ELECT MACH	36 MOTOR VEH	37 OTH TRANSP	38 O MFG PROD	39 ELECTRCITY	40 WATER
1 OTH AGRIC	0.	0.	0.	0.	0.	0.	0.	0.	0.	0.
2 RUBBER PLN	0.	0.	0.	0.	0.	0.	0.	0.	0.	0.
3 OIL PALM	0.	0.	0.	0.	0.	0.	0.	0.	0.	0.
4 LIVESTOCK	0.	0.	0.	0.	0.	0.	0.	0.	0.	0.
5 FORESTRY	0.	0.	0.	0.	0.	0.	0.	0.	0.	0.
6 FISHING	0.	0.	0.	0.	0.	0.	0.	0.	0.	0.
7 PETROL MIN	0.	0.	0.	0.	0.	0.	0.	0.	0.	0.
8 DAIRY PROD	0.	0.	0.	0.	0.	0.	0.	0.	0.	0.
9 VEG FRUIT	0.	0.	0.	0.	0.	0.	0.	0.	0.	0.
10 OIL & FATS	0.	0.	0.	0.	0.	0.	0.	0.	0.	0.
11 GRAIN MILL	0.	0.	0.	0.	0.	0.	0.	0.	0.	0.
12 BAKER COMP	0.	0.	0.	0.	0.	0.	0.	0.	0.	0.
13 OTH FOODS	0.	0.	0.	0.	0.	0.	0.	0.	0.	0.
14 ANMAL FEED	0.	0.	0.	0.	0.	0.	0.	0.	0.	0.
15 BEVERAGES	0.	0.	0.	0.	0.	0.	0.	0.	0.	0.
16 TOBACCO	0.	0.	0.	0.	0.	0.	0.	1368.	0.	0.
17 TEXTILES	0.	0.	0.	0.	0.	0.	0.	497.	0.	0.
18 WEARNG APL	0.	0.	0.	0.	0.	0.	44.	12.	0.	0.
19 SAWMILLS	0.	2549.	187.	0.	0.	0.	37.	3.	0.	0.
20 FURN FIXT	0.	1129.	99.	2757.	9.	0.	0.	2925.	0.	0.
21 PAPER PRNT	0.	0.	0.	2.	0.	0.	0.	0.	0.	0.
22 INDST CHEM	0.	0.	1506.	0.	10.	0.	0.	0.	0.	0.
23 PAINTS ETC	0.	0.	0.	0.	0.	0.	0.	3402.	0.	0.
24 OT CHM PRO	0.	0.	0.	0.	0.	0.	0.	0.	0.	0.
25 PETROL PRO	0.	0.	0.	172.	0.	0.	0.	0.	0.	0.
26 RUBBER PRO	0.	0.	0.	0.	0.	0.	0.	0.	0.	0.
27 RUBBER PRD	0.	3331.	0.	1.	0.	145.	0.	0.	0.	0.
28 PLSTIC PRD	0.	528.	335.	0.	1306.	0.	0.	22.	0.	0.
29 GLASS PROD	4172.	42.	2.	0.	0.	0.	0.	0.	0.	0.
30 CEMENT	8194.	0.	0.	0.	0.	0.	0.	0.	0.	0.
31 N METALLIC	178421.	23.	0.	0.	0.	235.	220.	1582.	0.	0.
32 BASIC MTL	20.	2760860.	54122.	10353.	5400.	235.	114.	894.	0.	1233.
33 OTH METAL	0.	12069.	417072.	611.	0.	10.	114.	894.	24.	0.
34 N ELEC MAC	23.	31952.	4345.	419855.	120190.	10.	9.	24.	0.	0.
35 ELECT MACH	0.	537.	936.	32813.	1972151.	0.	152.	1321.	0.	0.
36 MOTOR VEH	0.	8504.	0.	631.	0.	976184.	658.	0.	0.	0.
37 OTH TRANSP	0.	140.	0.	147.	6.	257.	268158.	0.	0.	0.
38 O MFG PROD	29.	33.	44.	1.	48096.	0.	2.	273252.	0.	0.
39 ELECTRCITY	0.	114.	8.	0.	0.	0.	0.	0.	868589.	0.
40 WATER	0.	0.	0.	0.	0.	0.	0.	0.	21470.	123853.
41 CNSTRCTION	791.	1802.	3440.	3367.	449.	19.	295.	729.	0.	369.
42 TRADE	417.	14470.	2037.	3978.	9171.	1151.	0.	5401.	0.	0.
43 HOTEL ETC	0.	0.	0.	0.	0.	0.	0.	0.	768.	0.
44 TRANSPORT	727.	363.	59.	90.	85.	0.	2740.	0.	0.	0.
45 COMMUNICAT	0.	0.	0.	0.	0.	0.	0.	0.	0.	0.
46 FINANCE	0.	0.	0.	0.	0.	0.	0.	0.	0.	0.
47 INSURANCE	0.	0.	0.	0.	0.	0.	0.	0.	0.	0.
48 DWELLINGS	35.	874.	722.	1295.	63.	119.	173.	77.	0.	14.
49 BUSIN SERV	68.	2395.	157.	123.	269.	263.	2.	645.	0.	4.
50 PRIV EDUC	0.	0.	0.	0.	0.	0.	0.	0.	0.	0.
51 PR HEALTH	0.	0.	0.	0.	0.	0.	0.	0.	0.	0.
52 CULT SERV	0.	0.	0.	0.	0.	0.	0.	0.	0.	0.
53 REPAIR VEH	0.	0.	0.	0.	0.	0.	0.	0.	0.	0.
54 PERSON SER	0.	0.	0.	0.	0.	0.	0.	0.	0.	0.
55 PUB ADMIN	0.	0.	0.	0.	0.	0.	0.	0.	0.	0.
56 GOV EDUC	0.	0.	0.	0.	0.	0.	0.	0.	0.	0.
57 GOV HEALTH	0.	0.	0.	0.	0.	0.	0.	0.	0.	0.
58 O GOV SERV	0.	0.	0.	0.	0.	0.	0.	0.	0.	0.
59 PRI NP SER	0.	0.	0.	0.	0.	0.	0.	0.	0.	0.
60 OTHER SERV	0.	0.	0.	0.	0.	0.	0.	0.	0.	0.
61 MISCELLAN	0.	0.	0.	0.	0.	0.	0.	0.	0.	0.
62 GROSS OUTP	192917.	2837815.	505531.	476246.	2157215.	978649.	273592.	291260.	890787.	125473.

JADUAL 1.1 – MATREKS 'MAKE' PADA NILAI–NILAI ASAS, 1978. KOMODITI X AKTIVITI (RIBU RINGGIT) – SAMB.

Table 1.1 – Make Matrix At Basic Values, 1978. Commodity x Activity (Thousand Ringgit) – Cont'd.

COL ROW	41 CNSTRCTION	42 TRADE	43 HOTEL ETC	44 TRANSPORT	45 COMMUNICAT	46 FINANCE	47 INSURANCE	48 DWELLINGS	49 BUSIN SERV	50 PRIV EDUC
1 OTH AGRIC	0.	0.	0.	0.	0.	0.	0.	0.	0.	0.
2 RUBBER PLN	0.	0.	0.	0.	0.	0.	0.	0.	0.	0.
3 OIL PALM	0.	0.	0.	0.	0.	0.	0.	0.	0.	0.
4 LIVESTOCK	0.	0.	0.	0.	0.	0.	0.	0.	0.	0.
5 FORESTRY	0.	0.	0.	0.	0.	0.	0.	0.	0.	0.
6 FISHING	0.	0.	0.	0.	0.	0.	0.	0.	0.	0.
7 PETROL MIN	0.	0.	0.	0.	0.	0.	0.	0.	0.	0.
8 DAIRY PROD	0.	0.	0.	0.	0.	0.	0.	0.	0.	0.
9 VEG FRUIT	0.	0.	0.	0.	0.	0.	0.	0.	0.	0.
10 OIL & FATS	0.	0.	0.	0.	0.	0.	0.	0.	0.	0.
11 GRAIN MILL	0.	0.	0.	0.	0.	0.	0.	0.	0.	0.
12 BAKER CONF	0.	0.	0.	0.	0.	0.	0.	0.	0.	0.
13 OTH FOODS	0.	0.	0.	0.	0.	0.	0.	0.	0.	0.
14 ANIMAL FEED	0.	0.	0.	0.	0.	0.	0.	0.	0.	0.
15 BEVERAGES	0.	0.	0.	0.	0.	0.	0.	0.	0.	0.
16 TOBACCO	0.	0.	0.	0.	0.	0.	0.	0.	0.	0.
17 TEXTILES	0.	0.	0.	0.	0.	0.	0.	0.	0.	0.
18 WEARNG APL	0.	0.	0.	0.	0.	0.	0.	0.	0.	0.
19 SAWMILLS	0.	0.	0.	0.	0.	0.	0.	0.	0.	0.
20 FURN FIXT	0.	0.	0.	0.	0.	0.	0.	0.	0.	0.
21 PAPER PRNT	0.	0.	0.	0.	0.	0.	0.	0.	0.	0.
22 INDST CHEM	0.	0.	0.	0.	0.	0.	0.	0.	0.	0.
23 PAINTS ETC	0.	0.	0.	0.	0.	0.	0.	0.	0.	0.
24 OT CHM PRD	0.	0.	0.	0.	0.	0.	0.	0.	0.	0.
25 PETROL PRD	0.	0.	0.	0.	0.	0.	0.	0.	0.	0.
26 RUBBER PRD	0.	0.	0.	0.	0.	0.	0.	0.	0.	0.
27 RUBBER PRD	0.	0.	0.	0.	0.	0.	0.	0.	0.	0.
28 PLSTIC PRD	0.	0.	0.	0.	0.	0.	0.	0.	0.	0.
29 GLASS PPOD	0.	0.	0.	0.	0.	0.	0.	0.	0.	0.
30 CEMENT	0.	0.	0.	0.	0.	0.	0.	0.	0.	0.
31 N METALLIC	0.	0.	0.	0.	0.	0.	0.	0.	0.	0.
32 BASIC MTL	0.	0.	0.	0.	0.	0.	0.	0.	0.	0.
33 OTH METAL	0.	0.	0.	0.	0.	0.	0.	0.	0.	0.
34 N ELEC MAC	0.	0.	0.	0.	0.	0.	0.	0.	0.	0.
35 ELECT MACH	0.	0.	0.	0.	0.	0.	0.	0.	0.	0.
36 MOTOR VEH	0.	0.	0.	0.	0.	0.	0.	0.	0.	0.
37 OTH TRANSP	0.	0.	0.	327.	0.	0.	0.	0.	0.	0.
38 O MFG PROD	0.	0.	0.	0.	0.	0.	0.	0.	0.	0.
39 ELECTRCITY	0.	0.	0.	0.	0.	0.	0.	0.	0.	0.
40 WATER	0.	0.	0.	232.	0.	0.	0.	0.	0.	0.
41 CNSTRCTION	5114762.	0.	0.	0.	0.	0.	0.	0.	0.	0.
42 TRADE	0.	5327363.	73423.	459.	0.	0.	0.	0.	0.	0.
43 HOTEL ETC	0.	0.	1352021.	0.	0.	0.	0.	0.	0.	36.
44 TRANSPORT	0.	0.	0.	2826986.	0.	0.	0.	0.	0.	0.
45 COMMUNICAT	0.	0.	0.	13.	452553.	0.	0.	0.	0.	430.
46 FINANCE	0.	0.	0.	0.	0.	660939.	0.	0.	0.	0.
47 INSURANCE	0.	0.	0.	0.	0.	0.	479386.	0.	0.	0.
48 DWELLINGS	0.	0.	11971.	12106.	0.	13134.	0.	2065036.	868.	559.
49 BUSIN SERV	0.	0.	57.	1830.	0.	0.	0.	0.	532874.	0.
50 PRIV EDUC	0.	0.	0.	0.	0.	0.	0.	0.	0.	0.
51 PR HEALTH	0.	0.	0.	0.	0.	0.	0.	0.	0.	62938.
52 CULT SERV	0.	0.	0.	0.	0.	0.	0.	0.	0.	0.
53 REPAIR VEH	0.	0.	0.	0.	0.	0.	0.	0.	0.	0.
54 PERSON SER	0.	0.	0.	0.	0.	0.	0.	0.	0.	0.
55 PUB ADMIN	0.	0.	0.	38.	0.	0.	0.	0.	0.	0.
56 GOV EDUC	0.	0.	0.	0.	0.	0.	0.	0.	0.	0.
57 GOV HEALTH	0.	0.	0.	0.	0.	0.	0.	0.	0.	0.
58 O GOV SERV	0.	0.	115.	0.	0.	0.	0.	0.	0.	0.
59 FRI MP SER	0.	0.	0.	0.	0.	0.	0.	0.	0.	0.
60 OTHER SERV	0.	0.	0.	0.	0.	0.	0.	0.	0.	0.
61 MISCELLAN	0.	0.	0.	0.	0.	0.	0.	0.	0.	0.
62 GROSS OUTP	5114762.	5327363.	1441287.	2841908.	452553.	674073.	478386.	2065036.	533742.	63959.

174

JADUAL 1.1 – MATRIKS 'MAKE' PADA NILAI–NILAI ASAS, 1978. KOMODITI X AKTIVITI (RIBU RINGGIT) – SAMB.

Table 1.1 – Make Matrix At Basic Values, 1978. Commodity x Activity (Thousand Ringgit) – Cont'd.

COL	51 PR HEALTH	52 CULT SERV	53 REPAIR VEH	54 PERSON SER	55 PUB ADMIN	56 GOV EDUC	57 GOV HEALTH O	58 GOV SERV	59 PRI NP SER	60 OTHER SERV
ROW										
1 OTH AGRIC	0.	0.	0.	0.	0.	0.	0.	2307.	0.	0.
2 RUBBER PLN	0.	0.	0.	0.	0.	0.	0.	1056.	0.	0.
3 OIL PALM	0.	0.	0.	0.	0.	0.	0.	597.	0.	0.
4 LIVESTOCK	0.	0.	0.	0.	0.	0.	0.	1801.	0.	0.
5 FORESTRY	0.	0.	0.	0.	0.	0.	0.	0.	0.	0.
6 FISHING	0.	0.	0.	0.	0.	0.	0.	0.	0.	0.
7 PETROL MIN	0.	0.	0.	0.	0.	0.	0.	0.	0.	0.
8 DAIRY PROD	0.	0.	0.	0.	0.	0.	0.	0.	0.	0.
9 VEG FRUIT	0.	0.	0.	0.	0.	0.	0.	0.	0.	0.
10 OIL & FATS	0.	0.	0.	0.	0.	0.	0.	471.	0.	0.
11 GRAIN MILL	0.	0.	0.	0.	0.	0.	0.	0.	0.	0.
12 BAKER CONF	0.	0.	0.	0.	0.	0.	0.	0.	0.	0.
13 OTH FOODS	0.	0.	0.	0.	0.	0.	0.	0.	0.	0.
14 ANIMAL FEED	0.	0.	0.	0.	0.	0.	0.	0.	0.	0.
15 BEVERAGES	0.	0.	0.	0.	0.	0.	0.	44.	0.	0.
16 TOBACCO	0.	0.	0.	0.	0.	0.	0.	0.	0.	0.
17 TEXTILES	0.	0.	0.	0.	0.	0.	0.	0.	0.	0.
18 WEARNG APL	0.	0.	0.	39.	0.	0.	0.	0.	0.	0.
19 SAWMILLS	0.	0.	0.	0.	0.	0.	0.	0.	0.	0.
20 FURN FIXT	0.	0.	0.	0.	1173.	0.	0.	152.	0.	0.
21 PAPER PRNT	0.	0.	0.	0.	20.	17.	0.	559.	0.	0.
22 INDST CHEM	0.	0.	0.	0.	0.	0.	0.	0.	0.	0.
23 PAINTS ETC	0.	0.	0.	0.	0.	0.	0.	0.	0.	0.
24 OT CHM PRD	0.	0.	0.	0.	0.	0.	619.	1.	0.	0.
25 PETROL PRD	0.	0.	0.	0.	0.	0.	0.	0.	0.	0.
26 RUBBER PRD	0.	0.	0.	0.	0.	0.	0.	0.	0.	0.
27 RUBBER PRD	0.	0.	0.	69.	0.	0.	0.	635.	0.	0.
28 PLSTIC PRD	0.	0.	0.	0.	0.	0.	0.	0.	0.	0.
29 GLASS PROD	0.	0.	0.	0.	0.	0.	0.	130.	0.	0.
30 CEMENT	0.	0.	0.	0.	0.	0.	0.	0.	0.	0.
31 N METALLIC	0.	0.	0.	0.	0.	0.	0.	0.	0.	0.
32 BASIC MTL	0.	0.	0.	7.	222.	0.	0.	0.	0.	0.
33 OTH METAL	0.	0.	0.	0.	0.	0.	0.	0.	0.	0.
34 N ELEC MAC	0.	0.	0.	0.	0.	0.	0.	0.	0.	0.
35 ELEC MACH	0.	0.	0.	123.	0.	0.	0.	0.	0.	0.
36 MOTOR VEH	0.	0.	0.	0.	0.	0.	0.	0.	0.	0.
37 OTH TRANSP	0.	0.	0.	0.	0.	0.	0.	0.	0.	0.
38 O MFG PROD	0.	0.	0.	0.	0.	0.	0.	32.	0.	0.
39 ELECTRCITY	0.	0.	0.	0.	52.	0.	0.	0.	0.	0.
40 WATER	0.	0.	0.	0.	0.	0.	0.	302.	0.	0.
41 CNSTRCTION	0.	0.	0.	0.	77.	0.	0.	0.	0.	0.
42 TRADE	197.	2.	0.	0.	77.	0.	0.	0.	0.	1312.
43 HOTEL ETC	0.	0.	0.	0.	911.	0.	0.	814.	0.	0.
44 TRANSPORT	0.	0.	0.	0.	2989.	0.	0.	4420.	0.	0.
45 COMMUNICAT	0.	0.	0.	0.	0.	0.	0.	0.	0.	0.
46 FINANCE	0.	0.	0.	0.	0.	0.	0.	0.	0.	0.
47 INSURANCE	0.	0.	0.	0.	0.	0.	0.	0.	0.	0.
48 DWELLINGS	1107.	1429.	0.	23.	41210.	44.	1281.	5975.	0.	229.
49 BUSIN SERV	0.	35422.	0.	0.	871.	211.	0.	1503.	0.	0.
50 PRIV EDUC	0.	0.	0.	0.	0.	0.	0.	0.	0.	0.
51 PR HEALTH	173730.	0.	0.	0.	0.	0.	0.	0.	0.	0.
52 CULT SERV	0.	267519.	0.	0.	0.	0.	0.	0.	0.	0.
53 REPAIR VEH	0.	0.	335624.	0.	0.	0.	0.	0.	0.	0.
54 PERSON SER	0.	0.	0.	19582.	0.	0.	0.	0.	0.	0.
55 PUB ADMIN	0.	0.	0.	0.	2945341.	0.	0.	4.	0.	0.
56 GOV EDUC	0.	0.	0.	0.	162.	1680169.	0.	0.	0.	0.
57 GOV HEALTH	0.	0.	0.	0.	0.	0.	622719.	164.	0.	0.
58 O GOV SERV	0.	0.	0.	0.	1486.	0.	0.	965926.	0.	0.
59 PRI NP SER	0.	0.	0.	0.	0.	0.	0.	0.	8701.	0.
60 OTHER SERV	0.	0.	0.	0.	0.	0.	0.	1097.	0.	153044.
61 MISCELLAN	0.	0.	0.	0.	0.	0.	0.	0.	0.	0.
62 GROSS OUTP	172114.	304452.	335624.	33843.	2994618.	1680441.	624619.	987990.	8701.	154585.

JADUAL 1.1 – MATRIKS 'MAKE' PADA NILAI–NILAI ASAS, 1978. KOMODITI X AKTIVITI (RIBU RINGGIT) – SAMB.

Table 1.1 – Make Matrix At Basic Values, 1978. Commodity x Activity (Thousand Ringgit) – Cont'd.

COL	61 MISCELLAN	62 GROSS OUTP
ROW		
1 OTH AGRIC	0.	1696162.
2 RUBBER FLW	0.	1264638.
3 OIL PALM	0.	834406.
4 LIVESTOCK	0.	915630.
5 FORESTRY	0.	1845936.
6 FISHING	0.	1626970.
7 PETROL MIN	0.	4083555.
8 DAIRY PROD	0.	777737.
9 VEG FRUIT	0.	397234.
10 OIL \ FATS	0.	1550790.
11 GRAIN MILL	0.	349823.
12 BAKER CON*	0.	818115.
13 OTH FOODS	0.	645637.
14 ANIMAL FEED	0.	327011.
15 BEVERAGES	0.	310794.
16 TOBACCO	0.	516034.
17 TEXTILES	0.	1010700.
18 WEARNG APL	0.	387236.
19 SAWMILLS	0.	1656273.
20 FURN FIXT	0.	136675.
21 PAPER PRNT	0.	552699.
22 INDST CHEM	0.	419646.
23 PAINTS ETC	0.	107137.
24 OT CHM PRD	0.	405225.
25 PETROL PRD	0.	1628218.
26 RUBBER FTD	0.	2538751.
27 RUBBER PRD	0.	528321.
28 PLSTIC PRD	0.	285979.
29 GLASS PROD	0.	219930.
30 CEMENT	0.	217573.
31 N METALLIC	0.	179736.
32 BASIC MTL	0.	2834509.
33 OTH METAL	0.	451630.
34 N ELEC MAC	0.	536629.
35 ELECT MACH	0.	2010024.
36 MOTOR VEH	0.	983169.
37 OTH TRANSP	0.	263834.
38 O MFG PROD	0.	322473.
39 ELECTRCITY	0.	863861.
40 WATER	0.	124337.
41 CNSTRCTION	0.	5213126.
42 TRADE	0.	5523933.
43 HOTEL ETC	0.	1354366.
44 TRANSPORT	0.	2955730.
45 COMMUNICAT	0.	452563.
46 FINANCE	0.	663939.
47 INSURANCE	0.	473316.
48 DWELLINGS	0.	2167937.
49 BUSIN SERV	0.	677237.
50 PRIV EDUC	0.	62934.
51 PR HEALTH	0.	170730.
52 CULT SERV	0.	267593.
53 REPAIR VEH	0.	305623.
54 PERSON SER	0.	195132.
55 PUB ADMIN	0.	2945333.
56 GOV EDUC	0.	1630311.
57 GOV HEALTH	0.	622933.
58 O GOV SERV	0.	967727.
59 PRI NP SER	0.	1731.
60 OTHER SERV	0.	153131.
61 MISCELLAN	143620.	143620.
62 GROSS OUTP	143620.	65075933.

JADUAL 1.2 – MATRIKS SERAPAN KOMODITI-KOMODITI DALAM NEGERI PADA NILAI-NILAI ASAS, 1978. KOMODITI X AKTIVITI (RIBU RINGGIT)

Table 1.2 – Absorption Matrix Of Discrete Commodities At Basic Values, 1978. Commodity x Activity (Thousand Ringgit)

COL / ROW	1 OTH AGRIC	2 RUBBER PLN	3 OIL PALM	4 LIVESTOCK	5 FORESTRY	6 FISHING	7 PETROL MIN	8 DAIRY PROD	9 VEG FRUIT	10 OIL & FATS
1 OTH AGRIC	20487.	0.	0.	0.	0.	0.	0.	250.	27610.	124484.
2 RUBBER PLN	0.	5262.	0.	0.	0.	0.	0.	0.	0.	0.
3 OIL PALM	1129.	0.	921.	0.	0.	0.	0.	0.	0.	642280.
4 LIVESTOCK	0.	0.	0.	0.	0.	0.	0.	327124.	658.	0.
5 FORESTRY	446.	59.	2951.	0.	58464.	0.	5239.	2.	100.	114.
6 FISHING	0.	0.	0.	0.	0.	0.	0.	95.	162394.	0.
7 PETROL MIN	102.	1106.	1333.	0.	0.	0.	10908.	0.	0.	0.
8 DAIRY PROD	0.	0.	0.	0.	0.	0.	0.	10674.	731.	0.
9 VEG FRUIT	0.	0.	0.	0.	0.	0.	0.	1692.	1401.	0.
10 OIL & FATS	0.	0.	1226.	25288.	0.	0.	0.	3941.	2347.	1036734.
11 GRAIN MILL	0.	0.	0.	51847.	0.	0.	0.	165.	773.	2003.
12 BAKER CONF	0.	0.	0.	0.	0.	0.	0.	15095.	32.	442.
13 OTH FOODS	0.	0.	0.	350.	0.	16272.	0.	83632.	22464.	146.
14 ANIMAL FEED	0.	0.	0.	285471.	0.	0.	0.	0.	0.	0.
15 BEVERAGES	0.	0.	0.	0.	0.	0.	0.	0.	0.	0.
16 TOBACCO	0.	0.	0.	0.	0.	0.	0.	0.	0.	0.
17 TEXTILES	1885.	0.	0.	0.	476.	4668.	463.	0.	99.	8173.
18 WEARNG APL	0.	0.	0.	0.	0.	0.	211.	81.	76.	69.
19 SAWMILLS	914.	3986.	943.	0.	704.	0.	4919.	33.	607.	525.
20 FURN FIXT	0.	0.	0.	0.	0.	0.	96.	0.	0.	0.
21 PAPER PRNT	916.	967.	1983.	0.	640.	0.	8674.	5451.	3146.	1749.
22 INDST CHEM	82123.	58504.	95575.	0.	0.	0.	1605.	0.	8.	1110.
23 PAINTS ETC	110.	393.	270.	0.	285.	0.	2848.	0.	85.	15.
24 OT CHM PRD	0.	268.	52.	0.	19.	0.	249.	54.	23.	0.
25 PETROL PRD	2509.	12834.	11199.	0.	26463.	73015.	105337.	1165.	2475.	14121.
26 RUBBER PRO	0.	10378.	0.	0.	0.	0.	0.	0.	0.	304.
27 RUBBER PRD	185.	379.	778.	0.	8205.	0.	8130.	0.	0.	283.
28 PLSTIC PRD	921.	1932.	0.	0.	0.	0.	147.	995.	4038.	2359.
29 GLASS PROD	34.	215.	591.	0.	0.	0.	80.	1527.	5313.	293.
30 CEMENT	407.	611.	2831.	0.	258.	0.	3282.	372.	212.	2257.
31 N METALLIC	60.	769.	3649.	0.	97.	0.	1012.	0.	0.	0.
32 BASIC MTL	681.	2324.	1401.	0.	1180.	0.	14196.	0.	0.	42.
33 OTH METAL	912.	7614.	4172.	596.	12285.	0.	3049.	38925.	25101.	28026.
34 N ELEC MAC	3155.	9526.	14360.	769.	20541.	0.	31085.	1084.	1868.	3934.
35 ELECT MACH	88.	173.	358.	0.	3851.	0.	3828.	0.	0.	129.
36 MOTOR VEH	204.	577.	868.	0.	4575.	0.	3374.	60.	41.	547.
37 OTH TRANSP	0.	0.	0.	0.	0.	8420.	0.	0.	0.	0.
38 O MFG PROD	100.	155.	467.	0.	110.	0.	897.	206.	196.	64.
39 ELECTRCITY	1233.	9299.	6190.	0.	366.	0.	97888.	2538.	3254.	9747.
40 WATER	811.	1054.	688.	0.	314.	0.	775.	801.	731.	2565.
41 CNSTRCTION	1959.	7565.	6689.	0.	2908.	0.	29399.	636.	703.	2098.
42 TRADE	24590.	10495.	41089.	51654.	37010.	31127.	82512.	47347.	25678.	61597.
43 HOTEL ETC	1467.	1150.	1697.	0.	5017.	0.	7273.	978.	1417.	2163.
44 TRANSPORT	1369.	12591.	8608.	7122.	3501.	1569.	42838.	33222.	13057.	51776.
45 COMMUNICAT	1097.	2261.	1548.	0.	1627.	0.	3475.	265.	986.	1959.
46 FINANCE	27.	0.	0.	0.	0.	0.	811.	156.	400.	1743.
47 INSURANCE	720.	4043.	4413.	0.	3255.	0.	11333.	550.	873.	4255.
48 DWELLINGS	57.	5.	0.	0.	645.	0.	17364.	1085.	1148.	556.
49 BUSIN SERV	114.	1219.	4153.	0.	2159.	0.	36100.	9642.	11336.	5868.
50 PRIV EDUC	0.	0.	0.	0.	0.	0.	0.	0.	0.	0.
51 PR HEALTH	0.	0.	0.	0.	0.	0.	0.	0.	0.	0.
52 CULT SERV	0.	0.	0.	0.	0.	0.	0.	0.	0.	0.
53 REPAIR VEH	1788.	2594.	3104.	0.	3662.	0.	29794.	558.	1668.	2768.
54 PERSON SER	0.	0.	0.	0.	0.	0.	0.	0.	0.	0.
55 PUB ADMIN	12.	0.	0.	0.	0.	0.	377.	72.	187.	813.
56 GOV EDUC	0.	0.	0.	0.	0.	0.	383.	0.	0.	0.
57 GOV HEALTH	0.	0.	0.	355.	0.	0.	0.	0.	0.	0.
58 O GOV SERV	159.	0.	0.	0.	0.	0.	0.	14.	0.	0.
59 PRI MP SER	0.	0.	0.	0.	0.	0.	0.	0.	0.	0.
60 OTHER SERV	0.	0.	0.	0.	0.	0.	0.	0.	0.	0.
61 TOT INT FR	155966.	190457.	225705.	423052.	198617.	135071.	569941.	549447.	323236.	2014111.
62 MISCELLAN	2943.	12934.	13078.	0.	0.	0.	0.	0.	0.	0.
63 N COMP IMP	0.	0.	0.	0.	0.	0.	0.	0.	0.	0.
64 TOT IMPRTS	45301.	103370.	143284.	139464.	84574.	38794.	212909.	137807.	17932.	44946.
65 COM TAXES	9779.	12125.	14313.	3457.	16020.	9196.	28462.	12081.	3954.	4486.
66 INVISB BAL	0.	0.	0.	0.	0.	0.	0.	0.	0.	0.
67 VALUE ADD	1586579.	2056602.	1337133.	317801.	1468903.	1443919.	3274955.	93234.	128033.	552810.
68 GRSS INPUT	1339868.	2375598.	1790013.	933774.	1766114.	1626970.	4096267.	792569.	473159.	2616353.

JADUAL 1.2 – MATRIKS SERAPAN KOMODITI–KOMODITI DALAM NEGERI PADA NILAI–NILAI ASAS, 1978. KOMODITI X AKTIVITI (RIBU RINGGIT) – SAMB.

Table 1.2 – Absorption Matrix Of Domestic Commodities At Basic Values, 1978. Commodity x Activity (Thousand Ringgit) – Cont'd.

COL / ROW	11 GRAIN MILL	12 BAKER CONF	13 OTH FOODS	14 ANNAL FEED	15 BEVERAGES	16 TOBACCO	17 TEXTILES	18 WEARING APL	19 SAWMILLS	20 FURN FIXT
1 OTH AGRIC	473991.	21174.	49825.	144.	1211.	51679.	5.	0.	0.	0.
2 RUBBER PLT	0.	0.	0.	0.	0.	0.	0.	0.	0.	284.
3 OIL PALM	0.	0.	0.	135.	0.	0.	0.	0.	0.	0.
4 LIVESTOCK	0.	2784.	292.	0.	0.	0.	0.	0.	0.	0.
5 FORESTRY	1119.	414.	975.	171.	23.	654.	17.	9.	635702.	1462.
6 FISHING	0.	202.	0.	0.	0.	0.	0.	0.	0.	0.
7 PETROL MIN	0.	0.	0.	0.	0.	0.	0.	0.	7.	3.
8 DAIRY PROD	0.	3686.	40.	0.	60.	0.	0.	2080.	0.	0.
9 VEG FRUIT	0.	107.	186.	1986.	0.	0.	0.	2.	0.	0.
10 OIL & FATS	157.	19299.	7467.	6696.	0.	20.	25.	0.	0.	0.
11 GRAIN MILL	3098.	50096.	13922.	37524.	719.	0.	0.	0.	805.	0.
12 BAKER CONF	0.	8975.	24.	0.	130.	0.	0.	0.	0.	0.
13 OTH FOODS	50.	22804.	13088.	971.	27773.	0.	782.	0.	0.	0.
14 ANNAL FEED	0.	0.	0.	12568.	0.	0.	0.	0.	0.	0.
15 BEVERAGES	0.	49.	0.	929.	489.	0.	0.	0.	0.	0.
16 TOBACCO	0.	0.	0.	0.	2.	10707.	0.	0.	0.	0.
17 TEXTILES	6981.	21.	450.	1193.	2.	23.	201801.	140700.	383.	323.
18 WEARING APL	27.	60.	130.	11.	201.	227.	341.	5420.	62.	10.
19 SAWMILLS	8.	192.	219.	0.	1195.	136.	787.	191.	126988.	40191.
20 FURN FIXT	0.	0.	0.	0.	0.	0.	0.	5.	0.	2620.
21 PAPER PRNT	281.	2843.	4759.	1033.	2769.	20529.	3380.	1774.	2126.	421.
22 INDST CHEM	0.	0.	930.	0.	883.	496.	5900.	0.	1228.	441.
23 PAINTS ETC	0.	0.	0.	0.	0.	0.	0.	10.	1360.	3428.
24 OT CHM PRD	0.	0.	1125.	2925.	34.	20.	3660.	35.	16129.	950.
25 PETROL PRD	3385.	3398.	12439.	744.	2012.	556.	9009.	540.	17512.	391.
26 RUBBER PRD	0.	0.	0.	0.	0.	0.	172.	0.	0.	0.
27 RUBBER PRD	410.	136.	127.	0.	0.	0.	904.	1617.	1291.	1118.
28 PLSTIC PRD	3907.	8393.	9922.	2310.	32.	3580.	1460.	4292.	174.	2682.
29 GLASS PROD	1.	39.	269.	0.	23770.	0.	5.	0.	1.	1065.
30 CEMENT	282.	119.	1218.	232.	514.	634.	1447.	144.	3225.	319.
31 N METALLIC	0.	0.	0.	0.	0.	0.	0.	0.	42.	0.
32 BASIC MTL	42.	23.	22.	0.	0.	0.	54.	0.	1234.	1590.
33 OTH METAL	528.	6635.	1945.	0.	4669.	298.	115.	123.	2096.	102.
34 N ELEC MAC	1123.	1436.	2261.	1412.	1846.	664.	2488.	1051.	11752.	149.
35 ELECT MACH	99.	63.	58.	0.	0.	0.	48.	0.	612.	0.
36 MOTOR VEH	139.	78.	292.	38.	88.	119.	286.	23.	1287.	27.
37 OTH TRANSP	0.	0.	0.	0.	0.	0.	0.	0.	0.	0.
38 O MFG PROD	42.	131.	141.	31.	221.	106.	567.	5891.	249.	102.
39 ELECTRICITY	3096.	3737.	13115.	1566.	2806.	1413.	34606.	3323.	21102.	2173.
40 WATER	250.	334.	1604.	76.	1331.	107.	2389.	612.	1460.	157.
41 CNSTRCTION	552.	833.	1258.	565.	587.	214.	1421.	385.	4044.	251.
42 TRADE	12190.	20571.	22045.	18734.	13702.	18433.	59856.	20331.	31803.	8170.
43 HOTEL ETC	1491.	1034.	2037.	801.	955.	698.	2977.	1614.	7955.	1084.
44 TRANSPORT	11445.	4211.	13791.	2462.	3874.	14840.	9527.	3808.	87705.	2993.
45 COMMUNICAT	673.	641.	798.	414.	650.	583.	2366.	1279.	3721.	450.
46 FINANCE	650.	376.	684.	401.	291.	238.	1859.	868.	1697.	297.
47 INSURANCE	964.	415.	385.	421.	751.	969.	3755.	771.	8566.	641.
48 DWELLINGS	452.	1407.	395.	223.	940.	209.	2460.	2862.	4962.	1335.
49 BUSIN SERV	1460.	3133.	4332.	2166.	12259.	18774.	4618.	2558.	9409.	2023.
50 PRIV EDUC	0.	0.	0.	0.	0.	0.	0.	0.	0.	0.
51 PR HEALTH	0.	0.	0.	0.	0.	0.	0.	0.	0.	0.
52 CULT SERV	0.	0.	1.	0.	2.	0.	0.	0.	23.	0.
53 REPAIR VEH	832.	1239.	1487.	847.	911.	321.	2131.	840.	5348.	390.
54 PERSON SER	0.	0.	0.	0.	0.	0.	0.	0.	0.	0.
55 PUB ADMIN	323.	175.	319.	187.	116.	111.	867.	405.	792.	118.
56 GOV EDUC	0.	0.	0.	0.	0.	0.	0.	0.	5.	0.
57 GOV HEALTH	0.	0.	0.	0.	0.	0.	0.	0.	0.	0.
58 O GOV SERV	0.	0.	0.	0.	0.	0.	0.	0.	0.	0.
59 PRI NP SER	0.	0.	0.	0.	0.	0.	0.	0.	0.	0.
60 OTHER SERV	0.	0.	0.	0.	0.	0.	0.	0.	0.	0.
61 TOT INTER	511324.	197872.	145937.	130121.	107856.	147385.	341085.	203540.	1012847.	77666.
62 MISCELLAN	0.	0.	0.	0.	0.	0.	0.	0.	0.	0.
63 N COMP INP	0.	0.	0.	0.	0.	0.	0.	0.	0.	0.
64 TOT IMPRT	176805.	58411.	333010.	195910.	53162.	138119.	326148.	53429.	65295.	10640.
65 COM TAXES	3811.	6040.	11218.	4242.	7750.	143284.	25604.	14312.	59694.	2789.
66 INVISD BAL	0.	0.	0.	0.	0.	0.	0.	0.	0.	0.
67 VALUE ADD	122737.	73801.	151567.	41571.	128319.	125391.	266920.	173364.	627924.	46801.
68 GRSS INPUT	813907.	336124.	641733.	333844.	297087.	524182.	979757.	444645.	1765764.	137896.

JADUAL 1.2 – MATRIKS SERAPAN KOMODITI–KOMODITI DALAM NEGERI PADA NILAI–NILAI ASAS, 1978. KOMODITI X AKTIVITI (RIBU RINGGIT) – SAMB.

Table 1.2 – Absorption Matrix Of Domestic Commodities At Basic Values, 1978. Commodity x Activity (Thousand Ringgit) – Cont'd.

COL	21 PAPER PRNT	22 INDST CHEM	23 PAINTS ETC	24 OT CHM PRD	25 PETROL PRD	26 RUBBER PRO	27 RUBBER PRD	28 PLSTIC PRD	29 GLASS PROD	30 CEMENT
ROW										
1 OTH AGRIC	0.	0.	0.	7.	0.	0.	0.	12.	0.	0.
2 RUBBER PLN	0.	0.	0.	271.	0.	1083663.	0.	0.	0.	0.
3 OIL PALM	0.	0.	0.	0.	0.	0.	0.	0.	0.	0.
4 LIVESTOCK	0.	0.	0.	0.	0.	0.	0.	0.	0.	0.
5 FORESTRY	36.	2290.	0.	2828.	2.	372.	115.	9.	4956.	131.
6 FISHING	0.	253.	0.	0.	0.	0.	0.	0.	0.	0.
7 PETROL MIN	0.	2760.	0.	3.	373352.	0.	171.	0.	6692.	17842.
8 DAIRY PROD	0.	0.	0.	4485.	0.	0.	0.	0.	0.	0.
9 VEG FRUIT	0.	0.	0.	0.	0.	0.	0.	0.	0.	0.
10 OIL & FATS	0.	0.	1523.	9239.	0.	1270.	0.	0.	0.	0.
11 GRAIN MILL	0.	11.	0.	1132.	0.	0.	0.	0.	2.	0.
12 BAKER CONF	0.	0.	0.	1.	0.	0.	0.	0.	0.	0.
13 OTH FOODS	0.	0.	0.	673.	0.	0.	0.	60.	0.	0.
14 ANMAL FEED	0.	0.	0.	0.	0.	0.	0.	0.	0.	0.
15 BEVERAGES	0.	0.	0.	0.	0.	0.	0.	0.	0.	0.
16 TOBACCO	0.	0.	0.	0.	0.	0.	0.	0.	0.	0.
17 TEXTILES	1178.	81.	0.	319.	0.	361.	5999.	2530.	6.	20.
18 WEARNG APL	53.	83.	55.	188.	24.	48.	2170.	203.	36.	25.
19 SAWMILLS	390.	126.	1010.	2108.	0.	2173.	417.	1364.	1127.	0.
20 FURN FIXT	1551.	0.	0.	0.	0.	0.	0.	9.	0.	0.
21 PAPER PRNT	63698.	1196.	390.	9356.	447.	1057.	3097.	2361.	1900.	3358.
22 INDST CHEM	694.	36068.	6784.	11957.	1899.	2165.	6029.	29205.	1231.	0.
23 PAINTS ETC	506.	0.	1006.	342.	56.	0.	11.	243.	616.	0.
24 OT CHM PRD	7432.	361.	543.	8631.	1089.	0.	15229.	1829.	0.	0.
25 PETROL PRD	3568.	9120.	2763.	3202.	46860.	6563.	7633.	1228.	13166.	29752.
26 RUBBER PRJ	0.	0.	0.	0.	0.	1261.	91959.	0.	0.	0.
27 RUBBER PRD	233.	0.	2.	0.	0.	286.	18290.	600.	556.	0.
28 PLSTIC PRO	4179.	7455.	61.	7606.	655.	2364.	2117.	703.	326.	164.
29 GLASS PROD	0.	127.	1.	1658.	0.	0.	14.	105.	4738.	0.
30 CEMENT	475.	1122.	224.	402.	370.	570.	888.	454.	1981.	2523.
31 N METALLIC	0.	1.	0.	0.	0.	0.	3.	0.	67.	0.
32 BASIC MTL	229.	620.	0.	3.	0.	42.	78.	341.	84.	0.
33 OTH METAL	625.	1823.	5910.	1377.	8832.	8.	1445.	60.	57.	0.
34 M ELEC MAC	2817.	1552.	237.	1771.	4774.	4352.	3997.	1369.	3061.	69.
35 ELECT MACH	92.	0.	0.	0.	0.	119.	117.	420.	256.	0.
36 MOTOR VEH	167.	207.	7.	65.	69.	216.	224.	140.	416.	255.
37 OTH TRANSP	0.	0.	0.	0.	0.	0.	0.	0.	0.	0.
38 O MFG PROD	727.	69.	59.	215.	40.	31.	388.	107.	86.	44.
39 ELECTRCITY	9273.	16428.	436.	3317.	6186.	10497.	12098.	10676.	6053.	21305.
40 WATER	699.	829.	57.	324.	701.	665.	749.	459.	286.	183.
41 CNSTRCTION	1697.	755.	95.	673.	398.	2550.	1481.	863.	1184.	27.
42 TRADE	51660.	29120.	7297.	23265.	20069.	57554.	25109.	19951.	10169.	15645.
43 HOTEL ETC	5448.	1631.	797.	2568.	351.	1221.	2585.	2294.	1288.	1124.
44 TRANSPORT	6965.	3692.	1064.	4776.	7172.	20178.	4123.	2957.	3945.	2020.
45 COMMUNICAT	4180.	785.	312.	1264.	218.	988.	1832.	1103.	570.	254.
46 FINANCE	1480.	490.	80.	946.	20.	661.	943.	1512.	471.	53.
47 INSURANCE	737.	1079.	313.	876.	987.	1754.	1319.	1368.	849.	586.
48 DWELLINGS	5979.	590.	806.	1492.	300.	946.	1891.	1633.	1032.	169.
49 BUSIN SERV	10055.	4710.	4354.	20181.	4009.	1279.	4364.	3833.	2423.	941.
50 PRIV EDUC	0.	0.	0.	0.	0.	0.	0.	0.	0.	0.
51 PR HEALTH	0.	0.	0.	0.	0.	0.	0.	0.	0.	0.
52 CULT SERV	123.	0.	6.	0.	0.	0.	0.	2.	11.	0.
53 REPAIR VEH	2102.	1137.	143.	1013.	598.	3238.	1876.	1412.	1708.	40.
54 PERSON SER	0.	0.	0.	0.	0.	0.	0.	0.	0.	0.
55 PUB ADMIN	690.	229.	37.	442.	0.	308.	439.	705.	220.	25.
56 GOV EDUC	11.	0.	0.	0.	0.	0.	0.	0.	0.	0.
57 GOV HEALTH	0.	0.	0.	0.	0.	0.	0.	0.	0.	0.
58 O GOV SERV	0.	0.	0.	0.	0.	20.	0.	0.	0.	0.
59 PRI NP SER	0.	0.	0.	0.	0.	0.	0.	0.	0.	0.
60 OTHER SERV	0.	0.	0.	0.	0.	0.	0.	0.	0.	0.
61 TOT INTER	191749.	125750.	35972.	128375.	479445.	1203680.	219196.	92111.	75468.	96555.
62 MISCELLAN	0.	0.	0.	0.	0.	0.	0.	0.	0.	0.
63 N COMP IMP	0.	0.	0.	0.	0.	0.	0.	0.	0.	0.
64 TOT IMPPTS	180375.	156302.	37520.	105295.	972122.	39465.	104296.	113157.	32606.	30934.
65 COM TAXES	17114.	10695.	1791.	9045.	3589.	2991.	14410.	8506.	3576.	3048.
66 INVISB BAL	0.	0.	0.	0.	0.	0.	0.	0.	0.	0.
67 VALUE ADD	264964.	122563.	30155.	135475.	177907.	204235.	197924.	93495.	110842.	78500.
68 GRSS INPUT	654202.	415370.	105440.	378790.	1632263.	1455371.	535826.	307269.	222492.	209037.

JADUAL 1.2 – MATRIKS SERAPAN KOMODITI-KOMODITI DALAM NEGERI PADA NILAI-NILAI ASAS, 1978. KOMODITI X AKTIVITI (RIBU RINGGIT) – SAMB.

Table 1.2 – Absorption Matrix Of Domestic Commodities At Basic Values, 1978. Commodity x Activity (Thousand Ringgit) – Cont'd.

COL	31	32	33	34	35	36	37	38	39	40
ROW	N METALLIC	BASIC MTL	OTH METAL	N ELEC MAC	ELECT MACH	MOTOR VEH	OTH TRANSP	O MFG PROD	ELECTRICITY	WATER
1 OTH AGRIC	0.	0.	0.	0.	0.	0.	0.	0.	0.	0.
2 RUBBER PLN	0.	0.	0.	0.	0.	0.	0.	0.	0.	0.
3 OIL PALM	0.	0.	0.	0.	0.	0.	0.	0.	0.	0.
4 LIVESTOCK	0.	0.	0.	0.	0.	0.	0.	0.	0.	0.
5 FORESTRY	487.	18771.	71.	643.	26.	11.	6.	681.	0.	0.
6 FISHING	0.	0.	0.	0.	0.	0.	0.	0.	0.	0.
7 PETROL MIN	7356.	1277145.	0.	31.	0.	0.	0.	0.	0.	0.
8 DAIRY PROD	0.	0.	0.	0.	0.	0.	0.	0.	0.	0.
9 VEG FRUIT	0.	0.	0.	0.	0.	0.	0.	0.	0.	0.
10 OIL & FATS	0.	0.	0.	0.	0.	0.	0.	933.	0.	0.
11 GRAIN MILL	0.	0.	0.	0.	0.	0.	0.	0.	0.	0.
12 BAKER CONF	0.	0.	0.	0.	0.	0.	0.	0.	0.	0.
13 OTH FOODS	0.	0.	0.	0.	0.	0.	0.	0.	0.	0.
14 ANMAL FEED	0.	0.	0.	0.	0.	0.	0.	0.	0.	0.
15 BEVERAGES	0.	0.	0.	0.	0.	0.	0.	0.	0.	0.
16 TOBACCO	0.	0.	0.	0.	0.	0.	0.	0.	0.	0.
17 TEXTILES	17.	95.	702.	0.	2024.	70.	38.	6352.	0.	0.
18 WEARNG APL	56.	262.	128.	162.	980.	293.	192.	48.	939.	38.
19 SAWMILLS	488.	1622.	827.	838.	374.	2392.	1353.	2938.	0.	0.
20 FURN FIXT	0.	0.	74.	0.	2789.	0.	3.	0.	0.	0.
21 PAPER PRNT	1317.	1431.	1747.	737.	9625.	1085.	128.	2837.	1148.	297.
22 INDST CHEM	0.	6778.	2182.	1190.	13600.	403.	694.	499.	0.	0.
23 PAINTS ETC	0.	2540.	1739.	3584.	785.	6531.	739.	327.	0.	0.
24 OT CHM PRD	7.	12.	835.	2.	4786.	1139.	23.	984.	32.	0.
25 PETROL PRD	1668.	10961.	2263.	1708.	3869.	1946.	499.	152.	256356.	970.
26 RUBBER PRD	0.	0.	0.	0.	0.	0.	0.	0.	0.	0.
27 RUBBER PRD	33.	1934.	258.	593.	1731.	28383.	7099.	19.	0.	737.
28 PLSTIC PRD	193.	533.	584.	2088.	13098.	321.	130.	3530.	33.	0.
29 GLASS PROD	223.	671.	138.	0.	68.	870.	0.	124.	0.	0.
30 CEMENT	22459.	1553.	617.	724.	2171.	708.	398.	197.	0.	0.
31 N METALLIC	1013.	836.	0.	236.	0.	120.	4.	0.	0.	0.
32 BASIC MTL	1005.	108979.	75659.	41414.	10044.	6362.	9658.	7736.	355.	1586.
33 OTH METAL	1289.	2606.	13361.	27.	2876.	2896.	547.	255.	140.	998.
34 N ELEC MAC	818.	10649.	1548.	19067.	7878.	1370.	4183.	1552.	1583.	5072.
35 ELECT MACH	0.	1255.	899.	8070.	158870.	5276.	1295.	19.	1091.	2053.
36 MOTOR VEH	48.	322.	113.	197.	476.	3300.	109.	60.	0.	305.
37 OTH TRANSP	55.	0.	0.	0.	0.	0.	1242.	0.	0.	0.
38 O MFG PROD	56.	256.	78.	87.	1083.	58.	39.	65341.	186.	39.
39 ELECTRCITY	1350.	13310.	4389.	1304.	17890.	2680.	1061.	3421.	706.	2710.
40 WATER	479.	1165.	326.	357.	2673.	260.	350.	310.	308.	333.
41 CNSTRCTION	576.	1570.	773.	629.	1575.	179.	107.	460.	14165.	1343.
42 TRADE	9126.	60737.	17705.	48628.	204987.	16680.	7804.	34288.	85029.	3988.
43 HOTEL ETC	1223.	4875.	3538.	3278.	5611.	1797.	1351.	1990.	7465.	178.
44 TRANSPORT	2922.	17668.	4910.	4632.	21792.	10275.	2027.	2417.	11525.	1030.
45 COMMNICAT	478.	1978.	1200.	1854.	6512.	816.	371.	1555.	4744.	68.
46 FINANCE	309.	4141.	1264.	1194.	2003.	814.	273.	283.	0.	0.
47 INSURANCE	389.	1361.	399.	392.	2342.	1000.	331.	1265.	3249.	31.
48 DWELLINGS	383.	2374.	2121.	2520.	3379.	1413.	470.	1541.	1051.	203.
49 BUSIN SERV	2743.	6372.	4565.	4323.	9863.	3858.	1029.	4099.	2908.	961.
50 PRIV EDUC	0.	0.	0.	0.	0.	0.	0.	0.	0.	0.
51 PR HSALTH	0.	0.	0.	0.	0.	0.	0.	0.	0.	0.
52 CULT SERV	0.	0.	0.	8.	0.	0.	0.	0.	0.	0.
53 REPAIR VEH	862.	2113.	1167.	944.	2067.	271.	176.	696.	2043.	528.
54 PERSON SRV	0.	0.	0.	0.	0.	0.	0.	0.	0.	0.
55 PUB ADMIN	144.	1933.	590.	556.	935.	179.	127.	132.	0.	0.
56 GOV EDUC	0.	0.	0.	0.	0.	0.	0.	0.	0.	5.
57 GOV HEALTH	0.	0.	0.	0.	0.	0.	0.	0.	0.	0.
58 O GOV SERV	0.	0.	0.	0.	0.	0.	0.	0.	0.	0.
59 PRI VP SER	0.	0.	0.	0.	0.	0.	0.	0.	0.	0.
60 OTHER SERV	0.	0.	0.	0.	0.	0.	0.	0.	0.	0.
61 TOT INTER	61961.	1575105.	171969.	173717.	537766.	103946.	41858.	147231.	195057.	28079.
62 MISCELLAN	0.	0.	0.	0.	0.	0.	0.	0.	0.	0.
63 N COMP IMP	0.	0.	0.	0.	0.	0.	0.	0.	0.	0.
64 TOT IMPRTS	49313.	440120.	163355.	134727.	1002637.	716981.	112010.	49695.	37196.	14655.
65 COM TAXES	2870.	512156.	12316.	19633.	83241.	29643.	5390.	5543.	12886.	1666.
66 INVISB BAL	0.	0.	0.	0.	0.	0.	0.	0.	0.	0.
67 VALUE ADD	78273.	310434.	157891.	149169.	533571.	129079.	112334.	88791.	445646.	85073.
69 GRSS INPUT	192917.	2837815.	505531.	476246.	2157215.	979649.	273592.	291260.	890787.	125473.

180

JADUAL 1.2 – MATRIKS SERAPAN KOMODITI–KOMODITI DALAM NEGERI PADA NILAI–NILAI ASAS, 1978. KOMODITI X AKTIVITI (RIBU RINGGIT) – SAMB.

Table 1.2 – Absorption Matrix Of Domestic Commodities At Basic Values, 1978. Commodity x Activity (Thousand Ringgit) – Cont'd.

COL ROW	41 CNSTRCTION	42 TRADE	43 HOTEL ETC	44 TRANSPORT	45 COMMUNICAT	46 FINANCE	47 INSURANCE	48 DWELLINGS	49 BUSIN SERV	50 PRIV EDUC
1 OTH AGRIC	0.	0.	52937.	560.	0.	0.	0.	0.	0.	0.
2 RUBBER PLN	0.	0.	0.	0.	0.	0.	0.	0.	0.	0.
3 OIL PALM	0.	0.	0.	0.	0.	0.	0.	0.	0.	0.
4 LIVESTOCK	0.	0.	76277.	118.	0.	0.	0.	0.	0.	0.
5 FORESTRY	19565.	0.	14.	161.	0.	0.	0.	0.	2.	3.
6 FISHING	0.	0.	131443.	336.	0.	0.	0.	0.	0.	0.
7 PETROL MIN	174248.	0.	0.	626.	0.	0.	0.	0.	0.	0.
8 DAIRY PROD	0.	0.	105091.	791.	0.	0.	0.	0.	0.	0.
9 VEG FRUIT	0.	0.	7891.	178.	0.	0.	0.	0.	0.	0.
10 OIL & FATS	0.	0.	19109.	31.	0.	0.	0.	0.	0.	0.
11 GRAIN MILL	0.	0.	8312.	70.	0.	0.	0.	0.	0.	0.
12 BAKER CONF	0.	0.	9956.	384.	0.	0.	0.	0.	0.	91.
13 OTH FOODS	0.	6348.	25387.	326.	0.	0.	0.	0.	0.	0.
14 ANMAL FEED	0.	0.	0.	0.	0.	0.	0.	0.	0.	0.
15 BEVERAGES	0.	0.	11901.	269.	0.	0.	0.	0.	4.	82.
16 TOBACCO	0.	0.	0.	170.	0.	0.	0.	0.	0.	0.
17 TEXTILES	0.	0.	1089.	4168.	234.	0.	0.	0.	0.	0.
18 WEARNG APL	50.	0.	933.	1295.	363.	7.	20.	0.	370.	11.
19 SAWMILLS	158629.	0.	2170.	1863.	696.	0.	0.	0.	0.	0.
20 FURN FIXT	0.	0.	0.	16.	9.	0.	0.	16.	0.	1428.
21 PAPER PRNT	6250.	200606.	2366.	6858.	1676.	11933.	2010.	144.	5773.	1055.
22 INDST CHEM	1592.	0.	0.	205.	4.	0.	0.	0.	0.	0.
23 PAINTS ETC	69348.	0.	7813.	195.	228.	0.	0.	0.	0.	0.
24 OT CHM PRD	509.	70.	3401.	821.	189.	225.	55.	0.	114.	29.
25 PETROL PRD	66022.	71378.	14498.	142413.	1551.	17.	68.	65.	1399.	96.
26 RUBBER PRO	0.	0.	0.	0.	0.	0.	0.	0.	0.	0.
27 RUBBER PRD	14295.	16522.	908.	48882.	525.	431.	0.	0.	352.	0.
28 PLSTIC PRD	3.	68165.	287.	691.	1392.	0.	0.	0.	0.	0.
29 GLASS PROD	121720.	0.	0.	289.	22.	0.	0.	0.	0.	0.
30 CEMENT	166139.	0.	0.	67.	0.	0.	0.	0.	0.	0.
31 N METALLIC	162351.	0.	0.	4.	68.	0.	0.	0.	0.	0.
32 BASIC MTL	147691.	124.	785.	1864.	330.	0.	0.	9.	46.	0.
33 OTH METAL	128162.	16487.	214.	1115.	975.	762.	190.	0.	424.	134.
34 N ELEC MAC	47598.	7551.	12529.	5374.	782.	6796.	51.	323.	2038.	745.
35 ELECT MACH	45152.	597.	818.	4373.	1465.	79.	0.	0.	161.	78.
36 MOTOR VEH	508.	151.	377.	25014.	35.	0.	0.	0.	147.	0.
37 OTH TRANSP	0.	0.	0.	32345.	0.	0.	0.	0.	0.	0.
38 O MFG PROD	661.	2517.	412.	1082.	329.	1113.	361.	42.	698.	189.
39 ELECTRCITY	16965.	55213.	89323.	9240.	6076.	12598.	916.	880.	4724.	976.
40 WATER	5655.	18935.	14759.	3528.	408.	4144.	104.	250.	466.	220.
41 CNSTRCTION	43941.	72845.	9034.	9550.	4770.	13027.	1075.	118502.	2486.	361.
42 TRADE	149894.	43638.	44383.	100025.	3414.	3633.	738.	87.	4429.	898.
43 HOTEL ETC	12864.	168160.	15539.	40488.	2742.	13739.	4948.	423.	13491.	281.
44 TRANSPORT	91453.	136399.	20050.	133315.	3500.	216.	1755.	630.	5954.	490.
45 COMMUNICAT	8870.	87532.	22696.	21003.	6862.	23775.	3932.	208.	8033.	511.
46 FINANCE	5700.	35924.	6838.	2263.	0.	152.	316.	201.	939.	17.
47 INSURANCE	21512.	23579.	4182.	48871.	0.	4415.	104246.	9777.	2126.	114.
48 DWELLINGS	59228.	189197.	41713.	29560.	555.	21446.	8750.	4253.	18883.	3937.
49 BUSIN SERV	1994.	84328.	21324.	23205.	955.	12392.	5670.	794.	18724.	1373.
50 PRIV EDUC	0.	0.	0.	0.	0.	0.	0.	0.	0.	0.
51 PR HEALTH	0.	0.	0.	0.	0.	0.	0.	0.	0.	0.
52 CULT SPPV	42.	0.	0.	0.	0.	0.	0.	0.	0.	0.
53 REPAIR VEH	15544.	25305.	11241.	75074.	561.	1761.	0.	20.	1736.	490.
54 PERSON SER	0.	0.	303.	4636.	1.	0.	0.	0.	0.	0.
55 PUB ADMIN	2658.	18258.	1189.	1055.	0.	71.	148.	118.	205.	8.
56 GOV EDUC	0.	0.	0.	6602.	1.	0.	0.	0.	0.	0.
57 GOV HEALTH	0.	0.	0.	0.	0.	0.	0.	0.	0.	0.
58 O GOV SERV	3128.	17344.	0.	598.	4.	1442.	0.	150.	98.	2.
59 PRI NP SER	0.	0.	0.	0.	0.	0.	0.	0.	0.	0.
60 OTHER SERV	0.	0.	0.	0.	0.	0.	0.	0.	0.	0.
61 TOT INTER	2499941.	1366743.	861096.	841153.	42682.	134394.	135353.	136892.	93322.	13569.
62 MISCELLAN	0.	0.	0.	0.	0.	0.	0.	0.	0.	0.
63 N COMP IMP	0.	0.	0.	0.	0.	0.	0.	0.	0.	0.
64 TOT IMPRT	929310.	209795.	115785.	459410.	34319.	11435.	44567.	90.	24968.	1838.
65 COM TAXES	114367.	23957.	52320.	48311.	1064.	1065.	328.	67.	3223.	447.
66 INVISB BAL	0.	0.	0.	0.	0.	0.	0.	0.	0.	0.
67 VALUE ADD	1571042.	3721968.	414186.	1492108.	374488.	527159.	298138.	1927987.	412229.	48105.
68 GRSS INPUT	5114762.	5327363.	1443287.	2941588.	452553.	674073.	478386.	2065036.	533742.	63959.

JADUAL 1.2 – MATRIKS SERAPAN KOMODITI–KOMODITI DALAM NEGERI PADA NILAI–NILAI ASAS, 1978. KOMODITI X AKTIVITI (RIBU RINGGIT) – SAMB.

Table 1.2 - Absorption Matrix Of Domestic Commodities At Basic Values, 1978. Commodity x Activity (Thousand Ringgit) – Cont'd.

COL	51 PR HEALTH	52 CULT SERV	53 REPAIR VEH	54 PERSON SER	55 PUB ADMIN	56 GOV EDUC	57 GOV HEALTH	58 O GOV SERV	59 PRI NP SER	60 OTHER SERV
ROW										
1 OTH AGRIC	0.	0.	0.	0.	5805.	1716.	2048.	2719.	0.	0.
2 RUBBER PLN	0.	0.	0.	0.	1.	115.	0.	10.	0.	0.
3 OIL PALM	0.	0.	0.	0.	15.	485.	0.	97.	0.	0.
4 LIVESTOCK	0.	0.	0.	0.	1064.	564.	1677.	120.	0.	0.
5 FORESTRY	3.	0.	8.	27.	70.	137.	34.	2588.	0.	0.
6 FISHING	0.	0.	0.	0.	2876.	1264.	2529.	1029.	0.	0.
7 PETROL MIN	0.	0.	0.	0.	0.	32.	2.	79.	0.	0.
8 DAIRY PROD	0.	0.	0.	0.	4222.	1881.	3771.	374.	0.	0.
9 VEG FRUIT	0.	0.	0.	0.	986.	540.	174.	245.	0.	0.
10 OIL & FATS	0.	0.	0.	0.	3257.	503.	489.	218.	0.	0.
11 GRAIN MILL	0.	0.	0.	0.	3010.	1244.	977.	459.	0.	0.
12 BAKER CONF	30.	0.	0.	0.	409R.	1002.	1250.	570.	0.	0.
13 OTH FOODS	0.	1.	0.	0.	9949.	1762.	1183.	932.	0.	0.
14 ANMAL FEED	0.	0.	0.	0.	233.	109.	1851.	453.	0.	0.
15 BEVERAGES	11.	0.	0.	0.	692.	726.	390.	61.	0.	0.
16 TOBACCO	0.	0.	0.	0.	0.	0.	0.	0.	0.	0.
17 TEXTILES	0.	27.	379.	30.	6355.	1490.	2013.	835.	0.	73.
18 WEARNG APL	108.	75.	0.	157.	14085.	902.	907.	1821.	0.	14.
19 SAWMILLS	0.	10.	978.	0.	939.	591.	323.	755.	0.	691.
20 FURN FIXT	0.	0.	0.	0.	425.	0.	0.	0.	0.	136.
21 PAPER PRNT	438.	4694.	52.	431.	18640.	21997.	2430.	10352.	0.	937.
22 INDST CHEM	0.	0.	1781.	17.	900.	921.	3282.	4544.	0.	0.
23 PAINTS ETC	0.	17.	2461.	47.	571.	238.	104.	250.	0.	0.
24 OT CHM PRO	9929.	131.	582.	512.	1891.	1838.	6271.	992.	0.	5313.
25 PETROL PRO	515.	625.	1458.	320.	39527.	810.	1461.	10150.	418.	84.
26 RUBBER PRO	0.	0.	0.	0.	0.	0.	0.	0.	0.	0.
27 RUBBER PRD	265.	156.	12165.	747.	1676.	437.	583.	2753.	0.	0.
28 PLSTIC PRO	810.	1.	0.	0.	0.	0.	0.	0.	0.	252.
29 GLASS PROD	0.	0.	0.	0.	334.	51.	5.	216.	0.	98.
30 CEMENT	0.	0.	0.	0.	124.	386.	47.	721.	0.	0.
31 N METALLIC	0.	4.	0.	0.	14.	51.	5.	155.	0.	0.
32 BASIC MTL	106.	28.	4370.	0.	3815.	495.	411.	1067.	0.	0.
33 OTH METAL	0.	333.	783.	2.	1718.	1065.	551.	1021.	0.	68.
34 N ELEC MAC	1374.	1478.	469.	152.	10787.	5084.	3630.	5565.	0.	521.
35 ELECT MACH	119.	2557.	2052.	417.	6747.	2631.	550.	1370.	0.	0.
36 MOTOR VEH	0.	71.	9147.	0.	343.	300.	61.	159.	0.	0.
37 OTH TRANSP	0.	0.	16687.	1962.	4803.	0.	0.	5002.	0.	0.
38 O MFG PROD	1384.	810.	15.	94.	4775.	2154.	7186.	2401.	0.	214.
39 ELECTRICITY	2489.	12572.	1475.	560.	31368.	12633.	13009.	11557.	591.	2591.
40 WATER	461.	1935.	491.	356.	11381.	3779.	2102.	2878.	144.	763.
41 CNSTRCTION	577.	3110.	0.	62.	150255.	12680.	10282.	140179.	526.	328.
42 TRADE	9042.	3019.	12503.	1301.	45613.	13514.	17598.	13386.	145.	3146.
43 HOTEL ETC	1426.	3429.	441.	62.	87095.	40579.	10052.	32965.	179.	576.
44 TRANSPORT	1190.	3855.	1331.	104.	52793.	9457.	9797.	20533.	96.	390.
45 COMMUNICAT	1500.	17918.	434.	36.	32873.	4549.	4202.	10395.	172.	514.
46 FINANCE	139.	315.	0.	8.	27.	0.	0.	943.	0.	20.
47 INSURANCE	574.	2275.	431.	31.	0.	0.	0.	226.	0.	136.
48 DWELLINGS	6440.	9930.	702.	614.	11642.	2282.	922.	15019.	197.	7215.
49 BUSIN SERV	5646.	14336.	139.	44.	30913.	7389.	2780.	31515.	0.	898.
50 PRIV EDUC	0.	0.	0.	0.	0.	0.	0.	0.	0.	0.
51 PR HEALTH	0.	0.	0.	0.	0.	0.	0.	0.	0.	0.
52 CULT SERV	0.	17131.	0.	0.	0.	0.	0.	0.	0.	0.
53 REPAIR VEH	954.	450.	157.	82.	16653.	1498.	2743.	12941.	297.	275.
54 PERSON SER	0.	1.	0.	230.	644.	519.	1368.	115.	0.	0.
55 PUB ADMIN	65.	430.	0.	0.	3.	0.	0.	0.	0.	9.
56 GOV EDUC	0.	0.	0.	0.	0.	0.	0.	0.	0.	0.
57 GOV HEALTH	0.	0.	0.	0.	0.	0.	0.	0.	0.	0.
58 O GOV SERV	68.	419.	0.	0.	24.	860.	2.	216.	0.	0.
59 PRI NP SER	0.	0.	0.	0.	0.	0.	0.	0.	0.	182.
60 OTHER SERV	0.	0.	0.	0.	0.	0.	0.	0.	0.	182.
61 TOT INTER	46183.	102303.	74953.	8910.	640813.	163183.	122258.	352753.	2765.	25454.
62 MISCELLAN	0.	0.	0.	0.	0.	0.	0.	2411.	0.	0.
63 N COMP INP	0.	0.	0.	0.	0.	0.	0.	0.	0.	0.
64 TOT IMPRTS	22959.	9271.	11625.	2777.	724359.	43720.	50217.	31779.	279.	11735.
65 COM TAXES	2635.	2956.	17503.	622.	19880.	4613.	7411.	8407.	471.	2691.
66 INVISB BAL	0.	0.	0.	0.	0.	0.	0.	0.	0.	0.
67 VALUE ADD	100317.	190922.	111741.	28934.	1598957.	1469928.	444733.	592640.	5186.	118715.
68 GRSS INPUT	172114.	314452.	315624.	41843.	2994614.	1690441.	624619.	987990.	8701.	158585.

182

JADUAL 1.2 – MATRIKS SERAPAN KOMODITI–KOMODITI DALAM NEGERI PADA NILAI–NILAI ASAS, 1978. KOMODITI X AKTIVITI (RIBU RINGGIT) – SAMB.

Table 1.2 – Absorption Matrix Of Domestic Commodities At Basic Values, 1978. Commodity x Activity (Thousand Ringgit) – Cont'd.

COL ROW	61 TOT INTER	62 BANK INT	63 PRIV CONS	64 GOVT CONS	65 STOCKS	66 INVESTMENT	67 EXPORTS	68 TOTAL FN D	69 TOTAL DES	70 TOT IMPRTS
1 OTH AGRIC	836668.	0.	491528.	0.	36617.	18806.	310951.	859898.	0.	0.
2 RUBBER PLN	1389606.	0.	986.	0.	4191.	169465.	390.	175032.	0.	0.
3 OIL PALM	645062.	0.	0.	0.	-10.	189333.	21.	189344.	0.	0.
4 LIVESTOCK	410678.	0.	523796.	0.	-4980.	0.	6106.	524922.	0.	0.
5 FORESTRY	765768.	0.	27468.	0.	61953.	0.	990747.	1080168.	0.	0.
6 FISHING	302420.	0.	1323153.	0.	476.	283.	638.	1324550.	0.	0.
7 PETROL MIN	1973998.	0.	0.	0.	-21894.	0.	2236451.	2214557.	0.	0.
8 DAIRY PROD	137886.	0.	616342.	0.	459.	0.	23093.	639894.	0.	0.
9 VEG FRUIT	15545.	0.	148929.	0.	501.	0.	232259.	381689.	0.	0.
10 OIL & FATS	1141761.	0.	221366.	0.	262590.	0.	1925072.	2409028.	0.	0.
11 GRAIN MILL	132769.	0.	691004.	0.	45976.	0.	19074.	756054.	0.	0.
12 BAKER CONF	42080.	0.	336015.	0.	314.	0.	39926.	376255.	0.	0.
13 OTH FOODS	134953.	0.	427038.	0.	5861.	0.	17835.	450734.	0.	0.
14 ANMAL FEED	100685.	0.	0.	0.	26193.	0.	155.	26348.	0.	0.
15 BEVERAGES	35553.	0.	247823.	0.	392.	0.	17026.	265241.	0.	0.
16 TOBACCO	10877.	0.	499551.	0.	5162.	0.	444.	505157.	0.	0.
17 TEXTILES	402731.	0.	365404.	0.	17324.	2430.	242811.	627969.	0.	0.
18 WEARNG APL	34031.	0.	222063.	0.	2898.	0.	127694.	353255.	0.	0.
19 SAWMILLS	569276.	0.	4323.	0.	-13017.	0.	1095691.	1086997.	0.	0.
20 FURN FIXT	9176.	0.	90463.	0.	772.	11912.	24352.	127499.	0.	0.
21 PAPER PPNT	467294.	0.	85336.	0.	-14332.	0.	14401.	85405.	0.	0.
22 INDST CHEM	383527.	0.	7421.	0.	-60.	0.	28758.	36119.	0.	0.
23 PAINTS ETC	109148.	0.	0.	0.	-4319.	0.	2358.	-1961.	0.	0.
24 OT CHM PRD	101231.	0.	253372.	0.	-3489.	0.	54111.	303994.	0.	0.
25 PETROL PRD	1056865.	0.	447113.	0.	9130.	0.	116110.	571353.	0.	0.
26 RUBBER PRO	104078.	0.	0.	0.	36618.	0.	2399059.	2434677.	0.	0.
27 RUBBER PBD	134604.	0.	221340.	0.	10129.	0.	112249.	343717.	0.	0.
28 PLSTIC PRD	164795.	0.	73464.	0.	12066.	0.	38653.	121183.	0.	0.
29 GLASS PROD	164687.	0.	46523.	0.	-2620.	0.	11390.	55293.	0.	0.
30 CEMENT	223696.	0.	0.	0.	-12958.	0.	6845.	-6113.	0.	0.
31 N METALLIC	170558.	0.	2077.	0.	-2581.	0.	8682.	8178.	0.	0.
32 BASIC MTL	668615.	0.	11618.	0.	48501.	37670.	2066105.	2165894.	0.	0.
33 OTH METAL	336727.	0.	44937.	0.	4800.	26340.	38826.	114903.	0.	0.
34 N ELEC MAC	121786.	0.	31943.	0.	-4444.	99652.	87692.	264843.	0.	0.
35 ELECT MACH	139205.	0.	132751.	0.	63040.	89311.	1365717.	1700819.	0.	0.
36 MOTOR VEH	55821.	0.	533605.	0.	11359.	377014.	6370.	928348.	0.	0.
37 OTH TRANSP	70516.	0.	160786.	0.	608.	34871.	3093.	199318.	0.	0.
38 O MFG PROD	105902.	0.	106550.	0.	-1998.	2479.	109540.	216571.	0.	0.
39 ELECTCITY	537296.	0.	212575.	0.	0.	0.	0.	212575.	0.	0.
40 WATER	103377.	0.	23010.	0.	0.	0.	1000.	24010.	0.	0.
41 CNSTRCTION	636016.	0.	0.	0.	0.	4526510.	0.	4526510.	0.	0.
42 TRADE	2157741.	0.	1931799.	0.	176.	705635.	709435.	3317044.	0.	0.
43 HOTEL ETC	562079.	0.	736237.	0.	0.	0.	6050.	792287.	0.	0.
44 TRANSPORT	1010127.	0.	895882.	0.	8.	39205.	905655.	1839750.	0.	0.
45 COMMUNICAT	111819.	0.	135445.	0.	0.	0.	35300.	140745.	0.	0.
46 FINANCE	80597.	578535.	1807.	0.	0.	0.	0.	590142.	0.	0.
47 INSURANCE	292311.	0.	170176.	0.	0.	0.	15900.	186076.	0.	0.
48 DWELLINGS	519493.	0.	1633494.	0.	0.	0.	0.	1648494.	0.	0.
49 BUSIN SERV	356347.	0.	33313.	0.	0.	49421.	38156.	120990.	0.	0.
50 PRIV EDUC	0.	0.	62934.	0.	0.	0.	0.	62934.	0.	0.
51 PR HEALTH	0.	0.	170730.	0.	0.	0.	0.	170730.	0.	0.
52 CULT SERV	17349.	0.	233106.	0.	0.	0.	144.	250250.	0.	0.
53 REPAIR VEH	252954.	0.	52670.	0.	0.	0.	0.	52670.	0.	0.
54 PERSON SER	7817.	0.	31765.	0.	0.	0.	0.	31765.	0.	0.
55 PUB ADMIN	33974.	0.	653.	2905756.	0.	0.	0.	2906409.	0.	0.
56 GOV EDUC	7007.	0.	37280.	1636044.	0.	0.	0.	1673324.	0.	0.
57 GOV HEALTH	155.	0.	21719.	600810.	0.	0.	0.	622529.	0.	0.
58 O GOV SERV	24568.	0.	5128.	913031.	0.	0.	0.	943159.	0.	0.
59 PRI VP SER	0.	0.	8701.	0.	0.	0.	0.	8701.	0.	0.
60 OTHER SERV	182.	0.	153891.	0.	0.	0.	68.	153959.	0.	0.
61 TOT INTER	21234557.	578535.	15071157.	6080641.	580411.	6378937.	15491903.	44181894.	0.	0.
62 MISCELLAN	17386.	0.	45683.	9551.	0.	0.	0.	106234.	0.	0.
63 N COMP INP	0.	0.	0.	0.	0.	0.	0.	0.	0.	0.
64 TOT IMPRTS	1731891.	0.	2642808.	0.	109191.	2657139.	0.	5409138.	0.	0.
65 COM TAXES	1431372.	6701.	1511686.	0.	33812.	345215.	1931101.	3828515.	0.	0.
66 INVISB BAL	0.	0.	251100.	0.	0.	0.	624339.	885439.	0.	-883200.
67 VALUE ADD	31016204.	-585236.	0.	0.	0.	0.	0.	-585236.	0.	0.
68 GRSS INPUT	55531410.	0.	19534234.	6090192.	723414.	9381291.	18046843.	53825978.	0.	-883200.

JADUAL 1.2 – MATRIKS SERAPAN KOMODITI-KOMODITI DALAM NEGERI PADA NILAI-NILAI ASAS, 1978. KOMODITI X AKTIVITI (RIBU RINGGIT) – SAMB.

Table 1.2 – Absorption Matrix Of Domestic Commodities At Basic Values, 1978. Commodity x Activity (Thousand Ringgit) – Cont'd.

COL	71	72	73
	RE-EXPORTS	COM TAXES	GRS OUTPUT
ROW			
1 OTH AGRIC	0.	0.	1696162.
2 RUBBER PLN	0.	0.	1264638.
3 OIL PALM	0.	0.	814406.
4 LIVESTOCK	0.	0.	935600.
5 FORESTRY	0.	0.	1845936.
6 FISHING	0.	0.	1626970.
7 PETROL MIN	0.	0.	4038555.
8 DAIRY PROD	0.	0.	777780.
9 VEG FRUIT	0.	0.	337234.
10 OIL & FATS	0.	0.	3550789.
11 GRAIN MILL	0.	0.	948823.
12 BAKER CONF	0.	0.	413335.
13 OTH FOODS	0.	0.	645687.
14 ANMAL FEED	0.	0.	327033.
15 BEVERAGES	0.	0.	300794.
16 TOBACCO	0.	0.	516034.
17 TEXTILES	0.	0.	1030700.
18 WEARNG APL	0.	0.	337286.
19 SAWMILLS	0.	0.	1636273.
20 FURN FIXT	0.	0.	136675.
21 PAPER PRNT	0.	0.	552599.
22 INDST CHEM	0.	0.	419646.
23 PAINTS ETC	0.	0.	137187.
24 OT CHM PRD	0.	0.	405225.
25 PETROL PRD	0.	0.	1623219.
26 RUBBER PRO	0.	0.	2518751.
27 RUBBER PRD	0.	0.	528321.
28 PLSTIC PRD	0.	0.	205978.
29 GLASS PROD	0.	0.	219980.
30 CEMENT	0.	0.	217573.
31 N METALLIC	0.	0.	179736.
32 BASIC MTL	0.	0.	2814509.
33 OTH METAL	0.	0.	451630.
34 N ELEC MAC	0.	0.	536629.
35 ELECT MACH	0.	0.	2010024.
36 MOTOR VEH	0.	0.	934169.
37 OTH TRANSP	0.	0.	269834.
38 O MFG PROD	0.	0.	322473.
39 ELECTRCITY	0.	0.	869361.
40 WATER	0.	0.	124387.
41 CNSTRCTION	0.	0.	5213126.
42 TRADE	49048.	0.	5523933.
43 HOTEL ETC	0.	0.	1354366.
44 TRANSPORT	5921.	0.	2955799.
45 COMMUNICAT	0.	0.	452563.
46 FINANCE	0.	0.	660939.
47 INSURANCE	0.	0.	478386.
48 DWELLINGS	0.	0.	2167387.
49 BUSIN SERV	0.	0.	677237.
50 PRIV EDUC	0.	0.	62934.
51 PR HEALTH	0.	0.	179730.
52 CULT SERV	0.	0.	267599.
53 REPAIR VEH	0.	0.	335624.
54 PERSON SER	0.	0.	39582.
55 PUB ADMIN	0.	0.	2945381.
56 GOV EDUC	0.	0.	1640331.
57 GOV HEALTH	0.	0.	622883.
58 O GOV SERV	0.	0.	967727.
59 PRI NP SER	0.	0.	9701.
60 OTHER SERV	0.	0.	154141.
61 TOT INTER	54969.	0.	65531410.
62 MISCELLAN	0.	0.	143620.
63 N COMP IMP	. 0.	0.	.
64 TOT IMPRTS	332961.	0.	15531990.
65 COM TAXES	697.	0.	5310584.
66 INVISB PAL	0.	0.	2239.
67 VALUE ADD	0.	0.	12410968.
68 GRSS INPUT	518627.	0.	119012911.

184

COL	1 OTH AGRIC	2 RUBBER PLN	3 OIL PALM	4 LIVESTOCK	5 FORESTRY	6 FISHING	7 PETROL MIN	8 DAIRY PROD	9 VEG FRUIT	10 OIL & FATS
ROW										
1 OTH AGRIC	1173.	0.	0.	10052.	0.	0.	0.	99.	3336.	3270.
2 RUBBER PLN	0.	0.	0.	0.	0.	0.	0.	0.	0.	0.
3 OIL PALM	6.	0.	0.	0.	0.	0.	0.	0.	0.	0.
4 LIVESTOCK	0.	0.	0.	3814.	0.	0.	0.	6446.	22.	0.
5 FORESTRY	0.	0.	0.	0.	2347.	0.	256.	0.	0.	0.
6 FISHING	0.	0.	0.	0.	0.	0.	0.	0.	0.	0.
7 PETROL MIN	0.	0.	0.	0.	0.	0.	1.	0.	1062.	4.
8 DAIRY PROD	0.	0.	0.	12133.	0.	0.	0.	105507.	0.	19.
9 VEG FRUIT	0.	0.	0.	0.	0.	0.	1.	1403.	722.	0.
10 OIL & FATS	0.	19.	0.	43093.	0.	0.	0.	529.	979.	10886.
11 GRAIN MILL	0.	0.	0.	61491.	0.	0.	0.	11.	215.	618.
12 BAKER CONF	0.	0.	0.	0.	0.	0.	0.	5042.	0.	37.
13 OTH FOODS	0.	0.	0.	125.	0.	0.	0.	7040.	2230.	52.
14 ANMAL FEED	0.	0.	0.	68535.	0.	0.	0.	0.	0.	0.
15 BEVERAGES	0.	0.	0.	0.	0.	0.	0.	0.	0.	0.
16 TOBACCO	0.	0.	0.	0.	0.	0.	0.	0.	0.	0.
17 TEXTILES	75.	0.	197.	0.	0.	4968.	263.	0.	0.	0.
18 WEABNG APL	0.	0.	0.	0.	526.	0.	87.	21.	15.	14.
19 SAWMILLS	0.	0.	0.	0.	0.	0.	0.	152.	0.	0.
20 FURN FIXT	0.	0.	0.	0.	0.	0.	0.	0.	0.	0.
21 PAPER PRNT	520.	947.	331.	0.	67.	0.	899.	6886.	3011.	1951.
22 INDST CHEM	74669.	79801.	118782.	0.	0.	0.	2410.	221.	1141.	2936.
23 PAINTS ETC	0.	709.	159.	0.	0.	0.	114.	0.	0.	0.
24 OT CHM PRD	55.	76.	0.	0.	1313.	0.	8690.	51.	0.	441.
25 PETROL PRD	1040.	3621.	4125.	0.	18019.	25989.	43969.	396.	849.	5334.
26 RUBBER PRO	0.	1.	0.	0.	0.	0.	0.	0.	0.	0.
27 RUBBER PRO	0.	0.	0.	0.	0.	0.	641.	0.	0.	0.
28 PLSTIC PRD	103.	227.	0.	0.	0.	0.	0.	41.	208.	202.
29 GLASS PROD	123.	0.	160.	0.	0.	0.	0.	475.	1227.	96.
30 CEMENT	0.	0.	333.	0.	0.	0.	962.	0.	0.	266.
31 N METALLIC	0.	0.	0.	0.	0.	0.	852.	0.	0.	0.
32 BASIC MTL	5514.	10183.	3694.	0.	3040.	0.	19291.	53.	17.	94.
33 OTH METAL	85.	734.	791.	0.	13777.	0.	5724.	2550.	1693.	1679.
34 N ELEC MAC	373.	3196.	5665.	206.	26132.	0.	33050.	763.	775.	12523.
35 ELECT MACH	63.	126.	257.	0.	18419.	0.	7947.	0.	0.	117.
36 MOTOR VEH	908.	2521.	3392.	0.	4736.	0.	14996.	359.	240.	2553.
37 OTH TRANSP	0.	0.	0.	15.	0.	7837.	0.	0.	0.	0.
38 O MFG PROD	94.	159.	398.	0.	99.	0.	29138.	160.	191.	66.
39 ELECTRCITY	0.	0.	0.	0.	0.	0.	0.	0.	0.	0.
40 WATER	0.	0.	0.	0.	0.	0.	0.	0.	0.	0.
41 CNSTRCTION	0.	0.	0.	0.	0.	0.	4228.	0.	0.	0.
42 TRADE	0.	0.	0.	0.	0.	0.	0.	0.	0.	0.
43 HOTEL ETC	0.	0.	0.	0.	0.	0.	0.	0.	0.	0.
44 TRANSPORT	0.	0.	0.	0.	0.	0.	0.	0.	0.	0.
45 COMMUNICAT	0.	0.	0.	0.	0.	0.	0.	0.	0.	0.
46 FINANCE	0.	0.	0.	0.	0.	0.	0.	0.	0.	0.
47 INSURANCE	0.	0.	0.	0.	0.	0.	0.	0.	0.	0.
48 DWELLINGS	0.	0.	0.	0.	0.	0.	0.	0.	0.	0.
49 BUSIN SERV	0.	0.	0.	0.	0.	0.	35470.	0.	0.	1789.
50 PRIV EDUC	0.	0.	0.	0.	0.	0.	0.	0.	0.	0.
51 PR HEALTH	0.	0.	0.	0.	0.	0.	0.	0.	0.	0.
52 CULT SERV	0.	0.	0.	0.	0.	0.	0.	0.	0.	0.
53 REPAIR VEH	0.	0.	0.	0.	0.	0.	0.	0.	0.	0.
54 PERSON SER	0.	0.	0.	0.	0.	0.	0.	0.	0.	0.
55 PUB ADMIN	0.	0.	0.	0.	0.	0.	0.	0.	0.	0.
56 GOV EDUC	0.	0.	0.	0.	0.	0.	0.	0.	0.	0.
57 GOV HEALTH	0.	0.	0.	0.	0.	0.	0.	0.	0.	0.
58 O GOV SERV	0.	0.	0.	0.	0.	0.	0.	0.	0.	0.
59 PRI 1P SER	0.	0.	0.	0.	0.	0.	0.	0.	0.	0.
60 OTHER SERV	0.	0.	0.	0.	0.	0.	0.	0.	0.	0.
61 TOT INTER	85301.	103370.	143284.	189464.	84574.	38794.	212909.	137807.	17932.	44946.
62 MISCELLAN	0.	0.	0.	0.	0.	0.	0.	0.	0.	0.
63 N COMP IMP	0.	0.	0.	0.	0.	0.	0.	0.	0.	0.
64 TOT IMPITS	85301.	103370.	143284.	189464.	84574.	38794.	212909.	137807.	17932.	44946.
65 COM TAXES	0.	0.	0.	0.	0.	0.	0.	0.	0.	0.
66 INVISB BAL	0.	0.	0.	0.	0.	0.	0.	0.	0.	0.
67 VALUE ADD	0.	0.	0.	0.	0.	0.	0.	0.	0.	0.
68 GRSS INPUT	0.	0.	0.	0.	0.	0.	0.	0.	0.	0.

185

JADUAL 1.3 – MATRIKS SERAPAN KOMODITI–KOMODITI IMPORT PADA NILAI–NILAI ASAS, 1978. KOMODITI X AKTIVITI (RIBU RINGGIT) – SAMB.

Table 1.3 Absorption Matrix Of Imported Commodities At Basic Values, 1978. Commodity x Activity (Thousand Ringgit) – Cont'd.

COL / ROW	11 GRAIN MILL	12 BAKER CONF	13 OTH FOODS	14 ANNAL FEED	15 BEVERAGES	16 TOBACCO	17 TEXTILES	18 WEARNG APL	19 SAWMILLS	20 FURN FIXT
1 OTH AGRIC	169097.	19792.	11979.	97105.	2387.	0.	119300.	0.	0.	0.
2 RUBBER PLN	0.	0.	0.	0.	0.	0.	0.	0.	0.	0.
3 OIL PALM	0.	0.	0.	0.	0.	0.	0.	0.	0.	0.
4 LIVESTOCK	0.	27.	0.	0.	0.	0.	0.	2.	0.	0.
5 FORESTRY	0.	0.	0.	0.	0.	0.	0.	0.	753.	0.
6 FISHING	0.	0.	0.	0.	0.	0.	0.	0.	0.	0.
7 PETROL MIN	0.	657.	592.	107.	0.	0.	0.	10.	0.	0.
8 DAIRY PROD	0.	2619.	505.	7244.	1529.	0.	0.	456.	0.	0.
9 VEG FRUIT	0.	587.	51.	78.	17.	0.	0.	0.	0.	0.
10 OIL & FATS	37.	76.	98.	59094.	8.	0.	285.	0.	0.	0.
11 GRAIN MILL	2096.	12987.	10320.	12319.	846.	0.	0.	0.	0.	0.
12 BAKER CONF	0.	536.	0.	0.	0.	0.	0.	0.	0.	0.
13 OTH FOODS	11.	13502.	256120.	57.	17764.	24.	291.	0.	0.	0.
14 ANNAL FEED	0.	0.	0.	0.	0.	0.	0.	0.	0.	0.
15 BEVERAGES	0.	0.	0.	0.	13279.	0.	0.	0.	0.	0.
16 TOBACCO	0.	0.	0.	0.	0.	74485.	0.	0.	0.	0.
17 TEXTILES	2477.	0.	2.	0.	0.	0.	124423.	33596.	385.	200.
18 WEARNG APL	6.	12.	0.	0.	39.	44.	66.	2967.	11.	0.
19 SAWMILLS	0.	0.	2.	0.	966.	0.	0.	493.	14934.	1685.
20 FURN FIXT	0.	0.	140.	0.	0.	0.	0.	0.	0.	548.
21 PAPER PRNT	193.	1249.	5609.	1184.	6315.	26294.	2188.	1717.	1179.	709.
22 INDST CHEM	85.	1515.	6083.	1237.	1184.	1420.	67485.	3516.	9291.	1464.
23 PAINTS ETC	0.	0.	0.	0.	0.	0.	0.	0.	279.	693.
24 OT CHM PRD	0.	14.	762.	6247.	39.	52.	992.	50.	4727.	225.
25 PETROL PRD	1135.	1044.	4750.	217.	789.	117.	3398.	159.	7159.	101.
26 RUBBER PRO	0.	0.	0.	0.	0.	0.	0.	0.	0.	0.
27 RUBBER PRD	0.	0.	0.	0.	0.	0.	0.	467.	0.	0.
28 PLSTIC PRD	162.	646.	787.	256.	0.	403.	0.	561.	318.	52.
29 GLASS PROD	0.	0.	0.	0.	4151.	0.	0.	0.	44.	580.
30 CEMENT	0.	0.	140.	0.	0.	74.	0.	0.	168.	0.
31 N METALLIC	0.	0.	0.	0.	0.	0.	0.	0.	72.	79.
32 BASIC STL	81.	55.	69.	0.	25.	15.	52.	15.	3689.	2786.
33 OTH METAL	0.	321.	43.	0.	1632.	32.	40.	31.	1425.	14.
34 N ELEC MAC	1500.	460.	4001.	489.	982.	1362.	1428.	194.	10215.	1290.
35 ELECT MACH	72.	45.	42.	0.	0.	0.	42.	0.	442.	0.
36 MOTOR VEH	156.	177.	1343.	227.	515.	687.	1313.	139.	4803.	156.
37 OTH TRANSP	0.	0.	0.	0.	0.	0.	0.	0.	0.	0.
38 O MFG PROD	43.	70.	136.	29.	194.	110.	482.	9056.	201.	58.
39 ELECTRICITY	0.	0.	0.	0.	0.	0.	0.	0.	0.	0.
40 WATER	0.	0.	0.	0.	0.	0.	0.	0.	0.	0.
41 CNSTRCTION	0.	0.	0.	0.	0.	0.	0.	0.	0.	0.
42 TRADE	0.	0.	0.	0.	0.	0.	0.	0.	0.	0.
43 HOTEL ETC	0.	0.	0.	0.	0.	0.	0.	0.	0.	0.
44 TRANSPORT	0.	0.	0.	0.	0.	0.	0.	0.	0.	0.
45 COMMNICAT	0.	0.	0.	0.	0.	0.	0.	0.	0.	0.
46 FINANCE	0.	0.	0.	0.	0.	0.	0.	0.	0.	0.
47 INSURANCE	0.	0.	0.	0.	0.	0.	0.	0.	0.	0.
48 DWELLINGS	0.	0.	0.	0.	0.	0.	0.	0.	0.	0.
49 BUSIN SERV	0.	0.	0.	0.	1000.	3000.	2362.	0.	5000.	0.
50 PRIV EDUC	0.	0.	0.	0.	0.	0.	0.	0.	0.	0.
51 PR HEALTH	0.	0.	0.	0.	0.	0.	0.	0.	0.	0.
52 CULT SERV	0.	0.	0.	0.	0.	0.	0.	0.	0.	0.
53 REPAIR VEH	0.	0.	0.	0.	0.	0.	0.	0.	0.	0.
54 PERSON SRV	0.	0.	0.	0.	0.	0.	0.	0.	0.	0.
55 POB ADMIN	0.	0.	0.	0.	0.	0.	0.	0.	0.	0.
56 GOV EDUC	0.	0.	0.	0.	0.	0.	0.	0.	0.	0.
57 GOV HEALTH	0.	0.	0.	0.	0.	0.	0.	0.	0.	0.
58 O GOV SERV	0.	0.	0.	0.	0.	0.	0.	0.	0.	0.
59 PRI VP SER	0.	0.	0.	0.	0.	0.	0.	0.	0.	0.
60 OTHER SERV	0.	0.	0.	0.	0.	0.	0.	0.	0.	0.
61 TOT INTER	176995.	59411.	303313.	195910.	51162.	108119.	326144.	53429.	65295.	10640.
62 MISCELLAN	0.	0.	0.	0.	0.	0.	0.	0.	0.	0.
63 N COMP IMP	0.	0.	0.	0.	0.	0.	0.	0.	0.	0.
64 TOT IMPRTS	176995.	59411.	303313.	195910.	51162.	109119.	326148.	53429.	65295.	10640.
65 COM TAXES	0.	0.	0.	0.	0.	0.	0.	0.	0.	0.
66 INVISBL BAL	0.	0.	0.	0.	0.	0.	0.	0.	0.	0.
67 VALUE ADD	0.	0.	0.	0.	0.	0.	0.	0.	0.	0.
68 GRSS INPUT	0.	0.	0.	0.	0.	0.	0.	0.	0.	0.

186

JADUAL 1.3 — MATRIKS SERAPAN KOMODITI-KOMODITI IMPORT PADA NILAI-NILAI ASAS, 1978. KOMODITI X AKTIVITI (RIBU RINGGIT) — SAMB.

Table 1.3 — Absorption Matrix Of Imported Commodities At Basic Values, 1978. Commodity x Activity (Thousand Ringgit) — Cont'd.

COL	21 PAPER PRNT	22 INDST CHEM	23 PAINTS ETC	24 OT CHM PRD	25 PETROL PRD	26 RUBBER PPO	27 RUBBER PRD	28 PLSTIC PRD	29 GLASS PROD	30 CEMENT
1 OTH AGRIC	0.	0.	0.	1300.	0.	0.	0.	0.	0.	0.
2 RUBBER PLN	0.	0.	0.	0.	0.	0.	0.	0.	0.	0.
3 OIL PALM	0.	0.	0.	0.	0.	0.	0.	0.	0.	0.
4 LIVESTOCK	0.	0.	0.	87.	0.	0.	0.	0.	0.	0.
5 FORESTRY	0.	35.	0.	1.	0.	0.	1219.	0.	0.	0.
6 FISHING	0.	0.	0.	0.	0.	0.	0.	0.	0.	0.
7 PETROL MIN	0.	15185.	8.	135.	922451.	0.	178.	0.	10084.	6528.
8 DAIRY PROD	0.	153.	0.	0.	0.	0.	0.	0.	0.	0.
9 VEG FRUIT	0.	0.	0.	0.	0.	0.	0.	0.	0.	0.
10 OIL & FATS	0.	4.	926.	554.	0.	0.	0.	13.	0.	0.
11 GRAIN MILL	0.	0.	0.	75.	0.	0.	0.	0.	0.	0.
12 BAKES CONF	0.	0.	0.	0.	0.	0.	0.	0.	0.	0.
13 OTH FOODS	0.	785.	0.	1751.	0.	1.	0.	25.	0.	0.
14 ANMAL FEED	0.	0.	0.	0.	0.	0.	0.	0.	0.	0.
15 BEVERAGES	0.	0.	0.	4.	0.	0.	0.	0.	0.	0.
16 TOBACCO	0.	0.	0.	0.	0.	0.	0.	0.	0.	0.
17 TEXTILES	82.	0.	0.	0.	0.	0.	34330.	3894.	0.	0.
18 WEARNG APL	11.	18.	10.	38.	5.	10.	26.	13.	8.	6.
19 SAWMILLS	29.	0.	0.	4312.	0.	0.	0.	0.	14.	0.
20 FURN FIXT	0.	0.	0.	0.	0.	0.	0.	0.	0.	0.
21 PAPER PRNT	160355.	1023.	322.	11974.	232.	3752.	3068.	2671.	2116.	4636.
22 INDST CHEM	3885.	123201.	31042.	73164.	10204.	29603.	44018.	96500.	6987.	245.
23 PAINTS ETC	67.	0.	246.	74.	155.	0.	0.	304.	1681.	5.
24 OT CHM PRD	7217.	1362.	0.	5826.	3391.	0.	3293.	0.	9.	122.
25 PETROL PRD	1137.	5889.	4856.	802.	27637.	2465.	2704.	446.	4842.	11035.
26 RUBBER PRD	0.	0.	0.	0.	0.	0.	1646.	0.	0.	0.
27 RUBBER PRD	0.	0.	0.	0.	0.	0.	3186.	0.	0.	0.
28 PLSTIC PRD	466.	742.	0.	257.	0.	245.	237.	6197.	0.	0.
29 GLASS PROD	0.	0.	0.	2348.	0.	0.	0.	0.	1707.	0.
30 CEMENT	0.	129.	0.	0.	0.	67.	105.	0.	77.	295.
31 N METALLIC	0.	0.	0.	0.	0.	0.	117.	3.	665.	0.
32 BASIC MTL	1385.	2237.	0.	12.	0.	83.	98.	217.	290.	0.
33 OTH METAL	362.	0.	384.	253.	467.	0.	3584.	26.	52.	0.
34 N ELEC MAC	1649.	2360.	86.	766.	3743.	2401.	4219.	1267.	2572.	6587.
35 ELECT MACH	66.	0.	0.	0.	0.	86.	61.	962.	184.	0.
36 MOTOR VEH	551.	1196.	40.	392.	393.	713.	1004.	493.	1267.	1475.
37 OTH TRANSP	0.	0.	0.	0.	0.	0.	0.	0.	0.	0.
38 O MFG PROD	633.	98.	0.	176.	52.	39.	353.	126.	51.	0.
39 ELECTRCITY	0.	0.	0.	0.	0.	0.	0.	0.	0.	0.
40 WATER	0.	0.	0.	0.	0.	0.	0.	0.	0.	0.
41 CNSTRCTION	0.	0.	0.	0.	0.	0.	0.	0.	0.	0.
42 TRADE	0.	0.	0.	0.	0.	0.	0.	0.	0.	0.
43 HOTEL ETC	0.	0.	0.	0.	0.	0.	0.	0.	0.	0.
44 TRANSPORT	0.	0.	0.	0.	0.	0.	0.	0.	0.	0.
45 COMMUNICAT	0.	0.	0.	0.	0.	0.	0.	0.	0.	0.
46 FINANCE	0.	0.	0.	0.	0.	0.	0.	0.	0.	0.
47 INSURANCE	0.	0.	0.	0.	0.	0.	0.	0.	0.	0.
48 DWELLINGS	0.	0.	0.	0.	0.	0.	0.	0.	0.	0.
49 BUSIN SERV	2490.	1955.	0.	1000.	3592.	0.	850.	0.	0.	0.
50 PRIV EDUC	0.	0.	0.	0.	0.	0.	0.	0.	0.	0.
51 PP HEALTH	0.	0.	0.	0.	0.	0.	0.	0.	0.	0.
52 CULT SERV	0.	0.	0.	0.	0.	0.	0.	0.	0.	0.
53 REPAIR VEH	0.	0.	0.	0.	0.	0.	0.	0.	0.	0.
54 PERSON SER	0.	0.	0.	0.	0.	0.	0.	0.	0.	0.
55 PUB ADMIN	0.	0.	0.	0.	0.	0.	0.	0.	0.	0.
56 GOV EDUC	0.	0.	0.	0.	0.	0.	0.	0.	0.	0.
57 GOV HEALTH	0.	0.	0.	0.	0.	0.	0.	0.	0.	0.
58 O GOV SERV	0.	0.	0.	0.	0.	0.	0.	0.	0.	0.
59 PRI MF SER	0.	0.	0.	0.	0.	0.	0.	0.	0.	0.
60 OTHER SERV	0.	0.	0.	0.	0.	0.	0.	0.	0.	0.
61 TOT INTER	180375.	156362.	37520.	105295.	972322.	39465.	104296.	113157.	32606.	30934.
62 MISCELLAN	0.	0.	0.	0.	0.	0.	0.	0.	0.	0.
63 N COMP INP	0.	0.	0.	0.	0.	0.	0.	0.	0.	0.
64 TOT IMPRTS	180375.	156362.	37520.	105295.	972322.	39465.	104296.	113157.	32606.	30934.
65 COM TAXES	0.	0.	0.	0.	0.	0.	0.	0.	0.	0.
66 INVISB BAL	0.	0.	0.	0.	0.	0.	0.	0.	0.	0.
67 VALUE ADD	0.	0.	0.	0.	0.	0.	0.	0.	0.	0.
68 GRSS INPUT	0.	0.	0.	0.	0.	0.	0.	0.	0.	0.

JADUAL 1.3   MATRIKS SERAPAN KOMODITI–KOMODITI IMPORT PADA NILAI–NILAI ASAS, 1978. KOMODITI X AKTIVITI (RIBU RINGGIT) – SAMB.

Table 1.3   Absorption Matrix Of Imported Commodities At Basic Values, 1978. Commodity x Activity (Thousand Ringgit) – Cont'd.

COI	31 METALLIC BASIC MTL	32 OTH METAL	33	34 N ELEC MAC	35 ELECT MACH	36 MOTOR VEH	37 OTH TRANSP O	38 MFG PROD	39 ELECTRCITY	40 WATER
ROW										
1 OTH AGRIC	0.	0.	0.	0.	0.	0.	0.	0.	0.	0.
2 RUBBER PLN	0.	0.	0.	0.	0.	0.	0.	0.	0.	0.
3 OIL PALM	0.	0.	0.	0.	0.	0.	0.	0.	0.	0.
4 LIVESTOCK	0.	0.	0.	0.	0.	0.	0.	0.	0.	0.
5 FORESTRY	0.	700.	0.	59.	0.	0.	0.	116.	0.	0.
6 FISHING	0.	0.	0.	0.	0.	0.	0.	0.	0.	0.
7 PETROL MIN	36532.	223718.	0.	0.	1219.	0.	0.	0.	0.	0.
8 DAIRY PROD	0.	0.	0.	0.	0.	0.	0.	0.	0.	0.
9 VEG FRUIT	0.	0.	0.	0.	0.	0.	0.	0.	0.	0.
10 OIL & FATS	0.	0.	0.	0.	0.	0.	0.	0.	0.	0.
11 GRAIN MILL	0.	0.	0.	2.	0.	0.	0.	0.	0.	0.
12 BAKE CONF	0.	0.	0.	0.	0.	0.	0.	0.	0.	0.
13 OTH FOODS	0.	0.	0.	0.	0.	0.	0.	0.	0.	0.
14 ANMAL FEED	0.	0.	0.	0.	0.	0.	0.	0.	0.	0.
15 BEVERAGES	0.	0.	0.	0.	0.	1.	0.	0.	0.	0.
16 TOBACCO	0.	0.	0.	0.	0.	0.	0.	0.	0.	0.
17 TEXTILES	17.	16.	12.	0.	848.	40.	1.	3255.	0.	0.
18 WEARNG APL	10.	51.	25.	32.	181.	57.	75.	10.	63.	11.
19 SAWMILLS	0.	1.	72.	21.	0.	23.	0.	13.	0.	0.
20 FURN FIXT	0.	0.	0.	0.	121.	0.	0.	0.	0.	0.
21 PAPER PRNT	1434.	911.	3455.	408.	7624.	987.	87.	2558.	116.	18.
22 INDST CHEM	1220.	3339.	1259.	134.	32452.	172.	349.	2815.	0.	2425.
23 PAINTS ETC	45.	411.	541.	166.	34.	1146.	47.	38.	0.	0.
24 OT CHM PRD	0.	6.	497.	5.	3067.	222.	4.	296.	0.	0.
25 PETROL PRD	722.	6443.	782.	1401.	1354.	760.	264.	158.	30995.	1035.
26 RUBBER PRO	0.	0.	0.	0.	0.	0.	0.	0.	0.	0.
27 RUBBER PRO	0.	268.	0.	6.	1367.	25.	0.	0.	0.	0.
28 PLSTIC PRD	0.	6.	55.	339.	1239.	30.	0.	384.	0.	0.
29 GLASS PROD	332.	4079.	8.	0.	4030.	502.	11.	1.	96.	0.
30 CEMENT	5364.	32.	73.	0.	222.	34.	0.	0.	0.	0.
31 N METALLIC	23.	534.	44.	93.	0.	305.	0.	138.	0.	0.
32 BASIC MTL	1405.	130310.	116923.	52450.	96724.	3822.	17145.	21999.	1092.	4147.
33 OTH METAL	136.	1418.	11040.	110.	801.	908.	545.	377.	584.	2302.
34 N ELEC MAC	2504.	4542.	1299.	64462.	1624.	873.	1436.	124.	7.	418.
35 ELECT MACH	13.	4332.	1596.	11808.	824127.	1375.	425.	64.	3784.	3938.
36 MOTOR VEH	279.	1501.	654.	817.	2346.	695390.	640.	176.	3.	275.
37 OTH TRANSP	18.	0.	0.	0.	0.	0.	90909.	0.	0.	0.
38 O MFG PROD	69.	134.	33.	1194.	17205.	72.	0.	17161.	456.	50.
39 ELECTRCITY	0.	0.	0.	0.	0.	0.	0.	0.	0.	0.
40 WATER	0.	0.	0.	0.	0.	0.	0.	0.	0.	0.
41 CNSTRCTION	0.	0.	0.	0.	0.	0.	0.	0.	0.	0.
42 TRADE	0.	5330.	377.	1020.	0.	125.	13.	0.	0.	0.
43 HOTEL ETC	0.	0.	0.	0.	0.	0.	0.	0.	0.	0.
44 TRANSPORT	0.	0.	0.	0.	0.	0.	0.	0.	0.	0.
45 COMMNICAT	0.	0.	0.	0.	0.	0.	0.	0.	0.	0.
46 FINANCE	0.	0.	0.	0.	0.	0.	0.	0.	0.	0.
47 INSURANCE	0.	0.	0.	0.	0.	0.	0.	0.	0.	0.
48 DWELLINGS	0.	0.	0.	0.	0.	0.	0.	0.	0.	0.
49 BUSIT SERV	0.	0.	1420.	0.	4000.	4000.	0.	12.	0.	0.
50 PRIV EDUC	0.	0.	0.	0.	0.	0.	0.	0.	0.	0.
51 PR HEALTH	0.	0.	0.	0.	0.	0.	0.	0.	0.	0.
52 CULT SERV	0.	0.	0.	0.	0.	0.	0.	0.	0.	0.
53 REPAIR VEH	0.	0.	0.	0.	0.	0.	0.	0.	0.	0.
54 PERSON SER	0.	0.	0.	0.	0.	0.	0.	0.	0.	0.
55 PUB ADMIN	0.	0.	0.	0.	0.	0.	0.	0.	0.	0.
56 GOV EDUC	0.	0.	0.	0.	0.	0.	0.	0.	0.	0.
57 GOV HEALTH	0.	0.	0.	0.	0.	0.	0.	0.	0.	0.
58 O GOV SERV	0.	0.	0.	0.	0.	0.	0.	0.	0.	0.
59 PRI NP SER	0.	0.	0.	0.	0.	0.	0.	0.	0.	0.
60 OTHER SERV	0.	0.	0.	0.	0.	0.	0.	0.	0.	0.
61 TOT INTER	49913.	413139.	163355.	134727.	1002637.	716991.	112010.	49695.	37196.	14655.
62 MISCELLAN	0.	0.	0.	0.	0.	0.	0.	0.	0.	0.
63 N COMP IMP	0.	1931.	0.	0.	0.	0.	0.	0.	0.	0.
64 TOT IMPRTS	49913.	440120.	163355.	134727.	1002637.	716991.	112010.	49695.	37196.	14655.
65 COM TAXES	0.	0.	0.	0.	0.	0.	0.	0.	0.	0.
66 INVISB PAL	0.	0.	0.	0.	0.	0.	0.	0.	0.	0.
67 VALU ADD	0.	0.	0.	0.	0.	0.	0.	0.	0.	0.
68 GRSS INPUT	0.	0.	0.	0.	0.	0.	0.	0.	0.	0.

JADUAL 1.3 – MATRIKS SERAPAN KOMODITI–KOMODITI IMPORT PADA NILAI–NILAI ASAS, 1978. KOMODITI X AKTIVITI (RIBU RINGGIT) – SAMB.

Table 1.3 – Absorption Matrix Of Imported Commodities At Basic Values, 1978. Commodity x Activity (Thousand Ringgit) – Cont'd.

COL / ROW	41 CNSTRCTION	42 TRADE	43 HOTEL ETC	44 TRANSPORT	45 COMMUNICAT	46 FINANCE	47 INSURANCE	48 DWELLINGS	49 BUSIN SERV	50 PRIV EDUC
1 OTH AGRIC	0.	0.	9540.	0.	0.	0.	0.	0.	0.	0.
2 RUBBER PLN	0.	0.	0.	0.	0.	0.	0.	0.	0.	0.
3 OIL PALM	0.	0.	0.	0.	0.	0.	0.	0.	0.	0.
4 LIVESTOCK	0.	0.	2089.	0.	0.	0.	0.	0.	0.	0.
5 FORESTRY	0.	0.	0.	0.	0.	0.	0.	0.	0.	0.
6 FISHING	0.	0.	0.	0.	0.	0.	0.	0.	0.	0.
7 PETROL MIN	750.	0.	0.	0.	0.	0.	0.	0.	0.	0.
8 DAIRY PROD	0.	0.	23354.	770.	0.	0.	0.	0.	0.	0.
9 VEG FRUIT	0.	0.	9662.	183.	0.	0.	0.	0.	0.	0.
10 OIL & FATS	0.	0.	31.	0.	0.	0.	0.	0.	0.	0.
11 GRAIN MILL	0.	0.	18341.	30.	0.	0.	0.	0.	0.	0.
12 BAKER CONF	0.	0.	0.	12.	0.	0.	0.	0.	0.	0.
13 OTH FOODS	0.	0.	4776.	78.	0.	0.	0.	0.	0.	0.
14 ANMAL FEED	0.	0.	0.	0.	0.	0.	0.	0.	0.	0.
15 BEVERAGES	0.	0.	23956.	405.	0.	0.	0.	0.	0.	4.
16 TOBACCO	0.	0.	0.	0.	0.	0.	0.	0.	0.	4.
17 TEXTILES	0.	0.	2085.	423.	103.	0.	0.	0.	0.	0.
18 WEARNG APL	10.	0.	170.	781.	120.	0.	5.	0.	70.	0.
19 SAWMILLS	11918.	0.	0.	48.	0.	0.	0.	0.	0.	30.
20 FURN FIXT	0.	0.	0.	0.	0.	0.	0.	0.	0.	0.
21 PAPER PRNT	1672.	7374.	322.	929.	241.	1256.	209.	0.	1858.	1237.
22 INDST CHEM	8827.	0.	0.	196.	68.	0.	0.	0.	0.	0.
23 PAINTS ETC	10255.	0.	366.	9.	10.	0.	0.	0.	0.	0.
24 OT CHM PRO	30.	0.	760.	183.	1.	0.	0.	0.	0.	0.
25 PETROL PRD	20150.	22267.	3392.	127731.	549.	4.	7.	28.	198.	12.
26 RUBBER PRO	0.	0.	0.	0.	0.	0.	0.	0.	0.	0.
27 RUBBER PRO	0.	172.	0.	13791.	0.	0.	0.	0.	0.	0.
28 PLSTIC PRO	11068.	771.	0.	446.	0.	0.	0.	0.	0.	0.
29 GLASS PROD	53839.	0.	1092.	158.	81.	0.	0.	0.	0.	0.
30 CEMENT	21109.	0.	0.	0.	0.	0.	0.	0.	0.	0.
31 N METALLIC	12932.	0.	0.	2.	8.	0.	0.	0.	0.	0.
32 BASIC MTL	366599.	341.	1043.	2931.	724.	174.	43.	33.	213.	22.
33 OTH METAL	77563.	6052.	189.	485.	200.	390.	98.	0.	228.	49.
34 N ELEC MAC	78507.	1951.	5585.	1021.	89.	0.	0.	29.	4400.	0.
35 ELECT MACH	163567.	699.	300.	2272.	4513.	72.	0.	0.	117.	248.
36 MOTOR VEH	458.	317.	341.	73900.	203.	0.	0.	0.	132.	0.
37 OTH TRANSP	0.	0.	0.	26578.	0.	0.	0.	0.	0.	0.
38 O MFG PROD	559.	1584.	335.	1079.	310.	1526.	296.	0.	1571.	236.
39 ELECTRICITY	0.	0.	0.	0.	0.	0.	0.	0.	0.	0.
40 WATER	0.	0.	0.	0.	0.	0.	0.	0.	0.	0.
41 CNSTRCTION	51477.	0.	0.	0.	0.	0.	0.	0.	0.	0.
42 TRADE	0.	61658.	0.	154.	0.	0.	0.	0.	0.	0.
43 HOTEL ETC	0.	0.	0.	0.	0.	0.	0.	0.	0.	0.
44 TRANSPORT	3000.	44694.	0.	122283.	0.	0.	0.	0.	0.	0.
45 COMMUNICAT	0.	0.	0.	0.	27120.	0.	0.	0.	0.	0.
46 FINANCE	0.	0.	0.	0.	0.	9000.	0.	0.	0.	0.
47 INSURANCE	0.	0.	0.	0.	0.	0.	39400.	0.	0.	0.
48 DRELLINGS	0.	0.	0.	0.	0.	0.	0.	0.	0.	0.
49 BUSIN SERV	15120.	61739.	8956.	12532.	0.	33.	4509.	0.	16181.	0.
50 PRIV EDUC	0.	0.	0.	0.	0.	0.	0.	0.	0.	0.
51 PR HEALTH	0.	0.	0.	0.	0.	0.	0.	0.	0.	0.
52 CULT SERV	0.	176.	0.	0.	0.	0.	0.	0.	0.	0.
53 REPAIR VEH	0.	0.	0.	0.	0.	0.	0.	0.	0.	0.
54 PERSON SER	0.	0.	0.	0.	0.	0.	0.	0.	0.	0.
55 PUB ADMIN	0.	0.	0.	0.	0.	0.	0.	0.	0.	0.
56 GOV EDUC	0.	0.	0.	0.	0.	0.	0.	0.	0.	0.
57 GOV HEALTH	0.	0.	0.	0.	0.	0.	0.	0.	0.	0.
58 O GOV SERV	0.	0.	0.	0.	0.	0.	0.	0.	0.	0.
59 PRI NP SER	0.	0.	0.	0.	0.	0.	0.	0.	0.	0.
60 OTHER SERV	0.	0.	0.	0.	0.	0.	0.	0.	0.	0.
61 TOT INTER	929310.	209795.	115785.	459410.	34319.	11455.	44567.	90.	24968.	1838.
62 MISCELLAN	0.	0.	0.	0.	0.	0.	0.	0.	0.	0.
63 N COMP IMP	0.	0.	0.	0.	0.	0.	0.	0.	0.	0.
64 TOT IMPPTS	929310.	209795.	115785.	459410.	34319.	11455.	44567.	90.	24968.	1838.
65 COM TAXES	0.	0.	0.	0.	0.	0.	0.	0.	0.	0.
66 INVISB BAL	0.	0.	0.	0.	0.	0.	0.	0.	0.	0.
67 VALUE ADD	0.	0.	0.	0.	0.	0.	0.	0.	0.	0.
68 GRSS INPUT	0.	0.	0.	0.	0.	0.	0.	0.	0.	0.

189

JADUAL 1.3 - MATRIKS SERAPAN KOMODITI-KOMODITI IMPORT PADA NILAI-NILAI ASAS. 1978. KOMODITI X AKTIVITI (RIBU RINGGIT) – SAMB.

Table 1.3 – Absorption Matrix Of Imported Commodities At Basic Values, 1978. Commodity x Activity (Thousand Ringgit) – Cont'd.

COL	51 PR HEALTH	52 CULT SERV	53 REPAIR VEH	54 PERSON SER	55 PUB ADMIN	56 GOV EDUC	57 GOV HEALTH	58 O GOV SERV	59 PRI NP SER	60 OTHER SERV
ROW										
1 OTH AGRIC	0.	0.	0.	0.	1208.	500.	365.	1099.	0.	0.
2 RUBBER PLN	0.	0.	0.	0.	0.	149.	0.	0.	0.	0.
3 OIL PALM	0.	0.	0.	0.	0.	0.	0.	0.	0.	0.
4 LIVESTOCK	0.	0.	0.	0.	3944.	9.	463.	266.	0.	0.
5 FORESTRY	0.	0.	0.	0.	0.	0.	0.	838.	0.	0.
6 FISHING	0.	0.	0.	0.	0.	0.	0.	0.	0.	0.
7 PETROL MIN	0.	0.	0.	0.	174.	0.	0.	0.	0.	0.
8 DAIRY PROD	0.	0.	0.	0.	5178.	1628.	3147.	671.	0.	0.
9 VEG FRUIT	0.	0.	0.	0.	1249.	998.	251.	503.	0.	0.
10 OIL & FATS	0.	0.	0.	0.	5.	0.	0.	0.	0.	0.
11 GRAIN MILL	0.	0.	0.	0.	3635.	1237.	1239.	539.	0.	0.
12 BAKER CONF	0.	0.	0.	0.	56.	38.	47.	3.	0.	0.
13 OTH FOODS	0.	0.	0.	0.	3088.	450.	139.	551.	0.	0.
14 ANMAL FEED	0.	0.	0.	0.	15.	0.	167.	117.	0.	0.
15 BEVERAGES	0.	0.	0.	0.	37.	53.	21.	0.	0.	0.
16 TOBACCO	0.	0.	0.	0.	0.	0.	0.	0.	0.	0.
17 TEXTILES	0.	21.	322.	24.	6608.	677.	1954.	839.	0.	126.
18 WEARIG APL	21.	14.	0.	0.	2487.	167.	169.	330.	0.	3.
19 SAWMILLS	0.	0.	0.	0.	0.	0.	0.	0.	0.	520.
20 FURN FIXT	0.	0.	0.	0.	195.	0.	93.	129.	0.	0.
21 PAPER PRNT	47.	674.	0.	53.	2952.	22629.	417.	1694.	232.	205.
22 INDST CHEM	0.	15.	385.	39.	1009.	1692.	4234.	10955.	0.	0.
23 PAINTS ETC	0.	4.	416.	0.	63.	70.	0.	21.	0.	0.
24 OT CHM PRD	21207.	287.	3312.	120.	92667.	1218.	21586.	1399.	0.	10588.
25 PETROL PRD	158.	147.	975.	70.	6920.	164.	871.	2634.	47.	46.
26 RUBBER PRO	0.	0.	0.	0.	0.	0.	0.	0.	0.	0.
27 RUBBER PRD	0.	0.	32.	0.	3547.	10.	12.	16.	0.	0.
28 PLSTIC PRD	0.	0.	0.	0.	0.	0.	0.	0.	0.	0.
29 GLASS PROD	0.	39.	109.	7.	39.	19.	3519.	168.	0.	0.
30 CEMENT	0.	0.	0.	0.	0.	0.	0.	0.	0.	0.
31 N METALLIC	0.	0.	383.	0.	0.	0.	0.	0.	0.	0.
32 BASIC MTL	240.	150.	10224.	82.	14061.	2314.	804.	2476.	0.	13.
33 OTH METAL	0.	152.	9468.	0.	3887.	1067.	242.	239.	0.	29.
34 N ELEC MAC	0.	138.	9490.	65.	231333.	12.	146.	1237.	0.	0.
35 ELEC MACH	137.	1973.	11360.	472.	41114.	2369.	505.	1348.	0.	0.
36 MOTOR VEH	0.	64.	34688.	0.	21741.	1731.	363.	963.	0.	0.
37 OTH TRANSP	0.	0.	1189.	1705.	191666.	0.	0.	0.	0.	0.
38 O MF; PROD	1179.	877.	0.	140.	6951.	2333.	9451.	1329.	0.	209.
39 ELECTRCITY	0.	0.	0.	0.	0.	0.	0.	0.	0.	0.
40 WATER	0.	0.	0.	0.	0.	0.	0.	0.	0.	0.
41 CNSTRCTION	0.	0.	0.	0.	0.	0.	0.	0.	0.	0.
42 TRADE	0.	0.	0.	0.	0.	0.	0.	0.	0.	0.
43 HOTEL ETC	0.	0.	0.	0.	0.	0.	0.	0.	0.	0.
44 TRANSPORT	0.	0.	0.	0.	0.	0.	0.	0.	0.	0.
45 COMMUNICAT	0.	0.	0.	0.	0.	0.	0.	0.	0.	0.
46 FINANCE	0.	0.	0.	0.	0.	0.	0.	0.	0.	0.
47 INSURANCE	0.	0.	0.	0.	0.	0.	0.	0.	0.	0.
48 DWELLINGS	0.	595.	0.	0.	0.	0.	0.	0.	0.	0.
49 BUSIN SERV	0.	595.	0.	0.	63600.	0.	0.	1403.	0.	0.
50 PRIV EDUC	0.	0.	0.	0.	0.	0.	0.	0.	0.	0.
51 PR HEALTH	0.	0.	0.	0.	0.	0.	0.	0.	0.	0.
52 CULT SERV	0.	3093.	0.	0.	2023.	33.	0.	5.	0.	0.
53 REPAIR VEH	0.	0.	0.	0.	0.	0.	0.	0.	0.	0.
54 PERSON SER	0.	0.	0.	0.	0.	0.	0.	0.	0.	0.
55 PUB ADMIN	0.	0.	0.	0.	0.	0.	0.	0.	0.	0.
56 GOV EDUC	0.	0.	0.	0.	0.	0.	0.	0.	0.	0.
57 GOV HEALTH	0.	0.	0.	0.	0.	0.	0.	0.	0.	0.
58 O GOV SERV	0.	0.	0.	0.	0.	0.	0.	0.	0.	0.
59 PRI NP SER	0.	0.	0.	0.	0.	0.	0.	0.	0.	0.
60 OTHER SERV	0.	0.	0.	0.	0.	0.	0.	0.	0.	0.
61 TOT INTER	22959.	8273.	31413.	2777.	724353.	43567.	50205.	31772.	279.	11735.
62 MISCELLAN	0.	0.	0.	0.	0.	0.	0.	0.	0.	0.
63 N COMP IMP	0.	0.	12.	0.	6.	153.	12.	7.	0.	0.
64 TOT IMPRTS	22959.	8273.	31425.	2777.	724359.	43720.	50217.	31779.	279.	11735.
65 COM TAXES	0.	0.	0.	0.	0.	0.	0.	0.	0.	0.
66 INVISB BAL	0.	0.	0.	0.	0.	0.	0.	0.	0.	0.
67 VALUE ADD	0.	0.	0.	0.	0.	0.	0.	0.	0.	0.
68 GRSS INPUT	0.	0.	0.	0.	0.	0.	0.	0.	0.	0.

JADUAL I.3 — MATRIKS SERAPAN KOMODITI-KOMODITI IMPORT PADA NILAI–NILAI ASAS, 1978. KOMODITI X AKTIVITI (RIBU RINGGIT) — SAMB.

Table 1.3 – Absorption Matrix Of Imported Commodities At Basic Values, 1978. Commodity x Activity (Thousand Ringgit) - Cont'd.

COL / ROW	61 TOT INTER	62 BANK INT	63 PRIV CONS	64 GOVT CONS	65 STOCKS	66 INVESTMENT	67 EXPORTS	68 TOTAL FN D	69 TOTAL DEM	70 TOT IMPRTS
1 OTH AGRIC	349501.	0.	211423.	0.	-1177.	0.	0.	210246.	0.	659747.
2 RUBBER PLN	149.	0.	0.	0.	0.	0.	0.	0.	0.	149.
3 OIL PALM	6.	0.	0.	0.	0.	0.	0.	0.	0.	6.
4 LIVESTOCK	17169.	0.	5476.	0.	0.	10876.	0.	16352.	0.	33521.
5 FORESTRY	6433.	0.	4395.	0.	53.	0.	0.	4448.	0.	10881.
6 FISHING	0.	0.	916.	0.	0.	0.	0.	916.	0.	916.
7 PETROL MIN	1219434.	0.	6558.	0.	22760.	0.	0.	29318.	0.	1248752.
8 DAIRY PROD	165012.	0.	89908.	0.	1699.	0.	0.	91607.	0.	256619.
9 VEG FRUIT	15705.	0.	148480.	0.	0.	0.	0.	148480.	0.	164185.
10 OIL & FATS	116676.	0.	8271.	0.	-372.	0.	0.	7899.	0.	124575.
11 GRAIN MILL	125321.	0.	303979.	0.	-646.	0.	0.	303333.	0.	428654.
12 BAKER CONF	5771.	0.	45549.	0.	0.	0.	0.	45549.	0.	51320.
13 OTH FOODS	308864.	0.	66006.	0.	-20284.	0.	0.	45722.	0.	354586.
14 ANMAL FEED	58834.	0.	0.	0.	2254.	0.	0.	2254.	0.	61088.
15 BEVERAGES	37764.	0.	53363.	0.	0.	0.	0.	53363.	0.	91127.
16 TOBACCO	74485.	0.	31571.	0.	1825.	0.	0.	33396.	0.	107881.
17 TEXTILES	222305.	0.	231286.	0.	3492.	6719.	0.	241497.	0.	463802.
18 WEARNG APL	8818.	0.	58846.	0.	1261.	0.	0.	60107.	0.	68921.
19 SAWMILLS	35233.	0.	3648.	0.	-1319.	0.	0.	2329.	0.	37562.
20 FURN FIXT	1086.	0.	12114.	0.	10.	1167.	0.	13291.	0.	14377.
21 PAPER PRNT	314991.	0.	49507.	0.	-6642.	0.	0.	42865.	0.	357856.
22 INDST CHEM	367955.	0.	12507.	0.	5639.	0.	0.	18146.	0.	386101.
23 PAINTS ETC	18298.	0.	1313.	0.	-567.	0.	0.	946.	0.	19244.
24 QT CHM PRD	202324.	0.	223397.	0.	569.	0.	0.	220966.	0.	423290.
25 PETROL PRD	410829.	0.	141896.	0.	32270.	0.	0.	174166.	0.	584995.
26 RUBBER PRO	1647.	0.	0.	0.	26245.	0.	0.	26245.	0.	27892.
27 RUBBER PRD	28542.	0.	32045.	0.	1908.	0.	0.	33953.	0.	62495.
28 PLSTIC PRD	26758.	0.	47134.	0.	5909.	0.	0.	53043.	0.	79801.
29 GLASS PROD	79102.	0.	40254.	0.	-1351.	0.	0.	38903.	0.	118005.
30 CEMENT	29460.	0.	0.	0.	-689.	0.	0.	-689.	0.	28771.
31 N METALLIC	16110.	0.	1448.	0.	1000.	7216.	0.	9664.	0.	25774.
32 BASIC MTL	982508.	0.	9354.	0.	10206.	72291.	0.	91851.	0.	1074359.
33 OTH METAL	153524.	0.	63260.	0.	6721.	10413.	0.	80394.	0.	233918.
34 N ELEC MAC	545947.	0.	70491.	0.	2701.	1590931.	0.	1664123.	0.	2210070.
35 ELECT MACH	1111319.	0.	232710.	0.	27160.	496557.	0.	756447.	0.	1867766.
36 MOTOR VEH	396084.	0.	149956.	0.	-9212.	172053.	0.	312797.	0.	1208881.
37 OTH TRANSP	319947.	0.	33725.	0.	-2769.	72071.	0.	103027.	0.	422974.
38 O MFG PROD	108590.	0.	132062.	0.	253.	159802.	0.	292117.	0.	400707.
39 ELECTRCITY	0.	0.	0.	0.	0.	0.	0.	0.	0.	0.
40 WATER	0.	0.	3500.	0.	0.	0.	0.	3500.	0.	3500.
41 CNSTRCTION	55705.	0.	0.	0.	0.	0.	0.	0.	0.	55705.
42 TRADE	69173.	0.	0.	0.	0.	0.	0.	0.	0.	69173.
43 HOTEL ETC	0.	0.	0.	0.	0.	0.	0.	0.	0.	0.
44 TRANSPORT	239977.	0.	113906.	0.	0.	0.	0.	113906.	0.	353883.
45 COMMUNICAT	27100.	0.	0.	0.	0.	0.	0.	0.	0.	27100.
46 FINANCE	8000.	0.	0.	0.	0.	0.	0.	0.	0.	8000.
47 INSURANCE	39400.	0.	0.	0.	0.	0.	0.	0.	0.	39400.
48 DWELLINGS	0.	0.	0.	0.	0.	0.	0.	0.	0.	0.
49 BUSIN SERV	272598.	0.	4110.	0.	0.	57043.	0.	61153.	0.	333751.
50 PRIV EDUC	0.	0.	0.	0.	0.	0.	0.	0.	0.	0.
51 PR HEALTH	0.	0.	0.	0.	0.	0.	0.	0.	0.	0.
52 CULT SERV	5330.	0.	274.	0.	0.	0.	0.	274.	0.	5604.
53 REPAIR VEH	0.	0.	0.	0.	0.	0.	0.	0.	0.	0.
54 PERSON SER	0.	0.	0.	0.	0.	0.	0.	0.	0.	0.
55 PUB ADMIN	0.	0.	0.	0.	0.	0.	0.	0.	0.	0.
56 GOV EDUC	0.	0.	0.	0.	0.	0.	0.	0.	0.	0.
57 GOV HEALTH	0.	0.	0.	0.	0.	0.	0.	0.	0.	0.
58 O GOV SERV	0.	0.	0.	0.	0.	0.	0.	0.	0.	0.
59 PRI NP SER	0.	0.	0.	0.	0.	0.	0.	0.	0.	0.
60 OTHER SERV	0.	0.	950.	0.	0.	0.	0.	950.	0.	950.
61 TOT INTER	9599780.	0.	2642808.	0.	109907.	2657139.	0.	5408854.	0.	15108634.
62 MISCELLAN	0.	0.	0.	0.	0.	0.	0.	0.	0.	0.
63 N COMP IMP	2111.	0.	0.	0.	284.	0.	0.	284.	0.	2395.
64 TOT IMPRTS	9731891.	0.	2642808.	0.	109191.	2657139.	0.	5409138.	0.	15111029.
65 COM TAXES	0.	0.	0.	0.	0.	0.	0.	0.	0.	0.
66 INVISB BAL	0.	0.	883200.	0.	0.	0.	0.	883200.	0.	883200.
67 VALUE ADD	0.	0.	0.	0.	0.	0.	0.	0.	883200.	883200.
68 GRSS INPUT	0.	0.	0.	0.	0.	0.	0.	0.	0.	0.

JADUAL 1.3   MATRIKS SERAPAN KOMODITI-KOMODITI IMPORT PADA NILAI–NILAI ASAS, 1978.   KOMODITI X AKTIVITI (RIBU RINGGIT) – SAMB.

Table 1.3 – Absorption Matrix Of Imported Commodities At Basic Values, 1978.   Commodity x Activity (Thousand Ringgit) – Cont'd.

COL	71	72	73
	R3-3XPORTS	COM TAXES	GRS OUTPUT
ROW			
1 OTH AGRIC	18361.	0.	0.
2 RUBB3R PLN	0.	0.	0.
3 OIL PALM	0.	0.	0.
4 LIVE3TOCK	557.	0.	0.
5 FOR E3TRY	278.	0.	0.
6 FISHING	710.	0.	0.
7 PETR3L MIN	873.	0.	0.
8 DAIRY PRO3	1584.	0.	0.
9 VEG FRUIT	19575.	0.	0.
10 OIL & FAT3	1090.	0.	0.
11 GRAIN MILL	1690.	0.	0.
12 BAKE3 CONF	2362.	0.	0.
13 OTH FOODS	4457.	0.	0.
14 ANMAL FE33	24.	0.	0.
15 BEVERAGES	21.	0.	0.
16 TOBACCO	334.	0.	0.
17 TEXTILES	13172.	0.	0.
18 WEARNG APL	13731.	0.	0.
19 SAWMILLS	6600.	0.	0.
20 FURN FIXT	1962.	0.	0.
21 PAPER PRNT	4612.	0.	0.
22 INDSI CHEM	5315.	0.	0.
23 PAINTS ETC	113.	0.	0.
24 OT CIM PRD	5954.	0.	0.
25 PETR3L PRD	17623.	0.	0.
26 RUBB3R PRD	62254.	0.	0.
27 RUBB3R PRO	1831.	0.	0.
28 PLSTIC PRO	404.	0.	0.
29 GLAS3 PROD	6466.	0.	0.
30 CEMENT	11.	0.	0.
31 N METALLIC	237.	0.	0.
32 BASIC MTL	12364.	0.	0.
33 OTH METAL	5328.	0.	0.
34 N ELEC MAC	35115.	0.	0.
35 ELECT MACH	39166.	0.	0.
36 MOTOR VEH	9149.	0.	0.
37 OTH TRANSP	107925.	0.	0.
38 O MF3 PROD	62929.	0.	0.
39 ELECTRCITY	0.	0.	0.
40 WATER	0.	0.	0.
41 CNSTRCTION	0.	0.	0.
42 TRAD3	110.	0.	0.
43 HOTEL ETC	0.	0.	0.
44 TRANSPORT	0.	0.	0.
45 COMMUNICAT	0.	0.	0.
46 FINANCE	0.	0.	0.
47 INSURANC3	0.	0.	0.
48 DWELLINGS	0.	0.	0.
49 BUSIN SERV	0.	0.	0.
50 PRIV EDUC	0.	0.	0.
31 PR H3ALTH	0.	0.	0.
52 CULT SERV	12.	0.	0.
53 REPAIR V3H	0.	0.	0.
54 PERSON SER	0.	0.	0.
55 PUB ADMIN	0.	0.	0.
56 GOV EDUC	0.	0.	0.
57 GOV HEALTH	0.	0.	0.
58 O GOV SERV	2.	0.	0.
59 PRI VP SER	0.	0.	0.
60 OTHER SERV	14.	0.	0.
61 TOT INTER	432915.	0.	0.
62 MISCELL AN	0.	0.	0.
63 N COMP IMP	10.	0.	0.
64 TOT IMPRTS	432825.	0.	0.
65 COM TAXES	0.	0.	0.
66 INVISB BAL	0.	0.	0.
67 VALU3 ADD	0.	0.	0.
68 GRSS INPUT	0.	0.	0.

XI. MEXICO

A. General information

The present report is based on volume seven of the *Series de Cuentas Nacionales de México*, entitled *Matriz de Insumo-Producto, Año de 1975* published by the Secretaría de Programación y Presupuesto de Mexico.

Input-output tables for Mexico have been compiled for the years 1950, 1960, 1970 and 1975. The present report refers to the 1975 table, which was compiled by the Secretaría de Programación y Presupuesto and the Banco de México, with technical assistance provided by the United Nations Development Programme and the Economic Commission for Latin America and the Caribbean. The 1970 and 1975 tables are not strictly comparable with those for 1950 and 1960 owing to different classifications of activities. The differences are the following: (*a*) industrial activities related to agriculture, except those that involve cleaning and packing of agricultural products, were transferred in the 1970 and 1975 tables from agriculture to manufacturing; (*b*) refining of non-ferrous metallic minerals and carbon were included in the 1970 and 1975 tables in mining together with extraction activities, while in the earlier tables such activities were covered in manufacturing; (*c*) the services of repair and maintenance that do not result in the production of parts of machinery and equipment were transferred in the 1970 and 1975 tables from manufacturing to services. To improve comparability of the 1970 and 1975 tables with the earlier tables, the latter ones were adapted to the more recent classification on the basis of a detail of 30 sectors.

The compilation of the 1975 input-output table was undertaken as part of a programme aimed at the improvement and updating of the system of national accounts estimates for 1975 onward. Complete equivalence exists between the input-output tables and the national accounts estimates of the corresponding aggregates.

The main deviations of the Mexican input-output table from the SNA recommendations include: (*a*) treatment of producers of government services; (*b*) treatment of education and health public services; (*c*) treatment of activities of private non-profit institutions; (*d*) breakdown of value added; (*e*) treatment of imports; and (*f*) commodity taxes are not recorded separately and therefore no valuation at approximate basic values can be derived.

B. Analytical framework

1. *Tables and derived matrices available*

The following basic tables were compiled:

(i) Input-output table of domestic transactions valued at producers' prices;

(ii) Imports matrix;

(iii) Input-output table of total transactions (i.e., domestic production plus imports) valued at producers' prices;

(iv) Input structure of subgroups of the food, beverages and tobacco sectors;

(v) Input structure of subgroups of the textiles, clothing and leather sectors;

(vi) Input structure of subgroups of the wood sectors;

(vii) Input structure of subgroups of the paper and printing sectors;

(viii) Input structure of subgroups of the chemicals, petroleum, rubber and plastics sector;

(ix) Input structure of subgroups of the non-metallic minerals sectors;

(x) Input structure of subgroups of the basic metal sectors;

(xi) Input structure of subgroups of the metal products, machinery and equipment goods sectors;

(xii) Input structure of subgroups of the health and education sectors;

(xiii) Input structure of subgroups of the government sector;

(xiv) Imports by type of good and subsectors of final demand categories;

(xv) Indirect taxes by type of taxes and economic sector of incidence.

On the basis of the data mentioned above, the following derived matrices were compiled:

(i') Technical coefficients based on table (i);

(ii') Inverse matrix of table (i);

(iii') Distribution coefficients based on table (i). Each element of matrix (ii) obtained by dividing the corresponding entry in the row of table (i) by the total demand for output of the relevant sector;

(iv') Technical coefficients based on table (ii);

(v') Technical coefficients based on table (iii).

All basic tables and derived matrices are presented at a level of disaggregation of 72 x 72 intermediate sectors.

2. *Valuation standards*

All basic tables are valued at producers' prices, defined as purchasers' prices less distribution margins. Imports are valued c i.f.

Exports are valued f.o.b.

3. *Statistical units and classification standards*

The establishment is the statistical unit generally used in the data collection process. Input-output tables (i) and (iii) are of the industry-by-industry type.

The overall classification of input-output sectors corresponds to a national classification system, specially devised for the purpose of compilation of the 1975 national accounts and input-output estimates. This special classification system was adopted on a temporary basis, to be used during the process of revision of the Mexican Catalogue of Economic

Activities (currently under way), and it generally coincides with the broader aggregates of ISIC, except for the coal and metallic non-ferrous mining sectors, which, in the Mexican classification system, also include the corresponding manufacturing activities.

The classification of the intermediate consumption quadrant differs from the SNA recommendations on input-output in that: (a) public health and educational services are recorded together with the same services provided by the private sector; (b) the activities of producers of government services - except health and education - are recorded in the final demand quadrant, under the government consumption category; (c) the activities of private non-profit institutions are recorded together with the corresponding activities of the private sector.

The definition and breakdown of final demand is in agreement with the SNA recommendations. Private consumption is defined on a domestic basis.

Value added is defined as in SNA, but its breakdown differs from the SNA recommendations in that operating surplus in the Mexican table also includes depreciation of fixed capital.

Imports are classified by destination only in table (i). In addition, imports are cross-classified by origin and destination in table (ii). Contrary to the SNA recommendations, no distinction is made between complementary and competitive imports.

4. *Treatment and presentation of selected transactions*

Secondary products and their associated input were not transferred. Secondary output were distinguished, however, during the compilation process and allocated to their respective destinations on the basis of market shares per product.

Non-monetary output (such as self-consumption of agricultural products, imputed housing rents etc.) and its corresponding input were generally recorded together with the monetary output and input in the corresponding input-output sector.

Second-hand products were restricted to intermediate type products only, such as metal scrap, glass and paper. Owing to data limitations, transactions in second-hand capital goods were not considered. The sales and purchases of second-hand goods are recorded as plus and minus items in the rows of those industries that are the characteristic producers of those products, except for the trade margins, which were included as output of the trade sector.

Output is generally defined on a gross basis, that is, it includes intra-sector consumption of goods and services.

As recommended in SNA, output of the financial sector is defined to include imputed service charges, which are defined as the difference between interests received and interests paid. The distribution of output of this sector also follows the SNA recommendations, that is, imputed services charges were allocated to a dummy sector which forms part of the "other services" sector of the input-output table.

Output of the insurance sector is defined as in SNA, that is, it excludes claims paid and includes net addition to the actuarial reserves by life insurance companies.

C. STATISTICAL SOURCES AND COMPILATION METHODOLOGY

Data collection is based on existing regular sources, the results of the 1975 Industrial, Trade, Transportation and Services Censuses, and special analyses carried out for the purpose of compilation of the table.

Although the 1975 table presents a level of disaggregation of 72 x 72 intermediate sectors, the basic information used for the compilation of the table was available at a much finer level of disaggregation. Output values were based on the analysis of data collected for 197 groups and 353 subgroups of economic activities. In addition, the tabulations used in the 1975 Industrial Census identify some 1,500 main products and raw materials. This high level of disaggregation allowed for the calculation of balances of supply and demand (measured in quantity terms) for the main products as well as for balances of output of each sector and its use by intermediate and final demand sectors. Such balances as well as the 1970 input-output table and the time series data available for the production sectors of the national accounts, were used as additional consistency checks of the results of the 1975 input-output table.

1. *Gross output and intermediate consumption*

(a) *Agriculture, livestock, forestry and fishing*

Output of the agricultural sector was estimated as the sum of the product of output of annual and permanent crops and their corresponding average rural prices. A total of 178 varieties of annual and permanent crops were considered. Most of the total agricultural production is covered in data provided by such agencies as Dirección General de Economía Agrícola, Dirección General de Distritos de Riego, Comisión Nacional de Fruticultura, Unión Nacional de Productores de Azúcar, and Instituto Mexicano del Café. The rest is mainly obtained from estimates based on the adjusted results of periodically conducted household surveys.

Data on intermediate input of the agriculture sector published in regular sources were relatively scarce. Therefore, special studies had to be carried out by the Dirección General de Economía Agrícola and other agencies.

Output and intermediate input of the livestock sector were obtained from data mainly provided by the Direcciones Generales de Ganadería, Avicultura y Especies Menores, Instituto Nacional de la Leche and the results of the 1968 National Household Surveys. The estimate of gross output of livestock was based on an estimation of the total animal population needed to satisfy total demand for livestock as obtained in the above-mentioned household surveys. This total demand for livestock was obtained by applying to each one of several types of livestock a model of biological evolution which takes into account the prevailing practices in animal rearing as well as the impact of known anomalies in the corresponding years. Livestock volumes so calculated were then multiplied by the corresponding average rural prices, which were compared to the extrapolated average prices in 1970 for further consistency of estimates. Two balances of supply and demand, one in quantity terms and another in terms of protein content, were also used as consistency checks.

Data on gross output and intermediate consumption of the forestry, hunting and fishing sectors were provided by the Subsecretaria Forestal y de la Fauna and the Departamento de Pesca, respectively. The special characteristics of the production process in timber-yielding activities were taken into account in the estimation of the input structure of the forestry sector. Similarly, subgroups of the hunting and fishing sectors were formed to allow for the existing varieties of products in the output of those sectors.

(b) *Mining and quarrying*

Data on the mining sector (except for natural gas and petroleum products) were mainly obtained from the results of the 1975 Industrial Census, mining and metal statistics and the Comisión de Fomento Minero. Census data include information on output, use of intermediate input, compensation of employees and other value added. Census data are valued at average purchasers' prices, which were transformed into producers' prices by deducting the corresponding distribution margins. Data on output and cost stucture of the natural gas and petroleum sectors were obtained from the accounting books of the government-owned petroleum company Petróleos Mexicanos (PEMEX).

(c) *Manufacturing*

Data on the manufacturing sector (except petroleum refining and petroleum products) were obtained from the results of the 1975 Industrial Census, annual industrial statistics and the Dirección General de Estadística. Only establishments with output values exceeding 1 million pesos were covered by the Census. Additional surveys were carried out to cover the remaining manufacturing establishments. Census data included estimates on quantity and value of production, intermediate consumption and compensation of employees of each establishment covered. The detailed level of disaggregation at which these data were available allowed for a consistency analysis of the census estimates of intermediate input and the known technical relationships existing between output and amount of raw materials used. Although two types of observation units (namely, the establishment and the ancillary unit responsible for administration activities) are used in the census, available data do not permit the separation of industrial and ancillary activities. However, a major improvement could be introduced in the 1975 input-output table with respect to the 1970 table, namely, the disaggregation of the content of such census items as "other incomes" and "other expenditures" into their main components (i.e., packing, advertising and repair and maintenance activities). This disaggregation was carried out on the basis of the information provided by direct research on these items.

Data on petroleum refining and petroleum products were provided by PEMEX. Output of those sectors was valued at the reported average prices for domestic sales and exports, which include the distribution margins charged by the distribution agencies of PEMEX. Therefore, the input of those distribution agencies was also added to the input structure of the petroleum refining and petroleum products sectors. Self-consumption of crude petroleum, natural gas and other products was valued at the prices used for PEMEX to calculate the unit costs of products of the sector.

(d) *Construction*

Gross output of the construction sector was estimated by extrapolating the sector's output in the 1970 table by means of the combined evolution of the following three indexes: index of quantity used of strategic domestic and imported input; index of prices of the just-mentioned input; and index of wages. The cost structure of the sector was determined by updating the sector's input coefficients in 1970, taking into account the evolution of prices of each intermediate input. Estimates so obtained were checked against available data on apparent consumption of strategic input.

(e) *Electricity, gas and water supply*

Gross output of this sector was estimated as the sum of net incomes obtained by the Comisión Federal de Electricidad and the Compañía de Luz y Fuerza del Centro from sales of electric power, taxes on electricity consumption and sales of gas and drinking water. Data on output and intermediate consumption were obtained from the accounting records of the agencies mentioned. The municipal services of water distribution remain included in government consumption.

(f) *Trade, hotels and restaurants*

Gross output of the trade sector was estimated indirectly by deducting transport margins from the estimated total distribution margins. Total distribution margins of each intermediate sector were obtained as the difference between the purchasers' and producers' prices of their corresponding intermediate input, on the basis of data on quantity, value and average prices of main products and raw materials collected in the 1975 Industrial Census. The same procedure was applied in the estimation of total distribution margins of government consumption and exports. In the case of private consumption and fixed capital formation, for which original data were collected at producers' prices, total distribution margins were estimated on the basis of data on average mark-ups of importers and trade dealers, provided by the 1970 and 1975 Trade Censuses, registers of controlled prices of the Secretaría de Comercio and direct research on trade in the metropolitan area of Mexico City. Intermediate input of the trade sector was estimated on the basis of data provided by the 1970 and 1975 Trade Censuses.

Output of hotel services was estimated from data provided by the Secretaría de Turismo, hotel associations and special research carried out by the Fondo Nacional de Fomento al Turismo, which include estimates of number of rooms, average annual occupation and average rates charged by category and type of establishment. Those estimates were compared to the indicators of tourism activity collected by the Banco de México, Dirección General de Estadística and other agencies. Cost structure estimates were mainly based on the 1970 and 1975 Trade Censuses data and on the results of special research carried out by the Asociación de Hoteles y Moteles de la Ciudad de México for the period 1975-1978.

Data on output of restaurants were collected on the basis of the assumption that output of restaurants was a fixed proportion of output of hotel services. This estimate was checked against the expenditure on restaurant services by tourists and resident households obtained in the Tourism and Family Income Expenditure Surveys carried out by the Banco de México, the Centro Nacional de Información y Estadísticas del Trabajo and the Dirección General de Estadística. Cost structure data were obtained from the Trade Census, the above-mentioned survey of hotels and motels in Mexico City and a survey of major taxpayers carried out by the Secretaría de Hacienda y Crédito Público for the period 1970-1974.

(g) Transportation, storage, communications

Different data collection methods were followed for each one of the two main components of the transportation sector, that is, public sector transportation enterprises and private sector freight and passenger transportation services. Reasonably good information was available on the public sector transportation, the output and cost structure of which were estimated directly on the basis of data provided by the Transportation Census and the following agencies: Ferrocarriles Nacionales de México, Ferrocarril del Pacífico, Tranvías y Trolebuses, Sistema de Transporte Colectivo (METRO) del D.D.F., Aeronaves de México y Cía. Mexicana de Aviación, Caminos y Puentes Federales de Ingreso y Servicios Conexos; Aeropuertos y Servicios Auxiliares; Servicios a la Navegación en el Espacio Aéreo Mexicano; and Almacenes Nacionales y Generales de Depósito. However, information on the second component of the sector, which represents almost 75 per cent of its total output, had to be obtained through indirect methods involving the estimation of number and types of vehicles licensed. In the case of passenger transportation, use was also made of data on number of days worked, income, expenditure, fuel consumption and number of passengers and of kilometres covered per unit and type of service. These data were provided by the Transportation Census. Since the comparison of census data with data available on licensed vehicles indicated an insufficient coverage of census data, the latter were adjusted by an index of average income and cost per unit in order to obtain total output and intermediate consumption of this subsector. In the case of private freight, data collection was further complicated by the absence of accurate data on number of vehicles used for this purpose. This number was estimated by applying the annual net increment in number of vehicles registered to the total number of vehicles registered in 1974. This total was distributed among input-output sector on the basis of an updated index of the 1970 input-output data on physical output of the agriculture, livestock, industrial and service sectors. Output of this subsector was first estimated at 1970 prices and then expressed in 1975 prices by means of an index of cost per load. This index was a combination of price indexes of the main intermediate input, labour and replacement cost of the vehicles, weighted by their relative importance in the 1970 cost structure. Intermediate consumption was estimated on the basis of census data and data obtained from a sample of transportation enterprises.

Data on output and cost structure of the communications sector were based on direct information provided by the Teléfonos de México and its subsidiaries, and the Dirección de Correos, Telégrafos y Telecomunicaciones, and include an imputation of franchise services which are consumed mainly by the Federal Government. Output was distributed among the input-output sectors on the basis of available global estimations carried out by the same Dirección, and on estimates based on direct inquiries.

(h) Financing and real estate

Most activities included in the financial services sector are regulated by the Central Bank and the Comisión Nacional Bancaria y de Seguros, which provided the required data on output and intermediate input. Data on most activities not covered by this Commission were based on the 1975 Services Census and on direct inquiries with the producers of the services.

Gross output of rentals of residential units was obtained by extrapolating the corresponding 1970 output. The extrapolation was based on a value index that combined the evolution of the amount of residential construction with the rent estimates used in the elaboration of the national consumer price index of the Banco de México. The estimate so obtained was compared to estimates of the same variable obtained in the 1975 and 1977 Family Income and Expenditure Surveys. Estimates of intermediate consumption were likewise based on the extrapolation of the 1970 input-output data adjusted by appropriate evolution indicators. Gross output of rentals of non-residential construction was estimated from the demand side by adding up the use of this type of service by each input-output sector. Intermediate consumption of non-residential construction was estimated as in the residential subsector.

(i) Services

Various data collection methods were used to estimate the input-output data of the five main groups of services included in the input-output table. Services provided by professionals (except medical doctors) were obtained by extrapolating the output and cost structures of the 1970 input-output table. These data were adjusted with a price index of intermediate input and labour and with data collected in the 1975 Services Census. In the case of advertising, and notary services, data were supplemented with direct inquiries on income, expenditures and employment to the main advertising agencies and notaries respectively. Data on education services were obtained from the expenditures required to provide them, in the case of public education; output of private education was obtained by extrapolating the 1970 input-output value according to a combined index of annual growth of the number of students and the evolution of average income per student, provided by direct inquiries to education establishments. The corresponding cost structure was obtained from the 1975 Services Census. Data on medical services were based on the expenditure required to provide them, in the case of public medical services. Output of private medical services was mainly based on an index combining data on income, expenditure, employment and number of patients cared for per day. These data were provided by the Dirección General de Estadística, and the 1975 Services Census. Data on the remaining services were obtained by combining information from the 1975 Services Census with statistics on income and expenditures of the main taxpayers compiled by the Secretaría de Hacienda y Crédito Público, demand data on repair and maintenance services and several indexes of the evolution of prices of output and level of activity.

(j) Value added

Value added was generally estimated as the difference between each sector's output and intermediate consumption. Value added was disaggregated into labour costs and net indirect taxes, and the residual was assigned to operating surplus. Data on net indirect taxes of each sector were compiled by means of special research carried out by the Government and based on data provided by the Federal Government, the Federal District and local and municipal governments. Data on labour costs were estimated as follows. In the agriculture and livestock sectors, labour costs were obtained as the product of estimated demand for labour and the corresponding average wages. In the fishing and hunting sectors, labour data were obtained by expanding those corresponding to the main species. Labour costs for the construction sector are based on the 1970 input-output table coefficients updated by an index of evolution of minimum wages. In the hotels and restaurants sector, labour costs were based on an estimate of employment per room in different types of establishments. The remaining labour data were generally obtained from the same sources as output and intermediate consumption data.

(k) *Final demand and imports*

Final demand data were obtained according to the commodity flow method. Private consumption was mainly estimated as a residual. Estimates so obtained were compared to direct data available from the Family Income and Expenditure Surveys referring to 1963, 1968, 1975 and 1977. Use was also made of direct information provided by enterprises in the electricity and communications sectors.

Government consumption data were provided by the Cuenta de la Hacienda Pública Federal, the Cuenta Pública del Distrito Federal and financial statistics of the state and municipal governments.

Gross fixed capital formation was estimated partly on the basis of direct information from statistical sources and for the remaining part on the use of the commodity flow method. The direct sources of information are the 1975 Censuses of Industry and Trade, the annual compilations of United States-Mexican trade (as published in the Anuario de Estadística de Comercio Exterior de los Estados Unidos - Mexicanos, by the Dirección General de Estadística), data compiled on investments by the Federal Government (as published by the Dirección General de Inversiones Públicas, 1975), and finally special surveys of trade outlets of capital goods, conducted in the metropolitan area of Mexico City.

Export and import data were provided by the Statistical Yearbook of Foreign Trade and the Balance of Payments, which include separate information on special transactions such as trade of precious metals, direct purchases in the domestic market by non-resident households etc. Imports data were also supplemented by direct information on imports of the main public sector agencies, lists of main importers, tariffs of the general import tax and the classification of imports by origin and destination elaborated for the 1970 input-output table.

MEXICO INPUT-OUTPUT TABLE FOR 1978:

TOTAL TRANSACTIONS
(million pesos at producers' values)

Translation of rows and buying sectors
1 Agriculture
2 Livestock
3 Forestry
4 Hunting and fishing
5 Coal and by-products
6 Crude petroleum and natural gas
7 Iron ore
8 Non-ferrous metal ores mining
9 Stone and clay mining and quarrying
10 Other non-metal minerals
11 Meat and dairy products
12 Canned fruits and vegetables
13 Wheat milling and wheat products
14 Wet corn milling and corn products
15 Coffee processing
16 Sugar and by-products

17 Oils and vegetable shortening
18 Animal foods
19 Other food products
20 Alcoholic beverages
21 Beer
22 Bottled soft-drinks
23 Tobacco and by-products
24 Soft fiber yarn and fabrics
25 Hard fiber yarn and fabrics
26 Other textile industries
27 Apparel
28 Leather and leather products
29 Sawmills
30 Other wood industries
31 Paper and paperboard
32 Printing and publishing
33 Petroleum refining
34 Basic petro-chemical industry
35 Industrial chemicals
36 Fertilizers
37 Synthetic resins, plastics and man-made fibers
38 Drugs and medicines
39 Soaps, detergents, perfumes and cosmetics
40 Other chemical industries
41 Oil cloth products
42 Plastic products
43 Glass and glass products
44 Cement
45 Other non-metallic mineral products
46 Iron and steel basic industries
47 Non-ferrous metal basic industries
48 Furniture and metal fixtures
49 Structural metal products
50 Other metal products
51 Machinery and equipment, except electrical machinery
52 Electrical machinery and apparatus
53 Electrical appliances and housewares
54 Electronic equipment and apparatus
55 Other electrical equipment and apparatus
56 Motor vehicles
57 Vehicle bodies and parts
58 Other transport equipment
59 Other manufacturing industries
60 Construction and installations
61 Electricity
62 Wholesale and retail trade
63 Restaurants and hotels
64 Transport
65 Communications
66 Financial services
67 Real estate letting
68 Professional services
69 Education services
70 Medical services
71 Recreational services
72 Other services
73 Net direct imports
74 Total domestic and imported input
75 Gross value added
    A. Compensation of employees
    B. Gross operating surplus
    C. Indirect taxes net of subsidies
76 Total gross production value

Translation of columns and selling sectors
1-72 Identical to rows 1-72 of the previous table
72A Imputed bank services
Total
Table 7 — Private consumption
Government consumption
Gross fixed capital formation
Increase in stock
Exports
Total

For table, see end of volume.

197

XII. NETHERLANDS

A. GENERAL INFORMATION

The present report is based on *Input-Output Tables for the Netherlands*, Statistical Studies No. 16, July 1963, and on *De Produktiestructuur van de Nederlandse Volkshuishouding, Deel VII, Input-Output Tabelleu 1972-1975*, both published by the Central Bureau of Statistics. This information was supplemented with that provided by direct communication between the Statistical Office of the United Nations Secretariat and the Netherlands Central Bureau of Statistics.

The first input-output tables for the Netherlands were compiled for the year 1938 and 1946. Since then, five series of annual input-output tables have been compiled for 1948-1957, 1958-1960, 1961-1964, 1968-1970, and 1972-1975. Tables within each series are comparable to each other. The latest input-output table available refers to 1977. The 1977 table and future tables are not comparable to the previous tables as several revisions have been introduced in order to make use in the national accounts and input-output tables of new and improved basic statistics. At the same time, the method of registration of producers of government services has been changed and the valuation of the table in approximate factor values has been altered to approximate basic values. A revision along the same lines of previous tables is being contemplated, so that in the future longer consistent time series may be expected.

Input-output tables constitute the basis of the national accounts system, and therefore both sets of estimates are mutually consistent.

B. ANALYTICAL FRAMEWORK

1. *Tables and derived matrices available*

Data are presented in the following basic tables:

(i) Input-output table valued at producers' prices;
(ii) Imports matrix;
(iii) Matrix of indirect taxes net of subsidies;
(iv) Matrix of indirect taxes minus subsidies other than commodity taxes;
(v) Input-output tables at approximate factor values until 1977 and at approximate basic values since 1977. The earlier tables in approximate factor values are derived as the difference between tables (i) and (iii), while the 1977 and later tables are computed as the difference between tables (i) and (iii), plus table (iv).

On the basis of these tables, the following derived matrices are compiled:

(i') Technical coefficients based on table (iv);
(ii') Inverse matrix based on the intermediate consumption quadrant of matrix (i');
(iii') Inverse matrix based on the value added quadrant of matrix (i');

(iv') Total requirements of value added components and of imports per categories of final demand;
(v') Disaggregation of matrix (iv') into direct and indirect requirements per categories of final demand.

All basic tables and derived matrices are compiled at a level of aggregation of 33 x 33 intermediate sectors.

2. *Valuation standards*

Producers' prices are defined to exclude distribution margins, which are considered to be payments for services rendered by the distribution sectors to the buying industries or final sectors. Imports are valued c.i.f. frontier and exports are valued f.o.b. As mentioned above, another valuation standard is also used, namely, approximate factor values, which are defined as producers' prices less indirect taxes net of subsidies. In the tables prior to 1977 no distinction is made between commodity aud other indirect taxes, so that goods and services flows can only be valued in approximate factor values. Starting with the 1977 table the distinction is made and a table in approximate basic values is actually presented.

3. *Statistical units and classification standards*

The establishment is the basic statistical unit adopted for rows and columns of the basic tables.

Establishments were generally classified according to ISIC. In general, industries distinguished in the tables correspond to the so-called major groups of the ISIC classification. However, in some cases (i.e., forestry and fishing) major ISIC groups were combined into a single industry because of their relative unimportance or to preserve the secrecy of the data relating to particular firms. Also, several major ISIC groups (i.e., food manufacturing, trade, community and business services, personal services and transportation) were disaggregated into several industries to make more efficient use of the available data.

The structure of the intermediate consumption quadrant differs from the SNA recommendations in that: (*a*) the activities of private non-profit institutions are not recorded separately, but generally together with the activities of producers of government services; (*b*) intermediate and primary input of the producers of government services was not recorded in the intermediate consumption quadrant; but in the government consumption column of the final demand quadrant;* (*c*) three dummy sectors have been included. One of them allocates along a row those goods and services for which the sector of origin cannot be identified. Another allocates in a column those goods and services (for instance, output of printing offices) for which it was impossible to

---

*Starting with the 1977 input-output table this practice has been changed, so that intermediate and primary input of producers of government services is included in the intermediate consumption quadrant.

identify their sector of destination. Finally, a "correction items" dummy sector has been set up to allow for statistical discrepancies among rows and columns and to adjust the concept of final private consumption to a national basis. Thus, along the row of this third dummy sector, purchases in the Netherlands by foreign residents are deducted from final private consumption and added to exports.

The breakdown of final demand differs from the SNA recommendations in that gross fixed capital formation is disaggregated into its government and enterprise components. Private consumption has been defined on a national basis.

The breakdown of value added differs from the SNA recommendations in that compensation of employees is disaggregated into wages and salaries and employers' contributions to social security. In addition, net indirect taxes are disaggregated into indirect taxes and subsidies to producers.

As recommended in SNA, a distinction is made between complementary and competitive imports. Competitive imports are cross-classified by origin and destination in the import matrix (table (iii)), while complementary imports are classified by sector of destination only in an additional row of the import matrix. In addition, all imports are classified by sector of destination in a row of table (i).

4. Treatment and presentation of selected transactions

In classifying the basic statistical material by industries an attempt was made to maintain a parallel classification of commodities and of industries. Thus, for an establishment producing several products that would come under more than one industry in the tables, an attempt was made to split up both the input and the output data for the establishment concerned. In practice, however, it is impossible to ensure that the commodity classification and the industrial classification coincide completely. Where certain establishments in a particular industry happened to produce one or more minor products which contributed only a very small part of the total value of production for that industry, no correction was made. However, in cases where it was thought that the statistical analysis for a particular industry would diverge widely from a commodity classification, the breakdown was calculated.

Intra-industry transactions are recorded on the main diagonal of the input-output table. In general, these are transactions between different establishments within the same industry. Internal transactions within the same establishment have been generally excluded.

Non-monetary output and its associated input have been recorded together with the monetary output and input in three corresponding input-output sectors: construction (own-account capital formation), agriculture (household consumption of own products by farmers) and ownership of dwellings.

Government services include public administration and defence, as well as government contributions to the operating costs of hospitals and similar institutions, and public and subsidized private education. As mentioned above, intermediate and primary input of government services has been recorded in the final demand quadrant in the input-output tables prior to 1977. However, the value of goods and services sold by the Government to other sectors (such as sales from surplus, movable stocks, rents of buildings, pilots' services) have been recorded in the "sales of goods and services by Government" row of the intermediate consumption quadrant. These sales have been deducted from the value of government current expenditures in accordance with the national accounts definition.

Output of the financial institutions is defined as recommended in SNA, that is, it includes imputed banking services defined as the difference of interest earned over interest paid. Actual banking charges are distributed to intermediate and final demand sectors along the banking and financial services row, while imputed charges are recorded with a minus sign in a dummy entry of the value added section of the banking and financial services column.

Output of the trade sector is defined to include gross trade and transportation margins of wholesale and retail enterprises and gross trade margins received by productive enterprises from their wholesale trade activities. Excluded from output of the trade sector are wholesale trade activities carried out by separate selling organizations of industrial enterprises; a few cases (i.e., bakers' and chemists' shops) of retail activities, which have been recorded as output of the corresponding industrial sectors; and those transportation margins that could be estimated separately.

5. Statistical sources and compilation methodology

Data collection is mainly based on annually collected production statistics (which provide information on output and input of a large number of sectors), data provided by specialized professional organizations and the results of non-agriculture censuses carried out every 10 years. In addition, use is made of information regarding government expenditures. These data are preliminarily classified according to 40 industries, the output of which is generally distributed over its various uses by applying the commodity flow method.

Work on the compilation of the input-output table is organized into several teams of sector specialists, each of which covers the output and input of one or more sectors. These teams are usually in close contact with each other whenever the production processes of their corresponding sectors are closely related. In addition, there are teams specialized in specific components of final demand and primary input.

The resulting partly distributed data are transferred to another special section which confronts the figures received from the sector specialists and composes the input-output table. Composition of the table consists mainly of the following:

(a) Allocation of output and input not already carried out by the sector specialists. This allocation is mainly based on: (i) input-output data not yet confronted which mostly relate to commodities with a multi-purpose character, (ii) analysis of product balances, (iii) gross percentage distribution of output obtained for previous years or from specific studies; and (iv) adjustments of private consumption estimates and of changes in stocks;

(b) Application of various consistency checks. These checks relate mainly to the results of private consumption and changes in stocks. Preliminary data on private consumption are checked against results based on trend of retail sales. Those on change in stocks are checked against (i) direct information available on changes in stocks for several sectors, (ii) data on actual stocks changes available for previous years; and (iii) *a priori* known constraints, such as zero value of stock changes in sectors such as services.

6. *Gross output and intermediate consumption*

Data on quantities of output and input of the agriculture sectors are mainly based on two sources: an annual census of farmers, supplemented with information provided by professional organizations, and the accounts of about 6,000 farms. From the second source, output and input per hectare are computed for various sizes and types of farms in about 60 regions of the country, and nation-wide estimates are obtained on the basis of this information and acreage figures for similar farms in each region. A number of adjustments are then made to reconcile the results obtained from both sources of data on agriculture.

The quantitative estimates obtained as described above are valued at the producers' prices provided by the Landouw Economisch Instituut, which are obtained as annual weighted averages of monthly prices quoted at representative markets. Trade margins classified by products and destination are then added to the producers' prices estimates. These margins consist of a percentage estimated by experts in the field.

Data on manufacturing, mining, gas, electricity and water consumption are mainly based on the annually collected production statistics and on a non-agriculture census of establishments conducted every 10 years.

Annual production statistics collect data on sales of medium size establishments (i.e., those with 10 to 50 employees), and on sales, changes in stocks, intermediate deliveries, purchases of raw materials, wages and salaries, social security contributions and employment of large establishments. Other costs are only covered for large establishments and no information at all is collected from establishments with less than 10 employees. Therefore, estimates from production surveys have to be supplemented with estimates of the output and the input of small establishments. These estimates are based on the ratio of employment in small and medium size establishments, or the ratio of wages earned in small and medium size establishments, combined with any information on differences in output and input structures between other large and small establishments.

The census of non-agriculture establishments, which is carried out every 10 years as mentioned above, covers all establishments with 20 or more employees and a sample of some 15,000 small establishments in manufacturing, transport and distribution. It excludes agriculture, government services and activities mainly carried out for household purposes such as laundries in hospitals. The main purpose of the census is to provide background or "statistical" information for benchmark years, and "dynamic" data (concerning production turnover, investment, wage totals etc.) which supplement the information gathered in the annual production statistics.

Data on the construction sector are partially based on the annual production statistics mentioned above, from which information mainly regarding intermediate input is obtained. However, since the construction sector is only covered by this source on a sample basis, additional information is required. This is provided by independent data available on output of buildings, roads etc. and output of other industries used in construction as input. Construction of buildings is covered by bi-monthly progress reports from municipalities, which describe the number of starts, finishes and production value of buildings over 10,000 guilders. Production value is estimated on the basis of the proportion of work finished, as determined by the local authorities. Production values in roads, waterworks etc. are reported by municipalities, provincial authorities and the Office of Public Works.

Data on financial institutions are mainly obtained from the income and expenditure statements of commercial banks gathered by the Netherlands Bank. A special adjustment is made to cover foreign establishments of commercial banks. The adjustment is made on the basis of the results of yearly inquiries. Income and expenditure data for all other types of banks are available from the Central Bureau of Statistics and the Netherlands Bank.

Life insurance companies publish annual reports in a standardized format which contains practically all information required for the purpose of compilation of input-output tables. Adjustments for activities abroad are based on the results of direct inquiries. Income and expenditure statistics for all large firms in other types of insurance are compiled by the Central Bureau of Statistics. Some rough adjustments are made to these data for small firms.

A variety of sources of different reliability is used to obtain estimates for the transportation sector. Information on air and train transport is derived directly from the few existing enterprises. Public transportation by bus and sea is covered by annual questionnaires. Road traffic and taxis transport estimates are mainly based on the number of registered cars. The latter estimates are not considered to be very reliable.

Information on the rest of the services sector is very scarce. Some of the subsectors (i.e., schools, hospitals etc.) are covered by direct government information and occasional censuses.

7. *Value added*

Data on wages of the agriculture sector are mainly provided by accident statistics adjusted upwards by a fixed percentage so as to include non-real wages. Social security payments are linked to wages through fixed percentages. In the manufacturing, mining, construction, public utilities and distribution sectors, labour costs including social security payments are provided by annual production statistics and the records of professional organizations.

Data on depreciation allowances are based on estimates of the expected average economic life of the various categories of capital goods and their replacement value in the period of depreciation. Since no information on the stock of capital goods is available, the above-mentioned estimates are based on information available on investment.

The totals of indirect taxes and subsidies are derived from government records. Breakdowns are based on production survey information regarding taxes paid by sector.

8. *Final demand and imports*

Estimates of private consumption are mainly obtained through the commodity flow method, which measures "potential" consumption, that is, the retail value of goods and services that become available for household consumption. From the rather detailed list of goods and services used in the commodity flow approach, groups are formed of commodities that sell through retail. Information on consumption of these groups of goods and services is provided by short-term indicators of retail sales. The trend of retail sale indicators, corrected when necessary with an extrapolation of the differences between the trends of potential consumption and of retail sales, is the basic source used for the estimation of private consumption.

Investment statistics are collected annually. Output of the construction sector provides the only direct information on gross fixed capital formation. The remaining of investment is derived as a result of the commodity flow method.

Government expenditures on consumption and investment are taken directly from central, provincial and local government accounts. The local government accounts are covered on a sample basis.

Changes in producers' stocks are estimated directly from the annual production statistics and are based on responses obtained from an annual sample of farmers on relationships between output, changes in stock and own consumption. The survey is conducted by the professional organizations concerned. Changes in stock in the trade sector are very difficult to cover and, as a consequence, they are estimated as a residual of the commodity flow method. Stocks and changes in stocks are in principle valued at replacement cost — finished products at producers' prices and raw materials at purchasers' prices. To approach this valuation as much as possible, questions on stocks are formulated in quantities and valued afterwards.

Data on exports and imports are obtained from the balance of payment statistics.

CLASSIFICATION OF INPUT-OUTPUT TABLES FOR 1970

(Translation of rows)

Input-output sectors	Industry and primary cost categories
1	Agriculture, forestry and fishing
2	Mining of coal
3	Other mining and quarrying (exclusive of crude oil and natural gas)
4	Manufacture of food (based on animal products)
5	Manufacture of food (based on other products)
6	Manufacture of beverages and tobacco products
7	Manufacture of textiles
8	Manufacture of wearing apparel (excluding footwear)
9	Manufacture of leather, footwear and leather products
10	Manufacture of wood products, including furniture
11	Manufacture of paper and paper products
12	Graphic industry and publishing companies
13	Petroleum industry (inclusive of crude oil and natural gas)
14	Chemical industry, rubber industry and synthetic materials processing industry
15	Manufacture of building materials, of earthenware and of glass
16	Manufacture of basic metals
17	Manufacture of metal products and of machinery and equipment
18	Manufacture of electrical machinery, apparatus, appliances and supplies
19	Manufacture of transport equipment
20	Manufacture of optical products, of professional, scientific, measuring and controlling instruments and other manufacturing
21	Public utilities (electricity, gas and water)
22	Construction
23	Wholesale and retail trade
24	Hotels, cafés and restaurants
25	Repair services
26	Sea and air transport
27	Other transport and storage
28	Communication
29	Banking and insurance
30	Ownership of dwellings
31	Business services
32	Medical and veterinary services
33	Culture and recreation
34	Other services
35	a. Goods and services not specified according to origin
	b. Sales of goods and services by Government
	c. Correction items
36	Total rows 1-35 c
37	Imports of goods and services
38	Indirect taxes
39	Subsidies to producers (–)
40	Wages and salaries
41	Employers' contributions to social insurance
42	Other income (including depreciation)
43	Interest margin banks
44	Total rows 37-43
45	Total rows 36-44

(Translation of columns)

Input-output sectors	Input of industries and final expenditures
1-33	Identical to rows 1-34
35	Not specified according to destination
36	Total columns 1-35
37	Export of goods and services
38	Private consumption expenditure
39	Government consumption expenditure
40	Gross investment in fixed assets of Government
41	Gross investment in fixed assets of enterprises
42	Increase in stocks and work in progress of enterprises
43	Total columns 37-42
44	Total columns 36 and 43

Quadrants	
I	Intermediary goods and services
II	Final production of industries
III	Total output of industries
IV	Primary costs of industries
V	Primary costs, also final goods and services
VI	Total primary costs
VII	Total costs of industries
VIII	Total final expenditure

NETHERLANDS
INPUT-OUTPUT TABLES
1975

Source: *De Produktiestructuur van de Nederlandse Volkshuidhouding, Deel VII, Input-Output Tabellen 1972-1975,* Central Bureau of Statistics, Netherlands.

Tabel 16. "Input-output" tabel voor de Nederlandse volkshuishouding in 1975 (op basis van het verbruik; miljoenen guldens)
(Directe berekening van de indirecte belastingen c.q. subsidies aan de kopers)

"Input" van bedrijfsklassen

"Output" van bedrijfsklassen	1	2	3	4	5	6	7	8	9	10	11	12	13	14	15	16	17	18
Intermediaire goederen en diensten (I)																		
Landbouw, bosbouw en visserij	1257	-	10996	1839	28	12	5	-	32	21		15	-	-	-	-	-	-
Delfstoffenwinning (excl. kolenmijnbouw en aardolie- en aardgaswinning)	16	-	8	4	-	-	-	1	-	-		30	191	-	-	-	-	-
Voedingsmiddelenindustrie (veehouderijprodukten)	6	-	1178	395	6	3	-	2	-	-		16	-	-	-	-	-	-
Voedingsmiddelenindustrie (overige produkten)	5318	-	211	3456	184	7	-	2	8	42		81	-	4	-	-	-	-
Dranken- en tabakverwerkende industrie	9	-	3	16	76	-	-	-	-	5		-	-	-	-	2	-	-
Textielindustrie	25	-	3	10	-	766	256	19	67	12		33	-	-	34	13	46	
Kledingindustrie	-	-	-	-	-	-	71	-	-	-		-	-	-	-	-	-	-
Leder- en schoenindustrie	2	-	-	1	-	-	13	40	9	-		-	-	-	1	5	0	
Hout- en meubelindustrie	34	-	4	41	18	2	-	2	227	18	2	38	26	1	63	8	213	
Papierindustrie	9	2	134	344	74	45	6	7	7	435	437	2	153	16	9	34	43	7
Grafische industrie en uitgeverijen	36	3	62	156	89	52	20	6	31	28	1766	28	278	20	22	98	98	35
Aardolie-industrie (incl. aardolie- en aardgaswinning)	143	10	60	75	14	12	5	3	25	13	21	278	1475	28	50	35	30	15
Chemische, rubber- en kunststofverw. ind. (incl. kolenmijnbouw)	509	7	57	137	57	91	14	19	112	109	86	773	2024	57	11	215	125	111
Bouwmaterialen-, aardewerk- en glasindustrie	21	-	3	42	49	21	-	-	11	-	-	-	27	253	29	16	27	6
Basismetaalindustrie	5	-	1	-	-	-	-	-	8	4	2	5	10	19	5602	630	137	227
Metaalprodukten- en machine-industrie	124	11	198	205	87	20	2	4	75	19	18	130	249	30	54	1544	153	609
Elektrotechnische industrie	8	-	-	3	2	3	-	-	5	1	2	10	14	1	17	240	113	227
Transportmiddelenindustrie	50	7	6	9	1	2	-	-	7	1	1	10	19	2	21	55	13	588
Optische en overige industrie	1	-	2	1	-	-	-	-	6	1	2	7	8	1	1	95	26	33
Openbare nutsbedrijven	301	43	136	276	44	100	9	7	47	146	40	88	1164	239	377	183	113	73
Bouwnijverheid en bouwinstallatiebedrijven	243	6	40	91	22	35	10	5	19	25	36	67	180	35	29	366	161	366
Groothandel en detailhandel	573	4	288	857	110	156	85	21	170	217	120	39	900	240	83	334	111	143
Hotels, cafés en restaurants	11	2	8	13	11	8	6	3	12	5	26	7	33	6	7	29	34	12
Reparatie van gebruiksgoederen	166	19	52	77	19	17	7	5	29	16	31	22	52	24	13	39	37	15
Zee- en luchtvaart	11	-	2	9	4	3	1	1	2	3	12	-	90	3	2	20	12	6
Overige transport- en opslagbedrijven	48	11	80	106	18	14	10	4	20	6	95	32	86	14	13	98	48	20
Communicatiebedrijven	79	6	41	87	27	19	9	5	33	17	98	23	79	16	21	55	64	27
Bank- en verzekeringswezen	130	5	33	73	26	24	8	4	20	15	28	32	130	15	43	73	67	42
Woningbezit	-	-	-	-	-	-	-	-	-	-	-	-	-	-	-	-	-	-
Zakelijke dienstverlening	131	6	40	98	34	37	15	7	41	27	261	76	174	24	19	83	57	32
Medische en veterinaire diensten	136	-	-	-	-	-	-	-	-	-	-	-	-	-	-	-	-	-
Cultuur en recreatie	-	-	3	35	23	6	1	-	1	-	85	-	69	-	-	8	10	5
Overige dienstverlening	6	-	27	52	12	18	8	4	7	8	21	4	55	15	7	27	35	14
a. Goederen en diensten niet naar herkomst verdeeld	-	-	8	-	-	11	-	-	-	17	90	25	110	40	-	159	80	50
b. Verkoop goederen en diensten door de overheid	32	7	32	42	-	-	1	-	1	3	3	3	10	8	1	14	7	1
c. Correctieposten	-	-	-	-	-	-	-	-	-	-	-	-	-	-	-	-	-	-
TOTAAL regels 1 t/m 34b	9448	149	13726	8550	1035	1484	583	179	1030	1313	3283	1316	7105	2378	6486	4493	1617	3211
Primaire kosten van bedrijven (IV)																		
Invoer van goederen en diensten	936	19	450	8222	875	1983	1192	169	927	1248	831	11136	5612	477	2346	4370	4662	2533
Afschrijvingen	1060	50	250	600	160	230	60	30	130	190	230	670	1360	270	480	530	380	240
Indirecte belastingen	240	3	239	215	55	24	14	2	31	34	60	19	164	32	54	90	73	44
Prijsverlagende subsidies (-)	-13	-1	-18	-83	-6	-8	-4	-1	-7	-3	-20	-10	-48	-4	-4	-17	-14	-6
Lonen en salarissen	1374	110	1261	2326	649	1081	499	212	1076	777	1812	538	3454	1030	1137	5016	3803	2060
Werkgeversbijdragen voor sociale verzekering	303	31	359	614	192	295	137	59	274	215	486	194	977	285	300	1315	990	569
Overige inkomens	6807	101	430	997	443	-22	-34	-29	180	-35	542	7952	1477	310	-15	1199	712	306
Restmarge banken	-	-	-	-	-	-	-	-	-	-	-	-	-	-	-	-	-	-
TOTAAL regels 36 t/m 43	10707	313	2971	12891	2368	3583	1838	462	2611	2426	3941	22479	12796	2400	4318	12503	10006	5766
Totale kosten van bedrijven (VII)																		
TOTAAL regels 35 en 44	20155	462	16697	21441	3403	5067	2421	641	3641	3638	7104	23815	19901	3732	10774	16996	11623	8977

204

	Finale financieringscategorieën								

19	20	21	22	23	24	25	26	27	28	29	30	31	32	33	34	35	36	37	38	39	40	41	42	43	Regelnummer
																Finale goederen en diensten voortgebracht door bedrijven (II)								Totale produktiewaarde van bedrijven (III)	
-	-	-	32	-	3	-	-	-	-	16	14	-	-	-	-	14270	4306	1822	77	-	-34	-286	5885	20155	1
-	-	26	-	-	-	-	-	-	-	-	-	-	-	-	9	285	122	9	43	-	2	1	177	462	2
4	-	-	22	206	-	5	-	-	-	78	12	-	2	1939	8352	6077	23	-	4	302	14758	16697	3
-	2	3	-	209	-	5	-	-	-	74	10	3	12	9635	5440	6010	38	-	13	305	11806	21441	4
-	-	-	-	264	-	26	-	-	-	3	-	-	7	411	1068	1874	22	-	5	23	2992	3403	5
-	-	41	32	20	9	6	27	2	-	-	24	1	9	-	1450	2535	1026	35	30	3	-20	3609	5067	6
-	-	17	-	-	-	-	-	-	-	-	-	-	-	-	88	1304	1052	4	-	1	-28	2333	2421	7
-	-	-	-	1	-	-	-	-	-	-	-	-	-	-	89	218	348	5	-	-19	552	641	8
6	1	882	23	-	11	3	14	6	-	-	-	-	1	-	1645	525	1064	70	131	234	-28	1996	3641	9
6	1	11	484	16	1	1	13	3	7	-	10	2	1	6	43	2289	1216	150	34	-	-	-51	1349	3638	10
21	26	120	660	18	8	38	99	58	237	-	107	79	40	84	57	4439	471	1686	470	-	3	35	2665	7164	11
5	4844	302	124	17	14	192	481	14	54	-	24	56	11	40	12	8561	13962	1109	287	-	163	-267	15254	23815	12
10	59	643	205	22	20	43	71	28	12	-	9	145	3	92	61	5537	13330	1210	119	-	65	-360	14364	19901	13
1	-	2246	19	8	-	4	-	-	-	-	-	4	-	19	31	2937	688	129	130	-	12	-64	895	3732	14
20	78	140	2	1	25	-	-	1	1	-	-	1	-	-	-	6919	3668	1	32	-	98	56	3855	10774	15
100	79	1589	112	15	244	10	138	36	74	28	11	62	6	21	5	6342	7079	534	280	368	2491	-98	10654	16996	16
97	153	104	6	1	134	5	86	27	16	-	1	37	-	1	1	1315	7806	1141	212	191	897	61	10308	11623	17
-	1	65	41	1	19	132	168	12	6	-	-	20	-	1	9	1267	6067	442	344	30	1214	-387	7710	8977	18
34	-	22	1	-	15	2	9	5	-	-	1	47	-	-	3	323	942	193	56	75	52	-	1318	1641	19
26	1700	224	386	136	78	19	217	41	139	-	61	244	38	99	10	8804	2	4596	523	-	264	-	5385	12189	20
12	98	2019	191	29	6	21	122	40	97	1324	28	132	22	44	-	5939	1238	759	1225	5585	14358	-	23165	29104	21
33	23	1240	268	117	84	56	157	24	28	-	14	99	3	36	-	6244	8384	19218	146	93	1176	-14	29003	35247	22
1	7	39	69	-	1	2	42	8	38	-	14	12	6	13	-	473	-	2819	123	-	-	-	2942	3415	23
3	19	107	297	4	3	10	368	21	46	-	12	28	3	23	-	1580	-	2247	119	-	-	-	2366	3946	24
-	3	14	162	-	1	75	21	23	24	-	11	5	1	9	48	514	4716	483	72	-	12	-	5283	5797	25
1	16	101	4682	19	3	168	134	72	116	-	32	20	8	27	21	6118	4056	1547	475	-	230	-	6308	12426	26
6	21	151	609	28	7	69	147	-	548	-	48	78	21	47	43	2531	125	1590	395	-	48	-	2158	4689	27
7	17	136	287	11	6	46	147	1	1573	64	21	37	3	28	-	3150	493	2470	111	-	-	-	3074	6224	28
-	-	-	-	-	-	-	-	-	-	-	-	-	-	-	-	9881	-	-	-	-	-	-	9881	9881	29
11	22	254	635	76	9	58	184	21	146	47	33	84	73	55	57	3127	318	667	572	265	1427	-	3249	6376	30
-	-	-	-	-	-	-	-	1	22	-	-	66	6	-	-	231	-	12270	572	-	-	-	12842	13073	31
-	-	-	28	11	-	-	3	-	5	-	-	11	41	4	-	303	4	1194	315	-	-	-	1513	1816	32
1	17	43	147	51	10	21	34	6	107	-	26	216	24	46	-	1063	458	5255	1221	-	-	-	6934	7997	33
-	70	-	-	-	-	71	135	50	40	-	-	40	-	7	-	963	1976	-650	21	-	-	-	1347	2310	34a
6	44	29	55	2	-	35	74	32	28	19	55	26	13	20	231	844	340	271	-1626	173	-	-	-844	-	b
-	-	-	-	-	-	-	-	-	-	-	-	-	-	-	-	3094	-3094								c
411	7303	10630	9484	1334	709	1100	2891	532	3564	1482	520	1746	358	737	664	109593	104303	87400	6543	6941	22738	-839	227086	336679	35
																Primaire kosten, tevens finale goederen en diensten (V)								Totale primaire kosten (VI)	
44	143	4901	2403	170	912	2157	855	74	655	-	67	442	65	171	1646	64738	5767	20716	710	134	9372	665	37364	102102	36
5	1540	590	1820	210	60	820	1710	590	140	2716	220	710	50	129	-	18240	993	14119	1142	1188	2962	-6	20298	19811	37
17	41	217	336	234	24	74	178	84	247	248	25	101	6	65	-	3392	993	14119	1142	1188	2962	-6	20298	23690	38
-	-7	-	-26	64	-2	-1	-2	-22	-26	-	-10	-6	-2	-8	-	-338	-1481	-1492	-137	-1	-20	-12	-3143	-3481	39
141	1501	8464	11100	1141	1308	1255	4702	2163	4555	-	1072	4782	674	4801	-	77726	-	-	20478	256	-	-	20734	98460	40
110	322	2753	2830	220	369	305	1250	471	1291	-	608	1517	218	1116	-	21363	-	-	7880	-	-	-	7880	29243	41
213	1338	1575	7210	108	565	88	862	801	2392	5441	1674	1581	499	793	-	48562								48562	42
-	-	-	-	-	-	-	-	-	-6597	-	-	-	-	-	-	-6597								-6597	43
1210	4886	18474	25761	2081	3237	4697	9535	4157	2660	8399	5856	11127	1458	7260	1646	227086	5179	33343	31646	1577	12314	647	84706	311792.	44
																Totale finale bestedingen (VIII)									
1641	12189	29104	35247	3415	3946	5797	12426	4689	6224	9881	6376	13073	1816	7997	2310	336679	109482	120743	38189	8518	35052	-192	311792		45

205

XIII. NORWAY

A. GENERAL INFORMATION

The present country chapter is based on *National Accounts of Norway, System and Methods of Estimation*, by Erling J. Flottum, published by the Central Bureau of Statistics in 1981, and "Compilation of input-output tables in Norway", by N. T. Furunes and S. L. Rogeberg, in *Compilation of Input-Output Tables*, Proceedings, edited by Jiri V. Skolka, Gouvieux, France, 1981.

Norway is one of the few countries that have compiled input-output tables as an integral part of national accounts based on the production approach (or commodity flow approach). Annual input-output tables are available on magnetic tapes but have been published only for a selected number of years. Input-output tables for Norway have been published for the years 1947, 1948, 1950, 1954, 1959 and 1964. Rectangular tables have been published for the years 1973 and 1976. Norway has followed all the essential points of the recommendations of SNA, published by the United Nations in 1968. The revised figures based on the 1968 SNA were published in 1973. Production and commodity accounts in the form of the make and the absorption matrices serve as the core of the Norwegian national accounts.

The main policy of the Central Bureau of Statistics is to establish primary statistics with a view to serving the needs of national accounts. This co-ordinating and integrating role assigned to the national accounts in relation to joint definitions, classifications etc. has facilitated the integration of input-output and national accounts. The importance of input-output has been helped by the institutionalization of modelling for national budgeting and macro-economic planning within the national accounts division of the Central Bureau of Statistics.

B. ANALYTICAL FRAMEWORK

1. *Tables and derived matrices available*

Two basic flow tables are compiled:
(i)   The make matrix;
(ii) The absorption matrix.
The absorption matrix is split into eight different value flows; the first four relate to the decomposition of the producers' value and the last four relate to the composition of the gross trade and transport margin:
(i')   Approximate basic value (on production and import);
(ii') Value added tax (on production and import);
(iii') Other commodity tax (on production and import);
(iv') Commodity subsidies (on production and import);
(v')   Approximate basic values (trade and transport margins);
(vi') Value added tax (in wholesale and retail trade);
(vii') Other commodity taxes (in wholesale and retail trade);

(viii') Commodity subsidies (on commodity in wholesale and retail trade).

Thus, Norway allows great flexibility in valuation; flows can be converted to producers' values and purchasers' values.

Flow tables are rectangular in the form of commodities by industries, with 161 industries (production sectors) and 1,750 commodities (groups of goods and services). No commodity-by-commodity or industry-by-industry matrices are provided. It is up to analysts to produce these tables based on the assumptions of their own choices.

2. *Valuation standards*

All tables are valued at approximate basic values, producers' values and purchasers' values.

3. *Statistical units and classification standards*

The classification of production sectors (industries), with the establishment as the statistical unit according to kind of economic activity, is based on the Standard Industrial Classification in official Norwegian statistics, which is in turn based on ISIC. The same industrial classification, although not as detailed, is also applied to fixed capital formation, but not for increase in stocks.

Norway has its own commodity classification, known as national accounts commodities (NA-commodities), obtained by aggregating more than 5,000 commodity groups. The classification is based on the principle that a commodity is only allocated to a specific category of use and in such a manner that an individual commodity within the NA-commodities is assumed to have the same trade and transport margins.

Establishments engaged in activities that could be classified under several industrial groups are classified under the activity that provides the largest contribution to total value added of the establishment.

The structure of the intermediate consumption quadrant closely follows the SNA recommendations. The activities of the producers of government services, which are grouped separately into central and local governments, and producers of private non-profit institutions are recorded in this quadrant. These government purchases are recorded net of government sales. Imputed charges of bank services are recorded as sales by the financing and insurance industry to a dummy sector. This dummy input flow is balanced by a negative operating surplus to make output of the dummy sector equal to zero.

The breakdown and definition of value added and final demand follow the SNA recommendations. Value added includes separate categories of compensation of employees, operating surplus, consumption of fixed capital, net indirect taxes and other net commodity taxes.

Gross capital formation and increase in stocks have commodity details only for private enterprises. Dwellings, expenses for major land improvement in agriculture and forestry, all expenses for oil drilling and oil exploration, and the part of the change in livestock relating to breeding stock, draught animals and dairy cattle are considered capital stock as recommended by SNA. The increase in livestock raised for slaughter is considered increase in stocks. Net sales of second-hand capital goods are also included. A correction row is set up to record purchases of residents abroad (for household consumption, capital formation and government consumption) net of sales to non-residents. No distinction is made between complementary and competitive imports.

4. Treatment and presentation of selected transactions

Characteristic and secondary products produced by each industry are presented in the form of the make matrix as recommended by SNA. In the make matrix, a dummy commodity is set up to record repair expenses and other unspecified intermediate consumption goods.

C. STATISTICAL SOURCES AND COMPILATION METHODOLOGY

Primary statistics for input-output and national accounts, such as annual agricultural statistics, forestry statistics, fishery statistics, industrial statistics, and statistics of the Housing Bank, are collected by the special subject-matter divisions within the Central Bureau of Statistics of Norway, which is also responsible for preparing input-output tables. The main method used for input-output compilation is the commodity flow method through balancing supply and uses of commodity in producers' values. Changes in stocks are treated more or less as residuals and therefore contain statistical errors. The production approach is used to compute value added for almost all industrial and trade sectors. By this approach, intermediate demand is subtracted from gross output to obtain value added. The income approach, by adding up income components to value added, is used to obtain value added in the government sectors and a few private service sectors such as education and research, welfare institutions and domestic services. Operating surplus is computed as a residual, given that values added and other components of value added are known.

Private final consumption expenditure has been determined in the main versions by the use of consumer surveys and other sources such as data on the supply of commodities and revised margin percentages. However, for estimating most categories of consumer goods on an annual basis, changes in the sales figures of annual wholesale and retail sales are used as value indicators. Even though annual consumer surveys are now available as additional sources of data, these figures have not been used for annual estimation of private final demand since they have shown large discrepancies from wholesale and retail trade statistics. Private consumption of expenditure on services is estimated by computing gross output in the service sectors.

1. Gross output

The output of the agriculture sector includes production for home consumption and services in connection with agriculture. As recommended by SNA, changes in livestock are divided into two categories: changes in breeding stock and dairy cattle are allocated to gross fixed capital formation and changes in livestock raised for slaughter are allocated to changes in stocks.

The output of forestry includes all work on felling and hauling and the collection of wild berries and plants.

The fishing sector includes ocean and coastal fishing consisting of the catch and landing of fish and shellfish, cleaning and icing of fish and other preparation activities aboard fishing vessels before delivery to processing plants or buyers. It also includes sealing and whaling and hatching and breeding of fish. The output of this industry also includes estimated values of catch for own consumption, own-account installation, repairs and maintenance of the fixed assets.

For mining and manufacturing industries, their outputs are calculated as suggested by SNA. Electricity, gas and water include both production and distribution activities.

Construction output does not include the digging of mine shafts or drilling for oil and natural gas if they are carried out on an own-account basis. The production of prefabricated houses, cottages, garages etc. to be erected in a location other than the production site is considered manufacturing industry, while the assembly work at the building site is classified into the construction sector.

The hotels and restaurants industry includes in its output its gross sales of goods and drinks, which comprise the costs of goods and beverages and the serving margins.

2. Value added, final demand

The classification of value added and final demand closely follows the SNA recommendations.

CLASSIFICATION OF INPUT-OUTPUT TABLES

Input-output sector — Goods and services

1. Crops
2. Livestock products
3. Agricultural services
4. Forestry products
5. Fish etc.
6. Mining and quarrying products
7. Crude petroleum
8. Prepared fish products
9. Prepared agricultural products
10. Other prepared foodstuffs
11. Beverages
12. Tobacco
13. Textile articles and wearing apparel
14. Leather, leather products, fur articles and footwear
15. Wood products, except furniture and fixtures of wood
16. Furniture and fixtures of wood
17. Products from manufacture of paper and paper products
18. Graphic products
19. Industrial chemicals
20. Other chemical products
21. Products of petroleum and coal
22. Rubber products
23. Plastic products
24. Ceramics
25. Glass, glass products and mineral products, not elsewhere classified
26. Iron, steel and ferro-alloys
27. Non-ferrous metals
28. Metal products
29. Machinery and oil and gas well machinery and tools
30. Electrical apparatus and supplies
31. Ships and boats
32. Other transport equipment
33. Professional and scientific instruments etc.
34. Other manufacturing products
35. Electricity
36. Water
37. Buildings and repair of buildings
38. Construction other than buildings
39. Crude oil and natural gas wells
40. Commissions etc.
41. Services from hotels and restaurants

NORWAY

INPUT-OUTPUT TABLES

1976

Source: Central Bureau of Statistics, Norway.

TABELL 8. VARE- OG TJENESTETILGANG. 100000 KR. 1976. HELE LANDET **INDUSTRIES (46)**

	PRODUKSJONSSEKTORER							
COMMODITIES (58) NR. VARER OG TJENESTER	JORD- BRUK	SKOG- BRUK	FISKE OG FANGST	BERG- VERKS- DRIFT	UT- VINNING AV RÅ- OLJE OG NATUR- GASS	FISKE- FORED- LING	NÆRINGS- MIDDEL- INDUSTRI	PRODUK- SJON AV DRIKKE- VARER
	01.	02.	03.	04.	05.	06.	07.	08.
01. PLANTEPRODUKTER............	44471	-	-	-	-	-	743	-
02. HUSDYRPRODUKTER...........	73365	-	-	-	-	7	178	-
03. TJENESTER I TILKNYTNING TIL JORDBRUK..............	7589	-	-	-	-	-	-	-
04. SKOGPRODUKTER..............	-	19274	-	-	-	-	-	-
05. FISK M.V.................	-	-	32063	-	-	133	75	-
06. BERGVERKSPRODUKTER........	-	-	-	15688	-	-	1	-
07. RÅOLJE OG NATURGASS.......	-	-	-	-	68182	-	-	-
08. FOREDLEDE FISKEPRODUKTER..	-	-	20	-	-	45920	232	6
09. FOREDLEDE JORDBRUKS-PRODUKTER................	594	-	345	-	-	455	109362	232
10. ANDRE NÆRINGSMIDLER.......	-	-	345	-	-	750	64246	76
11. DRIKKEVARER...............	-	-	-	-	-	1	55	19504
12. TOBAKKSVARER..............	-	-	-	-	-	-	-	-
13. TEKSTILVARER OG KLÆR......	1	-	-	-	-	-	-	-
14. LÆR, LÆR- OG SKINNVARER OG SKOTØY...................	-	-	-	-	-	-	-	-
15. TREVARER, UNNTATT MØBLER OG INNREDNINGER AV TRE....	-	-	-	-	-	1	-	-
16. MØBLER OG INNREDNINGER AV TRE....................	-	-	-	-	-	-	-	-
17. TREFOREDLINGSPRODUKTER....	-	-	-	-	-	-	-	-
18. GRAFISKE PRODUKTER........	-	-	-	-	-	-	-	-
19. KJEMISKE RÅVARER..........	-	-	-	29	-	-	115	24
20. KJEMISK-TEKNISKE PRODUKTER	-	-	-	-	-	11	131	-
21. OLJE- OG KULLPRODUKTER....	-	-	-	-	-	-	-	-
22. GUMMIPRODUKTER............	-	-	-	-	-	-	-	-
23. PLASTVARER...............	-	-	-	-	-	-	-	-
24. KERAMISKE PRODUKTER.......	-	-	-	-	-	-	-	-
25. GLASS, GLASSVARER OG MINE-RALSKE PRODUKTER ELLERS...	-	-	-	239	-	-	-	-
26. JERN, STÅL OG FERRO-LEGERINGER...............	-	-	-	6	-	-	-	-
27. IKKE-JERNHOLDIGE METALLER.	-	-	-	6	-	-	-	-
28. METALLVARER..............	-	-	-	-	-	-	13	-
29. MASKINER OG OLJE-PLATTFORMER...............	-	-	-	-	-	-	-	-
30. EL. APPARATER OG MATERIELL	-	-	-	-	-	-	-	-
31. FARTØYER.................	-	-	-	-	-	-	-	-
32. ANDRE TRANSPORTMIDLER.....	-	-	-	-	-	-	-	-
33. TEKNISKE OG VITENSKAPLIGE INSTRUMENTER M.V.........	-	-	-	-	-	-	7	-
34. ANDRE INDUSTRIPRODUKTER...	-	-	-	-	-	-	-	-
35. ELEKTRISITET.............	-	-	-	-	-	-	-	-
36. VANN...................	-	-	-	-	-	-	-	-
37. BYGG OG REPARASJONER AV BYGG....................	-	-	-	-	-	-	-	-
38. ANLEGG.................	-	-	-	-	-	-	-	-
39. BOREHULL FOR OLJE OG GASS.	-	-	-	-	-	-	-	-
40. PROVISJONER, M.V..........	-	-	-	-	-	-	-	-
41. HOTELL OG RESTAURANT-TJENESTER...............	-	-	-	-	-	-	-	-
42. TJENESTER FRA UTENRIKS SJØFART.................	-	-	-	-	-	-	-	-
43. PERSONTRANSPORTTJENESTER..	-	-	-	-	-	-	-	-
44. GODSTRANSPORTTJENESTER....	-	-	-	-	-	-	-	-
45. POST- OG TELETJENESTER....	-	-	-	-	-	-	-	-
46. BANK- OG FORSIKRINGS-TJENESTER...............	-	-	-	-	-	-	-	-
47. TJENESTER FRA BOLIGER OG FORRETNINGSBYGG.........	-	-	-	48	-	118	324	19
48. HELSE- OG VETERINÆR-TJENESTER................	-	-	-	-	-	-	-	-
49. UNDERVISNINGS- OG FORSKNINGSTJENESTER.......	-	-	-	-	-	-	-	-
50. FORRETNINGSMESSIGE TJENESTER................	-	-	-	36	4	62	199	6
51. ANDRE TJENESTER...........	-	-	-	-	-	-	-	-
52. IKKE MARKEDSFØRTE OFFENTLIGE TJENESTER......	-	-	-	-	-	-	-	-
53. VARER TIL REPARASJONER, USPESIFISERT VAREINNSATS M.V.....................	-	249	1014	1148	1480	1176	4079	147
54. VARER TIL INVESTERINGER, BYGG OG ANLEGG..........	-	-	-	-	-	-	-	-
55. VARER TIL INVESTERINGER, MASKINER OG TRANSPORT-MIDLER M.V.............	-	-	-	-	-	-	-	-
56. KORREKSJONER FOR MERVERDI-OG INVESTERINGSAVGIFT.....	-	-	-	-	-	-	-	-
57. KORR. FOR UTLENDINGERS KONSUM I NORGE OG KJØP/ SALG AV BRUKT REALKAP.....	-	-	-	-	-	-	-	-
58. LEIE AV PRODUKSJONS-FAKTORER MELLOM FYLKENE...	-	-	-	-	-	-	-	-
65. IALT..................	126020	19523	33442	29197	69666	48636	179723	20014

212

TABELL 8(FORTS.). VARE- OG TJENESTETILGANG. 100000 KR. 1976. HELE LANDET   INDUSTRIES (46)

	PRODUKSJONSSEKTORER (FORTS.)							
COMMODITIES (58) NR. VARER OG TJENESTER	PRODUK-SJON AV TOBAKKS-VARER.	PRODUK-SJON AV TEKSTIL-VARER OG KLÆR	PRODUK-SJON AV LÆR, LÆR- OG SKINN-VARER OG SKOTØY	PROD. AV TREVARER UNNTATT MØBLER OG INNREDN. AV TRE	PRODUK-SJON AV MØBLER OG INNRED-NINGER AV TRE	TRE-FOREDLING	GRAFISK PRODUK-SJON OG FORLAGS-VIRKSOM-HET	PRODUK-SJON AV KJEMISKE RÅVARER
	09.	10.	11.	12.	13.	14.	15.	16.
01. PLANTEPRODUKTER............	-	-	-	-	-	-	-	-
02. HUSDYRPRODUKTER............	-	4	1	-	-	-	-	-
03. TJENESTER I TILKNYTNING TIL JORDBRUK.............	-	-	-	-	-	-	-	-
04. SKOGPRODUKTER.............	-	-	-	451	-	-	-	-
05. FISK M.V................	-	-	-	-	-	-	-	-
06. BERGVERKSPRODUKTER........	-	-	-	-	-	-	-	44
07. RÅOLJE OG NATURGASS.......	-	-	-	-	-	-	-	-
08. FOREDLEDE FISKEPRODUKTER..	-	-	-	-	-	-	-	-
09. FOREDLEDE JORDBRUKS-PRODUKTER...............	-	-	-	-	-	-	-	-
10. ANDRE NÆRINGSMIDLER.......	-	-	-	-	-	-	-	-
11. DRIKKEVARER...............	-	-	-	-	-	-	-	12
12. TOBAKKSVARER..............	10438	-	-	-	-	-	-	-
13. TEKSTILVARER OG KLÆR......	-	55546	128	71	107	508	13	-
14. LÆR, LÆR- OG SKINNVARER OG SKOTØY.................	-	110	4607	-	-	-	-	-
15. TREVARER, UNNTATT MØBLER OG INNREDNINGER AV TRE....	-	19	-	69545	1350	-	-	-
16. MØBLER OG INNREDNINGER AV TRE....................	-	5	-	312	20947	-	-	-
17. TREFOREDLINGSPRODUKTER....	-	57	-	121	-	71447	218	212
18. GRAFISKE PRODUKTER........	-	-	-	2	-	338	58027	-
19. KJEMISKE RÅVARER..........	-	1	-	-	-	-	-	32394
20. KJEMISK-TEKNISKE PRODUKTER	-	-	2	-	-	16	-	1084
21. OLJE- OG KULLPRODUKTER....	-	-	-	9	-	143	-	-
22. GUMMIPRODUKTER............	-	20	47	-	-	-	-	19
23. PLASTVARER...............	-	230	12	13	121	243	5	93
24. KERAMISKE PRODUKTER.......	-	-	-	-	-	-	-	-
25. GLASS, GLASSVARER OG MINE-RALSKE PRODUKTER ELLERS...	-	11	-	32	404	27	-	15
26. JERN, STÅL OG FERRO-LEGERINGER...............	-	-	-	-	-	-	-	-
27. IKKE-JERNHOLDIGE METALLER.	-	5	-	-	-	235	-	99
28. METALLVARER..............	-	27	2	108	286	23	50	-
29. MASKINER OG OLJE-PLATTFORMER................	-	-	-	4	3	23	-	-
30. EL. APPARATER OG MATERIELL	-	-	7	-	77	-	17	11
31. FARTØYER.................	-	-	-	6	-	-	-	-
32. ANDRE TRANSPORTMIDLER.....	-	-	-	1	-	-	-	-
33. TEKNISKE OG VITENSKAPLIGE INSTRUMENTER M.V.........	-	111	-	-	9	-	-	-
34. ANDRE INDUSTRIPRODUKTER...	-	1	-	43	-	14	21	-
35. ELEKTRISITET.............	-	-	-	-	-	-	-	-
36. VANN...................	-	-	-	-	-	-	-	-
37. BYGG OG REPARASJONER AV BYGG....................	-	-	-	-	-	-	-	-
38. ANLEGG.................	-	-	-	-	-	-	-	-
39. BOREHULL FOR OLJE OG GASS.	-	-	-	-	-	-	-	-
40. PROVISJONER M.V...........	-	-	-	-	-	-	-	-
41. HOTELL OG RESTAURANT-TJENESTER................	-	-	-	-	-	-	-	-
42. TJENESTER FRA UTENRIKS SJØFART..................	-	-	-	-	-	-	-	-
43. PERSONTRANSPORTTJENESTER..	-	-	-	-	-	-	-	-
44. GODSTRANSPORTTJENESTER....	-	-	-	-	-	-	-	-
45. POST- OG TELETJENESTER....	-	-	-	-	-	-	-	-
46. BANK- OG FORSIKRINGS-TJENESTER................	-	-	-	-	-	-	-	-
47. TJENESTER FRA BOLIGER OG FORRETNINGSBYGG..........	10	76	13	79	18	21	366	12
48. HELSE- OG VETERINÆR-TJENESTER................	-	-	-	-	-	-	-	-
49. UNDERVISNINGS- OG FORSKNINGSTJENESTER.......	-	-	-	-	-	-	-	-
50. FORRETNINGSMESSIGE TJENESTER...............	-	8	1	20	-	14	33	162
51. ANDRE TJENESTER..........	-	-	-	-	-	-	-	-
52. IKKE MARKEDSFØRTE OFFENTLIGE TJENESTER......								
53. VARER TIL REPARASJONER, USPESIFISERT VAREINNSATS M.V....................	27	2429	250	5711	1137	4102	639	3392
54. VARER TIL INVESTERINGER, BYGG OG ANLEGG...........	-	-	-	-	-	-	-	-
55. VARER TIL INVESTERINGER, MASKINER OG TRANSPORT-MIDLER M.V..............	-	-	-	-	-	-	-	-
56. KORREKSJONER FOR MERVERDI-OG INVESTERINGSAVGIFT.....	-	-	-	-	-	-	-	-
57. KORR. FOR UTLENDINGERS KONSUM I NORGE OG KJØP/ SALG AV BRUKT REALKAP.....	-	-	-	-	-	-	-	-
58. LEIE AV PRODUKSJONS-FAKTORER MELLOM FYLKENE...	-	-	-	-	-	-	-	-
65. IALT.................	10475	58660	5070	75529	24459	77154	59389	37549

TABELL 8(FORTS.). VARE- OG TJENESTETILGANG. 100000 KR. 1976. HELE LANDET INDUSTRIES (46)

	PRODUKSJONSSEKTORER (FORTS.)							
COMMODITIES (58) NR. VARER OG TJENESTER	PRODUK-SJON AV KJEMISK-TEKNISKE PRODUKTER	RAFF. OG PROD. AV JORDOLJE OG KULL-PRODUKTER	PRODUK-SJON OG REPARA-SJON AV GUMMI-PRODUKTER	PRODUK-SJON AV PLAST-VARER	PRODUK-SJON AV KERAMISKE PRODUKTER	PROD. AV GLASS, GLASSVAR. OG MINE-RALSKE PRODUKTER	PROD. AV JERN, STÅL OG FERRO-LEGER-INGER	PROD. AV IKKE-JERN-HOLDIGE METALLER
	17.	18.	19.	20.	21.	22.	23.	24.
01. PLANTEPRODUKTER............	-	-	-	-	-	-	-	-
02. HUSDYRPRODUKTER............	-	-	-	-	-	-	-	-
03. TJENESTER I TILKNYTNING TIL JORDBRUK.............	-	-	-	-	-	-	-	-
04. SKOGPRODUKTER.............	-	-	-	-	-	-	-	-
05. FISK M.V...............	-	-	-	-	-	-	-	-
06. BERGVERKSPRODUKTER........	-	2247	-	-	-	699	318	
07. RÅOLJE OG NATURGASS.......	-	-	-	-	-	-	-	-
08. FOREDLEDE FISKEPRODUKTER..	-	-	-	-	-	-	-	-
09. FOREDLEDE JORDBRUKS-PRODUKTER.................	15	-	-	-	-	42	-	-
10. ANDRE NÆRINGSMIDLER.......	455	-	-	-	-	-	-	-
11. DRIKKEVARER.............	-	-	-	-	-	-	-	-
12. TOBAKKSVARER.............	-	-	-	-	-	-	-	-
13. TEKSTILVARER OG KLÆR......	-	-	28	417	-	-	-	-
14. LÆR, LÆR- OG SKINNVARER OG SKOTØY.................	7	-	-	7	-	-	-	-
15. TREVARER, UNNTATT MØBLER OG INNREDNINGER AV TRE...	-	-	-	15	-	2	-	1
16. MØBLER OG INNREDNINGER AV TRE.....................	1	-	-	773	-	-	-	-
17. TREFOREDLINGSPRODUKTER....	-	6	-	380	-	-	-	-
18. GRAFISKE PRODUKTER........	24	-	-	-	4	-	-	5
19. KJEMISKE RÅVARER..........	905	351	-	15	-	10	28	75
20. KJEMISK-TEKNISKE PRODUKTER	25047	28	-	3	-	78	40	467
21. OLJE- OG KULLPRODUKTER....	18	62254	-	-	-	-	-	49
22. GUMMIPRODUKTER............	74	-	4431	48	-	-	-	-
23. PLASTVARER...............	53	72	24	16896	81	34	17	18
24. KERAMISKE PRODUKTER.......	-	-	-	114	2045	1	-	-
25. GLASS, GLASSVARER OG MINE-RALSKE PRODUKTER ELLERS...	-	41	-	-	8	33513	-	4
26. JERN, STÅL OG FERRO-LEGERINGER..............	-	-	-	-	-	-	43133	155
27. IKKE-JERNHOLDIGE METALLER.	-	-	-	-	-	-	53	55255
28. METALLVARER...............	24	-	-	350	8	4	1288	126
29. MASKINER OG OLJE-PLATTFORMER.............	-	-	-	77	-	-	1560	4
30. EL. APPARATER OG MATERIELL	-	-	-	54	-	-	16	51
31. FARTØYER.................	-	-	-	74	-	-	868	1
32. ANDRE TRANSPORTMIDLER.....	14	-	-	2	-	52	149	-
33. TEKNISKE OG VITENSKAPLIGE INSTRUMENTER M.V.........	141	-	-	-	-	-	-	22
34. ANDRE INDUSTRIPRODUKTER...	2	-	30	37	-	-	-	8
35. ELEKTRISITET.............	-	-	-	-	-	-	-	-
36. VANN..................	-	-	-	-	-	-	-	-
37. BYGG OG REPARASJONER AV BYGG...................	-	-	-	-	-	-	-	-
38. ANLEGG.................	-	-	-	-	-	-	-	-
39. BOREHULL FOR OLJE OG GASS.	-	-	-	-	-	-	-	-
40. PROVISJONER M.V.........	-	-	-	-	-	-	-	-
41. HOTELL OG RESTAURANT-TJENESTER...............	-	-	-	-	-	-	-	-
42. TJENESTER FRA UTENRIKS SJØFART.................	-	-	-	-	-	-	-	-
43. PERSONTRANSPORTTJENESTER..	-	-	-	-	-	-	-	-
44. GODSTRANSPORTTJENESTER....	-	-	-	-	-	-	-	-
45. POST- OG TELETJENESTER....	-	-	-	-	-	-	-	-
46. BANK- OG FORSIKRINGS-TJENESTER...............	-	-	-	-	-	-	-	-
47. TJENESTER FRA BOLIGER OG FORRETNINGSBYGG.........	44	-	8	25	-	24	22	9
48. HELSE- OG VETERINÆR-TJENESTER...............	-	-	-	-	-	-	-	-
49. UNDERVISNINGS- OG FORSKNINGSTJENESTER.......	-	-	-	-	-	-	-	-
50. FORRETNINGSMESSIGE TJENESTER...............	-	-	-	1	-	21	2	52
51. ANDRE TJENESTER.........	-	-	-	-	-	-	-	-
52. IKKE MARKEDSFØRTE OFFENTLIGE TJENESTER.....	-	-	-	-	-	-	-	-
53. VARER TIL REPARASJONER, USPESIFISERT VAREINNSATS M.V...................	734	3966	751	372	25	1539	4121	1713
54. VARER TIL INVESTERINGER, BYGG OG ANLEGG.........	-	-	-	-	-	-	-	-
55. VARER TIL INVESTERINGER, MASKINER OG TRANSPORT-MIDLER M.V.............	-	-	-	-	-	-	-	-
56. KORREKSJONER FOR MERVERDI- OG INVESTERINGSAVGIFT.....	-	-	-	-	-	-	-	-
57. KORR. FOR UTLENDINGERS KONSUM I NORGE OG KJØP/ SALG AV BRUKT REALKAP.....	-	-	-	-	-	-	-	-
58. LEIE AV PRODUKSJONS-FAKTORER MELLOM FYLKENE...	-	-	-	-	-	-	-	-
45. IALT.................	27557	58955	5282	17650	2171	36019	51525	58012

214

TABELL 8(FORTS.). VARE- OG TJENESTETILGANG. 100000 KR. 1976. HELE LANDET INDUSTRIES (46)

PRODUKSJONSSEKTORER (FORTS.)

COMMODITIES (58) NR. VARER OG TJENESTER	PROD. AV METALL-VARER	PROD. AV MASKINER OG OLJE-PLATT-FORMER	PROD. AV ELEKTR. APPARATER OG MATERIELL	BYGGING AV FARTØYER	PROD. AV ANDRE TRANS-PORT MIDLER	PROD. AV TEKN. OG VITENSK. INSTRUM. M.V.	ANNEN IND.-PRODUK-SJON	KRAFT-OG VANN-FOR-SYNING
	25.	26.	27.	28.	29.	30.	31.	32.
01. PLANTEPRODUKTER............	-	-	-	-	-	-	-	-
02. HUSDYRPRODUKTER............	-	-	-	-	-	-	-	-
03. TJENESTER I TILKNYTNING TIL JORDBRUK............	-	-	-	-	-	-	-	-
04. SKOGPRODUKTER............	-	-	-	-	-	-	-	-
05. FISK M.V............	-	-	-	-	-	-	-	-
06. BERGVERKSPRODUKTER.......	-	-	-	-	-	-	-	-
07. RÅOLJE OG NATURGASS.......	-	-	-	-	-	-	-	-
08. FOREDLEDE FISKEPRODUKTER..	-	-	-	-	-	-	-	-
09. FOREDLEDE JORDBRUKS-PRODUKTER............	-	-	-	-	-	-	-	-
10. ANDRE NÆRINGSMIDLER.......	-	-	-	-	-	-	-	-
11. DRIKKEVARER............	-	-	-	-	-	-	-	-
12. TOBAKKSVARER............	-	-	-	-	-	-	-	-
13. TEKSTILVARER OG KLÆR.....	24	-	5	-	1	-	20	-
14. LÆR, LÆR- OG SKINNVARER OG SKOTØY............	7	-	-	-	-	-	3	-
15. TREVARER, UNNTATT MØBLER OG INNREDNINGER AV TRE....	59	7	-	4	-	-	78	-
16. MØBLER OG INNREDNINGER AV TRE............	373	-	200	-	38	-	4	-
17. TREFOREDLINGSPRODUKTER....	4	-	-	-	-	-	-	-
18. GRAFISKE PRODUKTER........	-	-	6	-	-	-	6	-
19. KJEMISKE RÅVARER.........	1	-	-	-	-	-	-	-
20. KJEMISK-TEKNISKE PRODUKTER	95	365	-	-	-	-	-	-
21. OLJE- OG KULLPRODUKTER....	-	-	-	-	-	-	-	-
22. GUMMIPRODUKTER............	-	-	-	-	-	-	2	-
23. PLASTVARER............	109	45	32	232	49	-	522	-
24. KERAMISKE PRODUKTER.......	-	-	36	-	-	-	-	-
25. GLASS, GLASSVARER OG MINE-RALSKE PRODUKTER ELLERS...	-	-	-	37	18	-	2	-
26. JERN, STÅL OG FERRO-LEGERINGER............	510	415	165	28	306	-	-	-
27. IKKE-JERNHOLDIGE METALLER.	1985	85	144	62	235	-	79	-
28. METALLVARER............	44434	4555	675	3419	327	-	360	-
29. MASKINER OG OLJE-PLATTFORMER............	2456	78890	1728	13783	122	441	9	-
30. EL. APPARATER OG MATERIELL	1762	2178	45622	60	5	54	57	-
31. FARTØYER............	259	3327	74	89375	143	-	-	-
32. ANDRE TRANSPORTMIDLER.....	325	549	37	12	13998	1	1	-
33. TEKNISKE OG VITENSKAPLIGE INSTRUMENTER M.V........	35	46	2472	9	1	1452	515	-
34. ANDRE INDUSTRIPRODUKTER...	272	4	413	45	-	-	5553	-
35. ELEKTRISITET............	-	-	-	-	-	-	-	91835
36. VANN............	-	-	-	-	-	-	-	4241
37. BYGG OG REPARASJONER AV BYGG............	-	-	-	-	-	-	-	-
38. ANLEGG............	-	-	-	-	-	-	-	-
39. BOREHULL FOR OLJE OG GASS.	-	-	-	-	-	-	-	-
40. PROVISJONER M.V............	-	-	-	-	-	-	-	-
41. HOTELL OG RESTAURANT-TJENESTER............	-	-	-	-	-	-	-	-
42. TJENESTER FRA UTENRIKS SJØFART............	-	-	-	-	-	-	-	-
43. PERSONTRANSPORTTJENESTER..	-	-	-	-	-	-	-	-
44. GODSTRANSPORTTJENESTER....	-	-	-	-	-	-	-	-
45. POST- OG TELETJENESTER....	-	-	-	-	-	-	-	-
46. BANK- OG FORSIKRINGS-TJENESTER............	-	-	-	-	-	-	-	-
47. TJENESTER FRA BOLIGER OG FORRETNINGSBYGG............	153	222	61	129	7	1	8	132
48. HELSE- OG VETERINÆR-TJENESTER............	-	-	-	-	-	-	-	-
49. UNDERVISNINGS- OG FORSKNINGSTJENESTER......	-	-	-	-	-	-	-	-
50. FORRETNINGSMESSIGE TJENESTER............	33	64	213	44	7	4	2	182
51. ANDRE TJENESTER............	56	856	8	19	425	-	-	-
52. IKKE MARKEDSFØRTE OFFENTLIGE TJENESTER......	-	-	-	-	-	-	-	-
53. VARER TIL REPARASJONER, USPESIFISERT VAREINNSATS M.V.	8014	29463	6039	4634	714	284	343	4111
54. VARER TIL INVESTERINGER, BYGG OG ANLEGG............	-	-	-	-	-	-	-	-
55. VARER TIL INVESTERINGER, MASKINER OG TRANSPORT-MIDLER M.V............	-	-	-	-	-	-	-	-
56. KORREKSJONER FOR MERVERDI- OG INVESTERINGSAVGIFT.....	-	-	-	-	-	-	-	-
57. KORR. FOR UTLENDINGERS KONSUM I NORGE OG KJØP/ SALG AV BRUKT REALKAP.....	-	-	-	-	-	-	-	-
58. LEIE AV PRODUKSJONS-FAKTORER MELLOM FYLKENE...	-	-	-	-	-	-	-	-
65. IALT............	61024	120071	57934	113901	16396	2237	7564	100501

TABELL 8(FORTS.). VARE- OG TJENESTETILGANG. 100000 KR. 1976. HELE LANDET INDUSTRIES (46)

	BYGGE- OG ANLEGGS-VIRKSOM-HET INKL. OLJE-BORING	VARE-HANDEL M.V.	HOTELL-OG RESTAU-RANT DRIFT	UTENRIKS SJØFART	ANNEN SAM-FERDSEL	BANK- OG FORSIKR.- VIRKSOM-HET	EIENDOMS-DRIFT	FORRET-NINGS-MESSIS TJENESTE-YTING
COMMODITIES (58) NR. VARER OG TJENESTER				PRODUKSJONSSEKTORER (FORTS.)				
	33.	34.	35.	36.	37.	38.	39.	40.
01. PLANTEPRODUKTER.............	-	18616	-	-	-	-	-	-
02. HUSDYRPRODUKTER.............	-	3705	-	-	-	-	-	-
03. TJENESTER I TILKNYTNING TIL JORDBRUK..............	-	-	-	-	-	-	-	-
04. SKOGPRODUKTER..............	-	6077	-	-	-	-	-	-
05. FISK M.V.................	-	-1335	-	-	-	-	-	-
06. BERGVERKSPRODUKTER........	-	5489	-	-	-	-	-	-
07. RÅOLJE OG NATURGASS.......	-	7223	-	-	-	-	-	-
08. FOREDLEDE FISKEPRODUKTER..	-	3554	-	-	-	-	-	-
09. FOREDLEDE JORDBRUKS-PRODUKTER..................	-	32927	-	-	-	-	-	-
10. ANDRE NÆRINGSMIDLER.......	-	18904	-	-	-	-	-	-
11. DRIKKEVARER..............	-	23688	-	-	-	-	-	-
12. TOBAKKSVARER..............	-	9289	-	-	-	-	-	-
13. TEKSTILVARER OG KLÆR......	-	39433	-	-	-	-	-	-
14. LÆR, LÆR- OG SKINNVARER OG SKOTØY.................	-	6432	-	-	-	-	-	-
15. TREVARER, UNNTATT MØBLER OG INNREDNINGER AV TRE....	-	6472	-	-	-	-	-	-
16. MØBLER OG INNREDNINGER AV TRE.....................	-	9450	-	-	-	-	-	-
17. TREFOREDLINGSPRODUKTER....	-	8655	-	-	-	-	-	-
18. GRAFISKE PRODUKTER........	-	7895	-	-	41	-	-	-
19. KJEMISKE RÅVARER..........	-	8751	-	-	-	-	-	-
20. KJEMISK-TEKNISKE PRODUKTER	-	14787	-	-	-	-	-	-
21. OLJE- OG KULLPRODUKTER....	-	42152	-	-	-	-	-	-
22. GUMMIPRODUKTER............	-	4629	-	-	-	-	-	-
23. PLASTVARER...............	-	5182	-	-	-	-	-	-
24. KERAMISKE PRODUKTER.......	-	1443	-	-	-	-	-	-
25. GLASS, GLASSVARER OG MINE-RALSKE PRODUKTER ELLERS...	-	7220	-	-	-	-	-	-
26. JERN, STÅL OG FERRO-LEGERINGER...............	-	11555	-	-	-	-	-	-
27. IKKE-JERNHOLDIGE METALLER.	-	5597	-	-	-	-	-	-
28. METALLVARER..............	-	18794	-	-	-	-	-	-
29. MASKINER OG OLJE-PLATTFORMER..............	-	33849	-	-	-	-	-	-
30. EL. APPARATER OG MATERIELL	-	26960	-	-	-	-	-	-
31. FARTØYER.................	-	5215	-	-	-	-	-	-
32. ANDRE TRANSPORTMIDLER.....	-	53125	-	-	-	-	-	-
33. TEKNISKE OG VITENSKAPLIGE INSTRUMENTER M.V..........	-	6490	-	-	-	-	-	-
34. ANDRE INDUSTRIPRODUKTER...	-	6208	-	-	-	-	-	-
35. ELEKTRISITET.............	-	39	-	-	-	-	-	-
36. VANN...................	-	-	-	-	-	-	-	-
37. BYGG OG REPARASJONER AV BYGG...................	243042	-	-	-	-	-	-	-
38. ANLEGG.................	107221	-	-	-	-	-	-	-
39. BOREHULL FOR OLJE OG GASS.	6759	-	-	-	-	-	-	-
40. PROVISJONER M.V..........	-	11874	-	-	-	-	-	-
41. HOTELL OG RESTAURANT-TJENESTER..............	-	-	49128	-	-	-	-	-
42. TJENESTER FRA UTENRIKS SJØFART................	-	-	-	175897	-	-	-	-
43. PERSONTRANSPORTTJENESTER..	-	-	-	-	46247	-	-	-
44. GODSTRANSPORTTJENESTER....	-	31	-	818	90293	-	-	-
45. POST- OG TELETJENESTER....	-	174	-	-	44078	-	-	-
46. BANK- OG FORSIKRINGS-TJENESTER.................	-	-	-	-	-	76065	-	-
47. TJENESTER FRA BOLIGER OG FORRETNINGSBYGG..........	-	-	-	-	-	1984	117454	-
48. HELSE- OG VETERINÆR-TJENESTER.................	-	-	-	-	-	-	-	-
49. UNDERVISNINGS- OG FORSKNINGSTJENESTER.......	-	-	-	-	-	-	-	-
50. FORRETNINGSMESSIGE TJENESTER................	90	64	-	-	2	-	-	57525
51. ANDRE TJENESTER..........	1933	-	-	-	-	-	-	-
52. IKKE MARKEDSFØRTE OFFENTLIGE TJENESTER......								
53. VARER TIL REPARASJONER, USPESIFISERT VAREINNSATS M.V.....................	1352	8057	-	-	6573	-	-	1000
54. VARER TIL INVESTERINGER, BYGG OG ANLEGG...........			-					
55. VARER TIL INVESTERINGER, MASKINER OG TRANSPORT-MIDLER M.V...............	-	-	-	-	-	-	-	-
56. KORREKSJONER FOR MERVERDI-OG INVESTERINGSAVGIFT.....	-	-26819	-	-	-	-	-	-
57. KORR. FOR UTLENDINGERS KONSUM I NORGE OG KJØP/ SALG AV BRUKT REALKAP.....	-	-	-	-	-	-	-	-
58. LEIE AV PRODUKSJONS-FAKTORER MELLOM FYLKENE...	-	-	-	-	-	-	-	-
65. IALT.................	360357	455831	49128	176715	187234	78049	117454	58528

MAKE MATRIX (continued)

COMMODITIES (58) NR. VARER OG TJENESTER	PRODUKSJONSSEKTORER (FORTS.)				GRUPPERINGSSEKTORER			
	SOSIAL OG PRIVAT TJENESTE-YTING	KORR. FPIE BANKTJ.	STATS- OG TRYGDE-FORVALT-NINGEN	KOMMUNE-FORVALT-NINGEN	GR. SEKT. FOR VARER TIL REP. OG USPES. VAREINNS. M.V.	GR. SEKT. FOR VARER TIL INVESTER-ING	IMPORT	I ALT
	41.	42.	43.	44.	45.	46.	55.	57.
01. PLANTEPRODUKTER............	-	-	-	-	-	-	23411	87241
02. HUSDYRPRODUKTER...........	-	-	-	-	-	-	571	77831
03. TJENESTER I TILKNYTNING TIL JORDBRUK..............	-	-	4	-	-	-		7593
04. SKOGPRODUKTER.............	-	-	76	-	-	-	3245	29123
05. FISK M.V.................	-	-	-	-	-	-	396	31329
06. BERGVERKSPRODUKTER........	-	-	-	-	-	-	10561	38047
07. RÅOLJE OG NATURGASS.......	-	-	-	-	-	-	42101	117505
08. FOREDLEDE FISKEPRODUKTER..	-	-	-	-	-	-	1133	50835
09. FOREDLEDE JORDBRUKS-PRODUKTER..	-	-	-	-	-	-	11231	155204
10. ANDRE NÆRINGSMIDLER.......	-	-	-	-	-	-	6865	91296
11. DRIKKEVARER..............	-	-	-	-	-	-	1815	50075
12. TOBAKKSVARER.............	-	-	-	-	-	-	835	20562
13. TEKSTILVARER OG KLÆR.....	-	-	-	-	-	-	38310	114612
14. LÆR, LER- OG SKINNVARER OG SKOTØY.................	-	-	-	-	-	-	6591	17764
15. TREVARER, UNNTATT MØBLER OG INNREDNINGER AV TRE....	-	-	-	-	-	-	7759	84342
16. MØBLER OG INNREDNINGER AV TRE.....	-	-	-	-	-	-	5344	37447
17. TREFOREDLINGSPRODUKTER....	-	-	-	-	-	-	10976	92076
18. GRAFISKE PRODUKTER........	-	-	-	-	-	-	3636	69945
19. KJEMISKE RÅVARER..........	-	-	-	-	-	-	25503	68202
20. KJEMISK-TEKNISKE PRODUKTER	-	-	-	-	-	-	15892	58046
21. OLJE- OG KULLPRODUKTER....	-	-	-	-	-	-	25657	130292
22. GUMMIPRODUKTER...........	-	-	-	-	-	-	6159	15428
23. PLASTVARER..............	-	-	-	-	-	-	7855	31938
24. KERAMISKE PRODUKTER......	-	-	-	-	-	-	1365	5004
25. GLASS, GLASSVARER OG MINE-RALSKE PRODUKTER ELLERS...	-	-	-	-	-	-	6460	48030
26. JERN, STÅL OG FERRO-LEGERINGER.............	-	-	-	-	-	-	28863	85130
27. IKKE-JERNHOLDIGE METALLER.	-	-	-	-	-	-	19493	83337
28. METALLVARER.............	-	-	-	-	-	-	26170	101043
29. MASKINER OG OLJE-PLATTFORMER.............	1403	-	-	-	-	-	79654	211046
30. EL. APPARATER OG MATERIELL	-	-	-	-	-	-	36283	113214
31. FARTØYER.................	24	-	-	-	-	-	104000	203366
32. ANDRE TRANSPORTMIDLER.....	-	-	-	-	-	-	42635	119901
33. TEKNISKE OG VITENSKAPLIGE INSTRUMENTER M.V.........	-	-	-	-	-	-	12321	23624
34. ANDRE INDUSTRIPRODUKTER...	-	-	-	-	-	-	6559	19210
35. ELEKTRISITET.............	-	-	-	-	-	-	169	92043
36. VANN...................	-	-	-	-	-	-	-	4241
37. BYGG OG REPARASJONER AV BYGG...................	-	-	-	-	-	-	-	243042
38. ANLEGG.................	-	-	-	-	-	-	-	107221
39. BOREHULL FOR OLJE OG GASS.	-	-	-	-	-	-	17170	23429
40. PROVISJONER M.V..........	-	-	-	-	-	-	6788	18662
41. HOTELL OG RESTAURANT-TJENESTER..............	-	-	-	-	-	-	-	49128
42. TJENESTER FRA UTENRIKS SJØFART...............	-	-	-	-	-	-	-	175897
43. PERSONTRANSPORTTJENESTER..	-	-	196	-	-	-	-	46443
44. GODSTRANSPORTTJENESTER....	-	-	1676	485	-	-	157	93460
45. POST- OG TELETJENESTER....	-	-	-	-	-	-	1329	45581
46. BANK- OG FORSIKRINGS-TJENESTER..............	-	-	-	-	-	-	2071	78135
47. TJENESTER FRA BOLIGER OG FORRETNINGSBYGG..........	-	-	-	-	-	-	-	121396
48. HELSE- OG VETERINÆR-TJENESTER..............	33142	-	776	7139	-	-	1	41058
49. UNDERVISNINGS- OG FORSKNINGSTJENESTER.......	6372	-	620	975	-	-	56	9023
50. FORRETNINGSMESSIGE TJENESTER..............	-	-	123	-	-	-	352	59329
51. ANDRE TJENESTER..........	74912	-	3626	6320	-	-	2761	90585
52. IKKE MARKEDSFØRTE OFFENTLIGE TJENESTER......	-	-	144254	196600	-	-	-	340863
53. VARER TIL REPARASJONER, USPESIFISERT VAREINNSATS M.V....................	1761	-	-	-	460654	1340	213637	790654
54. VARER TIL INVESTERINGER, BYGG OG ANLEGG..........	-	-	-	-	-	316874	-	316874
55. VARER TIL INVESTERINGER, MASKINER OG TRANSPORT-MIDLER M.V..............	-	-	-	-	-	334972	-	334972
56. KORREKSJONER FOR MERVERDI-OG INVESTERINGSAVGIFT.....	-	-	-	-	-	-	-	-26818
57. KORR. FOR UTLENDINGERS KONSUM I NORGE OG KJØP/SALG AV BRUKT REALKAP.....	-	-	-	-	-	-	-	
58. LEIE AV PRODUKSJONS-FAKTORER MELLOM FYLKENE...	-	-	-	-	-	-	-	
65. IALT...................	117514	-	151351	211528	460654	653186	964130	5535161

TABELL 9. VARE- OG TJENESTEANVENDELSE OG KOMP. I BRUTTOPRODUKTET. 100000 KR. 1976. HELE LANDET

	PRODUKSJONSSEKTORER							
NR. VARER OG TJENESTER OG KOMP. I BRUTTOPRODUKTET	JORD-BRUK	SKOG-BRUK	FISKE OG FANGST	BERG-VERKS-DRIFT	UT-VINNING AV RÅ-OLJE OG NATUR-GASS	FISKE-FORED-LING	NÆRINGS-MIDDEL-INDUSTRI	PRODUK-SJON AV DRIKKE-VARER
	01.	02.	03.	04.	05.	06.	07.	08.
01. PLANTEPRODUKTER.............	19776	-	-	-	-	17	27012	361
02. HUSDYRPRODUKTER.............	3278	-	-	-	-	2	61626	-
03. TJENESTER I TILKNYTNING TIL JORDBRUK...............	1641	972	-	-	-	-	-	-
04. SKOGPRODUKTER..............	-	74	-	-	-	2	175	-
05. FISK M.V.................	58	-	23	-	-	25367	318	-
06. BERGVERKSPRODUKTER........	356	-	85	282	-	102	185	-
07. RÅOLJE OG NATURGASS......	-	-	-	-	-	-	-	-
08. FOREDLEDE FISKEPRODUKTER..	49	-	237	-	1	7652	3315	24
09. FOREDLEDE JORDBRUKS-PRODUKTER..................	2241	-	41	-	-	610	42417	903
10. ANDRE NÆRINGSMIDLER.......	19915	-	-	-	-	360	6752	350
11. DRIKKEVARER..............	-	-	-	1	-	-	143	1091
12. TOBAKKSVARER.............	-	-	-	-	-	-	-	-
13. TEKSTILVARER OG KLÆR.....	42	-	197	1	-	-	-	-
14. LÆR, LÆR- OG SKINNVARER OG SKOTØY...................	-	-	-	-	-	-	-	-
15. TREVARER, UNNTATT MØBLER OG INNREDNINGER AV TRE....	312	-	11	-	-	-	-	-
16. MØBLER OG INNREDNINGER AV TRE......................	-	-	-	-	-	-	-	-
17. TREFOREDLINGSPRODUKTER....	337	-	44	53	-	-	9	-
18. GRAFISKE PRODUKTER........	-	-	-	-	-	-	250	-
19. KJEMISKE RÅVARER.........	5621	-	-	99	-	66	393	386
20. KJEMISK-TEKNISKE PRODUKTER	589	-	244	766	42	26	524	14
21. OLJE- OG KULLPRODUKTER....	1953	327	3790	838	320	1060	1394	174
22. GUMMIPRODUKTER...........	-	-	-	37	-	-	-	-
23. PLASTVARER..............	35	-	-	-	-	-	224	-
24. KERAMISKE PRODUKTER......	62	-	-	-	-	-	-	-
25. GLASS, GLASSVARER OG MINE-RALSKE PRODUKTER ELLERS...	499	-	-	57	-	-	46	-
26. JERN, STÅL OG FERRO-LEGERINGER...............	-	-	-	371	-	1	-	-
27. IKKE-JERNHOLDIGE METALLER.	14	-	-	-	-	-	66	-
28. METALLVARER..............	24	45	64	515	-	1	12	-
29. MASKINER OG OLJE-PLATTFORMER...............	-	-	-	180	-	-	-	-
30. EL. APPARATER OG MATERIELL	-	-	54	12	-	-	-	-
31. FARTØYER...............	-	-	-	-	-	-	-	-
32. ANDRE TRANSPORTMIDLER.....	-	-	-	-	-	-	-	-
33. TEKNISKE OG VITENSKAPLIGE INSTRUMENTER M.V.........	-	-	-	-	-	-	1	-
34. ANDRE INDUSTRIPRODUKTER...	1358	-	-	697	-	518	1090	141
35. ELEKTRISITET.............	1358	-	-	697	-	518	1090	141
36. VANN...................	-	-	-	-	-	-	-	-
37. BYGG OG REPARASJONER AV BYGG...................	-	-	-	-	-	-	-	-
38. ANLEGG..................	-	-	-	-	-	-	-	-
39. BOREHULL FOR OLJE OG GASS.	-	-	-	-	-	-	-	-
40. PROVISJONER M.V..........	-	-	-	-	-	-	-	-
41. HOTELL OG RESTAURANT-TJENESTER...............	-	-	-	-	-	-	-	-
42. TJENESTER FRA UTENRIKS SJØFART.................	-	-	-	-	-	-	-	-
43. PERSONTRANSPORTTJENESTER..	-	-	-	-	-	-	-	-
44. GODSTRANSPORTTJENESTER....	-	-	48	-	-	-	-	-
45. POST- OG TELETJENESTER....	-	-	-	-	-	-	-	-
46. BANK- OG FORSIKRINGS-TJENESTER...............	254	-	179	-	-84	-	-	-
47. TJENESTER FRA BOLIGER OG FORRETNINGSBYGG...........	-	-	-	130	50	264	813	43
48. HELSE- OG VETERINÆR-TJENESTER...............	454	-	-	-	-	-	-	-
49. UNDERVISNINGS- OG FORSKNINGSTJENESTER.......	152	-	-	24	-	-	68	-
50. FORRETNINGSMESSIGE TJENESTER...............	365	-	-	740	699	89	735	68
51. ANDRE TJENESTER..........	231	23	2	-	-	-	-	-
52. IKKE MARKEDSFØRTE OFFENTLIGE TJENESTER......								
53. VARER TIL REPARASJONER, USPESIFISERT VARFINNSATS M.V...................	8472	1175	6829	5181	7432	5140	21801	3892
54. VARER TIL INVESTERINGER, BYGG OG ANLEGG.........	-	-	-	-	-	-	-	-
55. VARER TIL INVESTERINGER, MASKINER OG TRANSPORT-MIDLER M.V.............	-	-	-	-	-	-	-	-
56. KORREKSJONER FOR MERVERDI-OG INVESTERINGSAVGIFT.....								
57. KORR. FOR UTLENDINGERS KONSUM I NORGE OG KJØP/SALG AV BRUKT REALKAP.....	-	-	-	-	-	-	-	-
58. LEIE AV PRODUKSJONS-FAKTORER MELLOM FYLKENE...	-	-	-	-	-	-	-	-
59. BRUTTOPRODUKT I ALT.......	57992	15905	21592	13200	61206	7357	10363	12573
60. LØNNSKOSTNADER...........	2611	4451	1456	5749	2447	8272	21141	3634
61. DRIFTSRESULTAT..........	49166	7452	12909	528	34466	525	9761	-253
62. KAPITALSLIT.............	14740	1354	5479	2812	15913	1396	4353	915
63. INDIREKTE SKATTER........	8776	2753	2366	641	8350	-1027	2579	9315
64. SUBSIDIER...............	-17131	-1139	-617	-529	-	-912	-27651	-39
65. IALT...................	126020	19523	__33442__	23191	69666	48634	179723	20014

TABELL 9(FORTS.). VARE- OG TJENESTEANVENDELSE OG KOMP. I BRUTTOPRODUKTET. 100000 KR. 1976. HELE LANDET

NR. VARER OG TJENESTER OG KOMP. I BRUTTOPRODUKTET	PRODUKSJON AV TOBAKKSVARER	PRODUKSJON AV TEKSTILVARER OG KLÆR	PRODUKSJON AV LÆR, LÆR- OG SKINNVARER OG SKOTØY	PROD. AV TREVARER UNNTATT MØBLER OG INNREDV. AV TRE	PRODUKSJON AV MØBLER OG INNREDNINGER AV TRE	TREFOREDLING	GRAFISK PRODUKSJON OG FORLAGSVIRKSOMHET	PRODUKSJON AV KJEMISKE RÅVARER
	09.	10.	11.	12.	13.	14.	15.	16.
01. PLANTEPRODUKTER............	1134	150	-	-	7	-	-	6
02. HUSDYRPRODUKTER............	-	656	192	-	-	-	-	-
03. TJENESTER I TILKNYTNING TIL JORDBRUK..............	-	-	-	-	-	-	-	-
04. SKOGPRODUKTER.............	-	20	6	13063	25	11770	-	25
05. FISK M.V..................	-	-	277	-	-	-	-	1
06. BERGVERKSPRODUKTER........	-	1	5	3	-	340	-	3171
07. RÅOLJE OG NATURGASS.......	-	-	-	-	-	-	-	-
08. FOREDLEDE FISKEPRODUKTER..	1	1	-	-	-	2	-	8
09. FOREDLEDE JORDBRUKSPRODUKTER..............	7	2	270	-	-	14	-	12
10. ANDRE NÆRINGSMIDLER.......	3	11	2	-	-	20	-	175
11. DRIKKEVARER..............	1	-	-	2	-	7	6	20
12. TOBAKKSVARER.............	5	-	-	-	-	-	-	-
13. TEKSTILVARER OG KLÆR.....	-	11653	287	109	1407	374	114	7
14. LÆR, LÆR- OG SKINNVARER OG SKOTØY................	-	838	829	-	1055	22	17	-
15. TREVARER, UNNTATT MØBLER OG INNREDNINGER AV TRE....	-	6	5	19142	3571	3615	4	7
16. MØBLER OG INNREDNINGER AV TRE......................	-	44	-	665	1720	-	-	-
17. TREFOREDLINGSPRODUKTER....	25	44	11	896	402	25271	7709	968
18. GRAFISKE PRODUKTER.......	-	301	-	602	100	190	10970	50
19. KJEMISKE RÅVARER..........	7	1311	88	733	94	1613	45	8218
20. KJEMISK-TEKNISKE PRODUKTER	7	736	80	414	390	961	917	778
21. OLJE- OG KULLPRODUKTER....	29	285	32	493	102	2308	187	3172
22. GUMMIPRODUKTER...........	-	17	209	31	44	63	19	-
23. PLASTVARER..............	-	204	45	169	612	711	27	-
24. KERAMISKE PRODUKTER.......	-	-	-	11	-	-	-	-
25. GLASS, GLASSVARER OG MINERALSKE PRODUKTER ELLERS...	-	59	1	1592	217	143	-	7
26. JERN, STÅL OG FERROLEGERINGER..............	-	9	-	187	96	-	1	1
27. IKKE-JERNHOLDIGE METALLER.	-	127	-	144	42	534	105	120
28. METALLVARER.............	-	324	131	1843	951	290	12	13
29. MASKINER OG OLJEPLATTFORMER................	-	61	-	7	25	4	1	-
30. EL. APPARATER OG MATERIELL	-	-	-	132	75	-	-	496
31. FARTØYER..............	-	-	-	-	-	-	-	14
32. ANDRE TRANSPORTMIDLER....	-	-	-	-	-	-	-	-
33. TEKNISKE OG VITENSKAPLIGE INSTRUMENTER M.V..........	-	-	-	-	2	8	645	-
34. ANDRE INDUSTRIPRODUKTER...	-	535	2	-	24	1	-	-
35. ELEKTRISITET.............	13	274	30	516	165	7383	269	2054
36. VANN....................	-	-	-	-	-	-	-	-
37. BYGG OG REPARASJONER AV BYGG....................	-	-	-	-	-	-	-	-
38. ANLEGG.................	-	-	-	-	-	-	-	-
39. BOREHULL FOR OLJE OG GASS.	-	-	-	-	-	-	-	-
40. PROVISJONER M.V..........	-	-	-	-	-	-	-	-
41. HOTELL OG RESTAURANTTJENESTER..............	-	-	-	-	-	-	-	-
42. TJENESTER FRA UTENRIKS SJØFART..............	-	-	-	-	-	-	-	-
43. PERSONTRANSPORTTJENESTER..	-	-	-	-	-	-	-	-
44. GODSTRANSPORTTJENESTER....	-	-	-	-	-	-	-	-
45. POST- OG TELETJENESTER....	-	-	-	-	-	-	-	-
46. BANK- OG FORSIKRINGSTJENESTER..............	-	-	-	-	-	-	-	-
47. TJENESTER FRA BOLIGER OG FORRETNINGSBYGG...........	42	273	33	274	122	170	725	18
48. HELSE- OG VETERINÆRTJENESTER..............	-	-	-	-	-	-	-	-
49. UNDERVISNINGS- OG FORSKNINGSTJENESTER.......	-	-	-	-	-	-	-	-
50. FORRETNINGSMESSIGE TJENESTER..............	11	94	15	375	77	172	375	72
51. ANDRE TJENESTER..........	-	-	-	-	-	-	1410	-
52. IKKE MARKEDSFØRTE OFFENTLIGE TJENESTER......	-	-	-	-	-	-	-	-
53. VARER TIL REPARASJONER, USPESIFISERT VAREINNSATS M.V..................	1015	5302	547	9927	3076	9212	8970	6991
54. VARER TIL INVESTERINGER, BYGG OG ANLEGG.........	-	-	-	-	-	-	-	-
55. VARER TIL INVESTERINGER, MASKINER OG TRANSPORTMIDLER M.V..........	-	-	-	-	-	-	-	-
56. KORREKSJONER FOR MERVERDIOG INVESTERINGSAVGIFT.....	-	-	-	-	-	-	-	-
57. KORR. FOR UTLENDINGERS KONSUM I NORGE OG KJØP/ SALG AV BRUKT REALKAP.....	-	-	-	-	-	-	-	-
58. LEIE AV PRODUKSJONSFAKTORER MELLOM FYLKENE...	-	-	-	-	-	-	-	-
59. BRUTTOPRODUKT I ALT.......	8175	15365	1973	26194	10058	16947	26821	11147
60. LØNNSKOSTNADER..........	830	11120	1569	16694	5920	14305	19933	7386
61. DRIFTSRESULTAT..........	-151	1703	145	5371	2614	1265	2672	209
62. KAPITALSLIT.............	130	1194	133	1654	492	3044	1967	4615
63. INDIREKTE SKATTER........	7757	1990	210	3835	1471	-1390	4913	-1030
64. SUBSIDIER...............	-	-662	-63	-360	-448	-278	-494	-422
65. IALT...................	10475	33650	5070	76528	24459	77156	59399	37549

219

ABSORPTION MATRIX (continued)

TABELL 9(FORTS.). VARE- OG TJENESTEANVENDELSE OG KOMP. I BRUTTOPRODUKTET. 100000 KR. 1976. HELE LANDET

PRODUKSJONSSEKTORER (FORTS.)

NR. VARER OG TJENESTER OG KOMP. I BRUTTOPRODUKTET	PRODUK-SJON AV KJEMISK-TEKNISKE PRODUKTER	RAFF. OG PROD. AV JORDOLJE OG KULL-PRODUKTER	PRODUK-SJON OG REPARA-SJON AV GUMMI-PRODUKTER	PRODUK-SJON AV PLAST-VARER	PRODUK-SJON AV KERAMISKE PRODUKTER	PROD. AV GLASS, GLASSVAR. OG MINE-RALSKE PRODUKTER	PROD. AV JERN, STÅL OG FERRO-LEGER-INGER	PROD. AV IKKE-JERN-HOLDIGE METALLER
	17.	18.	19.	20.	21.	22.	23.	24.
01. PLANTEPRODUKTER	77	36	-	-	-	1	-	-
02. HUSDYRPRODUKTER	-	-	-	-	-	-	-	-
03. TJENESTER I TILKNYTNING TIL JORDBRUK	-	-	-	-	-	-	-	-
04. SKOGPRODUKTER	52	2	179	-	-	-	-	-
05. FISK M.V.	253	-	-	-	-	-	-	1
06. BERGVERKSPRODUKTER	59	1885	11	1	73	3166	8680	2371
07. RÅOLJE OG NATURGASS	-	53714	-	-	-	-	-	-
08. FOREDLEDE FISKEPRODUKTER	21	2	-	1	1	10	-	-
09. FOREDLEDE JORDBRUKS-PRODUKTER	440	-	-	23	-	5	2	-
10. ANDRE NÆRINGSMIDLER	472	-	6	24	-	12	1	-
11. DRIKKEVARER	170	-	-	5	-	-	1	-
12. TOBAKKSVARER	-	-	-	-	-	-	-	-
13. TEKSTILVARER OG KLÆR	43	2	367	93	1	30	6	19
14. LÆR, LÆR- OG SKINNVARER OG SKOTØY	1	-	-	4	-	-	-	-
15. TREVARER, UNNTATT MØBLER OG INNREDNINGER AV TRE	4	-	-	58	-	71	245	2
16. MØBLER OG INNREDNINGER AV TRE	-	-	-	-	-	11	-	-
17. TREFOREDLINGSPRODUKTER	248	225	-	355	4	216	-	4
18. GRAFISKE PRODUKTER	50	200	-	10	6	-	-	-
19. KJEMISKE RÅVARER	4376	30	191	7055	7	571	269	11402
20. KJEMISK-TEKNISKE PRODUKTER	3409	263	370	306	19	349	169	237
21. OLJE- OG KULLPRODUKTER	535	4214	83	139	11	2329	6374	5520
22. GUMMIPRODUKTER	96	5	552	27	-	18	1	2
23. PLASTVARER	43	53	2	795	68	23	8	1
24. KERAMISKE PRODUKTER	-	-	-	-	4	5	-	-
25. GLASS, GLASSVARER OG MINE-RALSKE PRODUKTER ELLERS	79	76	-	142	68	5390	393	83
26. JERN, STÅL OG FERRO-LEGERINGER	36	-	20	25	-	811	5874	264
27. IKKE-JERNHOLDIGE METALLER	117	3	8	109	2	75	620	15148
28. METALLVARER	31	15	62	183	109	481	349	25
29. MASKINER OG OLJE-PLATTFORMER	13	2	-	20	-	51	66	74
30. EL. APPARATER OG MATERIELL	-	29	-	30	-	-	7	594
31. FARTØYER	-	-	-	-	-	13	1112	7
32. ANDRE TRANSPORTMIDLER	-	-	-	-	-	-	-	-
33. TEKNISKE OG VITENSKAPLIGE INSTRUMENTER M.V.	-	-	-	1	-	-	7	-
34. ANDRE INDUSTRIPRODUKTER	-	-	-	-	-	-	7	-
35. ELEKTRISITET	153	325	97	232	59	579	4125	4990
36. VANN	-	-	-	-	-	-	-	-
37. BYGG OG REPARASJONER AV BYGG	-	-	-	-	-	-	-	-
38. ANLEGG	-	-	-	-	-	-	-	-
39. BOREHULL FOR OLJE OG GASS	-	-	-	-	-	-	-	-
40. PROVISJONER M.V	-	-	-	-	-	-	-	-
41. HOTELL OG RESTAURANT-TJENESTER	-	-	-	-	-	-	-	-
42. TJENESTER FRA UTENRIKS SJØFART	-	-	-	-	-	-	-	-
43. PERSONTRANSPORTTJENESTER	-	-	-	-	-	-	-	-
44. GODSTRANSPORTTJENESTER	-	-	-	-	-	-	-	-
45. POST- OG TELETJENESTER	-	-	-	-	-	-	-	-
46. BANK- OG FORSIKRINGS-TJENESTER	-	-	-	-	-	-	-	-
47. TJENESTER FRA BOLIGER OG FORRETNINGSBYGG	253	10	50	136	7	120	97	70
48. HELSE- OG VETERINÆR-TJENESTER	-	-	-	-	-	-	-	-
49. UNDERVISNINGS- OG FORSKNINGSTJENESTER	-	-	-	-	-	-	-	-
50. FORRETNINGSMESSIGE TJENESTER	196	65	30	83	4	728	361	135
51. ANDRE TJENESTER	-	-	-	-	-	-	-	-
52. IKKE MARKEDSFØRTE OFFENTLIGE TJENESTER	-	-	-	-	-	-	-	-
53. VARER TIL REPARASJONER, USPESIFISERT VAREINNSATS M.V.	6923	4539	572	2650	375	5735	8320	5705
54. VARER TIL INVESTERINGER, BYGG OG ANLEGG	-	-	-	-	-	-	-	-
55. VARER TIL INVESTERINGER, MASKINER OG TRANSPORT-MIDLER M.V.	-	-	-	-	-	-	-	-
56. KORREKSJONER FOR MERVERDI- OG INVESTERINGSAVGIFT	-	-	-	-	-	-	-	-
57. KORR. FOR UTLENDINGERS KONSUM I NORGE OG KJØP/ SALG AV BRUKT REALKAP	-	-	-	-	-	-	-	-
58. LEIE AV PRODUKSJONS-FAKTORER MELLOM FYLKENE	-	-	-	-	-	-	-	-
59. BRUTTOPRODUKT I ALT	9599	4251	2682	7144	1353	15219	14539	11358
60. LØNNSKOSTNADER	5067	2101	1790	5650	1017	9067	13030	10473
61. DRIFTSRESULTAT	973	4564	455	174	121	3199	3236	3185
62. KAPITALSLIT	950	762	235	556	35	1742	1519	3402
63. INDIREKTE SKATTER	1620	-1076	248	776	180	2331	-3021	-5537
64. SUBSIDIER	-71	-100	-46	-14	-	-120	-333	-163
65. IALT	27550	49055	5233	17460	2171	36019	51625	58012

220

TABELL 9(FORTS.). VARE- OG TJENESTEANVENDELSE OG KOMP. I BRUTTOPRODUKTET. 100000 KR. 1976. HELE LANDET

NR. VARER OG TJENESTER OG KOMP. I BRUTTOPRODUKTET	PROD. AV METALL-VARER	PROD. AV MASKINER OG OLJE-PLATT-FORMER	PROD. AV ELEKTR. APPARATER OG MATERIELL	BYGGING AV FARTØYER	PROD. AV ANDRE TRANS-PORT MIDLER	PROD. AV TEKN. OG VITENSK. INSTRUM. M.V.	ANNEN IND.-PRODUK-SJON	KRAFT-OG VANN-FOR-SYNING
	25.	26.	27.	28.	29.	30.	31.	32.
01. PLANTEPRODUKTER	-	-	-	4	-	-	-	-
02. HUSDYRPRODUKTER	-	-	-	-	-	-	5	-
03. TJENESTER I TILKNYTNING TIL JORDBRUK	-	-	-	-	-	-	-	-
04. SKOGPRODUKTER	-	1	5	74	-	-	45	-
05. FISK M.V.	-	-	-	-	-	-	-	-
06. BERGVERKSPRODUKTER	3	29	6	74	-	-	-	31
07. RÅOLJE OG NATURGASS	-	-	-	-	-	-	-	-
08. FOREDLEDE FISKEPRODUKTER	-	4	-	-	-	-	-	-
09. FOREDLEDE JORDBRUKS-PRODUKTER	-	-	-	-	-	-	16	-
10. ANDRE NÆRINGSMIDLER	-	-	-	-	-	-	4	-
11. DRIKKEVARER	-	-	-	-	-	-	-	-
12. TOBAKKSVARER	-	-	-	-	-	-	-	-
13. TEKSTILVARER OG KLÆR	209	34	197	343	71	3	119	-
14. LÆR, LÆR- OG SKINNVARER OG SKOTØY	14	-	-	2	7	5	29	-
15. TREVARER, UNNTATT MØBLER OG INNREDNINGER AV TRE	137	172	52	1239	108	3	254	-
16. MØBLER OG INNREDNINGER AV TRE	322	13	247	198	12	-	1	-
17. TREFOREDLINGSPRODUKTER	90	9	247	49	28	-	30	-
18. GRAFISKE PRODUKTER	51	450	250	100	7	-	54	36
19. KJEMISKE RÅVARER	399	350	815	1417	58	5	327	-
20. KJEMISK-TEKNISKE PRODUKTER	641	1008	345	1010	88	5	53	-
21. OLJE- OG KULLPRODUKTER	431	471	274	448	174	9	33	446
22. GUMMIPRODUKTER	82	312	12	236	122	2	7	-
23. PLASTVARER	439	296	267	369	208	4	288	-
24. KERAMISKE PRODUKTER	1	64	660	179	3	-	-	-
25. GLASS, GLASSVARER OG MINE-RALSKE PRODUKTER ELLERS	330	315	91	747	257	13	110	-
26. JERN, STÅL OG FERRO-LEGERINGER	10224	7913	2207	11528	1471	40	57	-
27. IKKE-JERNHOLDIGE METALLER	5711	900	2161	2094	671	32	1201	-
28. METALLVARER	4498	7655	997	8492	448	28	203	-
29. MASKINER OG OLJE-PLATTFORMER	127	24458	305	9902	227	67	1	-
30. EL. APPARATER OG MATERIELL	592	2953	12660	3808	254	72	11	-
31. FARTØYER	7	1162	1	22388	9	-	-	-
32. ANDRE TRANSPORTMIDLER	20	170	-	-	2285	-	1	-
33. TEKNISKE OG VITENSKAPLIGE INSTRUMENTER M.V.	1	674	1028	869	5	533	-	-
34. ANDRE INDUSTRIPRODUKTER	42	-	21	16	-	-	173	-
35. ELEKTRISITET	535	484	279	490	118	9	53	33236
36. VANN	-	-	-	-	-	-	-	-
37. BYGG OG REPARASJONER AV BYGG	-	-	-	-	-	-	-	-
38. ANLEGG	-	-	-	-	-	-	-	-
39. BOREHULL FOR OLJE OG GASS	-	-	-	-	-	-	-	-
40. PROVISJONER M.V.	-	-	-	-	-	-	-	-
41. HOTELL OG RESTAURANT-TJENESTER	-	-	-	-	-	-	-	-
42. TJENESTER FRA UTENRIKS SJØFART	-	-	-	-	-	-	-	-
43. PERSONTRANSPORTTJENESTER	-	-	-	-	-	-	-	-
44. GODSTRANSPORTTJENESTER	-	-	-	-	-	-	-	-
45. POST- OG TELETJENESTER	-	-	-	-	-	-	-	-
46. BANK- OG FORSIKRINGS-TJENESTER	-	-	-	-	-	-	-	-
47. TJENESTER FRA BOLIGER OG FORRETNINGSBYGG	433	509	362	287	173	14	60	146
48. HELSE- OG VETERINÆR-TJENESTER	-	-	-	-	-	-	-	34
49. UNDERVISNINGS- OG FORSKNINGSTJENESTER	-	-	-	-	-	-	-	-
50. FORRETNINGSMESSIGE TJENESTER	175	971	218	262	20	4	18	145
51. ANDRE TJENESTER	-	-	-	-	-	-	-	-
52. IKKE MARKEDSFØRTE OFFENTLIGE TJENESTER	-	-	-	-	-	-	-	-
53. VARER TIL REPARASJONER, USPESIFISERT VAREINNSATS M.V.	8590	33390	8960	13604	1617	277	1145	9064
54. VARER TIL INVESTERINGER, BYGG OG ANLEGG	-	-	-	-	-	-	-	-
55. VARER TIL INVESTERINGER, MASKINER OG TRANSPORT-MIDLER M.V.	-	-	-	-	-	-	-	-
56. KORREKSJONER FOR MERVERDI-OG INVESTERINGSAVGIFT	-	-	-	-	-	-	-	-
57. KORR. FOR UTLENDINGERS KONSUM I NORGE OG KJØP/SALG AV BRUKT REALKAP	-	-	-	-	-	-	-	·
58. LEIE AV PRODUKSJONS-FAKTORER MELLOM FYLKENE	-	-	-	-	-	-	-	-
59. BRUTTOPRODUKT I ALT	26552	53315	25257	33512	7255	1112	3266	57363
60. LØNNSKOSTNADER	18994	24915	18375	32905	6513	839	2370	11207
61. DRIFTSRESULTAT	3064	5792	3903	8447	65	171	497	15751
62. KAPITALSLIT	1822	1692	1475	2155	429	53	158	15972
63. INDIREKTE SKATTER	3223	-2566	2949	-5776	599	65	288	12927
64. SUBSIDIER	-443	-235	-145	-1115	-55	-15	-57	-494
65. IALT	61025	120071	57354	113891	16396	2237	7564	100501

TABELL 9(FORTS.). VARE- OG TJENESTEANVENDELSE OG KOMP. I BRUTTOPRODUKTET. 100000 KR. 1976. HELE LANDET

N9. VARER OG TJENESTER OG KOMP. I BRUTTOPRODUKTET	BYGGE- OG ANLEGGS-VIRKSOM-HET INKL. OLJE-BORING	VARE-HANDEL M.V.	HOTELL-OG RESTAU-RANT DRIFT	UTENRIKS SJØFART	ANNEN SAM-FERDSEL	BANK- OG FORSIKR.-VIRKSOM-HET	FIENDOMS-DRIFT	FORRET-NINGS-MESSIG TJENESTE-YTING
	33.	34.	35.	36.	37.	38.	39.	40.
01. PLANTEPRODUKTER............	-	-	885	-	-	. -	-	-
02. HUSDYRPRODUKTER............	-	-	480	-	-	-	-	-
03. TJENESTER I TILKNYTNING TIL JORDBRUK...........	2855	-	-	-	171	-	-	-
04. SKOGPRODUKTER.............	1458	7	25	-	-	-	-	-
05. FISK M.V.................	-	-	499	-	-	-	-	-
06. BERGVERKSPRODUKTER........	7365	-	33	-	28	-	282	-
07. RÅOLJE OG NATURGASS.......	-	-	-	-	-	-	-	-
08. FOREDLEDE FISKEPRODUKTER..	-	28	248	-	-	-	-	-
09. FOREDLEDE JORDBRUKS-PRODUKTER................	238	-	6730	-	-	-	-	-
10. ANDRE NÆRINGSMIDLER.......	29	-	3039	-	-	-	-	-
11. DRIKKEVARER..............	-	-	4808	-	-	-	-	-
12. TOBAKKSVARER.............	-	-	-	-	-	-	-	-
13. TEKSTILVARER OG KLÆR......	2430	319	572	215	58	-	-	-
14. LÆR- LÆR- OG SKINNVARER OG SKOTØY................	-	-	-	-	-	-	-	-
15. TREVARER, UNNTATT MØBLER OG INNREDNINGER AV TRE....	46418	143	-	-	-	-	-	-
16. MØBLER OG INNREDNINGER AV TRE....................	4325	781	-	39	-	-	-	-
17. TREFOREDLINGSPRODUKTER....	4068	4000	-	-	-	-	-	-
18. GRAFISKE PRODUKTER........	-	3655	-	-	38	-	-	500
19. KJEMISKE RÅVARER.........	352	-	-	19	18	-	-	-
20. KJEMISK-TEKNISKE PRODUKTER	6396	-	-	858	298	-	-	57
21. OLJE- OG KULLPRODUKTER....	3858	3206	-	1290	8222	-	2495	-
22. GUMMIPRODUKTER............	562	-	-	10	-	-	-	-
23. PLASTVARER..............	5141	7225	163	100	97	-	-	-
24. KERAMISKE PRODUKTER.......	1297	-	230	27	-	-	-	-
25. GLASS, GLASSVARER OG MINE-RALSKE PRODUKTER ELLERS...	29534	20	163	-	-	-	-	-
26. JERN, STÅL OG FERRO-LEGERINGER...............	10433	-	-	-	-	-	-	-
27. IKKE-JERNHOLDIGE METALLER.	4329	-	-	43	-	-	-	-
28. METALLVARER.............	33610	564	246	188	-	-	-	-
29. MASKINER OG OLJE-PLATTFORMER.............	8886	208	-	-	-	-	-	-
30. EL. APPARATER OG MATERIELL	19656	-	-	45	32	-	-	-
31. FARTØYER...............	354	-	-	-	-	-	-	-
32. ANDRE TRANSPORTMIDLER.....	-	-	-	-	-	-	-	-
33. TEKNISKE OG VITENSKAPLIGE INSTRUMENTER M.V........	-	62	-	-	-	-	-	2
34. ANDRE INDUSTRIPRODUKTER...	269	-	102	-	-	-	-	-
35. ELEKTRISITET.............	754	-	-	-	844	396	3571	-
36. VANN...................	-	-	-	-	-	-	2770	-
37. BYGG OG REPARASJONER AV BYGG..................	-	-	-	-	-	-	-	-
38. ANLEGG.................	-	-	-	-	-	-	-	-
39. BOREHULL FOR OLJE OG GASS.	-	-	-	-	-	-	-	-
40. PROVISJONER M.V..........	-	-	-	-	-	-	-	-
41. HOTELL OG RESTAURANT-TJENESTER..............	-	-	-	-	-	-	-	-
42. TJENESTER FRA UTENRIKS SJØFART................	-	-	-	629	-	-	-	-
43. PERSONTRANSPORTTJENESTER..	-	-	-	642	477	-	-	-
44. GODSTRANSPORTTJENESTER....	-	12104	356	3621	8516	-	-	-
45. POST- OG TELETJENESTER....	-	-	-	-	1489	4154	-	-
46. BANK- OG FORSIKRINGS-TJENESTER................	-50	1025	-	1865	871	2039	936	-
47. TJENESTER FRA BOLIGER OG FORRETNINGSBYGG..........	118	11795	5271	137	2676	1667	-	1271
48. HELSE- OG VETERINÆR-TJENESTER................	-	-	-	-	-	-	-	-
49. UNDERVISNINGS- OG FORSKNINGSTJENESTER.......	-	-	-	-	-	-	-	-
50. FORRETNINGSMESSIGE TJENESTER................	6595	-	-	-	-	-	218	9
51. ANDRE TJENESTER.........	223	-	143	-	-	-	2625	-
52. IKKE MARKEDSFØRTE OFFENTLIGE TJENESTER......								
53. VARER TIL REPARASJONER, USPESIFISERT VAREINNSATS M.V...................	31944	73971	2950	93519	50748	16379	23001	19933
54. VARER TIL INVESTERINGER, BYGG OG ANLEGG.........								
55. VARER TIL INVESTERINGER, MASKINER OG TRANSPORT-MIDLER M.V..............								
56. KORREKSJONER FOR MERVERDI-OG INVESTERINGSAVGIFT.....								
57. KORR. FOR UTLENDINGERS KONSUM I NORGE OG KJØP/ SALG AV BRUKT REALKAP.....								
58. LEIE AV PRODUKSJONS-FAKTORER MELLOM FYLKENE...	-	-	-	-	-	-	-	-
59. BRUTTOPRODUKT I ALT........	122850	337718	22185	75465	112652	53414	81556	36555
60. LØNNSKOSTNADER..........	88291	124036	16130	45520	88316	31646	1197	20551
61. DRIFTSRESULTAT..........	13957	74083	2110	-22502	-9438	21550	51687	9171
62. KAPITALSLIT............	10424	13773	918	52748	27136	1783	28554	163
63. INDIREKTE SKATTER........	15140	201330	3277	702	15924	154	2595	6953
64. SUBSIDIER..............	-133	-11564	-250	-	-9286	-1429	-2287	-194
65. IALT.................	360357	455931	49120	176715	187234	73042	117454	58529

TABELL 9(FORTS.). VARE- OG TJENESTEANVENDELSE OG KOMP. I BRUTTOPRODUKTET. 100000 KR. 1976. HELE LANDET

	PRODUKSJONSSEKTORER (FORTS.)				GRUPPERINGSSEKTORER		KONSUM	
NR. VARER OG TJENESTER OG KOMP. I BRUTTOPRODUKTET	SOSIAL OG PRIVAT TJENESTE- YTING	KORR. FRIE BANKTJ.	STATS- OG TRYGDE- FORVALT- NINGEN	KOMMUNE- FORVALT- NINGEN	GR. SEKT. FOR VARER TIL REP. OG USPES. VAREINNS. M.V.	GR. SEKT. FOR VARER TIL INVESTER- ING	KONSUM I STATS- OG TRYGDE- FORVALT- NINGEN	KONSUM I KOMMUNE- FORVALT- NINGEN
	41.	42.	43.	44.	45.	46.	47.	48.
01. PLANTEPRODUKTER............	127	-	178	323	3500	-	-	-
02. HUSDYRPRODUKTER...........	48	-	25	151	-	480	-	-
03. TJENESTER I TILKNYTNING TIL JORDBRUK..........	-	-	11	-	1041	729	-	-
04. SKOGPRODUKTER.............	-	-	262	-	-	-	-	-
05. FISK M.V................	41	-	8	116	-	-	-	-
06. BERGVERKSPRODUKTER........	11	-	57	188	-	-	-	-
07. RÅOLJE OG NATURGASS.......	-	-	-	-	-	-	-	-
08. FOREDLEDE FISKEPRODUKTER..	22	-	2	61	-	-	-	-
09. FOREDLEDE JORDBRUKS- PRODUKTER........	560	-	164	1837	-	-	-	-
10. ANDRE NÆRINGSMIDLER.......	250	-	58	624	35	-	-	-
11. DRIKKEVARER..............	46	-	1	85	-	-	-	-
12. TOBAKKSVARER.............	-	-	-	-	-	-	-	-
13. TEKSTILVARER OG KLÆR......	315	-	1210	1161	1568	4057	-	-
14. LÆR, LÆR- OG SKINNVARER OG SKOTØY.............	-	-	129	-	-	32	-	-
15. TREVARER, UNNTATT MØBLER OG INNREDNINGER AV TRE.	57	-	335	134	1935	1478	-	-
16. MØBLER OG INNREDNINGER AV TRE......	-	-	-	-	382	8383	-	-
17. TREFOREDLINGSPRODUKTER....	52	-	385	188	12487	-	-	-
18. GRAFISKE PRODUKTER........	167	-	2872	3711	24150	-	-	-
19. KJEMISKE RÅVARER.........	1	-	498	160	119	-	-	-
20. KJEMISK-TEKNISKE PRODUKTER	1132	-	5550	3068	2273	-	-	-
21. OLJE- OG KULLPRODUKTER....	62	-	3810	1650	14523	-	-	-
22. GUMMIPRODUKTER...........	477	-	116	20	3935	541	-	-
23. PLASTVARER..............	180	-	556	548	2334	285	-	-
24. KERAMISKE PRODUKTER......	42	-	-	-	299	30	-	-
25. GLASS, GLASSVARER OG MINE- RALSKE PRODUKTER ELLERS...	31	-	-	112	1603	774	-	-
26. JERN, STÅL OG FERRO- LEGERINGER........	14	-	-	-	168	2679	-	-
27. IKKE-JERNHOLDIGE METALLER.	88	-	-	-	330	529	-	-
28. METALLVARER.............	81	-	421	48	5937	15876	-	-
29. MASKINER OG OLJE- PLATTFORMER......	-	-	193	67	25826	85106	-	-
30. EL. APPARATER OG MATERIELL	423	-	52	50	7166	24075	-	-
31. FARTØYER...............	1032	-	-	-	21557	118934	-	-
32. ANDRE TRANSPORTMIDLER.....	4071	-	-	-	8779	45006	-	-
33. TEKNISKE OG VITENSKAPLIGE INSTRUMENTER M.V......	250	-	284	195	1809	7549	-	-
34. ANDRE INDUSTRIPRODUKTER...	17	-	146	95	880	211	-	-
35. ELEKTRISITET..........	820	-	995	086	-	-	-	-
36. VANN.................	-	-	-	-	1471	-	-	-
37. BYGG OG REPARASJONER AV BYGG......	-	-	-	-	38449	204593	-	-
38. ANLEGG..............	-	-	-	-	32780	74441	-	-
39. BOREHULL FOR OLJE OG GASS.	-	-	-	-	-	19604	-	-
40. PROVISJONER M.V..........	630	-	-	-	6788	-	-	-
41. HOTELL OG RESTAURANT- TJENESTER.........	-	-	-	-	15482	-	-	-
42. TJENESTER FRA UTENRIKS SJØFART..........	-	-	-	-	1046	-	-	-
43. PERSONTRANSPORTTJENESTER...	-	-	-	-	14002	1344	-	-
44. GODSTRANSPORTTJENESTER....	-	-	-	-	50356	1127	-	-
45. POST- OG TELETJENESTER....	-	-	-	-	27510	-	-	-
46. BANK- OG FORSIKRINGS- TJENESTER.........	-	49587	-	-	14864	-	-	-
47. TJENESTER FRA BOLIGER OG FORRETNINGSBYGG........	3259	-	107	882	-	-	-	-
48. HELSE- OG VETERINÆR- TJENESTER.........	1	-	1078	1014	805	-	-	-
49. UNDERVISNINGS- OG FORSKNINGSTJENESTER.......	8	-	-	-	2838	-	-	-
50. FORRETNINGSMESSIGE TJENESTER........	-	-	605	344	35578	3074	-	-
51. ANDRE TJENESTER........	961	-	2098	187	36036	-	-	-
52. IKKE MARKEDSFØRTE OFFENTLIGE TJENESTER......	-	-	-	-	-	-	144254	196609
53. VARER TIL REPARASJONER, USPESIFISERT VAREINNSATS M.V..........	13175	-	35243	36833	40063	59067	-	-
54. VARER TIL INVESTERINGER, BYGG OG ANLEGG........	-	-	-	-	-	-	-	-
55. VARER TIL INVESTERINGER, MASKINER OG TRANSPORT- MIDLER M.V.......	-	-	-	-	-	-	-	-
56. KORREKSJONER FOR MERVERDI- OG INVESTERINGSAVGIFT.....	-	-	-	-	-	-26818	-	-
57. KORR. FOR UTLENDINGERS KONSUM I NORGE OG KJØP/ SALG AV BRUKT REALKAP.....								
58. LEIE AV PRODUKSJONS- FAKTORER MELLOM FYLKENE...								
59. BRUTTOPRODUKT I ALT........	80093	-49587	93899	156584	-	-	-	-
60. LØNNSKOSTNADER..........	54456	-	90201	145483	-	-	-	-
61. DRIFTSRESULTAT........	33365	-49587	-	-	-	-	-	-
62. KAPITALSLIT..........	4045	-	3698	10101	-	-	-	-
63. INDIREKTE SKATTER.......	9066	-	-	-	-	-	-	-
64. SUBSIDIER..............	-12736	-	-	-	-	-	-	-
65. IALT...............	117614	-	151351	211528	460656	653186	144254	196609

223

TABELL 9(FORTS.). VARE- OG TJENESTEANVENDELSE OG KOMP. I BRUTTOPRODUKTET. 100000 KR. 1976. HELE LANDET

NR. VARER OG TJENESTER OG KOMP. I BRUTTOPRODUKTET	KONSUM	BRUTTOINVESTERINGER						
	PRIVAT KONSUM	INVEST. I STATS- OG TRYGDE-FORVALT-NINGEN	INVEST. I KOMMUNE-FORVALT-NINGEN	INVEST. I BEDRIFTER	LAGER-ENDRING	EKSPORT	OVER-SKUDD/ UNDER-SKUDD	I ALT
	49.	50.	51.	52.	53.	54.	56.	57.
01. PLANTEPRODUKTER.............	31523	-	-	-	1886	138	-	87241
02. HUSDYRPRODUKTER.............	8068	-	-	-	167	2673	-	77831
03. TJENESTER I TILKNYTNING TIL JORDBRUK............	173	-	-	-	-	-	-	7593
04. SKOGPRODUKTER..............	2292	-	-	-	-894	452	-	29123
05. FISK M.V...................	5671	-	-	-	-2791	1457	-	31329
06. BERGVERKSPRODUKTER.........	230	-	-	-	-325	9274	-	38047
07. RÅOLJE OG NATURGASS........	-	-	-	-	-373	67165	-	117505
08. FOREDLEDE FISKEPRODUKTER...	6833	-	-	-	-1529	33871	-	53835
09. FOREDLEDE JORDBRUKS-PRODUKTER................	94829	-	-	-	-566	4412	-	155204
10. ANDRE NÆRINGSMIDLER........	51377	-	-	-	3189	4659	-	91295
11. DRIKKEVARER...............	43698	-	-	-	-464	434	-	50075
12. TOBAKKSVARER..............	20873	-	-	-	-491	175	-	20562
13. TEKSTILVARER OG KLÆR......	82149	-	-	-	-1578	6439	-	114612
14. LÆR, LÆR- OG SKINNVARER OG SKOTØY.................	13439	-	-	-	-42	1383	-	17764
15. TREVARER, UNNTATT MØBLER OG INNREDNINGER AV TRE...	414	-	-	-	4	5370	-	84342
16. MØBLER OG INNREDNINGER AV TRE....................	18512	-	-	-	-96	1931	-	37447
17. TREFOREDLINGSPRODUKTER....	4094	-	-	-	-2906	32524	-	92076
18. GRAFISKE PRODUKTER........	20405	-	-	-	-65	838	-	69948
19. KJEMISKE RÅVARER..........	318	-	-	-	1709	19053	-	68202
20. KJEMISK-TEKNISKE PRODUKTER	19424	-	-	-	-1680	5890	-	130292
21. OLJE- OG KULLPRODUKTER....	31759	-	-	-	6123	15439	-	15428
22. GUMMIPRODUKTER............	6685	-	-	-	-313	1501	-	31938
23. PLASTVARER...............	5793	-	-	-	650	4065	-	5004
24. KERAMISKE PRODUKTER.......	1693	-	-	-	-103	500	-	5004
25. GLASS, GLASSVARER OG MINE-RALSKE PRODUKTER ELLERS...	2030	-	-	-	8	3060	-	48030
26. JERN, STÅL OG FERRO-LEGERINGER...............	151	-	-	-	-2412	32871	-	85130
27. IKKE-JERNHOLDIGE METALLER.	49	-	-	-	-1799	49764	-	83337
28. METALLVARER..............	9530	-	-	-	-3772	10516	-	101043
29. MASKINER OG OLJE-PLATTFORMER..............	8092	-	-	-	10434	36643	-	211045
30. EL. APPARATER OG MATERIELL	23964	-	-	-	1167	14805	-	113214
31. FARTØYER.................	4212	-	-	-	682	31882	-	203366
32. ANDRE TRANSPORTMIDLER.....	44970	-	-	-	1168	4431	-	110901
33. TEKNISKE OG VITENSKAPLIGE INSTRUMENTER M.V.........	6495	-	-	-	711	2453	-	23624
34. ANDRE INDUSTRIPRODUKTER...	14679	-	-	-	41	1945	-	19210
35. ELEKTRISITET.............	25267	-	-	-	42	2843	-	92043
36. VANN....................	-	-	-	-	-	-	-	4241
37. BYGG OG REPARASJONER AV BYGG...................	-	-	-	-	-	-	-	243042
38. ANLEGG.................	-	-	-	-	-	-	-	197221
39. BOREHULL FOR OLJE OG GASS.	-	-	-	-	-	3825	-	23429
40. PROVISJONER M.V..........	2392	-	-	-	-	8862	-	18662
41. HOTELL OG RESTAURANT-TJENESTER.................	33666	-	-	-	-	-	-	49128
42. TJENESTER FRA UTENRIKS SJØFART.................	972	-	-	-	-	173250	-	175897
43. PERSONTRANSPORTTJENESTER..	23248	-	-	-	-	6730	-	46443
44. GODSTRANSPORTTJENESTER....	3408	-	-	-	-	13924	-	93460
45. POST- OG TELETJENESTER....	11330	-	-	-	-	1099	-	45581
46. BANK- OG FORSIKRINGS-TJENESTER.................	5565	-	-	-	-	1095	-	78135
47. TJENESTER FRA BOLIGER OG FORRETNINGSBYGG..........	98514	-	-	-	-	-	-	121396
48. HELSE- OG VETERINÆR-TJENESTER.................	37660	-	-	-	-	-	-	41055
49. UNDERVISNINGS- OG FORSKNINGSTJENESTER.......	4595	-	-	-	-	338	-	8023
50. FORRETNINGSMESSIGE TJENESTER.................	1674	-	-	-	-	4020	-	59329
51. ANDRE TJENESTER..........	44333	-	-	-	-	2583	-	90885
52. IKKE MARKEDSFØRTE OFFENTLIGE TJENESTER......	-	-	-	-	-	-	-	340863
53. VARER TIL REPARASJONER, USPESIFISERT VAREINNSATS M.V.	48018	-	-	-	7973	23381	-	700654
54. VARER TIL INVESTERINGER, BYGG OG ANLEGG.........	-	22513	46772	247593	-	-	-	315874
55. VARER TIL INVESTERINGER, MASKINER OG TRANSPORT-MIDLER M.V..............	-	3992	7145	323025	-	-	-	334072
56. KORREKSJONER FOR MERVERDI- OG INVESTERINGSAVGIFT.....	-	-	-	-	-	-	-	-26818
57. KORR. FOR UTLENDINGERS KONSUM I NORGE OG KJØP/ SALG AV BRUKT REALKAP.....	-19991	151	1067	-33954	-	51767	:	
58. LEIE AV PRODUKSJONS-FAKTORER MELLOM FYLKENE...	-	-	-	-	-	-	-	1707094
59. BRUTTOPRODUKT I ALT.......	-	-	-	-	-	-	-	999924
60. LØNNSKOSTNADER...........	-	-	-	-	-	-	-	260029
61. DRIFTSRESULTAT..........	-	-	-	-	-	-	-	253265
62. KAPITALSLIT............	-	-	-	-	-	-	-	313114
63. INDIREKTE SKATTER........	-	-	-	-	-	-	-	116241
64. SUBSIDIER..............	-	-	-	-	-	-	-	-116241
65. IALT..................	904954	26557	54984	533662	13757	701730	-	7242255

XIV. PAPUA NEW GUINEA

A. General information

The present report is based on *Monograph 5, An Input-Output Matrix for Papua New Guinea 1972/73,* published by the Institute of Applied Social and Economic Research of Papua New Guinea.

Input-output tables for Papua New Guinea have been compiled for 1969/70 and 1972/73. Different methodologies and data sources were used in each table. The present report refers to the 1972/73 table, which was compiled by the National Statistical Office with technical and financial assistance provided by the Office of Technical Co-operation of the United Nations Secretariat.

The national accounts series is calculated using an income and consumption approach. A revision of this methodology was implemented in 1974 with a view to allowing for a more extensive use of a production-based method of calculating GDP estimates. However, the compilation of the 1972/73 input-output table helped to highlight the deficiencies existing in the currently available production data. In general, the methodology followed in the compilation of the input-output table is in line with the methodology followed for the national accounts. However, a number of differences exist between the national accounts and input-output estimates as a result of the production approach and the wider range of sources of data used in the input-output table. A comparison of GDP estimates according to the national accounts and the input-output table shows a 3 per cent underrecording of GDP in the national accounts estimates. This difference is mainly because of the underevaluation of the national accounts estimates for compensation of employees, private consumption expenditure and imports of goods and services.

Major deviations from the SNA recommendations on input-output include: (*a*) the treatment of government health, education and welfare services; (*b*) the inclusion of two dummy sectors; (*c*) the disaggregation of final demand and value added; (*d*) the treatment and disaggregation of imports; (*e*) the exclusion of intra-industry transactions; and (*f*) the distribution of imputed financial charges.

B. Analytical framework

1. *Tables and derived matrices available*

Data are presented in five basic tables:
  (i)   Absorption table at purchasers' prices;
  (ii) Make table valued at purchasers' prices;
  (iii) Input-output table of the industry-by-industry type, valued at purchasers' prices;
  (iv) Imports absorption matrix;
  (v)   Rent matrix. This matrix provides an industry-by-industry flow analysis of rent paid and received. The reasons for compiling this table are explained below.

No derived matrices have been published.

All basic tables compiled are presented at a 68 x 68 level of aggregation of intermediate sectors.

2. *Valuation standards*

Transactions have been valued at purchasers' prices in all basic tables compiled. However, a research project conducted in an Australian university transformed the 1972/73 input-output table from purchasers' to approximate basic values. The Papua New Guinea statistician currently holds the information required to repeat this transformation whenever this is required. Imports are valued f.o.b., plus the mark-ups applied to derive the purchasers' value of imports. Exports are valued f.o.b.

3. *Statistical units and classification standards*

Industries are the statistical units adopted for columns of table (i), rows of table (ii), rows and columns of tables (iii) and (v) and columns of table (iv). The statistical unit adopted for rows of table (i), columns of table (ii) and rows of table (iv) is commodities.

Industries are classified according to the 1966 Australian Classification of Industries. Commodities follow the classification developed by Parker in his 1973 inter-industry study of Papua New Guinea.[1]

The classification of the intermediate consumption quadrant differs from the SNA recommendations in that (*a*) health, education and welfare services provided by the Government are distributed together with the same kind of services provided by industries; and (*b*) two dummy sectors are included: (i) unallocated rent, which records the minor amount of rental income earned by the goods-producing sectors, and (ii) business expenses, which include administrative expenditures that are too small to be allocated directly to the corresponding sector, expenditures on drinks and other entertainment expenses that have not been allocated to the amusements, hotels and cafés sector, and expenditures on administrative expenses paid to parent companies overseas.

The final demand quadrant presents a higher disaggregation than that recommended in SNA. Private consumption is disaggregated into its market and non-market components, and gross fixed capital formation is subdivided into government and private, with private gross capital formation further disaggregated into market and non-market. In addition, exports are subdivided into exports f.o.b. of commodities, exports of services, exports of other commodities (i.e., management and commissions for services provided to overseas buyers and transfers of emigrants' personal and household effects) and direct purchases by non-residents. Private consumption is defined on a national basis. All components of final demand are defined as recommended in SNA.

Value added is also disaggregated into a finer breakdown than that recommended in SNA. Compensation of employees is subdivided into its indigenous and non-indigenous

[1] M. L. Parker, "Papua New Guinea—an inter-industry study", **Research School of Pacific Studies**, Australian National University, Canberra, 1973.

components and the operating surplus is subdivided into market and non-market. Indigenous primary producers mainly producing cash crops, as well as their immediate families who assist them in their production activity, are assumed to receive a return for their labour from entrepreneurial income. These labour returns are thus included separately in operating surplus rather than in compensation of employees. This treatment applies both to indigenous small-holders and village industries in the market component of the economy, and to subsistence villagers in the non-market component. It should also be noted that, in agreement with the SNA recommendations, compensation of employees includes wages and salaries in kind such as housing provided to government employees at markedly reduced costs. In addition, a housing subsidy has been imputed. This has resulted in an increase of gross output, which has been treated as a sale from the corresponding input-output sectors to the government final consumption expenditure component of final demand.

Contrary to the SNA recommendations, the Papua New Guinea input-output tables do not present a distinction between competitive and complementary imports. All imports have been cross-classified by origin and destination in the import matrix, and by destination only in separate rows of the input-output table. Imports in this table have been subdivided into imports of merchandise (at both f.o.b. and c.i.f. values), freight and insurance, other imports services, imports of other commodities (which include repair work done overseas, administrative and management expenses overseas, rent paid overseas and immigrants' personal effects) and imports of other goods and services, which include expenditure by Papua New Guinea residents travelling overseas.

4. Treatment and presentation of selected transactions

As mentioned above, a pure industry-by-industry input-output table has been compiled on the basis of the information provided by the absorption and make tables. However, in the case of two types of secondary production, namely, rental income and own-account capital formation, the corresponding output and input have been retained in the industry sector in which they are produced. The reasons for adopting this approach is to preserve a direct link between the industry-by-industry matrix and the industry statistics collected and generally used. The influence of this secondary production is in most instances of such a minor nature that this treatment will probably not greatly impair the value of the pure input-output table. On the other hand, the Papua New Guinea statistician has enough information available to modify this treatment according to the users' convenience. In addition, an industry-by-industry rent matrix has been compiled describing the origin and destination of this component of secondary production.

Sales and purchases of second-hand goods are presented together in a "sales by final buyers" row of the input-output table, which is added to domestic production and imports to obtain total supply.

Non-market output of the agriculture and owner-occupied dwellings sectors have been recorded in separate rows with a single input, namely, operating surplus non-market component. Gross output of these sectors has been distributed along their corresponding rows to the private final consumption non-market component category of final demand.

Intra-industry transactions have been excluded from the table because of lack of data on this type of transaction. This procedure is in disagreement with the SNA recommendations on input-output.

Output of the financial and insurance sectors has been defined according to the SNA recommendations. Thus, output of financial institutions includes actual service charges as well as the imputed excess of property income received over property income paid for by banks; imputed output of ancillary insurance companies equals premiums less claims; and, for life insurance, a service charge is imputed which is equivalent to the excess of premiums received over the sum of claims paid, plus the net addition to actuarial reserves which accrues to policy holders. The distribution of financial output does not conform to the SNA recommendations, since the imputed service charges have been allocated to the input-output sectors and the final demand categories, together with actual service charges.

C. STATISTICAL SOURCES AND COMPILATION METHODOLOGY

Data collection is mainly based on regular statistical sources and the results of the Agricultural and Pastoral Census, and the Secondary Industries Census.

The methodology followed involved a detailed step-by-step exercise of gathering all the available information on commodity flows, completing a commodity flow analysis for the whole economy and translating this into an inter-industry flow matrix. Work commenced by quantifying all available supplies of goods and services into 100 commodity groups. These were distributed among producing industries and recorded in the make matrix. Concurrently, work progressed on the allocation of commodities as input into these industry sectors. This work could only proceed as the total cost of each industry sector was determined and after the primary input of compensation of employees, operating surplus and consumption of fixed capital, along with other indirect taxes net of subsidies, had been estimated. The allocation of commodity groups to the final demand sectors was undertaken as a separate exercise.

1. Gross output, intermediate consumption and primary input

(a) Agriculture

Data on the agriculture sectors were mainly obtained from the Agricultural and Pastoral Census, which collects quantity data on agriculture operations. These were supplemented with financial data gathered in the *Rural Industries Bulletin* and a number of *ad hoc* studies carried out to cover the operations of indigenous producers. The main agricultural sectors associated with exported and domestically consumed commodities such as copra, cocoa, coffee, rubber, tea, oil palm and cattle have been disaggregated into plantation and small-holder types of operations. The main sources of data for the plantation sectors have been the Papua New Guinea Bureau of Statistics, annual *Rural Industries Bulletins* and *International Trade Statistics Bulletins*, unpublished details from the Agricultural and Pastoral Census, various *ad hoc* studies conducted into the operations of particular producers, privately collected information from the

Department of Primary Industries, and company records and reports.

(b) Mining and quarrying

Sources of data on the mining and quarrying sectors include published and unpublished company records, records kept by the Department of Natural Resources, export statistics, cost structure information obtained from the input-output sector of the Australian Bureau of Statistics and direct correspondence with some companies.

(c) Manufacturing

Data on the manufacturing sectors are mainly obtained from the Secondary Industries Census. This source presented several problems. The questionnaire used in the census excludes management, sales and distribution costs and the census results have generally proved to be incompatible with other privately collected data. Therefore, it was necessary to undertake extensive re-editing and recording of the census questionnaires. This exercise uncovered a number of errors in the published results which had to be corrected. In general, the lack of suitable production statistics was overcome by a heavy reliance on company records, governmental reports and financial reports of various public authorities and commissions, *ad hoc* studies prepared for particular industries, taxation statistics etc.

(d) Electricity

The main sources of data for the electricity sector are the Electricity Commission Annual Report, and cost and receipt records relating to the operation of government-owned power houses.

(e) Construction

The building and construction sector includes various public sector maintenance and construction operations in addition to private contractors providing similar services. Output of the sector includes maintenance operations, including the imputed value for work performed by free and partially paid labour. Sources of data for the public sector operations range from published documents and reports to privately collected confidential files and papers. Private building and construction operations have been estimated indirectly, because of lack of data. An estimate of total demand for private contractors' services was first determined as the difference between total demand for construction services and demand for public sector services. Then, primary input was estimated on the basis of taxation statistics and the Department of Labour Employment Census. Finally, the value of intermediate input was estimated and checked against a number of indicators.

(f) Transport and communications

Aggregated statistics relating to the transport and storage sector are not available. Therefore, use has been made of a wide variety of data sources, including the Department of Transport Road Use and Freight Reports, government details of expenditure and receipts, published documents and privately collected company data.

The communications sector is dominated by the activities

of the Department of Posts and Telegraphs, although in 1972/73 the Australian Overseas Telecommunications Commission was responsible for telecommunications flowing in and out of the country. In addition to the usual published reports relating to these two organizations, access has also been obtained, through the departments concerned, to more detailed unpublished financial statements on revenue and operating costs.

(g) Trade

Output of the commerce sector has been derived from the demand in the economy for commercial services. Demand for commercial services has been calculated in a variety of ways depending on the sector and commodity group involved. For imported goods and much of the supply of domestic goods, retail and wholesale mark-ups have been determined after examination of the maximum mark-up rates set by the Prices Controller and after private discussions with a number of large retailing/wholesaling companies. Included in this sector are the regular wholesale and retail operators, export and import agents and various traders and distributing branches of larger overseas manufacturers. In calculating the value of operating costs, those parts of the sector (such as exports agents) that have peculiar cost structures have been dealt with separately. Moreover, co-operative stores for which some cost information is available, and indigenous trade stores for which a recent unpublished survey has been conducted by the Department of Business Development, have been treated individually when determining operating costs. For most wholesale and retail operators it has been necessary to rely on privately collected company records for some of the largest nation-wide operators. It has also been necessary to draw upon taxation statistics, results of the Department of Labour Employment Census (suitably modified for omissions) and the working papers used in the compilation of the 1973 input-output table for Papua New Guinea.

(h) Financial and real estate

Data on the financial institutions and insurance sector are obtained directly from company financial records. Included in this sector are the main trading and savings banks, the Papua New Guinea Development Bank and Investment Corporation, and the Reserve Bank of Australia (which operated as the central bank in Papua New Guinea in 1972/73). Also included are all the insurance (life and general) companies and agencies operating in Papua New Guinea and three main leasing companies.

Output of the real estate property and services sector has been mainly calculated in terms of rental income. Unpublished taxation statistics have been used to determine the total rent receipts from Papua New Guinea and overseas. Output in the form of fees charged by real estate agents, stockbrokers, auctioneers etc. could only be derived from the total demand for these types of services by the other sectors of the economy. Both published and unpublished information from taxation statistics and the Employment Census have been used to determine the primary input of this sector. Having obtained the value of total intermediate input by subtraction, various company records and reports have been used as a guide to the individual intermediate input.

Estimates of imputed gross rental income from owner-occupied dwellings are based on official national accounts estimates, which are derived as follows. A market value has been assigned to the owner-occupied dwellings included in the latest population census and an estimate of current annual rental value has been obtained based on a percentage of the market value of the stock of available houses (the stock being suitably allocated between various high- and low-cost housing groups). The operating costs associated with the estimated gross rental value of the owner-occupied dwellings are estimated using observed operating costs/gross rent ratios from taxation statistics sources. As estimates of gross rent obtained from the latter source were slightly higher than the estimate based on the first method, it was necessary to modify the official estimates of operating costs accordingly. In an attempt to retain the same official operating surplus estimate, the adjustment had to be made to intermediate input and other value added components only.

(i) Services

The education sector is basically composed of government-controlled and -administered education facilities, but also includes the education facilities operated by various missions. Output for this sector, where actual payment received from services is exceeded by expenditure in providing these services, is measured in terms of the total expenditure incurred in providing these services. The difference between total expenditure on these services and the actual cash receipts is treated as part of the final consumption expenditure of either the Government (for government-operated facilities) or private households and non-profit-making institutions servicing households (for mission-operated activities). The sources of data used in calculating sales of education services and total expenditure by this sector are government income and expenditure records such as the Appropriate Ordinance 1973/74, annual reports from institutions such as universities and the survey of religious organizations conducted by the Bureau of Statistics.

The health sector is basically composed of two parts: the operations of government and mission hospitals, aid posts and other assorted health services, on the one hand, and the operations of private doctors, dentists and veterinarians, on the other. For the government- and mission-operated health services, the main sources of data are government expenditure and receipts records, and the survey of religious organizations. Government health operations basically relate to expenditures associated with the Department of Health (excluding medical training facilities). The operations of private doctors, dentists and veterinarians have been estimated using taxation statistics in regard to claimed expenditure on medical services. In using this source, allowance has been made for medicaments included in the estimate and some attempt has also been made to allow for a slight exaggeration in the estimates provided by private persons when completing their tax returns. Indigenous persons who do not complete tax returns are regarded as not using the services provided by private medical practitioners but relying instead on government-provided medical services. As a check against this method of estimation, an attempt was made to derive a gross output for medical practitioners from unpublished tax statistics on income. From these two methods a mutually consistent estimate of total output has been derived.

Data on the amusement, hotels and cafés sector have been mainly obtained from tax statistics, the Employment Census, the Bureau of Statistics Survey of Retail Trade, government expenditure and receipts records, and privately obtained company records. The operations of hotels, clubs, restaurants and motels have been estimated as a single group because of the basic interrelation that exists among them. In the calculation of commercial mark-ups on aerated waters and alcoholic beverages, estimates have been derived of the mark-ups on these commodities which form part of the output of hotels, clubs and restaurants. This calculation has been based on company records of sales to these types of outlets as distinct from supermarkets and trade stores. Unpublished details obtained from the Survey of Retail Trade have been used to estimate the value of other takings. These results have also been used as an estimate of meals sold and accommodation services provided by industry groups in this survey which correspond to the amusement, hotels and cafés sector. This estimate of total output has been compared with some company reports and appears to be reasonably consistent. For the remaining part of this sector, which covers movie theatres, squash courts and other amusement-type activities, it has been necessary to rely on privately collected company records and unpublished Employment Census results.

The largest part of the personal services sector relates to the activities of household domestic servants. The estimated number of household domestic servants is derived from the 1971 Population Census, adjusted to 1972/73 in accordance with the movement in non-indigenous population since 1971. The services of household domestic servants are valued at the estimated average rate applying in 1972/73. The remaining part of this sector relates to the activities of laundries, dry-cleaners, hairdressers and similar types of services. Estimates of output and operating costs are obtained from completed Secondary Industries Census returns for dry-cleaning and laundry services. Unpublished details from the Survey of Retail Trade relating to "other retail takings" of hairdressers and other miscellaneous personal services provide an estimate of the output of the remaining part of this sector. Operating costs for this component of this sector have had to be estimated from the Employment Census.

Data on the other community and business services sector were obtained from taxation statistics and unpublished details obtained from the Employment Census. The sector includes the activities of the private practice of the legal profession, consultant engineers and surveyors, architects, accountants and auditors, advertising agencies and typing and copying agencies.

2. Final demand and imports

Private consumption expenditure has been estimated on the basis of a detailed product analysis conducted on each of the 100 commodity groups used in the compilation of the input-output table. As a cross-check on the estimates derived from this commodity approach, an estimate of consumption expenditure has been constructed using the Bureau of Statistics Survey of Retail Trade. In addition, use was made of the results of household expenditure surveys and a number of minor data sources. The results were adjusted to account for inflation and observed changes in consumption patterns between periods.

Data on government consumption have been obtained from national accounts estimates slightly modified in cases where noted discrepancies with other data sources existed. The non-market component has been derived from the national accounts.

Estimates of change in stocks have been derived in two ways: directly, from calculation of the supply and usage of domestically produced goods where sources of data permit an exact calculation of the quantity variation in stocks (e.g., the difference between copper concentrate production and export sales); and indirectly as a residual after the allocation of total commodity supplies to all using sectors. The official national accounts estimate was also used as a guide to the overall value of the change in stocks.

The main sources of data covering the gross fixed capital formation of general government are government records of receipts and expenditure, special surveys and investigations conducted into the expenditure of Australian Government departments operating in Papua New Guinea, and statistics on the activities of local government councils collected by the Commissioner for Local Government. Data on private capital formation were mainly obtained from the Survey of Capital Expenditure, the Rural Industries Bulletin (to cover own-account capital formation on rural holdings) and unpublished details from the Agriculture and Pastoral Census (to obtain the value of "new areas" of crops and plantations laboured by non-indigenous producers). The non-market estimate was obtained directly from the national accounts.

Data on exports and imports are mainly derived from the *International Trade Statistics Bulletin*.

For tables, see end of volume.

XV. SPAIN

A. GENERAL INFORMATION

The present country chapter is based on *La Estructura Productiva Española, Tablas Input-Output de 1975 y Análisis de las Interdependencias de la Económica Española*, published by the Fondo de la Investigación Economía y Social de las Cajas de Ahorro Confederadas.

Input-output tables have been compiled in Spain for the years 1954, 1958, 1962, 1966, 1970, 1975 and 1980. All input-output tables compiled since 1962 have followed the methodology established by the Statistical Office of the European Community (EUROSTAT) and therefore are basically comparable with each other, except for (a) methodological changes introduced on the basis of recommendations by EUROSTAT and (b) changes in the classification of intermediate sectors. Specifically, the 1962 and 1966 tables are directly comparable with each other since both follow the EUROSTAT methodology applied to the European Community Tables of 1959 and present the same classification of intermediate sectors. The 1970 and 1975 tables differ from each other and from previous tables in that their methodologies follow that applied to the European Community tables of 1965 and 1970-75 respectively, and in that intermediate sectors are classified according to ISIC and the General Industrial Classification of Economic Activities within the European Economic Communities (NACE), respectively. In addition to these benchmark tables, updated versions of the 1962, 1966 and 1975 tables are available for the years 1965, 1968 and 1979. Following the EUROSTAT recommendations, basic input-output tables are planned to be compiled every five years for all years ending in 0 or 5. The present report refers to the 1975 table. However, the tables presented at the end of the chapter are those of 1980, which also follow the EUROSTAT methodology.

The compilation of input-output tables is not integrated with the system of national accounts of the country. Different types of methodology are adopted in obtaining both sets of data. However, most aggregate estimates obtained in the table are fairly close to those obtained in the national accounts, with the exception of gross value added of several branches of economic activity. Differences in those estimates are mainly because of different treatments of financial services.

The Spanish input-output table conforms in many aspects to the EUROSTAT recommendation on input-output.[1] The Spanish table differs from the SNA recommendations on input-output in the following aspects: (a) definition and breakdown of value added; (b) treatment of secondary production; (c) treatment of transactions in scrapped and second-hand goods; (d) treatment of imports; (e) no imputed transactions of the banking sector are included; (f) distribution of output of the public administration and defence sec-

tor; (g) no valuation of transactions at approximate basic values is presented nor can it be derived; and (h) definition of final demand.

B. ANALYTICAL FRAMEWORK

1. *Tables and derived matrices available*

The only basic table available is an absorption table. Each entry in the intermediate consumption quadrant of this table is disaggregated into input of domestic origin, imported input, import duties associated to input imported and total input, which are obtained by adding up the first three components.

Several derived matrices based on this basic table, such as input coefficients and the inverse matrix, have been calculated but they have not been published. Summary measures published include: (a) tables of comparison of the following selected ratios of sectoral values in the years 1970 and 1975: value of domestic output at ex-factory prices over total supply (including imports), gross value added over total output at producers' prices; labour costs over gross value added; energy inputs over total output at producers' prices and over gross value added; inputs imported over total output at producers' prices, and over gross value added; competitive imports over total output at producers' prices and over total resources; and exports over imported inputs, over total output at producers' prices, over gross value added and over labour costs; (b) ratios for each sector of intermediate input over total input and of intermediate output over total output; and (c) linkage tables, including simple linkages (i.e., sum of the rows and columns of the inverse matrix based on domestic input-output coefficients) and their coefficients of variation; simple linkages weighted by their respective averages; and simple linkages weighted by the participation of each sector in total demand.

The basic table and the published summary measures are presented at a level of disaggregation of 127 x 127 intermediate sectors.

2. *Valuation standards*

Transactions in the absorption table are valued at producers' prices. Imports are valued c.i.f. plus import duties, in order to equate the value of imported goods to those domestically produced. Exports are valued f.o.b. Contrary to SNA recommendations, commodity taxes are not recorded separately and therefore no valuation at approximate basic values is available.

3. *Statistical units and classification standards*

The establishment is the statistical unit adopted for rows and columns. Establishments are classified according to a national classification system which closely follows the gen-

---

[1]See Statistical Office of the European Communities, *European System of Integrated Economic Accounts* (ESA), 2nd edition (Luxembourg, 1979).

eral Industrial Classification of Economic Activities used in the European Community for input-output tables (NACE/CLIO).

The classification of sectors in the intermediate consumption quadrant is in agreement with the SNA recommendations. The activities of producers of government services and of private non-profit institutions are differentiated from industrial activities according to criteria similar to those described in SNA and they are separately recorded in this quadrant. Services provided by private non-profit institutions are included in the non-market services sectors of the input-output table.

The breakdown and definitions of final demand and value added follow the SNA recommendations, except for (a) the definition of government consumption, which includes sales to non-government buyers, (b) the definition of value added, which includes interest actually paid by the intermediate sectors for loans received, and (c) the disaggregation of compensation of employees into wages and salaries, and employers' contribution to social security and similar schemes.

Private final consumption is defined on a domestic basis, that is, it includes consumption expenditures in the national territory by non-residents and excludes expenditures abroad by Spanish residents.

Contrary to SNA recommendations, no distinction is made between competitive and complementary imports. All imports and their associated import duties are cross-classified by type of commodity and destination and are recorded separately from domestic inputs in the absorption table, as mentioned above. In addition, imports (c.i.f. plus import duties) classified by commodity are recorded in a separate row of the absorption table.

4. *Treatment and presentation of selected transactions*

The treatment of secondary production differs from that recommended in SNA in that neither secondary products nor their associated input are transferred to their characteristic sectors.

The treatment of scrapped and second-hand goods is in conformity with the ESA recommendations and therefore differs from that of SNA. Both types of goods are dealt with in a recovery services sector. The column of this sector records the value of all inputs used in the process of demolition and treatment of demolition materials. The value of recovered goods is, however, considered to be neither an intermediate input of the recovery services sector nor an output of the sectors selling them. This value is recorded in the operating surplus row of the recovery sector. Gross output of the recovery sector includes (a) the value of demolition material and recovered goods sold by the recovery sector; (b) net purchases of existing durable consumer goods and recovered goods by non-market branches of general government and private non-profit institutions and by households; these purchases are recorded at the intersection of the row of recovery services with the collective consumption and private consumption columns, respectively; (c) net purchases of antiques and of existing fixed capital goods by all sectors, which are recorded in the column gross fixed capital formation; and (d) exports of existing goods, which are recorded in the exports columns.

Non-monetary output and its corresponding inputs have been included in the inputs and outputs of each intermediate sector.

Output of each intermediate sector is recorded gross, that is, it includes intra-sector consumption of characteristic goods, as well as intra-sector consumption of non-characteristic goods.

Contrary to SNA recommendations, the output of banking services is defined to include only the value of commissions actually charged for transactions. Imputed service charges, as measured by the difference between interest earned and paid by the banks, are excluded. Interest charged for loans granted therefore remains included in the value added of the intermediate sectors paying it. As a consequence of this treatment, the operating surplus of the banking sector presents a negative value.

Public administration and defence are included as a separate intermediate sector. Its output is distributed to each intermediate sector according to the charges paid by those sectors in return for public services obtained. Similarly, the delivery of public services to private final consumption is measured by the amount of charges directly paid by the families in return for the services obtained. The remaining output is allocated to the consumption of the public sector category of final demand. This treatment of the public administration and defence sector is in agreement with the European Economic Community recommendations on input-output.

Gross output of health and education services provided by the government is recorded in the non-market services sectors of the intermediate consumption quadrant, and is allocated in its entirety to the government consumption category of final demand. This procedure is in agreement with the SNA recommendations.

C. STATISTICAL SOURCES AND COMPILATION METHODOLOGY

Data collection is mainly based on regular statistical sources and on the results of the agriculture, livestock, trade and professional activities censuses.

1. *Gross output and intermediate consumption*

Data on agriculture and livestock activities are based on several benchmark livestock and agriculture censuses, and on statistics compiled by the Ministry of Agriculture for the year 1974-1979.

Data on fishing activities are provided by the Dirección General de Pesca.

Mining and manufacturing and data are obtained from the following publications: Mining Statistics; Output and Distribution of Coal, published by the Ministry of Industry; Industrial Statistics, published by the National Institute of Statistics; Industrial Production Statistics, Analysis of Results, and Investment and Stocks, published by the Trade Unions Statistical Service; Cement Industries Statistics; reports on the basic metal industries, published by the Union de Empresas Siderirurgicas (UNESID); annual report of the National Institute of Industry; reports on equipment goods published by the Servicio Comercial de Bienes de Equipo (SERCOBE); and information gathered from various enterprises.

Data on activities are compiled by the Ministry of Public Works and Urbanism.

232

Data on transport and communications are obtained from Statistics of Civil Flights; Statistics on Railroad Transportation, published by the Red Nacional de Ferrocarriles Españoles (RENFE) and Ferrocarriles de Via Estrecha (FEVE); Statistics on Transportation by Sea, published by the Subsecretaria de Marina Mercante del Ministerio de Comercio; Statistics on Transportation by Road, published by the National Institute of Statistics; annual report of the Telephone Company; and annual report of Mail and Telegraph Activities, published by the General Bureau of Communications.

Data on trade are obtained from several surveys carried out by the National Institute of Statistics, the Ministry of Commerce and the Instituto de Reforma de Estructuras Comerciales (IRESCO).

Data on services are based on tourism statistics, and on information provided by the Registro de la Seguridad Social.

2. *Value added*

Labour data are obtained from wage statistics compiled by the National Institute of Statistics and social security institutions such as the Instituto Nacional de Prevision (INP). Direct and indirect taxes and subsidies are estimated from the Public Administration Accounts compiled by the Ministry of the Treasury. The operating surplus was estimated from data on depreciation, profits, savings, dividends and interests of a sample of corporations analyzed by the Banco de Vizcaya, and from an analysis of large industrial corporations carried out by the Ministry of Industry.

3. *Final demand and imports*

Private final consumption data were taken from the family budget survey carried out by the National Institute of Statistics. Data on collective consumption were provided by the Public Administration Accounts. Public gross fixed capital formation data were obtained from the Ministry of Treasury. Data on changes in stocks and private gross fixed capital formation were obtained from a survey carried out by the Ministry of Industry and from statistics on investment and stocks gathered by the Trade Unions Statistical Service. Data on aggregate imports and exports were taken from Foreign Trade Statistics, published by the Customs General Bureau. Imports were disaggregated on the basis of information provided by the General Bureau of Planning and the Customs General Bureau.

SPAIN

INPUT-OUTPUT TABLES

1980

Source: *National Accounts ESA, Input-Output Tables
1980,* EUROSTAT.

1980 ESPAGNE

Column groups: **MIO PES** (B010) · **ECH.INTERM.** (B030–B110) · **TOUTES ORIGINES** (B130–B190) · **PRIX DEPART-USINE** (B210–B290)

	B010	B030	B050	B070	B090	B110	B130	B150	B170	B190	B210	B230	B250	B270	B290
010 PROD. AGRICULTURE	322290	-	-	-	3	-	10	120	6120	19	5	-	33	1	8
030 HOUILLE	-	23797	36251	-	-	-	2121	1397	919	276	53	-	33	139	126
050 COKE	-	-	64	-	63237	-	39873	1287	826	1092	41	-	44	11	-
070 PETROLE + PROD.GAZ N	64713	1199	1192	878048	168513	-	20271	62750	42081	4780	1637	42	1093	2267	1408
090 ELECTR.,GAZ,VAP.,EAU	31710	3657	2789	11130	68303	-	62957	29585	30292	12019	3053	257	4784	6239	3031
110 COMBUST. NUCLEAIRES	-	-	-	-	-	-	-	-	-	-	-	-	-	-	-
130 FERREUX ET NON FERR.	590	259	-	1961	451	-	670774	11820	6607	224848	44835	2572	64244	74080	25645
150 MIN. NON METALLIQUES	1646	4	15	802	283	-	13564	96716	26066	4856	1655	683	3351	4470	278
170 PRODUITS CHIMIQUES	104539	1223	22	755	1884	-	31721	24032	213133	10330	3166	905	12724	8185	4239
190 PRODUITS EN METAUX	11607	839	37	4027	3439	-	1535	6444	9455	48206	65051	1753	22534	81425	23909
210 MACHINES	28447	1751	-	5404	7265	-	11733	15081	4823	8367	91659	1050	5831	10046	4233
230 MACH. DE BUREAU,ETC.	-	-	-	-	-	-	344	196	89	838	-	25343	1664	696	-
250 MATERIEL ELECTRIQUE	2348	247	-	-	-	-	6273	1430	681	3340	1719	3674	67290	29724	2709
270 AUTOS ET PIECES	-	-	2	194	-	-	-	-	-	-	16694	-	-	168894	4529
290 AUTRES MOYENS TRANSP	5715	-	-	-	11146	-	-	-	-	-	-	-	-	-	24969
310 VIANDES ET CONSERVES	-	-	-	-	-	-	-	-	4829	-	-	-	-	-	-
330 LAIT, PROD. LAITIERS	-	-	-	-	-	-	-	-	298	-	-	-	-	-	-
350 AUTRES ALIMENTS	231490	-	-	-	-	-	-	-	9278	-	-	-	-	-	-
370 BOISSONS	-	-	-	-	-	-	-	-	2556	-	-	-	-	-	-
390 TABACS	-	-	-	-	-	-	-	-	-	-	-	-	-	-	-
410 TEXTILE, HABILLEMENT	4012	131	53	32	64	-	702	802	3368	1270	341	47	560	7151	560
430 CUIR, CHAUSSURES	757	1581	17	-	-	-	13	-	1	-	-	-	-	266	22
450 BOIS,MEUBLES EN BOIS	42	90	50	131	937	-	912	3521	2422	3876	1969	618	3539	3163	2716
470 PAPIER, IMPRIMES	5559	-	-	196	454	-	3128	10376	15403	3273	2042	536	3897	3179	957
490 CAOUTCHOUC,PLASTIQUE	-	6	5	40	104	-	686	2267	22262	8224	7535	1647	15288	38561	3428
510 AUTRES INDUSTRIES	2914	1849	213	790	2247	-	34	219	118	114	894	558	1113	1139	1341
530 CONSTRUCTION	8672	407	29	605	408	-	4078	3468	1586	2057	501	188	1654	360	58
550 RECUPER., REPARATION	56427	198	48	646	5533	-	48684	2242	1165	5949	8766	735	8146	4350	2221
570 COMMERCE	2121	1264	68	2305	1940	-	7596	13895	17088	17722	3277	584	3618	3509	1844
590 RESTAUR.,HEBERGEMENT	25418	301	774	2952	2274	-	2574	3863	5484	3846	6836	699	8375	16742	2401
610 TRANSPORT INTERIEUR	1614	176	312	1505	2837	-	12187	13902	19926	15458	637	32	570	1313	231
630 TR. MARITIME, AERIEN	5357	60	65	230	342	-	6065	4473	3736	1843	628	29	531	1406	130
650 SERV. ANNEXES TRANSP.	486	3350	43	402	857	-	769	879	1581	1521	1371	266	998	1834	396
670 COMMUNICATIONS	18809	3100	1416	11802	8345	-	798	1502	2508	2505	10990	1370	9873	14632	11389
690 CREDIT ET ASSURANCES	31902	33	386	8772	8395	-	12794	15675	20584	21527	6865	871	8386	8851	9383
710 SERV. AUX ENTREPRISES	370	32	-	43	486	-	6229	7157	13967	7647	1388	254	1462	464	426
730 LOCATION IMMOBILIERE	40	-	15	358	205	-	1089	2211	2456	1951	168	135	3879	780	293
750 ENSEIGN. RECH. MARCH	2021	42	-	-	-	-	941	240	4089	116	-	-	-	-	-
770 SANTE MARCHAND	-	-	-	-	-	-	-	-	-	-	-	-	-	-	-
790 SERV. MARCHANDS NDA	19	-	-	48	63	-	507	697	1280	1240	592	61	60	683	630
810 ADMINISTR.PUBLIQUE	-	-	-	-	-	-	-	-	-	-	-	-	-	-	-
850 ENS. RECH. NON-MARCH	-	-	-	-	-	-	-	-	-	-	-	-	-	-	-
890 SANTE NON-MARCHAND	-	-	-	-	-	-	-	-	-	-	-	-	-	-	-
930 SERV. NON-MARCH. NDA	-	-	-	-	-	-	-	-	-	-	-	-	-	-	-
990 TOTAL	971635	45664	43866	933178	360191	-	970962	338247	497077	419110	284368	44909	255574	494560	133510

1980 ESPAGNE — MIO PES — ECH.INTERM. — TOUTES ORIGINES — PRIX DEPART-USINE

	B310	B330	B350	B370	B390	B410	B430	B450	B470	B490	B510	B530	B550	B570	B590
010 PROD. AGRICULTURE	418405	115872	460576	73674	20984	23279	7033	34502	12717	12910	395	357	-	242	78682
030 HOUILLE	18	7	52	13	-	273	1	4	17	36	50	11	-	70	1633
050 COKE	23	-	423	42	-	7	11	11	64	5	5	-	-	-	3489
070 PETROLE + PROD.GAZ N	2848	2198	13438	5020	82	5368	579	3074	9645	2200	285	47762	3375	13925	75968
090 ELECTR.,GAZ,VAP.,EAU	4849	2478	11292	4182	234	12006	1522	6630	12095	6562	728	16826	5218	58525	-
110 COMBUST. NUCLEAIRES	-	-	-	-	-	-	-	-	-	-	-	-	-	-	-
130 FERREUX ET NON FERR.	486	519	390	12303	328	143	4	262	632	4920	11679	73450	6547	187	10581
150 MIN. NON METALLIQUES	2986	843	4293	5113	83	213	5865	1739	1403	532	423	402161	2614	11049	11384
170 PRODUITS CHIMIQUES	3968	2971	16708	6281	144	62631	1551	11307	23886	85219	5863	19927	200	5767	11487
190 PRODUITS EN METAUX	2214	1076	18304	2667	376	645	1088	9770	1802	1480	1417	141845	206	569	306
210 MACHINES	304	234	6169	162	29	7241	-	2705	4620	4372	438	20943	26922	1222	561
230 MACH. DE BUREAU,ETC.	254	87	439	-	-	-	62	15	155	377	37	4085	63810	1358	1353
250 MATERIEL ELECTRIQUE	-	-	263	-	-	385	-	324	299	337	1336	83600	5019	1123	-
270 AUTOS ET PIECES	-	-	-	-	-	-	24274	-	-	-	-	-	-	-	-
290 AUTRES MOYENS TRANSP	-	-	-	-	-	68	-	40	754	85	71	1758	-	-	-
310 VIANDES ET CONSERVES	1642	230	10143	15437	-	-	-	59	-	-	-	-	-	-	67688
330 LAIT, PROD. LAITIERS	98	1983	6738	14394	-	49	-	-	-	31	-	-	-	-	18026
350 AUTRES ALIMENTS	3205	6309	168765	-	-	-	-	-	-	-	-	-	-	-	85613
370 BOISSONS	57	87	930	241	-	-	-	-	-	-	-	-	-	-	180549
390 TABACS	-	-	-	-	-	-	3879	-	-	-	-	-	-	-	-
410 TEXTILE, HABILLEMENT	593	426	1860	3718	1154	232947	37913	5345	2012	9195	2290	7770	4432	2277	14696
430 CUIR, CHAUSSURES	-	-	87	-	18	8245	2052	339	158	787	205	-	564	684	245
450 BOIS,MEUBLES EN BOIS	949	5136	2976	5006	258	507	2661	102572	1072	941	1949	58482	470	2817	5007
470 PAPIER, IMPRIMES	4662	8847	15856	4174	6371	8290	13367	2655	176417	4333	2188	3558	765	37381	122
490 CAOUTCHOUC,PLASTIQUE	2940	-	10039	-	215	7122	267	3773	2119	4816	4074	25635	15966	13666	572
510 AUTRES INDUSTRIES	-	348	-	1204	-	1244	843	-	-	38	21267	1087	302	842	-
530 CONSTRUCTION	492	115	2787	6061	285	2468	259	1506	1154	915	393	4142	1269	36705	45646
550 RECUPER., REPARATION	252	1792	6508	5970	933	2451	7745	2879	14806	172	354	49986	13548	11805	1422
570 COMMERCE	37902	598	37015	2009	874	14957	1857	6549	6527	5863	2166	24959	727	23581	65977
590 RESTAUR.,HEBERGEMENT	1102	7110	4301	8924	302	6038	4756	4422	2612	2990	554	57682	4241	16959	21985
610 TRANSPORT INTERIEUR	17157	587	36010	666	1200	14698	313	8542	12822	7244	1488	6283	345	5052	426
630 TR. MARITIME, AERIEN	391	803	1977	753	72	1282	368	764	1356	1012	128	1859	1449	2828	893
650 SERV.ANNEXES TRANSP.	544	213	2223	672	89	1451	359	708	1651	1068	129	4319	2997	3360	27761
670 COMMUNICATIONS	758	1436	1731	4657	103	1748	5227	1254	1184	936	250	39470	1498	31471	17200
690 CREDIT ET ASSURANCES	4784	1586	12308	4547	158	18266	1826	9230	11743	15193	2132	56732	1449	50988	9066
710 SERV.AUX ENTREPRISES	2914	304	5407	1018	459	8897	426	3970	4342	7342	1411	4086	52	105537	4899
730 LOCATION IMMOBILIERE	272	37	1637	54	66	1192	10	667	1158	978	366	525	-	63944	-
750 ENSEIGN. RECH. MARCH	49	-	210	-	12	46	-	2	122	1865	-	277	600	52	-
770 SANTE MARCHAND	-	-	-	-	-	-	-	-	-	-	-	-	-	-	-
790 SERV. MARCHANDS NDA	410	212	737	556	49	526	207	459	505	770	141	-	-	5064	2446
810 ADMINISTR.PUBLIQUE	-	-	-	-	-	-	-	-	-	-	-	-	-	-	-
850 ENS. RECH. NON-MARCH	-	-	-	-	-	-	-	-	-	-	-	-	-	-	-
890 SANTE NON-MARCHAND	-	-	-	-	-	-	-	-	-	-	-	-	-	-	-
930 SERV. NON-MARCH. NDA	-	-	-	-	-	-	-	-	-	-	-	-	-	-	-
990 TOTAL	517528	165855	862505	189533	34878	444683	126315	226078	309849	185524	64207	1159662	176599	509050	775683

Group headings across the table: MIO PES — ECH.INTERM. — TOUTES ORIGINES — PRIX DEPART-USINE

	B610	B630	B650	B670	B690	B710	B730	B750	B770	B790	B810	B850	B890	B930	B990
010 PROD. AGRICULTURE	-	60	-	-	-	326	-	20	1203	1478	5582	41	1730	1924	1600601
030 HOUILLE	138	13	-	23	-	404	-	24	182	-	408	53	111	-	131890
050 COKE	-	-	-	-	-	-	-	-	-	-	-	-	-	-	43990
070 PETROLE + PROD.GAZ N	104309	63881	1821	552	1773	7238	1398	1393	1295	5816	13756	2374	2948	1487	1573323
090 ELECTR.,GAZ,VAP.,EAU	10850	555	2172	1655	3824	3186	2751	1544	2499	5033	9492	2364	4654	632	540132
110 COMBUST. NUCLEAIRES	-	-	-	-	-	-	-	-	-	-	-	-	-	-	-
130 FERREUX ET NON FERR.	369	-	601	30	-	51	-	28	395	7775	336	26	489	-	1222341
150 MIN. NON METALLIQUES	251	737	1497	71	-	1386	-	-	-	-	1443	35	-	622	601045
170 PRODUITS CHIMIQUES	748	340	490	214	-	249	-	646	9630	-	14710	711	23695	17	764933
190 PRODUITS EN METAUX	1357	952	2180	121	-	3884	-	107	376	177	26883	423	701	-	522033
210 MACHINES	397	95	95	-	-	-	-	-	24	-	17875	12	25	-	273574
230 MACH. DE BUREAU,ETC.	196	1052	503	494	3273	542	867	60	7188	1012	19398	397	7499	-	83734
250 MATERIEL ELECTRIQUE	3053	127	1638	1216	-	949	-	110	875	1289	1720	10	1784	19	277133
270 AUTOS ET PIECES	13802	74	236	47	-	418	-	-	-	-	6144	-	-	-	254633
290 AUTRES MOYENS TRANSP	23126	25453	889	-	-	706	-	-	1161	-	37930	-	2058	807	125650
310 VIANDES ET CONSERVES	-	73	-	-	-	-	-	-	461	-	3997	-	746	549	117081
330 LAIT, PROD. LAITIERS	-	31	-	-	-	-	-	-	1347	-	865	-	1986	657	29889
350 AUTRES ALIMENTS	-	116	-	-	-	-	-	5	480	-	6352	95	698	150	531458
370 BOISSONS	-	459	-	-	-	-	-	-	-	-	593	-	-	-	200897
390 TABACS	-	-	-	-	-	-	-	-	-	-	-	-	-	-	1154
410 TEXTILE, HABILLEMENT	839	515	385	377	-	370	-	92	862	652	812	61	3424	855	315979
430 CUIR, CHAUSSURES	84	178	118	88	-	72	-	14	40	157	568	-	60	233	51054
450 BOIS,MEUBLES EN BOIS	122	101	1209	-	-	-	-	30	40	667	629	158	59	55	207350
470 PAPIER, IMPRIMES	1638	672	2611	2297	17080	24777	799	2238	433	4514	16971	3709	568	3252	405886
490 CAOUTCHOUC,PLASTIQUE	19512	448	102	164	2020	1036	-	18	749	819	1656	88	1658	27	249095
510 AUTRES INDUSTRIES	152	56	260	533	-	224	444	278	43	788	2856	269	56	1	33870
530 CONSTRUCTION	15288	451	7219	333	21537	6503	330022	3171	1582	3517	48736	3630	2570	92	565115
550 RECUPER., REPARATION	21377	511	968	551	2402	5767	199	227	204	2178	114	1105	659	70	156255
570 COMMERCE	7957	2905	1007	42	10098	2288	20	457	2304	2153	9921	675	5043	1079	462973
590 RESTAUR.,HEBERGEMENT	3666	5016	502	5299	6511	4490	77	458	22	2285	11063	2049	362	12	144746
610 TRANSPORT INTERIEUR	6537	3158	6678	1202	5920	1798	-	349	1075	1530	22534	3257	1624	455	399001
630 TR. MARITIME, AERIEN	1583	1981	1755	45	1190	990	9	70	40	1192	7351	366	57	14	66429
650 SERV.ANNEXES TRANSP.	66416	42718	1161	1429	-	346	-	16	454	454	6169	-	-	14	148072
670 COMMUNICATIONS	3249	1728	3436	1331	37473	6936	2662	1190	1094	2480	9588	1957	725	547	162728
690 CREDIT ET ASSURANCES	18325	5700	6348	4089	561493	14138	25390	774	1395	2551	192	600	157	209	996948
710 SERV.AUX ENTREPRISES	4723	17712	3830	599	87050	5387	6000	3487	2148	5655	58669	2055	1621	925	540796
730 LOCATION IMMOBILIERE	1416	1040	1940	56	23465	8424	-	1805	3009	11350	5093	-	65	430	153731
750 ENSEIGN. RECH. MARCH	59	15	89	-	-	592	-	212	18	-	1623	-	-	-	16939
770 SANTE MARCHAND	-	-	-	-	-	-	-	341	-	-	184	-	-	-	2546
790 SERV. MARCHANDS NDA	4416	1594	278	1381	4001	35704	-	892	1994	3140	11352	5049	7180	-	95862
810 ADMINISTR. PUBLIQUE	-	-	-	-	-	-	-	-	-	-	-	-	-	-	-
850 ENS. RECH. NON-MARCH	-	-	-	-	-	-	-	-	-	-	-	-	-	-	-
890 SANTE NON-MARCHAND	-	-	-	-	-	-	-	-	-	-	-	-	-	-	-
930 SERV. NON-MARCH. NDA	-	-	-	-	-	-	-	-	-	-	-	-	-	-	-
990 TOTAL	335955	180517	52018	24239	789110	139181	370658	20056	44188	68662	383567	31569	75212	15134	14070866

1980 ESPAGNE

Code / Désignation	MIO PES F01	F02	F03	F09	EMPL.FINALS F19	F29	F41	F42	TOUTES ORIGINES F43	PRIX DEPART-USINE F49	F89	F99
010 PROD. AGRICULTURE	437478	–	–	437478	17421	60339	–	–	–	106536	621774	2222375
030 HOUILLE	8320	–	–	8320	–	3533	–	–	–	106	11959	143049
050 COKE	462	–	–	462	–	329	–	–	–	25	816	44806
070 PETROLE + PROD.GAZ N	431723	–	–	431723	16364	-2542	–	–	–	101672	547217	2120540
090 ELECTR.,GAZ,VAP.,EAU	179854	–	–	179854	–	-4586	–	–	–	2100	177368	717500
110 COMBUST. NUCLEAIRES	–	–	–	–	–	–	–	–	–	–	–	–
130 FERREUX ET NON FERR.	17894	–	–	17894	14684	5859	–	–	–	186439	192298	1414639
150 MIN. NON METALLIQUES	219504	–	–	219504	–	10391	–	–	–	73061	116030	717075
170 PRODUITS CHIMIQUES	95561	–	–	95561	138870	4125	–	–	–	117598	341227	1106160
190 PRODUITS EN METAUX	4831	–	–	4831	278488	17800	–	–	–	86456	338567	860720
210 MACHINES	19764	–	–	19764	54514	-2110	–	–	–	102005	383214	656788
230 MACH. DE BUREAU,ETC.	165658	–	–	165658	179239	988	–	–	–	18863	94129	177863
250 MATERIEL ELECTRIQUE	254556	–	–	254556	212694	5286	–	–	–	60832	411015	688148
270 AUTOS ET PIECES	17381	–	–	17381	106050	3611	–	–	–	152004	622865	877498
290 AUTRES MOYENS TRANSP	544818	–	–	544818	–	3703	–	–	–	36788	163922	289572
310 VIANDES ET CONSERVES	231649	–	–	231649	–	662	–	–	–	3906	549386	666467
330 LAIT, PROD. LAITIERS	608879	–	–	608879	–	2594	–	–	–	501	234744	264633
350 AUTRES ALIMENTS	114683	–	–	114683	17564	759	–	–	–	112742	722380	1253838
370 BOISSONS	110843	–	–	110843	1510	16927	–	–	–	34057	165667	366564
390 TABACS	431220	–	–	431220	85180	3620	–	–	–	2056	116519	117673
410 TEXTILE, HABILLEMENT	110911	–	–	110911	–	19823	–	–	–	68331	536938	852917
430 CUIR, CHAUSSURES	107891	–	–	107891	–	6924	–	–	–	62601	181946	233000
450 BOIS,MEUBLES EN BOIS	89200	–	–	89200	–	10486	–	–	–	27900	231457	438807
470 PAPIER, IMPRIMES	25615	–	–	25615	4939	5645	–	–	–	56827	151672	557558
490 CAOUTCHOUC.PLASTIQUE	110949	–	–	110949	3909	4955	–	–	–	42059	77568	326663
510 AUTRES INDUSTRIES	51305	–	–	51305	–	766	–	–	–	16606	132230	166100
530 CONSTRUCTION	300659	–	–	300659	1691666	–	–	–	–	–	1942971	2508086
550 RECUPER., REPARATION	1804493	–	–	1804493	-6444	–	–	–	–	567	294782	451037
570 COMMERCE	1250460	–	–	1250460	78251	–	–	–	–	76797	1959541	2422514
590 RESTAUR.,HEBERGEMENT	290809	–	–	290809	–	–	–	–	–	–	1250460	1395206
610 TRANSPORT INTERIEUR	60758	–	–	60758	17444	–	–	–	–	18863	327116	726117
630 TR. MARITIME, AERIEN	31799	–	–	31799	342	–	–	–	–	190995	252095	318524
650 SERV.ANNEXES TRANSP.	80051	–	–	80051	–	–	–	–	–	48659	80458	228530
670 COMMUNICATIONS	132986	–	–	132986	–	–	–	–	–	2895	90946	253674
690 CREDIT ET ASSURANCES	31156	–	–	31156	255521	–	–	–	–	28861	161847	1158795
710 SERV.AUX ENTREPRISES	1334739	–	–	1334739	–	–	–	–	–	37713	324390	865186
730 LOCATION IMMOBILIERE	123068	–	–	123068	–	–	–	–	–	–	1334739	1488470
750 ENSEIGN. RECH. MARCH	200025	–	–	200025	–	–	–	–	–	–	123068	140007
770 SANTE MARCHAND	304981	–	–	304981	–	–	–	–	–	–	200025	202571
790 SERV. MARCHANDS NDA	–	1231396	–	1231396	–	–	–	–	–	23811	328792	424654
810 ADMINISTR.PUBLIQUE	–	1231396	–	1231396	–	–	–	–	–	–	1231396	1231396
850 ENS. RECH. NON-MARCH	9662	323825	–	333487	–	–	–	–	–	–	333487	333487
890 SANTE NON-MARCHAND	–	374095	–	374095	–	–	–	–	–	–	374095	374095
930 SERV. NON-MARCH. NDA	139672	–	–	139672	–	–	–	–	–	–	139672	139672
990 TOTAL	10494267	1929316	–	12423563	3368206	179887	–	–	–	1901232	17072908	31943774

239

1980 ESPAGNE

	MIO PES				ENTREES PRIMAIRES					PRIX DEPART-USINE					
	B010	B030	B050	B070	B090	B110	B130	B150	B170	B190	B210	B230	B250	B270	B290
010 SALAIRES BRUTS	272371	47934	2451	16395	89393	-	121039	145629	128859	192786	105094	15666	129126	141693	80147
020 COTISATIONS SOCIALES	30346	18707	828	5082	26992	-	38433	42881	38282	54797	29441	4603	38464	43613	24925
030 EXCEDENT NET	799053	23828	4266	69523	169997	-	139828	132541	178513	126252	62403	6972	83250	60154	19983
070 VAL.AJOUTEE NETTE CF	1101770	90469	7545	91000	286382	-	299300	321051	345654	373835	196938	27241	250840	245460	125055
080 CONS. CAPITAL FIXE						-									
090 VAL.AJOUTEE BRUTE CF	1101770	90469	7545	91000	286382	-	299300	321051	345654	373835	196938	27241	250840	245460	125055
110 IMPOTS (PRODUCTION)	2315	1598	103	203244	25046	-	10792	12515	24992	15974	6763	1933	22270	59983	4377
120 SUBVENTIONS	30653	23529	1	3982	2417	-	38787	7514	24532	13249	14293	1287	9208	25023	3581
170 IMPOTS NETS	-28338	-21931	102	199262	22629	-	-27995	5001	460	2725	-7530	646	13062	34960	796
180 VAL.AJOUTEE NETTE PM	1073432	68538	7647	290262	309011	-	271305	326052	346114	376560	189408	27887	263902	280420	125851
190 VAL.AJOUTEE BRUTE PM	1073432	68538	7647	290262	309011	-	271305	326052	346114	376560	189408	27887	263902	280420	125851
270 TVA NON-DED. ECH.INT						-									
290 PRODUCTION EFFECTIVE	2045067	114202	51513	1223640	669202	-	1242267	664299	843191	795670	473776	72796	519476	774980	259361
310 PRODUITS FATALS	-108557	-3344	-10906	-10612	16302	-	-12386	-1983	10484	-9418	-7328	-	9811	15	-14118
330 VENTES RESIDUELLES	173	268	-	-	11168	-	-	-	1500	-	-	-	-	-	-
390 TOTAL DES TRANSFERTS	-108384	-3076	-10906	-10612	27470	-	-12386	-1983	11984	-9418	-7328	-	9811	15	-14118
410 SUBVENTIONS (EXPORT)						-									
490 PRODUCTION DISTRIB.	1936683	111126	40607	1212828	696672	-	1229881	662316	855175	786252	466448	72796	529287	774995	245243
510 IMPORTATIONS CAF CE						-									
520 IMPORTATIONS CAF PT						-									
590 TOTAL IMPORT. CAF	259741	31617	3823	907308	20828	-	163806	47697	215845	62912	155777	90525	123184	73163	40010
610 IMPOTS (IMPORT.CE)						-									
620 IMPOTS (IMPORT.PT)						-									
690 TOTAL IMPOTS(IMPORT)	25951	1106	376	404		-	20952	7062	35140	11556	34563	14542	35677	29340	4319
710 IMPORTATIONS PDD CE						-									
720 IMPORTATIONS PDD PT						-									
790 TOTAL IMPORT. PDD	285692	32723	4199	907712	20828	-	184758	54759	250985	74468	190340	105067	158861	102503	44329
870 T.V.A. (GREVANT)						-									
980 TOTAL RESSOURCES PDU	2222375	143849	44806	2120540	717500	-	1414639	717075	1106160	860720	656788	177863	688148	877498	289572

240

1980 ESPAGNE

MIO PES | ENTREES PRIMAIRES | PRIX DEPART-USINE

	B310	B330	B350	B370	B390	B410	B430	B450	B470	B490	B510	B530	B550	B570	B590
010 SALAIRES BRUTS	42029	21060	108641	51969	9619	166009	48445	95367	91813	71008	18642	681098	90556	530237	157571
020 COTISATIONS SOCIALES	12759	6238	31920	14785	2721	49140	14141	26178	27469	22393	5493	208064	27469	155678	47271
030 EXCEDENT NET	63575	32306	139346	66398	11869	143688	22835	57839	78914	55559	14457	351613	138127	1193840	397408
070 VAL.AJOUTEE NETTE CF	118363	59604	279907	133152	24209	358837	85421	179384	198117	148960	38592	1240775	256152	1879755	602250
080 CONS. CAPITAL FIXE	-	-	-	-	-	-	-	-	-	-	-	-	-	-	-
090 VAL.AJOUTEE BRUTE CF	118363	59604	279907	133152	24209	358837	85421	179384	198117	148960	38592	1240775	256152	1879755	602250
110 IMPOTS (PRODUCTION)	4032	2712	17293	38109	43252	14099	4124	8980	9142	6893	3427	43954	4168	40652	16886
120 SUBVENTIONS	564	124	11400	7373	9	13405	6641	3916	14005	7180	1680	1026	-	26443	613
170 IMPOTS NETS	3468	2588	5893	30736	43243	694	-2517	5064	-4863	-287	1747	42928	4168	14209	16273
180 VAL.AJOUTEE NETTE PM	121831	62192	285800	163888	67452	359531	82904	184448	193254	148673	40339	1283703	260320	1893964	618523
190 VAL.AJOUTEE BRUTE PM	121831	62192	285800	163888	67452	359531	82904	184448	193254	148673	40339	1283703	260320	1893964	618523
270 TVA NON-DED. ECH.INT	-	-	-	-	-	-	-	-	-	-	-	-	-	-	-
290 PRODUCTION EFFECTIVE	639359	228047	1148305	353421	102330	804214	209219	410526	503103	334197	104546	2443365	436919	2403014	1394206
310 PRODUITS FATALS	2920	24572	47697	-	-	231	13026	-3210	-2111	-31037	14033	64721	14118	-	1000
330 VENTES RESIDUELLES	-	-	-	-	-	-	-	-	6429	-	-	-	-	-	-
390 TOTAL DES TRANSFERTS	2920	24572	47697	353421	102330	231	13026	-3210	4318	-31037	14033	64721	14118	-	1000
410 SUBVENTIONS (EXPORT)	-	-	-	-	-	-	-	-	-	-	-	-	-	-	-
490 PRODUCTION DISTRIB.	642279	252619	1196002	353421	102330	804445	222245	407316	507421	303160	118579	2508086	451037	2403014	1395206
510 IMPORTATIONS CAF CE	-	-	-	-	-	-	-	-	-	-	-	-	-	-	-
520 IMPORTATIONS CAF PT	-	-	-	-	-	-	-	-	-	-	-	-	-	-	-
590 TOTAL IMPORT. CAF	23368	10585	51150	9253	8019	39120	8861	28325	43687	18811	43289			19500	
610 IMPOTS (IMPORT.CE)	-	-	-	-	-	-	-	-	-	-	-	-	-	-	-
620 IMPOTS (IMPORT.PT)	820	1429	6686	3890	7324	9352	1894	3166	6450	4692	4232				
690 TOTAL IMPOTS(IMPORT)	820	1429	6686	3890	7324	9352	1894	3166	6450	4692	4232				
710 IMPORTATIONS PDD CE	-	-	-	-	-	-	-	-	-	-	-	-	-	-	-
720 IMPORTATIONS PDD PT	-	-	-	-	-	-	-	-	-	-	-	-	-	-	-
790 TOTAL IMPORT. PDD	24188	12014	57836	13143	15343	48472	10755	31491	50137	23503	47521			19500	
870 T.V.A. (GREVANT)	-	-	-	-	-	-	-	-	-	-	-	-	-	-	-
980 TOTAL RESSOURCES PDU	666467	264633	1253838	366564	117673	852917	233000	438807	557558	326663	166100	2508086	451037	2422514	1395206

1980 ESPAGNE   MIO PES   ENTREES PRIMAIRES   PRIX DEPART-USINE

	B610	B630	B650	B670	B690	B710	B730	B750	B770	B790	B810	B850	B890	B930	B990
010 SALAIRES BRUTS	172638	67385	48808	97762	328909	106637	9196	113547	47446	111120	681965	213740	236186	107506	6015492
020 COTISATIONS SOCIALES	58274	19005	14792	22902	117106	31546	2759	35200	12782	33335	224744	70778	60784	15427	1768468
030 EXCEDENT NET	257851	41426	84251	90285	-111290	336148	1085261	29885	89478	104370	50317	17400	9413	1605	6730737
070 VAL.AJOUTEE NETTE CF	488763	127816	147851	210949	334725	474331	1097216	178632	149706	248825	957026	301918	306383	124538	14514697
080 CONS. CAPITAL FIXE	-	-	-	-	-	-	-	-	-	-	-	-	-	-	-
090 VAL.AJOUTEE BRUTE CF	488763	127816	147851	210949	334725	474331	1097216	178632	149706	248825	957026	301918	306383	124538	14514697
110 IMPOTS (PRODUCTION)	10834	4074	438	33710	28877	137235	14858	100	2377	49997	-	-	-	-	932128
120 SUBVENTIONS	110886	10507	9653	16653	829	90	-	59756	-	8438	-	-	-	-	509247
170 IMPOTS NETS	-100052	-6433	-9215	17057	28048	137145	14858	-59656	2377	41559	-	-	-	-	422881
180 VAL.AJOUTEE NETTE PM	388711	121383	138636	228006	362773	611476	1112074	118976	152083	290384	957026	301918	306383	124538	14937578
190 VAL.AJOUTEE BRUTE PM	388711	121383	138636	228006	362773	611476	1112074	118976	152083	290384	957026	301918	306383	124538	14937578
270 TVA NON-DED. ECH.INT	-	-	-	-	-	-	-	-	-	-	-	-	-	-	-
290 PRODUCTION EFFECTIVE	724666	301900	190654	252245	1151883	750657	1482732	139032	196271	359046	1340593	333487	381595	139672	29008444
310 PRODUITS FATALS	-	-	-	-	-4966	-	4966	-	-	-	-	-	-	-	-
330 VENTES RESIDUELLES	-	-	-	-	10	27718	772	975	6300	57464	-109197	-	-7500	-	-
390 TOTAL DES TRANSFERTS	-	-	-	-	-4956	27718	5738	975	6300	57464	-109197	-	-7500	-	-
410 SUBVENTIONS (EXPORT)	-	-	-	-	-	-	-	-	-	-	-	-	-	-	-
490 PRODUCTION DISTRIB.	724666	301900	190654	252245	1146927	778375	1488470	140007	202571	416510	1231396	333487	374095	139672	29008444
510 IMPORTATIONS CAF CE	1451	16624	37876	1429	11868	86196	-	-	-	8144	-	-	-	-	2663792
520 IMPORTATIONS CAF PT	-	-	-	-	-	-	-	-	-	-	-	-	-	-	-
590 TOTAL IMPORT. CAF	1451	16624	37876	1429	11868	86196	-	-	-	8144	-	-	-	-	2663792
610 IMPOTS (IMPORT.CE)	-	-	-	-	-	-	-	-	-	-	-	-	-	-	-
620 IMPOTS (IMPORT.PT)	-	-	-	-	-	615	-	-	-	-	-	-	-	-	271538
690 TOTAL IMPOTS(IMPORT)	-	-	-	-	-	615	-	-	-	-	-	-	-	-	271538
710 IMPORTATIONS PDD CE	-	-	-	-	-	-	-	-	-	-	-	-	-	-	-
720 IMPORTATIONS PDD PT	-	-	-	-	-	-	-	-	-	-	-	-	-	-	-
790 TOTAL IMPORT. PDD	1451	16624	37876	1429	11868	86811	-	-	-	8144	-	-	-	-	2935330
870 T.V.A. (GREVANT)	-	-	-	-	-	-	-	-	-	-	-	-	-	-	-
980 TOTAL RESSOURCES PDU	726117	318524	228530	253674	1158795	865186	1488470	140007	202571	424654	1231396	333487	374095	139672	31943774

1980 ESPAGNE MIO PES

Column groups: **ECH.INTERM.** (B070, B090, B110) — **ORIGINE INTERIEURE** (B130, B150) — **PRIX DEPART-USINE** (B170, B190, B210, B230, B250, B270, B290)

	B010	B030	B050	B070	B090	B110	B130	B150	B170	B190	B210	B230	B250	B270	B290
010 PROD. AGRICULTURE	318176	7554	31771	-	3	-	10	120	5302	19	5	-	33	1	8
030 HOUILLE	-	-	-	-	57135	-	2121	754	910	276	53	-	33	139	126
050 COKE	-	-	-	-	176	-	35805	1287	758	1092	41	-	44	11	-
070 PETROLE + PROD.GAZ N	61993	822	1169	69543	129451	-	17847	60610	38361	4683	1606	41	1073	2228	1382
090 ELECTR.,GAZ,VAP.,EAU	31710	3657	2789	11130	47481	-	62951	29585	30292	12019	3053	257	4784	6239	3031
110 COMBUST. NUCLEAIRES	-	-	-	-	-	-	-	-	-	-	-	-	-	-	-
130 FERREUX ET NON FERR.	533	243	-	1830	409	-	596636	9825	5746	181625	32903	1890	47354	55313	19608
150 MIN. NON METALLIQUES	1639	4	15	799	278	-	11775	87285	11080	3842	1445	581	2783	3673	234
170 PRODUITS CHIMIQUES	90301	1103	22	729	1733	-	27610	19311	81886	6927	2606	716	8857	7028	3635
190 PRODUITS EN METAUX	11198	817	37	3630	3236	-	1347	5871	8473	43299	63006	1584	21576	79052	22046
210 MACHINES	28440	1723	-	5318	7161	-	11545	14842	4746	8234	25133	1034	5738	9086	4166
230 MACH. DE BUREAU,ETC.	-	-	-	-	-	-	344	196	89	764	1662	77	1608	653	2010
250 MATERIEL ELECTRIQUE	1678	247	2	194	-	-	4637	1430	681	1985	9835	1306	24066	22816	3223
270 AUTOS ET PIECES	-	-	-	-	8427	-	-	-	-	-	-	-	-	-	-
290 AUTRES MOYENS TRANSP	5715	-	-	-	-	-	-	-	-	-	-	-	-	136992	8696
310 VIANDES ET CONSERVES	-	-	-	-	-	-	-	-	1726	-	-	-	-	-	-
330 LAIT, PROD. LAITIERS	-	-	-	-	-	-	-	-	220	-	-	-	-	-	-
350 AUTRES ALIMENTS	230993	-	-	-	-	-	-	-	6833	-	-	-	-	-	-
370 BOISSONS	-	-	-	-	-	-	-	-	2426	-	-	-	-	-	-
390 TABACS	-	-	-	-	-	-	-	-	-	-	-	-	-	-	-
410 TEXTILE, HABILLEMENT	3583	126	51	32	59	-	670	734	3147	1142	309	43	526	6829	521
430 CUIR, CHAUSSURES	757	638	17	-	-	-	13	-	1	-	-	-	-	261	21
450 BOIS,MEUBLES EN BOIS	41	84	47	120	880	-	903	3506	2421	3488	1646	607	3398	2975	2291
470 PAPIER, IMPRIMES	5071	-	774	184	430	-	3030	9567	14271	3127	1989	515	3544	3033	923
490 CAOUTCHOUC,PLASTIQUE	-	6	5	36	94	-	637	2198	21455	7777	7057	1511	14206	35571	3229
510 AUTRES INDUSTRIES	2914	1849	213	790	2247	-	30	200	109	103	894	558	1113	1139	1341
530 CONSTRUCTION	8672	68	29	605	408	-	4078	3468	1586	2057	501	188	1654	360	58
550 RECUPER., REPARATION	56427	407	48	646	5533	-	48684	2242	1165	5949	8766	735	8146	4350	2221
570 COMMERCE	2121	198	68	2305	1940	-	7596	13895	17088	17722	3277	584	3618	3509	1844
590 RESTAUR.,HEBERGEMENT	25418	1264	774	2952	2274	-	2574	3863	5484	3846	6836	699	8375	16742	2401
610 TRANSPORT INTERIEUR	1593	266	285	1476	2794	-	12187	13902	19926	15458	558	28	503	1136	206
630 TR. MARITIME, AERIEN	5010	176	65	230	342	-	5742	4220	3297	1652	628	29	531	1406	130
650 SERV.ANNEXES TRANSP.	486	60	43	402	857	-	769	879	1581	1521	1371	266	998	1834	396
670 COMMUNICATIONS	18809	3350	1416	11802	8345	-	798	1502	2508	2505	10990	1370	9873	14632	11389
690 CREDIT ET ASSURANCES	28085	2728	340	7723	7404	-	12794	15675	20584	21527	6045	767	7384	7794	8261
710 SERV.AUX ENTREPRISES	370	33	-	43	486	-	5481	6299	12292	6731	1388	254	1462	464	426
730 LOCATION IMMOBILIERE	40	32	15	358	205	-	1089	2211	2456	1951	168	135	3879	780	293
750 ENSEIGN. RECH. MARCH	2021	-	-	-	-	-	941	240	4089	116	-	-	-	-	-
770 SANTE MARCHAND	19	42	-	48	63	-	507	697	1280	1240	592	61	60	683	630
790 SERV. MARCHANDS NDA	-	-	-	-	-	-	-	-	-	-	-	-	-	-	-
810 ADMINISTR.PUBLIQUE	-	-	-	-	-	-	-	-	-	-	-	-	-	-	-
850 ENS. RECH. NON-MARCH	-	-	-	-	-	-	-	-	-	-	-	-	-	-	-
890 SANTE NON-MARCHAND	-	-	-	-	-	-	-	-	-	-	-	-	-	-	-
930 SERV. NON-MARCH. NDA	-	-	-	-	-	-	-	-	-	-	-	-	-	-	-
990 TOTAL	943813	27497	39222	122925	289851	-	801151	316414	334269	362677	194363	15636	187219	427529	104748

243

MIO PES

ECH.INTERM. — ORIGINE INTERIEURE — PRIX DEPART-USINE

	B310	B330	B350	B370	B390	B410	B430	B450	B470	B490	B510	B530	B550	B570	B590
010 PROD. AGRICULTURE	417095	115872	257490	71604	11531	9113	1507	20304	11334	3316	373	357	-	241	76818
030 HOUILLE	18	7	52	13	-	273	1	1	17	36	50	11	-	70	1633
050 COKE	23	-	423	42	-	7	1	11	64	5	5	-	-	-	3433
070 PETROLE + PROD.GAZ N	2795	2150	13178	4928	80	5273	568	3011	9464	2159	279	46876	3312	13682	75968
090 ELECTR.,GAZ,VAP.,EAU	4849	2478	11292	4182	234	12006	1522	6630	12095	6562	728	16826	5218	50525	-
110 COMBUST. NUCLEAIRES	-	-	-	-	-	-	-	-	-	-	-	-	-	-	-
130 FERREUX ET NON FERR.	-	494	377	10833	311	70	-	181	509	3893	9191	67423	5818	187	9536
150 MIN. NON METALLIQUES	477	718	3761	2885	78	211	4	1658	1107	436	357	384951	11058	10366	19527
170 PRODUITS CHIMIQUES	2402	2088	14080	5634	127	46939	4319	10256	17571	53247	4013	18548	2201	5006	10591
190 PRODUITS EN METAUX	3600	833	15555	2624	370	561	676	6985	1222	1304	1099	128319	197	560	301
210 MACHINES	2179	1389	6073	162	29	7125	1071	2662	4546	4294	431	20608	59	1222	561
230 MACH. DE BUREAU,ETC.	304	234	439	-	-	-	-	15	155	377	37	2802	-	1358	1353
250 MATERIEL ELECTRIQUE	254	87	263	-	-	385	62	324	299	337	668	49497	17824	966	-
270 AUTOS ET PIECES	-	-	-	-	-	-	-	-	-	-	-	-	55330	-	-
290 AUTRES MOYENS TRANSP	-	-	-	-	-	-	-	-	-	-	-	-	3694	-	-
310 VIANDES ET CONSERVES	-	201	9548	-	-	68	14615	40	-	85	71	76	-	-	65332
330 LAIT, PROD. LAITIERS	96	-	4724	15	-	-	-	56	703	-	-	-	-	-	17485
350 AUTRES ALIMENTS	3052	6251	162733	15283	-	49	-	-	-	31	-	1758	-	-	78323
370 BOISSONS	57	-	858	11926	-	-	-	-	-	-	-	-	-	-	172933
390 TABACS	-	-	-	-	-	-	-	-	-	-	-	-	-	-	-
410 TEXTILE, HABILLEMENT	559	83	1768	231	18	214687	3577	5016	1785	8254	1966	7239	4194	2097	13814
430 CUIR, CHAUSSURES	-	-	-	-	-	7944	33070	324	154	764	175	-	533	641	233
450 BOIS,MEUBLES EN BOIS	949	426	2976	3718	258	504	1717	81611	1070	640	1751	55406	470	2817	-
470 PAPIER, IMPRIMES	4375	4762	14758	4652	5877	7811	2522	2532	145543	4132	2048	3381	734	35711	4816
490 CAOUTCHOUC,PLASTIQUE	2853	8584	9736	4048	209	6502	9777	3340	1989	1444	3664	24405	14758	12954	118
510 AUTRES INDUSTRIES	-	-	-	-	-	866	241	1506	34	34	56	976	269	761	315
530 CONSTRUCTION	492	348	2787	1204	285	2468	843	2879	1154	915	393	-	1269	36705	45646
550 RECUPER., REPARATION	252	115	6508	6061	933	2451	259	6549	14806	172	354	4142	-	11805	1422
570 COMMERCE	37902	1792	37015	5970	874	14957	7745	4422	6527	5863	2166	49986	13548	4081	65977
590 RESTAUR.,HEBERGEMENT	1102	598	4301	2009	302	6038	1857	8542	2612	2990	554	24959	727	16959	21985
610 TRANSPORT INTERIEUR	17157	7110	36010	8924	1200	14698	4756	674	12822	7244	1488	57682	4241	5052	388
630 TR. MARITIME, AERIEN	323	487	1685	571	61	1098	266	708	1147	877	112	5670	345	2331	893
650 SERV.ANNEXES TRANSP.	544	803	2223	753	89	1451	368	1254	1651	1068	129	1859	-	3360	27761
670 COMMUNICATIONS	758	213	1731	672	103	1748	359	-	1184	936	250	4319	1449	31471	17200
690 CREDIT ET ASSURANCES	4784	1436	12308	4657	158	18266	5227	9230	11743	15193	2132	39470	2997	50988	7976
710 SERV.AUX ENTREPRISES	2568	1398	4757	4001	404	7827	1606	3494	3821	6461	1242	48492	1318	92895	4899
730 LOCATION IMMOBILIERE	272	304	1637	1018	66	1192	426	667	1158	978	366	4086	1449	63944	-
750 ENSEIGN. RECH. MARCH	49	37	210	54	12	46	10	2	122	1865	-	525	-	52	-
770 SANTE MARCHAND	-	-	-	-	-	-	-	-	-	-	-	-	-	-	-
790 SERV. MARCHANDS NDA	410	212	737	556	49	526	207	459	505	770	141	277	600	5064	2446
810 ADMINISTR.PUBLIQUE	-	-	-	-	-	-	-	-	-	-	-	-	-	-	-
850 ENS. RECH. NON-MARCH	-	-	-	-	-	-	-	-	-	-	-	-	-	-	-
890 SANTE NON-MARCHAND	-	-	-	-	-	-	-	-	-	-	-	-	-	-	-
930 SERV. NON-MARCH. NDA	-	-	-	-	-	-	-	-	-	-	-	-	-	-	-
990 TOTAL	512550	161510	641993	179230	23658	393160	99179	185346	268879	136682	36284	1070926	153612	471871	749683

1980 ESPAGNE — MIO PES

ECH.INTERM. · ORIGINE INTERIEURE · PRIX DEPART-USINE

Code	Secteur	B610	B630	B650	B670	B690	B710	B730	B750	B770	B790	B810	B850	B890	B930	B990
010	PROD. AGRICULTURE	-	58	-	-	-	325	-	20	1161	1473	5538	41	1674	1900	1332822
030	HOUILLE	138	13	-	23	-	404	-	21	182	-	408	47	111	-	104404
050	COKE	-	-	-	-	-	-	-	-	-	-	-	-	-	-	39791
070	PETROLE + PROD.GAZ N	98908	30197	1787	542	1740	7108	1372	1367	1271	5709	13408	2330	2919	1459	672114
090	ELECTR.,GAZ,VAP.,EAU	10850	555	2172	1655	3824	3186	2751	1544	2499	5033	9492	2364	4654	632	519304
110	COMBUST. NUCLEAIRES	-	-	-	-	-	-	-	-	-	-	-	-	-	-	1037583
130	FERREUX ET NON FERR.	341	661	539	30	-	44	-	26	364	-	313	26	452	-	550150
150	MIN. NON METALLIQUES	216	309	1464	66	-	1236	-	555	8822	5738	1388	33	21990	555	523688
170	PRODUITS CHIMIQUES	677	871	435	193	-	231	-	93	347	161	12830	641	658	17	469510
190	PRODUITS EN METAUX	1252	94	2080	119	-	3882	-	-	24	-	14348	389	25	-	195303
210	MACHINES	391	1052	95	-	3273	542	887	60	4106	1012	8228	12	3568	-	35875
230	MACH. DE BUREAU,ETC.	196	127	503	494	-	949	-	-	875	1289	6177	397	1784	19	165789
250	MATERIEL ELECTRIQUE	3053	65	1638	1216	-	379	-	110	-	-	1290	10	-	-	211650
270	AUTOS ET PIECES	12124	25453	208	42	-	706	-	-	-	-	5468	-	-	-	107980
290	AUTRES MOYENS TRANSP	23126	-	889	-	-	-	-	-	-	-	37858	-	-	-	99031
310	VIANDES ET CONSERVES	-	73	-	-	-	-	-	-	1094	-	3493	-	1979	791	25202
330	LAIT, PROD. LAITIERS	-	31	-	-	-	-	-	-	467	-	837	-	731	540	514118
350	AUTRES ALIMENTS	-	113	-	-	-	-	-	5	1221	-	6017	95	1806	641	190601
370	BOISSONS	-	459	-	-	-	-	-	-	476	-	593	-	692	150	-
390	TABACS	-	-	-	-	-	-	-	-	-	-	-	-	-	-	-
410	TEXTILE, HABILLEMENT	793	470	366	359	-	352	-	88	819	620	773	58	3303	813	291874
430	CUIR, CHAUSSURES	84	167	116	87	-	70	-	14	40	155	555	-	59	208	45689
450	BOIS,MEUBLES EN BOIS	122	101	1209	-	15838	-	767	30	40	667	629	158	59	55	180030
470	PAPIER, IMPRIMES	1576	649	2489	2167	-	22999	-	2128	414	4164	15407	3338	544	3091	360396
490	CAOUTCHOUC,PLASTIQUE	17972	424	99	148	1809	967	400	18	717	794	1602	85	1582	26	227993
510	AUTRES INDUSTRIES	137	50	234	533	21537	202	-	250	39	215	2525	242	2570	1	10403
530	CONSTRUCTION	15288	451	7219	333	-	6503	330022	3171	1582	3517	48738	3630	659	92	565115
550	RECUPER., REPARATION	21377	511	968	551	2402	5767	199	227	204	2178	114	675	5043	70	156255
570	COMMERCE	7957	2905	1007	42	10098	2288	20	457	2304	2153	9921	2049	362	1079	443473
590	RESTAUR.,HEBERGEMENT	3666	5016	502	5299	6511	4490	77	458	22	2285	11063	3257	1624	12	144746
610	TRANSPORT INTERIEUR	6537	3158	6678	1052	4912	1798	9	349	1075	1530	22534	302	52	455	399001
630	TR. MARITIME, AERIEN	1573	1810	1633	45	1190	820	-	59	37	981	6065	-	-	14	59112
650	SERV.ANNEXES TRANSP.	55892	19583	1161	-	-	346	-	16	-	454	5601	-	725	14	113498
670	COMMUNICATIONS	3249	1728	3436	-	37473	6936	2662	1190	1094	2480	9588	1957	157	547	161299
690	CREDIT ET ASSURANCES	18325	5700	6348	1331	549625	14138	25390	774	1395	2551	192	600	1427	209	985080
710	SERV.AUX ENTREPRISES	4157	12119	3371	3599	77306	4739	5281	3068	1890	4976	33835	1809	65	814	453985
730	LOCATION IMMOBILIERE	1416	1040	1940	599	23465	8424	-	1805	3009	11350	5093	-	-	430	153731
750	ENSEIGN. RECH. MARCH	59	15	89	56	-	592	-	212	18	-	1623	-	-	-	16939
770	SANTE MARCHAND	-	-	-	-	-	-	-	341	-	-	184	-	7180	-	2546
790	SERV. MARCHANDS NDA	4416	1594	278	1381	4001	-	-	892	1994	1920	11352	5049	-	-	94642
810	ADMINISTR.PUBLIQUE	-	-	-	-	-	-	-	-	-	-	-	-	-	-	-
850	ENS. RECH. NON-MARCH	-	-	-	-	-	-	-	-	-	-	-	-	-	-	-
890	SANTE NON-MARCHAND	-	-	-	-	-	-	-	-	-	-	-	-	-	-	-
930	SERV. NON-MARCH. NDA	-	-	-	-	-	-	-	-	-	-	-	-	-	-	-
990	TOTAL	315868	117622	50953	21962	765004	136127	369837	19348	39602	63405	315080	30699	68504	14634	11660722

		MIO PES			EMPL.FINALS			ORIGINE INTERIEURE			PRIX DEPART-USINE		
		F01	F02	F03	F09	F19	F29	F41	F42	F43	F49	F09	F99
010	PROD. AGRICULTURE	419565	–	–	419565	17421	60339	–	–	–	106536	603061	1936663
030	HOUILLE	6467	–	–	6467	–	149	–	–	–	106	6722	111126
050	COKE	462	–	–	462		329	–	–	–	25	816	40607
070	PETROLE + PROD,GAZ N	425220	–	–	425220	16364	-2542	–	–	–	101672	540714	1212828
090	ELECTR.,GAZ,VAP.,EAU	179854	–	–	179854	–	-4586	–	–	–	2100	177368	696672
110	COMBUST. NUCLEAIRES	–	–	–	–	–	–	–	–	–	–	–	–
130	FERREUX ET NON FERR.	–	–	–	–	–	5859	–	–	–	186439	192298	1229681
150	MIN. NON METALLIQUES	14975	–	–	14975	13739	10391	–	–	–	73061	112166	662316
170	PRODUITS CHIMIQUES	209764	–	–	209764	123709	4125	–	–	–	117598	331487	855175
190	PRODUITS EN METAUX	88777	–	–	88777	166419	17800	–	–	–	86456	316742	786252
210	MACHINES	4831	–	–	4831	10850	-2110	–	–	–	102005	271145	466440
230	MACH. DE BUREAU,ETC.	6220	–	–	6220		988	–	–	–	18863	36921	72796
250	MATERIEL ELECTRIQUE	143135	–	–	143135	154245	5286	–	–	–	60032	363498	529287
270	AUTOS ET PIECES	221969	–	–	221969	185761	3611	–	–	–	152004	563345	774995
290	AUTRES MOYENS TRANSP	14472	–	–	14472	82300	3703	–	–	–	36788	137263	245243
310	VIANDES ET CONSERVES	538680	–	–	538680		662	–	–	–	3906	543248	642279
330	LAIT, PROD. LAITIERS	224322	–	–	224322		2594	–	–	–	501	227417	252619
350	AUTRES ALIMENTS	568383	–	–	568383		759	–	–	–	112742	681884	1196002
370	BOISSONS	111836	–	–	111836		16927	–	–	–	34057	162820	353421
390	TABACS	96654	–	–	96654		3620	–	–	–	2056	102330	102330
410	TEXTILE, HABILLEMENT	409334	–	–	409334	15083	19823	–	–	–	68331	512571	804445
430	CUIR, CHAUSSURES	105521	–	–	105521	1510	6924	–	–	–	62601	176556	222245
450	BOIS,MEUBLES EN BOIS	105328	–	–	105328	83572	10486	–	–	–	27900	227286	407316
470	PAPIER, IMPRIMES	84553	–	–	84553		5645	–	–	–	56827	147025	507421
490	CAOUTCHOUC,PLASTIQUE	23214	–	–	23214	4939	4955	–	–	–	42059	75167	303160
510	AUTRES INDUSTRIES	86895	–	–	86895	3909	766	–	–	–	16606	108176	118579
530	CONSTRUCTION	51305	–	–	51305	1891666		–	–	–		1942971	2508086
550	RECUPER., REPARATION	300659	–	–	300659	-6444		–	–	–	567	294782	451037
570	COMMERCE	1804493	–	–	1804493	78251		–	–	–	76797	1959541	2403014
590	RESTAUR.,HEBERGEMENT	1250460	–	–	1250460			–	–	–		1250460	1395206
610	TRANSPORT INTERIEUR	289358	–	–	289358	17444		–	–	–	18863	325665	724666
630	TR. MARITIME, AERIEN	51451	–	–	51451	342		–	–	–	190995	242788	301900
650	SERV. ANNEXES TRANSP.	28497	–	–	28497			–	–	–	48659	77156	190654
670	COMMUNICATIONS	88051	–	–	88051			–	–	–	2895	90946	252245
690	CREDIT ET ASSURANCES	132986	–	–	132986			–	–	–	28861	161847	1146927
710	SERV. AUX ENTREPRISES	31156	–	–	31156	255521		–	–	–	37713	324390	778375
730	LOCATION IMMOBILIERE	1334739	–	–	1334739			–	–	–		1334739	1488470
750	ENSEIGN. RECH. MARCH	123068	–	–	123068			–	–	–		140007	140007
770	SANTE MARCHAND	200025	–	–	200025			–	–	–	23611	200025	202571
790	SERV. MARCHANDS NDA	298057	–	–	298057			–	–	–		321068	416510
810	ADMINISTR.PUBLIQUE		1231396	–	1231396			–	–	–		1231396	1231396
850	ENS. RECH. NON-MARCH	9662	323825	–	333487			–	–	–		333487	333487
890	SANTE NON-MARCHAND		374095	–	374095			–	–	–		374095	374095
930	SERV. NON-MARCH. NDA	139672	–	–	139672			–	–	–		139672	139672
990	TOTAL	10224070	1929316	–	12153386	3116601	176503	–	–	–	1901232	17347722	29000444

1980 ESPAGNE

Column groups: **MIO PES** (B010) · **ECH. INTERM.** (B030–B110) · **IMPORTATIONS** (B130–B170) · **PRIX DEPART-USINE** (B190–B290)

	B010	B030	B050	B070	B090	B110	B130	B150	B170	B190	B210	B230	B250	B270	B290
010 PROD. AGRICULTURE	4114	16243	-	-	-	-	-	643	818	-	-	-	-	-	-
030 HOUILLE	-	-	4480	-	6102	-	4068	-	-	-	-	-	-	-	-
050 COKE	-	-	63	-	-	-	-	-	68	-	-	-	-	-	-
070 PETROLE + PROD.GAZ N	-	-	-	808505	39062	-	2424	-	3720	-	-	-	-	-	-
090 ELECTR.,GAZ,VAP.,EAU	2720	377	23	-	20822	-	6	2140	-	97	31	1	20	39	26
110 COMBUST. NUCLEAIRES	-	-	-	-	-	-	-	-	-	-	-	-	-	-	-
130 FERREUX ET NON FERR.	57	16	-	131	42	-	74138	1789	861	43223	11932	682	16890	18767	6037
150 MIN. NON METALLIQUES	7	-	-	-	5	-	1789	9431	14986	1014	210	102	568	797	44
170 PRODUITS CHIMIQUES	14238	120	-	26	151	-	4111	4721	131247	3403	560	189	3867	1157	604
190 PRODUITS EN METAUX	409	22	-	397	203	-	188	573	982	4907	2045	169	958	2373	1863
210 MACHINES	7	28	-	86	104	-	188	239	77	133	66526	16	93	160	67
230 MACH. DE BUREAU,ETC.	-	-	-	-	-	-	-	-	-	-	-	25266	56	-	699
250 MATERIEL ELECTRIQUE	670	-	-	-	2719	-	1636	-	-	1355	6859	2368	43224	6908	1306
270 AUTOS ET PIECES	-	-	-	-	-	-	-	-	-	-	-	-	-	31902	16273
290 AUTRES MOYENS TRANSP	-	-	-	-	-	-	-	-	-	-	-	-	-	-	-
310 VIANDES ET CONSERVES	-	-	-	-	-	-	-	-	3103	-	-	-	-	-	-
330 LAIT, PROD. LAITIERS	-	-	-	-	-	-	-	-	78	-	-	-	-	-	-
350 AUTRES ALIMENTS	497	-	-	-	-	-	-	-	2445	-	-	-	-	-	-
370 BOISSONS	-	-	-	-	-	-	-	-	130	-	-	-	-	-	-
390 TABACS	429	5	2	-	5	-	32	68	221	128	32	4	34	322	39
410 TEXTILE, HABILLEMENT	-	-	-	-	-	-	-	-	1	-	-	-	-	5	1
430 CUIR, CHAUSSURES	-	943	-	-	-	-	-	-	-	-	-	-	-	-	-
450 BOIS,MEUBLES EN BOIS	1	-	3	11	57	-	9	15	1132	388	323	11	141	188	425
470 PAPIER, IMPRIMES	488	6	-	12	24	-	98	809	807	146	53	21	353	146	34
490 CAOUTCHOUC,PLASTIQUE	-	-	-	4	10	-	49	69	9	447	478	136	1082	2990	199
510 AUTRES INDUSTRIES	-	-	-	-	-	-	4	19	-	11	-	-	-	-	-
530 CONSTRUCTION	-	-	-	-	-	-	-	-	-	-	-	-	-	-	-
550 RECUPER., REPARATION	-	-	-	-	-	-	-	-	-	-	-	-	-	-	-
570 COMMERCE	-	-	-	-	-	-	-	-	-	-	-	-	-	-	-
590 RESTAUR.,HEBERGEMENT	-	-	-	-	-	-	-	-	-	-	-	-	-	-	-
610 TRANSPORT INTERIEUR	-	-	-	-	-	-	-	-	-	-	-	-	-	-	-
630 TR. MARITIME, AERIEN	21	35	27	29	43	-	323	253	439	191	79	4	67	177	23
650 SERV.ANNEXES TRANSP.	347	-	-	-	-	-	-	-	-	-	-	-	-	-	-
670 COMMUNICATIONS	-	-	-	-	-	-	-	-	-	-	-	-	-	-	-
690 CREDIT ET ASSURANCES	3817	372	46	1049	991	-	748	858	1675	916	820	104	1002	1057	1122
710 SERV.AUX ENTREPRISES	-	-	-	-	-	-	-	-	916	-	-	-	-	-	-
730 LOCATION IMMOBILIERE	-	-	-	-	-	-	-	-	-	-	-	-	-	-	-
750 ENSEIGN. RECH. MARCH	-	-	-	-	-	-	-	-	-	-	-	-	-	-	-
770 SANTE MARCHAND	-	-	-	-	-	-	-	-	-	-	-	-	-	-	-
790 SERV. MARCHANDS NDA	-	-	-	-	-	-	-	-	-	-	-	-	-	-	-
810 ADMINISTR.PUBLIQUE	-	-	-	-	-	-	-	-	-	-	-	-	-	-	-
850 ENS. RECH. NON-MARCH	-	-	-	-	-	-	-	-	-	-	-	-	-	-	-
890 SANTE NON-MARCHAND	-	-	-	-	-	-	-	-	-	-	-	-	-	-	-
930 SERV. NON-MARCH. NDA	-	-	-	-	-	-	-	-	-	-	-	-	-	-	-
990 TOTAL	27822	18167	4644	810253	70340	-	89611	21833	162808	56433	90005	29073	68355	67031	28762

247

1980 ESPAGNE   MIO PES

ECH.INTERM. IMPORTATIONS PRIX DEPART-USINE

	B310	B330	B350	B370	B390	B410	B430	B450	B470	B490	B510	B530	B550	B570	B590
010 PROD. AGRICULTURE	1310	-	203086	2070	9453	14166	5526	14198	1383	9594	22	-	-	1	1864
030 HOUILLE	-	-	-	-	-	-	-	-	-	-	-	-	-	-	-
050 COKE	53	48	260	92	2	95	11	63	181	41	6	886	63	243	56
070 PETROLE + PROD.GAZ N	-	-	-	-	-	-	-	-	-	-	-	-	-	-	-
090 ELECTR.,GAZ,VAP.,EAU	-	-	-	-	-	-	-	-	-	-	-	-	-	-	-
110 COMBUST. NUCLEAIRES	-	-	-	-	-	-	-	-	-	-	-	-	-	-	-
130 FERREUX ET NON FERR.	-	25	13	-	17	73	-	81	123	1027	2488	6027	-	-	-
150 MIN. NON METALLIQUES	9	125	532	1470	-	2	-	81	296	96	66	17210	729	683	1045
170 PRODUITS CHIMIQUES	584	883	2628	2228	5	15692	1546	1051	6315	31972	1850	1379	1008	761	1857
190 PRODUITS EN METAUX	368	243	2749	647	17	84	875	2785	580	176	318	13526	413	9	896
210 MACHINES	35	22	96	43	6	116	17	43	74	78	7	335	3	-	5
230 MACH. DE BUREAU,ETC.	-	-	-	-	-	-	-	-	-	-	-	-	-	-	-
250 MATERIEL ELECTRIQUE	-	-	-	-	-	-	-	-	-	-	-	1283	147	157	-
270 AUTOS ET PIECES	-	-	-	-	-	-	-	-	-	-	668	34103	-	-	-
290 AUTRES MOYENS TRANSP	-	-	-	-	-	-	-	3	51	-	-	9	-	-	-
310 VIANDES ET CONSERVES	1642	29	595	-	-	-	9659	-	-	-	-	-	9098	-	2356
330 LAIT, PROD. LAITIERS	2	1983	2014	-	-	-	-	-	-	-	-	-	8480	-	541
350 AUTRES ALIMENTS	153	58	6032	154	-	-	-	-	-	-	-	-	1325	-	7290
370 BOISSONS	-	-	72	2468	-	-	-	-	-	-	-	-	-	-	7616
390 TABACS	-	-	-	-	1154	-	-	-	-	-	-	-	-	-	-
410 TEXTILE, HABILLEMENT	34	4	92	10	-	18260	302	329	227	941	324	531	238	180	882
430 CUIR. CHAUSSURES	-	-	-	-	-	301	4843	15	4	23	30	-	31	43	12
450 BOIS.MEUBLES EN BOIS	-	-	-	-	-	3	335	20961	2	301	198	3076	-	-	-
470 PAPIER, IMPRIMES	287	374	1098	354	494	479	139	123	30874	201	140	177	31	1670	191
490 CAOUTCHOUC,PLASTIQUE	87	263	303	126	6	620	3590	433	130	3372	410	1230	1206	712	4
510 AUTRES INDUSTRIES	-	-	-	-	-	378	26	-	-	4	21211	111	33	81	257
530 CONSTRUCTION	-	-	-	-	-	-	-	-	-	-	-	-	-	-	-
550 RECUPER. REPARATION	-	-	-	-	-	-	-	-	-	-	-	-	-	-	-
570 COMMERCE	-	-	-	-	-	-	-	-	-	-	-	-	-	19500	-
590 RESTAUR.,HEBERGEMENT	-	-	-	-	-	-	-	-	-	-	-	-	-	-	-
610 TRANSPORT INTERIEUR	-	-	-	-	-	-	-	-	-	-	-	-	-	-	-
630 TR. MARITIME, AERIEN	68	100	292	95	11	184	47	90	209	135	16	613	-	497	36
650 SERV.ANNEXES TRANSP.	-	-	-	-	-	-	-	-	-	-	-	-	-	-	-
670 COMMUNICATIONS	-	-	-	-	-	-	-	-	-	-	-	-	-	-	-
690 CREDIT ET ASSURANCES	346	188	650	546	55	1070	220	476	521	881	169	8240	180	12642	1090
710 SERV.AUX ENTREPRISES	-	-	-	-	-	-	-	-	-	-	-	-	-	-	-
730 LOCATION IMMOBILIERE	-	-	-	-	-	-	-	-	-	-	-	-	-	-	-
750 ENSEIGN. RECH. MARCH	-	-	-	-	-	-	-	-	-	-	-	-	-	-	-
770 SANTE MARCHAND	-	-	-	-	-	-	-	-	-	-	-	-	-	-	-
790 SERV. MARCHANDS NDA	-	-	-	-	-	-	-	-	-	-	-	-	-	-	-
810 ADMINISTR.PUBLIQUE	-	-	-	-	-	-	-	-	-	-	-	-	-	-	-
850 ENS. RECH. NON-MARCH	-	-	-	-	-	-	-	-	-	-	-	-	-	-	-
890 SANTE NON-MARCHAND	-	-	-	-	-	-	-	-	-	-	-	-	-	-	-
930 SERV. NON-MARCH. NDA	-	-	-	-	-	-	-	-	-	-	-	-	-	-	-
990 TOTAL	4978	4345	220512	10303	11220	51523	27136	40732	40970	48842	27923	88736	22987	37179	26000

1980 ESPAGNE   MIO PES   ECH.INTERM.   IMPORTATIONS   PRIX DEPART-USINE

	B610	B630	B650	B670	B690	B710	B730	B750	B770	B790	B810	B850	B890	B930	B990
010 PROD. AGRICULTURE	-	2	-	-	-	1	-	-	42	5	44	-	56	24	267779
030 HOUILLE	-	-	-	-	-	-	-	3	-	-	-	6	-	-	27486
050 COKE	-	-	-	-	-	-	-	-	-	-	-	-	-	-	4199
070 PETROLE + PROD,GAZ N	5401	33684	34	10	33	130	26	26	24	107	348	44	29	28	901209
090 ELECTR.,GAZ,VAP.,EAU	-	-	-	-	-	-	-	-	-	-	-	-	-	-	20828
110 COMBUST. NUCLEAIRES	-	-	-	-	-	-	-	-	-	-	-	-	-	-	-
130 FERREUX ET NON FERR.	28	-	62	-	-	-	-	-	-	-	23	-	-	-	184758
150 MIN. NON METALLIQUES	35	76	33	-	-	7	-	2	31	-	55	2	37	-	50895
170 PRODUITS CHIMIQUES	71	31	55	5	-	150	91	91	808	2037	1880	70	1905	67	241245
190 PRODUITS EN METAUX	105	81	100	21	-	18	-	14	29	16	12535	34	43	-	52523
210 MACHINES	6	1	-	2	-	-	-	-	-	-	9647	-	-	-	78271
230 MACH. DE BUREAU,ETC.	-	-	-	-	-	-	-	-	3082	-	13221	-	3931	-	47859
250 MATERIEL ELECTRIQUE	-	-	-	-	-	-	-	-	-	-	430	-	-	-	111344
270 AUTOS ET PIECES	1678	9	28	5	39	-	-	-	-	-	676	-	-	-	42983
290 AUTRES MOYENS TRANSP	-	-	-	-	-	-	-	-	-	-	72	-	-	-	17670
310 VIANDES ET CONSERVES	-	-	-	-	-	-	-	-	67	-	504	-	79	16	18050
330 LAIT, PROD. LAITIERS	-	-	-	-	-	-	-	-	14	-	28	-	15	9	4687
350 AUTRES ALIMENTS	-	3	-	-	-	-	-	-	126	-	335	-	180	16	17340
370 BOISSONS	-	-	-	-	-	-	-	-	4	-	-	-	6	-	10296
390 TABACS	-	-	-	-	-	-	-	-	-	-	-	-	-	-	1154
410 TEXTILE, HABILLEMENT	46	45	19	18	-	18	-	4	43	32	39	3	121	42	24105
430 CUIR, CHAUSSURES	-	11	2	1	-	2	-	2	-	2	13	-	1	25	5365
450 BOIS,MEUBLES EN BOIS	-	-	-	-	-	-	-	-	-	-	-	-	-	-	27320
470 PAPIER, IMPRIMES	62	23	122	130	1242	1778	32	110	19	350	1564	371	24	161	45490
490 CAOUTCHOUC,PLASTIQUE	1540	24	3	24	-	69	-	-	32	25	54	3	76	1	21102
510 AUTRES INDUSTRIES	15	6	26	16	211	22	44	28	4	573	331	27	6	-	23467
530 CONSTRUCTION	-	-	-	-	-	-	-	-	-	-	-	-	-	-	-
550 RECUPER., REPARATION	-	-	-	-	-	-	-	-	-	-	-	-	-	-	-
570 COMMERCE	-	-	-	-	-	-	-	-	-	-	-	-	-	-	19500
590 RESTAUR.,HEBERGEMENT	-	-	-	-	-	-	-	-	-	-	-	-	-	-	-
610 TRANSPORT INTERIEUR	10	171	122	150	1008	170	-	11	3	211	1286	64	5	-	7317
630 TR. MARITIME, AERIEN	10524	23135	-	-	-	-	-	-	-	-	568	-	-	-	34574
650 SERV. ANNEXES TRANSP.	-	-	-	1429	-	-	-	-	-	-	-	-	-	-	1429
670 COMMUNICATIONS	-	-	-	-	11868	-	-	-	-	-	-	-	-	-	11868
690 CREDIT ET ASSURANCES	566	5593	459	490	9744	648	719	419	258	679	24834	246	194	111	86811
710 SERV.AUX ENTREPRISES	-	-	-	-	-	-	-	-	-	-	-	-	-	-	-
730 LOCATION IMMOBILIERE	-	-	-	-	-	-	-	-	-	-	-	-	-	-	-
750 ENSEIGN. RECH. MARCH	-	-	-	-	-	-	-	-	-	-	-	-	-	-	-
770 SANTE MARCHAND	-	-	-	-	-	-	-	-	-	1220	-	-	-	-	-
790 SERV. MARCHANDS NDA	-	-	-	-	-	-	-	-	-	-	-	-	-	-	1220
810 ADMINISTR.PUBLIQUE	-	-	-	-	-	-	-	-	-	-	-	-	-	-	-
850 ENS. RECH. NON-MARCH	-	-	-	-	-	-	-	-	-	-	-	-	-	-	-
890 SANTE NON-MARCHAND	-	-	-	-	-	-	-	-	-	-	-	-	-	-	-
930 SERV. NON-MARCH. NDA	-	-	-	-	-	-	-	-	-	-	-	-	-	-	-
990 TOTAL	20087	62895	1065	2277	24106	3054	821	708	4586	5257	68487	870	6708	500	2410144

249

1980 ESPAGNE

	MIO PIS			EMPL.FINALS			IMPORTATIONS			PRIX DEPART-USINE		
	F01	F02	F03	F09	F19	F29	F41	F42	F43	F49	F89	F99
010 PROD. AGRICULTURE	17913			17913							17913	285692
030 HOUILLE	1853			1853		3384					5237	32723
050 COKE												4199
070 PETROLE + PROD.GAZ N	6503			6503							6503	907712
090 ELECTR.,GAZ,VAP.,EAU												20828
110 COMBUST. NUCLEAIRES												
130 FERREUX ET NON FERR.												184758
150 MIN. NON METALLIQUES	2919			2919	945						3864	54759
170 PRODUITS CHIMIQUES	9740			9740							9740	250985
190 PRODUITS EN METAUX	6784			6784	15161						21945	74468
210 MACHINES					112069						112069	190340
230 MACH. DE BUREAU,ETC	13544			13544	43664						57208	105067
250 MATERIEL ELECTRIQUE	22523			22523	24994						47517	150861
270 AUTOS ET PIECES	32587			32587	26933						59520	102503
290 AUTRES MOYENS TRANSP	2909			2909	23750						26659	44329
310 VIANDES ET CONSERVES	6138			6138							6138	24188
330 LAIT, PROD. LAITIERS	7327			7327							7327	12014
350 AUTRES ALIMENTS	40496			40496							40496	57836
370 BOISSONS	2847			2847							2847	13143
390 TABACS	14189			14189							14189	15343
410 TEXTILE, HABILLEMENT	21886			21886	2481						24367	40472
430 CUIR, CHAUSSURES	5390			5390							5390	10755
450 BOIS,MEUBLES EN BOIS	2563			2563	1608						4171	31491
470 PAPIER, IMPRIMES	4647			4647							4647	50137
490 CAOUTCHOUC,PLASTIQUE	2401			2401							2401	23503
510 AUTRES INDUSTRIES	24054			24054							24054	47521
530 CONSTRUCTION												
550 RECUPER., REPARATION												
570 COMMERCE											19500	19500
590 RESTAUR.,HEBERGEMENT												
610 TRANSPORT INTERIEUR	1451			1451							1451	1451
630 TR. MARITIME, AERIEN	9307			9307							9307	16624
650 SERV.ANNEXES TRANSP.	3302			3302							3302	37876
670 COMMUNICATIONS												1429
690 CREDIT ET ASSURANCES												11868
710 SERV.AUX ENTRPRISES												86811
730 LOCATION IMMOBILIERE												
750 ENSEIGN. RECH. MARCH												
770 SANTE MARCHAND												
790 SERV. MARCHANDS NDA	6924			6924							6924	8144
810 ADMINISTR.PUBLIQUE												
850 ENS. RECH. NON-MARCH												
890 SANTE NON-MARCHAND												
930 SERV. NON-MARCH. NDA												
990 TOTAL	270197			270197	251605	3384					525186	2935330

FINAL USES Description	Code	EMPLOIS FINALS Libellé
Final consumption of households on the economic territory	01	Consommation finale des ménages sur le territoire économique
Collective consumption of general government	02	Consommation collective des administrations publiques
Collective consumption of private non-profit institutions	03	Consommation collective des administrations privées
Final consumption on the economic territory	09	Consommation finale sur le territoire économique
Gross fixed capital formation	19	Formation brute de capital fixe
Change in stocks	29	Variation des stocks
Exports of goods and services to EEC countries	41	Exportations de biens et services vers la Communauté
Exports of goods and services to third countries	42	Exportations de biens et services vers les pays tiers
Adjustment	43	Ajustement statistique
Total exports of goods and services	49	Exportations totales de biens et services
Final uses	89	Emplois finals
Total uses	99	Total des emplois

PRIMARY INPUTS Description	Code	ENTRÉES PRIMAIRES ET RESSOURCES Libellé
Gross wages and salaries	010	Salaires et traitements bruts
Employers' social contributions	020	Cotisations sociales à charge des employeurs
Net operating surplus	030	Excédent net d'exploitation
Net value added at factor cost	070	Valeur ajoutée nette au coût des facteurs
Consumption of fixed capital	080	Consommation de capital fixe
Gross value added at factor cost	090	Valeur ajoutée brute au coût des facteurs
Taxes linked to production (excluding VAT)	110	Impôts liés à la production (à l'exclusion de la TVA)
Subsidies	120	Subventions d'exploitation
Net taxes linked to production (excluding VAT)	170	Impôts liés à la production nets des subventions d'exploitation (à l'exclusion de la TVA)
Net value added at market prices	180	Valeur ajoutée nette aux prix du marché
Gross value added at market prices	190	Valeur ajoutée brute aux prix du marché
Actual output at producer prices	290	Valeur de la production effective aux prix départ usine
Transfer of ordinary by-products and adjacent products at approximate factor prices	310	Transferts de produits fatals ordinaires et de produits voisins aux prix de production
Transfer of incidental sales at approximate factor prices	330	Transferts de ventes résiduelles aux prix de production
Total transfers at approximate factor prices	390	Total des transferts aux prix de production
Subsidies linked to exports	410	Subventions d'exploitation liées à l'exportation
Distributed output at producer prices	490	Valeur de la production distribuée aux prix départ usine
Imports c.i.f. of similar products from CEE countries	510	Importations caf de produits similaires en provenance de la Communauté
Imports c.i.f of similar products from third countries	520	Importations caf de produits similaires en provenance des pays tiers
Total imports c.i.f. of similar products	590	Total des importations caf de produits similaires
Taxes linked to imports of similar products from EEC countries (excluding VAT)	610	Impôts liés à l'importation de produits similaires en provenance de la Communauté (à l'exclusion de la TVA)
Taxes linked to imports of similar products from third countries (excluding VAT)	620	Impôts liés à l'importation de produits similaires en provenance des pays tiers (à l'exclusion de la TVA)
Total taxes linked to imports of similar products (excluding VAT)	690	Total des impôts liés à l'importation de produits similaires (à l'exclusion de la TVA)
Imports of similar products from EEC countries at ex-customs prices	710	Importations de produits similaires en provenance de la Communauté aux prix départ douane
Imports of similar products from third countries at ex-customs prices	720	Importations de produits similaires en provenance des pays tiers aux prix départ douane
Total imports of similar products at ex-customs prices	790	Total des importations de produits similaires aux prix départ douane
VAT imposed on domestic and imported products	870	TVA grevant les produits nationaux et importés
Total resources	980	Total des ressources

BRANCHES AND SUB-BRANCHES Description	NACE-CLIO (R 44)	BRANCHES ET SOUS-BRANCHES Libellé
Agricultural, forestry and fishery products	010	Produits de l'agriculture, de la sylviculture et de la pêche
Coal, lignite (brown coal) and briquettes	030	Houille, lignite, agglomérés et briquettes
Products of coking	050	Produits de la cokéfaction
Crude petroleum, natural gas and petroleum products	070	Pétrole brut, gaz naturel, produits pétroliers
Electric power, gas, steam and water	090	Énergie électrique, gaz, vapeur et eau
Electric power, steam, hot water, compressed air	091	Énergie électrique, vapeur, eau chaude, air comprimé
Gas distributed by pipes	093	Gaz distribué
Water	095	Eau
Production and processing of radio active materials and ores	110	Minerais et produits de la transformation des matières fissiles et fertiles
Ferrous and non-ferrous ores and metals, other than radioactive	130	Minerais et métaux ferreux et non ferreux autres que fertiles et fissiles
Ferrous metals and minerals	131	Minerais et métaux ferreux
Non-ferrous metals and minerals	133	Minerais et métaux non ferreux
Non-metallic mineral products	150	Minéraux et produits à base de minéraux non métalliques
Chemical products	170	Produits chimiques
Metal products except machinery and transport equipment	190	Produits et métaux à l'exclusion des machines et du matériel de transport
Agricultural and industrial machinery	210	Machines agricoles et industrielles
Office and data processing machines, precision and optical instruments	230	Machines de bureau, machines pour le traitement de l'information, instruments de précision, d'optique et similaires
Electrical goods	250	Matériel et fournitures électriques
Motor vehicles	270	Véhicules et moteurs automobiles
Other transport equipment	290	Moyens de transport autres que véhicules automobiles
Meats, meat preparations and preserves, other products from slaughtered animals	310	Viandes, préparation et conserves de viande, autres produits de l'abattage
Milk and dairy products	330	Lait et produits laitiers
Other food products	350	Autres produits alimentaires
Beverages	370	Boissons
Tobacco products	390	Produits à base de tabacs
Textiles and clothing	410	Produits textiles, habillement
Leathers, leather and skin goods, footwear	430	Cuirs, articles en cuir et en peau, chaussures
Timber, wooden products and furniture	450	Bois et meubles en bois
Paper and printing products	470	Papier, articles en papier, articles imprimés
Rubber and plastic products	490	Produits en caoutchouc et en plastique
Other manufacturing products	510	Produits des autres industries manufacturières
Building and construction	530	Bâtiments et ouvrages de génie civil
Recovery and repair services	550	Récupération et réparation
Wholesale and retail trade	570	Services de commerce
Lodging and catering services	590	Services de restauration et hébergement
Inland transport services	610	Services de transport intérieur
Maritime and air transport services	630	Services de transports maritimes et aériens
Maritime transport and coastal services	631	Services de transports maritimes et par cabotage
Air transport services	633	Services de transports aériens
Auxiliary transport services	650	Services annexes des transports
Communication services	670	Services de communication
Services of credit and insurance institutions	690	Services des institutions de crédit et d'assurance
Business services provided to enterprises	710	Services fournis aux entreprises
Services of renting of immovable goods	730	Services de location de biens immobiliers
Market services of education and research	750	Services d'enseignement et de recherche marchands
Market services of health	770	Services de santé marchands
Recreational and cultural services, personal services, other market services n.e.c.	790	Services récréatifs et culturels, services personnels, autres services marchands n.d.a.
General public services	810	Services d'administration générale des administrations publiques
Non-market services of education and research provided by general government and private non-profit institutions	850	Services d'enseignement et de recherche non marchands des administrations publiques et privées
Non-market services of health provided by general government and private non-profit institutions	890	Services de santé non marchands des administrations publiques et privées
Domestic services and other non-market services n.e.c.	930	Services domestiques et autres services non marchands n.d.a
Total	990	Total

XVI. SWEDEN

A. General information

The present country chapter is based on *Input-Output tabeller för Sverige 1975, Statistika Meddelanden N 1980:3*, published by the Sveriges Officiella Statistik.

Input-output tables for Sweden have been compiled for the years 1957, 1964, 1968, 1969 and 1975. The National Central Bureau of Statistics has been in charge of the compilation of all input-output tables, except those referring to 1957. All input-output tables, (except those referring to 1957) have generally followed similar concepts and definitions, but differences among them exist regarding the underlying classification system and the methods of calculation, which have been continually improved. The present report refers to the 1975 table.

The Swedish input-output tables are generally based on the same data sources and follow similar definitions and methodology as those adopted in the national accounts. However, differences exist in the estimates of the aggregates obtained in both sets of data. The main difference refers to their coverage, which in the input-output table is restricted to industry-like activities. That is, the producion and distribution of goods and services other than commodities is not recorded in the table. Therefore, final government consumption as defined in SNA and value added of the government sector are excluded from the input-output estimate of GDP. In addition, minor differences exist due to the different level of detail at which data are presented in the tables and in the national accounts. Such differences are usually taken into account in revising the national accounts estimates.

The main differences between the Swedish input-output table and SNA recommendations on input-output refer to: (*a*) the treatment of activities of the government sector and of private non-profit institution; (*b*) the definition and disaggregation of value added; and (*c*) the treatment of imports.

B. Analytical framework

1. Data are presented in three basic tables:

(i) Absorption matrix valued at purchasers' prices. Only the intermediate consumption quadrant of the table is presented. The final demand quadrant is recorded in table (iii), while use of primary input is recorded only in the "pure" (i.e., commodity-by-commodity and industry-by-industry) input-output table (see derived table (i') below);

(ii) Make matrix valued at basic values;

(iii) Table of reconciliation of total supply and total demand valued at purchasers' prices. In this table, total supply at purchasers' prices is obtained by adding to the domestic production at approximate basic values recorded in the make table the corresponding distribution margins, commodity taxes net of subsidies, imports valued at c.i.f. and import duties.

On the basis of these tables, the following derived matrices are obtained:

(i') Commodity-by-commodity input-output table of domestic flows valued at approximate basic values. This matrix is obtained by first subtracting distribution costs and imports from table (i) and from the final demand side of table (iii), and then merging the matrix so obtained with the make matrix (table (ii)) on the basis of a constant industry technology assumption;

(ii') Commodity-by-commodity input-output table of imports;

(iii') Domestic input-output coefficients, based on matrix (i');

(iv') Domestic inverse matrix, based on matrix (iii');

(v') Imports inverse matrix, based on matrix (ii');

(vi') Industry-by-industry input-output table of domestic flows valued at purchasers' prices. This matrix is obtained on the assumption of a constant industry technology assumption;

(vii') Domestic input-output coefficients, based on matrix (vi');

(viii') Domestic inverse matrix, based on matrix (vii');

(ix') Total production of the commodities of each sector required by final demand categories; This matrix is presented in terms of both absolute and percentage values, and is obtained as the product of matrix (iv') and the final demand categories of matrix (i');

(x') Matrix of changes in the price level of each commodity group and each category of final demand associated with 1 per cent changes in the prices of components of value added.

All basic tables and derived matrices mentioned are presented at an 88 x 88 level of aggregation of intermediate sectors.

2. *Valuation standards*

As mentioned above, different valuation standards have been used for different basic tables and derived matrices. Imports are valued c.i.f. and exports are valued f.o.b.

3. *Statistical units and classification standards*

Commodities are the statistical units adopted for the columns of tables (ii), (ix') and (xi'), for rows of table (i) and (iii) and for rows and columns of derived matrices (i') through (v'). The statistical unit adopted for columns of table (i), rows of table (ii), and rows and columns of derived matrices (vi') through (viii') is the establishment.

Starting with the 1968 table, establishments are classified according to the Swedish Standard Industrial Classification of All Economic Activities, of which the 4-digit level corresponds to ISIC. Commodities are classified according to a Swedish adaptation of the international Customs Co-operation Council Nomenclature (CCCN).

The classification and structure of the intermediate consumption quadrant differ from the SNA recommendations in that the distribution of goods and services provided by the Government and by private non-profit institutions, and the intermediate consumption of these economic agents, are excluded from this quadrant. The intermediate consumption of the Government and of private non-profit institutions is recorded in the final demand quadrant. The distribution of government-marketed products is considered as a supply external to the production system, and is recorded in a row additional to the 88 rows referring to intermediate input-output sectors.

The definition of value added adopted in the Swedish input-output table differs from the SNA recommendations in that it excludes value added of the government sector, for reasons mentioned above. The disaggregation of value added also deviates from the SNA recommendations in that depreciation is included in the operating surplus category, rather than being recorded separately.

The definition and disaggregation of final demand are in agreement with the SNA recommendations. Private consumption has been defined on a domestic basis.

No classification of imports is recorded in the absorption table, in which imports are distributed to intermediate and final demand uses together with domestic flows. Imports allocated to domestic industries are recorded in a separate row of the industry-by-industry derived matrix (vi'). In addition, a cross-classification of imports by origin and destination is presented in the commodity by-commodity import matrix (ii'). The inverse of this import matrix is also available, as mentioned above. Contrary to the SNA recommendations, no distinction is made between competitive and complementary imports.

4. Treatment and presentation of selected transactions

Secondary products and their associated input are transferred to their characteristic sectors by merging the make and absorption tables on the basis of the assumption of a constant industry technology. Two types of "pure" input-output tables are obtained, one in terms of industries and another in terms of commodities.

Non-monetary production and the corresponding input have been covered. Non-monetary production is included in the output of each corresponding intermediate sector of the input-output table. Main non-monetary flows covered include: (a) farmers' own consumption of agricultural products; (b) gross rent of one- or two-dwelling buildings; and (c) value of own-account construction.

Output is defined gross, that is, it includes intra-sector consumption of characteristic goods.

As recommended in SNA, output of banking institutions is defined to include imputed service charges, that is, the difference between interest earned and paid by these institutions. Imputed service charges are recorded as intermediate consumption of a nominal industry within financial institutions.

5. Statistical sources and compilation methodology

Data collection is mainly based on regular statistical sources such as industrial and foreign trade statistics and current national accounts estimates. These basic data are adjusted in the light of additional information available.

Estimates are made with the help of a tentative procedure with several control totals and checks at aggregate levels. The model allows for the possibility of going back to detailed basic data which are available at a level of specification of 300 industries and commodities.

6. Gross output and intermediate consumption

Output and intermediate consumption of establishments belonging to ISIC major division 1 (i.e., agriculture, hunting, forestry and fishing) have been obtained from the Agricultural Council, the Forestry Council and tax returns on fishing. The Agricultural Council provides data on cost structure at a level of disaggregation of 300 commodities. The other sources mentioned provide data at a much more aggregated level and therefore judgemental criteria had to be applied to conform to the 300-commodities specification level. Output of fishing is based on data on landings of sea-fish provided by the national association of fishing boat owners. Similar data are available on fishing on inland lakes. Surveys on assessed income and expenditure of professional fishermen are used to calculate intermediate input.

Estimates of output and intermediate consumption of mining and manufacturing establishments are mainly based on industrial statistics, which are collected by means of an annual survey covering all establishments with five or more employees. Data on establishments with fewer than five employees are estimated on the basis of information provided by the Central Register of Enterprises and the Industrial Statistics on number of employees, and output and input per employee, respectively.

Industrial statistical data have two kinds of limitations. First, they only cover five types of aggregated intermediate input, namely, raw materials, wrapping materials, fuel, electrical energy and hired transportation. Secondly, the rate of coverage of commodity-specified input varies considerably, from over 90 per cent of the industries that produce raw materials to very low levels for the engineering industries.

To overcome these information gaps, the following measures were taken. Data on most intermediate inputs not covered by industrial statistics were obtained from estimates prepared acording to the commodity flow method for the national accounts. This is the case for the following input: water, rents, vehicles, fuel, office supplies and advertising expenditures, other services, car leasing, special input (such as government sales, input to non-profit organizations, etc.) and repairs. In addition, information gaps regarding the limited coverage of some industries were removed with the help of additional data specifying the allocation of raw materials to over 139 purchasing industries. Fuel consumption by establishments excluded from Industrial Statistics was allocated on the basis of additional information available from railway, sea and road transportation of goods.

Integrated information is available on electric energy, steam and hot water production. Almost all producers and distributors are covered by an annual survey giving output and input values. Data on all gas and the larger water works are also available through annual surveys.

The calculation of construction activities is subdivided into three parts, namely, construction enterprises, own-account construction and construction work on one- or two-dwelling buildings made by home-owners. Estimates of gross output and value added of the first two categories are based on information from the Enterprise Statistics and the related Statistics on Construction Enterprises. Output for home owners in 1975 was assumed to be the difference between output of categories 1 and 2 and the total investment value of one- or two-dwelling buildings. Input in 1975 was assumed to be 65 per cent of the output value.

As to trade, gross output defined as total trade margins is based on information on turnover values and margins. Wholesale and retail trade are calculated separately. Trade margins for different commodities are estimated mainly according to information from the National Price and Cartel Office. The sum of trade margins on commodities is adjusted to the total trade margin estimated for the National Accounts.

Information on the activity of banks and insurance companies is provided by the Bank Inspection Board and the National Private Insurance Inspectorate. As to dwellings, the output is the sum of real and imputed rents for multi-dwelling and one- or two-dwelling buildings and for secondary homes. Information on intermediate input is available in several surveys on receipts and costs of different dwellings and in the family expenditure survey.

The statistical sources on the remaining input-output sectors are very heterogeneous and incomplete. There is a survey on repair of motor-cars. For several activities, however, only turnover data and employment figures are available.

7. *Value added*

Value added of ISIC groups 1 to 4 has been calculated as the difference between gross output and intermediate consumption. Value added of the remaining groups is mainly estimated as the sum of the following items: compensation of employees, consumption of fixed capital, operating surplus and net indirect taxes.

8. *Final demand and imports*

Data on private consumption are mainly based on national accounts estimates, which are available at a level of disaggregation of about 60 commodities. Use was also made of preliminary work on input-output, which compiled about 2,000 commodity specifications. These balances were first recorded according to the 300-commodities specification level, and then aggregated into the 88 sectors of the input-output table.

Data on gross fixed capital formation are also obtained from national accounts estimates, which identify 27 investing industries and three subdivisions, namely, equipment, means of transportation and construction. In the input-output table no classification of gross investment by type of investment is included.

Changes in stocks are calculated for the following sectors: agriculture, forestry, mining and manufacturing, electricity, gas and water works and trade. Information on changes in stocks in agriculture, covering stocks of cereals and slaughter animals, is given by the National Agricultural Marketing Board. Values on changes in stocks in forestry are based on quantity changes of pulp- and saw-timber according to surveys on supply and use of commodities. A quarterly stocks inquiry covers a sample of all establishments with five or more employees in the mining, quarrying and manufacturing sectors. Respondents give the opening and closing values of their stocks, reporting separately on finished goods, raw materials and work in progress. To permit adjustments for stock appreciation, respondents also indicate the dates to which their valuations refer. A separate stocks inquiry is made among retail and wholesale traders. The quarterly survey covers retailers with 10 or more employees and wholesalers with 20 or more, but once a year the inquiry is extended to all trading establishments in order to obtain the blow-up factor. Stocks held by electricity and gas producers mainly consist of fuel. Those establishments provide quarterly returns of fuel stocks held.

Data on government consumption have been obtained from the records of defense equipment material supply and from national account estimates. The first source provides enough detail to classify defense equipment at the 300-commodities specification level. For data regarding the government consumption of non-defence goods, use has been made of preliminary work in the input-output table, which provided about 2,000 commodity balances. As in the case of private consumption, those commodity balances were first recorded at the 300-commodities specification level and then aggregated into the 88 sectors of the input-output table.

Data on imports and exports are obtained from Foreign Trade Statistics, 1975, which provide information on goods traded, and from the Central Bank, which provide information concerning service flows. The first source provides data at a very detailed level, and aggregation have been made first to the 300-commodities level of specification and then to the 88 level. The Central Bank's data have generally been allocated on the basis of the type of service concerned, except for unspecified items, which have been allocated as a residual. Imports are defined net of re-exports and exports are defined net of re-imports.

Foreign trade statistics also provide data on import duties and compensation charges. Import duties are also defined net of the refunds associated to re-exports. Those refunds were distributed proportionally at the 300-commodities level, since no more precise information was available.

CLASSIFICATION OF INPUT-OUTPUT TABLES FOR 1975

Input-output sectors	Industry
1	Agriculture and hunting
2	Forestry and logging
3	Fishing
4	Iron ore mining
5	Non-ferrous ore mining
6	Other mining and quarrying
7	Slaughtering, preparation of meat
8	Dairy products
9	Canning, preservation of fruit and vegetables
10	Canning of fish
11	Oils and fats
12	Grain mill production
13	Bakery products
14	Sugar
15	Cocoa, chocolates and sugar confectionary
16	Other food
17	Prepared animal feeds
18	Beverage industries
19	Tobacco manufacturing
20	Spinning and weaving
21	Textiles, other than clothing
22	Hoisery and knitted goods
23	Carpets, rugs, etc.
24	Clothing
25	Leather and shoes

26	Sawing, planing and preservation of wood
27	Wooden building materials
28	Other wooden materials
29	Wooden packaging products
30	Furniture and bedding
31	Pulp manufacturing
32	Paper and board manufacturing
33	Fireboard manufacturing
34	Packaging products of paper, board, etc.
35	Other paper and board products
36	Printing
37	Publishing
38	General chemicals
39	Fertilizers and pesticides
40	Plastics and synthetics fibres
41	Semi-finished plastic products
42	Paints
43	Pharmaceutical chemicals and preparations
44	Soap, detergents and toilet preparations
45	Chemical products, n.e.c.
46	Petroleum refining
47	Lubricating oils, greases, etc.
48	Rubber products
49	Plastic products
50	Pottery
51	Glass and glass products
52	Structural clay products
53	Cement, lime and plaster
54	Other non-metal mineral products
55	Iron and steel manufacturing
56	Ferro-alloys manufacturing
57	Iron and steel casting

58	Non-ferrous metals
59	Semi-finished non-ferrous metal products
60	Non-ferrous metal casting
61	Other metal goods
62	Mechanical engineering
63	Electrical machinery, etc.
64	Electronics and telecommunications
65	Domestic electrical appliances
66	Other electrical goods
67	Ship and boat building and repair
68	Manufacturing and repair of railroad equipment
69	Motor vehicles and parts
70	Bicycles and motorcycles
71	Manufacturing and repair of aircraft
72	Other vehicles
73	Instruments and photo equipment
74	Other manufacturing
75	Electricity and steam water supply
76	Gas manufacture and distribution
77	Water supply
78	Construction
79	Distributive trades
80	Restaurants and hotels
81	Transport and storage
82	Communication
83	Financial institutions and insurance
84	Housing
85	Management of other real estate
86	Business services
87	Repair of cars, households goods, etc.
88	Personal services

SWEDEN
INPUT-OUTPUT TABLES
1975

Source: *Input-Output Tabeller for Sverige 1975. Statistika Meddeladen N 1980:3,* Sveriges Officiella Statistik, Sweden.

aktivitets SNI	activity classification (see SNI)	lagerförändring	change in stocks
		löner enligt SNR	compensation of employees according to SNR
andel	share		
användning	use	löpande förbrukning	intermediate consumption except repairs
arbetsgivaravgifter = sociala avgifter	employers' contribution to social security		
arbetsställe	establishment	marknadspris	market price
avgifter	charges	mottagarpris	purchasers' price
avgår	less	marknadsprodukter	commodities
		matris	matrix
bidrag	subsidies	mervärdeskatt (moms)	value added tax (VAT)
bilaga	appendix		
BNP till marknadspris	GDP at market price	naturakonsumtion	consumption of own account production
bransch	industry		
bruttoinvestering	gross fixed capital formation	nettade avgifter	counterbalanced charges and subsidies
bränsle	fuel	näringslivet	the market economy
byggnad	construction		
		oallokerad	unallocated
differenssammanställning	compilation of differences	offentlig förbrukning	government intermediate consumption
differens SNR/input-output	difference SNR/input-output		
		offentliga sektorns försäljning	government sales
direktfördelning	direct allocation		
driftsöverskott	operating surplus	offentliga löner	government compensation of employees
ej varuanknutna indirekta skatter	non commodity indirect taxes	offentliga myndigheter	government
		ofördelade banktjäns-ter	unallocated service charge for banks
ej varuanknutna sub-ventioner	non commodity subsidies		
elkraft	electric energy	privat konsumtion (PK)	private consumption
emballage	wrapping materials	producentpris	basic value
enhet	unit	rad	row
export	exports	reparationer och un-derhåll	repairs and maintenance
faktorpris	factor value	restpost	residual
förbrukning per enhet slutlig användning	total consumption per unit final demand	råvaror	raw materials
fördelning på varu-grupper (= varuSNI)	allocation to commodity groups (= commodity classification)	sammanfattningstabell	condensed table
		skatt	tax
		slutlig användning	final demand
försvar	defence	SNI = svensk närings-grensindelning	SNI = Swedish Standard Industrial Classification of all Economic Activities (four digit level corresponds to ISIC)
försäljning	sales		
förädlingsvärde	value added		
grossist	wholesaler		
handelsmarginaler	trade margins	SNR (de svenska natio-nalräkenskaperna)	SNR = Swedish national accounts
hushåll	households		
hyror	rents	statistiskt nr	statistical number which is equal to CCC on the four digit level
icke varuanknutna skat-ter och subventioner	non commodity taxes and subsidies		
		subventioner	subsidies
import	imports	summa användning	total use
indirekta skatter	indirect taxes	särskilda varuskatter	special commodity taxes
införsel- och kompen-sationsavgifter	import and compensation charges		
		tillgång, tillförsel	supply
inhemsk produktion	domestic production	tjänster	services
inhemsk slutlig an-vändning	domestic final demand	total insats	total input
		totala produktionens fördelning på olika slag av slutlig an-vändning	total production allocated different types of final demand
insatsvaror	commodities for intermediate consumption		
intäkter	income		
investeringsvaror	commodities for formation of fixed capital	transporter	transports
		tullar	import duties
		tullrestitutioner	refund of import duties
jordbruksregleringen	the price regulation system of agriculture		
		varor och tjänster	commodities
		värden	value
kapitalförslitning	consumption of fixed capital		
kostnad	cost	övriga	other

INPUT-OUTPUT 1975

TABELL 1A   INSATS NÄRINGSLIVET FÖRDELAD ENLIGT AKTIVITETSSNI   MOTTAGARPRIS   MILJONER KR

VARUSNI	AKTIVITETSSNI	1 JORD BRUK	2 SKOGS BRUK	3 FISKE BRUK	4 JÄRNM. GRUVOR	5 A MET. A GRUVOR	6 A MIN. A GRUVOR	7 SLAK-TERIER	8 MEJE-RIER	9 VEG. K.IND.	10 FISK K.IND.	11 OLJE-IND.	12 KVAR-NAR	13 BAGE-RIER	14 SOCKER IND.	15 CHOKL. TILLV.
11	JORDBRUKSVAROR	371						2773	1981	201	5	243	637	42	310	87
12	SKOGSBRUKSVAROR	10	141							16	62			1		
13	FISK	15								5						
2301	JÄRNMALM			253												
2302	ANNAN MALM	55				7	2									
2900+	A MINERALER				26											
3111	KÖTT & CHARK	24		21				2441	778	102	1	16		4	30	30
3112	MJÖLK ETC.							52	9	6		15		13	24	24
3113	VEG. KONSERVER	9						1	4	144	12			25		
3114	FISKKONSERVER									1	103					
3115	OLJOR & FETTER	21						77	44	35	35	531		92	18	18
3116	MJÖL							5		16			19	461	2	2
3117	BRÖD															
3118	SOCKER	26						4	13		7	1		124		80
3119	CHOKL. & KONF.								12			2		30	238	62
3121	A LIVSMEDEL			3				15	5	81	4	1	1	89		27
3122	FODERMEDEL	1833								31	1					
3130	DRYCKER										1					
3140	TOBAK															
3211	GARN & VÄVNADER												11			
3212	TEXTILSÖMNAD															
3213	TRIKÅVAROR															
3214/9	ANNAN TEXTIL	23	55	17	20	20		20	20				4			
3220	KLÄDER	10														
3231+	LÄDER & SKOR			3		20	1	1	6							
3234	SÅGAT TRÄ		30													
33111	TRÄHUS & BYGGSN															
33119	FANER & SPÅNSK.			13												
33112/9	Ö TRÄVAROR	20	5								14					
3320	TRÄMÖBLER															
34111	PAPPERSMASSA	24	6	2				7	152	13		14	3	18	2	6
34115	PAPPER & PAPP						2	78	36	52	6		8	61	19	52
34113	TRÄFIBERPLATTOR					2		5	39	5			1	8	1	2
3412	PAPPFÖRPACKN.	4	7	1		2	1	8	5	5	1	6	1	5	1	5
3419	Ö PAPPERSVAROR	7	5			3		6	5	4	1	1		4	1	2
34201	GRAFISKA VAROR	5				13	2	9	85	9	1	20		4	4	3
34204	FÖRLAGSVAROR					6										
3511	KEMIKALIER	1102	20	21			1	36	11	5		3	1	6	1	2
3512	GÖDSELMEDEL								5			5	2			
35131	BASPLAST															
35132	PLAST,HALVFAB.			9												
3521	FÄRGER	18					9	38	2	20	3	19	3	32	26	2
3522	LÄKEMEDEL	15					23	2	48	2	1	4	1	2	3	9
3523	TVÄTTMEDEL						1	1	6							
3529	Ö KEM-VAROR	339	61	49			3	30	2	32	3	14	6	43	3	12
3530	BENSIN EO ETC.	20	20						84		2					
3540	SMÖRJMEDEL	25	25													
3550	GUMMIVAROR	2	2													
3560	PLASTVAROR															

#	VAKUSNI	AKTIVITETSSNI	JORD BRUK	SKOGS BRUK	FISKE	JXRNM. GRUVOR	A MET. GRUVOR	A MIN. GRUVOR	SLAK-TERIER	MEJE-RIER K.IND.	VEG. K.IND.	FISK K.IND.	OLJE-IND.	KVAR-NAR	BAGE-RIER	SOCKER IND.	CHOKL. TILLV.
50	3610	PORSLIN															
51	3620	GLAS															
52	3691	TEGEL															
53	3692	CEMENT	28			48	3										
54	3699	BEARB. MINERAL	10			20	20		2	2	54		1	2	3		1
55	37101	JARN & STÅL															
56	37102	FERROLEGERINGAR															
57	37103	JXRNGJUTGODS															
58	37201/	ANNAN METALL															
59	37203	A MET.HALVFAB.						4	4	4	4	5	20				2
60	37204	A MET.GJUTGODS															
61	381	METALLVAROR	27	163		53	31	6	19	7	48	23	3	1	11	4	12
62	382	MASKINER	292	119		96	31	30	10	5	2	1		3	3	9	1
63	3831	ELMOTORER															
64	3832	TELEMATERIAL				2											
65	3833	HUSH.ELAPP.															
66	3839	Ö EL-VAROR				10	3		2	2	1		1	1	1	2	1
67	3841	FARTYG & BÅTAR			23												
68	3842	RXLSFORDON				10	4										
69	3843	BILAR															
70	3844	MC & CYKLAR															
71	3845	FLYGPLAN															
72	3849	Ö TRANSP.MEDEL															
73	3850	INSTRUMENT															
74	3900	Ö VAROR			5												
75	41018.3	EL & VXRME	245			87	30	21	33	21	12	2	9	8	24	8	7
76	4102	GAS		24		1	11			6	1	1	1	1	2		
77	4200	VATTEN	1071						6	12	8	4	2	1	18	4	1
78	5000	BYGGNADER		63		36	11	3	24	1	1	1	3	1	1		6
79	61/62	HANDELSTJXNSTER				2	1	1	4	2	2		1		1	1	2
80	63	HOTELL&REST.TJ.				26		77	60	85	15	3	16	4	39	1	11
81	71	TRANSPORTTJXNST	101	558		417	1	2	9	6	9		2		6	2	4
82	72	POST & TELETJ.	9	9		5	2	2	9	6	9		2		6	2	5
83	81/82	BANK & FÖRS.TJ.	124	34	4	22	11	4	29	18	17	4	4	3	21		11
84	831BO	BOSTADSHYROR															
85	831AN	Ö HYROR															
86	832/3	UPPDRAG	114	59		7	1	3	29	18	6	2	4	3	10	3	4
87	9511/3	BIL- & HH.REP.	121	15	2	14	9	2	67	43	35	5	9	6	46	11	21
88	9 ÖVR	Ö PRIV.TJXNSTER	51			14	5	1	19	21	5	3		2	24		3
89		OFF MARKN.PROD	3	3		4	1	1	19	1	5	1	1	1	10	2	4
90	1-9	SUMMA INSATS	6180	1425	131	1321	281	226	5952	3624	1015	319	973	734	1285	662	520
		FÖRXDLINGSVXRDE	5590	6288	157	1564	237	781	1821	1041	557	177	271	206	1184	278	367
		PRODUKTION PP	11770	7713	288	2885	518	1007	7773	4665	1572	496	1244	940	2469	940	887

TABELLENS KOLUMNSUMMOR ÖVERENSSTÄMMER BORTSETT FRÅN EV AVRUNDNINGSFEL MED RADSUMMORNA I TABELL 2 GENOM TILLÄGG AV FÖRXD-
LINGSVÄRDEN TILL PRODUCENTPRIS. FÖRXDLINGSVÄRDETS FÖRDELNING PÅ ICKE VARUANKNUTNA INDIREKTA SKATTER, LÖNER OCH DRIFTS-
ÖVERSKOTT INKLUSIVE KAPITALFÖRSLITNING REDOVISAS I TABELL 3.

INPUT - OUTPUT 1975

TABELL 1A INSATS NÄRINGSLIVET FÖRDELAD ENLIGT AKTIVITETSSNI   MOTTAGARPRIS   MILJONER KR

VARUSNI	AKTIVITETSSNI	16 Ö. LIVS IND.	17 FODER M.IND.	18 DRYCK. TILLV.	19 TOBAKS IND.	20 GARN & VÄVIND	21 T.SÖM NADIND	22 TRIKÅ- TILIND	23 Ö TEX- TILIND	24 BEKLÄD NADIND	25 LÄDER& SKOIND	26 SÅG- VERK	27 TRÄHUS BYGGSN	28 A TRÄ- M.IND.	29 Ö TRÄ- V.IND.	30 MÖBEL- IND.
1 11	JORDBRUKSVAROR	797	413	91	143	35					30	3389	167	152	78	2
2 12	SKOGSBRUKSVAROR										7					4
3 13	FISK															
4 2301	JÄRNMALM															
5 2302	ANNAN MALM															
6 2900+	A MINERALER									2	79					3
7 3111	KÖTT & CHARK	48	9			1				2						
8 3112	MJÖLK ETC.	13	8													
9 3113	VEG. KONSERVER	9			6											
10 3114	FISKKONSERVER		23													
11 3115	OLJOR & FETTER	15	232	1		1										
12 3116	MJÖL	30	140	1												
13 3117	BRÖD															
14 3118	SOCKER	18	8	66												
15 3119	CHOKL. & KONF.	3														
16 3121	A LIVSMEDEL	97	3	19												
17 3122	FODERMEDEL		157													
18 3130	DRYCKER			147	3											
19 3140	TOBAK															
20 3211	GARN & VÄVNADER	6				441	119	303	161	695	9					132
21 3212	TEXTILSÖMNAD						10	2		8						
22 3213	TRIKÅVAROR						3	25	3	106	5					25
23 3214/9	ANNAN TEXTIL					57			38	14		2				
24 3220	KLÄDER									103						
25 323/4	LÄDER & SKOR									118	4					58
26 3311	SÅGAT TRÄ										171	385	659	72	151	136
27 33112	TRÄHUS & BYGGSN											13	548	20	66	4
28 33119	FANER & SPÅNSK.											5	140	2	7	178
29 3312/9	Ö TRÄVAROR			4					7				5			21
30 3320	TRÄMÖBLER								3							213
31 34111	PAPPERSMASSA								79	1						
32 34112	PAPPER & PAPP	2		2	32							3	9		2	12
33 34113	TRÄFIBERPLATTOR								16	2			99	3	4	3
34 3412	PAPPFÖRPACKN.	40	22	11	34	1					7					
35 3419	Ö PAPPERSVAROR	2		2	3	12			2	9	13	7	5	1	2	1
36 34201	GRAFISKA VAROR	2	1	3	1	5			2	6	2	7	11	1	1	6
37 34204	FÖRLAGSVAROR	2		32	11	4			17	2	2	5	9			5
38 3511	KEMIKALIER	8	50	7		49					26	18				19
39 3512	GÖDSELMEDEL								87			2			8	
40 35131	BASPLAST	2	10			93	30	18	17	10	2		10	96		132
41 35132	PLAST,HALVFAB.		1	4			28			16	5		1			106
42 3521	FÄRGER								5		2	20	46		26	45
43 3522	LÄKEMEDEL	1		86		1										
44 3523	TVÄTTMEDEL	1		2												
45 3529	Ö KEM-VAROR	11	11	31		12	5	10	1	3	9	3	30	1	5	18
46 3530	BENSIN EO ETC.	10	11	1	2	43	2	1	10	24	12	62	2	17	2	4
47 3540	SMÖRJMEDEL	2	2	2		8	2		4	9	2	10		1		2
48 3550	GUMMIVAROR								7			3				
49 3560	PLASTVAROR	17	5	29		3		5	2	26		1	6	2	2	14

261

AKTIVITETSNI / VARUSNI

kod	kod2	varu	Ö.LIVS IND.	FODER M.IND.	DRYCK- TILLV.	TOBAKS IND.	GARN & VÄVIND	T.SÖM NADIND	TRIKÅ- IND.	Ö TEX- TILIND	BEKLÄD NADIND	LÄDER& SKOIND	SÅG- VERK	TRÄHUS BYGGSN	A TRÄ- M.IND.	Ö TRÄ- V.IND.	MÖBEL- IND.
50	3010	PORSLIN											2		2		4
51	3620	GLAS												41			
52	3691	TEGEL			62		7										
53	3692	CEMENT															
54	3699	BEARB. MINERAL	2	2	10								6	167	2	2	5
55	37101	JÄRN & STÅL										2	9	6	2	5	10
56	37102	FERROLEGERINGAR										1					
57	37103	JÄRNGJUTGODS															
58	37201/	ANNAN METALL															
59	37201/	A MET,HALVFAB.	14													4	3
60	37204	A MET,GJUTGODS			5									1			
61	381	METALLVAROR	46	3	181	1	2	5	1		8	38	85	187		67	129
62	382	MASKINER	2	3	5	2	69	1	10		6	6	29	5		3	2
63	3831	ELMOTORER															1
64	3832	TELEMATERIEL															4
65	3833	HUSH.ELAPP.															
66	3839	Ö EL-VAROR		1	1		2			1		1	15	4	2	6	3
67	3841	FARTYG & BÅTAR															
68	3842	RÄLSFORDON															
69	3843	BILAR															
70	3844	MC & CYKLAR															
71	3845	FLYGPLAN															
72	3849	Ö TRANSP.MEDEL															
73	3850	INSTRUMENT															
74	3900	Ö VAROR											1				
75	4101&3	EL & VÄRME	8	9	11	2	23	3	6	9	29	7	87	32	21	5	16
76	4102	GAS							6		12						
77	4200	VATTEN	3	1	1					1	2	1	4	3	3	4	2
78	5000	BYGGNADER	2	2	10	2	14	1	1	5	6	2	39	18	5	2	9
79	61/62	HANDELSTJÄNSTER		1			9	2	3	5	9	6	47	5	1		13
80	63	HOTELL&REST.TJ.			1	1	2		8	10	4	1	3	5			39
81	71	TRANSPORTTJÄNST	20	15	28		16	4	10	2	24	7	105	72	11	11	
82	72	POST & TELETJ.	8	2	4	3	6	2	4	4	10	2	9	13	2	6	7
83	81/82	BANK & FÖRS.TJ.		5	13		11	3	6		18	5	23	31	4		17
84	831BO	BOSTADSHYROR	7	6	6	2	7	2	4	4	12	4	18	12	2	2	7
85	831AN	Ö HYROR	17	10	34	8	43	10	20	19	65	19	52	80	10	12	42
86	834/3	UPPDRAG	6	8	25		8	1	1	3	2	3	38	13	1	4	3
87	9511/3	BIL- & HH.REP.	3	3	5		6	1	4	3	16	4	19	17	3	3	10
88	9 ÖVR	Ö PRIV.TJÄNSTER	1	1	1		1	1	1	1	4	1	3	5	1	1	3
89		OFF MARKN.PROD															
90	1-9	SUMMA INSATS	1266	1177	943	256	931	302	474	548	1384	494	4524	2466	441	496	1474
		FÖRÄDLINGSVÄRDE	478	298	771	225	691	225	212	330	1273	385	2140	1978	323	394	1245
		PRODUKTION PP	1744	1475	1714	481	1622	527	686	878	2657	879	6664	4444	764	890	2719

262

INPUT - OUTPUT 1975

TABELL 1A   INSATS NÄRINGSLIVET FÖRDELAD ENLIGT AKTIVITETSSNI   MOTTAGARPRIS   MILJONER KR

VARUSNI	AKTIVITETSSNI	31 MASSA-IND.	32 PAPPER IND.	33 T-FIB-PL.IND	34 P-FÖRP IND.	35 Ö PPR-V.IND.	36 GRAF.IND.	37 FÖR-LAG	38 KEM.IND.	39 GÖDSEL M.IND.	40 BASPL.IND.	41 PLAST HF.IND	42 FÄRG-TILLV.	43 LÄKE-M.IND.	44 TVÄTT-M.IND.	45 Ö KEM.PR.IND
11	JORDBRUKSVAROR														3	1
12	SKOGSBRUKSVAROR	2279	1746	14												
13	FISK									1		3	1		3	12
2301	JÄRNMALM															
2302	ANNAN MALM															
2900+	A MINERALER	31	74						157	107	6	2	2		16	6
3111	KÖTT & CHARK										6	2		1		30
3112	MJÖLK ETC.										1			1		1
3113	VEG. KONSERVER															
3114	FISKKONSERVER										7					
3115	OLJOR & FETTER								3			1	8	5	32	9
3116	MJÖL															
3117	BRÖD															
3118	SOCKER													5		
3119	CHOKL. & KONF.															
3121	A LIVSMEDEL	5	36						74		1			1		16
3122	FODERMEDEL															
3130	DRYCKER															
3140	TOBAK															
3211	GARN & VÄVNADER	20	70				3				5	2				1
3212	TEXTILSÖMNAD															
3213	TRIKÅVAROR	20	34													
3214/9	ANNAN TEXTIL															
3220	KLÄDER & SKOR															
323/4	LÄDER & SKOR															
33111	SÅGAT TRÄ	748	400	94								1				7
33112	TRÄHUS & BYGGSN		20													
33119	FANER & SPÅNSK.															
3312/9	Ö TRÄVAROR	15	69	3			2					1				
3320	TRÄMÖBLER															
34111	PAPPERSMASSA	80	1422	3	2	14			9		46	6				
34112	PAPPER & PAPP	3	252	9	377	62	765				1	25	1		1	10
34113	TRÄFIBERPLATTOR															
3412	PAPPFÖRPACKN.	10	49	3	13	8	7		4	10	20	14	23	23	53	30
3419	Ö PAPPERSVAROR	7	6	1	292	305	641	3983	1	3	5	4	6	1		10
34201	GRAFISKA VAROR	4	14	1	3	2	283	19	9	1	2	3	3	9	5	4
34204	FÖRLAGSVAROR	4	9	1	2	1	34		3					35	32	3
3511	KEMIKALIER	373	223		5		6		593	256	582	148	175	75	118	97
3512	GÖDSELMEDEL								8	103				1		16
35131	BASPLAST	10	99	20	72	64	8		4	1	54	440	176	32	5	68
35132	PLAST, HALVFAB.				22	10	1				1	3	2	5	3	2
3521	FÄRGER			2		2							54			
3522	LÄKEMEDEL													124		
3523	TVÄTTMEDEL								3	2	2		1	1	1	2
3529	Ö KEM-VAROR	4							134							4
3530	BENSIN EO ETC.	200	33	36	25	14	191		433	30	33	23	103	3	52	139
3540	SMÖRJMEDEL	9	298	1	11	14	41		5	2	9	2	12	13	12	31
3550	GUMMIVAROR		13		3	2	12		6				2	2	13	37
3560	PLASTVAROR	1	2		9	11	13		26	9	4	4	9	33	19	15

263

VARUSNI AKTIVITETSSNI	MASSA-IND.	PAPPER IND.	T-FIB. PL.IND.	P-FÖRP IND.	Ö PPR-V.IND.	GRAF. IND.	FÖR-LAG	KEM. IND.	GÖDSEL M.IND.	BASPL. IND.	PLAST HF.IND.	FÄRG-TILLV.	LÄKE-M.IND.	TVÄTT-M.IND.	Ö KEM. PR.IND.
3610 PORSLIN															
3620 GLAS															
3691 TEGEL															1
3692 CEMENT	13							5					23	2	
3699 BEARB. MINERAL	9	6	1			1		4		7		1			2
37101 JÄRN & STÅL	20	13	1	4		1		2				4			
37102 FERROLEGERINGAR		20						1							
37103 JÄRNGJUTGODS															
37201/ ANNAN METALL				7		2		6			10	1			2
37203 A MET.HALVFAB.				1	1			5			5	1			58
37204 A MET.GJUTGODS															
381 METALLVAROR	89	53		5	2	45		18	5	7	1	37	4	3	43
382 MASKINER	88	59	3	2	3	18		74	9	20	19	4	4	3	6
3831 ELMOTORER															
3832 TELEMATERIEL															
3833 HUSH.-ELAPP.															
3839 Ö EL-VAROR	28	53	3	1	1	2		25	1	3	2	1	1		1
3841 FARTYG & BÅTAR															
3842 RÄLSFORDON															
3843 BILAR															
3844 MC & CYKLAR															
3845 FLYGPLAN															
3849 Ö TRANSP.MEDEL															
3850 INSTRUMENT	1	1		2		2		1					2		1
3900 Ö VAROR	244	432	25			3					18				
41U1&3 EL & VÄRME	244	432	25	11	15	33		220	12	36	18	5	13	3	13
4102 GAS						1									
4200 VATTEN	4	5		1		4									
5000 BYGGNADER	46	34	3	5	2	26		2	2	1	1	1	6	3	1
61/62 HANDELSTJÄNSTER	96	79	7	3	21	6		15	2	5	10	4	7	2	10
63 HOTELL&REST.TJ.	2	5	1	1	1	21		18	1	14	6	3	3	3	12
71 TRANSPORTTJÄNST	15	31	3	19	6	113	207	14	1	1	21	10	10	14	20
72 POST & TELETJ.	6	13	2	4	2	53		4	2	9	4	4	9	4	5
81/82 BANK & FÖPS.TJ.	40	83	6	21	9	56		10	3	6	8	7	14	7	9
831BO BOSTADSHYROR										4	8				
831AN Ö HYROR	18	23	1	4	3	20		7	2	6	3	3	3	2	4
832/3 UPPDRAG	50	88	8	28	13	551	142	28	8	20	26	26	51	22	32
9511/3 BIL- & HH.REP.	13	9	1	1		18		12	3	3	4	3		1	1
9 ÖVR Ö PRIV.TJÄNSTER	14	22	1	4	1	36	86	6		1	2	2	4	1	5
OFF MARKN.PROD	2	5		1	1	21		2				3	3		
1-9 SUMMA	4617	5900	248	953	593	3039	4437	1960	575	920	825	699	528	424	782
FÖRÄDLINGSVÄRDE	2811	3499	185	641	402	3850	1064	1051	188	355	561	363	675	312	585
PRODUKTION PP	7428	9399	433	1594	995	6889	5501	3011	763	1275	1386	1062	1203	736	1367

INPUT - OUTPUT 1975

TABELL 1A INSATS NÄRINGSLIVET FÖRDELAD ENLIGT AKTIVITETSSNI   MOTTAGARPRIS   MILJONER KR

#	VARUSNI	AKTIVITETSSNI	46 PETROL RAFF.	47 SMÖRJ- M.IND.	48 GUMMI- IND.	49 PLAST- IND.	50 PORS- LININD.	51 GLAS- BRUK	52 TEGEL- BRUK	53 CEMENT Ð IND.	54 MIN. V.IND.	55 JÄRNV. STÅLV.	56 FERRO- LEGIND	57 JÄRN- GJUTER	58 METALL VERK	59 MET A HF.IND	60 A MET- GJUTER
1	11	JORDBRUKSVAROR			39												
2	12	SKOGSBRUKSVAROR															
3	13	FISK															
4	2301	JÄRNMALM										674					
5	2302	ANNAN MALM									1	80					
6	2900+	A MINERALER	4065	284	3		41	12	7	4	228	46	139	12	286	5	6
7	3111	KÖTT & CHARK					2		33	83			11		13		
8	3112	MJÖLK ETC.			1				2								
9	3113	VEG. KONSERVER															
10	3114	FISKKONSERVER															
11	3115	OLJOR & FETTER			2												
12	3116	MJÖL															
13	3117	BRÖD															
14	3118	SOCKER															
15	3119	CHOKL. & KONF.															
16	3121	A LIVSMEDEL															
17	3122	FODERMEDEL															
18	3130	DRYCKER															
19	3140	TOBAK															
20	3211	GARN & VÄVNADER			6						5					2	
21	3212	TEXTILSÖMNAD															
22	3213	TRIKÅVAROR															
23	3214/9	ANNAN TEXTIL			56	4						50					
24	3220	KLÄDER															
25	323/4	LÄDER & SKOR			11												
26	33111	SÅGAT TRÄ			1			1	1		3				1		
27	33112	TRÄHUS & BYGGSN															
28	33119	FANER & SPÅNSK.															
29	3312/9	Ð TRÄVAROR			9		2	7	2	5	10	50	1	6	2	5	6
30	3320	TRÄMÖBLER										15					
31	34111	PAPPERSMASSA		8	1	2					22	3					
32	34112	PAPPER & PAPP				30										10	
33	34113	TRÄFIBERPLATTOR															
34	3412	PAPPFÖRPACKN.			2	38	4	10	4	2	10						
35	3419	Ð PAPPERSVAROR				1					1	3					
36	34201	GRAFISKA VAROR	5	4	5	15	10	6	3		13	24		2	2	3	3
37	34204	FÖRLAGSVAROR	1	1	5	4	2	1	1	2	7	18	1	1	1	2	1
38	3511	KEMIKALIER	22	4	72	69	17	60	15	1	69	104	17	3	97	23	
39	3512	GÖDSELMEDEL															
40	35131	BASPLAST			149	450	3	2	2		15	20		1			
41	35132	PLAST,HALVFAB.		1	15	222	1	1	1		2	1		7			
42	3521	FÄRGER					6	1	1								
43	3522	LÄKEMEDEL															
44	3523	TVÄTTMEDEL															
45	3529	Ð KEM-VAROR	82	15	15	3	16	41	31	139	103	26	2	1	28	16	5
46	3530	BENSIN EO ETC.	236	250	30	23				139	44	353	2	17	14	2	15
47	3540	SMÖRJMEDEL	2	25	5	5				9	3	744	56	14			1
48	3550	GUMMIVAROR			204						1	1					
49	3560	PLASTVAROR		8		27	4	9	2	2	14	2					

265

Table: Input-output matrix (insats), columns = receiving industries.

Nr	VARUSNI	AKTIVITETSSNI	PETROL RAFF.	SMÖRJ M.IND.	GUMMI IND.	PLAST IND.	PORS LININD	GLAS BRUK	TEGEL BRUK	CEMENT IND.	Ö MIN V.IND.	JÄRNV STÅLV.	FERRO LEGIND	JÄRN GJUTER	METALL VERK	A MET HF.IND	A MET GJUTER
50	3610	PORSLIN															
51	3620	GLAS						72									
52	3691	TEGEL					8										
53	3692	CEMENT							5								
54	3699	BEARB. MINERAL	2	3	2	4	1	1		2	3	186	2	2	6	1	1
55	37101	JÄRN & STÅL		1		1		3		3	400	2636	9		1	2	1
56	37102	FERROLEGERINGAR									140	957	2	106	1	23	
57	37103	JÄRNGJUTGODS				10					154		9	12	2		
58	37201	ANNAN METALL			1						8	40	2	50	149	1136	138
59	37203	A MET.HALVFAB.				1					8			6		207	6
60	37204	A MET.GJUTGODS									10	402	1	6			34
61	381	METALLVAROR	13	29	50	2	13	1	1	6	33	214	1	7	96	20	12
62	382	MASKINER	21	5	14	30	1		2	7	10	413	11	11	15	30	9
63	3831	ELMOTORER									1						
64	3832	TELEMATERIEL															
65	3633	HUSH.ELAPP.															
66	3839	Ö EL-VAROR	2	1	4	4	1	1	1	4	7	121	2	2	7	3	1
67	3841	FARTYG & BÅTAR															
68	3842	RÄLSFORDON															
69	3843	BILAR															
70	3844	MC & CYKLAR															
71	3845	FLYGPLAN															
72	3849	Ö TRANSP.MEDEL															
73	3850	INSTRUMENT															
74	3900	Ö VAROR			1										1	70	
75	4101&3	EL & VÄRME	13	7	25	40	9	21	9	37	41	283	68	30	67	22	11
76	4102	GAS										30					
77	4200	VATTEN	2								3	7					
78	5000	BYGGNADER	5	5	10	10	9	4		3	3	84	1	1	4	1	1
79	61/62	HANDELSTJÄNSTER	14	2	10	7	2	4	3	1	24	84	4	7	6	7	6
80	63	HOTELL&REST.TJ.	1	1	3	3	1	13	1	1	5	11		1	1	12	
81	71	TRANSPORTTJÄNST	1	4	22	32	8	3	1	4	4	146	19	0	7	1	3
82	72	POST & TELETJ.	2	2	8	7	3	2	6	2	98	30		2	2	24	2
83	81/82	BANK & FÖRS.TJ.	15	13	14	14	6	7	2	4	11	95	2	10	6	4	5
84	83IBO	BOSTADSHYROR							4							12	
85	83IAN	Ö HYROR	8	2	6	6	2	2	1	2	13	35		3	3	6	2
86	832/3	UPPDRAG	12	11	54	40	21	15	13	12	71	169	2	13	11	22	10
87	9511/3	BIL- & HH.REP.	1	5	5	3	3	2	2	4	37	17		1	2	1	
88	9 ÖVR	Ö PRIV.TJÄNSTER	3		3	8	2	3	1	1	13	36				4	1
89		OFF MARKN.PROD				3	1	1	1	1	1						
90	1-9	SUMMA INSATS	4527	690	870	1118	200	303	157	342	1662	8303	367	341	839	1677	282
		FÖRÄDLINGSVÄRDE	50	199	993	863	275	364	196	277	1655	3147	242	454	272	436	225
		PRODUKTION PP	4577	889	1863	1981	475	667	353	619	3317	11450	609	795	1111	2113	507

INPUT-OUTPUT 1975

TABELL 1A INSATS NÄRINGSLIVET FÖRDELAD ENLIGT AKTIVITETSSNI   MOTTAGARPRIS   MILJONER KR

VARUSNI	AKTIVITETSSNI	61 MET.- V.IND.	62 MASKIN IND.	63 ELMOT. IND.	64 TELE- M.IND.	65 HHEL- V.IND.	66 Ö EL- V.IND.	67 VARV ETC.	68 RXLS- F.IND.	69 BIL-IND. KELIND.	70 MC&CY- KELIND.	71 FLYGPL IND.	72 Ö TRPT M.IND.	73 INSTR. TILLV.	74 A IND. TILLV.	75 EL&VXR MEVERK	
11	JORDBRUKSVAROR																1
12	SKOGSBRUKSVAROR																2
13	FISK	5												1	4		3
2301	JÄRNMALM																4
2302	ANNAN MALM	183	1												8	4	5
2900+	A MINERALER	2	7	1											6		6
3111	KÖTT & CHARK						5	1		9							7
3112	MJÖLK ETC.																8
3113	VEG. KONSERVER																9
3114	FISKKONSERVER																10
3115	OLJOR & FETTER																11
3116	MJÖL																12
3117	BRÖD																13
3118	SOCKER																14
3119	CHOKL. & KONF.																15
3121	A LIVSMEDEL																16
3122	FODERMEDEL																17
3130	DRYCKER																18
3140	TOBAK																19
3211	GARN & VÄVNADER	12						10	10	60				2	7		20
3212	TEXTILSÖMNAD							5	5	103							21
3213	TRIKÅVAROR														1		22
3214/9	ANNAN TEXTIL		6				10	34		25				7	6		23
3220	KLÄDER		80					1						2	3		24
323/4	LÄDER & SKOR	26	14														25
3311	SÅGAT TRÄ		12			2		112		102					40	3	26
33112	TRÄHUS & BYGGSN		70					55		1		70					27
33119	FANER & SPÅNSK.	1	3							3					2		28
3312/9	Ö TRÄVAROR	31		14			25	4	10	319	1	1	1	2	5	5	29
3320	TRÄMÖBLER	93	60					15								3	30
34111	PAPPERSMASSA																31
34112	PAPPER & PAPP	5	8	11	3		20	2	2	24		2			14		32
34113	TRÄFIBERPLATTOR									1					1		33
3412	PAPPFÖRPACKN.	38	68	5	30	9	14	2	2	30	1	2		6	6	3	34
3419	Ö PAPPERSVAROR	6	11	2	3	2	12	18		4		17		7	3	24	35
34201	GRAFISKA VAROR	44	91	15	27	1	8	13		31	1	13		7	3	18	36
34204	FÖRLAGSVAROR	28	60	12	20	5	38	13	1	22				5	4	128	37
3511	KEMIKALIER	46	58	1						46							38
3512	GÖDSELMEDEL	47	33	2	52	5	161	53	10	2		10			22		39
35131	BASPLAST	17	32		2		91	160		4					9		40
35132	PLAST_HALVFAB.	170	70	10	10	5	15	112	5	54	5	15			33		41
3521	FÄRGER													6			42
3522	LÄKEMEDEL																43
3523	TVÄTTMEDEL																44
3529	Ö KEM-VAROR	119	13	8	17	3	4	7	10	54	1	21	1	1	2		45
3530	BENSIN EO ETC.	160	182	2	2	2	61	37	10	105	1	2	1	8	15	1119	46
3540	SMÖRJMEDEL	19	38	25			8	10	1	21	10	10		3	3		47
3550	GUMMIVAROR	3	223	1			46	12		471		1		10	8	3	48
3560	PLASTVAROR	49	289		112	5	19	3		195		1		3	9	2	49

No.	VARUSNI	AKTIVITETSSNI	MET.-V.IND.	MASKIN IND.	ELMOT. IND.	TELE-M.IND.	HHEL-V.IND.	Ö EL-V.IND.	VARV ETC.	RÄLS-F.IND.	BIL-IND.	MC&CY-KELIND.	FLYGPL IND.	Ö TRPT M.IND.	INSTR. TILLV.	A IND. TILLV.	EL&VÄR MEVERK
50	3610	PORSLIN	31	25	20		10	5	16		141				8		1
51	3620	GLAS		10	5			21			1						
52	3691	TEGEL															
53	3692	CEMENT		2													
54	3699	BEARB. MINERAL	27	70	32	2	10	8	66	20	18	8	9	17	29	2	25
55	37101	JÄRN & STÅL	2252	1556	113	96	38	34	963		888						42
56	37102	FERROLEGERINGAR	19	31	1	1				13	3						89
57	37103	JÄRNGJUTGODS	70	545	5	2	5	63	107		223	1	2		3		2
58	37201	ANNAN METALL	166	47	7		16	344	5		23	1	3		1		31
59	37203	A MET.HALVFAB.	390	93	32	144	3	11	35	1	133	5	7		12		3
60	37204	A MET.GJUTGODS	21	85	2	4	14	48	21		64		3		16		46
61	381	METALLVAROR	1910	1681	68	24	5	77	720	16	735		131	1	22		12
62	382	MASKINER	195	4142	110	14	52	44	640	82	727		180		19		
63	3831	ELMOTORER	14	317	287	132	17	5	66	11	213		1		15		
64	3832	TELEMATERIEL		75	50	1398	72	10	7				31				
65	3833	HUSH-ELAPP.															
66	3839	Ö EL-VAROR	138	26	390	233	35	234	73	2	4	5	6		29		109
67	3841	FARTYG & BÅTAR		111					653	10	438			32			
68	3842	RÄLSFORDON								20	5	8					
69	3843	BILAR	3	144					110		3844	27					
70	3844	MC & CYKLAR															
71	3845	FLYGPLAN											460				
72	3849	Ö TRANSP.MEDEL															
73	3850	INSTRUMENT	21	113	10	2		6	20		124	1	36		286		
74	3900	Ö VAROR	2	5		22	3			5	2			6	6	34	205
75	4101&3	EL & VÄRME	139	138	20			35	38		67	1	13				8
76	4102	GAS	2	1													
77	4200	VATTEN	8	12	2	3	4	2	4		8	3	1		1		
78	5000	BYGGNADER	57	112	16	35	5	18	57	6	65	3	13	1	5	3	499
79	61/62	HANDELSTJÄNSTER	68	220	22	63	1	14	60	1	143		2	1	18	6	
80	63	HOTELL&REST.TJ.	18	38	7	13	6	33	8	2	14	1	8	1	3	2	11
81	71	TRANSPORTTJÄNST	161	246	21	53	2	13	38	2	140	1	23	2	12	10	20
82	72	POST & TELETJ.	47	101	20	35	3	19	21	2	39		20	1	9	4	28
83	81/82	BANK & FÖRS.TJ.	71	137	25	44			36	4	54		27		12	5	31
84	831BO	BOSTADSHYROR	37	55	7	15	1	8	17	2	38	3	6		3		
85	831AN	Ö HYROR	196	358	108	182	9	73	125	12	255	3	119	3	49	29	65
86	832/3	UPPDRAG	49	31	2	5	1	9	9	1	21		8		9		56
87	9511/3	BIL- & HH.REP.	52	86	12	23	1	1	24	3	42		11		5	5	117
88	9 ÖVR	Ö PRIV.TJÄNSTER	17	38	7	12	1	10	8	1	14		8		3	2	11
89		OFF MARKN.PROD															
90	1-9	SUMMA INSATS	7284	12088	1508	2824	351	1695	4629	264	10170	85	1296	64	632	533	2529
		FÖRÄDLINGSVÄRDE	7353	10435	1282	3372	265	1545	3045	353	5086	76	1210	69	774	450	5350
		PRODUKTION PP	14637	22523	2790	6196	616	3240	7674	617	15256	161	2512	133	1406	983	7879

INPUT - OUTPUT 1975

TABELL 1A INSATS NÄRINGSLIVET FÖRDELAD ENLIGT AKTIVITETSSNI   MOTTAGARPRIS   MILJONER KR

RAD NR	VARUSNI	AKTIVITETSSNI	76 GAS-VERK	77 VATTEN VERK	78 BYGGN. IND.	79 VARU-HANDEL	80 HOTELL & REST	81 SAM-FÄRDS. & TELE	82 POST & TELE	83 BANK & FÖRS	84 BOST. FÖRV.	85 A FAST FÖRV.	86 UPPDR. VERKS.	87 BIL- & HH.REP	88 Ö PRIV TJÄNST	89 SUMMA INSATS
1	11	JORDBRUKSVAROR			50		186								47	8529
2	12	SKOGSBRUKSVAROR			91					1	25	5	1			8142
3	13	FISK					50				13					133
4	2301	JÄRNMALM														927
5	2302	ANNAN MALM														713
6	2900+	A MINERALER		5	462						10	5			42	5846
7	3111	KÖTT & CHARK					681	91							11	3573
8	3112	MJÖLK ETC.					175	60							7	1189
9	3113	VEG. KONSERVER					120								6	361
10	3114	FISKKONSERVER					116								3	263
11	3115	OLJOR & FETTER					46								2	1195
12	3116	MJÖL					28	61							9	786
13	3117	BRÖD					128	60							2	216
14	3118	SOCKER					28									701
15	3119	CHOKL. & KONF.														101
16	3121	A LIVSMEDEL					157								9	594
17	3122	FODERMEDEL														1990
18	3130	DRYCKER					410	30							9	600
19	3140	TOBAK														
20	3211	GARN & VÄVNADER			5		20	50		10					10	2101
21	3212	TEXTILSÖMNAD			20	25			5							237
22	3213	TRIKÅVAROR				55										137
23	3214/9	ANNAN TEXTIL			212		22	30	15						22	611
24	3220	LÄDER & SKOR			10									23		538
25	323J+	LÄDER & SKOR				50										406
26	3311	SÅGAT TRÄ			846	50		64			75	5	20		50	4034
27	33112	TRÄHUS & BYGGSN			3344											4274
28	33119	FANER & SPÅNSK.			412			132	20							830
29	3312/9	Ö TRÄVAROR			119	67									45	791
30	3320	TRÄMÖBLER				50	10									711
31	34111	PAPPERSMASSA			78	44	2	94	3	12	2	2	61	3	14	1592
32	34112	PAPPER & PAPP														2366
33	34113	TRÄFIBERPLATTOR			102											225
34	3412	PAPPFÖRPACKN.				340	2								125	1478
35	3419	Ö PAPPERSVAROR			142	55	31	10	4	16	3	3	14	3	20	1698
36	34201	GRAFISKA VAROR		2	119	266	19	72	113	51		41	708	27	174	6433
37	34204	FÖRLAGSVAROR		2	89	418	14	51	23	46		31	880	20	331	2431
38	3511	KEMIKALIER		15	2									13	33	3990
39	3512	GÖDSELMEDEL													90	1371
40	35131	BASPLAST														2565
41	35132	PLAST,HALVFAB.			648	13					25	5				1526
42	3521	FÄRGER			420											1255
43	3522	LÄKEMEDEL		5			13	62						20		193
44	3523	TVÄTTMEDEL			15	13	26	33	30	4	50	5	53		13	307
45	3529	Ö KEM-VAROR			214	21	152	35	84	92	1	72	74	20	50	1541
46	3530	BENSIN EO ETC.	57		948	1366		2229			398			109	319	11160
47	3540	SMÖRJMEDEL			160	40		119						10	15	1611
48	3550	GUMMIVAROR		7	113	155		300			3	2	1		20	1717
49	3560	PLASTVAROR			137	159	75	16	4	16			15	3		1706

VARUSNI	AKTIVITETSSNI	GAS- VATTEN VERK	VATTEN VERK	BYGGN. IND.	VARU- HANDEL	HOTELL & REST	SAM- FÄRDS.	POST & TELE	BANK & FORS	BOST. FÖRV.	A FAST FÖRV.	UPPDR. VERKS.	BIL- & HH.REP	Ö PRIV TJÄNST	SUMMA INSATS	RAD NR
3610	PORSLIN			330		60							6		425	50
3620	GLAS			81	39	72									727	51
3691	TEGEL			380											600	52
3692	CEMENT	2		64											622	53
3699	BEARB. MINERAL			2951						28					3701	54
37101	JÄRN & STÅL			317											9391	55
37102	FERROLEGERINGAR			20											1052	56
37103	JÄRNGJUTGODS														1082	57
37201/	ANNAN METALL			1	22									10	2232	58
37203	A MET.HALVFAB.			580											2269	59
37204	A MET,GJUTGODS			10											266	60
381	METALLVAROR	2	12	3820	234	16	197	14	5	61	12	5	20	46	11870	61
382	MASKINER			958	129			10	5			1	70	2	9034	62
3831	ELMOTORER			50									30		1238	63
3832	TELEMATERIEL			183	150									34	1975	64
3833	HUSH.ELAPP.			471											591	65
3839	Ö EL-VAROR		12	632	125	15	52	45		50	5		30	18	3131	66
3841	FARTYG & BÅTAR						368								1054	67
3842	RÄLSFORDON						432								471	68
3843	BILAR				110								1335		5586	69
3844	MC & CYKLAR														27	70
3845	FLYGPLAN														587	71
3849	Ö TRANSP.MEDEL						127								2	72
3850	INSTRUMENT			2	12	11	2	2	4	1	1	24	2	12	686	73
3900	Ö VAROR			10	40		7	7	7			91		9	359	74
410&3	EL & VÄRME	1	40	17	488	62	177	45	33	291	70	57	44	116	4763	75
4102	GAS			95											44	76
4200	VATTEN	20								267	153			20	580	77
5000	BYGGNADER	7	139				714			3629	815		19	119	10084	78
61/62	HANDELSTJÄNSTER			56	227			1785							1179	79
63	HOTELL&REST.TJ.	1	2		290	9	84	13	58	11	9	50	12	87	928	80
71	TRANSPORTTJÄNST	2	2	1389	4378	23	3172	203	101	3	3	93	3	23	12626	81
72	POST & TELETJ.	2		142	526	22	183	54	138	33	16	131	32	208	2362	82
81/82	BANK & FÖRS.TJ.	3	1	217	249	30	241	25	6045*	170	130	122	22	59	8761	83
831B0	BOSTADSHYROR															84
831AN	Ö HYROR			155	1960	419	170	156	636	101	50	1679	25	599	6365	85
832/3	UPPDRAG		5	504	1401	52	408	111	733	12	7	1432	54	424	9313	86
9511/3	BIL- & HH.REP.		3	343	445	25	1024	37	16			56	23	68	2733	87
9 ÖVR	Ö PRIV.TJÄNSTER	1	1	218	312	75	164	108	26	1124	162	56	24	367	3510	88
UFF	MARKN.PROD			58	318	9	119	13	55		20	49	12	83	983	89
1-9	SUMMA INSATS	69	281	22811	14588	3397	11240	2923	8110	6388	1628	5644	2018	3820	218871	90
	FÖRÄDLINGSVÄRDE	27	490	20018	25557	2480	10069	3551	2906	17785	5744	6813	2961	7752	204071	
	PRODUKTION PP	96	771	42829	40145	5877	21309	6474	11016	24173	7372	12457	4979	11572	423572	

*FÖRDELADE BANKTJÄNSTER (=RÄNTENETTOT) INGÅR MED ETT VÄRDE AV 5978 MKR.

TABELL 2   PRODUKTION AV MARKNADSPRODUKTER FÖRDELAD ENLIGT VARUSNI OCH AKTIVITETSSNI

PRODUCENTPRIS   MILJONER KR

	AKTIVITETSSNI	VARUSNI	1 JORDBR VAROR	2 SKOGS VAROR	3 FISK	4 JÄRN-MALM	5 ANNAN MALM	6 A MINE RALER	7 KÖTT CHARK	8 MJÖLK ETC.	9 VEG. KONS.	10 FISK KONS.	11 OLJOR FETTER	12 MJÖL	13 BRÖD	14 SOCKER	15 CHOK-LAD
1	11	JORDBRUK	11772														
2	12	SKOGSBRUK		7713													
3	13	FISKE			288												
4	2301	JÄRNMALMSGRUVOR				2876		6									
5	2302	A MET.GRUVOR				1	493	23									
6	2900+	STENBROTT,A.GR.						966									
7	3111	SLAKTERIINDUSTRI	17						7668		10		19		1		
8	3112	MEJERIINDUSTRI	3							4371	58	4	127	4			
9	3113	FRUKTKONSÉRVIND.	11						253		1071	58	17	20	2		4
10	3114	FISKKONSERVIND.							1		13	481					9
11	3115	OLJE- & FETTIND								29			1184				
12	3116	KVARNINDUSTRI												914			4
13	3117	BAGERIINDUSTRI												1	2445		
14	3118	SOCKERINDUSTRI							5	2	1					861	9
15	3119	CHOKL.KONF.IND.	7												1		
16	3121	Ö.LIVSM.IND	3						83	16	7	3	9	7	2		848
17	3122	FODERMEDELSIND.							3		48	3	14	1	15		10
18	3130	DRYCKESVARUIND.									24			1			
19	3140	TOBAKSINDUSTRI															
20	3211	GARN & VÄVIND.															
21	3212	TEXTILSÖMNADINU															
22	3213	TRIKÅVARUIND.															
23	3214/9	Ö TEXTILIND.															
24	3220	BEKLÄDNADSIND.															
25	323/4	LÄDER & SKOIND.															
26	33111	SÅGVERK		7													
27	33112	TRÄHUSINDUSTRI															
28	33119	A TRÄMTRL.IND.															
29	3312/9	Ö TRÄVARUIND.															
30	3320	TRÄMÖBELIND.															
31	34111	MASSAINDUSTRI						1									
32	34112	PAPPERSINDUSTRI															
33	34113	TRÄFIBERPL.IND.															
34	3412	PAPPFÖRP.IND.															
35	3419	Ö PPR-VARUIND.															
36	34201	GRAFISK IND.															
37	34204	FÖRLAG															
38	3511	KEMIKALIEIND.															
39	3512	GÖDSELMED.IND.						4					45				
40	35131	BASPLASTIND.															
41	35132	PLAST.HF.IND.						1	3								
42	3521	FÄRGINDUSTRI									1						
43	3522	LÄKEMEDELSIND.															
44	3523	TVÄTTMEDELSIND.															
45	3529	Ö KEM.INDUSTRI							8		2		7				
46	3530	PETROL.RAFF.															
47	3540	SMÖRJM.IND.															
48	3550	GUMMIVARUIND.															
49	3560	PLASTVARUIND.						27									

AKTIVITETSSNI / VARUSNI	JORDBR VAROR	SKOGS VAROR	FISK	JÄRN- MALM	ANNAN MALM	A.MINE RALER	KÖTT CHARK	MJÖLK ETC.	VEG. KONS.	FISK KONS.	OLJOR FETTER	MJÖL	BRÖD	SOCKER	CHOK- LAD
50 3o10 PORSLINSIND.															
51 3o20 GLASINDUSTRI															
52 3o91 TEGELINDUSTRI															
53 3o92 CEMENTIND.						14									
54 3699 Ö MIN.VARUIND.						26									
55 37101 JÄRN-&STÅLVERK															
56 37102 FERROLEG.VERK															
57 37103 JÄRNGJUTERIER					18										
58 37201/ ICKEJÄRNMET.IND															
59 37203 A MET.HF.IND.															
60 37204 A MET.GJUTERI															
61 381 METALLVARUIND.															
62 382 MASKININD.															
63 3831 ELMOTORIND.															
64 3832 TELEPROD.IND															
65 3o33 MH-ELAPP.IND.															
66 3839 Ö ELVARUIND.															
67 3841 VARV ETC.															
68 3842 RÄLSFORDONSIND.															
69 3o43 BILINDUSTRI															
70 3844 MC- & CYKELIND.															
71 3845 FLYGPLANSIND.															
72 3849 Ö TRPT.MED.IND.															
73 3850 INSTRUM.INDUSTRI															
74 3900 A TILLV.IND.															
75 4101&3 EL & VÄRMEVERK															
76 4102 GASVERK															
77 4200 VATTENVERK															
78 5000 BYGGNADSIND.															
79 o1/62 VARUHANDEL															
80 o3 HOTELL & REST.															
81 71 SAMFÄRDSEL															
82 72 POST & TELE															
83 81/82 BANK & FÖRSÄKR.															
84 831BO BOST.FÖRVALTN.															
85 831AN A FASTIGH.FÖRV.															
86 832/3 UPPDRAGSVERKS.															
87 9511/3 BILREP. ETC.															
88 9 ÖVR Ö PRIV.TJ.															
89 1-9 SUMMA PRODUKTION	11811	7720	288	2878	512	1008	8024	4421	1236	548	1422	950	2464	862	884

KOLUMNSUMMORNA I TABELL 2 MOTSVARAS AV VÄRDENA I PRODUKTIONSKOLUMNEN I TABELL 1. RADSUMMORNA ÄR IDENTISKA MED KOLUMNSUMMORNA
I TABELL 1A OCH KAN EFTER AGGREGERING ANKNYTAS TILL PRODUKTIONSVÄRDEN FÖR NÄRINGSGRENAR ENLIGT SNR.
AVVIKELSER ATT DÄRVID BEAKTA FRAMGÅR AV AVSNITT 6. VÄRDE I DIAGONALCELL DIVIDERAT MED RADSUMMA GER "SPECIALISERINGSGRAD" OCH MED
KOLUMNSUMMA "TÄCKNINGSGRAD" (JÄMFÖR AVSNITT 4).

INPUT-OUTPUT 1975

TABELL 2   PRODUKTION AV MARKNADSPRODUKTER FÖRDELAD ENLIGT VARUSNI OCH AKTIVITETSSNI

PRODUCENTPRIS   MILJONER KR

AKTIVITETSSNI	VARUSNI	16 ANDRA LIVSM.	17 FODER-MEDEL	18 DRYCK	19 TOBAK	20 GARN & VÄVN. TEXTIL	21 TEXTIL SÖMNAD	22 TRIKÅ-VAROR	23 ANNAN TEXTIL	24 KLÄDER SÖMNAD	25 LÄDER & SKOR	26 SÅGAT TRÄ	27 TRÄHUS SNICK.	28 FANER& SPÅNSK	29 Ö TRÄ-VAROR	30 TRÄ-MÖBLER	
11	JORDBRUK																1
12	SKOGSBRUK																2
13	FISKE																3
2301	JÄRNMALMSGRUVOR																4
2302	A MET.GRUVOR																5
2900+	STENBROTT,A.GR.																6
3111	SLAKTERIINDUSTRI	80	43														7
3112	MEJERIINDUSTRI	126	7	4													8
3113	FRUKTKONSERVIND	1	1	4													9
3114	FISKKONSERVIND.																10
3115	OLJE- & FETTIND	4															11
3116	KVARNINDUSTRI	23															12
3117	BAGERIINDUSTRI		5														13
3118	SOCKERINDUSTRI	9	69														14
3119	CHOKL.KONF.IND.	13															15
3121	Ö.LIVSM.IND	1520	11	7													16
3122	FODERMEDELSIND.	10	1431														17
3130	DRYCKESVARUIND.	8		1681													18
3140	TOBAKSINDUSTRI				481												19
3211	GARN & VÄVIND.					1420	44	21	95	4	4					19	20
3212	TEXTILSÖMNADINU						487	1	1	5							21
3213	TRIKÅVARUIND.					36	7	844	661	3							22
3214/9	Ö TEXTILIND.					32	4	2		7							23
3220	BEKLÄDNADSIND.						4	306	4	2318	802						24
323/4	LÄDER & SKOIND.						4	1	1	9	2						25
33111	SÅGVERK											6370	131	15	99	23	26
33112	TRÄHUSINDUSTRI											123	4170	36	11	18	27
33119	A TRÄMTRL.IND.											24	11	711	3	4	28
3312/9	b TRÄVARUIND.						14					23	8	2	788	21	29
3320	TRÄMÖBELIND.						12		10			3	26		4	2566	30
34111	MASSAINDUSTRI																31
34112	PAPPERSINDUSTRI								32			21					32
34113	TRÄFIBERPL.IND.																33
3412	PAPPFÖRP.IND.																34
3419	Ö PPR-VARUIND.							1	1								35
34201	GRAFISK IND.									2					2		36
34204	FÖRLAG																37
3511	KEMIKALIEIND.		3														38
3512	GÖDSELMED.IND.																39
35131	BASPLASTIND.	1							13								40
35132	PLAST.HF.IND.												7	2	4	11	41
3521	FÄRGINDUSTRI		4														42
3522	LÄKEMEDELSIND.		2														43
3523	TVÄTTMEDELSIND.																44
3529	Ö KEM.INDUSTRI	6															45
3530	PETROL.RAFF.																46
3540	SMÖRJM.IND.																47
3550	GUMMIVARUIND.						11		9	17	24				1	2	48
3560	PLASTVARUIND.					1			2	2	1					5	49

273

AKTIVITETSSNI / VARUSNI	ANDRA LIVSM.	FODER- MEDEL	DRYCK	TOBAK	GARN & VÄVN.	TEXTIL SÖMNAD	TRIKÅ- VAROR	ANNAN TEXTIL	KLÄDER	LÄDER & SKOR	SÅGAT TRÄ	TRÄHUS SNICK.	FANER& SPÅNSK	TRÄ- VAROR	TRÄ- MÖBLER
50 3610 PORSLINSIND.															
51 3620 GLASINDUSTRI															
52 3691 TEGELINDUSTRI															
53 3692 CEMENTIND.															
54 3699 Ö MIN.VARUIND.															1
55 37101 JÄRN-&STÅLVERK															
56 37102 FERROLEG.VERK															
57 37103 JÄRNGJUTERIER															
58 37601/ ICKEJÄRNMET.IND															
59 37203 A MET.HF.IND.															
60 3720A A MET.GJUTERI														26	8
61 381 METALLVARUIND.						1	9	15				1	2	1	231
62 382 MASKININD.						2									1
63 3831 ELMOTORIND.															
64 3832 TELEPROD.IND												1			
65 3833 HH.ELAPP.IND.												3			
66 3839 Ö ELVARUIND.															
67 3841 VARV ETC.							6			3					
68 3842 RXLSFORDONSIND.									2						
69 3843 BILINDUSTRI							4			4				2	5
70 3844 MC- & CYKELIND.															
71 3845 FLYGPLANSIND.															
72 3849 Ö TRPT.MED.IND.															
73 3850 INSTRUM.INDUSTRI									7		1				
74 3900 A TILLV.IND.									2					2	1
75 41014.3 EL & VÄRMEVERK															
76 4102 GASVERK															
77 420U VATTENVERK															
78 5000 BYGGNADSIND.															
79 61/62 VARUHANDEL															
80 63 HOTELL & REST.															
81 71 SAMFÄRDSEL															
82 72 POST & TELE															
83 81/82 BANK & FÖRSÄKR.															
84 831B0 BOST.FÖRVALTN.															
85 831AN A FASTIGH.FÖRV.															
86 832/3 UPPDRAGSVERKS.															
87 9511/3 BILREP. ETC.															
88 9 ÖVR Ö PRIV.TJ.															
89 1-9 SUMMA PRODUKTION	1802	1578	1696	481	1494	604	1176	845	2378	844	6568	4359	769	945	2918

274

TABELL 2   PRODUKTION AV MARKNADSPRODUKTER FÖRDELAD ENLIGT VARUSNI OCH AKTIVITETSSNI   PRODUCENTPRIS   MILJONER KR

AKTIVITETSSNI / VARUSNI		31 PAPPER MASSA & PAPP	32 PAPPER & PAPP	33 PAPPER TRÄFI-BERPL.	34 PAPP-FÖRP.	35 PPR-VAROR	36 GRAF. VAROR	37 FÖRLAG VAROR	38 KEMI-KALIER	39 GÖDSEL MEDEL	40 BAS-PLAST HALVF.	41 PLAST HALVF.	42 FÄRGER	43 LÄKE-MEDEL	44 TVÄTT-MEDEL	45 Ö KEM-VAROR
1	11 JORDBRUK															
2	12 SKOGSBRUK															
3	13 FISKE															
4	2301 JÄRNMALMSGRUVOR															
5	2302 A MET.GRUVOR															
6	2900+ STENBROTT.A.GR.															
7	3111 SLAKTERIINDUSTRI								1							
8	3112 MEJERIINDUSTRI															1
9	3113 FRUKTKONSERVIND.															
10	3114 FISKKONSERVIND.															
11	3115 OLJE- & FETTIND								1							
12	3116 KVARNINDUSTRI															
13	3117 BAGERIINDUSTRI															
14	3118 SOCKERINDUSTRI															
15	3119 CHOKL.KONF.IND.															3
16	3121 Ö.LIVSM.IND.					9			6							10
17	3122 FODERMEDELSIND.													3	1	1
18	3130 DRYCKESVARUIND.									9						
19	3140 TOBAKSINDUSTRI															
20	3211 GARN & VÄVIND.										1					
21	3212 TEXTILSÖMNADINU															
22	3213 TRIKÅVARUIND.															
23	3214/9 Ö TEXTILIND.					140								13		3
24	3220 BEKLÄDNADSIND.															
25	323/4 LÄDER & SKOIND.															
26	33111 SÅGVERK			6		2										
27	33112 TRÄHUSINDUSTRI															
28	33119 A TRÄMTRL.IND.															
29	3312/9 Ö TRÄVARUIND.															
30	3320 TRÄMÖBELIND.										8					
31	34111 MASSAINDUSTRI		7063	196		9				70						
32	34112 PAPPERSINDUSTRI		939	6663		270	1395	11		45						
33	34113 TRÄFIBERPL.IND.				428											
34	3412 PAPPFÖRP.IND.		15	2		1284	69	42					75			
35	3419 Ö PPR-VARUIND.		3	4	2	10	932	32					1			
36	34201 GRAFISK IND.		3			4	51	6793					5			
37	34204 FÖRLAG								5501							
38	3511 KEMIKALIEIND.									2350	48	255			11	26	136
39	3512 GÖDSELMED.IND.									45	714						
40	35131 BASPLASTIND.						26			124	1	1036	16	4			51
41	35132 PLAST.HF.IND.				2		1			119		88	1010				3
42	3521 FÄRGINDUSTRI									1	2	3		982	1058	9	33
43	3522 LÄKEMEDELSIND.									28	8	71			3	16	15
44	3523 TVÄTTMEDELSIND.									3	9			2		689	28
45	3529 Ö KEM.INDUSTRI									24	20	30	5	25	1	15	1166
46	3530 PETROL.RAFF.																5
47	3540 SMÖRJM.IND.													1			4
48	3550 GUMMIVARUIND.										3		34				
49	3560 PLASTVARUIND.					25	17	6				26	74				6

	AKTIVITETSSNI / VARUSNI	PAPPER MASSA	PAPPER & PAPP	TRÄFI-BERPL.	PAPP-FÖRP.	Ö PPR-VAROR	GRAF. VAROR	FÖRLAG VAROR	KEMI-KALIER	GÖDSEL MEDEL	BAS-PLAST	PLAST HALVF.	FÄRGER	LÄKE-MEDEL	TVÄTT-MEDEL	Ö KEM-VAROR
50	3610 PORSLINSIND.															
51	3620 GLASINDUSTRI															
52	3691 TEGELINDUSTRI															
53	3692 CEMENTIND.												4			
54	3699 Ö MIN.VARUIND.				1											1
55	37101 JÄRN-&STÅLVERK									9			4			3
56	37102 FERROLEG.VERK															1
57	37103 JÄRNGJUTERIER															
58	37201/. ICKEJÄRNMET.IND								59							6
59	37203 A MET.HF.IND.								4							6
60	37204 A MET.GJUTERI															
61	381 METALLVARUIND.				5		9		11				6			154
62	382 MASKININD.						1						13		7	169
63	3831 ELMOTORIND.															
64	3832 TELEPROD.IND															
65	3833 HH.ELAPP.IND.															
66	3839 Ö ELVARUIND.								2		2		1			
67	3841 VARV ETC.															
68	3842 RÄLSFORDONSIND.															
69	3843 BILINDUSTRI															7
70	3844 MC- & CYKELIND.															
71	3845 FLYGPLANSIND.															195
72	3849 Ö TRPT.MED.IND.															
73	3850 INSTRUM.INDUSTRI															2
74	3900 A TILLV.IND.												1			3
75	41016.3 EL & VÄRMEVERK															
76	4102 GASVERK															
77	4200 VATTENVERK															
78	5000 BYGGNADSIND.															
79	61/62 VARUHANDEL															
80	63 HOTELL & REST.															
81	71 SAMFÄRDSEL															
82	72 POST & TELE															
83	81/82 BANK & FÖRSÄKR.															
84	831B0 BOST.FÖRVALTN.															
85	831AN A FASTIGH.FÖRV.															
86	832/3 UPPDRAGSVERKS.															
87	9511/3 BILREP. ETC.															
88	9 ÖVR Ö PRIV.TJ.															
89	1-9 SUMMA PRODUKTION	8043	6872	432	1608	2641	6896	5501	2891	825	1521	1250	1020	1089	764	2018

TABELL 2   PRODUKTION AV MARKNADSPRODUKTER FÖRDELAD ENLIGT VARUSNI OCH AKTIVITETSSNI

PRODUCENTPRIS   MILJONER KR

AKTIVITETSSNI	VARUSNI	46 BENSIN EO ETC	47 SMÖRJ-MEDEL	48 GUMMI-VAROR	49 PLAST-VAROR	50 PORS-LIN	51 GLAS	52 TEGEL	53 CEMENT	54 BEARB. MINER.	55 JÄRN & STÅL	56 FERRO-LEGER.	57 JÄRN-GJUTG.	58 ANNAN METALL	59 A MET. HALVF.	60 A MET. GJUTG.
1	11 JORDBRUK															
2	12 SKOGSBRUK															
3	13 FISKE															
4	2301 JÄRNMALMSGRUVOR															
5	2302 A MET.GRUVOR									2						
6	2900+ STENBROTT.A.GR.								16	19						
7	3111 SLAKTERIINDUSTRI															
8	3112 MEJERIINDUSTRI															
9	3113 FRUKTKONSERVIND															
10	3114 FISKKONSERVIND.															
11	3115 OLJE- & FETTIND															
12	3116 KVARNINDUSTRI															
13	3117 BAGERIINDUSTRI															
14	3118 SOCKERINDUSTRI															
15	3119 CHOKL.KONF.IND.															
16	3121 Ö.LIVSM.IND				1											
17	3122 FODERMEDELSIND.															
18	3130 DRYCKESVARUIND.															
19	3140 TOBAKSINDUSTRI															
20	3211 GARN & VÄVIND.									22						
21	3212 TEXTILSÖMNADIND									1						
22	3213 TRIKÅVARUIND.				6											
23	3214/9 Ö TEXTILIND.				1											
24	3220 BEKLÄDNADSIND.			2												
25	323/4 LÄDER & SKOIND.															
26	33111 SÅGVERK															
27	33112 TRÄHUSINDUSTRI.															
28	33119 A TRÄMTRL.IND.				2											
29	3312/9 Ö TRÄVARUIND.			2	6											
30	3320 TRÄMÖBELIND.						6									
31	34111 MASSAINDUSTRI		14								2					
32	34112 PAPPERSINDUSTRI															
33	34113 TRÄFIBERPL.IND.		10													
34	3416 PAPPFÖRP.IND.				54										3	
35	3419 Ö PPR-VARUIND.				4											
36	34201 GRAFISK IND.				12											
37	34204 FÖRLAG	99														
38	3511 KEMIKALIEIND.			1											1	
39	3512 GÖDSELMED.IND.															
40	35131 BASPLASTIND.								1							
41	35132 PLAST.HF.IND.		6	5	107						8				27	
42	3521 FÄRGINDUSTRI															
43	3522 LÄKEMEDELSIND.		1													
44	3523 TVÄTTMEDELSIND.		20	5												
45	3529 Ö KEM.INDUSTRI		52		5									1		
46	3530 PETROL.RAFF.	4519	784	1688	6											
47	3540 SMÖRJM.IND.	43		4	1524											
48	3550 GUMMIVARUIND.										1				1	
49	3560 PLASTVARUIND.															

	Kod	AKTIVITETSSNI \ VARUSNI	BENSIN EO ETC	SMÖRJ- MEDEL	GUMMI- VAROR	PLAST- VAROR	PORS- LIN	GLAS	TEGEL	CEMENT	BEARB. MINER.	JÄRN & STÅL	FERRO- LEGER.	JÄRN- GJUTG.	ANNAN METALL	A MET. HALVF.	A MET. GJUTG.
50	3610	PORSLINSIND.				2	443										
51	3620	GLASINDUSTRI						654									
52	3691	TEGELINDUSTRI							341		2						
53	3692	CEMENTIND.							6	578	9	1					
54	3699	Ö MIN.VARUIND.							1	19	3133	3					
55	37101	JÄRN-&STÅLVERK										9665		108		22	
56	37102	FERROLEG.VERK											582				
57	37103	JÄRNGJUTERIER												645			
58	37201/	ICKEJÄRNMET.IND										5			922	120	
59	37203	A MET.HF.IND.													149	1810	
60	37204	A MET.GJUTERI													1		402
61	381	METALLVARUIND.				45		1				609		29	31	50	11
62	382	MASKININD.				4						376		166	6		5
63	3831	ELMOTOPIND.										5		8	4		
64	3832	TELEPROD.IND.				3						1		9	12	1	
65	3833	HH.ELAPP.IND.												2	1		
66	3839	Ö ELVARUIND.				8					30	26		7	5	3	
67	3841	VARV ETC.			1	6						1			1		
68	3842	RÄLSFORDONSIND.															
69	3843	BILINDUSTRI			1	10						46		16	5	58	1
70	3844	MC- & CYKELIND.															
71	3845	FLYGPLANSIND.															
72	3849	Ö TRPT.MED.IND.										1		5			
73	3850	INSTRUM.INDUSTRI			3	7								1	1		2
74	3900	A TILLV.IND.				4											
75	41063	EL & VÄRMEVERK															
76	4102	GASVERK															
77	4200	VATTENVERK															
78	5000	BYGGNADSIND.															
79	61/62	VARUHANDEL															
80	63	HOTELL & REST.															
81	71	SAMFÄRDSEL															
82	72	POST & TELE															
83	81/82	BANK & FÖRSÄKR.															
84	831B0	BOST.FÖRVALTN.															
85	831AN	A FASTIGH.FÖRV.															
86	832/3	UPPDRAGSVERKS.															
87	9511/3	BILREP. ETC.															
88	9 ÖVR	Ö PRIV.TJ.															
89	1-9	SUMMA PRODUKTION	4662	887	1712	1822	446	662	349	595	3256	10738	582	992	1141	2095	421

I N P U T - O U T P U T   1 9 7 5

TABELL 2   PRODUKTION AV MARKNADSPRODUKTER FÖRDELAD ENLIGT VARUSNI OCH AKTIVITETSSNI

PRODUCENTPRIS   MILJONER KR

#	AKTIVITETSSNI	VARUSNI	61 METALL VAROR	62 MASKIN VAROR	63 ELEKTR MOTOR	64 TELE- MTRL.	65 HUSH.- ELAPP.	66 Ö EL- VAROR	67 FARTYG BÅTAR	68 RÄLS- FORDON	69 BILAR	70 MC & CYKLAR	71 FLYG- PLAN	72 Ö TRPT MEDEL	73 INSTRU MENT	74 ÖVR. VAROR	75 EL. & VÄRME
1	11	JORDBRUK															
2	12	SKOGSBRUK															
3	13	FISKE															
4	2301	JÄRNMALMSGRUVOR															
5	2302	A MET.GRUVOR															
6	2900+	STENBROTT.A.GR.															
7	3111	SLAKTERIINDUSTRI															
8	3112	MEJERIINDUSTRI															
9	3113	FRUKTKONSERVIND															
10	3114	FISKKONSERVIND.															
11	3115	OLJE- & FETTIND															
12	3116	KVARNINDUSTRI															
13	3117	BAGERIINDUSTRI															
14	3118	SOCKERINDUSTRI															
15	3119	CHOKL.KONF.IND.															
16	3121	Ö.LIVSM.IND															
17	3122	FODERMEDELSIND.															
18	3130	DRYCKESVARUIND.															
19	3140	TOBAKSINDUSTRI															
20	3211	GARN & VXVIND.	1														
21	3212	TEXTILSÖMNADIND	2								1					2	
22	3213	TRIKÅVARUIND.															
23	3214/9	Ö TEXTILIND.															
24	3220	BEKLÄDNADSIND.														1	
25	323/4	LÄDER & SKOIND.									2						
26	33111	SÅGVERK	4													1	
27	33112	TRÄHUSINDUSTRI									2				2		
28	33119	A TRÄMTRL.IND.	22	1													
29	3312/9	B TRÄVARUIND.	20	33							1					5	
30	3320	TRÄMÖBELIND.				19										1	69
31	34111	MASSAINDUSTRI															1
32	34112	PAPPERSINDUSTRI															
33	34113	TRÄFIBERPL.IND.															3
34	3412	PAPPFÖRP.IND.	17	6												21	
35	3419	Ö PPR-VARUIND.		1												1	
36	34201	GRAFISK IND.	9	1											1	4	
37	34204	FÖRLAG															
38	3511	KEMIKALIEIND.		7													
39	3512	GÖDSELMED.IND.															
40	35131	BASPLASTIND.															
41	35132	PLAST.HF.IND.		1													
42	3521	FÄRGINDUSTRI														10	
43	3522	LÄKEMEDELSIND.													3		
44	3523	TVÄTTMEDELSIND.															
45	3529	Ö KEM.INDUSTRI	15			1		3							2	1	
46	3530	PETROL.RAFF.															
47	3540	SMÖRJM.IND.															
48	3550	GUMMIVARUIND.													7	21	
49	3560	PLASTVARUIND.	86	36	119	11		7	2		5				8	1	

AKTIVITETSSNI	VARUSNI	METALL VAROR	MASKIN	ELEKTR MOTOR	TELE-MTRL.	HUSH.-ELAPP.	ÖVR EL-VAROR	FARTYG BÄTAR	RÄLS-FORDON	BILAR	MC & CYKLAR	FLYG-PLAN	ÖVR TRPT MEDEL	INSTRU MENT	ÖVR. VAROR	EL. & VÄRME
3610	PORSLINSIND.						25									
3620	GLASINDUSTRI	9														
3691	TEGELINDUSTRI															
3692	CEMENTIND.															
3699	ÖVR MIN.VARUIND.	1	8													
37101	JÄRN-&STÅLVERK	1349	238	3		15	1			9		9	4			
37102	FERROLEG.VERK	9														
37103	JÄRNGJUTERIER	30	101							7						
37201/	ICKEJÄRNMET.IND															
37203	A MET.HF.IND.	105	8				23			30					13	
37204	A MET.GJUTERI	17	38				8									
381	METALLVARUIND.	12142	614	21	12	58	11	11	2	122	1	1	5	26	35	
382	MASKININD.	402	20222	70	50	315	9	88	56	203	48	23	48	55	38	
3831	ELMOTORIND.	5	12	1857	350		427			9				113	3	
3832	TELEPROD.IND.	39	22	28	5697		67			24				39		
3833	HH.ELAPP.IND.	12	32	68		435	14			12						
3839	ÖVR ELVARUIND.	28	16	113	37	14	2948			1				29	2	
3841	VARV ETC.	82	269	10				6927	44	206	2		1	2	4	
3842	RÄLSFORDONSIND.	15	2					407	595							
3843	BILINDUSTRI	129	358	5	5	1	7		4	14044	5	31	2	5	5	
3844	MC- & CYKELIND.	2						5		1	150		2		6	
3845	FLYGPLANSIND.	2	368				31					1696				
3849	ÖVR TRPT.MED.IND.	6	4							75			51	57	8	
3850	INSTRUM.INDUSTRI	25	35	10	34	3	8			25		19	1	1191	1	
3900	A TILLV.IND.	88											15		779	
4101&3	EL & VÄRMEVERK															7879
4102	GASVERK															
4200	VATTENVERK															
5000	BYGGNADSIND.															
61/62	VARUHANDEL															
63	HOTELL & REST.															
71	SAMFÄRDSEL															
72	POST & TELE															
81/82	BANK & FÖRSÄKR.															
8310	BOST.FÖRVALTN.															
831AN	A FASTIGH.FÖRV.															
832/3	UPPDRAGSVERKS.															
9511/3	BILREP. ETC.		349													
9 ÖVR	ÖVR PRIV.TJ.															
1-9	SUMMA PRODUKTION	14675	22758	2304	6223	841	3588	7440	701	14783	206	1779	124	1544	962	7952

INPUT-OUTPUT 1975

TABELL 2   PRODUKTION AV MARKNADSPRODUKTER FÖRDELAD ENLIGT VARUSNI OCH AKTIVITETSSNI   PRODUCENTPRIS   MILJONER KR

AKTIVITETSSNI	VARUSNI	76 GAS	77 VATTEN	78 BYGG-NÄDER	79 HANDEL TJÄNST	80 HOTELL RESTTJ	81 TRPT-TJÄNST	82 POST-TELETJ	83 BANK & FÖRSTJ	84 BOST. HYROR	85 ÖVR. HYROR	86 UPP-DRAG	87 BIL- & HH.REP	88 Ö PRIV TJÄNST	89 SUMMA PROD	RAD NR
11	JORDBRUK														11772	1
12	SKOGSBRUK														7713	2
13	FISKE														288	3
2301	JÄRNMALMSGRUVOR														2884	4
2302	A MET.GRUVOR														517	5
2900+	STENBROTT,A.GR.											2			1007	6
3111	SLAKTERIINDUSTRI											14			7773	7
3112	MEJERIINDUSTRI														4662	8
3113	FRUKTKONSERVIND														1572	9
3114	FISKKONSERVIND.														497	10
3115	OLJE- & FETTIND											21		1	1244	11
3116	KVARNINDUSTRI														938	12
3117	BAGERIINDUSTRI														2471	13
3118	SOCKERINDUSTRI														939	14
3119	CHOKL,KONF.IND.														887	15
3121	Ö. LIVSM.IND														1743	16
3122	FODERMEDELSIND.											3			1473	17
3130	DRYCKESVARUIND.														1714	18
3140	TOBAKSINDUSTRI														481	19
3211	GARN & VÄVIND.														1620	20
3212	TEXTILSÖMNADIND														527	21
3213	TRIKAVARUIND.												4		885	22
3214/9	Ö TEXTILIND.												1		877	23
3220	BEKLÄDNADSIND.											5	19		2657	24
323/4	LÄDER & SKOIND.												57		879	25
33111	SÄGVERK											11			6661	26
33112	TRÄHUSINDUSTRI			71											4443	27
33119	A TRÄMTRL.IND.											10			763	28
3312/9	Ö TRÄVARUIND.				1										888	29
3320	TRÄMÖBELIND.				1										2717	30
34111	MASSAINDUSTRI														7428	31
34112	PAPPERSINDUSTRI											2		5	9398	32
34113	TRÄFIBERPL.IND.														433	33
3412	PAPPFÖRP.IND.														1595	34
3419	Ö PPR-VARUIND.														996	35
34201	GRAFISK IND.											1			6887	36
34204	FÖRLAG											1			5501	37
3511	KEMIKALIEIND.			27											3013	38
3512	GÖDSELMED.IND.														762	39
35131	BASPLASTIND.														1274	40
35132	PLAST.HF.IND.														1385	41
3521	FÄRGINDUSTRI														1060	42
3522	LÄKEMEDELSIND.														1203	43
3523	TVÄTTMEDELSIND.														735	44
3529	Ö KEM.INDUSTRI														1364	45
3530	PETROL.RAFF.														4576	46
3540	SMÖRJM.IND.	25													889	47
3550	GUMMIVARUIND.											18		29	1863	48
3560	PLASTVARUIND.														1979	49

AKTIVITETSSNI / VARUSNI	GAS	VATTEN	BYGG-NADER	HANDEL TJÄNST	HOTELL RESTTJ	TRPT-TJÄNST	POST & TELETJ	BANK & FÖRSTJ	BOST. HYROR	ÖVR. HYROR	UPP-DRAG MH.REP	BIL- & MH.REP	ÖVR PRIV TJÄNST	SUMMA PROD	RAD NR
3610 PORSLINSIND.														474	50
3620 GLASINDUSTRI														666	51
3691 TEGELINDUSTRI			2											352	52
3692 CEMENTIND.														619	53
3699 Ö MIN.VARUIND.	13		117										1	3318	54
37101 JÄRN-&STÅLVERK											23		1	11450	55
37102 FERROLEG.VERK														609	56
37103 JÄRNGJUTERIER														794	57
37201/ ICKEJÄRNMET.IND													3	1110	58
37203 A MET.HF.IND.														2114	59
37204 A MET.GJUTERI														507	60
381 METALLVARUIND.			272								16		35	14635	61
382 MASKININD.											39	22	88	22527	62
3831 ELMOTORIND.														2790	63
3832 TELEPROD.IND											80		179	6196	64
3833 MH.ELAPP.IND.												29		616	65
3839 Ö ELVARUIND.														3241	66
3841 VARV ETC.											23		53	7674	67
3842 RXLSFORDONSIND.														617	68
3843 BILINDUSTRI												109		15256	69
3844 MC- & CYKELIND.														161	70
3845 FLYGPLANSIND.											27		60	2512	71
3849 Ö TRPT.MED.IND.												40		134	72
3850 INSTRUM.INDUSTRI											4	36	9	1406	73
3900 A TILLV.IND.												87		982	74
410143 EL & VÄRMEVERK	96													7879	75
4102 GASVERK														96	76
4200 VATTENVERK		771												771	77
5000 BYGGNADSIND.			42428											42829	78
61/62 VARUHANDEL				39925							401	220		40145	79
63 HOTELL & REST.					5877									5877	80
71 SAMFÄRDSEL						21152				38			119	21309	81
72 POST & TELE							6316			158				6474	82
81/82 BANK & FÖRSÄKR.								10664		352				11016	83
831B0 BOST.FÖRVALTN.									24173					24173	84
831AN A FASTIGH.FÖPV.										7372				7372	85
832/3 UPPDRAGSVERKS.											12458			12458	86
9511/3 BILREP. ETC.												4630		4979	87
9 ÖVR Ö PRIV.TJ.													11571	11571	88
1-9 SUMMA PRODUKTION	134	771	42919	39925	5877	21152	6316	10664	24173	7920	13158	5254	12155	423572	89

XVII. UNITED STATES

A. GENERAL INFORMATION

The present description is mainly based on Philip M. Ritz, "Definitions and Conventions of the 1972 input-output study", issued by the Bureau of Economic Analysis, July 1980. The tables were published (in a 496 x 496 aggregation) in *The Detailed Input-Output Structure of the United States Economy 1972*, United States Department of Commerce, Bureau of Economic Analysis, 1979, in two volumes: vol. I, *The Use and Make of Commodities by Industries;* vol. II, *Total Requirements for Commodities and Industries*. A less detailed version (85 x 85 aggregation) was published in the *Survey of Current Business*, vol. 59, No. 2 (February 1979) and vol. 59, No. 4 (April 1979).

The development of the input-output tool of economic analysis and the actual construction of the first input-output tables for the United States were the work of Professor Wasily Leontief. Such tables were compiled for the years 1919, 1929 and 1939 and were published in the *Structure of the American Economy 1919-1939*. The next set of input-output tables was compiled by the Bureau of Labour Statistics for the year 1947, and was published in 1952. None of those tables were integrated with the National Product and Income Accounts, which were annually prepared by the Bureau of Economic Analysis. Later input-output work was transferred to the bureau, which published tables for 1958, 1963 and 1967. These were consistent with the US National Income and Product Accounts for those years. The Bureau also revised the 1947 input-output study into a format that was consistent with the other input-output studies. The present report describes the 1972 input-output tables, which are the latest ones that have been published and on which information is available with regard to concepts, statistical sources and compilation methodology. The Bureau of Economic Analysis prepared a table for 1977, similar to the 1972 table with regard to concepts, table, structure, sources and statistical methodology. Results were published in May 1984.

The 1972 tables differ in various respects from previous input-output studies. The classification system used is modified in detail and coverage of individual activity and commodity categories in comparison with previous classification schemes. There are also some differences in the treatment of secondary products. A distinction is made in the present study between competitive and complementary imports. This distinction was not available in previous studies. Two types of dummy industries for office supplies and for business travel, entertainment and gifts, which were used in earlier tables as a channel for commodities that could not be separately identified among the intermediate inputs of industries, were eliminated due to improved basic data. On the other hand, a separate industry was introduced for eating and drinking places in order to arrive at a more homogeneous input structure for the column of retail trade in which this activity was previously included.

The input-output tables for 1972 are compiled within the framework of the National Income and Product Accounts, as mentioned above. This implies that the input-output estimates at the aggregate level are fully consistent with those of the National Income and Product Accounts. However, differences remain with regard to the industrial breakdown of those aggregates, particularly value added. One reason is that the two systems have adopted different classification units for some of the transactions. For example, where value added in the national accounts is compiled from the income side, property income which is available from the company accounts is classified on the basis of enterprise units. The input-output tables on the other hand arrive at value added from the production side as the difference between gross output and intermediate consumption per sector. Since in the latter calculation property income is only implicitly accounted for in the difference between the two aggregates per sector, this value added component is implicitly classified on the basis of the establishment as a unit of classification. Furthermore, since the input-output tables require more detail in the industrial breakdown than the national accounts, additional statistical sources are used, which results in further minor differences between some of the estimates obtained in both sets of data. A similar difference occurs with regard to the activity breakdown of changes in business inventories. In the national income and product accounts which breakdown is based on stocks held by establishments, that is, it is an industrial breakdown. In the 1972 input-output tables the classification of changes in business inventories appears in the absorption matrix, and therefore it reflects a distribution of the stocks by types of commmodities. Any discrepancy in the activity allocation of this category between the accounts and the input-output tables is caused by stocks of secondary products which are held by particular industries in addition to their stocks of characteristic products, and by stocks of characteristic products which are held as secondary products by other industries.

There are several differences between the concepts and classifications of the United States input-output tables and the input-output recommendations of SNA. Most reflect conceptual differences between the SNA national accounting recommendations and the United States framework of National Income and Product Accounts; others are differences that only pertain to input-output tables. They concern the definitions of gross output of producers of government services, the classification of producers of government services and government enterprises and their distinction, as well as the classification of producers of private non-profit services. Two dummy sectors are included that adapt the input-output concepts to those used in the National Income and Product Accounts. Furthermore there are differences with regard to the value added breakdown and the definition and allocation of imputed banking and insurance services. Changes in stocks are differently valued and have different coverage from what is recommended in SNA. Complementary imports are valued in foreign port values instead of c.i.f. values. Commodity taxes are not separately distinguished in the absorption or make matrices, so that approximate basic values cannot be derived. Finally, neither the United States tables nor the National Income and Product Accounts identify public gross fixed capital. Capital formation is limited to the non-government sectors only.

B. ANALYTICAL FRAMEWORK

1. *Tables and derived matrices available*

The results of the 1972 input-output study are presented in two basic tables:

    (i)   Absorption matrix;

    (ii) Make matrix;

and in the following five derived matrices:

    (i')   Matrix of input coefficients based on the absorption matrix, (table (i));

    (ii') Inverse matrix of total commodity output required per commodity used in final demand. This matrix is based on an input-output table that is derived from the absorption and make matrices (tables (i) and (ii)) after transfer of secondary production;

    (iii') Inverse matrix of total required industry output per commodity used in final demand. As table (iii), this inverse matrix is based on an input-output table that is derived after transfer of all secondary products;

    (iv') Matrix of percentage distribution of total demand for commodities by use, based on table (i);

    (v') Matrix of percentage distribution of commodity output per producing industry, is based on the make matrix of table (ii).

Tables (i) and (ii) and derived matrices (ii') and (iii') are available at three different levels of aggregation: 85 x 85, 365 x 365, and 496 x 496. Actually, derived matrices (ii') and (iii') are not presented in the 496 x 496 level of aggregation, but have been adjusted to respectively 489 x 485 and 487 x 487, because industry categories are not matched with corresponding commodity categories or vice versa. Table (i) is not available at the 496 x 496 level of aggregation. Tables (iv') and (v') are only presented in an 85 x 85 level of aggregation.

2. *Valuation standards*

All tables are compiled in producers' prices. Contrary to the SNA recommendations, commodity taxes are not separated in the make or absorption matrices and therefore no valuation in approximate basic values can be derived. The valuation of imports also differs from what is recommended in the SNA. In line with the valuation in producers' prices, imports exclude transoceanic trade and transport margins, that is, they are valued in foreign port values and not c.i.f. as recommended in SNA. However, in practice, this deviating treatment was only accorded to complementary imports. It was not applied to competitive imports, which were valued c.i.f. for two reasons. First, foreign port valuation would require an accompanying distribution of the transoceanic margins to the sectors of destination of the imported goods, which is not feasible because in the use matrix no distinction is made between domestically produced and imported goods in the individual intermediate and final demand categories. Furthermore, foreign port valuation would not well reflect

the competitiveness of the domestically produced goods versus the imported goods, since actually c.i.f. values are competing with producers' values of domestically produced goods and not foreign port values.

3. *Statistical units and classification standards*

A cross-classification of activity and commodity categories is used in the absorption and make matrices (tables (i) and (ii)) as recommended in SNA. The same applies to the derived tables. The establishment is the unit of classification in the activity breakdown. The establishment is defined as "an economic unit generally at a single physical location where business is conducted or where services or industrial operations are performed. Where distinct and separate economic activities are performed at a single physical location, each distinct activity should be treated as a separate establishment. Establishments defined in this manner generally produce more than one type of commodity. However, in two sectors, commodities and industries come very close, that is, in agriculture and construction. In both sectors, the activities are defined on the basis of the products produced (in agriculture: vegetables, fruits, food grains, etc. and in construction: new residential structures, industrial buildings, office buildings, hotels, etc.).

Establishments are classified according to the United States Standard Industrial Classification (SIC).[1] Since commodities are defined as the characteristic products of the corresponding industry, a one-to-one correspondence usually exists between the industrial categories distinguished and the commodities. In this sense, it can be said that commodities are also classified according to SIC categories. However, there are exceptions to this statement, as explained in the following paragraph.

There are products that are not characteristic to any industry or industries that only produce products that are characteristic of other industries. Examples of the first type are scrap, used and second-hand goods, as well as complementary imports, which are shown as separate commodity categories in the absorption matrix, but are not matched by corresponding industries in the columns of that table. There are several examples of the second type of discrepancy: the forest activity produces commodities that are characteristic products of the activity forestry and fishing products; federal, state and local utilities that are separately distinguished as activities under government enterprises produce commodities that are characteristic of private utilities that produce electricity, gas, water and sanitary services and are classified elsewhere; another activity under government enterprises is the local government passenger transit, which produces commodities that are characteristically produced by activities distinguished under the main heading of transportation and warehousing. Finally there is the Commodity Credit Corporation as a separate activity under government enterprises, which has only input and no output, so that no commodity category corresponds with this industry.

The intermediate consumption quadrant differs from the SNA recommendations in that a dummy sector known as "rest of the world industry" is introduced in order to elimi-

---

[1]The relationship between SIC and ISIC can be found in "Correlation between the United States and ISIC", Technical Paper No. 1, Office of Federal Statistical Policy and Standards, Office of Management and Budget, October 1979.

nate discrepancies between the National Income and Product Accounts and the input-output tables with regard to two concepts used in the accounts: gross national product and final consumption. To arrive at GNP instead of GDP (which is the concept used in the input-output tables for the industrial sectors), included in the rest of the world industry column are entries for factor incomes from abroad, (i.e., compensation of United States residents working in the United States for foreign governments or international organizations, plus earnings of United States residents working abroad, plus receipts of income on foreign investments), and for factor incomes that are paid to abroad, that is, wages and salaries paid to foreigners working in the United States and private payments of income on foreign assets. The factor incomes received are shown at the intersection of the rest of the world row and exports column, while factor incomes paid are entered as a negative item in the intersection of the same row and the import column. The difference between the two flows, which should be added to GDP in order to arrive at GNP, is recorded in the value added section of the rest of the world. To arrive at private final consumption, as presented in the accounts, travel expenditures in the United States by foreign residents working in the United States for foreign governments or international organizations, expenditures by other foreign workers working in the United States, expenditures in the United States by foreign crews and remittances in kind are shown as negative entries in the intersection of the rest of the world industry row and the column of private final consumption expenditure and as positive entries in the intersection of the same row and the exports column. Similarly, there is an adjustment of government final consumption expenditure by entering government sales to abroad as a negative item in the intersection of the rest of the world industry row and the government final consumption expenditure column and as a positive item in the intersection of the same row and the exports column.

Another deviation from SNA is that a dummy sector known as "inventory valuation adjustment" was introduced in order to account for the difference between historical and current cost accounting. The changes in the stocks in the individual rows of the absorption matrix refer to changes in the book value of those stocks between 1971 and 1972. Such changes therefore do not only include actual changes in the goods held in stock, but changes in their value from one period to the next. Therefore, in the intersection of the inventory valuation adjustment row and the changes in business inventories column, an overall negative adjustment has been introduced which reflects the inflation component that is present in the changes of inventories registered in the individual rows. The same adjustment is made in the column of this dummy industry and its intersection with the property type income row of value added. This is the same adjustment that is applied to the changes of business inventories in the United States National Income and Product Accounts.

There are additional differences from the SNA recommendations with regard to the classification of industries versus producers of government services and producers of private non-profit services to households. The United States input-output table does not make a distinction between industries and non-profit institutions in the industrial breakdown. In line with the treatment in the United States National Income and Product Accounts, they are jointly distributed with the industrial activity categories. On the other hand, the United States presentation makes an additional distinction in the case of public activities. It not only separate producers of government services, but also introduces separate rows and columns for government enterprises. Only the part of government services represented by wages and salaries of government employees is recorded in the intermediate consumption quadrant, under the heading "government industry". The presentation of government enterprises is much more detailed. A distinction is made in the first place between federal and state and local government enterprises, and, in addition, between types of government enterprises such as postal service, public utilities, passenger transit, Commodity Credit Corporation and others. Two criteria distinguish the government enterprises from the producers of government services included in government industry. First, a minimum of 50 per cent of the cost should be covered by sales of goods and services and furthermore the output should exceed $10 million. To distinguish government enterprises from the private ones included in the remaining categories of the table, an additional criteria is introduced which states that more than 50 per cent of the capital stock should be held by a government agency or corporation.

There are several discrepancies from the SNA recommendations with regard to the breakdown, coverage and valuation of the final demand categories. First, no distinction is made within the government purchases of goods and services between final consumption expenditure and gross capital formation. Instead, government purchases of goods and services have been broken down in final demand by level of Government (federal, state and local) and by type of government services (in the case of federal Government: defense; non-defence, and for state and local governments: education; health, welfare and sanitation; safety). Related to this is the different coverage of changes in business inventories, which do not include changes in strategic stocks held by the government. Also, stocks are valued differently, as mentioned in (para. 12). Finally, private final consumption expenditure is not fully compatible with the national concept of the SNA, as purchases by United States residents abroad are not included. These purchases are treated as complementary imports.

The breakdown of value added differs from the SNA recommendations in that consumption of fixed capital, subsidies and operating surplus are not identified separately in the tables, but are instead replaced by a single category called property type income. This is due to lack of separate data on these components of value added at the establishment level.

As recommended in SNA, a distinction is made between complementary and competitive imports. Competitive imports are classified by commodity groups and distributed to intermediate and final demand categories together with the production of domestic industries. To arrive at the correct level of domestic gross output per commodity item, competitive imports are recorded as negative entries in a separate column of the absorption matrix along with the final demand columns. Complementary imports, on the other hand, are distributed in a separate row to their destination in intermediate or final demand. Furthermore, the total of complementary imports is shown as a negative entry in the intersection of this row and the above-mentioned import column. This implies that the import column includes all imports, competitive as well as complementary, and that the total of the complementary imports row is zero. Imports are not recorded in the make matrix. There are three categories of non-comparable imports. The first one concerns goods and services of which there is no significant domestic production, which includes such goods as bananas, coffee and spices, as well as the government import of certain stockpile materials and other purchases directly abroad. The second category includes items that are produced and used outside the United States, such as personal travel abroad, port expenditures abroad, film company distribution and other expenses abroad, international commmunication costs and also such items as consular fees and royalties, which in SNA would not be dealt with as commodity-type services. Whether particular commodity groups belong to the group of competitive or complementary imports is based on information from the United States Tariff Commission, documented in its Summaries of Trade and Tariff Information.

4. *Treatment and presentation of selected transactions*

As recommended in SNA, secondary products and their corresponding inputs are transferred to the input-output sectors to which they characteristically belong. Transfers of output and input are carried out according to two methods. One group of secondary products is transferred to the characteristic industry, using the so-called commodity technology assumption that the input structure of the transferred products is the same as that of the input structure of the characteristic industry to which those products are transferred. This transfer is not fully mechanical in the sense that some other information on the input structure of these products is available and used. This method has been applied for the transfer of own-account construction work, including government own-account construction, to the construction categories, of manufacturing in trade and service industries to the appropriate manufacturing categories, of retail trade in service industries to trade industries, of services in the trade industries to the service industries, of non-characteristic production of services from one service industry to another, of wholesale trade activities regarding resales of unprocessed goods in manufacturing to wholesale trade industries, of rental activities of all industries to the real estate industry, and of electricity produced and sold by mining, manufacturing and railroad industries to utilities. For a second group of secondary products, output and input were transferred mechanically, using the industry technology assumption that the input structure is the same as that of the respective industries that produce these secondary products. This method was applied to the remaining secondary products. The transfers of the first group of secondary products is reflected in the presentation of the make and absorption matrices (tables (i) and (ii)) and in the tables that are directly derived from these matrices (tables (i'), (iv') and (v')). In other words, this type of secondary production is not shown in the off-diagonal elements of the make matrix nor in the input of the producing industries of the absorption matrix, because those tables have been compiled after transfer of this group of secondary products. On the other hand, the transfer of the second group of secondary products is not reflected in the two tables, which implies that output is shown in the off-diagonal elements of the make matrix and input remains included in the input columns of the industries that produce those secondary products. The industry technology assumption for these groups of products was only used when the inverse

commodity by commodity and industry by commodity matrices (tables (ii') and (iii')) were derived. Those matrices are based on an implicit input-output table that is derived from the make and absorption matrices, while applying the industry technology assumption to the transfer of the second group of secondary products.

The only type of secondary products that is not transferred according to either one of the above methods, is scrap. These types of products, which are not characteristic of any industry's production, are lumped together with second-hand and used goods and presented in a separate row of the absorption matrix and in a separate column of the matrix. In the inverse total requirement matrix this production has been either handled in a separate row and column (table (ii')) or deleted altogether (table (iii')). This is contrary to the SNA recommendations, which deal with these products as plus and minus items in the appropriate row sectors.

Several types of non-monetary production are included in the tables. These refer to agricultural, forestry and fishery products produced, imputed banking and insurance service charges and imputed rents of owner-occupied non-farm and farm dwellings, as well as of owner-occupied buildings by non-profit institutions. No rent imputations have been included for buildings owned and occupied by government agencies. Outside the agricultural sector, products that are produced and used by the same establishment are generally not recorded. For instance, electricity produced and used by the same mining or manufacturing establishment is not included. It is only included if it is sold and therefore has a market value. The only exception to this general rule is own-account construction activities including the activities of maintenance and repair facilities of railroads, which are considered to be secondary production activities even if the output is used in the same establishment. The valuation and coverage generally agrees with the SNA guidelines, except for imputed financial and insurance services. There are two types of differences regarding these services. One type concerns their definition, the other their distribution. The imputed banking services relate to commercial banks, regulated investment companies, mutual savings banks, Federal Reserve Banks, savings and loan associations and credit unions. The imputed service charge is equal to interest and dividends received, minus interest paid on deposits, and for mutual savings banks also minus profits and dividends paid. The output of life insurance companies is based on actual expenses, including an imputed interest, which is the difference between interest and dividends received minus interest and dividends paid and minus profits. The SNA definition of life insurance output, which includes reference to premiums and claims and additions to the mathematical reserves are not explicitly adhered to. With regard to non-life insurance output, the definition is the same as in SNA, that is, the difference between premiums received and benefits paid. Insurance output defined in this manner does not cover any of the transactions with foreign consumers. Banking services are not allocated, as recommended in SNA to a nominal sector but are distributed to intermediate and final demand categories in proportion to the case deposits held by those sectors.

Trade output covers, in addition to the trade margins, agents' and brokers' commissions as well as some miscellaneous fees related to exports. It covers not only the output of the trade sector proper, but also trade activities of manufacturing and mining companies in so far as these are related to resales of unprocessed commodities. Wholesale trade activities of those companies that cover the goods that are produced by those companies are not separated but remain included respectively with mining and manufacturing. Trade activities that take place in the services sector are transferred and included in the retail part of the trade sector, while other services and manufacturing activities performed by the trading companies are excluded. Eating and drinking places are also excluded and transferred to a separate industry category. The trade margins, furthermore, include various types of indirect taxes levied on the commodities that are channelled through trade. These are customs revenues from import duties (which are added to the output of the wholesale trade), state and local government general sales taxes (which are added to retail trade), federal excise taxes collected and remitted at the trade level, and various other wholesale and retail taxes, such as those levied on gasoline, aviation fuel, diesel fuel, tobacco and liquor. Similarly, gross output of transport includes, in addition to the transport margins, transport services not involved in the distribution of goods, such as transportation of passengers and existing movable property such as construction equipment, from one location to another. The trade and transport margins are allocated to the sectors that use the commodities. The remaining trade and transport output is allocated directly to the purchasing sectors.

Contrary to the SNA recommendations, gross output of government services included in the government industry sector is defined as the sum of its value added components only, and does not include the purchased goods and services for intermediate consumption. Value added covers compensation of all government employees, except those engaged in own-account construction activities which are covered in the construction columns of the table. The gross output of the government industry thus defined is allocated to the relevant final demand categories of government purchases. There they are included together with other purchases of goods and non-factor services and with the transferred output of government own-account construction activity, to arrive at a total for government purchases of goods and services.

C. STATISTICAL SOURCES AND COMPILATION METHODOLOGY

The benchmark information that is used for the compilation of the 1972 input-output tables is obtained from the 1972 census programme which covered manufacturing, mineral industries, construction, trade and transport and selected services. This information was supplemented with administrative data from government and other regulatory sources. Also, data from the Internal Revenue Service were used as an important source of information, particularly for some of the services sectors. The following broad methodology of compilation of data was adopted for the estimation of the cells of the use matrix:

(a) For each of the 496 industries, control totals for industry output were established, covering characteristic as well as secondary products. In addition, preliminary subtotals were estimated for intermediate purchases of goods and services and value added;

(b) Estimates were prepared for the distribution of each

commodity to intermediate and final demand categories. This distribution was done at the level of the major groups in SIC and in some cases finer groupings. Use was made of distributional information contained in economic censuses, reports of other government agencies, trade association data, engineering specifications, and so on;

(c) Similar sources were used to prepare independent estimates of individual commodity input to each industry;

(d) The independent output and input data were generally calculated in different valuations: output in producers' prices and inputs in purchaser's prices. To arrive at comparable valuations, input was revalued into producers' prices with the help of detailed information on trade and transport margins;

(e) The two independent input and output estimates were compared and, where they differed, were reconciled, either by selecting the more reliable estimate or by developing a new estimate. This was carried out by means of an iterative process consisting of various stages of revisions and new estimates, resulting in usually very small discrepancies between the two estimates;

(f) Before final balancing, the total value added for all industries together — that is, gross output minus intermediate consumption — is compared with independently derived value added totals, which are calculated as the sum of factor and non-factor payments. Based on this comparison, some adjustments are applied to value added, as well as inter-industry transactions, to assure consistency between the independently developed value added totals;

(g) Final balancing between value added and final demand totals is ultimately accomplished by somewhat arbitrary proration or similar procedures.

1. *Gross output and intermediate consumption*

Initial input-output estimates were prepared in the United States Department of Agriculture and were based on the regular data collection programme of the Economics, Statistics and Cooperatives Services of that Department, as reflected in the publication *The Farm Economic Situation*. In addition, use was made of the 1971 Survey of Farmers Expenditures, the 1969 Census of Agriculture and, to some extent, the 1972 Census of Manufactures, Mineral Industries and Business regarding information on the consumption of specific farm products by manufacturing industries. Non-purchased feed and seed estimates were based on production and farm disposition reports and the output of livestock products was based on livestock inventory data.

The values of fishery sales and output were obtained from the National Marine Fisheries Service and the value of wild fur catch and production from the Fish and Wildlife Service of the Department of the Interior. The value of sales of standing timber was derived from the 1972 Census of Manufactures, as far as those products are used in the lumber and wood products industries, while the output of crude gums, seedlings and other forest products was obtained from the Forest Service. Much of the input information was based on allocations of products from other industries, except for estimates of intermediate input of commercial fishery vessels which are based on operating cost data compiled by the National Marine Fisheries Service and benchmarked to the 1967 Census of Commercial Fisheries.

The output control totals for agriculture, foresry and fishery services were obtained by estimating separately the value of the various services that are included. Totals for agricultural services in 1972 were derived by interpolation between the 1969 and 1974 censuses of agricultural services. Output of forestry services was estimated by blowing up payroll information from the unemployment insurance of the Department of Labor, using receipts to payroll ratios derived from Internal Revenue Services (tax) data. Also some input information could be derived from the censuses of agricultural services and other input information is based on data published by the Department of Agriculture. Most of the agricultural and forestry services were assigned as input to the agricultural industry categories based on descriptions of the services in question; some specific services were allocated as input to other sectors (real estate) or final demand (private final consumption).

Estimates of output and input of the mining industry were largely based on the 1972 Census of Mineral Industries. Input were also based on a special survey of materials input into mining conducted together with the 1972 census. The census output was adjusted to exclude value added by resales, rental and royalty receipts and receipts from electric energy sales. The result is the total characteristics production of the mining industry, which has to be supplemented by secondary mining production in other industries and competitive imports of mining products in order to arrive at total supply. Adjustments were also made to the input in order to exclude capital purchases which were combined with current purchases in the census data. To supplement the input estimates, a study based on Bureau of Mining data was made of the purchase patterns of individual mining operations.

The main source of information for new construction as well as maintenance and repair, is the value-put-in-place series prepared by the Bureau of Census. The series is based on periodic surveys of builders and owners which collect information on progress and expenditures for construction work. Federal government-assisted projects and construction programmes of public utilities are regularly covered through accounting records, and other non-residential and residential construction through a monthly sample of building permits and contract awards. A special survey covers residential construction in rural areas and annual estimates of construction on farms are provided by the Ministry of Agriculture. The 1967 Census of Mineral Industries supplied the benchmark information on construction cost for oil and gas drilling, which is extrapolated with the help of annual data on footage drilled and annual cost per foot. The information was recorded in a detail of 33 new construction activities and 17 maintenance and repair activities. Data on material input by type of construction were developed in three stages. First, estimates for each type of construction were developed independently of the others. Secondly, the fixed amount of each construction material was allocated to each of the construction activities in conformity with the patterns established in the first phase. Finally, the second distribution was reviewed and adjusted in order to arrive at acceptable estimates. The input structure used in the first phase was based on studies that analysed the use of individual materials as a proportion of total value of construction in each of the 50 construction categories distinguished. Service input such as architectural and engineering services and equipment rental were developed from data provided by

government agencies and also from the 1972 Census of Selected Services. Other services were distributed according to the volume of construction activity. New private public construction was included in the appropriate column for government purchases. The distribution of maintenance and repair construction output to intermediate consumption in industries and government purchases was determined by type of construction.

Much of the data required for the manufacturing sector were obtained directly from the 1972 Census of Manufacturers. Output controls and input are generally prepared at the 496-industry level, while distribution of output was carried out in even more detail. To arrive at output of the manufacturing sectors, the following additions and exclusions were made: exclusion of construction-type installation work by employees of manufacturing establishments; addition of manufacturers' excise tax to arrive at producers' values; exclusion of items purchased for resale; exclusion of electric energy sales; exclusion of gross rents and royalty receipts; adjustment for net depletion of inventories of primary products held outside the industry; addition of receipts of selected services to foreigners based on estimates of the balance-of-payments accounts. As a result, gross output of characteristic products of the manufacturing industry is obtained. To this should be added competitive imports and manufacturing products that are produced as secondary products in other industries in order to arrive at total supply of manufacturing products. Also, some adjustments are made for small producers that are not covered in the 1972 Census. The major source of intermediate purchases of manufacturing industries was also the above-mentioned census. This provides detailed information on about 70 per cent of the total value of materials used by manufacturing plants. Furthermore, in conjunction with the 1972 Census, a special survey was conducted of 135 four-digit manufacturing activities, covering chemical, machinery and metal, and some other industries, which allowed for a substantial reduction of the "all other materials" category of the census. Among the other information used were data on product shipments, trade publications, technical periodicals and consultations with industry experts. Distribution of the commodities of the manufacturing industries to destinations was based on a very detailed grouping of commodity categories, using the characteristics of commodities in the application of the commodity flow method. In cases where no direct information was available, products were allocated to users in proportion to the distribution of closely related items.

Gross output and intermediate input of the electricity and gas were estimated on the basis of data provided respectively by the Federal Energy Regulatory Commission and the American Gas Association and, as far as water distribution and sanitary servicse are concerned, on the basis of Statistics on Income, compiled and published by the Internal Revenue Service. Fuel expenses by type of fuel for the generation of electric power were obtained as the product of quantity input provided by the United States Department of Energy and prices obtained from the Edison Electric Institute. The private consumption component of the use of electricity, gas and water production and distribution services was estimated on the basis of administrative records of the Federal Energy Regulatory Commission, the Rural Electrification Administration, the American Gas Association, and of the American Water Works Association. In addition, use was made, as far as the water distribution is concerned, of data provided in the Census of Housing. Industrial use was mainly derived from the 1972 Censuses of Manufactures and Mineral Industries, and from the Water Use Survey conducted in conjunction with the censuses. Steam output was distributed on the basis of data from individual steam producing companies, and the services of water irrigation were entirely allocated to agriculture. The distribution of output of sanitary services relied heavily on data on pollution abatement expenditures, which are collected annually by the United States Department of Commerce, Bureau of the Census.

The gross output and input components of trade were estimated as follows:

(a) Wholesale margins. Gross margins as well as operating expenses including profits in wholesale trade and including operating expenses of manufacturers' sales branches were derived from the 1972 Census of Business. These were adjusted for secondary production in trade and outside trade in order to arrive at the total supply of wholesale trade services. Thus, the estimated gross output is used as a control total for the wholesale trade sector. Given this total, the allocation of the margins to the individual commodity rows of the use matrix was then estimated. For manufacturing products, mark-up rates — selected from rates computed for different kinds of wholesale business — were applied to the flow of commodities into the wholesale channels, based on information from the 1967 Census of Manufactures, which was extrapolated to 1972. For non-manufactured products, margins as well as flows of goods to the wholesale channels were estimated on the basis of the 1972 Census of Wholesale Trade. The latter census provided in general information on mark-up and margin rates for all commodities that are channelled through wholesale trade, classified by different kinds of wholesale business. After having estimated in the above manner the subtotals for the margins per commodity row, these were adjusted on a *pro rata* basis in order to add up to the control total for gross output of the wholesale trade as a whole. The distribution of the margin subtotals per row to the individual commodity flow elements was generally done proportionally, assuming that for each destination of the commodity in intermediate and final demand there is the same relative mix between commodities that pass through wholesale channels and commodities that are purchased directly from the producer.

(b) Retail margins. Gross output of retail trade as well as input information was derived from the 1972 Census of Business. Gross output thus estimated again served as a control total. Retail trade margins were derived for about 75 kinds of retail business from published and unpublished data collected by the Bureau of Census for the 1972 retail trade business report. The most appropriate margins were applied to the merchandise line sales reported in the 1972 Census of Retail Trade. Two adjustments were applied, that is, one in order to arrive from the merchandise categories of the census at the commodity categories of the input-output table, and a second one which was a *pro rata* adjustment in order to arrive at the estimated control total for gross output of retail trade as a whole. Distribution of the retail margins among commodities was determined on the basis of the nature of the commodities, whose distribution would involve the levying of retail margins. Generally, this is the case of only private final consumption expenditure. For some products, such as

construction materials, gasoline, automobile parts and farm implements, retail activities also cover destinations in intermediate consumption. The general procedure was initially to allocate the total retail margin per commodity row to private final consumption expenditure. If this resulted in disproportionately high retail margins for this destination, an adjustment was made by calculating reduced margins for other purchasers of the commodity group in question who were assumed to purchase also through retail outlets.

(c) Sales taxes and customs duties are also included in the trade margins. These taxes were also distributed in the form of margins to be levied on the commodity flows. Information was obtained from published reports of the Treasury Department with regard to customs duties. With regard to sales taxes, information was obtained from the Internal Revenue Service. Allocation of the taxes and duties to commodity rows and individual elements of those rows was done according to the applicability of the tax law.

(d) A fourth element of the gross output of trade is the agents' and brokers' fees and miscellaneous fees on exports. Agents' and brokers' fees are estimated on the basis of information from the 1972 Census of Wholesale Trade and the fees on exports are derived from Balance of Payment Statistics. Their allocation is somewhat different from the allocation of the earlier described margins. Agents' and brokers' fees are generally allocated directly to the seller of the commodity, except for fees levied on such products as cocoa and green coffee, which are included with the wholesale margins on imports. Fees on exports are directly allocated to the export column.

Separate estimates of gross output and intermediate consumption of the transport sector are made for railroad, water, air and pipeline transportation, as well as for local and suburban transit and inter-urban passenger transportation, trucking, warehousing and stockyards, and transportation services. Estimates are mainly based on the accounting and operating reports of regulatory agencies, such as the Interstate Commerce Commission, the American Transit Association and the Civil Aeronautics Board. Additional sources such as the 1972 Census of Transportation and Business and the 1972 Census of Selected Services were used to make adjustments in the coverage of gross output for those units that do not report to the regulatory agencies. Estimates of the intermediate consumption pattern of the regulated portion for the several types of transportation activities were applied to the unregulated portion of the industry as well. The transport margins that are levied on commodity flows are obtained from the Interstate Commerce Commission Freight Commodity Statistics and from the 1972 Census of Transportation. Particular transport margins were assigned to particular commodity rows of the use matrix depending on the type of transport services involved, and then distributed to the sectors using those commodities in proportion to the value of the commodities consumed. In some particular cases, where additional information was available, this mechanical allocation method was adjusted to take into account special circumstances. The non-margin component of transportation gross output was allocated directly to the sectors that use that output.

Gross output and intermediate input of the remaining services categories — telephone and telegraph, radio and television, finance and insurance, real estate and rental services, and other services such as hotels, restaurants, advertising, professional services, eating and drinking places, amusement services, automobile repair, medical and educational services and services of non-profit organizations — are obtained from a variety of sources. Partly, these cover the 1972 census data of business and selected services. It also includes the administrative records of the Federal Communications Commission as far as telephone, telegraph and radio and television broadcasting services are concerned, and the Federal Insurance Corporation and the Federal Reserve Board with regard to the financial sectors. Another important source that is used for many of the services not covered by regulatory agencies is the Statistics of Income, published by the Internal Revenue Service, and income tax returns. The latter source is used to cover insurance agents, real estate and rental services and automobile repair services. Some of the reports of the regulatory agencies also provided information on the distribution of the services to intermediate and final demand categories. This applies to telephone and telegraph services. For other services, distribution keys have been utilized. For example, actual banking services were distributed to intermediate sectors on the basis of bonded indebtedness according to information provided by the Federal Reserve. Imputed banking charges were distributed on the basis of cash deposits held, using the same Federal Reserve source. The Statistics of Income, published by the Internal Revenue Service, provided the basis for the distribution of real estate and rental services. Business services were allocated on the basis of specific characteristics of those services. Some services, such as those of eating and drinking places, amusement and medical and educational services, were allocated nearly 100 per cent to private final consumption expenditure owing to their particular characteristics.

Government enterprises, which stands for a separate set of entries in the input-output table, cover the United States Postal Service, federal and state and local electric utilities, local government passenger transit and the Commodity Credit Corporation. Gross output and input of the federal government enterprises are derived from the annual government budget, combined statement of receipts and expenditures and the Monthly Treasury Bulletin. Output and input for state and local government enterprises are derived from state and local government budgetary data. The United States Postal Service is covered through its own accounting records, and information on the utilities is provided by the Federal Energy Regulatory Commission.

2. *Value added, final demand and imports*

Value added estimates derived as the difference between gross output and intermediate consumption per industry as explained above, were compared with independently derived value added totals, calculated as the sum of factor and non-factor payments.

Data on private final consumption expenditure and private gross fixed capital formation were derived as a result of the commodity flow method. Most of the detail required for the effective use of this method was based on the 1972 Census of Manufactures. Little use was made of the 1972/73 Consumer Expenditure Survey for two reasons. First, much of the work on the input-output table was completed before the survey results were made available. Secondly, definitions in the survey do not always conform with the definition of personal consumption expenditure used in the United States National Income and Products Accounts. With regard to capital formation, three criteria were used to identify capital equipment: duration of more than one year, not defined as part of construction and charged to the capital account under normal industry accounting procedures. These criteria were applied in consultation with industry experts and tax consultants. In addition to capital equipment, output of the construction industry was included in the capital formation.

Changes in the book value of stocks are generally estimated independently on the basis of information from the 1972 Census of Manufactures. The census information distinguishes between inventories of finished goods, work-in-progress and stocks of materials. The change in the value of the inventories in finished products of the respective industries as well as their recorded work-in-progress were assumed to be changes in stocks of commodities that are characteristic of the industries in question. Changes in inventories of materials recorded in the census were assumed to be changes in the stocks of materials purchased for intermediate consumption by the purchasing industry. These stock changes were included in the rows of those commodities that are used as intermediate consumption in the purchasing industry. Changes in stocks of trade were developed by kind of wholesale or retail business using Census Bureau Data. Those changes were all assumed to concern finished products and were allocated to the respective commodity rows of the use matrix, depending on the merchandise lines of the kinds of business that were distinguished in trade. Recorded in the intersections of the retail and wholesale trade rows and the changes in stocks column were the trade margins that were charged to the commmodities that were added to or taken from trade inventories.

Control totals for government compensation of employees and government purchases of goods and services are derived from three major sources: the Treasury's Combined Statement of Receipts, Expenditures and Balances; the Budget of the United States to cover federal government purchases; and the Census of Governments and Government Finances to cover the state and local government purchases. For the commodity breakdown of the purchases of goods and services additional sources are used. For the Federal Government, these include the 1967 Census of Manufactures which classifies sales by class of customer, the Current Industrial Reports of the Bureau of Census, the Census Bureau's Shipments of Defense-Oriented Industries, and information from the Department of Defense covering Military Prime Contract Awards by Service category and Federal Supply Classification. To cover the breakdown of purchases from non-manufacturing industries, use was made of reports of the National Science Foundation, the General Services Administration and the Commodity Credit Corporation.

UNITED STATES
INPUT-OUTPUT TABLES
1977

Source: *Survey of Current Business*, Vol.59, No.2,
May 1984, U.S. Department of Commerce.

Table 1.—The Use of Commodities

[Millions of dollars

Commodity number	For the distribution of output of a commodity, read the row for that commodity / For the composition of inputs to an industry, read the column for that industry	Livestock and livestock products	Other agricultural products	Forestry and fishery products	Agricultural, forestry, and fishery services	Iron and ferroalloy ores mining	Nonferrous metal ores mining	Coal mining	Crude petroleum and natural gas	Stone and clay mining and quarrying	Chemical and fertilizer mineral mining	New construction	Maintenance and repair construction	Ordnance and accessories	Food and kindred products
	Industry number	1	2	3	4	5	6	7	8	9	10	11	12	13	14
1	Livestock and livestock products	8,905	1,336		213										36,148
2	Other agricultural products	13,769	2,498		162				2						15,638
3	Forestry and fishery products			32	16										1,457
4	Agricultural, forestry, and fishery services	1,900	2,520	457	60		(*)	4	(*)	(*)	2	225	433	(*)	2
5	Iron and ferroalloy ores mining					174									
6	Nonferrous metal ores mining					10	286								
7	Coal mining	11	2			9	10	2,451		7	2				76
8	Crude petroleum and natural gas								2,302					4	
9	Stone and clay mining and quarrying	1	148		1		11	2		169	27	1,074	969		24
10	Chemical and fertilizer mineral mining		(*)								101				10
11	New construction														
12	Maintenance and repair construction	326	675	299	83	23	12	113	2,718	30	26	224	79	53	865
13	Ordnance and accessories			5								11	1	483	
14	Food and kindred products	11,237		65	56		1	(*)	5	1	1	8	2	(*)	33,222
15	Tobacco manufactures														
16	Broad and narrow fabrics, yarn and thread mills		16				1	24			4			1	
17	Miscellaneous textile goods and floor coverings	18	96	47	27							1,060	264	(*)	11
18	Apparel						1	9	11	3	1	25	7	6	12
19	Miscellaneous fabricated textile products		36	6	39							44	36		48
20	Lumber and wood products, except containers	9	9			3	26	69			2	16,086	2,245	16	22
21	Wood containers	2	166		10									11	56
22	Household furniture											89	29		
23	Other furniture and fixtures											365	87		
24	Paper and allied products, except containers	83	38	(*)	5	(*)	(*)	6	3	29	5	541	283	3	1,828
25	Paperboard containers and boxes	1	85	(*)	61		(*)	2	1	1	(*)	6	2	15	3,832
26	Printing and publishing	10	13	(*)	4	(*)	1	4	11	1	1	4	1	18	921
27	Chemicals and selected chemical products	136	6,648	135	703	43	125	213	398	69	67	399	261	29	1,141
28	Plastics and synthetic materials													13	48
29	Drugs, cleaning and toilet preparations	113							3		(*)	62	30	1	915
30	Paints and allied products		2						9			1,573	1,251	2	
31	Petroleum refining and related industries	505	2,670	115	264	49	68	338	259	154	55	4,771	2,447	40	733
32	Rubber and miscellaneous plastics products	289	312	2	35	33	55	139	20	50	10	1,678	1,343	61	1,803
33	Leather tanning and finishing														1
34	Footwear and other leather products	24			2				2			2	1	(*)	
35	Glass and glass products	5		(*)	2	(*)	(*)	(*)	7	1	(*)	152	113	1	2,981
36	Stone and clay products		61		8	2	21	75	11	3	1	12,630	3,480	11	51
37	Primary iron and steel manufacturing	6	6			48	103	82	413	36	22	4,569	1,081	284	9
38	Primary nonferrous metals manufacturing					3	12	43		14	3	2,782	770	230	1
39	Metal containers														5,841
40	Heating, plumbing, and structural metal products	6	8		4				37	16	7	13,229	4,452		
41	Screw machine products and stampings	20				8	20	146	13	8		97	42	61	409
42	Other fabricated metal products	80	123	18	19	36	47	100	307	53	9	4,117	2,044	91	511
43	Engines and turbines			8	27	22	29	109	144	43	23			18	
44	Farm and garden machinery	267	503	7	18										
45	Construction and mining machinery					68	105	752	231	186	48	304	35		
46	Materials handling machinery and equipment					12	11	51		29	5	628	245		1
47	Metalworking machinery and equipment			(*)	1	1	3	3	25	5	(*)	35	12	57	
48	Special industry machinery and equipment														111
49	General industrial machinery and equipment	15	17	4	1	19	24	170	169	42	11	857	138	64	48
50	Miscellaneous machinery, except electrical	33	42	(*)	2	3	16	56	130	22	5	36	13	51	80
51	Office, computing, and accounting machines				(*)										
52	Service industry machines											2,135	975		34
53	Electric industrial equipment and apparatus	7	7			4	14	77	243	21	9	1,199	442	53	
54	Household appliances								1			581	300		(*)
55	Electric lighting and wiring equipment	4	2	(*)	2	(*)	1	12	14	2	1	2,758	971	1	11
56	Radio, TV, and communication equipment				(*)		(*)	1	4			586	188	686	3
57	Electronic components and accessories													153	
58	Miscellaneous electrical machinery and supplies	72	293	(*)	21	(*)	5	6	9	4	1	158	49	3	2
59	Motor vehicles and equipment	44	43	3	30	38	5	4	5	41	3	83	36	17	7
60	Aircraft and parts			(*)	4									309	
61	Other transportation equipment			158	5	1	3					2			
62	Scientific and controlling instruments		1	(*)	(*)	(*)	2	6	22	1	(*)	486	212	5	23
63	Optical, ophthalmic, and photographic equipment			(*)	3	(*)	(*)	(*)	3	1	(*)	13	5	24	10
64	Miscellaneous manufacturing	6	8	(*)	4	7	3	7	12	8	3	390	129	6	19
65	Transportation and warehousing	921	777	43	188	43	51	128	205	56	28	4,377	1,507	122	4,446
66	Communications, except radio and TV	139	179	3	1	2	4	13	65	8	3	704	348	47	365
67	Radio and TV broadcasting														
68	Electric, gas, water, and sanitary services	410	1,092	17	104	214	184	283	750	248	267	603	230	119	2,067
69	Wholesale and retail trade	2,081	2,882	141	482	77	106	474	373	146	46	17,064	6,290	165	10,269
70	Finance and insurance	848	812	24	94	11	41	125	321	73	53	1,843	467	35	829
71	Real estate and rental	1,136	5,627	1	294	25	57	327	4,512	112	33	451	176	47	530
72	Hotels; personal and repair services (exc. auto)	67	65	6	16	2	5	17	44	30	7	253	66	18	378
73	Business services	218	1,014	44	172	48	67	427	712	179	76	14,161	1,030	289	4,775
74	Eating and drinking places	8	10	24	73	4	9	21	279	20	14	150	49	81	425
75	Automobile repair and services	154	153	18	121	23	52	89	137	29	22	983	185	10	336
76	Amusements				182			1	5	1	1	1	(*)		3
77	Health, educ., & social serv. and nonprofit org.	374	22	6	12	3	5	16	28	5	3	4	2	4	52
78	Federal Government enterprises	7	8	4	29	3	8	7	13	6	7	84	26	7	219
79	State and local government enterprises			2	10	1	2	2	6	5	2	44	13	3	124
80	Noncomparable imports	(*)	6	1	(*)	1	13	5	112	1	2	3	1		4,504
81	Scrap, used, and secondhand goods					3	12	9			10	15	26	3	3
82	Government industry														
83	Rest of the world industry														
84	Household industry														
85	Inventory valuation adjustment														
I	Total intermediate inputs	44,264	31,028	1,702	3,666	1,085	1,626	7,011	15,089	1,987	1,038	116,824	35,895	3,832	138,320
VA	Value added	8,028	34,046	2,768	4,161	975	1,671	9,642	33,994	2,793	1,121	73,870	37,745	5,048	50,880
88	Compensation of employees	3,149	5,275	555	2,640	603	1,172	5,584	3,570	1,430	433	58,410	31,962	3,689	25,372
89	Indirect business taxes	1,123	1,361	190	142	96	147	374	2,169	182	53	1,844	947	112	6,402
90	Property-type income	3,757	27,411	2,023	1,379	276	353	3,684	28,255	1,182	635	13,617	4,835	1,247	19,107
T	Total industry output	52,292	65,074	4,470	7,827	2,059	3,297	16,653	49,083	4,780	2,159	190,694	73,640	8,879	189,200

See footnote at end of table.

by Industries, 1977

at producers' prices]

Tobacco manufactures	Broad and narrow fabrics, yarn and thread mills	Miscellaneous textile goods and floor coverings	Apparel	Miscellaneous fabricated textile products	Lumber and wood products, except containers	Wood containers	Household furniture	Other furniture and fixtures	Paper and allied products, except containers	Paperboard containers and boxes	Printing and publishing	Chemicals and selected chemical products	Plastics and synthetic materials	Drugs, cleaning and toilet preparations	Paints and allied products	Petroleum refining and related industries	Rubber and miscellaneous plastics products	Leather tanning and finishing	Commodity number
15	16	17	18	19	20	21	22	23	24	25	26	27	28	29	30	31	32	33	
	101	67										116		31					1
	1,869	35										27		59		2			2
2,446			26						20			135		11	2	18			3
	1	(*)	236				(*)	(*)	1	(*)	(*)	119	(*)	(*)	(*)	(*)	(*)	(*)	4
			51		3,750									6					5
									3			516	1	10					6
7	31	3	5	1	6	(*)	4	1	202	4	3	259	101	12				1	7
												1,465	309		45	60,050	53		8
									110			248		16	34	210	15		9
									16			995		2	2	6	6	2	10
																			11
18	165	34	130	25	208	4	67	42	396	108	174	539	180	112	45	818	235	7	12
	(*)	9	(*)	5	3							(*)		45			(*)		13
4	2	7				(*)	30	2	230	3	15	359	45	620	161	35	10	509	14
																			15
2,628									455		26						598		16
	8,899	1,428	8,578	2,420	76		639	3	217		59	26		94		20	919		17
2	265	60	750				190	147	9	2	5	59		10	(*)	1	11		18
	5	123	8,638	99	279		42	6	2	1	1	5	4	1	2	1	5		19
(*)		13	532	279	12	(*)	30	3	2		1	26	10	4		23	102		20
	3	1	11		11,936	168	1,268	429	2,687		1	53					5		21
5					2	5	9	3	2										22
							22	2	1										23
								50	1									(*)	24
155	35	45	147	26	20	(*)	22	10	7,014	5,300	8,043	597	313	230	12	197	426		25
78	201	46	162	68	72	31	117	78	549	557	129	239	187	643	49	292	483	11	26
125	13	7	43	16	17	1	18	8	37	14	4,839	90	10	102	33	12	33	1	27
15	610	282	78	15	464		27	43	1,284	304	1,010	15,048	7,264	2,662	1,606	2,950	2,004	117	28
	4,170	1,888	1,343	73	20	3	44	2	921	135	7	495	856	92	424	25	7,465	40	29
12	50	12	105						60			212	94	2,119	16	382	12		30
	2	3	(*)		168		111	56	11	24	14	93	41	43	78	4	22	17	31
41	204	55	187	17	425	5	60	31	1,108	152	249	1,424	414	291	125	7,754	501	(*)	32
258	266	253	181	213	227	(*)	509	258	897	28	322	442	414	996	21	146	1,876	83	33
			174	79			37	2			4	4				1	5		34
					9		54	10	1	(*)	2	25	(*)	1	(*)	4	207		35
(*)	82	24	6	1	43	1	43	20	1	(*)	1	104	15	13	67	26	141	4	36
1	7	2	1		194		245	709	73		7	316	(*)	(*)	26	171	453		37
1	1	2			29	3	71	102	1	78	16	1,031	7	4	48	45	49		38
		40			14			44			38	528	67	591	338	344			39
1												7				31			40
					121		63	100			1	6		128	10	125			41
					310		581	220	282	65	83	144	28	207	25	207	223	(*)	42
63	4		25	1	784	2											9		43
																			44
																			45
					7				(*)								2		46
(*)	21		2		19		9	21	18	52	9	15	7	9	1	6	97	1	47
3	12	4	9	3	87	1	8	12	131	53	220	547	7			144	74		48
	154	90	72	6	32		1	21	21		1	187	35	54	(*)		11	2	49
3			5		23	2	16	22	45	22	21	39	18	13	5	17	120		50
	35	12	26	6	81						1								51
																			52
					23							66							53
					23			18				24					4		54
			31						(*)		1	(*)		1	(*)	(*)	32	(*)	55
(*)	3	(*)	3	(*)	15	(*)	1	2	3	1	4	3	1	2	(*)	(*)	1		56
(*)	(*)	(*)	1		1		1	1	(*)	(*)	4						13	(*)	57
	7													3			7		58
(*)	1		2		11		(*)	1	2	1	6	(*)	1			102	28	(*)	59
(*)	1	(*)	3		47	(*)	1	1	4	2	9			2	3				60
(*)																			61
					2														62
1	5	(*)	5	1	8	(*)	6	1	14	3	4	57	10	23	1	20	28	(*)	63
(*)	3		6		6	(*)	2	1	8	3	458	10	2	7	7	5	8	(*)	64
1	6	1	591	16	14	(*)	12	1	5	3	130	6	2	17		19	19	(*)	65
88	276	192	345	96	896	14	229	134	1,383	559	1,308	2,508	544	603	227	3,292	1,067	31	66
8	126	16	350	26	53	2	57	31	88	34	602	153	30	109	16	173	110	2	67
41	617	147	321	61	512	6	103	80	1,575	153	389	3,605	627	265	47	2,378	813	23	68
137	1,202	337	1,584	389	1,781	31	577	279	2,273	251	1,827	2,335	711	1,153	271	1,559	1,255	86	69
89	89	32	238	50	242	9	147	78	153	41	467	337	68	230	41	573	237	5	70
30	70	27	294	78	109	3	85	61	157	64	767	406	147	464	35	249	319	3	71
7	36	13	123	42	52	2	36	21	124	17	336	153	45	95	24	43	75	13	72
634	777	164	817	156	467	14	392	278	836	169	2,677	1,754	559	4,134	203	1,652	956	20	73
17	108	24	176	35	105	4	61	34	99	51	1,021	358	91	352	49	231	211	4	74
23	44	13	79	15	140	2	55	34	100	39	193	65	63	48	16	78	76	2	75
1	(*)		2		1		11	3	3	(*)	12	8	5	5	1	1	3		76
5	28	1	23	26	43	2	22	10	22	2	93	58	18	102	7	58	61	1	77
30	39	17	166	19	27	1	26	22	42	17	848	57	12	69	16	71	45	3	78
3	13	5	8		5	(*)	2	1	34	4	11	24		12		28	8	4	79
1	12	127	21	53	5		16	1	26	6	22	259	24	233	46	185	544	1	80
22	56								508			40					3		81
																			82
																			83
																			84
																			85
6,986	20,699	6,151	25,968	5,178	23,797	316	6,175	3,482	24,307	8,366	26,490	38,727	13,486	17,435	4,224	84,608	22,277	992	I
5,867	8,142	2,720	15,459	2,920	14,681	186	4,124	2,911	14,081	4,805	23,494	18,770	6,439	11,371	2,030	14,287	17,089	561	VA
1,118	6,122	1,500	11,971	2,086	8,643	157	3,197	2,073	8,674	3,107	16,661	9,630	4,506	5,629	1,101	5,205	10,728	347	88
2,423	237	89	164	29	336	7	73	42	604	180	576	812	347	369	72	5,273	1,230	6	89
2,326	1,783	1,131	3,324	805	5,702	21	854	796	4,803	1,519	6,257	8,328	1,586	5,373	857	3,809	5,131	208	90
12,853	28,841	8,871	41,427	8,098	38,477	501	10,299	6,394	38,388	13,172	49,984	57,497	19,926	28,806	6,254	98,895	39,366	1,552	T

Table 1.—The Use of Commodities

[Millions of dollars

Commodity number	For the distribution of output of a commodity, read the row for that commodity / For the composition of inputs to an industry, read the column for that industry	Footwear and other leather products	Glass and glass products	Stone and clay products	Primary iron and steel manufacturing	Primary nonferrous metals manufacturing	Metal containers	Heating, plumbing, and structural metal products	Screw machine products and stampings	Other fabricated metal products	Engines and turbines	Farm and garden machinery	Construction and mining machinery	Materials handling machinery and equipment	Metalworking machinery and equipment
	Industry number	34	35	36	37	38	39	40	41	42	43	44	45	46	47
1	Livestock and livestock products														
2	Other agricultural products			2											
3	Forest and fishery products														
4	Agricultural, forestry, and fishery services		(*)	1	1	(*)	(*)	(*)	(*)	1	(*)	(*)	(*)		(*)
5	Iron and ferroalloy ores mining			6	3,237										
6	Nonferrous metal ores mining			7	46	2,344		28							
7	Coal mining	1	1	283	3,178	21	(*)	1	5	5	1	4	7	1	2
8	Crude petroleum and natural gas				27										
9	Stone and clay mining and quarrying		166	1,443	218	8		3		6					
10	Chemical and fertilizer mineral mining		3	88	53	1									
11	New construction														
12	Maintenance and repair construction	21	84	418	1,313	232	63	361	195	201	75	43	98	28	50
13	Ordnance and accessories			21	12										
14	Food and kindred products	21	1	20	8	4	(*)	4	2	4	1	1	2	1	2
15	Tobacco manufactures														
16	Broad and narrow fabrics, yarn and thread mills	222		119		21									
17	Miscellaneous textile goods and floor coverings	249		(*)		2				2					
18	Apparel	17	4	6	16	3	1	3	3	11	4	1	1	1	3
19	Miscellaneous fabricated textile products		1	1	1	1			28						
20	Lumber and wood products, except containers	37	80	149	89	79	12	54	48	128		32	15	6	9
21	Wood containers	1	57	(*)	11	17		24	20	2		1	3	2	7
22	Household furniture														
23	Other furniture and fixtures				2									2	
24	Paper and allied products, except containers	46	11	333	12	21	7	26	66	7	19	3	3	2	3
25	Paperboard containers and boxes	76	422	113	54	59	30	101	119	251	34	26	4	2	53
26	Printing and publishing	13	20	22	27	22	123	25	20	31	8	9	14	6	17
27	Chemicals and selected chemical products	48	413	589	1,699	818	6	43	100	495	1	3	14	2	69
28	Plastics and synthetic materials	86		211		472	23	14	44	89					
29	Drugs, cleaning and toilet preparations	15		18	2	(*)	7	14	11	12					
30	Paints and allied products		15	47	17	31	193	89	71	162	5	32	23	6	18
31	Petroleum refining and related industries	9	144	489	808	467	26	129	48	131	60	24	41	27	79
32	Rubber and miscellaneous plastics products	367	48	142	77	234	16	187	117	656	39	336	318	80	64
33	Leather tanning and finishing	1,112													
34	Footwear and other leather products	241	3	(*)	4	(*)									
35	Glass and glass products		713	22	2	11	(*)	213	16	34	(*)		(*)		(*)
36	Stone and clay products	3	109	3,279	504	125	5	53	23	91	73	25	109	15	127
37	Primary iron and steel manufacturing	2	1	182	13,116	285	2,557	5,700	5,318	3,791	1,373	1,432	2,880	634	1,181
38	Primary nonferrous metals manufacturing	(*)	5	183	1,270	16,056	1,201	2,549	814	1,709	439	101	114	93	301
39	Metal containers			3	4	2	355	14	10						
40	Heating, plumbing, and structural metal products				8			544			6	150	328	70	87
41	Screw machine products and stampings	18	20	13	214	93	6	763	672	450	279	207	111	56	80
42	Other fabricated metal products	55	6	307	523	274	89	851	343	1,119	147	116	190	75	113
43	Engines and turbines			3	20			1		39	1,253	773	596	75	
44	Farm and garden machinery												837		
45	Construction and mining machinery			151									1,376	7	
46	Materials handling machinery and equipment	(*)		2	19	14								224	
47	Metalworking machinery and equipment	7	45	23	410	383	37	146	251	206	162	76	126	42	706
48	Special industry machinery and equipment	4	56	3	59	12		8							
49	General industrial machinery and equipment	(*)	3	15	630	261	1	156	16	30	239	491	1,113	313	272
50	Miscellaneous machinery, except electrical	12	39	52	343	145	24	131	632	175	326	220	108	87	303
51	Office, computing, and accounting machines				11										
52	Service industry machines				2			57							
53	Electric industrial equipment and apparatus		13	6	433	127	1	244	36	113	114	66	242	183	356
54	Household appliances			6				2							
55	Electric lighting and wiring equipment	1	7	22	9	8	(*)	5	14	2	1	12	1	(*)	15
56	Radio, TV, and communication equipment	(*)	1	(*)	(*)	(*)	(*)	1	(*)	1		(*)	(*)		
57	Electronic components and accessories									6					4
58	Miscellaneous electrical machinery and supplies		1	1	3	1	(*)	1		4		141	78	1	7	1
59	Motor vehicles and equipment		1	61	2	3	1	16	43	2	64	242	235	1	2
60	Aircraft and parts				4										
61	Other transportation equipment														
62	Scientific and controlling instruments	2	15	7	76	19	1	47	5	9	1	1	2	1	22
63	Optical, ophthalmic, and photographic equipment	(*)	4	11	12	3	2	6	5	9	5	3	5	2	6
64	Miscellaneous manufacturing	71	1	31	13	9	1	17	4	12	1	2	9	4	5
65	Transportation and warehousing	76	285	1,842	2,704	1,332	214	468	343	411	128	157	218	50	135
66	Communications, except radio and TV	31	28	89	70	66	9	115	117	128	27	22	81	18	43
67	Radio and TV broadcasting							7							
68	Electric, gas, water, and sanitary services	39	593	1,172	3,046	1,642	116	256	264	431	90	107	161	37	149
69	Wholesale and retail trade	194	321	786	3,350	2,089	327	1,185	707	1,048	410	808	1,050	273	415
70	Finance and insurance	64	53	198	323	238	53	169	100	223	40	36	75	21	74
71	Real estate and rental	42	103	188	194	134	49	168	93	155	30	50	52	29	77
72	Hotels; personal and repair services (exc. auto)	29	20	52	114	64	23	133	41	68	14	11	22	8	24
73	Business services	218	214	639	947	584	109	579	439	705	173	134	334	98	273
74	Eating and drinking places	42	42	148	135	103	40	149	65	133	30	33	65	24	83
75	Automobile repair and services	14	37	106	44	76	15	64	58	64	28	9	15	12	37
76	Amusements	(*)	1	(*)	4	2	1	7	1	1	1	1		1	1
77	Health, educ., & social serv. and noprofit org.	2	6	19	19	6	6	18	32	20	3	3	3	2	12
78	Federal Government enterprises	47	17	36	66	31	3	37	19	39	10	18	19	9	16
79	State and local government enterprises	(*)	3	7	16	8	2	5	5	11	2	2	3	1	4
80	Noncomparable imports	(*)	42	67	153	125	2	8	5	18	6	14	31	4	19
81	Scrap, used, and secondhand goods		43		1,923	1,559		42		28	26	13	7		19
82	Government industry														
83	Rest of the world industry														
84	Household industry														
85	Inventory valuation adjustment														
I	Total intermediate inputs	3,554	4,322	14,263	41,680	30,756	5,758	16,003	11,392	13,498	6,031	6,610	10,224	2,637	5,337
VA	Value added	2,549	4,769	11,259	23,555	10,623	3,031	10,891	8,597	12,602	4,318	4,954	7,500	2,170	7,820
88	Compensation of employees	2,008	3,519	6,987	19,099	6,853	1,790	7,445	6,485	7,946	2,825	3,064	5,116	1,449	5,380
89	Indirect business taxes	25	140	465	1,041	491	48	290	176	233	108	84	221	46	116
90	Property-type income	516	1,111	3,808	3,414	3,280	1,193	3,157	1,936	4,423	1,384	1,806	2,162	675	2,323
T	Total industry output	6,103	9,091	25,522	65,234	41,379	8,789	26,894	19,989	26,101	10,349	11,564	17,724	4,807	13,157

See footnote at end of table.

by Industries, 1977—Continued

[at producers' prices]

Special industry machinery and equipment	General industrial machinery and equipment	Miscellaneous machinery, except electrical	Office, computing, and accounting machines	Service industry machines	Electric industrial equipment and apparatus	Household appliances	Electric lighting and wiring equipment	Radio, TV, and communication equipment	Electronic components and accessories	Miscellaneous electrical machinery and supplies	Motor vehicles and equipment	Aircraft and parts	Other transportation equipment	Scientific and controlling instruments	Optical, ophthalmic, and photographic equipment	Miscellaneous manufacturing	Transportation and warehousing	Communications, except radio and TV	Commodity number
48	49	50	51	52	53	54	55	56	57	58	59	60	61	62	63	64	65	66	
																1	1		1
																19	4		2
																6	(*)		3
(*)	(*)	(*)	(*)	(*)	1		(*)	1	(*)		1			(*)	(*)	(*)	3	1	4
										6									5
										4				1					6
(*)	2	1	(*)	3	3	5	2	2	1	3	43	3	3	1	5	2	4		7
																	79		8
											2			(*)		26			9
			10																10
																			11
42	80	32	43	45	113	62	39	79	89	35	270	116	59	47	44	106	4,621	1,927	12
								(*)			(*)	1	(*)			1		(*)	13
2	2	2	3	1	3	1	1	3	2	1	3	3	3	40	1	29	73		14
																			15
						36	13				28	45	9	125		325	2		16
1	77	17			3					3	244		256	97	7	54	62		17
1	5	1	1	2	2	1	1	13	11	1	15	5	16	18	1	16	93	36	18
	1	1									2,298	50	85			63	74		19
24	33	3		37	24	57	19	17		1	134	12	842	25		430	17		20
2	7	1		20	10	16		13			6	4	(*)	70	3	7	(*)		21
								324	21		231	8	77						22
						6													23
3	38	3	73	13	114	36	2	42	41	3	106	7	25	117	271	328	75	35	24
10	58	51	61	87	81	176	149	72	64	57	98	3	13	105	74	359	37	9	25
13	18	12	32	13	28	12	10	163	22	269	42	41	22	47	13	263	117	8	26
118	9		2	47	62	59	200	120	165	70	67	215	17	57	94	759	344	523	27
			1								187	16	98	112	93	523			28
						1	3				7			1	(*)	38			29
	5			3		46	90	24	20	(*)	413	34	137	13	1	110	23	29	30
49	132	33	61								256	139	128	83	55	146	8,795	119	31
135	167	14	584	239	261	537	225	990	612	217	5,040	136	297	462	370	582	968	67	32
																38			33
								1		(*)						55		1	34
13	(*)	(*)	(*)	(*)	9	64	290	26	262	5	1,043	4	103	60	99	12	21	2	35
36	103	110	23	64	9	147	70	33	26	138	19	411	42	213	39	26	53	12	36
765	2,036	623	124	938	1,161	894	511	152	125	228	9,471	718	1,993	240	43	465	290	(*)	37
250	531	267	240	864	1,191	475	549	738	719	1,029	2,077	1,022	473	485	302	993	96	62	38
														5					39
109	128		136	98	50			160	25	12	6	42	888	29	5	3			40
66	206	52	276	310	275	244	242	263	255	122	8,130	272	204	308	84	109	65	72	41
160	187	122	195	252	185	270	174	361	362	218	2,736	217	334	239	110	255	421	24	42
90	97	25		39	66						991		655			4	185	98	43
																			44
											15		63						45
4											17		2			5			46
113	230	135	56	108	121	39	64	79	67	64	316	275	98	69	13	29	60		47
262													3			9			48
301	975	103	18	240	72	57	3	14	1	61	680	176	492	17	24	7	267	40	49
237	293	669	55	167	77	32	26	101	49	32	981	299	248	74	22	50	124	11	50
			2,554		29			38			(*)	9		49		4			51
5				603							1,164		97			24	12		52
337	599	43	470	886	1,361	560	147	192	48	92	214	50	222	223	34	68	180		53
				132					5		206					16			54
1	1	1	43	60	89	109	162	178	31	40	469	2	133	29	16	21	39	9	55
(*)	1	(*)	2	(*)	343	(*)	(*)	1,653	2	(*)	732	1,197	146	1	(*)	9	46	1,252	56
17	33		1,450		343		113	4,742	2,123	292	206	486	5	430	544	121	29	266	57
	(*)	50	20	(*)	1	1	161	14	2	376	1,783	63	47	25	10	9	59	9	58
6		15	2	(*)	1		1	26	1	2	31,780	16	587	2	1	2	331	146	59
		22			25					15	1	4,537	28				657		60
																			61
2	25	2	11	167	19	279	2	33	5	3	195	213	50	513	19	5	43	7	62
5	7	5	10	5	14	2	6	66	14	5	16	131	9	10	479	12	24	11	63
2	3	3	12	24	12	51	2	13	6	1	30	9	27	49	3	1,107	115	49	64
106	197	130	203	177	260	141	138	303	241	197	1,155	438	302	168	199	472	16,634	254	65
54	106	40	87	47	72	25	25	147	73	21	65	142	75	83	71	161	994	946	66
																			67
82	184	110	106	115	210	137	96	199	211	111	775	265	174	125	86	188	1,043	451	68
448	717	185	778	738	936	560	494	1,296	767	409	4,840	554	1,102	598	407	1,208	2,587	233	69
69	98	61	163	46	176	63	91	119	140	99	382	325	97	72	74	178	1,766	456	70
51	97	84	146	49	146	33	46	891	104	73	155	133	264	108	77	287	1,349	853	71
19	36	28	173	33	75	30	45	233	106	50	75	314	32	31	45	67	282	112	72
194	402	457	540	261	369	430	219	979	443	187	1,786	896	363	431	494	906	3,931	1,338	73
52	141	63	161	58	115	46	57	225	158	52	144	504	68	117	119	140	1,018	169	74
13	39	43	24	9	25	12	12	31	47	19	734	49	36	118	30	53	2,343	105	75
	5		9	(*)	(*)	(*)		5	7	13	15	11	19	18	9	10	32	2	76
4	16	14	9	10	7	9	5	32	20	3	90	35	7	30	45	54	192	54	77
22	32	13	24	6	28	34	14	104	28	6	132	83	23	34	17	75	147	170	78
1	4	2	5	3	4	2	2	5	5	3	22	5	2	4	3	6	108	37	79
11	12	1	124	1	44	12	4	107		11	309	30	3	56	14	527	2,877	900	80
20	8	11					14		40		214		(*)			48			81
																			82
																			83
																			84
																			85
4,323	8,196	3,663	9,181	7,068	8,693	6,316	4,459	15,556	7,831	4,620	84,028	14,195	12,932	6,284	5,220	11,338	54,891	10,559	I
4,392	8,000	4,744	6,611	4,888	9,033	4,226	3,830	13,322	6,881	4,254	33,657	12,181	8,708	7,005	6,561	8,407	71,319	42,308	VA
3,144	5,444	3,856	4,940	3,132	6,507	2,440	2,311	11,688	5,584	2,993	23,069	10,580	7,411	4,905	3,472	5,417	49,595	18,364	88
94	134	117	111	94	138	67	50	256	156	89	1,649	192	142	103	120	211	4,338	5,571	89
1,153	2,422	771	1,560	1,662	2,387	1,719	1,470	1,379	1,142	1,172	8,939	1,410	1,156	1,997	2,970	2,780	17,386	18,373	90
8,714	16,196	8,407	15,793	11,956	17,725	10,542	8,289	28,878	14,711	8,874	117,685	26,376	21,640	13,288	11,782	19,745	126,210	52,867	T

Table 1.—The Use of Commodities

[Millions of dollars at

Commodity number	For the distribution of output of a commodity, read the row for that commodity / For the composition of inputs to an industry, read the column for that industry	Radio and TV broadcasting	Electric, gas, water, and sanitary services	Wholesale and retail trade	Finance and insurance	Real estate and rental	Hotels; personal and repair services (exc. auto)	Business services	Eating and drinking places	Automobile repair and services	Amusements	Health, educ., and social serv. and nonprofit org.	Federal Government enterprises	State and local government enterprises
Industry number		67	68	69	70	71	72	73	74	75	76	77	78	79
1	Livestock and livestock products													
2	Other agricultural products			20		15	3	8	444		35	85	7	
3	Forestry and fishery products						23	9	692		662	87	124	2
4	Agricultural, forestry, and fishery services	(*)	7	613	3	1,463	39	5	741	(*)	64	81	17	13
5	Iron and ferroalloy ores mining													
6	Nonferrous metal ores mining													
7	Coal mining		6,065											
8	Crude petroleum and natural gas		13,148			5						16	578	619
9	Stone and clay mining and quarrying													
10	Chemical and fertilizer mineral mining											1		
11	New construction													6
12	Maintenance and repair construction	30	3,712	2,560	350	19,891	599	462	534	347	666	3,540	211	4,760
13	Ordnance and accessories		(*)	4		(*)		78	(*)			2	(*)	(*)
14	Food and kindred products	4	5	327	1	1	97	66	24,794	2	295	2,218	490	1
15	Tobacco manufactures													
16	Broad and narrow fabrics, yarn and thread mills			1			148				31	25	5	
17	Miscellaneous textile goods and floor coverings			58			20	2	16	11	19	13	2	3
18	Apparel	(*)	4	77		2	382	29		36	79	335	1	11
19	Miscellaneous fabricated textile products			32	80	1	391	7	48	(*)	31	324	53	3
20	Lumber and wood products, except containers		59	414		3	68		14		64	28		
21	Wood containers			19										
22	Household furniture						2							
23	Other furniture and fixtures										2	1		
24	Paper and allied products, except containers	4	43	2,230	387	53	147	400	340	21	17	906	45	23
25	Paperboard containers and boxes	(*)	4	690	1		46	28	610	1	(*)	60	15	(*)
26	Printing and publishing	14	64	1,547	1,642	301	224	1,555	92	12	62	3,266	168	54
27	Chemicals and selected chemical products	7	320	26	6	179	134	224	48	4	30	2,166	5	231
28	Plastics and synthetic materials													
29	Drugs, cleaning and toilet preparations		1	136	6	4	532	164	113		4	3,183	17	15
30	Paints and allied products						1	42		310		10	1	(*)
31	Petroleum refining and related industries	6	8,099	5,055	431	333	447	928	225	698	160	1,482	198	864
32	Rubber and miscellaneous plastics products	1	60	1,058	54	232	332	296	675	97	64	1,369	21	45
33	Leather tanning and finishing											(*)		
34	Footwear and other leather products	(*)	1	87	8	2	31	4	1	(*)	17	20	9	1
35	Glass and glass products	(*)	1	104	7	1	94	20	136	181	(*)	152	1	1
36	Stone and clay products		8	66	2	12	149	101	381	2		32	1	60
37	Primary iron and steel manufacturing			9	1		2	3				7	1	(*)
38	Primary nonferrous metals manufacturing		19				5		10		3	7	6	1
39	Metal containers		4	115				30				4	2	1
40	Heating, plumbing, and structural metal products		19			94						4	2	1
41	Screw machine products and stampings		46				21	53	283	1,479	8	92	36	5
42	Other fabricated metal products	(*)	87	276	11	4	98	152	53	1,184	13	103	8	6
43	Engines and turbines		617					68					4	22
44	Farm and garden machinery			9		39		215		33				60
45	Construction and mining machinery							245						(*)
46	Materials handling machinery and equipment		5	104				122				(*)	1	(*)
47	Metalworking machinery and equipment	(*)	13	41				105		6	(*)		1	2
48	Special industry machinery and equipment			15				71	67				1	9
49	General industrial machinery and equipment		41	2	4	3		230		3			8	4
50	Miscellaneous machinery, except electrical	(*)	22	204			18	56	150	313	3	9	8	118
51	Office, computing, and accounting machines		3	29	70	3	595	460				13	4	(*)
52	Service industry machines		(*)	289			34	25	149	335	13	11	8	6
53	Electric industrial equipment and apparatus		105	3			14	98		105		(*)		168
54	Household appliances		(*)	35	40	26	308	41	(*)		(*)	20	6	24
55	Electric lighting and wiring equipment	1	84	44	14	31	17	71	36	100	15	115	11	41
56	Radio, TV, and communication equipment	21	4	77	19	(*)	33	33	1	53	5	56	6	4
57	Electronic components and accessories	175	3	10	49		525	467				99	1	10
58	Miscellaneous electrical machinery and supplies	(*)	5	101	12	35	8	58	8	236	1	322	5	17
59	Motor vehicles and equipment	1	22	337	21	13	11	78	12	5,044	20	44	25	58
60	Aircraft and parts													
61	Other transportation equipment	1	5	60	18		2	155	(*)	4	78	5	14	53
62	Scientific and controlling instruments	1	72		8	2	21	21	(*)	7	(*)	1,455	1	5
63	Optical, ophthalmic, and photographic equipment	110	31	172	100	36	262	773	3	1	103	585	12	14
64	Miscellaneous manufacturing	4	28	573	240	49	690	240	174	16	90	476	39	25
65	Transportation and warehousing	80	2,052	6,806	950	208	251	1,826	1,327	1,010	379	2,098	1,360	338
66	Communications, except radio and TV	62	326	5,584	2,525	510	632	2,619	449	455	243	1,868	119	71
67	Radio and TV broadcasting	57						118						
68	Electric, gas, water, and sanitary services	67	21,426	7,452	1,272	2,040	1,732	908	1,793	473	503	3,391	217	3,331
69	Wholesale and retail trade	41	1,111	4,973	421	673	934	1,253	5,006	4,516	266	2,447	253	339
70	Finance and insurance	72	773	5,603	25,270	6,970	705	1,260	982	282	374	1,467	51	100
71	Real estate and rental	351	480	14,918	2,938	17,816	1,781	3,750	2,563	745	1,125	9,443	351	175
72	Hotels; personal and repair services (exc. auto)	64	156	1,557	643	71	674	1,166	464	95	242	1,052	59	45
73	Business services	289	968	29,408	8,706	5,242	2,206	9,514	3,248	1,178	1,917	7,758	525	433
74	Eating and drinking places	131	107	6,547	1,219	317		1,837	158	100	280	1,790	85	161
75	Automobile repair and services	6	142	5,507	383	151	338	1,138	125	173	316	1,007	121	50
76	Amusements	1,823	6	779	3		18	132	807	(*)	3,328	331	27	(*)
77	Health, educ., & social serv. and nonprofit org.	21	102	379	505	87	285	522	156	24	139	2,932	10	24
78	Federal Government enterprises	8	314	1,724	2,200	553	143	1,010	117	23	48	903	289	61
79	State and local government enterprises	11	18	207	27	38	49	29	61	29	10	100	11	4
80	Noncomparable imports	32	3	371	255	2	11	272	43		56	30	508	
81	Scrap, used, and secondhand goods						19			206				1
82	Government industry													
83	Rest of the world industry													
84	Household industry													
85	Inventory valuation adjustment													
I	Total intermediate inputs	3,493	60,801	109,461	50,908	57,928	16,660	35,558	47,871	20,325	11,882	59,443	6,160	12,492
VA	Value added	4,976	44,794	274,967	78,314	218,010	29,762	99,028	38,156	22,778	12,674	102,792	13,456	10,470
88	Compensation of employees	2,745	11,999	162,000	52,675	6,677	16,709	53,217	26,068	10,818	7,157	82,877	14,129	7,550
89	Indirect business taxes	174	4,875	53,161	5,505	47,706	1,717	1,300	3,349	1,126	1,370	551		
90	Property-type income	2,057	27,921	59,806	20,133	163,627	11,336	44,512	8,739	10,834	4,147	19,364	−673	2,919
T	Total industry output	8,470	105,596	384,429	129,222	275,938	46,422	134,586	86,027	43,103	24,556	162,235	19,616	22,962

*Less than $500,000.

by Industries, 1977—Continued

producers' prices]

Government industry (82)	Rest of the world industry (83)	Household industry (84)	Inventory valuation adjustment (85)	Total intermediate use	Personal consumption expenditures (91)	Gross private fixed investment (92)	Change in business inventories (93)	Exports (94)	Imports (95)	Federal Gov't purchases: Total	National defense (96)	Nondefense (97)	State and local gov't purchases: Total	Education (98)	Other (99)	Total final demand	Total commodity output	Commodity number
				47,384	2,511		−1,183	199	−360	6	1	5	48	24	24	1,219	48,603	1
				38,279	7,726		1,832	12,523	−1,047	3,496		3,496	367	191	177	24,897	63,176	2
				6,346	788		34	214	−1,302	−828		−828	−81	4	−85	−1,175	5,170	3
				8,095	353			24	−3	61	4	57	392	165	227	828	8,923	4
				3,548			−437	326	−1,173	−49	−49					−1,335	2,213	5
				3,257		374	57	203	−728	−16	−16	(*)				−110	3,147	6
				14,121	215		161	2,096	−86	31	22	9	109	49	60	2,525	16,646	7
				77,477		116	690	202	−35,062	100	1	99	−39		−39	−33,955	43,523	8
				4,930	20		79	181	−286	−2	−2		−39		−39	−47	4,883	9
				1,298	2		39	228	−231	3		3	87		87	128	1,426	10
						150,890			1	7,450	2,361	5,089	32,354	5,585	26,769	190,694	190,694	11
				57,525				26		3,350	2,265	1,086	12,739	4,351	8,388	16,115	73,640	12
				621	630	22	115	1,530	−99	5,978	5,157	821	45		45	8,220	8,841	13
				75,195	113,507		1,617	7,308	−8,358	604	161	443	2,983	2,045	938	117,660	192,855	14
				2,628	8,437		365	1,664	−272							10,195	12,823	15
				24,338	882		1,082	1,148	−1,075	55	50	5	59	27	32	2,152	26,489	16
				5,948	2,045	892	187	342	−402	16	2	14	21	4	17	3,101	9,049	17
				10,305	33,194		2,472	733	−5,865	344	344		288	7	281	31,167	41,472	18
				4,675	4,068		222	332	−255	73	54	20	187	35	152	4,627	9,303	19
				38,243	548	11	1,329	1,928	−3,537	23	18	5	72	49	23	373	38,616	20
				525			8	10	−40	5	3	2				−17	508	21
				571	8,642	725	360	203	−475	54	9	45	56	40	16	9,566	10,137	22
				830	566	4,325	131	91	−269	105	23	82	664	411	253	5,612	6,442	23
				31,919	5,307		739	2,150	−3,725	128	32	96	1,180	525	654	5,779	37,698	24
				12,359	192		181	178	−13	43	26	17	92	40	52	673	13,033	25
				16,718	10,237		596	702	−360	332	138	195	3,624	2,117	1,507	15,131	31,849	26
				56,407	1,149	541	1,083	6,273	−4,370	1,275	1,071	204	906	330	576	6,857	63,263	27
				20,775			259	1,734	−495	37	34	3	2	2	(*)	1,538	22,313	28
				8,541	16,921		600	1,703	−1,338	330	198	132	1,970	239	1,731	20,184	28,725	29
				5,600	168		148	162	−8	3	(*)	3	119	102	17	594	6,194	30
				57,315	38,595		3,046	2,693	−11,366	1,875	2,043	−169	3,956	1,795	2,160	38,799	96,114	31
				32,019	6,444	58	1,366	1,532	−2,527	309	213	96	590	137	453	7,772	39,791	32
				1,531			18	166	−175	1	(*)	1				10	1,541	33
				575	7,610		209	144	−2,493	24	17	7	28		28	5,522	6,097	34
				7,909	829		163	503	−466	16	7	9	282	87	195	1,327	9,236	35
				24,239	1,123		717	604	−1,247	66	22	44	87	36	51	1,349	25,589	36
				67,833	11	5	1,274	1,580	−7,256	157	119	38	21	4	16	−4,209	63,623	37
				42,579	48	106	1,007	1,512	−4,747	178	88	90	18	1	17	−1,878	40,702	38
				8,256			29	164	−55	54	54					295	8,551	39
				20,918	374	3,055	902	1,126	−251	890	634	256				6,096	27,014	40
				18,120	798		368	1,059	−618	104	72	32	161	124	38	1,871	19,992	41
				23,522	2,038	1,591	830	1,466	−1,757	408	288	120	174	95	78	4,751	28,273	42
				6,184	207	1,663	423	1,993	−468	751	725	25	112		112	4,681	10,865	43
				1,956	105	8,410	661	1,240	−1,057	21	17	4	80	20	60	9,460	11,416	44
				3,596		8,692	603	4,421	−814	156	127	29	329		329	13,386	16,982	45
				1,546		2,984	104	427	−201	113	76	36	3	1	1	3,430	4,976	46
				5,267	281	7,507	400	1,087	−953	198	116	82	59	39	20	8,580	13,846	47
				2,074	92	5,209	227	2,354	−1,248	84	64	20	28	26	1	6,745	8,818	48
				9,451		5,080	474	2,214	−994	283	193	90	48		48	7,105	16,556	49
				8,038	40	29	184	157	−92	102	36	66	34	17	17	454	8,492	50
				3,873	420	7,432	558	3,476	−1,550	1,217	867	351	373	235	138	11,926	15,798	51
				6,264	432	2,986	317	1,155	−133	89	54	36	276	217	59	5,122	11,386	52
				10,298	91	5,854	586	2,072	−1,488	795	552	242	115	48	67	8,024	18,321	53
				1,775	7,014	1,607	174	657	−965	33	28	5	78	32	46	8,597	10,371	54
				5,964	1,318	97	361	460	−240	67	47	21	171	128	43	2,234	8,199	55
				6,836	8,328	10,620	703	2,498	−5,716	4,794	4,395	400	269	183	86	21,497	28,333	56
				12,720	529	35	490	2,468	−2,226	715	454	261	60	20	40	2,069	14,790	57
				4,335	2,003	1,491	383	859	−763	164	83	81	141	19	122	4,277	8,612	58
				39,822	46,124	30,854	4,368	10,963	−18,253	976	685	291	2,050	651	1,399	77,084	116,906	59
				5,597	427	2,777	186	7,159	−760	9,795	9,166	629	8		8	19,592	25,189	60
				2,465	7,063	8,323	597	975	−1,284	2,997	2,846	151	247	29	218	18,917	21,382	61
				4,395	1,927	4,570	484	1,976	−1,395	1,107	708	398	567	60	508	9,236	13,631	62
				3,687	2,379	4,188	177	1,510	−1,713	679	276	404	792	380	412	8,013	11,700	63
				5,775	12,684	1,283	913	1,295	−3,833	83	58	25	836	518	318	13,263	19,038	64
				75,440	33,210	1,976	1,020	9,756	−332	3,315	2,728	587	3,879	2,373	1,506	52,823	128,264	65
				23,404	22,394	3,385		985		1,063	502	562	1,636	851	785	29,464	52,868	66
				182	344											344	526	67
				75,722	41,824			276	−2,200	1,524	862	662	5,311	2,466	2,845	46,734	122,456	68
				112,682	222,550	24,668	2,980	12,416	5,376	2,125	1,584	542	3,374	1,254	2,121	273,489	386,171	69
				58,752	65,533		630	(*)	−524	613	7	606	3,574	184	3,390	69,826	128,578	70
				79,438	181,314	10,747		3,705		700	236	464	3,338	446	2,892	199,805	279,243	71
				10,924	33,938			29		557	380	177	681	−294	975	35,205	46,129	72
				131,330	13,863		3,481	81	−100	7,053	2,666	4,387	6,343	2,324	4,019	30,640	161,969	73
				22,153	67,477			2	−11	194	129	66	−2,067	−2,762	695	65,685	87,839	74
				17,170	25,437		7			189	48	141	694	153	541	26,210	43,380	75
				7,666	16,018		145	444		189	132	57	159	134	25	16,917	24,583	76
				7,093	135,932		75			3,838	764	3,074	15,078	−757	15,835	154,923	162,016	77
				10,702	2,692		193			175	140	35	478	48	431	3,538	14,240	78
				1,259	3,576		1			43	33	10	83	44	39	3,702	4,961	79
				13,377	8,727	17	35		−26,610	4,436	3,406	1,030	17	15	2	−13,377		80
				4,949	5,502	−10,297	−102	1,558	−264	−55	−24	−31	959	212	747	−2,699	2,250	81
										65,523	42,213	23,309	138,411	77,533	60,878	203,934	203,934	82
					−7,221			40,119	−9,117	−317	−14	−303				23,464	23,464	83
					5,930											5,930	5,930	84
							−18,582									−18,582	−18,582	85
																		I
203,934	23,464	5,930	−18,582														1,976,563	VA
203,934	−40	5,930															1,165,555	88
																	165,958	89
	23,504		−18,582														645,051	90
203,934	23,464	5,930	−18,582		1,246,481	314,926	21,700	182,043	−184,154	143,363	92,825	50,538	252,204	105,492	146,712	1,976,563		T

Table 2.—The Make of Commodities

[Millions of dollars

#	Industry \ Commodity	1 Livestock and livestock products	2 Other agricultural products	3 Forestry and fishery products	4 Agricultural, forestry, and fishery services	5 Iron and ferroalloy ores mining	6 Nonferrous metal ores mining	7 Coal mining	8 Crude petroleum and natural gas	9 Stone and clay mining and quarrying	10 Chemical and fertilizer mineral mining	11 New construction	12 Maintenance and repair construction	13 Ordnance and accessories	14 Food and kindred products	15 Tobacco manufactures
1	Livestock and livestock products	48,594		72	398										3,184	
2	Other agricultural products		63,176	628	664										433	
3	Forestry and fishery products			4,470												
4	Agricultural, forestry, and fishery services				7,827											
5	Iron and ferroalloy ores mining					2,044	16			(*)	(*)					
6	Nonferrous metal ores mining					165	3,120	4	(*)	6	6					
7	Coal mining						5	16,636	(*)	12	2					
8	Crude petroleum and natural gas						4	2	43,385	(*)						
9	Stone and clay mining and quarrying					5	1	4	1	4,607						
10	Chemical and fertilizer mineral mining						1			7	1,284				(*)	
11	New construction											190,694				
12	Maintenance and repair construction												73,640			
13	Ordnance and accessories													7,974		
14	Food and kindred products	9													188,562	
15	Tobacco manufactures															12,803
16	Broad and narrow fabrics, yarn and thread mills															
17	Miscellaneous textile goods and floor coverings															
18	Apparel															
19	Miscellaneous fabricated textile products															
20	Lumber and wood products, except containers														4	
21	Wood containers														(*)	
22	Household furniture															
23	Other furniture and fixtures															
24	Paper and allied products, except containers													6	(*)	18
25	Paperboard containers and boxes															
26	Printing and publishing															
27	Chemicals and selected chemical products								50		140			6	307	2
28	Plastics and synthetic materials															
29	Drugs, cleaning and toilet preparations														12	
30	Paints and allied products														294	
31	Petroleum refining and related industries									44						
32	Rubber and miscellaneous plastics products								2					15	29	
33	Leather tanning and finishing														1	
34	Footwear and other leather products															
35	Glass and glass products															
36	Stone and clay products									201						
37	Primary iron and steel manufacturing									3				23		
38	Primary nonferrous metals manufacturing													2		
39	Metal containers					(*)								2		
40	Heating, plumbing, and structural metal products													8		
41	Screw machine products and stampings													21		
42	Other fabricated metal products													30		
43	Engines and turbines													15	1	
44	Farm and garden machinery													14		
45	Construction and mining machinery															
46	Materials handling machinery and equipment													4		
47	Metalworking machinery and equipment													13		
48	Special industry machinery and equipment													27		
49	General industrial machinery and equipment													4		
50	Miscellaneous machinery, except electrical													4		
51	Office, computing, and accounting machines													2		
52	Service industry machines													3		
53	Electric industrial equipment and apparatus													5	9	
54	Household appliances															
55	Electric lighting and wiring equipment													9		
56	Radio, TV, and communication equipment													17		
57	Electronic components and accessories													282		
58	Miscellaneous electrical machinery and supplies													23		
59	Motor vehicles and equipment													15		
60	Aircraft and parts													280		
61	Other transportation equipment													20		
62	Scientific and controlling instruments													21		
63	Optical, ophthalmic, and photographic equipment													1	9	
64	Miscellaneous manufacturing													6	(*)	
65	Transportation and warehousing				34										(*)	
66	Communications, except radio and TV															
67	Radio and TV broadcasting															
68	Electric, gas, water, and sanitary services								86							
69	Wholesale and retail trade															
70	Finance and insurance															
71	Real estate and rental															
72	Hotels; personal and repair services (exc. auto)															
73	Business services															
74	Eating and drinking places															
75	Automobile repair and services															
76	Amusements															
77	Health, educ., & social serv. and nonprofit org.															
78	Federal Government enterprises															
79	State and local government enterprises															
82	Government industry															
83	Rest of the world industry															
84	Household industry															
85	Inventory valuation adjustment															
T	Total commodity output	48,603	63,176	5,170	8,923	2,213	3,147	16,646	43,523	4,883	1,426	190,694	73,640	8,841	192,855	12,823

For the distribution of industries producing a commodity, read the column for that commodity

For the distribution of commodities produced by an industry, read the row for that industry

See footnote at end of table.

by Industries, 1977

at producers' prices]

Note: Columns are numbered 16–35. A "(*)" entry denotes a value of less than half the unit shown. Blank cells contain no entry. The far-right column gives the industry (row) number.

16 Broad and narrow fabrics, yarn and thread mills	17 Misc. textile goods and floor coverings	18 Apparel	19 Misc. fabricated textile products	20 Lumber and wood products, except containers	21 Wood containers	22 Household furniture	23 Other furniture and fixtures	24 Paper and allied products, except containers	25 Paperboard containers and boxes	26 Printing and publishing	27 Chemicals and selected chemical products	28 Plastics and synthetic materials	29 Drugs, cleaning and toilet preparations	30 Paints and allied products	31 Petroleum refining and related industries	32 Rubber and misc. plastics products	33 Leather tanning and finishing	34 Footwear and other leather products	35 Glass and glass products	Industry number
																				1
																				2
				102																3
																				4
																				5
																				6
																				7
											62				3,264					8
											1				31					9
											822									10
																				11
																				12
																2				13
				(*)		1	1	34	11	6	239	3	160		(*)	60				14
	1	8	1	4			1	5												15
25,911	193	272	937			9	19	39		9		1,214	(*)	3	5	46		1	3	16
119	8,370	26	47	45		(*)	12	47		14	8	41	2	3	1	80	(*)	1		17
131	29	41,029	141				11			8					18	6			19	18
121	15	25	7,811	5		6	3	36	1		52	1	3	1	3	14	3		5	19
2	2		1	38,019	38	21	23	56	9	(*)						35				20
																2				21
(*)	7		18	44	(*)	9,915	18				3					19		4	66	22
	15		43		1	28	6,111				5					27		1	1	23
3	97		77	1				36,570	60	223	199		4		15	280			11	24
	3		2					61	12,754	32	5		20		15	133		1		25
	13		8				8	296	35	31,158	49					19	4			26
			10					83			50,675	3,004	1,006	80	1,139	38	4			27
140	176		91								1,428	17,407	81	28		492				28
		6	14	5							975	94	27,055	29	60	34				29
	1										105	121	6	5,983	2	5				30
5			1				12				6,943	101	79	12	91,504	16		1	3	31
36	84	33	30	17	1	39	10	77	20	24	285	191	44	8	3	37,553	1	31	4	32
	1															2	1,534	1		33
	28	1										15				14		5,989		34
		1	4								65	15	9	8		18		(*)	8,964	35
	16											55			1	70			36	36
3			4								259					3				37
		1									286		4			72			64	38
			2								7					13			4	39
											92				2	56		1	31	40
			3								3	7		7	1	28			1	41
4			2				23				16	8	13	13	11	108	(*)	3	1	42
			23				3									5				43
			10				3			6	21					4				44
							6				34					17				45
							1									1				46
		1	1				4			(*)	5	20	14		1	23				47
1										2	20	3	5	1	8	7				48
3	1	2	17	17	(*)		2			1	33	3	2	1	1	46			5	49
2			4	1							19	3				3				50
			2					29			6					35		1		51
			10								35	8				9			(*)	52
			2					7			25		13			23			4	53
											4					20			(*)	54
	6		3	3			9	9			6	7			(*)	9		1	9	55
4	13		3				1	2			6	6		6		24				56
							15	9			14					27		5		57
	5		3	2			4	5			29		3	7	17	9			(*)	58
											2					6				59
		15	22	2			69	33		9						60				60
		4	11	12			18	9								4		3	(*)	61
1	1	4	2	7		1	9	18	27	3	53	14	104	10	3	21	(*)	15	24	62
3	1	16	39	21		36	4	17	3	47	82	58	131	2	1	59			(*)	63
											131					134				64
																				65
																				66
																				67
											143				30					68
																				69
																				70
																				71
																				72
																				73
																				74
																				75
																				76
																				77
										(*)	41									78
																				79
																				82
																				83
																				84
																				85
26,189	9,049	41,472	9,303	38,616	508	10,137	6,442	37,698	13,033	31,849	63,263	22,313	28,725	6,194	96,114	39,791	1,541	6,097	9,236	T

Table 2.—The Make of Commodities

[Millions of dollars

For the distribution of industries producing a commodity, read the column for that commodity

For the distribution of commodities produced by an industry, read the row for that industry

Ind. no.	Commodity	Stone and clay products	Primary iron and steel mfg.	Primary nonferrous metals mfg.	Metal containers	Heating, plumbing, and structural metal products	Screw machine products and stampings	Other fabricated metal products	Engines and turbines	Farm and garden machinery	Construction and mining machinery	Materials handling machinery and equip.	Metalworking machinery and equip.	Special industry machinery and equip.	General industrial machinery and equip.	Misc. machinery, except electrical
	Commodity number	36	37	38	39	40	41	42	43	44	45	46	47	48	49	50
1	Livestock and livestock products															
2	Other agricultural products															
3	Forestry and fishery products															
4	Agricultural, forestry, and fishery services															
5	Iron and ferroalloy ores mining															
6	Nonferrous metal ores mining															
7	Coal mining															
8	Crude petroleum and natural gas	8														
9	Stone and clay mining and quarrying	130														52
10	Chemical and fertilizer mineral mining	45														
11	New construction															
12	Maintenance and repair construction															
13	Ordnance and accessories		17	2	1	49	16	16	29		1		(*)	22	3	8
14	Food and kindred products				16	6	36	2		1				13		
15	Tobacco manufactures				17											
16	Broad and narrow fabrics, yarn and thread mills	50						3						22		
17	Miscellaneous textile goods and floor coverings			6				5						13	3	
18	Apparel					(*)								(*)		
19	Miscellaneous fabricated textile products	(*)														
20	Lumber and wood products, except containers	9	1	2		52	(*)	9			1	2	4	1	2	(*)
21	Wood containers							47			2	1			1	1
22	Household furniture											1				
23	Other furniture and fixtures		10	7		21	5	26			6		5			
24	Paper and allied products, except containers	1	3			18	5	10			2	6	2	3	5	3
25	Paperboard containers and boxes	17				5		144						12	5	
26	Printing and publishing				10	12	15	21					6	2	1	
27	Chemicals and selected chemical products	101	6			7		54					7	11		
28	Plastics and synthetic materials		5	42		11	10	68			16	1	11	94	11	1
29	Drugs, cleaning and toilet preparations	11						11					9			
30	Paint and allied products	9						12						3	23	
31	Petroleum refining and related industries					1										
32	Rubber and miscellaneous plastics products	108			40					1				4	5	
33	Leather tanning and finishing	92	29	13	2	34	25	103			21	7	11	92	26	40
34	Footwear and other leather products	2				1	1	6		1			2	1		
35	Glass and glass products	3	1			6	2	8		1			5	5		1
36	Stone and clay products	24,677	5			29	1	29		4	3	1	24	4	22	1
37	Primary iron and steel manufacturing	10	61,732	300		155	130	1,657		36	20	4	75	6	84	19
38	Primary nonferrous metals manufacturing	44	329	39,474	13	88	12	328		2			81	11	48	4
39	Metal containers				8,360	17		1					7	1		
40	Heating, plumbing, and structural metal products	27	68	72	8	25,411	64	150	30	37	25	46	27	24	88	41
41	Screw machine products and stampings	3	67	38	41	75	18,543	94	26	30	15	12	318	9	51	9
42	Other fabricated metal products	21	233	63	8	100	109	24,164	28	36	40	29	161	54	113	59
43	Engines and turbines		8	2		70	10	18	9,479	8			31	12	64	7
44	Farm and garden machinery		119	(*)		52	17	32	49	10,765	277	13	10	25	36	4
45	Construction and mining machinery	2	102			81	7	164	300	105	16,233	170	27	16	163	17
46	Materials handling machinery and equipment		20			17	5	16	6	14	49	4,456	19	25	51	10
47	Metalworking machinery and equipment	4	90	5		24	25	110	9	59	28	21	12,373	56	56	21
48	Special industry machinery and equipment	16	32	5	1	54	11	29	9	15	17	29	75	8,057	105	8
49	General industrial machinery and equipment	2	49	42		82	27	227	128	25	47	21	52	70	14,786	68
50	Miscellaneous machinery, except electrical	8	17	11	1	12	5	20	23		4	5	4	15	59	7,933
51	Office, computing, and accounting machines		3			24	26	83					18	18	75	7
52	Service industry machines	3	26	45	6	82	6	54			16	1	12	13	104	10
53	Electric industrial equipment apparatus	22	26	59		14	7	28		98	3	15	38	8	73	4
54	Household appliances		21	59	9	59	111	15			18			1	63	3
55	Electric lighting and wiring equipment	6	41	58		22	39	44			18	10	1	3	5	6
56	Radio, TV, and communication equipment	8	11	86		15	2	62			4	4	5	27	10	18
57	Electronic components and accessories	11	20	24		24	32	26	9			6	27	55	53	10
58	Miscellaneous electrical machinery and supplies	4	25	171		(*)	2	7				5	10	(*)	15	57
59	Motor vehicles and equipment	48	445	123	3	109	570	138	175	83	86	55	134	20	72	40
60	Aircraft and parts	10	57	6		54	42	66	386	20	48	20	28	50	136	8
61	Other transportation equipment		14			85	6	28	68	89	44	5	35	7	43	7
62	Scientific and controlling instruments		3	26		31	17	67		14			7	6	50	13
63	Optical, ophthalmic, and photographic equipment	8				4	7	7			7	6		8	22	13
64	Miscellaneous manufacturing	37	8	14	3	14	21	56			6	1	15	6	13	7
65	Transportation and warehousing															
66	Communications, except radio and TV															
67	Radio and TV broadcasting															
68	Electric, gas, water, and sanitary services															
69	Wholesale and retail trade															
70	Finance and insurance															
71	Real estate and rental															
72	Hotels; personal and repair services (exc. auto)															
73	Business services															
74	Eating and drinking places															
75	Automobile repair and services															
76	Amusements															
77	Health, educ., & social serv. and nonprofit org.															
78	Federal Government enterprises															
79	State and local government enterprises	25														
82	Government industry															
83	Rest of the world industry															
84	Household industry															
85	Inventory valuation adjustment															
T	Total commodity output	25,589	63,623	40,702	8,551	27,014	19,992	28,273	10,865	11,416	16,982	4,976	13,846	8,818	16,556	8,492

See footnote at end of table.

by Industries, 1977—Continued

at producers' prices]

Office, computing, and accounting machines	Service industry machines	Electric industrial equipment and apparatus	Household appliances	Electric lighting and wiring equipment	Radio, TV, and communication equipment	Electronic components and accessories	Misc. electrical machinery and supplies	Motor vehicles and equipment	Aircraft and parts	Other transportation equipment	Scientific and controlling instruments	Optical, ophthalmic, and photographic equipment	Miscellaneous manufacturing	Transportation and warehousing	Communications, except radio and TV	Radio and TV broadcasting	Electric, gas, water, and sanitary services	Wholesale and retail trade	Finance and insurance	Industry number
51	52	53	54	55	56	57	58	59	60	61	62	63	64	65	66	67	68	69	70	
																				1
														15						2
																				3
																				4
																				5
																				6
																				7
																	2,307			8
																				9
																				10
																				11
																				12
	2	13	1	1	251	4	1	45	332	51	5	4	10							13
	8		3										14							14
													(*)							15
											31		22							16
	1	1			5			2			5		9							17
(*)					1			4	1	2	21		27							18
			1	(*)	6	1		11		10	6		16							19
											7		14							20
16			42	3	4	7		4			16	5	22							21
10	6		2	3	5		2	5	5	4	20	5	17							22
130		2		2	1	125	4	7			31	78	150							23
													(*)							24
31				11							7	20	61							25
2	11	1		5	73	50		5		1	86	231	38							26
											9	23								27
	1		4		4		25				97		45							28
												1	2							29
													2							30
16	5	10	14	16	6	23	6	63	19	18	34	9	76							31
								3					2							32
								1	1		6	1	12							33
		5	5					12			11		6							34
5	(*)	11		20	10	10	3	7	7	4	13	5	13				44			35
9		9		62	6			154		5		3	1							36
		41	3	19	11	14	44	173	6	7	8		11							37
				1				8												38
8	56	38	48	12	13	3	20	80	46	42	37		13							39
8	13	32	105	14	10	19	19	55	7	20	8	1	33							40
7	21	59	24	25	15	18	14	40	17	17	140		42							41
8	12	381	8		9		3	138	27	4	16									42
	5	2	11	5	5			25	9	34	5		4							43
	10	37			19			124	2	22	32		10							44
9	2	8			3		2	49	4	15	5									45
15	8	27	5	4	4	11	(*)	43	13	4	27	1	9							46
33	28	6	5	2	3	3	2	20	1	36	26	2	4							47
34	67	53	35	18	7	29	3	134	14	19	32	4	5							48
1	6	5	4	3	3	4	11	157	13	1	4	2	2							49
14,436	1	5	12	11	55	434	30		31	20	125	60	44							50
11	10,661	11	188	10	11	7	30	516		1	22		12							51
51	20	16,583	14	93	77	202	22	38	5	5	106	16	(*)							52
	266	43	9,700	7	23		19	25	9		12		13							53
19		95		7,481	75	79	34	112		8	15	41	11							54
145	6	165	7	38	27,150	410	5	63	31		126	28	12							55
593		77	6	86	199	13,128	46	20	28		50	5	32							56
21	7	112	1	29	30	31	7,953	285	20		16	3	2							57
25	127	162	78	71	3		217	114,240	50	72	44	1	24							58
34	24	43		26	144	34		54	24,423	126	101		34							59
	7	84	(*)	2	6	10		138	23	20,816	9		11							60
52	6	119	37	63	87	55	32	41	17	5	12,107	96	35							61
53	1	10	5	58	53	46	12	7	17		116	11,048	16							62
6	1	1	5	9	21	7	4	4	6	11	40	1		18,101						63
														124,842			1,264			64
															52,867					65
																526	105,282			66
																		384,429		67
																			128,495	68
																				69
																				70
																				71
																				72
																				73
																				74
																				75
																				76
														103	1		2,262	971	21	77
														3,304			11,298	772	61	78
																				79
																				82
																				83
																				84
																				85
15,798	11,386	18,321	10,371	8,199	28,333	14,790	8,612	116,906	25,189	21,382	13,631	11,700	19,038	128,264	52,868	526	122,456	386,171	128,578	T

Table 2.—The Make of Commodities by Industries, 1977—Continued

[Millions of dollars at producers' prices]

Industry number	For the distribution of industries producing a commodity, read the column for that commodity / For the distribution of commodities produced by an industry, read the row for that industry	Real estate and rental	Hotels; personal and repair services exc. auto	Business services	Eating and drinking places	Automobile repair and services	Amusements	Health, educ., and social serv., and nonprofit org.	Federal Government enterprises	State and local government enterprises	Scrap, used, and secondhand goods	Government industry	Rest of the world industry	Household industry	Inventory valuation adjustment	Total industry output
Commodity number		71	72	73	74	75	76	77	78	79	81	82	83	84	85	
1	Livestock and livestock products															52,292
2	Other agricultural products						44									65,074
3	Forestry and fishery products						56									4,470
4	Agricultural, forestry, and fishery services															7,827
5	Iron and ferroalloy ores mining															2,059
6	Nonferrous metal ores mining															3,297
7	Coal mining															16,653
8	Crude petroleum and natural gas															49,083
9	Stone and clay mining and quarrying															4,780
10	Chemical and fertilizer mineral mining															2,159
11	New construction															190,694
12	Maintenance and repair construction															73,640
13	Ordnance and accessories															8,879
14	Food and kindred products			1							4					189,200
15	Tobacco manufactures															12,853
16	Broad and narrow fabrics, yarn and thread mills										27					28,841
17	Miscellaneous textile goods and floor coverings										54					8,871
18	Apparel			1												41,427
19	Miscellaneous fabricated textile products			(*)												8,098
20	Lumber and wood products, except containers			(*)												38,477
21	Wood containers										17					501
22	Household furniture										1					10,299
23	Other furniture and fixtures			2							2					6,394
24	Paper and allied products, except containers			1							2					38,388
25	Paperboard containers and boxes			9							67					13,172
26	Printing and publishing			23							97					49,984
27	Chemicals and selected chemical products			18,105							95					57,497
28	Plastics and synthetic materials										41					19,926
29	Drugs, cleaning and toilet preparations			1							5					28,806
30	Paints and allied products										4					6,254
31	Petroleum refining and related industries										15					98,895
32	Rubber and miscellaneous plastics products			1							9					39,366
33	Leather tanning and finishing															1,552
34	Footwear and other leather products			(*)												6,103
35	Glass and glass products			1												9,091
36	Stone and clay products															25,522
37	Primary iron and steel manufacturing															65,234
38	Primary nonferrous metals manufacturing										379					41,379
39	Metal containers										142					8,789
40	Heating, plumbing, and structural metal products										128					26,894
41	Screw machine products and stampings			1							77					19,989
42	Other fabricated metal products			1							204					26,101
43	Engines and turbines			2							76					10,349
44	Farm and garden machinery										13					11,564
45	Construction and mining machinery										9					17,724
46	Materials handling machinery and equipment										21					4,807
47	Metalworking machinery and equipment										4					13,157
48	Special industry machinery and equipment			(*)							10					8,714
49	General industrial machinery and equipment										3					16,196
50	Miscellaneous machinery, except electrical										24					8,407
51	Office, computing, and accounting machines										12					15,793
52	Service industry machines			3							17					11,956
53	Electric industrial equipment and apparatus			1							37					17,725
54	Household appliances										36					10,542
55	Electric lighting and wiring equipment			1							18					8,289
56	Radio, TV, and communication equipment										17					28,878
57	Electronic components and accessories										82					14,711
58	Miscellaneous electrical machinery and supplies										41					8,874
59	Motor vehicles and equipment										22					117,685
60	Aircraft and parts										275					26,376
61	Other transportation equipment										19					21,640
62	Scientific and controlling instruments			1							26					13,288
63	Optical, ophthalmic, and photographic equipment										19					11,782
64	Miscellaneous manufacturing			793							27					19,745
65	Transportation and warehousing			1		1					4					126,210
66	Communications, except radio and TV										68					52,867
67	Radio and TV broadcasting			7,944												8,470
68	Electric, gas, water, and sanitary services															105,596
69	Wholesale and retail trade									54						384,429
70	Finance and insurance			727												129,222
71	Real estate and rental	275,938														275,938
72	Hotels; personal and repair services (exc. auto)	256	46,112	55												46,422
73	Business services	814	17	133,755												134,586
74	Eating and drinking places				86,027											86,027
75	Automobile repair and serv.					43,103										43,103
76	Amusements			322			24,234									24,556
77	Health, educ., & social serv. and nonprofit org.			220				162,016								162,235
78	Federal Government enterprises	126			1,812		40		14,240							19,616
79	State and local government enterprises	2,110				276	209			4,907						22,962
82	Government industry											203,934				203,934
83	Rest of the world industry												23,464			23,464
84	Household industry													5,930		5,930
85	Inventory valuation adjustment														-18,582	-18,582
T	Total commodity output	279,243	46,129	161,969	87,839	43,380	24,583	162,016	14,240	4,961	2,250	203,934	23,464	5,930	-18,582	

* Less than $500,000.

XVIII. YUGOSLAVIA

A. GENERAL INFORMATION

The present report is based on *Inter-Industry Relations of the Economy in the Socialist Federal Republic of Yugoslavia in 1974*, published by Savezni Zavod Za Statistiku, 1978.

Input/output tables for Yugoslavia have been compiled for the years 1955, 1958, 1962, 1964, 1966, 1968, 1970, 1972, 1974 and 1976. The tables for 1955 and 1958 have 29 producing sectors and five sectors of final demand. Since 1962, the number of sectors has increased to 98 production activities, with the same five sectors of final demand.

Yugoslavian statistics on national income and input-output are based on the System of Balances of the National Economy (MPS) adopted by the member states of the Council for Mutual Economic Assistance. (See part one for more information on MPS.) Accordingly, economic activities of the input-output tables of Yugoslavia include only material production sectors such as agriculture, mining, construction, manufacturing, goods and transportation, communication, trade and catering. Non-material service activities such as health care, education and financial and banking services are not included in the intermediate demand matrix, but in the final demand sectors as expenses on goods and material services. Similar to SNA but different from the MPS convention is the treatment of depreciation; it is included in the quadrant of value added. As a result of this treatment, gross investment instead of net investment is entered in final demand.

B. ANALYTICAL FRAMEWORK

1. Tables and derived matrices available

The following tables are compiled for 1974:

(*a*) The transaction matrix and the corresponding matrix of technical coefficients and the matrix of total direct and indirect input requirement (the Leontief inverse). The tables of different levels of aggregation are also provided. Included are the tables of 8, 16, 29, 50 and 98 sectors;

(*b*) The import matrix by origin and destination and the corresponding matrix of domestic input coefficients, matrix of import coefficients and matrix of total direct and indirect domestic input requirements. Only the tables at more aggregated level are provided. Included are tables of 8, 16 and 29 sectors.

2. Valuation standards

All tables for 1974 are valued at producers' prices and in ex-customs values for imports which are equal to c.i.f. value

taxes. The latter treatment is different from the SNA convention which registers imports in c.i.f. values. Indirect taxes are included as part of trade margin and turnover tax on imports is treated as indirect taxes.

3. Statistical units and classification standards

The unit of classification used is the "economic-technical" unit concept, which is similar to the SNA concept of the establishment. Data on output and input of secondary products are collected at the initial stage in the preparation of input-output tables. Therefore no mechanical methods are needed later for the separation of secondary products. The tables become basically industry-by-industry tables.

4. Treatment and presentation of selected transactions

Reflecting the MPS concepts, the production segment of the input-output tables includes only material production sectors.

Final demand includes:

(*a*) Personal consumption of goods and material services;

(*b*) General consumption of goods and material services, which consists of all the consumption of goods and material services by non-material service sectors;

(*c*) Gross investment;

(*d*) Exports;

(*e*) Increase in stocks.

Value added includes:

(*a*) Personal income (wages and salaries and other compensation);

(*b*) Accumulation and funds which are also called other incomes (expenses on non-material services, turnover taxes, allocation to special funds etc.);

(*c*) Depreciation;

(*d*) Decrease in stocks;

(*e*) Imports of commodities that are comparable to those produced by the corresponding sectors.

In the tables following the SNA method, the row of decrease in stocks and the row of imports are placed in the final demand columns as negative values.

The sector "arts and crafts" comprises many products produced in an "artisan way" in different economic sectors.

Undistributed amounts which do not exceed 10 per cent of the total control amount are checked and then distributed proportionally to previously distributed amounts.

303

Table 2—1. Production and distribution by groups of branches of economic activities. Producer's prices. — Thousand dinars.

Column headings:

1. Energetika — Energy
2. Metalurgija — Metallurgy
3. Proizvodnja i prerada nemetala — Production and processing of non-metals
4. Prerada metala — Processing of metals
5. Proizvodnja hemijskih proizvoda i papira — Manufacture of chemicals and paper
6. Prerada drveta — Manufacture of wood
7. Proizvodnja tekstila, kože i gume — Manufacture of textile, leather and rubber
8. Proizvodnja prehrambenih proizvoda i duvana — Manufacture of food products and tobacco
9. Ostala industrija — Miscellaneous manufacturing industries
10. Poljoprivreda i ribarstvo — Agriculture and fisheries
11. Šumarstvo — Forestry
12. Vodoprivreda — Operation of irrigation systems and kindred activities
13. Građevinarstvo — Construction
14. Saobraćaj i veze — Transport and communications
15. Trgovina — Trade
16. Ugostiteljstvo i turizam — Catering and tourism
17. Zanatske usluge i opravke — Arts and crafts services and repairs
18. Komunalne delatnosti — Public utilities
19. Ostale proizvodne usluge — Other productive services
20. Stari materijal i otpaci — Scrap and waste
21. Svega (1—20) — All (1—20)
22. Povećanje zaliha — Increase of stocks
23. Bruto-investicije — Gross investment
24. Izvoz — Exports
25. Lična potrošnja — Personal consumption
26. Opšta potrošnja — General consumption
27. Svega — All
28. Finalna potrošnja — Final consumption
29. Raspodeljena sredstva — Distributed resources

Stub:

Primaoci — Industry consuming
Davaoci — Industry producing

22. Amortizacija — Depreciation
23. Čisti lični dohoci — Net personal incomes
24. Višak proizvoda — Accumulation and funds
25. Proizvodnja (21+22+23+24) — Production (21+22+23+24)
26. Smanjenje zaliha — Decrease of stocks
27. Uvoz — Imports
28. Raspoloživa sredstva (25+26+27) — Available resources (25+26+27)

YUGOSLAVIA
INPUT-OUTPUT TABLES
1976

Source: *Inter-Industry Relations of the Economy in the Socialist Federal Republic of Yugoslavia in 1974. Savezni Zavod Za Statistiku.*

PROIZVODNJA I RASPODELA PO GRUPAMA GRANA
DELATNOSTI U CENAMA PROIZVODJAČA
INPUT-OUTPUT TABELA

TABELA 2-1.
U HILJADAMA DINARA

PRIMAOCI / DAVAOCI		ENERGE-TIKA	META-LURGIJA	PROIZVO-DNJA I PRERADA NEMETALA	PRERADA METALA	PROIZ.HE-MIJSKIH PROIZVODA I PAPIRA	PRERADA DRVETA	PROIZVOD-NJA TEKS-TILA.KOŽE I GUME
		1	2	3	4	5	6	7
ENERGETIKA	1							
UKUPNO		24042328	7709104	3298952	3251020	3792999	854755	1773159
DOMAĆA PROIZVODNJA		11556122	7148226	3138839	3102063	3513456	829282	1721419
UVOZ		12486206	560878	160113	148957	279543	25474	51740
METALURGIJA	2							
UKUPNO		762494	44195156	736391	27981186	1132880	356609	193907
DOMAĆA PROIZVODNJA		545985	38017589	500438	20592959	417493	337464	125455
UVOZ		216509	6177567	235953	7288227	715387	19145	68452
PROIZVODNJA I PRERADA NEMETALA	3							
UKUPNO		292052	1684843	4400278	1573785	1713492	243514	134010
DOMAĆA PROIZVODNJA		263845	1094603	3426041	1225189	424296	148535	99363
UVOZ		28207	590240	974237	448596	1289196	94979	34647
PRERADA METALA	4							
UKUPNO		2589080	2053490	1256515	50584362	1729799	1453223	1564701
DOMAĆA PROIZVODNJA		1951728	1246332	1045008	39343946	1250056	1189110	1153578
UVOZ		637352	807158	211507	11240416	479743	254113	411123
PROIZV.HEMIJSKIH PROIZVODA I PAPIRA	5							
UKUPNO		918763	1030135	1380541	5086392	29277731	2077598	7973948
DOMAĆA PROIZVODNJA		424725	533576	1104438	3576164	17247046	1611701	4145124
UVOZ		494038	496559	276103	1510228	12030685	465897	3828824
PRERADA DRVETA	6							
UKUPNO		113154	121890	251599	1253664	173274	6714692	280291
DOMAĆA PROIZVODNJA		111770	117869	234361	995218	151212	6116362	275246
UVOZ		1384	4021	17238	358446	22062	593330	5045
PROIZVODNJA TEKSTILA,KOŽE I GUME	7							
UKUPNO		150556	150398	208605	1518104	555529	1044624	33379594
DOMAĆA PROIZVODNJA		116843	78303	173119	1294535	437291	885667	28797235
UVOZ		33713	72095	35486	223569	118238	158957	4582359
PROIZV.PREHRAMB.PROIZVODA I DUVANA	8							
UKUPNO		1797	15967	557	4606	509562	502	2560625
DOMAĆA PROIZVODNJA		1702	15967	369	3545	249766	459	1626963
UVOZ		95	0	188	1061	259796	43	933662
OSTALA INDUSTRIJA	9							
UKUPNO		109915	74277	94099	502787	638453	112537	465542
DOMAĆA PROIZVODNJA		109489	73464	85110	478141	615770	110651	414531
UVOZ		426	833	8989	24646	22683	1886	51011
POLJOPRIVREDA I RIBARSTVO	10							
UKUPNO		0	0	0	0	256894	2859	3208129
DOMAĆA PROIZVODNJA		0	0	0	0	165690	0	30542
UVOZ		0	0	0	0	91204	2859	3177587
ŠUMARSTVO	11							
UKUPNO		99267	71542	64980	97632	1801560	4492056	106024
DOMAĆA PROIZVODNJA		99140	69884	47554	78341	1315427	4225355	105521
UVOZ		127	1658	17426	9291	486133	255700	503
VODOPRIVREDA	12							
UKUPNO		62831	21719	21278	50756	28898	75564	38501
DOMAĆA PROIZVODNJA		62831	21719	21278	50756	28898	75566	38501
UVOZ		0	0	0	0	0	0	0
GRAĐEVINARSTVO	13							
UKUPNO		384842	156816	399902	1262494	167523	272507	225817
DOMAĆA PROIZVODNJA		384842	156816	399902	1262494	167523	272507	225817
UVOZ		0	0	0	0	0	0	0
SAOBRAĆAJ I VEZE	14							
UKUPNO		2274979	2355211	1471435	2368545	2107771	1393735	1593267
DOMAĆA PROIZVODNJA		2274979	2355211	1471435	2368545	2107771	1393735	1593267
UVOZ		0	0	0	0	0	0	0
TRGOVINA	15							
UKUPNO		1559565	1614902	1164819	6489680	2208908	1216629	2174068
DOMAĆA PROIZVODNJA		1559565	1614902	1164819	6489680	2208908	1216629	2174068
UVOZ		0	0	0	0	0	0	0
UGOSTITELJSTVO I TURIZAM	16							
UKUPNO		0	0	0	0	0	0	0
DOMAĆA PROIZVODNJA		0	0	0	0	0	0	0
UVOZ		0	0	0	0	0	0	0
ZANATSKE USLUGE I OPRAVKE	17							
UKUPNO		1040047	1922894	908507	3208733	1191974	456459	699707
DOMAĆA PROIZVODNJA		1040047	1922894	908507	3208733	1191974	456459	699707
UVOZ		0	0	0	0	0	0	0
KOMUNALNE DELATNOSTI	18							
UKUPNO		230678	472642	148030	1120963	672722	144506	691121
DOMAĆA PROIZVODNJA		230678	472642	148030	1120963	672722	144505	691121
UVOZ		0	0	0	0	0	0	0
OSTALE PROIZVODNE USLUGE	19							
UKUPNO		606412	473751	135702	1010955	536169	167563	515747
DOMAĆA PROIZVODNJA		606412	473751	135702	1010955	536169	167563	515747
UVOZ		0	0	0	0	0	0	0
STARI MATERIJAL I OTPACI	20							
UKUPNO		25797	2946668	43354	655540	379591	55828	158433
DOMAĆA PROIZVODNJA		25797	2155931	43216	548537	294520	55829	130545
UVOZ		0	790737	138	7003	84981	0	27888
SVEGA (1-20)	21							
UKUPNO		35264557	67071405	15985544	108511214	48875629	21125762	57736591
DOMAĆA PROIZVODNJA		21366500	57569659	14048166	87250774	32995978	19239380	44563750
UVOZ		13898057	9501746	1937378	21260440	15879651	1887382	13172841
AMORTIZACIJA	22	9671900	3843800	2279000	5609600	4006100	1344500	3274900
ČISTI LIČNI DOHOCI	23	6942200	4715300	5724700	25394100	6628000	6299000	14074500
VIŠAK PROIZVODA	24	13364788	6030957	5767308	30563903	8909881	6094730	13211205
PROIZVODNJA (21+22+23+24)	25	65243445	81661462	29756552	170078817	68399610	34855992	88297196
SMANJENJE ZALIHA	26	0	144150	301060	0	0	0	0
UVOZ	27	17062363	16174594	4476002	60658640	23377039	1454921	7126421
RASPOLOŽIVA SREDSTVA (25+26+27)	28	82305808	97980206	34533614	230737457	91776649	36310913	95423617

MEDJUSOBNI ODNOSI PRIVREDNIH DELATNOSTI
SFR JUGOSLAVIJE U 1976.GODINI

PROIZVODNJA I RASPODELA PO GRUPAMA GRANA
DELATNOSTI U CENAMA PROIZVODJAČA
INPUT-OUTPUT TABELA

TABELA 2-1.
U HILJADAMA DINARA

PRIMAOCI / DAVAOCI	PROIZV. PREHRAMB. PROIZVODA I DUVANA	OSTALA INDUS-TRIJA	POLJO-PRIVREDA I RIBAR-STVO	ŠUMAR-STVO	VODO-PRIVREDA	GRADJE-VINAR-STVO	SAOBRA-ĆAJ I VEZE
	8	9	10	11	12	13	14
ENERGETIKA 1							
UKUPNO	2298102	133422	2876467	144891	69112	2103907	5241671
DOMAĆA PROIZVODNJA	2238675	129814	2731777	138668	66643	2037157	3178526
UVOZ	59427	3608	144690	6223	2469	66750	2063145
METALURGIJA 2							
UKUPNO	359875	354909	92239	24252	27823	5974930	463104
DOMAĆA PROIZVODNJA	121280	303574	52816	23846	27138	5715467	276342
UVOZ	238595	51335	39423	406	685	259463	186762
PROIZVODNJA I PRERADA NEMETALA 3							
UKUPNO	1112948	24006	247160	47710	109247	16027367	300266
DOMAĆA PROIZVODNJA	1065992	15850	218356	47485	108947	15626666	286927
UVOZ	46956	8156	28804	225	300	400701	13339
PRERADA METALA 4							
UKUPNO	2108659	193129	2174631	301211	76366	6978847	6390813
DOMAĆA PROIZVODNJA	1970174	114117	1800037	277585	60551	6483292	5406176
UVOZ	136485	79012	374594	23626	15815	495555	984637
PROIZV.HEMIJSKIH PROIZVODA I PAPIRA 5							
UKUPNO	4649169	3584846	6963450	115335	18766	1299911	446733
DOMAĆA PROIZVODNJA	3624331	2947147	6808660	113002	18427	1093708	414859
UVOZ	1024838	737699	154790	2333	339	195203	31874
PRERADA DRVETA 6							
UKUPNO	244081	47138	258781	57701	17394	5755484	169771
DOMAĆA PROIZVODNJA	241674	45700	253298	57412	17384	5652682	169523
UVOZ	2407	1438	5483	289	0	112802	248
PROIZVODNJA TEKSTILA,KOŽE I GUME 7							
UKUPNO	668947	76032	408335	98421	14932	517522	1504299
DOMAĆA PROIZVODNJA	619913	53737	367091	86831	12835	453709	1326116
UVOZ	49034	22295	41244	11590	2097	63813	178183
PROIZV.PREHRAMB.PROIZVODA I DUVANA 8							
UKUPNO	26427883	45597	7430001	20739	464	3	20987
DOMAĆA PROIZVODNJA	23381977	34376	6906842	20739	464	0	20984
UVOZ	3045906	11221	523159	0	0	0	3
OSTALA INDUSTRIJA 9							
UKUPNO	645425	734753	65298	22550	5653	147809	289322
DOMAĆA PROIZVODNJA	642789	726834	64781	22549	5653	145654	286410
UVOZ	2636	7919	517	1	0	2155	2912
POLJOPRIVREDA I RIBARSTVO 10							
UKUPNO	41771175	43327	43721854	101766	0	3	15936
DOMAĆA PROIZVODNJA	36122097	35396	43304544	101585	0	0	15936
UVOZ	5649078	7931	417310	181	0	0	0
ŠUMARSTVO 11							
UKUPNO	41999	18237	361440	487480	3366	647949	16081
DOMAĆA PROIZVODNJA	36403	18237	326623	486086	3366	647949	15939
UVOZ	5596	0	34817	1394	0	0	142
VODOPRIVREDA 12							
UKUPNO	74885	6016	516924	18343	141710	537494	68297
DOMAĆA PROIZVODNJA	74885	6016	516924	18343	141710	537494	68297
UVOZ	0	0	0	0	0	0	0
GRADJEVINARSTVO 13							
UKUPNO	226430	29250	231459	140614	97705	30190119	450993
DOMAĆA PROIZVODNJA	226430	29250	231459	140614	97705	30190119	450993
UVOZ	0	0	0	0	0	3	0
SAOBRAĆAJ I VEZE 14							
UKUPNO	2681175	220364	1432297	171041	79064	7074227	9261029
DOMAĆA PROIZVODNJA	2681175	220364	1432297	171041	79064	7074227	6413783
UVOZ	0	0	0	0	0	0	2847246
TRGOVINA 15							
UKUPNO	3845801	338197	3181446	125792	51809	6873592	2941673
DOMAĆA PROIZVODNJA	3845801	338197	3181446	125792	51809	6873592	2941673
UVOZ	0	0	0	0	0	0	0
UGOSTITELJSTVO I TURIZAM 16							
UKUPNO	0	0	0	0	0	0	0
DOMAĆA PROIZVODNJA	0	0	0	0	0	0	0
UVOZ	0	0	0	0	0	0	0
ZANATSKE USLUGE I OPRAVKE 17							
UKUPNO	1250889	114312	1634508	213175	74028	1973683	3019730
DOMAĆA PROIZVODNJA	1250889	114312	1634508	213175	74028	1973683	3009730
UVOZ	0	0	0	0	0	0	10000
KOMUNALNE DELATNOSTI 18							
UKUPNO	468946	41306	181536	34674	39708	520579	248861
DOMAĆA PROIZVODNJA	468946	41306	181536	34674	39708	520579	248861
UVOZ	0	0	0	0	0	0	0
OSTALE PROIZVODNE USLUGE 19							
UKUPNO	798976	162912	232596	32795	23812	767734	1932841
DOMAĆA PROIZVODNJA	798976	162912	232596	32795	23812	767734	331177
UVOZ	0	0	0	0	0	0	1601664
STARI MATERIJAL I OTPACI 20							
UKUPNO	99831	26582	31834	2115	575	84344	40822
DOMAĆA PROIZVODNJA	99831	26582	31834	2115	575	84106	40822
UVOZ	0	0	0	0	0	238	0
SVEGA (1-20) 21							
UKUPNO	89775196	6294335	72042256	2160635	851524	87473497	32823229
DOMAĆA PROIZVODNJA	79512238	5363721	70277425	2114337	829819	85882817	24903074
UVOZ	10262958	930614	1764831	46268	21705	1596680	7920155
AMORTIZACIJA 22	2840400	504300	6076900	976900	172100	3452449	12154700
ČISTI LIČNI DOHOCI 23	8728700	2296100	65246621	4511979	703000	33221445	20556700
VIŠAK PROIZVODA 24	13615206	2759620	19327379	2535674	783309	27218089	16202115
PROIZVODNJA (21+22+23+24) 25	114959502	11854355	162693156	10185158	2509933	151381479	81736744
SMANJENJE ZALIHA 26	0	0	0	0	0	0	0
UVOZ 27	7944384	1370123	11692204	838927	0	0	3427973
RASPOLOŽIVA SREDSTVA (25+26+27) 28	122903886	13224478	174385360	11024085	2509933	151381479	85164717

PROIZVODNJA I RASPODELA PO GRUPAMA GRANA
DELATNOSTI U CENAMA PROIZVODJAČA
INPUT-OUTPUT TABELA

TABELA 2-1.
U HILJADAMA DINARA

DAVAOCI / PRIMAOCI		TRGOVI-NA	UGOSTI-TELJ-STVO I TURIZAM	ZANATSKE USLUGE I OPRAVKE	KOMJNAL-NE DE-LATNOSTI	OSTALE PROIZVOD-NE USLUGE	STARI MATERIJAL I OTPACI	SVEGA (1-20)
		15	16	17	18	19	20	21
ENERGETIKA	1							
UKUPNO		1638654	966782	1426494	1912927	291197	0	63825944
DOMAĆA PROIZVODNJA		1590701	941956	1382946	1870780	283054	0	47600104
UVOZ		47953	24826	43548	42147	8143	0	16225840
METALURGIJA	2							
UKUPNO		68456	6426	894370	156315	95307	0	83776629
DOMAĆA PROIZVODNJA		53008	5535	697619	148700	95337	0	68058015
UVOZ		15448	891	196751	7615	0	0	15718614
PROIZVODNJA I PRERADA NEMETALA	3							
UKUPNO		146820	94231	301410	183586	55596	0	28792321
DOMAĆA PROIZVODNJA		144521	92291	256028	173184	55098	0	24773207
UVOZ		2299	1940	45382	10402	508	0	4019114
PRERADA METALA	4							
UKUPNO		1096392	264837	4433642	471669	338762	0	86060128
DOMAĆA PROIZVODNJA		1091060	262481	4083556	440648	337414	0	69506849
UVOZ		5332	2356	350086	31021	1348	0	16553279
PROIZV.HEMIJSKIH PROIZVODA I PAPIRA	5							
UKUPNO		873887	272919	706690	140782	332963	0	67239559
DOMAĆA PROIZVODNJA		738579	245828	622279	117637	296279	0	45683509
UVOZ		135308	27091	84411	23145	36685	0	21556050
PRERADA DRVETA	6							
UKUPNO		318517	51029	532391	65035	24554	0	16460430
DOMAĆA PROIZVODNJA		318517	51029	525551	65034	24548	0	15324390
UVOZ		0	0	6840	1	6	0	1136040
PROIZVODNJA TEKSTILA,KOŽE I GUME	7							
UKUPNO		409683	136629	1026756	62166	57126	0	41988258
DOMAĆA PROIZVODNJA		374951	127133	981565	56165	53217	0	36296256
UVOZ		34732	9496	45191	6001	3909	0	5692002
PROIZV.PREHRAMB.PROIZVODA I DUVANA	8							
UKUPNO		533536	11862322	1152015	2	0	0	50587162
DOMAĆA PROIZVODNJA		533536	11862322	1152014	2	0	0	45812027
UVOZ		0	0	1	0	0	0	4775135
OSTALA INDUSTRIJA	9							
UKUPNO		535280	154095	46061	46485	593608	0	5283949
DOMAĆA PROIZVODNJA		535280	154095	44791	46374	593582	0	5155928
UVOZ		0	0	1270	111	26	0	128021
POLJOPRIVREDA I RIBARSTVO	10							
UKUPNO		379775	1002219	574397	0	0	0	91078330
DOMAĆA PROIZVODNJA		379775	1002219	571696	0	0	0	81729480
UVOZ		0	0	2701	0	0	0	9348850
ŠUMARSTVO	11							
UKUPNO		109442	17789	58254	8001	1013	0	8484112
DOMAĆA PROIZVODNJA		109442	17789	57949	4541	1013	0	7667560
UVOZ		0	0	305	3460	0	0	816552
VODOPRIVREDA	12							
UKUPNO		12727	55005	23089	18779	21243	0	1794061
DOMAĆA PROIZVODNJA		12727	55005	23089	18779	21243	0	1794061
UVOZ		0	0	0	0	0	0	0
GRAĐEVINARSTVO	13							
UKUPNO		588649	204523	179256	213147	117556	0	35539601
DOMAĆA PROIZVODNJA		588649	204523	179256	213147	117556	0	35539601
UVOZ		0	0	0	0	0	0	0
SAOBRAĆAJ I VEZE	14							
UKUPNO		1620441	567927	444588	326677	905637	0	38849410
DOMAĆA PROIZVODNJA		1620441	567927	444588	326677	905637	0	36002164
UVOZ		0	0	0	0	0	0	2847246
TRGOVINA	15							
UKUPNO		682916	1132402	2281899	293582	158528	0	38341208
DOMAĆA PROIZVODNJA		682916	1132402	2281899	293582	158528	0	38341208
UVOZ		0	0	0	0	0	0	0
UGOSTITELJSTVO I TURIZAM	16							
UKUPNO		0	0	0	0	0	0	0
DOMAĆA PROIZVODNJA		0	0	0	0	0	0	0
UVOZ		0	0	0	0	0	0	0
ZANATSKE USLUGE I OPRAVKE	17							
UKUPNO		1195239	420369	1894188	381497	247463	0	21847402
DOMAĆA PROIZVODNJA		1195239	420369	1894188	381497	247463	0	21837402
UVOZ		0	0	0	0	0	0	10000
KOMUNALNE DELATNOSTI	18							
UKUPNO		465958	280224	149950	552895	263360	0	6728659
DOMAĆA PROIZVODNJA		465958	280224	149950	552895	263360	0	6728659
UVOZ		0	0	0	0	0	0	0
OSTALE PROIZVODNE USLUGE	19							
UKUPNO		515525	133501	124070	244202	891274	0	9306537
DOMAĆA PROIZVODNJA		515525	133501	124070	244202	891274	0	7704873
UVOZ		0	0	0	0	0	0	1601664
STARI MATERIJAL I OTPACI	20							
UKUPNO		73337	6209	23243	3936	2333	0	4660282
DOMAĆA PROIZVODNJA		73337	6209	23243	3936	2333	0	3749297
UVOZ		0	0	0	0	0	0	910985
SVEGA (1-20)	21							
UKUPNO		11265234	17629438	16272763	5081683	4397520	0	700643982
DOMAĆA PROIZVODNJA		11024162	17562838	15496277	4957780	4346895	0	599304590
UVOZ		241072	66600	776486	123903	50625	0	101339392
AMORTIZACIJA	22	3228700	1855400	1209352	1085300	650800	254962	64514062
ČISTI LIČNI DOHOCI	23	22922500	7767200	9891655	2908700	6322600	1415892	256250892
VIŠAK PROIZVODA	24	88056214	8463461	7688709	3047435	9430100	2459180	285519263
PROIZVODNJA (21+22+23+24)	25	125472648	35715499	35062479	12123118	20801020	4141034	1306928199
SMANJENJE ZALIHA	26	0	0	0	0	0	0	445210
UVOZ	27	0	2028401	10000	386	2076100	910985	160629463
RASPOLOŽIVA SREDSTVA (25+26+27)	28	125472648	37743900	35072479	12123504	22877120	5051019	1468002872

308

PROIZVODNJA I RASPODELA PO GRUPAMA GRANA
DELATNOSTI U CENAMA PROIZVODJAČA
INPUT-OUTPUT TABELA

TABELA 2-1.
U HILJADAMA DINARA

PRIMAOCI / DAVAOCI	POVEĆANJE ZALIHA	BRUTO INVES- TICIJE	IZVOZ	POTROŠNJA LIČNA	OPŠTA	SVEGA	FINALNA POTROŠNJA	RASPO- DELJENA SREDSTVA
	22	23	24	25	26	27	28	29
ENERGETIKA 1								
UKUPNO	903156	0	1783237	12302619	3490852	15793471	18479864	82305808
DOMAĆA PROIZVODNJA	706104	0	1783237	11831576	3322424	15154000	17443341	65243445
UVOZ	197052	0	0	471043	168428	639471	836523	17062363
METALURGIJA 2								
UKUPNO	2113590	0	9544751	0	2545196	2545196	14203577	97990206
DOMAĆA PROIZVODNJA	1747272	0	9544791	0	2455534	2455534	13747597	81805612
UVOZ	366318	0	0	0	89662	89662	455980	16174594
PROIZVODNJA I PRERADA NEMETALA 3								
UKUPNO	436160	0	2201131	1986768	1117234	3104002	5741293	34533614
DOMAĆA PROIZVODNJA	323925	0	2201131	1733676	1025673	2759349	5284405	30057612
UVOZ	112235	0	0	253092	91561	344653	456888	4476002
PRERADA METALA 4								
UKUPNO	11291000	74204020	26465022	20315836	12401451	32717287	144477329	230737457
DOMAĆA PROIZVODNJA	9744889	37747403	26465022	17431189	9183465	26614654	100571968	170078817
UVOZ	1546111	36456617	0	2884647	3217986	6102633	44105361	60658640
PROIZV.HEMIJSKIH PROIZVODA I PAPIRA 5								
UKUPNO	1509390	0	9093157	6822570	7111973	13934543	24537090	91776649
DOMAĆA PROIZVODNJA	1078405	0	9093157	6118543	6425996	12544539	22716101	68399610
UVOZ	430985	0	0	704027	685977	1390004	1820989	23377039
PRERADA DRVETA 6								
UKUPNO	589670	1161513	6366145	10639989	1093166	11733155	19950483	36310913
DOMAĆA PROIZVODNJA	568799	1129084	6366145	10388902	1078672	11467574	19531602	34855992
UVOZ	20871	32429	0	251087	14494	265581	318881	1454921
PROIZVODNJA TEKSTILA,KOŽE I GUME 7								
UKUPNO	2791629	14018	15410864	32920295	2298553	35218848	53435359	95423617
DOMAĆA PROIZVODNJA	2598572	6313	15410864	31787670	2197521	33985191	52000940	88297196
UVOZ	193057	7705	0	1132625	101032	1233657	1434419	7126421
PROIZV.PREHRAMB.PROIZVODA I DUVANA 8								
UKUPNO	4911231	0	7402616	54321616	5681241	60002877	72316724	122903886
DOMAĆA PROIZVODNJA	4632017	0	7402616	51671179	5441663	57112842	69147475	114959502
UVOZ	279214	0	0	2650437	239598	2890035	3169249	7944384
OSTALA INDUSTRIJA 9								
UKUPNO	838077	55432	555875	5575612	915533	6491145	7940529	13224478
DOMAĆA PROIZVODNJA	799314	0	555875	4550562	792576	5343238	6698427	11854355
UVOZ	38763	55432	0	1025050	122857	1147907	1242102	1370123
POLJOPRIVREDA I RIBARSTVO 10								
UKUPNO	6944190	1773475	3529455	69088250	1971560	71059910	83337030	174385360
DOMAĆA PROIZVODNJA	6522761	1770835	3529455	67224624	1916001	69140625	80963676	162693155
UVOZ	421429	2640	0	1863626	55659	1919285	2343354	11692204
ŠUMARSTVO 11								
UKUPNO	41345	315811	748718	1173746	260353	1434099	2539973	11024085
DOMAĆA PROIZVODNJA	41345	315811	748718	1151371	260353	1411724	2517598	10185158
UVOZ	0	0	0	22375	0	22375	22375	938927
VODOPRIVREDA 12								
UKUPNO	0	0	0	0	715872	715872	715872	2509933
DOMAĆA PROIZVODNJA	0	0	0	0	715872	715872	715872	2509933
UVOZ	0	0	0	0	0	0	0	0
GRAĐEVINARSTVO 13								
UKUPNO	1482298	106190400	1367026	0	6802154	6802154	115841878	151391479
DOMAĆA PROIZVODNJA	1482298	106190400	1367026	0	6802154	6802154	115841878	151381479
UVOZ	0	0	0	0	0	0	0	0
SAOBRAĆAJ I VEZE 14								
UKUPNO	842804	702833	19431735	22353620	2984315	25337935	46315307	85164717
DOMAĆA PROIZVODNJA	842804	702833	19431735	21772893	2984315	24757298	45734580	81736744
UVOZ	0	0	0	580727	0	580727	580727	3427973
TRGOVINA 15								
UKUPNO	2566997	6526976	3898015	69067213	5072239	74139452	87131440	125472648
DOMAĆA PROIZVODNJA	2566997	6526976	3898015	69067213	5072239	74139452	87131440	125472648
UVOZ	0	0	0	0	0	0	0	0
UGOSTITELJSTVO I TURIZAM 16								
UKUPNO	0	0	8322630	29298990	122280	29421270	37743900	37743900
DOMAĆA PROIZVODNJA	0	0	8322630	27270589	122280	27392869	35715499	35715499
UVOZ	0	0	0	2028401	0	2028401	2028401	2028401
ZANATSKE USLUGE I OPRAVKE 17								
UKUPNO	117250	0	155403	11801722	1150702	12952424	13225077	35072479
DOMAĆA PROIZVODNJA	117250	0	155403	11801722	1150702	12952424	13225077	35062479
UVOZ	0	0	0	0	0	0	0	10000
KOMUNALNE DELATNOSTI 18								
UKUPNO	0	0	17768	3183230	2193847	5377077	5394845	12123504
DOMAĆA PROIZVODNJA	0	0	17768	3182844	2193847	5376691	5394459	12123118
UVOZ	0	0	0	386	0	386	386	386
OSTALE PROIZVODNE USLUGE 19								
UKUPNO	148035	6889550	877862	3094796	2560340	5655136	13570583	22877120
DOMAĆA PROIZVODNJA	148035	6435532	877862	3094796	2539922	5634718	13096147	20801023
UVOZ	0	454018	0	0	20418	20418	474436	2076100
STARI MATERIJAL I OTPACI 20								
UKUPNO	109814	0	203425	0	77498	77498	390737	5051019
DOMAĆA PROIZVODNJA	109814	0	203425	0	77498	77498	390737	4140034
UVOZ	0	0	0	0	0	0	0	910985
SVEGA (1-20) 21								
UKUPNO	37636636	197834028	117374875	353946872	60566479	414513351	767358890	1468002872
DOMAĆA PROIZVODNJA	34030601	160825187	117374875	340079349	55758807	395838156	708068819	1307373409
UVOZ	3606035	37008841	0	13867523	4807672	18675195	59290071	160629463

XIX. ZAMBIA

A. GENERAL INFORMATION

The present report is based on *National Accounts and Input-Output Tables 1973*, published by the Central Statistical Office of Zambia.

Input-output tables have been compiled approximately every two years since 1965. The present report describes the latest table available, which refers to 1973, compiled by the Central Statistical Office with technical assistance provided by the Office of Technical Co-operation of the United Nations Secretariat. In 1971, two major methodological changes were introduced: (*a*) "make" tables were compiled and (*b*) the compilation of import matrices was discontinued since the data available were considered to be insufficient.

Input-output tables are compiled jointly with the national accounts. Both sets of accounts are based on the same conventions and definitions and use the same data base.

Main deviations from the SNA recommendations include: (*a*) the inclusion of the dummy sector "unspecified" activities; (*b*) disaggregation of value added; (*c*) treatment of imports; (*d*) evaluation standards; (*e*) treatment of secondary production; and (*f*) distribution of output of the financial sector.

B. ANALYTICAL FRAMEWORK

1. *Tables and derived matrices available*

Two basic tables are compiled: an absorption matrix and a make matrix, both of which are valued at producers' prices. Neither input-output tables nor derived matrices are available. The row and column totals of each intermediate sector generally record different figures for the following reasons:

(*a*) Row totals refer to commodity output, while column totals refer to industry output. Therefore, only sectors producing all and only characteristic products could be expected to show equal row and column totals;

(*b*) Column totals refer to domestic output, while row totals refer to total supply, that is, domestic supply plus imports.

2. *Valuation standards*

Transactions are valued at producers' prices which exclude distribution margins. Imports are valued c.i.f. (import duties are recorded in a separate row) and exports are valued f.o.b. Contrary to the SNA recommendations, commodity taxes are not recorded separately and therefore no valuation at approximate basic values can be derived.

3. *Statistical units and classification standards*

Commodities are the statistical units adopted for row data, while establishments are taken as the units for column data. Commodities and establishments (industries) are defined as in SNA.

Commodities and industries are classified according to a national system which generally follows the ISIC classification.

The classification of the intermediate consumption quadrant differs from the SNA recommendations in that: (*a*) a dummy sector of "unspecified" activities is included to account for statistical errors and omissions; (*b*) the distribution of output of private non-profit institutions and of producers of government services are recorded together in a row describing the consumption of goods and services other than commodities. However, in agreement with the SNA recommendations, input into those two sectors (that is, private non-profit institutions and producers of government services) are recorded in two separate columns.

Final demand is disaggregated as recommended in SNA. Categories of final demand are also defined as in SNA. Private consumption is defined on a national basis.

The breakdown of value added recommended in SNA is adopted, except for subsidies which are recorded together with indirect taxes. Categories of value added are defined as in SNA.

Imports are distributed together with domestic output in the absorption matrix. No imports classification is presented in the absorption matrix. However, a commodity classification of imports is provided in the make matrix. Imports in this table are disaggregated into c.i.f. values and import duties. Contrary to the SNA recommendations, no distinction is made between competitive and complementary imports.

4. *Treatment and presentation of selected transactions*

Neither outputs of secondary products nor their corresponding inputs are transferred to their characteristic sectors. This is contrary to the SNA recommendations. The extent and pattern of secondary production are described in the "make" matrix.

Intermediate inputs which are used and produced by the same sector and are characteristic products of a different sector (such as electricity used and produced by mining industries, trade and transportation activities carried out by manufacturer etc.) are not recorded as commodity inputs. Instead, the inputs needed for their production are recorded.

Scrap generated as part of the production process is treated as any other secondary product. Sales of second-hand goods are treated as recommended in SNA.

Domestic output of industries is recorded gross, that is, it includes intra-sector consumption of characteristic and secondary products.

Non-monetary output (such as own-consumption of traditional farmers, imputed rents of owner-occupied homes etc.) and its corresponding input have been recorded together with the monetary output and input in the corresponding input-output sector.

Output of the financial sector is defined as in SNA but it is distributed to input-output sectors in proportion to their domestic output, which is contrary to the SNA recommendations.

The input structure of the government sector mostly refers to its production of goods and services other than commodities and includes such activities as public administration, defence, health, education, social services and promotion of economic growth. Output of this sector is measured as recommended in SNA and is allocated to private and to government final consumption. The output share allocated to private consumption is equal to the value of government commodity and non-commodity sales. As recommended in SNA, government services are recorded in the intermediate consumption quadrant.

C. STATISTICAL SOURCES AND COMPILATION METHODOLOGY

Data were obtained from existing regular sources and the results of the 1971 Agriculture Census and the Annual Census of Industrial Production. No special surveys were carried out for the purpose of compiling the input-output table.

1. Gross output and intermediate consumption

(a) Agriculture, forestry and fishing

Data for marketed production of main crops were obtained from the Quarterly Agricultural Statistical Bulletin (Ministry of Lands and Agriculture), the Annual Agricultural and Pastoral Production Surveys (APPS) of Commercial Farms and the 1970-1971 Census of Agriculture. Data on prices and values were also obtained from Household Budget Surveys, Monthly Surveys of Prices etc. Data on input became available for the first time through the 1972 APPS of Commercial Farms.

For the subsistence sector covering own-consumed production of traditional farms, use was made of APPS (non-commercial farms), supplemented by the Household Budget Surveys of rural areas. Estimates for this sector are considered to be less than satisfactory, since APPS (non-commercial farms) only covers main crops, and since annual changes are still based on the assumption of volume changes associated with population growth and mark-ups for price increases.

(b) Mining, manufacturing, electricity, water and construction

Data were mainly obtained from the Annual Census of Industrial Production. Response rates for this survey vary from full response in the metal mining sector to low rate of response in the construction sector.

(c) Services

Data were obtained from the Annual National Income Inquiry covering all large and medium-sized enterprises.

Small units are covered on a sample basis. The coverage of the "informal" sector is considered to be less than satisfactory, except for bars and domestic services. Unorganized trading activity, small repair shops etc. are still practically left out.

Regarding the government sector, data contained in *Financial Statistics of the Government Sector*, issued by the Central Statistical Office, supplemented by special tabulations, were used. Data for the central Government are processed through the computer, while for local governments, estimates are made on the basis of replies received from them.

2. Value added

Employment data are collected from the establishments through employment inquiries conducted by the Central Statistical Office. Grossing-up factors for non-responding units are worked out on the basis of employment data reported by the responding units. In the estimation for services sectors, grossing-up is done after carefully comparing employment data of companies responding to both the employment inquiry and the national income inquiry.

Estimates for consumption of fixed capital are usually obtained from the financial provisions for depreciation computed by enterprises on the basis of historical costs and expected economic lifetime of their fixed assets. However, efforts are made to obtain estimates on the basis of replacement costs (as recommended in SNA) for as many sectors as possible.

3. Final demand and imports

Data on private consumption expenditure are derived from the publication *Urban Household Budget Survey in Low Cost Housing Areas, 1966-1968*, supplemented by preliminary estimates from Household Budget Surveys conducted in urban and rural areas during 1974-1975. Estimates of the total number of households were based on population projections prepared by the Central Statistical Office. Data in this column also include statistical discrepancies found in the process of compilation of the table.

Transactions with the rest of the world are taken from the Balance-of-Payments Statistics, 1973, issued by the Central Statistical Office. Details on imports and exports of commodities are obtained from the Annual Statement of External Trade, published by the Central Statistical Office.

ZAMBIA
INPUT-OUTPUT TABLES
1973

Source: *National Accounts and Input-Output Tables
1973*, Central Statistical Office of Zambia.

Zambia

Reference year: 1973

Entries in table: Total flows, absorption matrix

Source: Central Statistical Office, *National Accounts and Input-Output Tables, 1973* (Lusaka, 1980)

Computerized: UNIDO

Currency units: Kwacha of Y 1973
Scale factor: 100,000

Pricing system: Producers' current prices
Intermediate sectors: 30 × 30
Treatment of trade margins: Intermediate demand row 17 and column 17

Treatment of imports: Rows 38, 39 and 40 in primary inputs
Availability of import matrix: Not available

Total number of rows: 41
Statistical unit of quadrant 1: Commodity

Total number of columns: 39
Statistical unit of quadrant 1: Industry

Fourth quadrant: Not occupied

Absorption Table of Zambia for the Year 1973 (Revised)

ZAMBIA 1973 FLOWS in hundred thousand kwacha of Y 1973 PRODUCERS CURRENT PRICES

INDUSTRY: COMMODITY	1 Agriculture, Forest. & Fishg.	2 Metal Mining	3 Other Mining	4 Food Manufacturing	5 Beverages and Tobacco	6 Textiles and Wearing Apparel
* TOTAL TRANSACTIONS *						
1 Agricult.Forestry & Fishing	89	1	0	471	33	38
2 Metal Mining	0	0	0	0	0	0
3 Other Mining	7	37	0	2	1	0
4 Food Manufacturing	57	7	0	100	25	4
5 Beverages and Tobacco	3	28	3	1	46	1
6 Textiles and Wearing Apparel	3	131	4	8	4	134
7 Wood and Wood Products	0	18	2	17	0	0
8 Paper.-Prod.,Printg.& Publ.	0	20	0	17	14	3
9 Rubber Products	10	84	2	7	1	3
10 Chemicals & Chem. Prods	138	573	5	30	12	45
11 Non-Metallic Mineral Prods.	0	25	0	0	0	0
12 Basic Metal Products	0	462	5	12	60	9
13 Fabricated Metal Products	0	10	0	0	0	2
14 Other Manufacturing Industr.	12	207	2	9	6	2
15 Electricity,Gas and Water	0	218	0	2	1	0
16 Construction	8	298	3	0	0	0
17 Wholesale and Retail Trade	20	45	0	10	2	20
18 Hotels and Restaurants	0	63	2	0	0	0
19 Rail Transport	0	20	3	39	12	7
20 Road Transport	20	14	1	1	6	7
21 Other Transport	0	64	0	35	1	0
22 Posts and Telecommunications	0	8	0	30	17	15
23 Financial Inst. & Insurance	0	90	0	0	2	3
24 Real Estate	0	0	0	0	4	1
25 Business Services	0	10	0	0	0	0
26 Education	0	54	0	0	0	0
27 Health	0		0	0	0	0
28 Recreational & Cultural Svc.	0		0	0	0	0
29 Personal & Household Serv.	0		0	0	0	0
30 Statistical Adjustments	40	54	2	-50	2	2
31 Total Intermediate Inputs	420	2313	55	758	215	309
32 Gross Fxd Capital Consumpt	222	1417	34	124	73	98
33 Compensation of Employees	1333	2763	2	86	82	54
34 Indirect Taxes less Subsidie	-17		0	-89	562	
35 Operating Surplus	55	852	33	29	18	13
36 Gross Value Added	1593	5032	89	170	735	187
37 Gross Output	2013	7345	124	928	950	478
38 Imports CIF.	86	0	240	283	27	428
39 Import duties	2		0	28	24	100
40 Imports incl Duties	88	0	241	311	51	528
41 Total Resources	2101	7345	365	1237	1001	1004

Absorption Table of Zambia for the Year 1973 (Revised)

ZAMBIA 1973   FLOWS in hundred thousand kwacha of Y 1973   PRODUCERS CURRENT PRICES

INDUSTRY:	7 Wood and Wood Products	8 Paper.-Prod. Printg.& Publ.	9 Rubber Products	10 Chemicals & Chem. Prods	11 Non-Metallic Mineral Prods	12 Basic Metal Products
* TOTAL TRANSACTIONS *						
COMMODITY						
1 Agricult.Forestry & Fishing	41	0	0	0	0	0
2 Metal Mining	0	0	0	0	0	0
3 Other Mining	0	0	0	0	27	0
4 Food Manufacturing	-1	2	2	253	3	0
5 Beverages and Tobacco	5	2	3	30	4	0
6 Textiles and Wearing Apparel	18	66	26	50	5	2
7 Wood and Wood Products	2	4	0	2	1	9
8 Paper.-Prod.,Printg.& Publ.	13	0	0	121	8	3
9 Rubber Products	0	0	3	2	14	0
10 Chemicals & Chem. Prods	7	3	0	13	18	2
11 Non-Metallic Mineral Prods	0	1	2	7	5	0
12 Basic Metal Products	2	0	0	24	8	0
13 Fabricated Metal Products	0	8	2	2	0	0
14 Other Manufacturing Industr.	0	0	0	53	7	2
15 Electricity,Gas and Water	5	2	1	8	3	3
16 Construction	0	8	2	50	1	0
17 Wholesale and Retail Trade	4	5	8	3	7	0
18 Hotels and Restaurants	3	0	4	24	0	2
19 Rail Transport	0	0	0	0	0	3
20 Road Transport	0	0	0	0	0	0
21 Other Transport	0	0	0	0	0	0
22 Posts and Telecommunications	0	0	0	3	2	0
23 Financial Inst.& Insurance						
24 Real Estate						
25 Business Services						
26 Education						
27 Health						
28 Recreational & Cultural Svc.						
29 Personal & Household Servc.						
30 Statistical Adjustments						
31 Total Intermediate Inputs	102	107	88	829	138	29
32 Gross Fxd.Capital Consumpt.	38	46	24	83	66	14
33 Compensation of Employees	15	19	35	50	-4	-1
34 Indirect Taxes less Subsidie	1	0	4	1	1	0
35 Operating Surplus	7	6	7	43	25	2
38 Gross Value Added	61	71	70	177	88	27
37 Gross Output	163	178	138	806	224	58
38 Imports CIF	36	115	89	662	89	238
39 Import duties	1	7	5	91	8	2
40 Imports incl. Duties	37	122	94	753	97	240
41 Total Resources	200	300	232	1559	321	298

316

Absorption Table of Zambia for the Year 1973 (Revised)

ZAMBIA 1973 FLOWS in hundred thousand kwacha of Y 1973 PRODUCERS CURRENT PRICES

INDUSTRY: COMMODITY	13 Fabricated Metal Products	14 Other Manufact. Industries	15 Electricity Gas and Water	16 Construction	17 Wholesale and Retail Trade	18 Hotels and Restaurants
* TOTAL TRANSACTIONS *						
1 Agricult.Forestry & Fishing	0	0	0	1	8	12
2 Metal Mining	39	0	0	0	0	0
3 Other Mining	2	0	1	45	7	0
4 Food Manufacturing	7	0	0	1	5	4
5 Beverages and Tobacco		0	2	130	16	14
6 Textiles and Wearing Apparel	56	0	0	54	100	5
7 Wood and Wood Products	0	0	0	2	10	4
8 Paper.-Prod.Printg & Publ		0	0	78	21	0
9 Rubber Products	5	0	2	178	8	2
10 Chemicals & Chem. Prods	13	0	6	56	40	0
11 Non-Metallic Mineral Prods	4	0	4	244	50	1
12 Basic Metal Products	160	1	0	16	0	0
13 Fabricated Metal Products	124	0	9	167	38	1
14 Other Manufacturing Industr	16	1	0	7	18	0
15 Electricity, Gas and Water	8	0	0	154	1	2
16 Construction	2	0	0	127	7	0
17 Wholesale and Retail Trade		0	4	5	24	2
18 Hotels and Restaurants		0	0	47	0	2
19 Rail Transport	59	0	2	13	12	0
20 Road Transport	2	0	2	48	10	0
21 Other Transport		0	7	17	28	0
22 Posts and Telecommunications	10	0	0	70	43	0
23 Financial Inst. & Insurance	3	0	9	0	81	1
24 Real Estate	27	0	0	7	147	1
25 Business Services	24	1	0	93	5	1
26 Education		0	0	0	0	1
27 Health		0	0	0	0	0
28 Recreational & Cultural Svc	0	0	0	0	0	0
29 Personal & Household Servc	0	0	0	7	3	1
30 Statistical Adjustments	11	0	0	93	6	0
31 Total Intermediate Inputs	584	5	59	1397	535	87
32 Gross Fxd.Capital Consumpt	181	3	119	655	722	92
33 Compensation of Employees	107	3	120	225	827	81
34 Indirect Taxes less Subsidie		0	2		-203	5
35 Operating Surplus	23	0	61	74	88	3
36 Gross Value Added	292	6	302	957	1432	181
37 Gross Output	878	11	361	2354	1987	268
38 Imports CIF	1870	42	73	0	0	0
39 Import duties	96	8	0	0	0	0
40 Imports incl. Duties	1966	50	73	0	0	0
41 Total Resources	2842	81	434	2354	1987	268

Absorption Table of Zambia for the Year 1973   (Revised)

ZAMBIA 1973   FLOWS in hundred thousand kwacha of Y 1973   PRODUCERS CURRENT PRICES

INDUSTRY:	19 Rail Transport	20 Road Transport	21 Other Transport	22 Posts and Telecommunic	23 Financial Inst. & Insurance	24 Real Estate
TOTAL TRANSACTIONS						
COMMODITY						
1 Agricult.Forestry & Fishing	0	0	0	0	0	0
2 Metal Mining	0	0	0	0	0	0
3 Other Mining	2	8	5	0	0	5
4 Food Manufacturing	0	0	0	0	0	0
5 Beverages and Tobacco	3	8	2	0	5	5
6 Textiles and Wearing Apparel	4	5	2	3	0	9
7 Wood and Wood Products	0	1	0	0	1	19
8 Paper.-Prod.Printg & Publ	1	2	3	0	1	0
9 Rubber Products	0	5	0	0	0	14
10 Chemicals & Chem. Prods	8	15	4	0	4	27
11 Non-Metallic Mineral Prods	0	85	0	0	0	2
12 Basic Metal Products	9	14	8	0	0	27
13 Fabricated Metal Products	3	46	8	2	2	1
14 Other Manufacturing Industr	0	4	0	8	0	10
15 Electricity.Gas and Water	3	0	7	8	2	29
16 Construction	7	0	0	0	0	18
17 Wholesale and Retail Trade	0	30	7	0	5	100
18 Hotels and Restaurants	7	0	0	5	0	3
19 Rail Transport	8	0	2	1	1	5
20 Road Transport	3	28	9	0	0	6
21 Other Transport	2	23	7	2	2	18
22 Posts and Telecommunications	7	12	3	0	9	24
23 Financial Inst. & Insurance	0	1	8	0	9	0
24 Real Estate	8	4	12	9	9	0
25 Business Services	2	0	0	3	0	0
26 Education	0	0	0	0	0	0
27 Health	0	0	0	0	0	0
28 Recreational & Cultural Svc.	0	0	0	0	0	0
29 Personal & Household Serv.	8	18	7	0	3	3
30 Statistical Adjustments	2	9	2	3	2	15
31 Total Intermediate Inputs	95	314	135	57	124	253
32 Gross Fxd.Capital Consumpt	129	147	78	81	194	50
33 Compensation of Employees	-21	75	-5	-10	297	172
34 Indirect Taxes less Subsidie	-75	6	0	0	-4	-4
35 Operating Surplus	28	68	20	13	48	144
36 Gross Value Added	101	296	93	85	535	362
37 Gross Output	196	810	228	142	858	815
38 Imports CIF.	0	215	199	0	0	0
39 Import duties	0	215	199	0	0	0
40 Imports incl. Duties	0	215	199	0	0	0
41 Total Resources	198	825	427	142	859	815

318

ZAMBIA 1973

FLOWS in hundred thousand kwacha of Y 1973

PRODUCERS CURRENT PRICES

INDUSTRY:	25 Business Services	26 Education	27 Health	28 Recreational & Cultural Svc	29 Personal & Household Svc	30 Statistical Adjustment
* TOTAL TRANSACTIONS * COMMODITY						
1 Agricult. Forestry & Fishing	0	0	0	0	0	0
2 Metal Mining	0	0	0	0	0	0
3 Other Mining	0	0	0	0	0	0
4 Food Manufacturing	0	1	1	0	1	0
5 Beverages and Tobacco	5	0	0	0	2	0
6 Textiles and Wearing Apparel	0	0	0	0	0	0
7 Wood and Wood Products	8	0	0	0	1	0
8 Paper.-Prod.,Printg.& Publ.	6	0	0	0	0	0
9 Rubber Products	0	0	0	0	2	0
10 Chemicals & Chem. Prods	0	0	0	1	0	0
11 Non-Metallic Mineral Prods	6	0	0	0	0	0
12 Basic Metal Products	0	0	0	0	3	0
13 Fabricated Metal Products	6	0	0	0	1	0
14 Other Manufacturing Industr	0	0	0	0	0	0
15 Electricity, Gas and Water	18	1	0	4	0	0
16 Construction	3	0	0	0	4	0
17 Wholesale and Retail Trade	0	0	0	0	0	0
18 Hotels and Restaurants	0	0	0	0	4	0
19 Rail Transport	2	0	0	0	4	0
20 Other Transport	8	0	0	0	3	0
21 Other Transport	3	1	0	0	0	0
22 Posts and Telecommunications	0	0	0	0	0	0
23 Financial Inst. & Insurance	0	0	0	0	0	0
24 Real Estate	33	0	0	2	0	0
25 Business Services	0	0	0	0	0	-58
26 Education	0	0	0	0	0	0
27 Health	0	0	0	0	0	0
28 Recreational & Cultural Svc.	1	2	0	0	1	0
29 Personal & Household Servc.	1	0	0	0	5	58
30 Statistical Adjustments						
31 Total Intermediate Inputs	102	2	2	1	92	0
32 Gross Fxd.Capital Consumpt	193	-	2	12	61	000
33 Compensation of Employees	85	00	20	40	4	000
34 Indirect Taxes less Subsidie	20	00	0	2	18	000
35 Operating Surplus	25	0		2		
36 Gross Value Added	303	1	4	18	83	0
37 Gross Output	405	3	8	29	175	343
38 Imports CIF	237	17	00	00	00	9
39 Import duties	0	0	0	0	0	
40 Imports incl. Duties	237	17	0	0	0	352
41 Total Resources	642	20	8	29	175	352

Absorption Table of Zambia for the Year 1973   (Revised)

ZAMBIA 1973   FLOWS in hundred thousand kwacha of Y 1973   PRODUCERS CURRENT PRICES

COMMODITY	31 Total Intermed Consumption	32 Private Consumption	33 Government Consumption	34 Gr.Fxd Capital Formation	35 Changes in Stocks	38 Export (f.o.b.)
* TOTAL TRANSACTIONS *						
1 Agricult.Forestry & Fishing	710	1317	70	12	-97	80
2 Metal Mining	39	0	0	0	181	7092
3 Other Mining	408	0	0	0	21	12
4 Food Manufacturing	240	809	128	0	21	12
5 Beverages and Tobacco	184	788	34	0	-4	
6 Textiles and Wearing Apparel	530	368	59	0	-12	13
7 Wood and Wood Products	92	21	2	74	-2	0
8 Paper.-Prod.Printg.& Publ.	199	36	87	2	-5	8
9 Rubber Products	204	15	0	0	8	0
10 Chemicals & Chem. Prods	1272	92	87	1	117	0
11 Non-Metallic Mineral Prods	285	16	7	0	25	0
12 Basic Metal Products	278	0	0	0	14	43
13 Fabricated Metal Products	1112	82	107	1504	-7	5
14 Other Manufacturing Industr.	47	9	1	0	1	2
15 Electricity, Gas and Water	319	48	55	0	0	4
16 Construction	228	0	233	1800	-8	0
17 Wholesale and Retail Trade	620	497	48	581	37	0
18 Hotels and Restaurants	21	196	45	0	0	70
19 Rail Transport	71	20	8	0	0	
20 Road Transport	339	89	69	20	12	214
21 Other Transport	161	0	152	4	3	82
22 Posts and Telecommunications	82	20	40	0	0	0
23 Financial Inst. & Insurance	413	49	159	0	0	0
24 Real Estate	200	468	10	0	0	0
25 Business Services	610	1	3	74	0	10
26 Education	19	0	2	0	0	0
27 Health	0	3	0	0	0	0
28 Recreational & Cultural Svc.	0	35	141	0	0	0
29 Personal & Household Serv.	86	25		0	0	4
30 Statistical Adjustments	284	-9	2	41	24	48
31 Total Intermediate Inputs	8993	5000	1529	4229	420	7804
32 Gross Fxd.Capital Consumpt.	4817					
33 Compensation of Employees	6475	297	1506	0	0	0
34 Indirect Taxes less Subsidie	2218			0	0	0
35 Operating Surplus	1701	4	412	0	0	0
36 Gross Value Added	13311	302	1919	0	0	0
37 Gross Output	22304	5302	3448	4229	420	7804
38 Imports CIF	5290	0	0	0	0	0
39 Import duties	381	0	0	0	0	0
40 Imports incl. Duties	5671	0	0	0	0	0
41 Total Resources	27975	5302	3448	4229	420	7804

320

Absorption Table of Zambia for the Year 1973   (Revised)

ZAMBIA 1973

FLOWS in hundred thousand kwacha of Y 1973

PRODUCERS CURRENT PRICES

	TOTAL TRANSACTIONS * COMMODITY	37 Total Final Demand	38 Stat Adjust for Indust./Commod	39 Total Resources
1	Agricult. Forestry & Fishing	1392	-1	2101
2	Metal Mining	7253	53	7345
3	Other Mining	38	-79	365
4	Food Manufacturing	968	-29	1237
5	Beverages and Tobacco	819	-2	1001
6	Textiles and Wearing Apparel	452	-2	1004
7	Wood and Wood Products	96	12	300
8	Paper,-Prod. Printg.& Publ.	101	-4	232
9	Rubber Products	24	-18	1559
10	Chemicals & Chem. Prods	305	8	321
11	Non-Metallic Mineral Prods.	48	4	296
12	Basic Metal products	14	-57	2842
13	Fabricated Metal Products	1787	-1	61
14	Other Manufacturing Industr.	-3	7	434
15	Electricity, Gas and Water	2131	-5	2354
16	Construction	1174	173	1967
17	Wholesale and Retail Trade	241	8	268
18	Hotels and Restaurants	108	17	198
19	Rail Transport	404	82	825
20	Road Transport	250	16	427
21	Other Transport	60	-1	142
22	Posts and Telecommunications	208	38	659
23	Financial Inst. & Insurance	478	-61	615
24	Real Estate	189	-157	842
25	Business Services	5	-4	20
26	Education	8	-2	8
27	Health	38	7	29
28	Recreational & Cultural Svc.	170	-81	175
29	Personal & Household Servc.	106	-18	352
30	Statistical Adjustments			
31	Total Intermediate Inputs	18982	0	27975
32	Gross Fxd Capital Consumpt.	1803	0	6720
33	Compensation of Employees	0	0	8475
34	Indirect Taxes less Subsidie	2	0	2220
35	Operating Surplus	416	0	2117
36	Gross Value Added	2221	0	15532
37	Gross Output	21203	0	43507
38	Imports CIF	0	0	5290
39	Import duties	0	0	381
40	Imports incl. Duties	0	0	5871
41	Total Resources	21203	0	49178

321

Litho in United Nations, New York   03600   United Nations publication
86-40556—October 1987—4,200   Sales No. E.86.XVII.15
ISBN 92-1-161268-3   ST/ESA/STAT/SER.X/7